THE ROCK HISTORY READER

This eclectic compilation of readings tells the history of rock as it has been received and explained as a social and musical practice throughout its six decade history. This third edition includes new readings across the volume, with added material on the early origins of rock 'n' roll as well as coverage of recent developments, including the changing shape of the music industry in the twenty-first century. With numerous readings that delve into the often explosive issues surrounding censorship, copyright, race relations, feminism, youth subcultures, and the meaning of musical value, *The Rock History Reader* continues to appeal to scholars and students from a variety of disciplines.

New to the third edition:

- Nine additional chapters from a broad range of perspectives
- Explorations of new media formations, industry developments, and the intersections of music and labor
- For the first time, a companion website providing users with playlists of music referenced in the book

Featuring readings as loud, vibrant, and colorful as rock 'n' roll itself, *The Rock History Reader* is sure to leave readers informed, inspired, and perhaps even infuriated—but never bored.

Theo Cateforis is Associate Professor of Music History and Cultures in the Department of Art and Music Histories at Syracuse University. He is the author of *Are We Not New Wave? Modern Pop at the Turn of the 1980s.*

THE ROCK HISTORY READER

Third Edition

edited by **Theo Cateforis**

Routledge
Taylor & Francis Group

NEW YORK AND LONDON

Third edition published 2019
by Routledge
52 Vanderbilt Avenue, New York, NY 10017

and by Routledge
2 Park Square, Milton Park, Abingdon, Oxon, OX14 4RN

Routledge is an imprint of the Taylor & Francis Group, an informa business

First edition published by Routledge 2007

Second edition published by Routledge 2013

Library of Congress Cataloging-in-Publication Data
Names: Cateforis, Theo, editor.
Title: The rock history reader / edited by Theo Cateforis.
Description: Third edition. | New York : Routledge, 2018. | Includes index.
Identifiers: LCCN 2018034023 (print) | LCCN 2018038100 (ebook) |
ISBN 9781315394824 (ebook) | ISBN 9781138227705 (hardback) |
ISBN 9781138227712 (pbk.)
Subjects: LCSH: Rock music—History and criticism.
Classification: LCC ML3534 (ebook) | LCC ML3534 .R6333 2018 (print) |
DDC 781.6609—dc23
LC record available at https://lccn.loc.gov/2018034023

ISBN: 978-1-138-22770-5 (hbk)
ISBN: 978-1-138-22771-2 (pbk)
ISBN: 978-1-315-39482-4 (ebk)

Typeset in Minion Pro
by Florence Production Ltd, Stoodleigh, Devon, UK
Printed by CPI Group (UK) Ltd, Croydon CR0 4YY

Visit the companion website: www.routledge.com/cw/cateforis

Contents

Preface

Rock music has been with us now, by one name or another, for nearly three-quarters of a century. It is an utterly familiar presence. We hear it in commercials, movie soundtracks and political campaigns, and we are constantly reminded of its privileged cultural status through frequent lists of the "100 greatest rock songs of all time." The music even has its own Hall of Fame and Museum, populated by a cluster of towering icons, many of whom have had book-length academic studies devoted to their life and works. As it has become engrained in our environment, rock music has also become a subject deemed worthy of study in higher education. Browse the course listings for most universities or colleges and chances are good that you will find a "History of Rock" or "Rock Music" class listed somewhere in their catalog. Currently there are approximately half a dozen rock music textbooks in circulation, some of them on their seventh or eighth editions. *The Rock History Reader*, now in its third edition, joins these textbooks in its efforts to provide students, instructors and scholars of rock music with an anthology of historically based readings. The concern of this book lies not with simply reinforcing a canon of great artists and their creations, but rather revealing the various ways in which rock music has been explained and received throughout its history.

Organization

The Rock History Reader is modeled after the types of annotated source reading collections that have long been a staple of scholarship and pedagogy in the Humanities. Within the realm of music history anthologies, the book follows most closely the purpose and design set forth by Oliver Strunk's *Source Readings in Music History* and Piero Weiss and Richard Taruskin's *Music in the Western World: A History in Documents*. These anthologies bring to life, via primary sources, the often contentious issues, arguments, conflicts and creative tensions that have defined music as a social practice throughout the ages. I have, at one time or another, required both these collections in classes that I have taught, and as years of student testimonies have proven, such books are truly invaluable teaching tools.

The purpose of this anthology is twofold: on one hand, it offers vivid and detailed eyewitness accounts that extend beyond the scope of what a textbook can reasonably provide; on the other hand, the selected readings are designed to encourage reflection, debate and classroom discussions. To this end, in many places I have included multiple perspectives of the same subject: a critique of Elvis Presley followed by the singer's response, a debate over Madonna's true significance for feminists and two differing perspectives on the criteria for admission to the Rock & Roll Hall of Fame. In other instances, such as the Parents Music Resource Center's congressional statement on rock music's explicit and graphic content and popular music studies scholar David Shumway's lament about the vanishing presence of the rock star, I have chosen readings whose deliberately polemical nature is intended to foster dialogue about rock's various meanings.

Throughout the book I have taken several steps to present the readings as part of rock's specific historical narrative. All the readings are arranged chronologically by decade, and each selection is prefaced by a detailed introductory note that sets the background context, explains the significance of key figures in the reading and highlights issues for discussion. In some cases I have also identified relevant readings of interest for further research. Readers will notice as well that there are various places *within* the printed texts where I have added explanatory footnotes. I have done so wherever I felt that certain terminology or references seemed to require further clarification. In order to avoid confusion, all my annotations are found as numbered footnotes, while all the notes that belong to the original reprint texts (specifically Chapters 34, 37, 45 and 77) are placed in brackets and then listed as endnotes at the conclusion of the appropriate chapter.

Readership

I am well aware that those who might use a book such as *The Rock History Reader* will likely come from an array of disciplinary backgrounds, a reality reflected in the variety of rock textbooks themselves, which range from the detailed music analyses of Joe Stuessy and Scott Lipscomb's *Rock and Roll: Its History and Stylistic Development* to David Szatmary's more sociologically oriented *Rockin' In Time: A Social History of Rock-and-Roll*. With this diversity in mind, I have employed a number of different criteria in selecting the *Reader*'s contents. Many readings focus on the music of a specific artist or group like Elvis Presley, the Beatles, Brian Wilson, Bruce Springsteen, Radiohead and Vampire Weekend. While others deal more broadly with an entire genre or style, such as Motown, punk, progressive rock, heavy metal and emo. In many cases I have chosen readings that directly address social and cultural issues such as censorship, race relations, youth subcultures and the importance of identity as it relates to gender and sexual formations. And I have also sought readings that place an emphasis on rock's relationship with such technological formations as television, radio and social media. On the whole, I have tried to maintain a balance in the book's contents, so that the readings are not overly centered on rock's "classic" first quarter century, but spread equally through its later decades as well.

Background

The Rock History Reader is by no means the only book to present an anthology of writings about rock. It draws its inspiration from many previous collections, and it is important that they be acknowledged here. The first is Jonathan Eisen's 1969 anthology *The Age of Rock: Sounds of the American Cultural Revolution*. An excellent survey of the first major wave of rock journalism, Eisen's book—which he quickly followed with two others, *The Age of Rock 2* and *Twenty-Minute Fandangos and Forever Changes: A Rock Bazaar*—was one of my first introductions to the golden age of late 1960s rock writing. Eisen's long out-of-print books are distinguished by their uniformly high quality, and when initially compiling the *Rock History Reader* I had to resist the temptation to fill my 1960s chapters with authors and material cribbed solely from his collections. I consider it a measure of great restraint that in the end only two such selections found their way into my anthology. Three later collections—Clinton Heylin's *The Penguin Book of Rock & Roll Writing* (1992), William McKeen's *Rock and Roll is Here to Stay: An Anthology* (2000) and David Brackett's *The Pop, Rock, and Soul Reader: Histories and Debates* (2005, 2009, 2014)—proved to be particularly helpful as well. All these books venture beyond the realm of rock criticism, adding selections from fiction, autobiography and the efforts of rock historians like Charlie Gillett and Peter Guralnick. As such they broadened my conception of what an anthology of rock writings could be.

In addition to these books, I have returned most often to two anthologies of source materials: one of them a collection of rock writings, the other a jazz history reader. The first, and probably lesser known of these, is Michael J. Budds and Marian Ohman's 1993 publication *Rock Recall: Annotated Readings in American Popular Music from the Emergence of Rock and Roll to the Demise of the Woodstock Nation*. A truly ambitious project, their book brings together a staggering total of over two hundred entries relating to the 1950s and 1960s, drawn primarily from the popular press and various autobiographies and biographies. Their extensive research paved a path for my own exploration into these decades, and in two cases I have reprinted selections that I initially encountered in their collection: Jeff Greenfield's "But Papa, It's My Music, I Like It" and Chester Anderson's "Notes for a New Geology."

The second of these anthologies, Robert Walser's *Keeping Time: Readings in Jazz History* (1999, 2014), is a text that I always require in my jazz history classes, and from which I have learned a great deal. For example, unlike many readers, Walser's book includes a number of rather substantial and lengthy entries. Readings like these are important for they enable students to see how an author develops a sustained commentary on a narrow topic. Following Walser's lead, I have incorporated similar such pieces into *The Rock History Reader* wherever possible. Part of what also distinguishes *Keeping Time* from other anthologies is Walser's willingness to include articles from academics. As with jazz, scholarly writings on rock contribute in significant ways to the music's history and discourse, and it is crucial that they be represented. I have tried, to the extent that I can, to do so in my own reader. One such selection comes from Walser himself, with his musicological examination of heavy metal virtuosity, "Highbrow, Lowbrow, Voodoo Aesthetics."

Beyond these aforementioned anthologies, I have turned to many other sources in assembling this latest iteration of the *Rock History Reader*. In some cases I have incorporated source material that I encountered through the research of other popular music scholars. To name just two: Michael James Roberts' book *Tell Tchaikovsky the News: Rock 'n' Roll, the Labor Question, and the Musicians' Union, 1942–1968* and Kyle Devine's work on the history of loudness. Elsewhere I have benefitted greatly from the ever-growing list of digital databases and archives that house reprinted texts and page scans from past pop and rock magazines and trade publications. Were it not for the voluminous holdings of *AmericanRadioHistory.com*, *Entertainment Industry Magazine Archive*, *Music Magazine Archive*, *Rock's Backpages* and other such collections, this anthology would look quite different.

Given the vast amount of available material on rock, the task of assembling a reader is a daunting one that can easily spiral out of control into a seemingly endless search for the perfect primary source. In the end, I had to balance my impossible desire to examine every possible rock-related source with the inevitability of approaching publication deadlines. As a result, I cannot help but see the *Rock History Reader* as incomplete. Having fretted over its selections for so long, I am ever aware of its gaps, of the musicians missing from its pages and the absence or under-representation of certain genres, geographies and topical issues. The rationale for these omissions runs the gamut. Some articles or essays that I considered including were simply too lengthy to fit within the book's limited space. In other cases my pursuit of certain pieces met with insurmountable copyright restrictions or prohibitive permission fees.

That a book of this nature should have holes, however, is to be expected. Rock's history at this point is so expansive and well chronicled that even were this book twice its length, I would still be voicing the same apologies. To this end *The Rock History Reader* is perhaps best considered not as a standalone document, but in concert with the larger wealth of writing about rock and its ever-changing history. My one hope is that what I have contributed to this discourse leaves the reader feeling informed, inspired, or even infuriated, but never bored. After all, a music as loud, vibrant and colorful as rock deserves a group of writings as equally enjoyable and engaging.

Changes to This Third Edition

Those familiar with the previous editions of the *Rock History Reader* will notice some minor, but nonetheless significant changes with this new edition. First, and most importantly, the contents have been expanded, with an additional nine more chapters than its predecessor. The majority of these entries concern recent developments in rock and are located in the closing sections devoted to the 2000s and 2010s. The opening 1950s section has been lengthened as well, with two new chapters.

Readers of the second edition will also notice that a few selections have not carried over to the third edition (though in one notable instance I was able to *return* a selection from the first edition—taken from Chuck Berry's autobiography—that had been unavailable for the second edition). In some cases, despite my efforts, I simply was unable to secure permission this time around for pieces that were integral to the *Rock History Reader*. In other instances, I decided for pedagogical purposes to leave out certain readings that had not worked as effectively in the classroom as I had hoped. Wherever possible I have attempted to replace these readings with new ones that cover a similar sliver of rock history. The feedback that I received from other rock instructors who have used the book was also important, and helped to determine some of the new selections. In response to their recommendations, I have added more material on music and labor (musicians' unions in the 1960s, musician royalties in the digital age), industry developments (rock festivals, the rise of MTV, Spotify) and new media formations (Twitter, crowdfunding sites) that has enriched the third edition greatly.

Acknowledgments

I would like to begin by reiterating my thanks to those whose assistance, guidance and inspiration helped make the previous editions of the *Rock History Reader* a reality. While I have not repeated all the names from the first two editions' acknowledgments section here, suffice to say that the book you hold in your hands continues to bear their imprint. For this third edition, I would first like to thank my editor at Routledge, Genevieve Aoki, whose enthusiasm and patience in shepherding this project to the finish line was truly invaluable. Thanks also goes to Peter Sheehy at Routledge for his help in various matters.

Routledge solicited numerous anonymous reviews of the second *Rock History Reader*, and these aided me greatly as I considered my revisions. While I could not act upon all their suggestions, I took the reviewers' comments seriously and whenever possible and appropriate implemented them in the third edition. In addition, numerous colleagues, primarily from the International Association for the Study of Popular Music (IASPM) and Society for American Music (SAM) communities, provided helpful advice, leads and conversation, in some cases offering specific recommendations for materials. I am particularly indebted to Christa Bentley, David Blake, Patrick Burke, Jason Hanley, Barney Hoskins, Elizabeth Lindau, Lauren Onkey, Steve Waksman and Brian Wright.

At Syracuse University, I would specifically like to thank the many students who have taken my rock music class over the years. As the audience whose responses to the *Rock History Reader*'s contents have been the most immediate and often brutally honest, their opinions have contributed vitally to my own assessment of this book. I would also like to thank our music librarian, Rachel Fox Von Swearingen, whose continual support in purchasing books and database/journal subscriptions has been a tremendous boon to this project. My deep appreciation also goes to the library staff at Interlibrary Loan who assisted in procuring dozens of titles for my research.

Lastly, my largest thanks goes to my family. As always, I am indebted to my wife Margaret Martin for putting up with my pack rat tendencies as I have cluttered our house with stacks of rock music magazines and miscellanea in the name of research. This book would not have been possible without her understanding and encouragement. Thanks goes to our two children, Lester and Rhoda, and for the many moments of joy, laughter, play and learning I shared with them while assembling this book, all of which served as reminders of the more important things in life. Lastly, a final thanks to our cat Mokolo, who spent countless mornings warming my lap as I was preparing this book during the cold of Syracuse's winter.

I

THE 1950s

1

Du-Wop

Johnny Keyes

Named for the nonsense syllables that were a central part of their vocal harmony arrangements, du-wop or doo-wop groups of young African American male singers were a constant presence on the R&B charts throughout the 1950s and a major influence on the rise of rock 'n' roll. In these selections from his memoir of the 1950s doo-wop era, Johnny Keyes of the Magnificents (best known for their 1956 hit "Up on the Mountain") recounts his formative experiences as a young singer. Like most doo-wop groups, the Magnificents came together in an urban setting, on the south side of Chicago, and Keyes explains how the specific spaces and places of this environment—from its street corners and apartments to its barber shops and musical venues—helped shape doo-wop's unique sound and visual style.[1] While we remember doo-wop mostly for its vocals, Keyes points out that in the recording studio and on stage the Magnificents and other groups were always interacting with, and dependent upon, the support of older big-band jazz musicians—a cross-generational collaboration that could sometimes result in disastrous miscommunications and power plays. Keyes' observations remind us that rock 'n' roll was not simply the province of the young, but rather a style performed by *both* teenagers and adults versed in many different musical languages.

Street Songs, Street Singers

Who They Were and What They Did

> "Eeeyo, eeeeh! Red ripe watermelons here.
> Get your watermelons here. Eeeyo, eeeh!
> Red ripe watermelons here. Get your watermelons here."

Usually three boys rode on the horse-drawn wagon, sometimes four counting the driver. You could hear them singing as they made their way slowly up and down the neighborhood streets on the South Side of Chicago in the 40s. It was one of the sounds of summer. The wagons would be piled high with the dark green melons. It seemed the street songs of watermelon hucksters could be heard for blocks. After all, everyone had their windows up to keep cool. There weren't very many air conditioners in the apartments, nor many automobile horns to compete with either.

---

1 For more on the history of doo wop in Chicago, see Robert Puter, *Doowop: The Chicago Scene* (Urbana: University of Illinois Press, 1996).

In the winter, many of these wagons were used to sell coal. But, the song of the coal sellers lacked the easy, melodic wail that the watermelon hucksters' tune had. Besides not too many people had their windows raised during the harsh Chicago winters. But, there was "music" in the streets of Chicago's South Side, in one form or another, for as long as I can remember.

Another interesting and entertaining form of street music was the hambone, a syncopated sound made by slapping the hands against the thighs and chest. If you're good, the mouth was added to the rhythm pattern. A rhyme went along with the hambone beat. This rhyme was spoken in a sing-song cadence, not unlike the vocals of the rap records of the 80s, with the ex-watermelon sellers slapping their thighs on the steps of the school and the front steps of the neighborhood buildings. These hamboners were the forerunners of the vocal groups. They got off the steps and took their acts to the legendary corners, underneath the street lamps.

There were very little gang problems in the 50s, by today's standards. Gangs seldom killed anything but time. One reason may be the fact that street kids competed on more than one level. It's true that there was a lot of fighting over territorial rights, or the capital offense of talking to the wrong girl. That one would get you hurt seriously, sometimes mortally. But, in addition to the combat, they would compete on the softball diamond or the street corner. Every gang had within its ranks a softball team and a singing Group, made up of six or seven cats. It was similar to belonging to a club within a club, a fraternity within a fraternity.

A Group singer, who for some reason found himself "visiting" out of his neighborhood, was seldom attacked by the gangs that inevitably surrounded him as he was leaving the girl's house. Escaping is hard to do, so you're trapped. A Group singer would be allowed to go on his way if he identified himself and was believed, or was recognized as belonging to another gang.

For instance, if you were approached by gang members as you were leaving a young lady's house in the vicinity of 57th and Wentworth, La Condors' territory, and you happened to live in Van Dykes' turf, around 42nd and Calumet, an explanation would definitely be in order.

From time to time, the gang would invite the alleged Group singer to "hit a tune" with a couple of the fellas, an obvious ploy to weed out imposters. That was a fairly simple challenge because everyone knew the same songs. The most common were, "Ling, Ting, Tong," by the 5 Keys, "The Wind," by the Diablos, "Hey Mrs. Fannie,"[2] by the Clovers, "Sunday Kind of Love," by the Harptones, "Hey Senorita," by the Penguins and "Good Lovin'," by the Clovers.

But the down side of it was if they called a tune and you were not a Group singer or were no good at improvisation, you better be good at running because there was going to be trouble. It was either "hit a tune" or get hit in the head.

Commuters standing on the El platform, waiting for the Jackson Park B or Englewood A trains, could usually spot a Group of teenagers huddled together underneath the lamp that spotlighted the Group as well as the sign that read Indiana Avenue. Chances are they would be singing one of the aforementioned songs. If they were sounding good or believed they were, this vocalizing would be resumed when they boarded the train and found seats together in the rear of the car.

This form of entertainment slowly replaced the blind man with the bottle-neck guitar, who sang either blues or religious songs. He was usually accompanied by a small boy who passed a hat among the commuters on the train as it rattled and lurched up and down the tracks to and from downtown Chicago.

The only intermission for the commuters came after the El plunged into the darkness of the subway. It was too noisy down there for anyone to hear the music, so the duo usually got off at the first stop and boarded another train headed in the opposite direction.

---

2 The song was recorded and released as "Hey Miss Fannie."

Streetcar passengers were treated to another form of music. Casey Jones would entertain the riders with his trained chicken, but neither Casey Jones nor the chicken would sing.[3] As I remember it, the chicken would drink beer from a cup and the old man would talk to the chicken and invite the audience to join in the fun. He had a tin cup that his young assistant would pass among the captive audience before the act began. "No dime, no show," he would repeat to the crowd. He had more smarts than many of his contemporaries and quite a few of the performers who came along later, including the Du-Wop singers and everybody else who complained that they were shortchanged in their show business careers.

In the 50s, buses slowly replaced streetcars, and the back of the bus was the ideal place for the Du-Wop Group to serenade the passengers. This was also a good place to test the Group's new material or warm up in preparation for pending talent shows and/or auditions. Most of them were located downtown.

Plus, the men's room of any office building had the best echo in the world, as far as the 50s Du-Wop Group was concerned. And, the boy's bathroom in high school was used for something other than smoking cigarettes and washing your hands. This area furnished the best echo chamber for singing slow songs with "woooo" in the background. All of that tile and porcelain was tailor-made for singing "Most of All," by the Moonglows, "The Wind," by Nolan Strong and the Diablos, or "Baby I Need You," by the El Dorados.

The vestibule of an apartment building was a good place too, especially in the winter time after school. But the all-time favorite combination stage and theater-in-the-round was on the corner, underneath the street lamp.

*   *   *

[The 50s R&B Groups] were called Du-Wops because they sang du-wop in the background of some of their songs. But let's discuss why they sang that particular phrase. One answer might be found in listening to the old masters, the Mills Brothers in particular. You'll recall that these early recordings featured the Group singing with only a hollow-box guitar for accompaniment. That was enough because they were self-contained in a manner of speaking—all music came from them. The harmony, the horn arrangements were made with their mouths. When the vocal groups of the early 50s got together for rehearsal, we had no back-up musicians, except in rare instances. There were a few Groups who had their own piano players, but these were the exceptions. Most of us sang acapella, and there was another reason for that stemming from the fact that you rehearsed in your parents' homes. In those days, parents tolerated only so much noise in the house. (When I say house, I really mean apartment.) The neighbors wouldn't be too pleased at seeing four or five singers and three or four other people carrying musical instruments getting ready to "make music." But, mainly it was the home folks who wouldn't tolerate it. I can just hear my old man now . . .

"Where do you think you're going with all of those folks?"
"Rehearsal."
"Rehearsal? What rehearsal?!!"
"Hey, this is no auditorium, music hall or night club . . . in the first place, there are too many of you, and in the second place, your group can't sing anyway. Hey, wait a minute, where's he going with those drums? Johnny, come over here and let me explain something to you . . . Have you lost your absolute mind?"

---

3 Casey Jones (real name Anderson Punch) was a famous street performer on Chicago's south side, who trained chickens to dance to his accordion and harmonica playing.

"Huh?"

"Huh Hell!"

"This is a family home, not the International Amphitheatre! It's bad enough I have to put up with you and your group yellin' and stomping up dust in my front room, but now you're bringing in some more bums with more noise makin' junk. Boy you need your head examined."

"We're just going to run through a few songs for a couple of hours or so," I explained.

"Get goin'! Take it to the park or somebody else's house, and take that 'band' with you."

The point I'm making is that there was a noise factor involved so that if you had backup musicians, you'd better not bring them to rehearsal unless your folks and the neighbors were on vacation. So we were forced into taking a more pragmatic course of action . . . making music with our mouths, imitating some of the musical instruments we weren't allowed to bring to the homefront rehearsals. First, the bass singer performed the same function as the bass player in a band. He set the tempo, after first getting the pitch pipe, similar to the one a music teacher used in school to set the Glee Club in motion. The first tenor, second tenor and baritone singers sang the phrase doo-wop in harmony, the sound of trombones was produced. Muted trumpet sounds were mimicked by singing the phrase . . . shoo-be-doo, and . . . duba-bop-bop. Sometimes the horn section would be divided. The bass singer doubled with the first tenor (or trumpet) and the remaining voices would blend, producing the sound of three trombones, a trumpet, and baritone sax. They would then be creating an ensemble thing [check out the intro to "Starlite" by the Moonglows] . . . oooowah—ooowah, or they often used Ba-Ba-Ba-Bop. These phrases or figures could be sung in ballads or medium and up tempo numbers. But most of the time the background singers would imitate the music they heard violins play . . . wooooooh or ooooooh sustained underneath the lead singer's vocal. Obviously these weren't the only things that Vocal Groups did behind the lead singer. Of course, they would sing actual words; one example can be heard in the old standby, "Sunday Kind of Love," as sung by the Harptones. On this ballad, the group would alternate between actually singing the intro in harmony along with the Lead Singer, then after the retard, the lead would be sung straight, with the background singing the string parts we mentioned earlier. (Ooooooohs) in the bridge the words were sung again in harmony around the lead, and the bass singer finishes the verse alone with the string sounds underneath leading into the last verse . . .

> Lead voices: I do my Sunday dreaming . . .
> and all my Sunday scheming . . .
> every minute, every hour, every day
> I'm hoping to discover
> a certain kind of lover—ooh
> Bass: who will show me the way . . .

*   *   *

The Style

Description

There's been a lot of talk concerning the different trends in popular music. Each trend had within it a target Group that was labeled. The artists who were the focal point of the 80s were called punks. Hence, the music was called punk rock. In the 70s, there were artists who combined rock music with country music. That segment of the industry became known as country/rock and the people who performed it were country/rock artists. Of course, disco music was another major force of the 70s, and the performers were known as disco recording artists. The 60s had its hard rock, acid rock, psychedelic rock, heavy metal rock and pop rock.

Each of these was a separate industry within the music industry. I suppose one of the reasons for this was the unique marketing angle each of these segments presents. The punk rock of the 80s generated sales for safety pins, magenta hair dye and black clothing, while the country/rock industry sold a lot of cowboy hats, silver belt buckles, satin shirts and fancy boots. The disco craze was responsible for the sale of white suits, black shirts and light sequined dresses. And everybody remembers the black light posters, lava lamps, incense, granny glasses, bell-bottom pants and tie-dyed T-shirts that flooded the country in the 60s.

But during the 50s, the dawn of rock 'n' roll, the Du-Wop Groups and the single arts of that period didn't have the benefit of these marketing tools. Maybe it was because rhythm and blues music was the art form from which all of the other forms were derived. And maybe a lot of the clothing that is associated with these trends came from the 50s era also. Perhaps the reason the Groups didn't get a lot of the high-powered publicity gimmicks and media hype that artists of today enjoy was because the limited budgets of the small, independent record labels didn't allow for it. And maybe there were no T-shirts to advertise the Groups' name on the front and company logo on the back because in the 50s, T-shirts were still considered to be underwear.

But, still there existed a style among the performers in Du-Wop show business, and it was as legitimate as any of the other forms that came later. Never mind that there was no marketing strategy to label and package it for the masses. The companies just cut the records and put them in the hands of disc jockeys, who played them on the radio. The people heard the records and if they liked what they heard, they went to the record shops and bought them. If the public liked the performer's act, they bought the next release. So, for the most part, the Du-Wop Group did its own advertising. These Groups rode around the country in station wagons that had their name painted on the side.

They had a certain style. We'll call it the Du-Wop style. There were Du-Wop gigs, Du-Wop contracts, and Du-Wop fans. Part of the Du-Wop style had to do with the artist's processed hair. It was long, wavy and shiny. Sometimes it was worn parted on one side. Other times it was combed to the front and called a "quo vadis." Whatever shade or style, all of the Groups in Chicago and on the East Coast wore processed hair. The exceptions were a couple of Groups on the West Coast, such as the Penguins or Don Julian and the Meadowlarks.

Every major city had at least one barber shop, sometimes two, that could fix hair, I mean have you leaving the shop looking like a star. Chicago had three, the House of Nelson on Cottage Grove, Mopp City across the street from Nelson's and a block down on the other side of Cottage Grove, and last but not least, Bill Buck's All Stars, on 36th and Cottage Grove.

Bill Buck's was next door to the poolroom and it had a restaurant in the back plus a lounge. The lounge had the usual magazines and books. A TV set was there, of course. Some of the people who came through there on a regular basis were Sam Cooke, Johnnie Taylor, The Soul Stirrers, Otis Rush, the 4 Buddies and a few DJs. It would take the better part of the day to get your hair fixed. I guess the process was so named because getting it done was such a very long process.

In preparing to go onstage, baby oil would be combed through the hair and makeup would be applied to the face. For many years, nut-brown face powder was used by the Groups. But, there were several Groups in the business that used greasepaint. Once commercial liquid makeup found its way into the dressing rooms, it wasn't long before nut-brown face powder was on its way out.

The Groups, in taking care of their hair, automatically started to take better care of their skin. They wore no hair on their faces. They were clean shaven, but sometimes a slight moustache could be drawn on the upper lip with an eyebrow pencil. The finishing touch would be a little Revlon Dark-Dark dabbed on the face and smoothed out lightly.

Then, when you get on stage and the flesh-colored spotlight hits the Group, the girls get to check out the contrast of the black silk-like hair with the smooth, velvet-like complexions. It made an impressive picture on stage.

*   *   *

Musicians

Peaceful Coexistence within Groups

Big band gigs were beginning to get scarce in the 50s. The trend had changed in music and the big night clubs that were prevalent in the last three decades in Chicago were closing their doors one by one. Gone were the days when the Club DeLisa, Chez Paree and the Grand Terrace employed big house bands.

Chicago, at one time, had a wealth of movie theaters where the bands could perform, in addition to the featured movie. There were the Chicago and Oriental theaters downtown, the Stratford on 63rd Street, the Grand on 31st and State and, of course, the Regal on 47th and South Parkway. Let's not forget the ballrooms, like the Aragon, located on the north side and the Trianon and Pershing ballrooms on the south side. The Regal was the one remaining movie house that continued to have stage shows, and the Trianon and Pershing also had shows on a regular basis.

The big bands were selling a few records, but the only two that come to mind are, "The Bunny Hop," by Ray Anthony's band and "Hand Clappin," by Red Prysock. The new music of the 50s, rock 'n' roll, was identified with small combos. The instrumentals that were selling were made by Bill Haley and the Comets, Bill Doggett and Sil Austin.

But, the emergence of the Du-Wop Groups provided a lot of session work for musicians. And most of the stage shows, with the exception of Larry Steele's "Smart Affairs," were rock 'n' roll shows.[4] There was a lot of work backing up the Groups because few of them had their own back-up musicians.

Most of the musicians were in their 30s and 40s, while the Groups were mostly teenagers, or in their early 20s. This made for a lot of generation gaps, and quite a few cultural gaps as well. But, for the most part, the Groups got along with the musicians. Although, they could read music, or fake it, and we could not, we still had to work together, especially when it came to making records.

Much of the work was already done by the Groups as was previously mentioned, which brought the material as well as the arrangements to the pre-session rehearsals. We wrote songs, arranged them, voiced the chords in the background, rehearsed the songs acapella and set the tempo and the key.

Most of the time, we then sang the songs for our peers, who, after all, were the target audience for our record sales. Very few people who were the same age as the musicians bought our records anyway. All of this ground work was laid before we even met the backup combo.

When we arrived at rehearsal, the bandleader would say, "OK, let's hear the first one. Run through it for us, mistakes and all, so we can see what's happening." We would be singing the first song and the conversation would begin between them like we weren't even there.

---

4 Larry Steele's "Smart Affairs" was a renowned black entertainment revue that featured many of the top jazz and big band musicians of the 1950s.

> "What are they doing?" one of them would ask the piano player.
>
> "Sounds like they're doing a flatted fifth on the turnaround."
>
> "Oh yeah, I got it. Where do they go in the bridge?"
>
> "To Australia somewhere, sounds like to me. Let me hear that bridge again lead singer."

We didn't know the language of music. We call the bridge the middle of the song, which it sometimes was. So, we would start at the beginning and sing it all the way through again. Every now and then, they would change key or force us to transpose it into a key that was more comfortable for *them* to play. After the key was established and they figured out the pattern of the tune, they were home free.

Now, the amazing thing about all of this was that after everything was over and the record was finished and ready for distribution, the bandleader's name would be on the label as the arranger. He would only have written the lead sheet. Of course, that, along with the session costs of studio rental, engineer, scale for the accompaniment,[5] whiskey for the band, sandwiches they ate, etc., were deducted from our royalties. We had no problem with those charges. But, we thought it was odd to be charged for the arrangements, the arrangements we brought to them. They actually charged us for work we brought to them. And believed that they had convinced us that we should be grateful. We weren't that young and gullible.

Some musicians were able to hide their resentment of the Groups a little better than others. But, for the most part, we were aware of it. It wasn't so much what they said as the way they said it sometimes.

> "What have we here? Oh yeah, some more birds doing that same tune in the same key."

But we had to be very diplomatic when we addressed them in a rehearsal before a theater gig that lasted five days or more. We might even have to address the bandleader as an orchestra leader. If there were more than six of them on the bandstand, they weren't a band anymore, they became an orchestra. Never mind that they referred to your Group as hummers or birds. The implications being, of course, that all vocal Groups were named after birds like the Flamingos, Ravens, Cardinals, and Crows.

If we were thought to be disrespectful or sarcastic, there was always the chance that our music would be played wrong. Our slow tunes could be played up-tempo and the up-tempo ones would become ballads. This seldom happened on the theater gigs, but it occurred many times on the one-nighters for several reasons.

One occasion might be the one-night stand at an auditorium. You're booked as part of a package, a singer, a band (his band) and your Group. You go on first, of course, followed by the singer.

You know you're in trouble when you come to the rehearsal, meet the band and they tell you it's not necessary for them to rehearse your stuff.

> "Hi, we're the Magnificents and here's a list of the tunes we'll probably need to run through before the show. This is the order we're gonna do them. See, this first one . . ."
>
> "Hey man, this is cool. This will work. I got it. Oh, yeah, we know all of these. No sweat."
>
> "Well, this last tune is kind of strange. It's got a funny intro, and there's a spot in the middle that has a clean break."

---

5 "Scale," here, most likely refers to the set union wages of the musicians' pay scale.

"Now, Junior, don't worry about that. We play that one all the time. Like I told you, no sweat. We got you."

That's exactly what he meant, too. They had us. They did just what I mentioned earlier—the slow one's fast, the fast one's slow, including the main tune, the one everybody wanted to hear us sing.

Source: Johnny Keyes, *Du-Wop* (Chicago: Vesti Press, 1987), pp. 1–4, 6–9, 12–14, 35–38.

2

"Miss Rhythm" Speaks Out

Ruth Brown on R&B and Covers

Singer Ruth Brown (1928–2006), whose title of "Miss Rhythm" signified her importance to the growing R&B field in the early 1950s, was one of the first artists to bring prominence to the independent label Atlantic Records. As she discusses in these excerpts from her 1996 autobiography, black artists like herself were at a decided disadvantage in the 1950s. Not only were they limited in their access to channels of distribution, such as radio and television, but their very songs were often duplicated virtually unchanged by white singers, whose versions were then promoted in wider marketplaces, and for greater sales. The flood of cover versions that floated between rhythm and blues, rock 'n' roll, and pop in the 1950s proved to be a point of serious contention for black singers like her and LaVern Baker (1929–1997), who as Brown mentions, formally complained of the inequality that she faced competing with white cover singers like Georgia Gibbs.[1] On one bitter occasion, Baker even went so far as to name Gibbs as the recipient of her flight insurance, reasoning that if any tragedy were to befall her, Gibbs would be without a source of further revenue. For all the deep resentment and pain that singers like Brown and Baker felt, at the same time Brown acknowledges that she did not view all covers as unwanted encroachments. As long as the recording "contributed" to the song, it was welcome.

Any real money I made came from touring, and I was always out there promoting the records. Back then any record by a black artist needed every ounce of help it could get. The expression "R&B chart" was another way in the later forties and early fifties to list "race and black" as well as "rhythm and blues" records. And the reason so few discs by black artists crossed over to the Billboard's mainstream chart was simple: it was compiled from white-owned radio station playlists featuring music by white artists, with our list catering to blacks. As Jerry Wexler, Herb's successor at Atlantic, put it when asked if it was difficult to get R-and-B records played on general-audience stations in the early fifties, "*Difficult* would have been easy. It was *impossible*."[2]

It very gradually became less so, of course, as R-and-B artists broke through the barriers by the sheer strength and quality of their music. But it took time, and throughout my biggest hit-making period I was forced to stand by as white singers like Georgia Gibbs and Patti Page duplicated my records note for note and were able to plug them on top television shows like *The Ed Sullivan Show*, to which I had no access.

---

1 For more on LaVern Baker's reactions to the cover versions of her songs, see Chip Deffaa's chapter on her in *Blue Rhythms: Six Lives in Rhythm and Blues* (Urbana and Chicago: University of Illinois Press, 1996).

2 "Herb" is Herb Abramson, the co-founder of Atlantic Records. Jerry Wexler succeeded him at Atlantic in 1953, when Abramson was drafted into the Army.

Chuck Willis wrote "Oh, What a Dream" especially for me, and it was my favorite song, but it was Patti Page, with an identical arrangement, who got to sing it on national television. Even topical stuff like my "Mambo Baby" had a Georgia Gibbs duplicate rushed out. My labelmate and good friend LaVern Baker, who joined Atlantic in '53, suffered the same fate on her original of "Tweedle Dee"—another note-for-note copy by Her Nibs Miss Gibbs. There was no pretense, either, that they were anything but duplicates. Mercury actually called up Tommy Dowd on the day they were cutting "Tweedle Dee" and said, "Look, we've got the same arrangement, musicians and tempo, we might as well have the same sound engineer too."

It was tough enough coming up with hit sounds, therefore doubly galling to see them stolen from under our noses. Few seemed to stop and question the morality of this, least of all the publishers, to whom it was a case of the more the merrier. LaVern for one did, protesting to her congressman over her treatment at Mercury's hands, but then as now, there was no copyright protection on arrangements.

I was denied sales abroad as well, although I knew nothing of this at the time. "Abroad," as far as the feedback from Atlantic's accounting department was concerned, could have been the moon. Having made number three on Billboard's R-and-B chart in the States, and actually crossing over to their pop charts as well, reaching number twenty-five, my version of "Lucky Lips" was ignored in Britain. The number itself hit there years later in a 1963 version by Cliff Richard. Naturally the lyrics were suitably amended for him, for "When I was a little girl my curls were long and silky" sounded pretty ridiculous even for me. Cliff took the tune to number four on the British charts, well into his unprecedented run of over one hundred chart entries that continues—and deservedly so—to this day. Why he's not bigger in the U.S. I'll never know.

*   *   *

My gripe would never be with legitimate covers, or subsequent versions like Cliff Richard's, but with bare-faced duplicates, with no artistic merit whatsoever. Everybody in the business accepted covers as fair game. There were umpteen versions of songs like "Hey, There," "Stranger in Paradise" and "Around the World," and you chose your favorite version based not only on the singer, but on the different treatments and arrangements on offer. I covered several songs myself, like "Be Anything (But Be Mine)," originated by Winnie Brown with the Lionel Hampton Orchestra, and Larry Darnell's "I'll Get Along Somehow," but they were never by any stretch of the imagination mere duplicates. We *contributed* to the songs.

Source: Ruth Brown with Andrew Yule, *Miss Rhythm: The Autobiography of Ruth Brown, Rhythm and Blues Legend* (New York: Donald I. Fine Books, 1996), pp. 76–78, 110.

3

Leiber & Stoller

TED FOX

As songwriters and "independent producers" for artists ranging from the Coasters and the Drifters to Big Mama Thornton and Elvis Presley, Jerry Leiber (1933–2011) and Mike Stoller (born 1933) were responsible for many of the rock 'n' roll era's most enduring hits. In this 1985 interview conducted by music writer and longtime Buckwheat Zydeco manager Ted Fox, the two songwriters discuss their formative years and the stories behind some of their most famous songs, giving insight along the way into the creative process behind many R&B and early rock 'n' roll recordings. As Fox points out, Leiber and Stoller's situation also throws the unusual racial dynamics surrounding 1950s rock 'n' roll into sharp relief. Songs like "Kansas City" and "Hound Dog" are often taken to be forms of "authentic" black musical expression, yet their authors were two nineteen-year-old white Jewish teenagers, both of whom felt a powerful attraction to the culture and music of African Americans. Much like Johnny Otis (1921–2012), the white musician, producer, and composer of "Willie and the Hand Jive," whose immersion among African Americans led him to feel "black by persuasion," Leiber and Stoller's experiences prove that notions of race in America have been informed as much by culture as they have by the color of one's skin.

Let's talk about how you got together.

Leiber: I was writing songs with a drummer, and going to Fairfax High School in Los Angeles. The drummer lost interest in writing songs and suggested I call Mike Stoller, whom he had worked with in a pickup dance band. I called Mike. He said he was not interested in writing songs. I said I thought it would be a good idea if we met anyway.

Mike, you were really into jazz and modern classical at that time, no?

Stoller: I was a very big modern jazz fan really. At the time Jerry called me, 1950, I was very into Charlie Parker and Thelonious Monk and Dizzy. And through modern jazz I got interested in Stravinsky and Bartók. When I lived in New York—before I moved to California when I was sixteen—I used to hang out on 52nd Street.

Didn't you take piano lessons with James P. Johnson?

Stoller: I did when I was ten or eleven. Four or five lessons. That was my earliest love, boogie-woogie and blues piano. But the thing that cemented our relationship was when Jerry showed me his lyrics and I saw that they were blues in structure. Most of them had a twelve-bar structure—a line, then ditto marks, then the rhyming line. So it wasn't difficult for me to relate to it and go back to my first love, which was Pine Top Smith and Meade Lux Lewis, and Albert Ammons.

Jerry, were you more rhythm and blues oriented?

Leiber: Boogie-woogie, rhythm and blues. I was working in a record shop on Fairfax Avenue after school. But actually I was exposed to boogie-woogie when I was a little kid in Baltimore. My mother had a grocery store just on the border of the black ghetto. She had many black customers.

It seems like an almost fateful encounter. You were both so heavily into black culture.

Stoller: We were, but my background was a bit different. I went to an interracial summer camp, which was very unusual in those days. Starting in 1940, I went there every summer for eight years. I heard the older black kids playing the upright piano in the barn. A couple of them played very good boogie-woogie. I tried to emulate what I'd heard.

When you first started, were there songwriters you tried to emulate or whom you admired?

Leiber: I was trying to imitate certain styles—sounds that I heard on records. Some of the writers I was imitating, I found out later were actually the performers.

You both were totally into the black scene in L.A. at that time. You had black girlfriends, and would go to the black clubs.

Leiber: Oh yeah. We lived a kind of black existence. I'd say eighty percent of our lives were lived that way. It's an interesting thing. I sometimes look back on it and I think, why did I do that? I think that somehow or other I was alienated from my own culture and searching for something else. My father died when I was five. My mother was a refugee from Poland. I don't know what fragments of tradition there were left in my family, but they were so slight, there was little to go on.

Did you feel that way, too, Mike?

Stoller: No, not exactly. My family life was very warm, very emotionally comfortable. My mother and father were very supportive. My mother in particular was very supportive of me, and later of Jerry as well. But I must have felt somewhat alienated from my white peers. I felt there was something more special about not only the music I heard, that came from black people, but the black people themselves who made the music. I belonged to a social club in Harlem when I was about thirteen or fourteen.

Leiber: The black neighborhood was groovy, and I was accepted there right away. Part of it was my mother's doing. Her store was the only store within ten blocks of the ghetto that extended credit to black families. So I was a welcome person in the black neighborhood.

This translated itself immediately and automatically into the stuff you were writing, didn't it? Your songs became authentic black songs of the period.

Leiber: Leroi Jones, writing about us in the sixties, said that we were the only authentic black voices in pop music. [Laughs.] He changed his tune a few years later when he became [Amiri] Baraka. We were flattered. Actually I think we wanted to be black. Being black was being great. The best musicians in the world were black. The greatest athletes in the world were black, and black people had a better time. As far as we were concerned the worlds that we came from were drab by comparison.

Jerry Wexler said in his interview with me that he supported the separation of black and white music into the pop and rhythm and blues charts because he felt that created more opportunity for black artists. How do you feel about that?

Stoller:	I never thought about it that way. I always felt that it was sad, in the early days especially, that artists like Ray Charles and Lloyd Price and Big Mama Thornton weren't exposed to a wider audience.
Leiber:	If they had had exposure on the major stations, then Georgia Gibbs wouldn't have been able to make all those covers of all those great records by Ruth Brown and LaVern Baker.
Stoller:	And Pat Boone, who was covering Fats Domino records and Little Richard records . . .
Leiber:	. . . wouldn't have happened. If Richard was played on all the Top 40 stations, nobody could have sold another record of anything he made. Could anybody cover Elvis Presley?
Stoller:	The point is that today people are still buying and listening to Little Richard, Fats Domino, and Laverne Baker. Nobody is buying their songs in a cover version by Pat Boone. Nobody wants to hear a Georgia Gibbs' record or The Crew Cuts' record [of The Chords' original "Sh-Boom"]. What I imagine Jerry Wexler meant was that within a smaller and separate pool you could support more new fish. But I think the black fish in that smaller pool were being denied an ocean in which they could have very well survived.

Let's talk about how you two worked together as songwriters.

Leiber:	Often, in the early days, I'd stalk around Mike's room. There'd be an upright piano against one of the walls. I'd just walk around and smoke and mumble, and he would jam until I would just get struck by some notion. Then I'd start yelling some kind of line. If Mike dug it, he would pick it up somewhere. Sometimes Mike would yell out some lines, too.
Stoller:	It was like spontaneous combustion, like Jackson Pollock. You threw a lot of paint at the canvas. I would just play riffs and Jerry would shout lines, almost like automatic writing.

Mike, it's been said you had an almost encyclopedic grasp of musical styles, and you could throw out ideas from everything you'd digested over the years.

Stoller:	I think that's somebody else's description.
Leiber:	I think it is true, although I don't think he was conscious of it. We used to just use shorthand after a while, sort of make signs. I'd say, "More Fats" [Domino] or "More Richard" [Little Richard] or "More Amos" [Milburn], "More Charles" [Ray Charles]. All these were signals for different styles pianistically. If I was talking about Toussaint [Allen Toussaint], it meant New Orleans.
Stoller:	If he said Fats, it generally meant triplets.
Leiber:	Hard triplets, at a certain tempo.

*   *   *

Let's talk about "Kansas City." Wasn't it first titled "K.C. Loving?"

Stoller:	It was written for Little Willie Littlefield. We called it "Kansas City," but Ralph Bass came to us and said, "You know, 'K.C.' is the hip thing, so I'm going to change the title of your song to 'K.C. Loving.'" We said "Okay. Just put it out!"

It's so authentic sounding, but different, it's not just a twelve-bar blues.

Stoller:	Actually it *is* a twelve-bar blues, but it's a *melodic* one, as opposed to a traditional blues melody, which is basically just a series of inflections. I wanted to write something that,

if it was played on a trumpet or a trombone, people could say it was a particular song, instead of that's a blues in E flat or F. I wanted something you could listen to instrumentally, and say, "I know that song."

Most people then, and probably to this day, think the song is traditional. How do you feel about that?

Stoller: At first when that happened we felt we had achieved something, that we had written something good enough to be thought of as traditional.

Leiber: At the time we were writing it, Mike and I had a little bit of an argument, and Mike turned out to be right. I didn't want it to have a melody. I wanted it to have a traditional straight blues contour, that any blues singer would sing in his own style with just the changes and the words. Mike said, "I don't want to do that, I want to write a melody. I want this to have a real identity." I said, "The other way it's much more flexible." He said, "Well, man, you're writing the words and I'm writing the music, and I'm going to write the music the way I hear it." [Laughter.]

At this point, and until the "Hound Dog" session with Big Mama Thornton in 1952, your records were being produced by other people. . . .

Stoller: Yeah. In the case of "Kansas City" we went out to Maxwell Davis' house. He was an A&R man, producer, arranger, songwriter, horn player. And he was the house musical director for Aladdin Records. He also made records for Modern, Specialty, and other labels, including Mercury.

Leiber: If he were alive today, he'd be making a million dollars a second. He was wonderful. There were four or five guys around the country at this time who had this ability.

Stoller: Like Jesse Stone, who worked for Atlantic, or Bumps Blackwell, who worked for Specialty. But up until that time, after we performed a song for an artist, we frequently went to the studio. At first it was like, "You guys can stay here, but be quiet." Later we began to express some ideas to whomever was running the session. Sometimes they'd use some of the ideas. After all, when you're working with the blues, which is pretty repetitive, you need as many ideas as you can get to make it a little different. We would be invited to the studio with songs after a while. Ralph would call us to bring songs to the studio. We would run them down with artists like Little Esther or Bobby Nunn or Little Willie Littlefield with Johnny Otis' band, and discuss how they ought to go. They would be worked out on the session. Sometimes we'd bring three songs with us and write a fourth during the session. When we did "Kansas City," it was the first time we had the opportunity to really spend time before the session laying out the ideas with an arranger who actually wrote down the ideas, as opposed to the way we had worked with Johnny Otis, where the charts were head arrangements done on the spot.

During this time when your material was being produced by others, were you happy with the way it was coming out?

Leiber: A lot of the stuff was misinterpreted. So we started to involve ourselves more and more in the making of arrangements and the running of sessions until we got to a point where we could run our own sessions. After a while they were calling us to produce records.

Stoller: "Hound Dog" was the first record we produced, although unofficially. Johnny Otis had played drums at the rehearsal. He had the snares turned off and was playing some old Southern, Latin-sounding kind of beat. On the actual recording date, he had his road drummer playing because Johnny was supposed to be running the session for Don Robey of Peacock Records. It wasn't happening. So Jerry said, "Johnny, get on the drums the way you were." Johnny said, "Who's gonna run the session?" and we said, "We will." Jerry went into the booth and directed from there. I stayed on the floor and worked with the musicians. There were only two takes, and both of them were good, but the second was better than the first.

You were known, along with Jerry Wexler and Ahmet Ertegun at Atlantic, for doing as many takes as necessary to get the song right, and for rehearsing your artists before entering the studio with them. That was pretty unusual in rhythm and blues at that time, wasn't it?

Stoller: I think so.

Leiber: We took a lot more time than the Biharis's and the Mesners' did. They'd do two, three, four, five takes and good-bye. We'd lay in there for two hours on a side if we had to. But we almost always got four sides in the allotted three hours—two A sides and two B sides. In fact, "Searchin'," which we did in the last six minutes of a session as a B side, was the fourth song of the session and we just *had* to get it.[1] I mean if we had come out of a session with only three sides, we'd have felt like failures. We were very thorough. We would rehearse for three weeks before a session, eight hours a day. Every lick was planned. The only thing we would leave to chance on the session was the feel, and the tempo. Sometimes Mike would take a note or two out of a bass pattern because it was too cluttered, or add a note or two. We knew what kind of a beat the drummer was going to lay down because we knew the drummer. We knew more or less how the piano player was going to play because Mike was playing piano. So we knew pretty much what to expect. The only thing we were looking for was that magic, that thing that comes together when everything is cooking.

Stoller: I used to write out some kind of road map for all the musicians. When it came to The Coasters, it took lots of preparation. Harmony was not their forte, and I used to rehearse them for weeks till they could remember who had which note.

Were the musicians available for this kind of extended rehearsal?

Stoller: No, no. We never rehearsed the musicians, only the vocal group. The musicians came to the studio where we had these little charts written out for them so that they wouldn't have to start learning from scratch what the bass pattern was, whether we had a four- or eight-bar intro, or where the break chorus came.

Source: Ted Fox, *In the Groove: The People Behind the Music* (New York: St. Martin's Press, 1986), pp. 157–61, 163–67.

---

1 "Searchin'" is from a 1957 session with The Coasters. It resulted in the group's first hit on the pop singles chart.

4

"Leer-ics"

A Warning to the Music Business

ABEL GREEN

There is little doubt that one of the appeals of R&B in the early 1950s was its sometimes coarse and earthy depiction of sexuality, often approached through cleverly deployed slang. While young fans may have flocked to these songs, many detractors within the industry saw R&B "leer-ics" as a dangerous and intrusive presence. *Variety*'s ominously titled "A Warning to the Music Business," issued under the name of editor-in-chief Abel Green, asks that the music business claim a self-policing responsibility for its products. The editorial is purposefully vague, mentioning neither any specific songs nor artists, nor even R&B itself. But for any reader who had been following other articles and letters within the magazine's pages, it was clear that the perceived threat extended to renegade disc jockeys, payola, the influence of BMI, and, tacitly, R&B's obvious racial dimension. *Variety*'s "Warning" proved to be wildly influential, as wire services picked up the editorial, turning it into a national news item. It was followed by two further *Variety* editorials that helped set the stage for the controversies that would accompany rock 'n' roll's explosion the following year in 1956.[1]

Music "leer-ics" are touching new lows and if the fast-buck songsmiths and musicmakers are incapable of social responsibility and self-restraint then regulation—policing, if you will—will have to come from more responsible sources. Meaning the phonograph record manufacturers and their network daddies. These companies have a longterm stake rather than a quick turn-around role. It won't wash for them to echo the cheap cynicism of the songsmiths who justify their "leer-ic" garbage by declaring "that's what the kids want" or "that's the only thing that sells today."

What are we talking about? We're talking about "rock and roll," about "hug," and "squeeze," and kindred euphemisms which are attempting a total breakdown of all reticences about sex. In the past such material was common enough but restricted to special places and out-and-out barrel-houses. Today "leer-ics" are offered as standard popular music for general consumption, including consumption by teenagers. Our teenagers are already setting something of a record in delinquency without this raw musical idiom to smell up the environment still more.

The time is now for some serious soul-searching by the popular music industry. This is a call to the conscience of that business. Don't invite the Governmental and religious lightning that is sure to strike. Forget the filthy fast buck. Nor is it just the little music "independents" who are heedless of responsibility.

---

1 Abel Green, "Leer-ics: Part II," *Variety*, March 2, 1955, p. 49 and "Leer-ics: Part III," *Variety*, March 9, 1955, p. 49.

The major diskeries, with the apparently same disregard as to where the blue notes may fall, are as guilty. Guiltier, perhaps, considering the greater obligation—their maturer backgrounds—their time-honored relations with the record-buying public.

The most casual look at the current crop of "lyrics" must tell even the most naive that dirty postcards have been translated into songs. Compared to some of the language that loosely passes for song "lyrics" today, the "pool-table papa" and "jellyroll" terminology of yesteryear is polite palaver. Only difference is that this sort of lyric then was off in a corner by itself. It was the music underworld—not the mainstream.

For the music men—publishers and diskeries—to say that "that's what the kids want" and "that's the only thing that sells nowadays," is akin to condoning publication of back-fence language. Earthy dialog may belong in "art novels" but mass media have tremendous obligation. If they forget, they'll hear from authority. Seemingly that is not the case in the music business.

Before it's too late for the welfare of the industry—forgetting for the moment the welfare of young Americans—VARIETY urges a strong self-examination of the record business by its most responsible chief executive officers. A strong suspicion lingers with VARIETY that these business men are too concerned with the profit statements to take stock of what's causing some of their items to sell. Or maybe they just don't care. A suspicion has been expressed that even the network-affiliated and Hollywood-affiliated record companies brush things off with "that's the music business." This is illogical because it is morally wrong and in the long run it's wrong financially.

Today's "angles" and sharp practices in the music business are an intra-trade problem. Much of it, time-dishonored. The promulgation and propagation of a pop song, ever since there was a Tin Pan Alley, was synonymous with shrewdness, astuteness and deviousness that often bordered on racketeering in its subornation of talent, subsidy, cajolery and out-and-out bribery.

In its trade functions no trade paper, VARIETY included, wants to be accused of "blowing the whistle." But the music business is flirting with the shrill commands of an outer influence if it doesn't wake up and police itself.

This is not the first time VARIETY has spotlighted the pyramiding evils of the music business as it operates today. One of the roots is the payola. If some freak "beat" captures the kids' imagination, the boys are in there quick, wooing, romancing, cajoling the a&r men.

Here is where the responsible chief officers of the major diskeries should come in. They can continue to either blind themselves, as apparently seems to be the case, or they can compel their moral obligations to stand in the way of a little quick profit. This has an accumulative force, because their own radio outlets can limit the exploitation of this spurious stuff. Not only the commodities of their own affiliation, but others.

Some may argue that this is a proposal of "censorship." Not at all. It is a plea to ownership to assume the responsibilities of ownership and eliminate practices which will otherwise invite censorship. In short, chums, do it yourself or have it done for you. You're not going to get or have it done for you.

Source: Abel Green, "A Warning to the Music Business," *Variety*, February 23, 1955, p. 2.

5

Chuck Berry
In His Own Words

Widely acknowledged as one of the early rock 'n' roll era's most important performers and songwriters, Chuck Berry (1926–2017) blazed a path through the 1950s that paved the way for countless future rock musicians. In the excerpts that follow from his 1987 autobiography, Berry narrates in the voice of one of the many young African American musicians who were hoping to make a living off their craft at that time, only to be met with densely worded recording contracts, crooked managers, and harsh touring conditions. In the first passage Berry describes his entryway into the rock 'n' roll business in 1955 via Muddy Waters (1915–1983), and the specific circumstances surrounding the genesis and recording of "Maybellene," his first hit single for Chicago's famed Chess Records. "Maybellene," which, as Berry explains, was inspired by the traditional folk song "Ida Red,"[1] was his first effort to "sing country-western," and the first of many songs that he intended as integrationist endeavors, deliberate attempts to appeal to rock 'n' roll's broad, diverse youth community. Along those lines, Berry, in his typically inventive language, concludes his autobiography by invoking the idealized image of a United States where "all races and nationalities" have merged into one "Americanese" people.

It was a hot Friday typical of summer in the Gateway City. It was only May, but in Missouri the month doesn't matter. When it decides to be hot it just does it. Dad, Hank, and I had been disassembling an old frame bungalow in the suburbs of St. Louis but I'd asked for this day off because I had an urge to hit the road again in the new station wagon.

Ralph Burris, my high-school classmate and long-time friend, had agreed to take off with me to visit his mother in Chicago. We arrived at sundown in the equally hot but windy city and drove directly to Ralph's mother's home to pay our respects, ate a well-prepared supper, then hit the streets to paint Chicago's Southside. Starting on 47th Street at Calumet, we hit most of the blues joints, bar after bar, spending time only in those that had live music.

I saw Howlin' Wolf and Elmore James for the first time on 47th Street, a tour I'll never lose memory of. I didn't want to leave the place where Elmore James was performing but Ralph had seen these artists before and insisted that we try other places. At the Palladium on Wabash Avenue we looked up and found the marquee glowing with MUDDY WATERS TONIGHT. Ralph gave me the lead as we ran up the stairs to the club, knowing I sang Muddy's songs and that he was my favorite blues singer. We paid our fifty-cents admission and scrimmaged forward to the bandstand, where in true living color I saw Muddy Waters.

---

1 In his autobiography, Berry refers to the song as both "Ida Red" and "Ida May."

He was playing "Mo Jo Working" at that moment and was closing the last set of the night. Once he'd finished, Ralph boldly called out from among the many people trying to get Muddy's autograph and created the opportunity for me to speak with my idol. It was the feeling I suppose one would get from having a word with the president or the pope. I quickly told him of my admiration for his compositions and asked him who I could see about making a record. Other fans of Muddy's were scuffling for a chance to just say hi to him, yet he chose to answer my question.

Those very famous words were, "Yeah, see Leonard Chess. Yeah, Chess Records over on Forty-seventh and Cottage." Muddy was the godfather of blues. He was perhaps the greatest inspiration in the launching of my career. I was a disciple in worship of a lord who had just granted me a lead that led to a never-ending love for music. It was truly the beginning as I continued to watch his most humble compliance in attempting to appease his enthused admirers. The way he communicated with those fans was recorded in my memory, and I've tried to respond in a similar way to fans of my own.

(Somewhere, somebody wrote in their column that on the occasion when I met Muddy he allowed me to play with his band. It has always hurt me when a writer replaces the truth with fictitious dramatic statements to increase interest in his story. I was a stranger to Muddy and in no way was I about to ask my godfather if I could sit in and play. He didn't know me from Adam on that eve and Satan himself could not have tempted me to contaminate the father's fruit of the blues, as pure as he picked it. Furthermore, I had wonders about my ability as a professional musician, singer, or anything else when in the presence of someone like the great Muddy Waters.)

I had planned to drive home to St. Louis that Sunday afternoon but, with anticipations of a chance at recording, I decided to stay over in Chicago until Monday. I couldn't believe I would be making connections with the Chess Record Company after being lucky enough to speak with Muddy, too.

Monday morning early I drove over to 4720 Cottage Grove Avenue[2] to the Chess Record Company and watched from a store across the street for the first person to enter the door. After a lady entered, a man came in dressed in a business suit, so I ran across Cottage Grove to challenge my weekend dream. While I was posing just inside the office door, he looked up from scanning mail and said, "Hi, come on in," then left for a further office.

Before I started my well-rehearsed introduction, I saw a black girl receptionist (Adella, as I remember) and asked her if I could speak with Mr. Leonard Chess. I was getting more of the shivers as I glanced through the big window into the studio. She told me that the man I had followed in was himself Leonard Chess, and he reentered the outer office and beckoned me into his. He listened to my description of Muddy's advice and my plans and hopes, asking occasional questions regarding my expectations. Finally he asked if I had a tape of my band with me.

I had been taping at home on a seventy-nine-dollar, quarter-inch, reel-to-reel recorder that I'd purchased in contemplation of such an audition. I told him I was visiting from St. Louis, but could return with the tapes (which I hadn't truly made yet) whenever he could listen to them. He said he could hear them within a week and I left immediately for St. Louis. He had stood all the while I was talking to him with a look of amazement that he later told me was because of the businesslike way I'd talked to him.

After I traveled down from U.S. Highway 66, I contacted Johnnie Johnson and Ebby Hardy and began arranging rehearsals. Johnnie, Ebby, and I had been playing other people's music ever since we started at the Cosmo, but for this tape I did not want to cover other artist's tunes. Leonard Chess

---

2 Berry is slightly off. Chess Records was located at 4750 S. Cottage Grove Avenue.

had explained that it would be better for me if I had original songs. I was very glad to hear this because I had created many extra verses for other people's songs and I was eager to do an entire creation of my own. The four that I wrote may have been influenced melodically by other songs, but, believe me, the lyrics were solely my own. Before the week had ended, I brought fresh recorded tapes to the ears of the Chess brothers in Chicago.

Chess was in the heart of the Southside of Chicago amid a cultural district I knew all too well. Leonard told me he had formerly had a bar in the neighborhood as well, which accounted for his easy relations with black people. When I carried the new tape up I immediately found out from a poster on the office wall that Muddy, Little Walter, Howlin' Wolf, and Bo Diddley were recording there. In fact Bo Diddley dropped by the studio that day.

Leonard listened to my tape and when he heard one hillbilly selection I'd included called "Ida May," played back on the one-mike, one-track home recorder, it struck him most as being commercial. He couldn't believe that a country tune (he called it a "hillbilly song") could be written and sung by a black guy. He said he wanted us to record that particular song, and he scheduled a recording session for May 21, 1955, promising me a contract at that time.

I went back to St. Louis to do more carpenter work with Dad but also with a plan to cut a record with a company in Chicago. Each time I nailed a nail or sawed a board I was putting a part of a song together, preparing for the recording session to come. At the Cosmo Club I boasted of the records we were going to make soon and we took the lead in popularity over Ike Turner's band, our main rivals at the time in the East St. Louis music scene.

Muddy Waters was in the St. Louis area one night around this time and visited the Cosmopolitan Club. Enthralled to be so near one of my idols, I delegated myself to chaperone him around spots of entertainment in East St. Louis. Ike Turner was playing at the Manhattan Club and since he was my local rival for prestige I took Muddy there to show Ike how big I was and who I knew. When we got to the Manhattan Club, Muddy preceded Johnnie, Ebby, and myself up to the box office and announced, "I'm Muddy Waters." The cashier said, "A dollar fifty." Muddy just reached in his pocket and forked it out with no comment. That incident remains on my mind unto this very day. From that experience I swore never to announce myself in hopes of getting anything gratis, regardless of what height I might rise to in fame.

I took Muddy to my house that night, introduced him to Toddy, who was a devout lover of his music long before I came into her life with mine, and took a photo of him holding my guitar.[3] May his music live forever, he will always be in first place at the academy of blues, my man, "McKinley Morganfield," Muddy Waters.

Finally the day came and I drove back to Chicago with my little band, on time, as I'd promised Leonard Chess. According to the way Dad did business, I was expecting Leonard to first take me into his office and execute the recording contracts. But instead he said he wanted to get "that tune" on tape right away. So we unloaded my seven-month-new red Ford station wagon and Phil Chess took the three of us into the studio and placed us around, telling us how we should set up for the session. I could see right away that Leonard was the brains of the company because he was busy making decisions and dictating to the five or six employees there. Phil ran around making friends and seeing that everybody was jockeyed into position for the flow of productions during the day.

I was familiar with moving in and away from the microphone to project or reduce the level of my voice but was not aware that in a studio that would be done by the engineer during the song. Having as much knowledge about recording as my homemade tapes afforded me was a big help,

---

3 "Toddy" is Berry's wife, Themetta "Toddy" Suggs.

but I listened intently and learned much from the rehearsal of the tunes with Phil instructing us. I tried to act professional although I was as frightened and green as a cucumber most of the time.

The studio was about twenty feet wide and fifty feet long with one seven-foot baby-grand piano and about twelve microphones available. I had used only one for the tape I'd come to audition with and eight were used for our four-piece session. There was a stack of throw rugs, a giant slow-turning ceiling fan, and two long fluorescent lights over a linoleum tile floor. Leonard Chess was the engineer and operated the Ampex 403 quarter-inch monaural tape recorder. Through the three-by-four-foot studio control-room window we watched him, or sometimes his brother Phil, rolling the tape and instructing us with signs and hand waving to start or stop the music.

The first song we recorded was "Ida May." Leonard suggested that I should come up with a new name for the song, and on the spot I altered it to "Maybellene."

Leonard had arranged for a lyricist/musician, Willie Dixon, who'd written many of Muddy's tunes, to sit in on the session, playing a stand-up bass to fill out the sound of the music. Electric bass instruments were yet to come and Willie, stout as he was, was a sight to behold slapping his ax to the tempo of a country-western song he really seemed to have little confidence in.

Each musician had one mike, excepting the drummer, who had three. I had one for the guitar and one for my vocal, which I sat down to sing because a chair was there and I thought that was how it was supposed to be done. We struggled through the song, taking thirty-five tries before completing a track that proved satisfactory to Leonard. Several of the completions, in my opinion, were perfectly played. We all listened to the final playback and then went on to record the next song which was "Wee Wee Hours." By then it was midafternoon. Around eight-thirty that night we finished the recording session. "Maybellene," "Wee Wee Hours," "Thirty Days," and "You Can't Catch Me" were the songs completed. Leonard sent out for hamburgers and pop and we lingered an hour picnicking, an ordeal that became a ritual with Leonard bearing the tab.

It was nearly ten o'clock when we went into Leonard's office and sat down for the first time to execute the contract he'd promised. The recording contract he handed me seemed to be a standard form, having no company-name heading at the top. It was machine printed on one side of the single sheet of paper. The other paper he gave me was a publishing contract, a segment of the music business I was totally ignorant of. It was printed on a double sheet, but I didn't understand most of the terms and arrangements of publishing either. I did see the word *copyright* several times as I read through it and thus figured if it was connected with the United States government, it was legitimate and I was likely protected. I remembered when I was a child, Dad had talked about getting a patent for a perpetual-motion apparatus that he'd invented, telling us nobody could take your achievements from you when they're patented and copyrighted.

Anyway, I read it word for word. Some of the statements were beyond my knowledge of the record business, such as the "residuals from mechanical rights," the "writer and producer's percentages," and the "performance royalties and publisher fees," but I intentionally would frown at various sections to give the impression that a particular term (I actually knew nothing of) was rather unfavorable. From the white of my eyes I could detect Leonard watching my reaction closely all the while I was reading, which made me think I was being railroaded. In fact, the corner of my left eyeball was checking out his response to my reaction, yet still knowing full well I'd sign the darn thing anyway. I slowly read on, finally signing it at last. I took my single-page copy, shook hands, and bade happy farewells to what was now "my" record company, loaded up, and drove off into the night with Johnnie and Ebby to St. Louis.

As we drove home through the black night more songs were sprouting in my head. As easy as it seemed now that the session was over, another four were bound to come forth.

Back home I continued to enjoy the local action at the Cosmo Club. The immediate future looked stable enough to support the little family I'd started. Melody was approaching two years old,

Ingrid was nearing four, and I had been married nigh six years, a veteran at paying monthly bills. Toddy and I were looking forward to Ingrid being enrolled in grade school that September. I was feeling no pain, playing three nights a week at the Cosmo Club and, except for the half day I took off to go to Poro College of Cosmetology to study hairdressing, I was working with Dad during the day. Our bank account had risen to fourteen hundred dollars, with the Ford station wagon payments paid to date and the house installment note one month ahead.

Days and weeks passed with no word from anyone about the recording session. No mail or phone calls followed to reveal any results of the contract I had with the Chess Company. I sat and waited, wondering if all the time and effort was in some trash can or did it actually take a lifetime to organize these things.

Ike Turner was sizzling at the Manhattan Club in East St. Louis just a couple of blocks from the Cosmopolitan Club. By then Ike had recorded "I'm Tore Up," and it was just beginning to be heard making its air way back toward the ears of the home folks. People were asking when was our record coming out and we had nothing to answer. Albert King, another artist from the St. Louis area who sported a left-hand guitar, began climbing to the Ike and Chuck level.

Suddenly from the mouths of babes came remarks that they'd heard "Maybellene" on the radio and shortly after I picked it up while driving home from Dad's house in the station wagon. There is no way to explain how you feel when you first hear your first recording for the first time in your first new car. I told Toddy as soon as I reached home and we celebrated as you can imagine how!

Johnnie told me that while coming home from the Cosmopolitan Club one hot night he was tuning the radio for some blues and on station WGN in Chicago heard the unmistakable rhythmic bounce of "Maybellene" being played over and over. WGN was a big rock station, bringing a linked-up program by a New York disk jockey.

On July 19, a phone call came from Leonard Chess informing me to expect a visit from a Mr. Jack Hook,[4] an affiliate of his, who was bringing a contract from the Gale Booking Agency for me to sign. I picked up this mediator at the St. Louis airport, brought him home, discussed the booking-agency contract, and signed it, keeping my copy. The exciting thing in the contract was that the Gale Booking Agency was to assure me of forty thousand dollars' worth of work each year for three years!

I was feeling so good about the way things were falling in place, I began wondering if I would die in a few weeks. I couldn't believe I had the chance to earn such a sum in such a short period. Themetta and I stayed up until 4 A.M. reading over the contract for flaws and mistakes, but found none. Plus it had no obligation on my part that I felt I could not uphold. I would be earning the money if only I got to the concert, played, and sang. I knew I'd make it to them on time even if I had to hire a police escort.

So now we knew the session was processed and records made. Would they sell? What was next? When would we see them on the jukebox?

What had happened was that Leonard Chess had sent our recordings to one of his promotion affiliates, Alan Freed, a big disk jockey in New York whose program was on the network going to major cities of the U.S. It was sent to him as a test run to determine which of the four tunes got the best response.[5] "Maybellene" took priority over not only the four Chuck Berry songs, but over all the records sent from other record companies for play that week. The phone lines from Alan Freed's radio audience were jammed with repeated requests for "another spin" of "Maybellene."

---

4 Jack Hooke.

5 For his services, Chess listed Freed as one of "Maybellene"'s co-authors, guaranteeing him a slice of the song's royalties.

Alan Freed was unknown to me at that time, but I was to become a distinct disciple. Leonard released "Maybellene" as a single, with "Wee Wee Hours" on the flip side.

I showed the Gale Agency contract to my folks, who wished me well. The fulfillment of the contract, traveling and performing, would put an end to the ritual of carpenter work with Dad. During the following days, up to the last day working with Dad, people would often mention that they'd heard a song and ask if I was the "Berry" who recorded it. Rapidly "Maybellene" rose to number one on the charts and there were many phone calls from Gale and Chess telling me what to expect in the coming weeks.[6]

One such call from Leonard Chess culminated in an opportunity to go and play three thirty-minute shows with the trio on the fifth, sixth, and seventh of August 1955 at the Peacock Lounge in Atlanta, Georgia, for a total of five hundred dollars. I swallowed the opportunity, not letting on that I'd walk down to Georgia and play all week for half that bread. The Ford station wagon was loaded three days before we left and without tricks, treats, or trouble, I pulled my red wagon up in front of the Royal Peacock Lounge. The marquee on the front of the building blazed with names from the show, reading, the FOUR FELLOWS, MISS WIGGLES, and CHUCK BERRY. Seeing my name there reminded me that my mother had once predicted that "Maybe someday your name will be in lights."

We registered at Mr. B. B. Beaman's Savoy Hotel on Auburn Avenue, shaved, shivered, and shot over to the gig to find out when and what we were supposed to do. Evidently we were liked and enjoyed since they requested "Maybellene" six times one night, and we played it as many. When the club owner paid me the five hundred dollars, it reminded me of making the down payment on 3137 Whittier, our little home, which was the largest amount I'd handled up to then.

That was our first professional road gig and after it we returned to the Cosmo and twenty-one dollars a night. A farewell party for our little combo was held there on August 14, the eve of our departure for a week-long gig in Cleveland. The entire family, including my dad, was present. My brother Paul, without a drop in him (he doesn't drink either), made his debut singing "On Top of Old Smokey" along with me during the country-western segment of the program. It was the first time my dad had ever chosen to be in such unholy surroundings and to date, as far as I know, it was his last. Nevertheless his attitude while there would have never given light to his indifference. "When in Rome," Dad always told the children, "do as the Romans." He seemed to be happy for my prospects but I could sense he had reservations about my ability to handle the wicked world he envisioned me headed into.

Then it was on the road, going to Cleveland and Gleason's Bar in the little red wagon. The bar was a jazz hangout and I thought we didn't go over too well, particularly with "Maybellene." At Gleason's Bar I received telegrams from the Gale Agency telling us to continue on around the lake to Vermilion and Youngstown, Ohio; Lynn and Roxbury, Massachusetts; and to Linden, New Jersey, doing two shows in each city, with the exception of Youngstown, where three nights were booked. We did it in great spirit, learning as we went how to manage the traveling.

A big entry, near to four hundred pounds, a friend of Jack Hook's named Teddy Roag, came into my ventures on this swing.[7] Teddy was organized by Jack Hook to arrange my schedules and assist my trio while traveling up the New England coast. The tour itself was a great education for me as to what a "concert" was, what a box office was actually for, and how to register into a hotel. I was unaccustomed to hotels, having never up to then experienced any out-of-town sleeping

---

6 "Maybellene" was No. 1 on the R&B chart. It reached No. 5 on the pop singles chart.

7 Teddy Roag is Chuck Berry's poetic pseudonym for his manager Teddy Reig (1918–1984), who is characterized in the book by his corrupt "rogue" like tendencies.

accommodations other than rooming houses. I also learned about percentages of gross-attendance income. My nightly fee then was 60 percent of the gross box-office intake with a minimum guarantee of $150. Teddy Roag, my acting manager, somehow always managed to see to it that the attendance was just at the brink of entering the 60 percent range, never into it.

I was a fair wizard at math in high school and could eyeball the dance houses to estimate attendance. Most nights I determined that there was enough attendance to carry into percentages, but when I mentioned this once I was told I'd have to prove it, so I didn't question anymore. I couldn't think of any way to support my judgment or monitor the attendance. The figures that Roag would return with, after sometimes over an hour of counting the gross paid attendance, would reach me on a handwritten statement and would usually show us just a few dollars under the amount that would have started my overage payable. Teddy had a habit of snapping his fingers and saying, "Damn, we almost made it."

Before I came to realize Teddy's tactics, he had been for weeks advising me that I needed his expert management and that he was available for the job. I should have known the big beer-bellied bully did not like rock 'n' roll enough to be traveling along without any compensation but the prospect of the job he hoped to get. I'd heard of managers for Marian Anderson and Joe Louis and thought having one was the professional thing to do, so I agreed and accepted him, signing him as my manager while still wondering about his integrity. Almost immediately after I signed him he stopped showing up at most concerts except when we'd be playing near where he lived.

After a concert in Lynn, Massachusetts, in 1955, he handed me a hundred-dollar bill, but without the usual written statement, saying, "How's that?" That night the crowd had to number over twelve hundred and the admission was $1.50 so it must have grossed at least $1,500 excluding freebies. We should have earned near to $750 aside from the guarantee of $150, but I could not have proved it. I pondered dearly how to overcome being vulnerable to such swindles. Since I had no other way to know the attendance I had to trust the promoters and my manager, who all knew each other very well.

*   *   *

Forgive me for using my own word, *hospitaboo*, which is meant to represent *hospitality* with *taboo* or in other words *how do you do but don't-you-dare*. I feel that the greatest hospitality on the entire globe is found in the Southland of the United States. There is no other place, at least that I've been, where friendliness and consideration for others are perpetuated more. But be that as it may, when it comes to matters of race the type of hospitality practiced by most southern people seems to fit the compound word I've improvised.

Remember that my view, the only true view I can see with, is through the black eyes that I have. As I toured far from St. Louis, I saw and I wondered, then reasoned and felt, then realized and believed. But I don't know any truths about racial matters but what I have seen.

Two buses were parked at the stage door of the Apollo when we closed the two-week engagement on September 16, 1955. Teddy Roag had given me a list of cities that the Gale Booking Agency had lined up for me as part of a tour that included Arthur Prysock; the Four Fellows; the Spaniels; the Cleftones; a comedian, Clay Tyson; Queenie Owens; an upside-down dancer known as Miss Wiggles; my group; and Buddy Johnson and his orchestra, featuring Ella Johnson. We all felt pretty much at home since all of the acts were black and there weren't likely to be any internal racial problems.

My heart sang when I viewed the list because I had been to only a couple of the cities listed. The instructions informed us that a bus ride plus hotel reservations would be provided, which left me only to ride, get dressed, sing, and peep then eat, meet fans, hide and sleep. It was for sure going to be exciting to be on the road with all of these recording stars who, just a month before, I had only heard sing on radio and records. Now I was going to be practically living with them.

At 3:30 A.M. the buses rolled across the George Washington Bridge and down the New Jersey Turnpike. Buddy's eighteen-piece orchestra, the roadies, the valets, and the equipment occupied the second bus and I was with the rest of the artists on the leading bus. I saw things going on among them that I had never known about a month before. I saw my first live gambling, a bold and blazing crap game in the aisle of the bus that carried on until dawn. When I woke up at the announcement of a breakfast stop, only three were left in the game and maybe twenty thousand dollars had changed hands in the aisle.

On we rode, snacking, arguing, singing, and still sleeping half the day until we reached the auditorium in Youngstown, Ohio, where the tour was to begin. We went directly to a hotel where I learned fast to rush to be first checking in to get the better rooms of those reserved collectively. At eight o'clock that evening the Buddy Johnson Show opened the Nu Elms Ballroom in Youngstown.

Many of the places we played on that first tour did not have enough dressing rooms or toilets for such a large show. Things were just getting started with rock 'n' roll and a lot of places weren't prepared for shows on a grand scale. This ballroom was one such and we all had to share the few dressing rooms. The fans were not restricted from freely coming backstage, visiting the artists, and whatnot. Whatnots were real nice then, since the management knew not what would be going on backstage. I thought the older artists knew all the fans who would come backstage and chat with them so I would leave the room when chats became whisperingly soft.

All first shows are bummers as far as everybody getting tight with the orchestra and getting coordinated with the time schedule of the show itself. Considering all, the Youngstown date went well with a near full house in attendance. After the final act of the show that night, everybody who knew the ropes let their hair down and the good times rolled in the hotel rooms.

I found that the custom of travel was to lay over on a night after we had traveled a long way that day. The following noon took us south to the Municipal Auditorium in Charleston, West Virginia; then we traveled on to the Skating Rink in Kyle, Virginia, and to the City Auditorium in Raleigh, North Carolina, where we began to bump into bits of biased behavior. The danger deferred any desire for drumming up any dilly-dally down in Dixie. Up to then I had never spent much time in the southern states, though I had constantly heard of things that occurred there from my father. Now I was traveling through the Heart of Dixie, where heeding his advice would behoove me to behave better than a Baptist bishop.

We played the Recreation Center in Kingston, North Carolina, on September 20, followed by Columbia, South Carolina, then the Duval Armory in Jacksonville, Florida. That is where southern habit hit home. My memory of how it went down remains vivid. We had to stay in a private boardinghouse and dined collectively on soul food. The conditions were good, I might add, except that they were the only legal accommodations available.

Once we got to the Duval Armory that evening, the conditions radically changed. "You boys this" and "You boys that" was the language used until an elderly stagehand started to address one of the band members with his customary term. It wasn't a nice or necessary name for a neatly dressed black guy, but then the addressee was hip to the old man's concept. After the obvious readdressing of the slip-lipped word to "ni-boy," the trombone player replied, "Yahzza, we need da platform over 'ere."

Just before they were to open the doors for the spectators, four of the maintenance guys came out and roped off the armory with white window cord. They looped and tied it to each seat down the center aisle, making it an off-limits zone that neither coloreds nor whites could tread. They didn't, we didn't, no one else didn't during the entire show although the armory was jam-packed with standing room sold as well. That six-foot-wide aisle, holding the choicest views in the place, stayed clear as a whistle.

At the close of the show, twice as many young whites as blacks rushed toward the stage, climbed on, and began socializing with us. After mumbling to ourselves the whole evening about the conditions we performed under, we overwelcomed them, extending hugs and some kisses. We knew the authorities were blazing angry with them for rushing on stage and at us for welcoming them, but they could only stand there and watch young public opinion exercise its reaction to the boundaries they were up against. Almost as if it was rehearsed they hugged, kissed, greeted, or shook a hand and filed off to the exits untouched by the helpless, amazed security.

I'd been hearing of this sort of racial problem for years from my father, except his stories were more severe. The difference that I could conceive between his stories and my observation showed that some progress had taken place in race relations.

On to Mobile, where the same attitudes prevailed. We were determined, at least I was, to bring those southerners to accept us for what we thought we were: northern artistic performers and not Yankee black lord-knows-what. When my turn came, I skipped on stage and belted out my song, "Maybellene." I put everything I had into it: a hillbilly stomp, the chicken peck, and even ad-libbed some southern country dialect.

Contrary to what I expected, I received far greater applause from the white side of the ropes than the black side, where I noticed only a chuckle or two. Okay, I thought, with my mind on getting next to my brethren and sisteren. There was truth showing up in what Leonard Chess had told me about "Wee Wee Hours," which was on the B side, selling mostly in the rhythm-and-blues market. On the other hand, "Maybellene" had hit in the pop charts, identifying the popular or the white market. When songs were so posted in the trade charts it seemed to serve as a guide to help disk jockeys and merchants direct their respective businesses. Thanks to the trade magazines, by the time any new recording reached the broadcasting or merchandising market, it had already been "Anglopinionated," my own word for being "white worthy" of broadcasting.

Determined to retaliate, I bowed longer to the bored black side than I lingered on the left, let my fingers crawl into the introduction, and poured out the pleading guitar passage of "Wee Wee Hours," hoping to pierce the perfect passion of my people. It seemed to be going homeward as I continued to pour on the profound pleadings. I began hearing the "uhmms" and "awws" as I approached the kissing climax and how beautifully the black side began to moan. I knew I was getting next to them. It was just like we were all then boarding da' ol' ribba-boat, about to float into a land of flawless freedom.

The palms of black and white were burning as the producer signaled me to exit. My act was scheduled for only two songs and my ad-libbing during "Wee Wee Hours" had carried me overtime, which was frowned at in such a regulated show. But I was thrilled and dragged my feet walking off stage as the applause simmered.

That night when the concert ended, it seemed the whole police force had surrounded our bus. Over a dozen patrolmen were lined up forming a path for the show people to walk through. The isolation ignited ill feelings in the fans as well as the artists, who vented their feelings by ridiculing the conditions in disguised voices. My father's stories came to mind as I watched the officers taking the abuse and I thought, do in Rome as the Romans do. Fear that the police would reciprocate led me to board the bus. As it turned out, nothing happened except bragging on the bus as we continued the tour westward.

* * *

I have been asked many times, "Where did you get the idea to write that song, Chuck?" Off hand, I wouldn't know, but I always refer to the story within the song, which usually recalls my inspiration. Or sometimes the melodic lines bring me in sync with the time and place where the tune got its origin. The embarrassing thing is that sometimes when I have been asked about a song's origin I have made up a reason that is dramatic enough to get by the question. But the origins have varied under different circumstances or with different interviewers.

"Maybellene" was my effort to sing country-western, which I had always liked. The Cosmo clubgoers didn't know any of the words to those songs, which gave me a chance to improvise and add comical lines to the lyrics. "Mountain Dew," "Jambalaya," and "Ida Red" were the favorites of the Cosmo audience, mainly because of the honky-tonk gestures I inserted while singing the songs.

"Maybellene" was written from the inspiration that grew out of the country song "Ida Red." I'd heard it sung long before when I was a teenager and thought it was rhythmic and amusing to hear. I'd sung it in the yard gatherings and parties around home when I was first learning to strum the guitar in my high-school days. Later in life, at the Cosmo Club, I added my bit to the song and still enjoyed a good response so I coined it a good one to sing.

Later when I learned, upon entering a recording contract, that original songs written by a person were copyrighted and had various rewards for the composer, I welcomed the legal arrangement of the music business. I enjoyed creating songs of my own and was pleased to learn I could have some return from the effort. When I wrote "Maybellene" I had originally titled it "Ida May," but when I took the song to Chess Records I was advised to change its title. That was simple because the rhythmic swing of the three syllables fit with many other names. The music progression itself is close to the feeling that I received when hearing the song "Ida Red," but the story in "Maybellene" is completely different.

The body of the story of "Maybellene" was composed from memories of high school and trying to get girls to ride in my 1934 V-8 Ford. I even put seat-covers in it to accommodate the girls that the football players would take riding in it while I was in class. Just to somehow explain the origin of the lyrics of "Maybellene," it could have been written from a true experience, recalling my high-school days thus:

> As I was watching from the windowsill,
> I saw pretty girls in my dream De Ville
> Riding with the guys, up and down the road
> Nothin' I wanted more'n be in that Ford
> Sittin' in class while they takin' rides
> Guys in the middle, girls on both sides
>
> Oh Pretty girl, why can't it be true
> Oh Pretty girl, that it's me with you
> You let football players do things I want to do.
>
> Girls in my dream car, door to door
> My Ford bogged down wouldn't hold no more
> Ring goes the last school bell of the day
> Hurrying outside, see 'em pullin' away
> Backseat full even sittin' on the hood
> I knew that was doing my motor good
>
> Oh Pretty girl, why can't it be true
> Oh Pretty girl, that it's me with you
> You let football players do things I want to do.
>
> The guys come back after all that fun
> Walking with the pretty girls, one by one
> My heart hangin' heavy like a ton a lead

Feelin' so down I can't raise my head
Just like swallowin' up a medicine pill
Watching them girls from the windowsill.

These lines were written just to provide an example of the true depiction of an event. This differs from the improvised writing of a song, which does not necessarily, if ever, coincide with a true story but mostly just goes along the pattern or close to the train of events. I have never, in my life, met or even known of any woman named "Maybellene." The name actually was first brought to my knowledge from a storybook, when I was in the third grade, of animals who bore names. Along with Tom the cat and Donald the duck, there was Maybellene the cow. Not offending anybody, I thought, I named my girl character after a cow.[8] In fact, the girl was to be two-timing, so it would have been worse if I had used a popular name.

Source: Chuck Berry, *Chuck Berry: The Autobiography* (New York: Harmony, 1987), pp. 97–109, 121–26, 141, 143–45.

---

8 Berry's pianist, Johnnie Johnson, alternately claimed that they took the name Maybellene from a Maybelline mascara box that was in the Chess studio, altering the spelling to avoid any copyright infringement.

6

Elvis Presley and "The Craze"

JOHN CROSBY

When Elvis Presley (1935–1977) rocketed into the national spotlight in 1956 on the wings of the rock 'n' roll phenomenon, his popularity and notoriety were aided in no small part by his numerous television appearances. Presley performed with his group six times on the Dorsey Brothers' CBS Stage Show between January and March, helping to send his first RCA single, "Heartbreak Hotel," to the top of the charts. But it was not until Presley's June 5 appearance on NBC's Milton Berle show that the young singer from Memphis drew the ire of incredulous and indignant television critics. Abandoning his guitar for the first time and engaging in a series of exaggerated motions and dance steps, Presley playfully gyrated his way through a burlesque version of "Hound Dog" that the band had worked up during a brief stint playing in Las Vegas. The reaction came swift from influential critics like John Crosby of the *New York Herald Tribune*, who bemoaned both the faddish appeal of Presley's music as well as the negative effects that his suggestive bodily movements were having on a nation of impressionable teenagers. Critics have voiced similar concerns throughout other eras of American history. From the ragtime and close-contact "animal dances" of the 1910s to the "freak dancing" and "twerking" of recent decades, youth dance crazes have long served as the very center of indecency debates. At their roots, all of these instances have arisen as responses to the importation of African American musical forms and dances into white society.

One thing about Elvis Presley, the convulsive shouter of rock 'n' roll songs—if that's what they are: this may be the end of rock 'n' fall and just conceivably a return to musical sanity. I mean where do you go from Elvis Presley?

The best description of Presley's performance on the Milton Berle show came from the chairman of the music department of Bryant High School, Harry A. Feldman, who wrote Berle: "The guest performer, Elvis Presley, presented a demonstration which was in execrable taste, bordering on obscenity. The gyrations of this young man were such an assault to the senses as to repel even the most tolerant observer.

"When television entrepreneurs present such performers to millions of viewers and pronounce them great, when such deplorable taste is displayed in the presentation of primitive, shoddy and offensive material, one begins to understand the present day attitude of our youth. We in the classroom can do very little to offset the force and impact of these displays in our efforts to stem the tide toward a cultural debacle."

About the only guy who ever summed up Elvis "The Pelvis" any better than that was the California policeman who, after watching him writhe around a stage, commented: "If he did that on the street, we'd arrest him."

The last appearance of this unspeakably untalented and vulgar young entertainer brought forth such a storm of complaints both from press and public that I imagine any entertainer would hesitate to try him again on television. Even gentle old Ben Gross of "The Daily News" of New York blew his top over this one. I doubt that in the thirty odd years he's been writing that column Ben has ever gotten quite so angry.

But, as I say, where do you go from Elvis, short of open obscenity which is against the law? Popular music has been in a tailspin for years now and I have hopes that with Presley it has touched bottom and will just have to start getting better.

Where did the degeneration of popular music start? You'd probably get a dozen different answers from a dozen different people. My own theory is that it started just before the war when the radio networks battled ASCAP over the price they were asked to pay for the use of songs. ASCAP pulled its music off the air and, since every composer of note was a member, music on the air consisted either of stuff in the public domain or perfectly dreadful new music.

Everyone and his Aunt Agatha thinks he can write songs and during that deplorable period, they all trotted them out. Songs that ordinarily would not have got past the receptionist at any reputable music publishers were not only published but played on the air. The public, particularly the teen-age public, got a taste for bad music that it hasn't lost to this day. The good composers—Irving Berlin, Rodgers and Hammerstein and the like—had their songs forced off the air and with a few exceptions their songs are still off it.

I am heartened by the fact that television is beginning to make fun of this absurdity. The other night "The Hit Parade" did an unavoidable version of "Heartbreak Hotel"—after all, it was *on* the hit parade—with all the singers dressed as Charles Addams monstrosities.

That same evening Goodman Ace on the Perry Como show wrote a very nice piece for his announcer. He enunciated a rock 'n' roll lyric—than which there is nothing more inane—without benefit of music (if that's what it is) in the style of a commencement address. It went something like this.

> "Digga boom"
> "Digga boom."
> "Digga"
> "Boom."

And Bob Hope came out with a blistering little parody on hillbilly music which I found very entertaining. If there's anything that will knock this craze into oblivion, it's laughter—and the laughter has started.

Source: John Crosby, "The Craze," *New York Herald Tribune*, June 18, 1956, Section Two, p. 1.

7

"Elvis Defends Low-Down Style"

KAYS GARY

Elvis Presley weathered a tremendous storm of criticism in the immediate wake of his controversial June 5, 1956, appearance on the Milton Berle television show. As such, it was perhaps to be expected that the singer would eventually defend himself in the press. That moment finally occurred three weeks after the Berle show when Presley, who was on tour in Charlotte, North Carolina, opened up in an interview conducted with the local newspaper. To the charges of obscenity that John Crosby of the *New York Herald Tribune* and others had thrown at him, Presley responded by calling attention to the double standard that allowed the sexual objectification of actress Debra Paget, who had been on the Berle show as well, to pass without comment. As to the music itself, Presley acknowledged his debt to the blues and musicians like Arthur "Big Boy" Crudup (1905–1974), establishing a mark of authenticity that doubtless held little sway with his critics. On a different note, Presley also expressed his interest in the ballad style of Eddie Fisher and Perry Como, a path that he would pursue on his very next hit, the romantic title song to his 1956 film debut, *Love Me Tender*.

Elvis Presley is a worried man. Some, that is, for a man with four Cadillacs and a $40,000 weekly pay check. Critics are saying bad things about him. It has been especially rough during the past three weeks. And that is why he bucked his manager's orders to stay away from newsmen in Charlotte Tuesday until showtime. That is why he refused to stay in the seclusion of his hotel room. At 4:10 he couldn't stand it any longer, and with "Cousin Junior" left the room.[1]

He walked quickly to a restaurant a few doors away for a barbecue, flirtation with a few women and a 30-minute round of pool next door.

"Sure I'll talk. Sit down. Most of you guys, though, been writin' bad things about me, man!"

His knees bounced while he sat. His hands drummed a tattoo on the table top. Eyes, under long lashes, darted from booth to booth, firing rapid winks at the girls who stared at him. "Hi ya, baby," he breathed. And she flopped back in the booth looking like she'd been poleaxed.

"This [John] Crosby guy, whoever he is, he says I'm obscene on the Berle show. Nasty. What does he know?"

"Did you see the show? This Debra Paget is on the same show. She wore a tight thing with feathers on the behind where they wiggle most. And I never saw anything like it. Sex? Man, she bumped and pooshed out all over the place. I'm like Little Boy Blue. And who do they say is obscene? Me!"

"It's because I make more money than Debra. Them critics don't like to see nobody win doing any kind of music they don't know nothin' about."

---

1 "Cousin Junior" is Presley's cousin, Junior Smith, who was accompanying him on the trip.

And he started to eat. The waitress brought his coffee. Elvis reached down and fingered the lace on her slip.

"Aren't you the one?"

"I'm the one, baby!"

Presley says he does what he does because this is what is making money. And it is music that was around before he was born.

"The colored folks been singing it and playing it just like I'm doin' now, man, for more years than I know. They played it like that in the shanties and in their juke joints, and nobody paid it no mind 'til I goosed it up. I got it from them. Down in Tupelo, Mississippi, I used to hear old Arthur Crudup bang his box the way I do now, and I said if I ever got to the place where I could feel all old Arthur felt, I'd be a music man like nobody ever saw."

Yep, some of the music is low-down.

"But, not like Crosby means. There is low-down people and high-up people, but all of them get the kind of feeling this rock 'n' roll music tells about."

Elvis says he doesn't know how long rock and roll will last.

"When it's gone, I'll switch to something else. I like to sing ballads the way Eddie Fisher does and the way Perry Como does. But the way I'm singing now is what makes the money. Would you change if you was me?"

Investments? "I haven't got to the place for investments. I put it in the bank, man, because I don't know how long it will last." How about the Cadillacs? "Yeah, that's right, I got me four Cadillacs. I keep two at home and two with me. One pink and one white." He never reads his fan mail. "I got nine secretaries in Madison, Tenn., to do that. If I meet somebody on the road I want to keep knowing I give 'em my home address."

Little Rosie Tatsis walked up to the booth and held out a trembling hand. Elvis gave her an autograph. "Look, I'm shaking all over," she tittered. And the grown-up girls in the next booth swapped long, searching looks.

Elvis fingered the collar of his shirt, opened half-way down his chest.

"Some people like me. There's more people than critics." The people who like him, he said, include Eddie Fisher, Como, Liberace, Kate Smith, Bob Hope and Guy Lombardo. And there are more. Lots more.

"When I sang hymns back home with Mom and Pop, I stood still and I looked like you feel when you sing a hymn. When I sing this rock 'n' roll, my eyes won't stay open and my legs won't stand still. I don't care what they say, it ain't nasty."

Source: Kays Gary, "Elvis Defends Low-Down Style," *The Charlotte Observer*, June 27, 1956, p. 1B.

8

"Experts Propose Study of 'Craze'"

Milton Bracker

Among the public events that brought widespread notoriety to rock 'n' roll were Alan Freed's stage shows. When more than 15,000 teenagers descended upon midtown Manhattan on February 22, 1957, to attend Freed's all-day Washington's Birthday extravaganza at the Paramount Theatre, there was little doubt that the sizable crowds would draw the media's attention. As the day's events unfolded and reports surfaced of unruly youth, damaged storefront property, and the efforts of police to control the crowd, Freed's spectacle mushroomed into a full-blown sensationalized story. During the mid-1950s newspapers routinely trotted out "stylized and stereotypical" depictions of these events, bolstered by the pronouncements of authority figures and diagnoses of "socially accredited experts"—all of which fed a growing "moral panic" among parents.[1] For their own coverage of the Paramount show and rock 'n' roll "craze," the *New York Times* called on the "expert" opinion of Doctor Joost A. M. Meerloo, a Columbia University instructor of psychiatry and author of books on mass delusion and totalitarian brainwashing.[2] Given Meerloo's interests, it comes as little surprise that he characterizes rock 'n' roll's effects on youth in terms of a contagious disease, drug addiction, Fascist mind control, and social depersonalization. As reports of rock 'n' roll riots continued to proliferate in the media, such portrayals became more and more common.

Psychologists suggested yesterday that while the rock 'n' roll craze seemed to be related to rhythmic behavior patterns as old as the Middle Ages, it required full study as a current phenomenon.

One educational psychologist asserted that what happened in and around the Paramount Theatre yesterday struck him as "very much like the medieval type of spontaneous lunacy where one person goes off and lots of other persons go off with him."

A psychopathologist, attending a meeting of the American Psychopathological Association at the Park Sheraton Hotel feared that this was just a guess.

Others present noted that a study by Dr. Reginald Lourie of Children's Hospital, Washington indicated in 1949 that 10 to 20 per cent of all children did "some act like rocking or rolling." The study went into detail on the stimulating effects of an intensified musical beat.

Meanwhile, a parallel between rock 'n' roll and St. Vitus Dance has been drawn by Dr. Joost A. M. Meerloo, associate in psychiatry at Columbia University in a study just completed for publication.

---

1 Stanley Cohen, *Folk Devils and Moral Panics: The Creation of the Mods and Rockers* 3rd Edition (London and New York: Routledge, 2002), p. 1.

2 See specifically *Delusion and Mass-Delusion* (New York: Nervous and Mental Disease Monographs, 1949) and *The Rape of the Mind: The Psychology of Thought Control, Menticide, and Brainwashing* (Cleveland: World Publishing Company, 1956). Meerloo would go on to publish his thoughts on dance and rock 'n' roll in *The Dance, from Ritual to Rock and Roll—Ballet to Ballroom* (Philadelphia: Chilton Co., 1960).

Dr. Meerloo described the "contagious epidemic of dance fury" that "swept Germany and spread to all of Europe" toward the end of the fourteenth century. It was called both St. Vitus Dance (or Chorea Major), he continued, with its victims breaking into dancing and being unable to stop. The same activity in Italy, he noted was referred to as Tarantism and popularly related to a toxic bite by the hairy spider called tarantula.

"The Children's Crusades and the tale of the Pied Piper of Hamelin" Dr. Meerloo went on "remind us of these seductive, contagious dance furies."

Dr. Meerloo described his first view of rock 'n' roll this way: Young people were moved by a juke box to dance themselves "more and more into a prehistoric rhythmic trance until it had gone far beyond all the accepted versions of human dancing."

Sweeping the country and even the world, the craze "demonstrated the violent mayhem long repressed everywhere on earth," he asserted.

He also saw possible effects in political terms: "Why are rhythmical sounds and motions so especially contagious? A rhythmical call to the crowd easily foments mass ecstasy: 'Duce! Duce! Duce!' The call repeats itself into the infinite and liberates the mind of all reasonable inhibitions ... as in drug addiction, a thousand years of civilization fall away in a moment."

Dr. Meerloo predicted that the craze would pass "as have all paroxysms of exciting music." But he said that the psychic phenomenon was important and dangerous. He concluded in this way: "Rock 'n' roll is a sign of depersonalization of the individual, of ecstatic veneration of mental decline and passivity.

"If we cannot stem the tide with its waves of rhythmic narcosis and of future waves of vicarious craze, we are preparing our own downfall in the midst of pandemic funeral dances.

"The dance craze is the infantile rage and outlet of our actual world. In this craze the suggestion of deprivation and dissatisfaction of deprivation and dissatisfaction is stimulated and advertised day by day. In their automatic need for more and more, people are getting less and less."

"The awareness of this tragic contradiction in our epoch," Dr. Meerloo said, "must bring us back to a new assessment of what value and responsibility are."

Source: Milton Bracker, "Experts Propose Study of 'Craze'," *New York Times*, February 23, 1957, p. 12.

9

Earl Palmer and the Heartbeat of Rock 'n' Roll

TONY SCHERMAN

The 1950s rock 'n' roll sound emerged from a variety of sources, among them the integral contributions of such studio musicians as New Orleans drummer Earl Palmer (1924–2008). In the passages excerpted here from Tony Scherman's collaborative biography, *Backbeat*, Palmer recalls his time playing with Dave Bartholomew (born 1920) and Little Richard (born Richard Penniman, 1932). Bartholomew was an important New Orleans songwriter, producer and bandleader whose ensembles were among the first to navigate the transition from jazz to rhythm and blues. As Palmer reminds us, the majority of jazz musicians in these bands, who were highly sought after for studio sessions, did not come to rock 'n' roll naturally. It was most of all commercial considerations, as well as their encounters and musical interactions in the studio with dynamic young performers such as Little Richard, that helped shape the driving rhythms that would come to define the rock 'n' roll big beat. While Palmer discusses Richard's sexuality directly (Richard had been a female impersonator and drag queen at the prominent New Orleans club the Dew Drop Inn), it is important to remember that Richard's gay identity was not a matter of public record in the 1950s; rather, it was what could be called an "open secret."[1] Not until decades later, following the societal advances of gay liberation, would popular musicians from the 1950s such as Little Richard openly declare their gay sexuality.

Dave Bartholomew was just a guy with a band that wasn't really doing anything, but musicians considered it the best band in New Orleans. Dave came from Edgard, out in the country. His folks had a little money, they were fancy blacks for those days; some were doctors and stuff.

My Uncle Dave Oxley was Dave Bartholomew's drummer, so when Bartholomew tried to hire me I said, "I can't do that, my Uncle Dave's in the band."

"No he ain't, I just fired him."

I called Uncle Dave. He said, "Go ahead on, you go ahead on, I ain't never working for the sumbitch again." My Uncle Dave was a big, big man that didn't take shit off no one. Dave Bartholomew could get mean sometime and I guess he'd went over the line with Uncle Dave.

---

1 Film critic and historian David Ehrenstein has written about the "open secret" as it pertains to movie stars in his influential study *Open Secret: Gay Hollywood 1928–1988* (New York: William Morrow, 1998). For more on Little Richard's background in New Orleans's gay black culture, see Marybeth Hamilton, "Sexual Politics and African-American Music; Or, Placing Little Richard in History," *History Workshop Journal*, 46 (1998): 160–76.

Dave Bartholomew was a hell of a trumpet player. I called him Leather Lungs. Remember that growling sound Earl Bostic got on alto? Dave played that way. They overblew the note, man, got a growl out of the horn. Dave was just strong, Powerful. But he was mainly a good showman, never ashamed of clowning. He had an awful lot of personality, hustled his ass off, and was a sumbitch that didn't take no for an answer.

I'd bought my first drums from Harold Dejan, I think he'd bought them from Big Foot Bill Phillips. Whatever I paid I'm sure was more than what Harold gave Big Bill. It was a big white set with a nude woman and a twenty-five-watt bulb inside. Horrible set, man. The cymbals sounded like garbage-can covers. When Dave hired me I went down to Morris Music Shop on Rampart Street to get some new cymbals. I didn't know nothing about cymbals. I said, "Give me those." I thought they were great because they were brand-new and shiny. Dave said, "If you don't get out of here with those, those—go get some cymbals, man!" I borrowed some from Placide Adams, and Dave said, "That's better." There was a lot of talk about them cymbals. New Orleans people— always making more out of something than it is. Do something dumb and they'll make it the dumbest thing they saw in their life.

But by the time you got in Dave's band, you knew you were a musician. Mr. Clarence Hall, Joe Harris, Meyer Kennedy was on saxophones, and later Red Tyler. Frank Fields on bass. Fred Land, "Pilou," on piano, then Salvador Doucette. Ernest McLean on guitar. Theard Johnson sang but Dave did more vocals than anyone. I sang, too—hell yeah! I'd sing a song like "Sunday Kind of Love," "Portrait of Jenny," ballads, tunes that had changes Theard couldn't hear. Theard sang your big black male vocalist songs, the Billy Eckstine, Roy Hamilton-type songs. Later on Tommy Ridgley replaced him.

*   *   *

Dave kept that band very commercial. He didn't want no bebop rhythm section, the drummer dropping bombs—people were dancing out there. Our satisfaction came from our arrangements— we voiced the horns as modern as we could. I'd sneak in a bomb and Dave would flash me a dirty look and say, "Uh-uh, Chief." I knew I was doing wrong, but I was bending him.

Tyler and McLean and I always snuck in a little bebop. We was all trying to play bebop, playing it the best we could. The hell bebop wasn't a mass movement! Maybe not as popular as rock and roll, because it was too musical for the common lay ear. But young musicians all over the country was getting into bebop. I'm talking about black kids mostly—white kids' families didn't want them playing that nigger music. Bebop was nigger jazz.

I made much more of a name in the other music, but ask yourself: If I was one of the beginners of rhythm and blues, what was I playing before? I'm a jazz drummer. Jazz is all anybody played until we started making those records. The backbeat came about because the public wasn't buying jazz, so we put something in that was simpler and that's what made the difference.

*   *   *

The first time I felt like a page was being turned was Little Richard. I hadn't heard anything like this before. He went into that *ding-ding-ding-ding* at the piano and I thought, "This sumbitch is wild!"

Richard wasn't a star when he met us but I *thought* he was. He walked into J&M like he was coming offstage: that thick, thick powder makeup and the eye liner and the lipstick and the hair everywhere in big, big waves.[2] Walked in there like something you'd never seen. And meeting him all them times since, I still get the same feeling.

---

2 J&M is the New Orleans recording studio where Palmer accompanied such artists as Fats Domino and Little Richard.

I don't remember exactly what I said; something like, "What the fuck is this?" Not who, *what.* "Gus," I said to Tyler, "what the fuck is this?"

And Red said, "Wow! Go on in there, child!" That was a New Orleans term—you'd put your hand on your hip, stick out your little finger and bend it a little. It meant, "He's round the bend, this is a fag." But Richard was so infectious and so unhiding with his flamboyancy, he sucked us right in. We got laughing with him instead of at him. I never thought Richard was crazy, never thought he didn't know exactly what he was doing. I just thought, "What the fuck is this?"

I'd go anywhere with Richard now, but at that time everybody was a little concerned about being seen with somebody that looked and acted so gay. He didn't need us anyway, he had his own entourage. Young black guys, all nice-looking younger dudes. We'd be joking: "Which of them's gonna fuck him tonight?" Richard liked to record right after a show, when he was wired. Came in the studio with a briefcase full of bills and set it up on the piano. I remember Lee Allen dipping his fingers in it and pulling bills out and laughing. Richard looked at Lee and say, "Lee, will you get *out* of that bag!" I said, "Play your cards right, Lee, and you could walk away with the whole bag," and Richard said, "Shut up, Earl!"

Dave didn't produce any of Richard's sessions, Bumps Blackwell did, and I usually led the band. Bumps's job was not very difficult. Richard always knew just what he wanted to do, and we knew how to do it. Bumps had kind of a slick L.A.-cat attitude in the beginning. We cut that real short, curbed it right away.

Bumps and Richard argued all the time, which we attributed to the fact that Richard was a temperamental gay dude and Bumps was kind of overbearing. Bumps was afraid of Art Rupe, too.[3] "Pappy," him and Richard called Rupe. "I don't know how Pappy's going to like this." That was Bumps. "*Fuck* Pappy." That would be Richard.

What I remember about those sessions is how physical they were. You got to remember how Richard played—can you imagine matching that? I'll tell you, the only reason I started playing what they come to call a rock-and-roll beat came from trying to match Richard's right hand. *Ding-ding-ding-ding!* Most everything I had done before was a shuffle or slow triplets. Fats Domino's early things were shuffles. Smiley Lewis's things were shuffles. But Little Richard moved from a shuffle to that straight eighth-note feeling. I don't know who played that way first, Richard or Chuck Berry. Even if Chuck Berry played straight eights on guitar, his band still played a shuffle behind him. But with Richard pounding the piano with all ten fingers, you couldn't so very well go against that. I did at first—on "Tutti Frutti" you can hear me playing a shuffle. Listening to it now, it's easy to hear I should have been playing that rock beat.

Richard's music was exciting as a sumbitch. I'm not talking about the quality of it. It wasn't quality music. It wasn't no chords, it was just blues. "Slippin' and Slidin'" sounded like "Good Golly Miss Molly" and they both sounded like "Lucille." It was exciting because he was exciting. Richard is one of the few people I've ever recorded with that was just as exciting to watch in the studio as he was in performance. He was just that kind of personality, on edge all the time, and full of energy. But I never remember him angry with anyone. He was a sweet-tempered guy. Still is. Whenever I'm around that way, I stop at the Continental Hotel where he lives, go up and see him, sit down and talk a while. Always come away with a pocketful of little Bible booklets.

Source: Tony Scherman, *Backbeat: The Earl Palmer Story* (New York: Da Capo Press, 2000), pp. 73–74, 74–75, 89–91.

---

3 Rupe was the owner of the noted Los Angeles-based independent label Specialty Records, which released all of Little Richard's singles between 1955 and 1957, before the singer left rock 'n' roll for the ministry.

10

The Rock 'n' Roll Audience

"But Papa, It's My Music, I Like It"

JEFF GREENFIELD

One of the ways in which the media asserted control over rock 'n' roll in the 1950s was through its depictions of the music's young audience. Often presented as a homogenous crowd, or simply a haven for delinquency, rock 'n' roll fans were rarely accorded any agency within the mainstream press. Jeff Greenfield's 1971 reminiscences of his experiences as an adolescent in New York City during the late 1950s offers a more personalized account of rock 'n' roll's impact on its young fans. Greenfield, a New York mayoral speechwriter who would later go on to a distinguished career as a political commentator, touches on a number of points. Most notably he describes the ways in which radio and live performances served to create an imagined community, unifying a disparate group of young rock 'n' roll fans, separated by class, race, and ethnicity. Much of Greenfield's article describes the important role of Alan Freed (1921–1965), the disc jockey often credited with popularizing the phrase "rock and roll." Freed's live shows at both the Brooklyn and New York Paramount Theaters routinely drew crowds of 4,000 to 5,000 teenagers (and many more who could not be admitted). The first performance that Greenfield attended, during "Washington's Birthday of 1957," was part of a ten-day marathon run of shows that attracted a total of 65,000 spectators. These shows which, as Greenfield describes, involved the destruction of property and demonstrative dancing, drew extensive media coverage and acted as lightning rods for the mounting concerns about rock 'n' roll's supposedly pernicious effects.

TERROR. Perhaps you think you can define it. It is sitting in a jet fighter cockpit, plummeting to a crash landing in a hostile country. It is losing footing on a mountain ledge in the midst of a blizzard. It is walking down a deserted city street in the dead of night, with the sudden, certain sound of footsteps behind you.

No, that is not terror. I will tell you what terror is. Terror is waiting on line at 6:30 in the morning on a school holiday in 1957 for the Brooklyn Paramount to open for Alan Freed's rock and roll revue.

You have been up since 5:30 on your first day of vacation, Christmas or Easter (Hanukkah or Passover in my set). You have staggered into the darkness, found your friend Alan (another normal, neurotic Jewish kid) and weaved your way into the subway. There you pass interminable time, speeding past unfamiliar stops, emerging into the sullen dawn in downtown Brooklyn (down-town *Brooklyn*?). There, about a block away, is the Brooklyn Paramount, a huge movie palace built to hold the thousands who do not go out to movies anymore. On the marquee are big red letters: "Ten Days Only! Alan Freed's All-Star Rock 'n' Roll Revue!"

You walk to the theater, past the shuttered luncheonettes and cheap clothing stores. There is already a knot of kids waiting on line, even though the doors will not open for 2 hours and 45 minutes. And now you will begin to learn the meaning of terror.

These people are different. They do not look the way I do. They do not talk the way I do. I do not think they were born the same way I was. All of the males are six feet, seven inches tall. The last six inches is their hair, carefully combed into a pompadour. They are lean, rangy, even scrawny (except for one who is very, very fat). They have the hard faces of the children of the working poor. They read auto specs at night, not college catalogues. They wear St. Christopher medals, white T-shirts with their cigarette packs held in the left sleeve which is rolled up to the muscles. They have muscles.

The girls are all named Fran. They have curlers in their hair and scarves tied around their heads. They chew gum. They wear jeans and sweaters, and their crucifixes bounce on their breasts, some of which are remarkable examples of stress under pressure.

The conversation is guttural, half-sentences and grunts, with innuendos and veiled hints of lubricity. "Eh, that party, eh, Fran? Remember, heh, heh? Nah, she don' remember nuthin'." Fran is giggling, blushing. There is about these people an overwhelming sense of physical force, the same sense exuded by the students of Ascension High who chased the Jews home from school every afternoon: they hit other people a lot. Every joke, every insult, every question, is followed by open-handed jabs to the face, punches on the arm, slaps which barely miss being punches. It is like watching Leo Gorcey and Huntz Hall in the Bowery Boys movies.

At this point, there is only one stark thought in my mind: what in God's name am I doing here? These people are going to kill me and steal my five-dollars and I will not be found for days. Consequently, the strategy of waiting on line at the Paramount is clear. You do not talk with your friend about your grades on the Social Studies test. You do not talk about where you are going to college. You do not engage in precocious arguments about socialism. You keep your big mouth shut.

The vow of silence makes time go slowly, so you look at the posters over the theater entrance: the pictures of the stars blown up on cardboard, the names spelled out in letters glittering from the gold and silver dust. There is Buddy Holly and the Crickets; the Cleftones, in white dinner jackets and red slacks; Jo-Ann Campbell, "the blonde bombshell" who wears high-heeled shoes and very tight skirts, and whose biggest hand comes when she turns her back to the audience.

If you talk at all, it is in grunts to the others. "Yeah, Frankie Lyman, I saw him—seen him—last year. You heard the new Fats Domino?" You wait for the doors to open, for the sanctuary of the dark theater, for the Terror to go away.

What were we waiting for, those dark mornings? The singers and their songs, yes; but there were shows that were clinkers. Alan Freed paid mediocre fees to his talent, splitting the net with his partners and himself. Sometimes he could not pull in the big names, and he was left with headliners who had recorded a single hit that everyone knew would not be repeated. No, it was something else. We waited for Alan Freed and what he was for the children of the 1950's. And waited because of something in each of us: an unspoken, undetected yearning for a sense of unity; an urge to join and celebrate this music that was ours as a community; an impulse that a decade later swept our younger brothers and sisters out of mainstream America.

Alan Freed had come out of Middle America in the mid-1950's, rising from $43-a-week obscurity in New Castle, Pa., to regional prominence in Akron, Ohio, and later Cleveland. He took music that had been played only on black radio stations and sold in black neighborhoods—race music, it was called—and played this black music for white kids.

Freed played this music with an infectious on-the-air spirit, emphasizing the heavy afterbeat by slamming a telephone book with the palm of his hand, shouting encouragement to the frenzy of a tenor saxophone, clanging a cowbell. And somewhere between Akron and Cleveland, he chose to label the sound with a term heard again and again in the bluntly sexual lyrics of rhythm and blues, in titles like "My Baby Rocks Me With a Steady Roll,"[1] or "All She Wants to Do Is Rock." He called it rock and roll. It had a good beat. You could dance to it.

The country was finding out in 1954 that Alan Freed knew what the kids wanted to hear. Rock and roll conquered young white America that year. Slowly at first, then regularly, rhythm and blues songs began selling outside the racial barriers, winning places on mainstream pop music charts. "I Understand" by the Four Tunes; "One Mint Julep" by the Clovers; "Gee" by the Crows; "Cryin' in the Chapel" by Sonny Till and the Orioles—all sold well. All were copied—"covered" is the polite music term—by white artists who imitated the distinctive arrangements note for note: a legal if shady practice, since arrangements could not be protected by copyright. But despite the imitations, the kids were often buying the original versions. Because those were the versions with the beat.

The first Alan Freed show in New York was during Christmas of 1954, at the Brooklyn Academy of Music. It grossed $150,000—an unheard-of sum for live shows. But it was nothing compared to his Labor Day show in 1955 which pulled in $254,000. Freed, now a $75,000-a-year disk jockey on WINS, had gone into partnership with the station—which may account for its indifference to his plugs over his radio show—and the 10-day affair netted $125,000. Disk jockeys all over the country began promoting rock and roll stage shows, and in New York, the seasons were marked by the Brooklyn Paramount—Christmas, Easter, Labor Day, Christmas.

Each night, sprawled on my bed on Manhattan's Upper West Side, I would listen to the world that Alan Freed created. To a 12- or 13-year-old, it was a world of unbearable sexuality and celebration; a world of citizens under 16, in a constant state of joy or sweet sorrow.

Freed would read "dedications" to the songs from faraway places with strange-sounding names: Bayside, New Dorp, Huntington, Erasmus, Riverdale.

"To John from you-know-who. I want you, but you want her. Listen to the words of this song—and go back to her."

"To Mike from Fran. Going steady for six weeks . . . and forever."

"To the kids of Miss Epstein's class. Good luck—and may our friendships never be broken."

Somewhere, somewhere there really were candy stores with juke boxes, where the kids ate Pop's hamburgers and danced after school the way they did in those Jane Withers movies. Somewhere, there were parties with close dancing (Bill Haley and the Comets cut a song called "Dim, Dim the Lights" which had more sexual implications than "I Am Curious (Yellow)"). Somewhere there were kids who spent their time with each other, touching and laughing and running around to all this music . . .

"Turn that damn thing down!"

My father has always been a fair and gentle man, but in the face of Little Richard or Fats Domino he abandoned himself to rage.

"You're going to turn your brain to mush!"

Francis of Assisi become Spiro Agnew. My adolescence is a continuing re-play: the door swinging open, the dark, furrowed brow, the flash of anger, the sullen retreat. Like a river of troubled water, rock and roll music was the boundary of a house divided.

Worse, there was a fifth column, a corner of my mind which told me: you know, of course, they're right. It is crap and your brain is turning to mush. One of the authentic scars of my life—far more vivid than a broken date or a broken zipper—is buying a rock and roll album with my

---

1 Greenfield is most likely referring to the blues standard "My Man Rocks Me (with One Steady Roll)," originally recorded in 1922 by Trixie Smith.

parents during a shopping trip to Union Square. We walked into a record store, and there it was, on Specialty Records: "Here's Little Richard." On a yellow background, a tight shot of a Negro face bathed in sweat, the beads of perspiration clearly visible, mouth wide open in a rictus of sexual joy, hair flowing endlessly from the head.

"Oh my God," my mother said.

Come on, I thought, let's just buy it and get out of here, come on . . .

"We better play it first," my father said.

The saleslady smiled indulgently. From the phonograph, ripping through the store, came the shouted opening to "Long Tall Sally": "Gonna tell Aunt Mary 'bout Uncle John! Says he got the misry but he has a lotta fun! Oh baby, who-o-ooh baby . . ."

"Jesus Christ," my father said.

I muttered something vague about "authentic gospel roots . . . tradition of Afro-American . . . folk . . ." but what I was saying inside was something else: look, it's my music, I like it, and you're not supposed to listen to it anyway.

And that, after all, is what I was doing on line outside the Brooklyn Paramount on a chilly dawn, surrounded by six-foot, seven-inch hoodlums who were going to kill me. It was a refuge from ridicule, a liberated zone where everyone else liked the same crap I did. In those days before the Beatles, before scholarly studies of rock in Partisan Review, before even Presley, Ed Sullivan was not presenting rock and roll stars. They were rarely seen on television outside local teen bandstand shows, and when they did appear it was an embarrassment. They did not belong there, vulnerable to our elders' outrage. They belonged here—apart from Them and with Us.

This whole sense of self-defense was part of the magic attraction of rock and roll. Night after night, Alan Freed would indignantly answer editorials in the Brooklyn Tablet or the Daily Mirror that accused rock and roll of filth or fostering juvenile delinquency—the latter an accusation heard with more frequency after "The Blackboard Jungle" reached the screen, opening with the music of "Rock Around the Clock."

"It's the one per cent of the bad kids who are making it rough for the 99 per cent of the good kids." Freed would say, and the theme became part of our cause. When Freed began to make rock and roll movies in the mid-1950's—with plots out of the I've-got-a-great-idea-let's-put-on-a-dance-and-build-the-new-gym school—he stressed this theme that goods kids liked rock and roll music. But the adult anger, the fury, the ban on rock shows in Boston and Bridgeport and New Haven, pulled us into a kind of sect. To journey to Brooklyn was not simply going to a show: it was an act of faith.

Of course, nobody knew that or talked like that at the time. There was no self-conscious Woodstock spirit, no notion that this was a way we could live out our lives. We knew we had to grow up sometime, to be like Them, We were here because . . . well, it had a good beat and you could dance to it.

Actually, my first journey was not out to Brooklyn, but to the safer regions of the New York Paramount on Times Square. Alan Freed had taken a big gamble, breaking the four-month cycle to put on a show during Washington's Birthday of 1957. To shorten the odds on conquering the citadel of Dorsey, Goodman, and Sinatra, Freed had booked two big acts: Frankie Lyman and the Teenagers, and the Platters. And he chose this occasion for the premiere of his movie, "Don't Knock the Rock," with Bill Haley and the Comets and Little Richard.

My friend Alan and I got there about 6:30 a.m. The line already went past McBride's Ticket Service's plate glass window, down 43rd street toward the offices of The New York Times. By the time the doors opened, the line was blocks long. The show broke all of Sinatra's records. It also broke McBride's plate glass window. The kids danced in the aisles. They stomped so hard to the beat that the Fire Department evacuated the balcony. They cheered the good-guy grown-up in the movie who said, "I don't see anything wrong with the music. I kinda like it." They told Middle America—through pictures in *Life* magazine—that the conquest was complete.

At about 9 a.m. at the Brooklyn Paramount, a ticket-taker, alone and afraid in a world he never made, edges into the booth. The line begins to rock, slowly, ominously. The doors open. Ushers flank the line, chanting "Admission is $1.50. Have your money ready please. Admission is . . ."

The enormous, cavernous theater is filled as it has not been since television. The horrible Western or mystery movie begins. The movie ends. Cheers. The newsreel comes on. Groans and boos. The newsreel ends. Cheers. *Another* newsreel—a feature on pet shows or women's fashions—comes on. Boos and shouts. The newsreel ends. Cheers. The lights go out. There is movement behind the curtain. Anticipatory shrieks. The announcer: "And now—the Brooklyn Paramount is proud to present—Alan Freed and his Rock and Roll Revue!" Yaaaayyyy!

The lights go on, red and blue and yellow, as the Alan Freed All-Star 18-piece orchestra plays "Night Train," one of Freed's trademarks. The band—as Freed has told us innumerable times—has great stars, sax men Sam the Man Taylor, Big Al Sears, Panama Francis. The song ends and Freed comes out to enormous cheers, grinning widely from a slightly misshapen face, permanent reminder of an auto crash in 1954 and the plastic surgery. His voice is raspy, electrically charged.

"Hiya!"

"Hiiii!"

"This is Alan Freed, the ol' king of rock 'n' roll."

The acts. In a sense, they are all the same. Four or five singers, outlandishly dressed, in flaming red dinner jackets, purple pants, yellow shirts. There are always two mikes—one for the lead singer, one for the rest of the group, including (always) a bass singer who supplies the do-bobba, doo-bobba line, one falsetto, to surround the reedy lead voice with logistical support.

The steps. They defy description. In a tribute to symmetry, the guy on the right puts out his right hand, the guy on the left puts out his left hand, the guy in the middle puts out both hands. Fingers snap and wave, in mirror-image perfection. Now the hands switch, the feet shuffle in tempo. The tenor sax break begins. The singers whirl around; they do splits. They gesture with the words.

"You know"—point out

"In my heart"—point to the heart

"I pray"—hands together in prayer

"We'll never part"—hands separate, heads shake no

No group, no matter how big, did more than six or seven songs (although Little Richard, in his last show before a four-year retirement, was on-stage for 40 minutes). It kept the shows short enough to do six or seven a day, which hiked the grosses. But nobody minded. Few of the groups had been in existence long enough to have a long string of songs, and the more groups that appeared, the better the shows.

And all the while, back at the radio show, a constant hype was kept up by Paul Sherman—the solid, straight, square d.j. who subbed for Freed. Sherman, whose voice went up 20 decibels during his stint on Freed's slot, would tell us endlessly that "Alan's at the Brooklyn Paramount theater right now, in an un-be-*liev*-a-ble show, you've just got to go see it." If you were home listening, if you hadn't seen the show, you felt like everybody in the world was at a party except you.

Alan Freed was driven off the air in 1959 in the wake of the payola scandals. He had given himself authorship credit—and a royalty share—on many songs he hadn't really written and, as the best-known jockey, Freed was the scapegoat. He left New York for the West Coast, where he found and lost several jobs. In early 1965, as the Beatles first swept America, Freed was indicted for perjury. He died at 43 of a liver ailment before the month was out.

The Brooklyn Paramount is no longer a theater. It's part of Long Island University. There is nothing there to remind anybody that Alan Freed once existed.

In late 1969, I went to the shiny new Felt Forum in Madison Square Garden for a Fifties rock and roll revival. As I approached the entrance, I felt the Terror. The Others were there, a little plumper, a turtleneck or two where T-shirts used to be, but with the pompadours, the grunts, the hostility still in place. They had all married Fran. A lot of them wore American flags and Honor America buttons. I hid my peace button instinctively. Terror does not die easily.

But we went in together and when the M.C. announced that this show was being dedicated to Alan Freed we applauded together, and when the Five Satins came out and sang "In the Still of the Night," we sang with them and stood together and cheered together until they sang it again.

Source: Jeff Greenfield, "'But Papa, It's My Music, I Like It'," *New York Times*, March 7, 1971, pp. HF1, 6.

11

The History of Chicano Rock

RUBÉN GUEVARA

Singer and songwriter Rubén Guevara (born 1942) is perhaps best known for his doo-wop and R&B group Ruben & the Jets, who gained a measure of notoriety in the 1970s through their association with Frank Zappa. But Guevara has also been one of the most active historians of Chicano Rock, producing a variety of musical exhibitions and album releases that draw on his own Mexican American heritage. His landmark 1985 essay, "A View from the Sixth Street Bridge," was one of the first attempts to sketch a detailed social and musical history of Chicano contributions to the history of rock.[1] As Guevara describes, the emergence and blossoming of Chicano Rock in the years between World War II and the British Invasion resulted from both the strong Mexican presence in Los Angeles and a distinctive cultural intermingling. Similar to New York's Spanish Harlem, Mexicans and African Americans in southern California found themselves in close proximity, settling together in affordable neighborhoods and sharing their music with one another. Meanwhile, white disc jockeys like Hunter Hancock (1916–2004) helped spread the new sounds over the airwaves of stations like KFVD and KGFJ, and entrepreneurs like Billy Cardenas (born 1938) looked to promote artists as part of a "Chicano Motown" sound.

ROOTS

What is Chicano rock? First we have to understand "Chicano": as a word, a concept, an expression of a people's history. Nobody is sure of the exact genesis of the term, although it can be traced back to the state of Chihuahua in Mexico, where the upper classes used it as a term of contempt for the poor. But "Chicano!" as an epithet was transformed into "Chicano!" as a statement of pride and defiance by student activists in the sixties. Where *Hispanic, Mexican-American*, and *Latino* are neutral, purely descriptive words—census talk—*Chicano* not only says what you are but that you're proud to be it. It doesn't mean Latino in general but the Southwest in particular. The best of many worlds rolled into one.

Los Angeles, City of the Angels, was founded in 1781 by Felipe de Neve and initially settled by Mexicans, blacks, Anglos, and the local Gabrielino Indians. The Mexicans who "immigrated" to L.A. didn't have to cross an ocean or a continent, only an invisible line on a map that separates regions that once were one, still irreversibly connected by longstanding familial, historical, and cultural ties. L.A.'s roots run deep and the roots are Mexican.

---

1 See also Steven Loza, *Barrio Rhythm: Mexican American Music in Los Angeles* (Urbana: University of Illinois Press, 1993), David Reyes and Tom Waldman, *Land of a Thousand Dances: Chicano Rock 'n' Roll from Southern California* (Albuquerque: University of New Mexico Press, 1998) and Roberto Avant-Mier, *Rock the Nation: Latin/o Identities and the Latin Rock Diáspora* (New York: Continuum, 2010).

The first great wave of immigrants came in the 1870s from Sonora, Mexico, settling in what is now Chinatown. The area was called Sonora-town and eventually grew into what is now called The Flats along the L.A. River. Around the turn of the century, Mexicans moved into Boyle Heights, which was mostly Jewish, and into Lincoln Heights, which was mostly Italian. Then came the second great wave during the Mexican Revolution of 1910. By 1923, Whittier Boulevard had been built, and by 1930 there were over 100,000 Mexicans living in Los Angeles.

In what was to become a constant pattern of push/pull, immigration/deportation, open/shut, during the Depression 64,000 residents—one third of whom were U.S. citizens—were removed from their homes and jobs and sent back to Mexico. This was called "repatriation." Depressing times for real, but at least there was music. In the mid-thirties, teens would go to party at playgrounds and parks. The music was usually traditional Mexican folk, boleros, and mariachi. Later in the decade, dance halls became popular. There was the Bowery Ballroom downtown at Ninth and Grand, where Sal's Deluxe Big Band, probably the first Chicano dance band, used to play. It was a horn band playing swing, jitterbug, and traditional Mexican music—sort of like Bob Wills from the other side of the Rio Grande. Two of the other popular house bands at the Bowery, the George Brown Band and the Irwin Brothers, were black. But since there were still very few blacks in L.A., the crowd was mostly Chicanos.

The Forties: You Might As Well Jump

In East L.A., as in so many other places, the link between swing and early R&B and rock & roll was jump blues. Jump evolved in the thirties from Harlem bands like those of Cab Calloway and the Kansas City groups of Count Basie and Louis Jordan. In Los Angeles the leading early practitioners were Roy Milton and the Solid Senders. When it became financially impossible to maintain a big swing orchestra, Milton cut his band down to ten pieces. Singer-turned-drummer-turned-conductor Roy Milton instructed his drummer to accent the 2 and 4 beats of a bar. Thus, the back beat of rock was born.[2] By the end of the war it was being heard across the country as the Kansas City refugee reached national prominence with his 1945 hit "R. M. Blues," on Specialty Records.

Zoot Music, Zoot Riots

Although thousands of Mexican families had called the City of Angels home for four generations, East L.A. remained separate and most unequal from the dominant mainstream Anglo parts of the city. This was due to social and economic discrimination, the language barrier, and the need for new arrivals from Mexico to have an area where they had some chance to escape the long arm of immigration officials. Such environments force people to build a protective shell from behind which they can secure, preserve, and expand their music, art, and culture.

One expression of that in East Los was the emergence of the Pachuco in the early forties. Pachucos were Chicano gang members who wore the outlandish zoot suit as a statement of defiance to the Anglo establishment. Pachucos originally came from El Paso (El Chuco) and were identifiable by a small cross with three dots or rays tattooed on the left hand between the thumb and first finger.

Pompadoured, in his tailored "drapes," strutting with his girlfriend, and swinging his long gold chain, he cut a most impressive figure. The girls—Pachucas—would wear their hair stacked and

---

2 This is but one of many claims to the origination of the back beat. See, for example, chapter 9 in this book, "Earl Palmer and the Heartbeat of Rock 'n' Roll."

sported modified zoot coats called "fingertips." The Pachuco was L.A.'s first modern rebel, the epitome of cool. Unfortunately, he was too cool.

With the outbreak of World War II, southern California was thrown into a state of hysterical paranoia. The war against Japan was perceived by many as a war against all people of color, at home and abroad. In 1942, following the shipment of hundreds of thousands of Japanese-Americans to internment camps, the tension between white servicemen stationed in California and Pachucos began to increase. As Luis Rodriguez wrote in the *L.A. Weekly*, "By mid-1943, anti-Chicano sentiment in Los Angeles reached its height, spurred on by newspaper articles about a 'huge Mexican crime wave,' 'zoot suit gangsters,' and a new breed of 'scum' known as Pachucos. In June, sailors rampaged out of L.A. Harbor and into Chicano neighborhoods, where they grabbed and beat lone 'zooters,' leaving them in bloody heaps to be arrested by the police. As a result, whole neighborhoods on the Eastside turned into armed camps, battles ensued, and there were an estimated 112 casualties.

"The riots were 'officially' stopped when the naval officer in charge ordered the sailors back to base. By then the Chicanos had gained support from black, Filipino, and even a few Anglo brothers."

The bitter irony of the event was that the U.S. government, with the advent of the war, had stopped deporting Mexicans and instead began drafting them into the armed forces, where they won more medals per capita than any other nationality.

While East L.A. was and is an enclave, the isolation of the community was only one side of the story of the development of Chicano rock. The flip side was the impact of technological change, reflected in the development of an unlikely pair: modern farming and the radio. It was the advent of modern methods of agriculture in the early 1940s that drove millions of blacks off the land in the South, and many were attracted to California by the relatively well-paying jobs in the burgeoning war industries.

The blacks settled in Mexican neighborhoods in East and South Central L.A. because that was where they could afford to live. Conversely, Anglos who lived nearby moved out because they could afford to. Blacks and Chicanos, isolated together, began to interact and, in large numbers, they listened to the same radio stations. For instance, there was Hunter Hancock ("Ol' H.H.") on KFVD. He had a show on Sundays called "Harlem Matinee," which featured records by Louis Jordan, Lionel Hampton, and locals Roy Milton, Joe and Jimmy Liggins, and Johnny Otis.

Johnny Otis moved to L.A. in 1943 from Tulsa, via Oakland, and by the end of the war was a mover and a shaker on the jump blues scene. When Johnny first played the Angelus Hall in 1948, introducing black jump blues to the Eastside, he caused quite a sensation. His swing didn't just swing. It jumped! And the Eastside jumped right along with him. Chicano jump bands began to form—the first was the Pachuco Boogie Boys, led by Raul Diaz and Don Tosti. They had a local hit, "Pachuco Boogie," which consisted of a jump-type shuffle with either Raul or Don rapping in *Galo* (Pachuco street slang: half Spanish, half English) about getting ready to go out on a date. Very funny stuff and another candidate for the title of the first rap record.

Pioneer record companies that would later help to spread R&B around the world were formed right and left in L.A. in the forties. Among them were Art Rupe's Specialty Records, Jules Bihari's Modern, and 4 Star, Exclusive, Aladdin, and Imperial.

East Coast musicians such as Tito Puente and Machito made appearances in Los Angeles in the mid-forties, introducing Afro-Cuban dance music that would later evolve into salsa. However, these out-of-towners performed mostly for Anglo show biz audiences in Hollywood clubs. Few Chicanos attended, not only because of the economic barrier a night on the town presented, but because the Latin musical traditions of countries such as Mexico, which didn't have slavery, are very different from those, such as Cuba or Brazil, that did.

The Fifties: At the Pachuco Hop

The fifties brought the Korean War, the Bracero Program (importation of temporary farm labor from Mexico), and the arrest and deportation of Mexican union and community organizers. In 1954 alone over a million Chicanos were deported. This continued a pattern that is still very much a part of life in the Southwest. When times are good, Mexican workers are allowed across the border into the United States, where they form a pool of cheap and easily controlled labor. But when times are hard, their contribution is forgotten and they are rounded up like animals and sent packing. But the fifties also saw the merging of diverse currents into something called rock & roll. This took place not only in Memphis, Chicago, and New Orleans, but in East L.A. as well.

DJs in L.A. played an important part in the development of local and regional sounds that often became a part of national hits. In 1952, Hunter Hancock broke a smokin' sax instrumental called "Pachuco Hop" by a black musician who lived on the Eastside, Chuck Higgins. A few years later, Hancock moved to KGFJ, which was the first local station to broadcast an all-black playlist seven days a week. A massive audience in East L.A. tuned in on each and every one of those days. At about the same time, DJs like Art Laboe and Dick "Huggy Boy" Hugg started playing jump and doo-wop on the radio.

Black jump sax players heard on the radio, such as Joe Houston, Big Jay McNeely, and Chuck Higgins, were a big influence on Chicano jump sax kingpins Li'l Bobby Rey and Chuck Rios. In the mid-fifties, a record came out on Laboe's Starla label entitled "Corrido Rock," by the Masked Phantom Band, which featured Rey. It's an instrumental with a couple of saxes playing a harmony Norteño riff over a fast rockin' back beat, predating Los Lobos by better than twenty years. Li'l Bobby went on to record "Alley Oop" with the Hollywood Argyles, while Chuck Rios and the Champs had a national hit in 1958 with the instrumental "Tequila."

In 1956 Johnny Otis discovered Li'l Julian Herrera, a singer who was Hungarian by birth but had been raised by Chicano parents. Herrera, heavily influenced by Jesse Belvin and Johnny Ace, was the first Eastside R&B star. With Johnny Otis, he cowrote "Lonely Lonely Nights," which became a major local hit. It's an elegant and beautiful doo-wop ballad, very much in the black style, but something about it—the accent, the voice, the *attitude*—made it different. It was Chicano rock. Otis introduced Li'l Julian to his growing audience at the legendary El Monte Legion Stadium, which became *the* dance hall in the late fifties and early sixties.

A typical weekend dance at the Legion would pack in crowds that were 90 percent Chicano, 10 percent Anglo. The dancers sported khaki pants with a Sir Guy shirt and a charcoal gray suit coat, one button roll, and spitshined French-toed shoes. The girls had stacked hair and wore white shoes called "bunnies," black tight short skirts, and feathered earrings. A lot of Anglo kids copied not only the styles but the dances, the most popular of which were the Pachuco Hop, Hully Gully, and the Corrido Rock.

Of all the dances, the Corrido was the wildest, sort of an early form of slam dancing. Two or three lines would form, people arm-in-arm, with each line consisting of 150 to 250 people. With the band blasting away at a breakneck rocking tempo, the lines took four steps forward and four steps back, eventually slamming into each other (but making sure that no one got hurt). The *corrido* is an old Mexican traditional folk story/song and dance that goes back to at least the mid-1800s, still very popular at weddings and dances today.

An evening at the Legion always ended with tight, slow dancing, called scrunching, usually to ballads by locals like "Handsome" Mel Williams or Vernon Green and the Medallions. After the dance, it was out to the parking lot for the grand finale. Where's the party? *Quien tiene pisto? Mota?* Who's got the booze? Weed? Rumors would fly all night as to which gangs were going to throw *chingasos*—come to blows. The Jesters Car Club from Boyle Heights, which dominated the Eastside, would parade around the parking lot in their lavender, maroon, or gray primered cars, wearing T-Timer shades (blue- or green-colored glass in square wire frames). In what was an inviolable ritual every weekend, the police would eventually break everything up and we'd caravan back to the Foster's Freeze at Whittier and Mott or to Johnnies' at Whittier and Ditman.

The Sixties: The Golden Age of the Eastside Sound

The success of Ritchie Valens, a seventeen-year-old kid from the barrio in Pacoima, with "La Bamba" and "Donna" in 1958 sent a strong signal to aspiring Chicano musicians, myself included, that we could make it, too. It served to convince several independent producers that it might be worth their while to help us. By the early 1960s, bands were forming left and right and East L.A.'s golden age had begun.

Frequent "Battle of the Bands" shows held at East L.A. College were the focus of the action. The Motown sound was a very heavy influence on Eastside bands in spite of the fact that the relatively friendly relations between blacks and Chicanos that had existed in the immediate postwar era had been deteriorating for some time. The civil rights movement had, in some ways, awakened us to the reality that our two cultures were very different. Neighborhoods began to separate on the basis of race. Towards the late 1950s, serious gang problems began to surface between blacks and Chicanos, and in the 1960s affirmative action programs often wound up pitting us against each other for jobs. But one thing did unite us: Motown. Whether it was Marvin Gaye, the Temptations, or Mary Wells, it sounded good at the end of a day of hard work or no work, regardless of the color of your skin. There were even a few Eastside bands, such as the Mixtures and Ronnie and the Pomona Casuals, composed of blacks, whites, and Chicanos.

Independent producer Billy Cardenas envisioned a "Chicano Motown" label. To that end, he brought the Premiers to the attention of Eddie Davis, the most important Eastside producer. The collaboration resulted in a remake of the Don and Dewey chestnut "Farmer John," which reached Number 19 on the national charts in 1964. As Cardenas expanded his promotion of dances featuring Eastside bands to several different ballrooms (including the Shrine, which later would become the rough equivalent of the Fillmore), the pace began to quicken. Cannibal and the Headhunters became a staple on the ballroom circuit and then had a national Top 30 hit with their version of Chris Kenner's "Land of a Thousand Dances" in April of 1965. Later that year they opened for the Beatles on their American tour, with King Curtis backing them up.

Cannibal and the Headhunters' arch rivals at the battles of the bands were Thee Midniters. Fronted by the dynamic Li'l Willie G (Garcia), who drew his inspiration from James Brown, Thee Midniters recorded "Land of a Thousand Dances" before either Cannibal or Wilson Pickett, reaching Number 67 on the *Billboard* chart. They peaked later in the year when they released their anthemic instrumental "Whittier Boulevard" and appeared at the Rose Bowl before 38,000 people along with the Turtles, Herman's Hermits, and the Lovin' Spoonful.

Several other Eastside bands, such as Ronnie and the Pomona Casuals and the Salas Brothers, had local and regional hits. The big records from the Eastside became hits because they were dance tunes, party tunes, keeping right up with Motown's dance-oriented records, but without the slickness. Billy Cardenas did succeed artistically with his "Chicano Motown" concept, but not commercially. He was unable to build a commercial enterprise that could guarantee national distribution and promotion, and that limited the Eastside sound to a regional phenomenon. It was in some ways parallel to what happened with surf music. The more polished Beach Boys had across-the-board success, but very talented but looser bands with more emphasis on the local aspects of the subculture, like Dick Dale and the Del-Tones or the Challengers, never built any base of popularity outside southern California. Although there was little contact between surfers and the Eastside (except for fights at the beaches), there is no denying that almost all surf instrumentals are based on "Malagueña."[3]

The golden age of the Eastside sound was nearly as short-lived as Ritchie Valens' career. Nineteen sixty-four and 1965 were a brief but glorious high point, but we were done in not only by a lack of polish or promotion but also by the British invasion, which, ironically, exerted quite an influence on later records by groups like Thee Midniters. I well remember a night in late 1965 when my band and I were booed at the Hullabaloo, an important Hollywood club. The audience wanted to hear Beatles hits and nothing else. My experience was all too typical.

Another factor was the escalation of the war in Vietnam. Many Eastside musicians were drafted, a true irony when you consider that Ringo Starr has attributed the success of the British Invasion to the end of the draft in England, which allowed British kids to pursue careers as musicians.

Finally, the rock & roll business was becoming more nationally organized as the independent labels and producers that gave birth to the music got swallowed up by the major record companies. In turn, the majors began to merge with each other. This meant that decisions about who would be signed and who would tour and be promoted were made at a national level. The increasing rigidity of radio formats began to blur the local and regional distinctions on the dial and, as a result, made it much harder for a local act to build a base on hometown radio as a stepping-stone to the stars. In a country where most media executives continue to doubt the existence of the massive Latin market, success was made just that much more elusive for us.

The golden age of the Eastside sound was over well before the Tet offensive of 1968 put the Vietnam War on the minds of all Americans, including a million-plus East Los Angelenos.

Source: Rubén Guevara, "The View from the Sixth Street Bridge: The History of Chicano Rock," in Dave Marsh, ed., *The First Rock & Roll Confidential Report* (New York: Pantheon, 1985), pp. 113–21.

---

3 Composed by Cuban pianist and songwriter Ernesto Lecuona in 1927, "Malagueña" is a popular Latin music standard that has been recorded by numerous surf bands.

12

"Music Biz Goes Round and Round

It Comes Out Clarkola"

PETER BUNZEL, *LIFE* MAGAZINE

The Congressional hearings on payola that grabbed headlines throughout late 1959 and 1960 cast a dark cloud over rock 'n' roll, suggesting that the music had soared to popularity on the wings of illegal industry practices. As Peter Bunzel's report for *Life* magazine points out, payola, loosely defined as "pay for play," had been an established part of the music business dating back to the late nineteenth century. Concerns over payola, however, had begun to escalate in the mid-1950s on two fronts. First, the American Society of Composers, Authors & Publishers (ASCAP) accused its rival licensing organization, Broadcast Music International (BMI)—home to the majority of rock 'n' roll songwriters—of forcing its songs onto the airwaves, and successfully lobbied Congress into hearing their claims. Second, and more significantly, the 1959 scandal surrounding rigged television quiz shows offered Congress a readymade platform to extend a formal investigation into the music industry. The central figure in the payola hearings, Dick Clark (1929–2012), the host of ABC's *American Bandstand*, bore the most public scrutiny of any of those brought forward to testify. As the *Life* article intimates, despite the conflict of interests between his corporate holdings and broadcasting practices, Clark's clean image and fervent fan base virtually guaranteed that he would escape the committee's wrath. The many comparatively anonymous disc jockeys who admitted to accepting bribes, however, were less fortunate. In the end, though, the Congressional hearings did little to abolish payola. By the early 1970s, another payola scandal had rocked the music industry, and major investigations into payola have occurred nearly every decade since. This raises the question: in an industry defined by market competition, where does one draw the line between legitimate business practices and abuses of the system? And what effect, if any, does payola have on today's listening audience?

Back in September 1958 a roly-poly Tulsa boy named Billy Jay Killion came home from high school and wanted to watch Dick Clark's television program, *American Bandstand*. His mother, who didn't particularly care for rock 'n' roll music, was all set to watch a different program, so she told Billy "No." He seethed the whole night long. Then in the morning Billy took out a rifle and shot his mother dead.

Millions of American teen-agers feel just as strongly about Dick Clark, though no others have vented their feelings so violently. Last week their loyalty was put to the supreme test, for Clark was up before Congress to answer for mayhem of another kind. For six months the Harris Committee had been investigating payola in music and broadcasting, and had developed a greedy image of the whole industry. A long succession of disk jockeys admitted taking payments from music companies.

But the one man the committee had always been gunning for was Dick Clark, the biggest disk jockey of all and a symbol, in giant screen, of the whole questionable business.

"I have never," Clark told the committee, "agreed to play a record in return for payment in cash or any other consideration." This statement seemed more and more astonishing to the committee as Clark went on to admit that in the last three years he had parlayed his position into a whopping personal fortune of $576,590. "Plugola," "royola" and "Clarkola," the committeemen variously called it.

But their skepticism did not alter Clark's mien as he sat on the stand giving off the same air of proper respectability he does on TV. He wore a blue suit, button-down shirt and black loafers. Every strand of his hair was neatly lacquered into place. His voice had the bland, dulcet tone of the TV announcer that he is.

A Most Important Commercial

His tone was appropriate, for 30-year-old Richard Wagstaff Clark was delivering the most important commercial of his life. He is out to sell his highly select adult audience the same moralistic image of himself that he has convincingly sold to the nation's teen-agers. It was an image he had peddled not only on the air but in a book of adolescent etiquette called *Your Happiest Years*. In this work he made a strong pitch for neatness and good manners, pausing briefly for little homilies: "Don't make the mistake of thinking those TV cameras are branches of the United States mint. Contrary to popular opinion, dollar bills don't come out of them like bread from a bakery oven."

Clark himself made the mistake he warned his public against, but it turned out fine for him. After all, he was in a unique spot to profit by his error. Most disk jockeys perform on radio. Clark is on TV. Most others are only on local stations. He is on a national network and he reaches some 16 million people with his stock in trade, rock 'n' roll. This form of music is alien to most adults, for whom it has all the soothing charm of a chorus of pneumatic drills. "But we love it," said a teen-age girl from Charleston, W. Va., who attended the Clark hearings. "When I hear a Beethoven symphony, I don't feel anything. When I hear our kind of music, I feel something way down deep, like oatmeal."

Payola as a Compliment

The same adults who disparage rock 'n' roll unwittingly helped get it going. When long-playing records came in, grown-ups stopped buying single records. Manufacturers of singles had to aim their products at teen-age taste and rock 'n' roll became the staple. The singles are easy and cheap to make and 600 record companies are expelling a constant flow. But the big problem is selling them.

First the records get a test run in such "break-out" cities as Cleveland, Boston or Detroit to see which can be sold—or which the public can be conned into buying. A sure way to boost the songs has been to put money on the line to disk jockeys. Many deejays were proud to be bribed, for, in their curious little fraternity, payments became a status symbol. "Payola comes to the top disk jockeys, not the others," said one. "If you are in show business, don't you want to be at the top? Isn't this the greatest compliment?"

A large number of fraternity brothers felt the same way, for the Federal Trade Commission estimates that 250 disk jockeys accepted the compliment. Generally the recipients deny that there is any connection between paying and playing. But remarked Congressman John Moss of the committee, "Some kind of telepathic communication seems to take place. By intellectual osmosis between the disk jockey and the record manufacturer, money is passed and records get played."

Actually the committee should not be so surprised at payola. It is old stuff in the music business. In Victorian England, before he teamed up with William Gilbert, a young composer named Arthur Sullivan dashed off a song called *Thou'rt Passing Hence.* He got it performed in public by giving a share of the royalties to Sir Charles Santley, a leading baritone of the time. Sir Charles was still collecting his payoff when the tune was played at Sullivan's funeral.

In the U.S., in the 1890s, the music publishers paid to have their songs played in beer gardens. Later, top stars like Al Jolson and Eddie Cantor were offered enormously tempting payola deals— and in the '30s maestros of big-name bands got a cut of the royalties for playing new tunes on network radio.

Until the payola scandals broke, disk jockeys had no pangs of conscience about benefiting from a practice with such a tradition. Payola was simply the way they did business and they imagined that everyone else did it that way too. "This seems to be the American way of life," said Boston's Stan Richards, "which is a wonderful way of life. It is primarily built on romance: 'I'll do for you. What will you do for me?'"

What Dick Clark did for music people was to give them a pre-sold market and what they gave him in return was a windfall. He did not rely on conventional cash payola but worked out a far more complex and profitable system. It hinged on his numerous corporate holdings which included financial interests in three record companies, six music publishing houses, a record pressing plant, a record distributing firm and a company which manages singers. The music, the records and the singers involved with these companies gained a special place in Clark's programs, which the committee said gave them systematic preference.

A statistical breakdown showed how his system worked. In a period of 27 months Clark gave far less air time to a top star like Elvis Presley than to a newcomer named Duane Eddy, one of the several singers whom he has helped make into a star. Clark had no stake in Presley. But firms in which he held stock both managed and recorded Eddy. During the same 27 months Clark played only one record by Bing Crosby (the almost mandatory *White Christmas*) and none at all by Frank Sinatra. "You sought to exploit your position as a network personality," said Moss. "By almost any reasonable test records you had an interest in were played more than the ones you didn't." Replied Clark, "I did not consciously favor such records. Maybe I did so without realizing it."

"You Laid It On"

Nor did Clark neglect revenues from copyright ownership. He owned 160 songs, and of these 143 came to him as outright gifts, much as Gilbert's *Thou'rt Passing Hence* came to Santley. "Once you acquired an interest," said Moss, "then you really laid it on."

A shining example was a record called *16 Candles.* Before getting the copyright, Clark spun it only four times in 10 weeks, and it got nowhere. Once he owned it, Clark played it 27 times in less than three months and it went up like a rocket. Each time the record was purchased Clark shared in the profits to the merry tune of $12,000. This pattern was duplicated with a song called *Butterfly*— and for his trouble the publisher gave him $7,000.

Many of his deals afforded Clark a special tax break. In May 1957 he invested $125 in the Jamie Record Company, which was then $450 in the red. Once he was a stockholder, Clark found Jamie records very attractive. By plugging them on his show he helped make many of them hits. When he sold out last December for $15,000, Clark had a cool profit of $11,900, and he could declare it all as capital gains. Clark granted the accuracy of these figures but explained, "I followed the ground rules that existed." He was familiar with the rules from another angle. Although he denied *he* had taken payola he admitted, paradoxically, that one of his record companies had passed out payola to get its wares plugged.

Coming back again and again to rock 'n' roll, the committee members strongly implied that Clark had deliberately foisted it on teen-agers. "I don't know of any time in our history when we had comparably bad, uniformly bad music," said Moss. Clark replied, "Popular music has always become popular because of young people. You can't force the public to like anything they don't want. If they don't want it, it won't become a hit."

Clark's soft sell made him an effective, if slippery, witness. At the end Chairman Oren Harris remarked, "You're not the inventor of the system or even its architect. You're a product of it." Then showing as much perspicacity as any 15-year-old, the congressman added, "Obviously you're a fine young man."

This encomium was sweet music to teen-agers who came to the hearing to see their hero in his hour of travail. Seated in the front row were two sisters from West Orange, N.J., whose parents had brought them to Washington to view the sights. To them the loveliest sight of all was Dick Clark.

"I don't care if he took payola," said Karen Katz, 13. "He gets to us as kids. The reason *16 Candles* took off is because we liked it. They say he didn't play enough Bing Crosby. Look, his show isn't for grandmothers. And Frank Sinatra, who needs him?"

The final verdict on Clark rests in part with teen-agers like Karen, but even more with his many sponsors. If they decide that his value as a pitchman has been hurt, then they will drop him like a cracked record. Already the danger signals are up. "We aren't happy about this thing," said the account executive for Hollywood Candy Bars, "and neither are any of the other ad agencies. We want to keep our noses clean."

The American Broadcasting Company is playing it cautious, waiting to see which way the wind will blow. Its stake in Clark is huge, for the network carries both of his shows, and each year they bring $6 million in advertising revenue. At least one disk jockey, a Miami man, says that ABC has already lined him up as Clark's replacement, just in case—and he is waiting for word to catch the next plane north.

But the sponsors had better think twice before dropping Clark. The teen-agers feel an almost fanatical bond with him. An investigator for the committee named James Kelly ran into this fanaticism right in his own family. Kelly's wife has a 15-year-old sister and they used to be great pals. But ever since Kelly started prying into Dick Clark's affairs, the girl has cut him absolutely dead.

Source: Peter Bunzel, "Music Biz Goes Round and Round: It Comes Out Clarkola," *Life,* May 16, 1960, pp. 118–22. LIFE and the LIFE logo are registered trademarks of Time Inc. Used under license.

II

THE 1960s

13

"The King of Surf Guitar"

DAVE SCHULPS

The surf music craze that swept across America in the early 1960s is remembered today for many things: its idealization of a youthful west coast California lifestyle, memorably depicted in the Beach Boys' 1963 single "Surfin' USA," and its popular instrumental hits, many of which—such as the Chantays' "Pipeline," the Surfaris' "Wipe Out," and the Marketts' "Surfer's Stomp"—were titled after surfing slang and dances. Surf music's most lasting legacy, however, may be the way it helped transform the electric guitar, both through its close association with the southern California Fender guitar company and the novel ways that guitarists began approaching the instrument, utilizing a percussive, staccato picking action. No one emerged as a greater influence and icon of this new movement than Dick Dale (born Richard Anthony Mansour, 1937), the acknowledged "King of the Surf Guitar." In this 1993 interview with journalist Dave Schulps for *BAM*, the California *Bay Area Music* magazine, Dale recalls his early musical inspirations and his experiences playing at the Rendezvous Ballroom in Balboa that led to the development of surf music. While surf music and the many popular 1960s *Beach Party* movies that followed in its wake helped disseminate a vision of California as a paradise predominantly populated by young white teens, Dale's comments—which draw attention to his Lebanese heritage, and the powerful influence of jazz drumming and middle-eastern melodies like "Miserlou" on his guitar style—point to the greater ethnic and cultural diversity that fueled the surf music movement.

On His Entrance into the Music Business

I never stepped into the business. I was pushed into the business by my dad, God bless him. He was a precision machinist for Hughes Aircraft, and he saw that I had a talent, playing all these different instruments, and he kind of tricked me into "Hey, get up on this stage and back this guy up and you can do this and do that in these little country bars," when I was underage. And then I'd win all these contests. He'd tell the guy to get off and I'd stand there and look like a jerk unless I did something. I was doing what I call rockabilly—this was like in 1954—because Hank Williams was my big hero, and I always wanted to be a cowboy singer.

On Pioneering Southern California's Teenage Rock 'n' Roll Scene

I went into this coffee shop and saw this kid playing on a piano. Billy Barber—he's passed on now. We got together and I talked to the owner of the Rinky Dink Ice Cream parlor in Balboa. I asked him if we could play there on the weekend and he said, "All right, I'll give you about six or seven dollars for the three of you." I got a raise to 12 bucks when I added a drummer. When I wanted a little more, he fired me. Meanwhile, the place became packed to see me, so when I left there, I went next door to that big ballroom and that was the first place we hit—the Rendezvous Ballroom in Balboa.

My dad got a hold of the people who owned the ballroom. They had closed it because Stan Kenton had lost about $80,000 trying to bring jazz back for the second time. We convinced them to reopen it, but we couldn't reopen it unless we got permits from the city to have teenage dancing.

I went down to Balboa with my very dear friend Ray Samra.[1] We were bikers at the time, and I was president of the Sultans of Southwest LA. So we rode on down and we ended up getting permits from the city. Cities were not allowing teenage dances or gatherings, unless it was a high school graduation and it was a horn band. Anybody who picked up a guitar was considered evil in the eyes of the principals or the PTAs. So we had a meeting at night with the Parent Teachers Association, with the principals of the schools, with the city fire and police departments. We had to convince them, "Hey, this is where your kids could go, to this big ballroom. And at least they're not out in the street." That was the first permit issued in California to have teenage dances for profit. They said we had to make sure people wore ties. Did you ever see surfers with bare feet wearing ties? We stood at the door and gave them all ties so they could come in! Opening night, I had 17 of the kids I was surfing with there, and I was playing everything from "Sunny Side of the Street" to Guy Lombardo stuff to Hank Williams, and the beat that I'd developed strumming made it sound like a big band sound, although I called it rockabilly.

On Developing His Guitar Style

I was listening to all types of music and drumming on the canisters. Listening to Harry James and Guy Lombardo and Gene Krupa. That's where I developed my percussive rhythm style from. Gene Krupa got his theory from the natives of the jungle. They would keep it simple and keep it driving, so they would mesmerize themselves into their fertility dances. Then they'd all be into this sexual dancing and end up making love or whatever they did. He learned that keeping that rhythm strong and building from the bottom up and on the down-stroke are the keys to pleasing an audience.

I've always maintained that, no matter how much I was criticized by musicians or critics or whatever because I didn't go into the patterns of a thousand scales . . . to me, keeping that driving beat creates this monster effect of hypnosis, of mesmerism. So what I do is I take people on a ride of sound when I play. That's why it's so difficult for me to play the same song the same way twice, because the audience affects me to such a point at each show that I'm riding on this curve of power, thunder, mesmerism, and sound. I've taken the ABC's of music and, you might say, thrown it out the window and only kept timing. That's why Mick Fleetwood said to me at the end of one of my shows, "My God, you are the most fuckin' percussive guitar player I have ever heard." And I said, "Mick, it's because I got this theory from where it all originated from."

On His Theory of Playing

To me, timing and continuity in your timing are the most important things, especially if it's staccato. Creating this machine gun staccato-style of playing is like fighting in an arena or throwing a barrage of punches [in] martial arts, or like coming off the top of a 15-foot wave, or like being in a cage

---

1 Samra was actually Dale's cousin, who performed with him at the Rinky Dink Ice Cream Parlor beginning in 1959. He would later go on to play the bass in Dale's band, the Del-Tones.

with an 800-pound tiger. The strength is so awe-inspiring, so humbling, that it's like standing next to the Andes Mountains. Then you find out who you really are. You're nothing. It's like being on the edge of these huge greatnesses in life that are uncontrollable. That's the way I feel when I am performing with that guitar, and that's why those picks melt so much on those 60-gauge strings, because I'm digging them in so hard to get this perfection in timing and thunderous sound.

*   *   *

On His Middle-Eastern Musical Roots

My relatives on my father's side were born in Beirut, Lebanon. In the Boston area, those were the people who lived under the subways. They'd all sit out on the stairs and play Arabic music. My uncle played an Arabic drum. A bell-shaped, metal [drum] with an open end on one end and a skin stretched across the other. And the beat would be *"doom-duh-duh, duh-duh-duh, doom-duh-duh."* I get chills just doing that sound. The oud players would play with a turkey quill and do things that were just . . . *spasmodic!* It just had such a beautiful sound to me.

On the Origin Of "Miserlou"

At the end of the very first night in Balboa, I said, "OK, we'll be back tomorrow night," and a kid came up to me—he was probably 10 years old—and he says, "Can you play something on your guitar on one string?" Whatever possessed him to ask me that, I don't know. I said, "Come back tomorrow and I'll have something," just to get him away. I went home that night and I just about cried myself to sleep, because I was going to be found out that I was a fake. I couldn't play on one string. I didn't know what I was going to do. I stayed up all night trying to figure it out, and then a light came on and I said, "Hey, you know those Arabic songs that your uncles used to play, and there's one called 'Miserlou.'" Well, I wondered how I could make it sound like a big band was playing it, and I went *"deeew"*—slid down the string and I was, *"deow, digga, digga, digga, digga"* and I doubled it and tripled it and quadrupled it. And that's how the staccato of Dick Dale was created—by a 10-year-old kid asking me if I could play something on a single string. I always wanted to please people.

On the Birth of the Fender Showman

I went up to Leo Fender one time and said, "I'm Dick Dale. I'm going to be playing at the Rendezvous Ballroom and I have no money, and I'd appreciate it if you could help me." He just took a liking to me, 'cause I guess I was honest to him, and he said, "Take this guitar and tell me what you think of it." At the same time, they were just perfecting the Telecaster, 'cause it had a bunch of bugs in it, and Leo brought in a man named Freddy Taveras, who was with Harry Owens' Royal Hawaiians, to iron out those bugs. Freddy was the real mastermind with Leo.

With the amplifier, he only had 10-inch speakers, because they'd built it for the country people and they didn't need a lot of power. It was just easy, kick-back stuff. But I had a theory. I wanted my guitar to sound like Gene Krupa, but it wouldn't sound that way because the speakers would just rattle and they'd tear, and then they didn't have enough power to push it. At that time, we weren't miking our speakers. We just used a mike to sing through, and that's how we played to 4000 people. I kept telling Leo, "I need a bigger and fatter sound," 'cause when 500 to 1000 people come in, I'd lose the thickness.

I wanted a big, thick, fat sound with an edge on it. Turn up the bass so it's bass-y, then turn up the treble so it puts an edge on it. So we kept blowing up speakers! I mean, they were catching on fire. The amp wasn't matching the speaker and the speaker wasn't matching the amp. Then the speakers would freeze. I was hitting them so hard that they would just stop. We blew up about 48 speakers and amplifiers, until we walked through Lansing Company.

I can remember the three of us down at their warehouse going, "We gotta get bigger windings. We gotta get a stronger voice coil. We gotta put something on the edge of the speakers." So we ended up putting rubberization on the edge of the speaker, and that stopped it from tearing along the edges, and from going crooked and locking in at the cone. And we then made the windings and the contacts bigger and thicker and put in a better magnet. And the D130 15" F, meaning Fender, was born.

I'm still playing through the identical speakers from those years and I think I've reconed two of them. One of them I used for so long that it rotted out inside. I had them reconed. There are new speakers on the market, but not one sounds like these. To get the thickness of sound, Leo would bring me into the factory and I'd plug into the amps and they'd sound loud as loud could be, but I'd start playing and the thickness just wasn't there. One day Leo and Freddy came to the show and afterwards they understood what I was saying. They went back and created this output transformer that favored all three ranges—mid, low, and high. It gave it a sweet, warm sound, and the tubes gave it that distortion sound you could never get from a transistor. We came up with the Fender Showman amplifier eventually, and when we came up with the twin speakers in one box, it became the Dual Showman.

On the Fender Stratocaster

To me, the Stratocaster is the finest guitar in the whole wide world, because there was a theory of sound that we were trying to get. What makes thick sound? Freddy Taveras told me, and he was a genius, "If you could put strings across a telephone pole and put electric pick-ups on it, you would have the most phenomenal, thick, fat sound you've ever heard in your life." It's got to be a thick piece of wood, 'cause a hollow guitar makes one sound and only one sound, and it cannot be changed. Even if you change pickups, it's still hollow.

The Stratocaster is the Rolls Royce. We made it as thick as could be. We carved out the back so it would fit against people who had protruding stomachs—they were worried about that—without losing the sound. The Fender Precision bass was designed along the same lines.

On Surf and Reverb

The reverb has nothing to do with surfing music. On my first surfing album, *Surfer's Choice*, was a picture of me surfing under the pier at San Clemente at about 7:30 in the morning. We sold about 80,000 of those on our own—at concerts—before it was taken over by Capitol. It was on Del Tone Records.[2] When that album came out, the kids were already calling me the "King of the Surf Guitar." Everything I ever did was named by kids. They named "Let's Go Trippin'," "Surf Beat," all those names. I always thought it was good luck to take things that people give you and use it. Good karma. On that first album, not one song had reverb, and yet I was already the King of the Surf Guitar. Four thousand kids a night, 80,000 albums sold.

I was singing on a radio program in Santa Ana—KWIZ or something like that. Thirty minutes. It was called *Dick Dale and His Rhythm Wranglers*, a country thing we did three or four times, and I believe one time I had Larry Carlton as a little kid playing the guitar. I'd sing a song and when I

---

2 Del Tone was the independent label that Dale's father, Jim Monsour, formed to release his son's records.

heard myself over the air it was so terrible, because I didn't have a natural vibrato like a classical singer would have. I died. I said, "I'm never going to do that again. I'm not going to sing onstage." And I wondered what I was going to do. I didn't want echo—didn't want it to repeat. I just wanted sustain—to hang. And I started thinking, the Wurlitzer organs had reverberation units in them. So we stole the idea of taking the reverb unit from a Wurlitzer and we put it in a separate box and I'd sing through it and it would sustain. It was really, really neat. At the same time, I said, "Wait a minute! Let's see what it sounds like with the guitar." Henceforth, the reverb. But I'd already recorded the *Surfer's Choice* album—"Miserlou," "Let's Go Trippin'," all those songs, and not one had reverb on it. What might have confused people was the heavy, heavy, hard percussion of the staccato picking I was doing.

Source: Dave Schulps, "The King of Surf Guitar Lives!," *Bay Area Music* magazine, August 13, 1993, pp. 23–25.

14

Phil Spector and the Wall of Sound

Ronnie Spector

Sandwiched between rock 'n' roll's supposed decline at the end of the 1950s and the rejuvenating arrival of the Beatles on America's shores in 1964, the explosive rise in popularity of early 1960s girl group music has often been trivialized and overlooked within mainstream histories of rock. And to the extent that rock histories have celebrated girl groups like the Ronettes, it has often been to praise the innovations of their Svengali-like male producers or the songwriting teams that provided them with their hits.[1] Lead singer Ronnie Spector of the Ronettes speaks from the perspective of the performer in the two following passages from her 1990 autobiography *Be My Baby*, offering a little-seen window into the complex creative processes and inordinate power relationships behind the girl group phenomenon. In the first excerpt, Spector describes the genesis of the group's breakout hit, "Be My Baby," recorded in 1963 at Gold Star Studios in Los Angeles. The second excerpt rejoins the Ronettes in 1965, at which point their career was already in a state of decline (they would break up the next year). Reading these two passages from *Be My Baby*, it is hard to believe that Ronnie Spector (born Veronica Bennett, 1943) and her producer, Phil Spector (born 1939), were separated in age by only four years. Even though the two were romantically involved during the Ronettes' meteoric rise to success, Spector held a firm control over the young singer, inserting her as the final jigsaw puzzle piece in his celebrated "wall of sound." Ronnie would eventually marry Spector in 1968 only to divorce him in 1974.

When we returned from California, the Ronettes went right back to work. Even though our Colpix singles had all flopped, we were always in demand as a live group. By 1963, all three of us were out of high school and playing with rock and roll variety shows like Clay Cole's Twisterama Revue. The following we developed at those shows—along with the fans we made at Murray the K's Brooklyn Fox revues—were all that kept us going before we met Phil.

Even before we ever had a hit record, we had a hard core of fans who followed us from show to show, and for some reason, a lot of them seemed to be gay men or lesbians. I'm not sure why. Maybe it was because we were half-breeds, and the gay crowd sensed that the Ronettes were outsiders just like they were.[2] Whatever the reason, there was something about our style that spoke to a lot of

---

1 In recent decades there have been some attempts to redress this imbalance as scholars have directed more emphasis to how girl groups and their singers provided a strong point of identification for adolescent female audiences. See in particular, Susan J. Douglas. "Why The Shirelles Mattered," in *Where The Girls Are: Growing Up Female With the Mass Media* (New York: Times Books, 1994), 83–99, and Jacqueline Warwick, *Girl Groups, Girl Culture: Popular Music and Identity in the 1960s* (New York: Routledge, 2007).

2 Throughout her autobiography Spector refers to all of the Ronettes (herself, her sister Estelle, and their cousin Nedra Talley) as half-breeds. Spector's mother was part "black and Cherokee," and her father was white; Nedra's father was Spanish.

gay people, because they've always been there for us. Even today I meet gay guys who saw the Ronettes at the Cafe Wha or the Bazaar in the Village, and they can still name every song we did at a show that happened twenty-five years ago.

In that long stretch before "Be My Baby," our live shows were the only place our fans could hear us. Even after Phil recorded our first song out in California, he refused to release it. When I asked him when "Why Don't They Let Us Fall in Love" was coming out, he answered without missing a beat.

"Never," he said.

I was shocked. I thought it was a pretty good record. But Phil just shook his head. "It's a good song," he told me. "But it's not a number-one record."

By this time I really believed that Phil actually could predict a number-one song, and I thought that was fantastic. "I'm still working on your first million-seller," he teased, "and it's almost finished. If you're a real nice girl, I might let you come over to my house to hear it."

I'd never been in a penthouse before—Phil's or anyone else's. So naturally, when I walked in I couldn't resist peeking into all the closets and poking around behind all the closed doors. I opened one door and was surprised to find a bedroom where six or seven pairs of women's shoes were scattered all over the floor. When I asked Phil who they belonged to, he nearly turned pink.

"Will you stop snooping around where you don't belong?" he snapped. I think it was the first time I ever saw Phil lose his temper.

"Okay, honey," I said. "I'm sorry." He must've noticed the hurt look in my eyes, because he softened his tone immediately.

"Those are my sister Shirley's shoes," he explained. "She stays here sometimes when she's in New York. Now," he said, changing the subject, "why don't you go into the other bedroom and watch TV? Jeff and Ellie are going to be here any minute to work on the song, and we don't want to be disturbed."

Phil was still very hush-hush about our relationship at that point, and he didn't want his writing partners to know I was there.[3] I didn't complain. I was too thrilled. I thought it was the greatest thing in the world to be sitting in the bedroom while my boyfriend wrote my first hit record in the next room. But what did I know? I also believed those were his sister's shoes spread out all over the floor.

If I had any doubts, I was too busy listening to what was going on in the living room to worry about them. I put my ear to the wall and tried to hear what Phil, Ellie Greenwich, and Jeff Barry were singing. It was hard to hear the words over Ellie's piano playing, but when they came around to the chorus, I could hear all three of them loud and clear. "Be my, be my baby," they sang. "Be my baby, now." I thought it was catchy, and I couldn't help wondering if that was what a number-one record sounded like.

Phil and I rehearsed that song for weeks before he would let me fly out to California to record it. But when that morning came, I knew the words to "Be My Baby" backwards and forwards.

I got up really early so my mother and I could catch the plane. Since I was going to sing lead, Phil wouldn't need Estelle and Nedra to do their backgrounds until later, so they stayed behind in New York for a few more weeks. I remember the morning I left, Estelle stuck her head out from under the sheets and said, "Don't forget to fill out the airplane insurance forms when you get to the airport." Airport insurance was a big thing with my family. Whenever one of my uncles would drop me off at the airport, it was always straight to the insurance stands.

---

3 At that time Spector was still married to his first wife, Annette Merar.

My mother and I got in a cab, and I sang "Be My Baby" all the way out to LaGuardia. I wanted to be so perfect, I couldn't rehearse it enough. I even made my mother wait in the airport bathroom with me while I sang through it a few times more. We must've stayed in there a little too long, because by the time we got out we'd missed our plane.

Then my mother did something I'd never seen her do before. She sat down and sighed. Right there in the airport waiting room, she just let out a big sigh like she was real tired all of a sudden. "Ronnie, sit down here with me," she said, patting the brown cushion of the airport couch. "I think you're at the age where you can go out there and sing "Be My Baby' all by yourself now, so I don't think I'm gonna go all the way out there to California with you this time." Then I kissed her good-bye and got on the next plane all by myself.

When I landed in California, Phil picked me up at the airport in his big limousine and drove me straight to Gold Star Studios. Gold Star's Studio A was old and really tiny, but that was the only place he ever recorded anymore, because he knew he could get sounds out of that room that he couldn't get anywhere else. It had something to do with the acoustics. The room was so small, the sound seemed to bounce off the walls, creating a natural echo that made every song recorded there sound fuller.

And Phil loved that, because he was always experimenting with ways to make his sound as big as possible. Instead of having one guitarist playing rhythm, he would have six. Where someone else might use one piano, Phil would have three. He'd have twin drum sets, a dozen string players, and a whole roomful of background singers. Then he'd record everything back on top of itself to double the sound. Then he'd double it again. And again. And again and again, until the sound was so thick it could have been an entire orchestra. That's what Phil was talking about when he told a reporter that his records were like "little symphonies for the kids."

Watching Phil record the background music for "Be My Baby," I finally understood what he meant when he stopped me that time and said, "That's it! That's the voice I've been looking for." He knew from the first second he heard me that my voice was exactly what he needed to fill in the center of this enormous sound. Phil had been trying to construct this giant wall of sound ever since he got started in the record business, and when he heard me, he knew my voice was the final brick.

I was always surprised at how much Phil used me when he had singers like Fanita James and Darlene Love around. When I'd hear them singing with those great big gospel voices, I'd start to wonder what was so special about my little voice. But I have to give Phil credit. He loved the way I sang, and he knew exactly what to do with my voice. He knew my range. He knew my pitch. He even knew which words sounded best coming out of my mouth. He knew that "Be My Baby" was a perfect song for me, so he constructed the whole record around my voice from the ground up.

It took about three days to record just my vocals for "Be My Baby." I was so shy that I'd do all my vocal rehearsals in the studio's ladies' room, because I loved the sound I got in there. People talk about how great the echo chamber was at Gold Star, but they never heard the sound in that ladies' room. And, between doing my makeup and teasing my hair, I practically lived in there anyway. So that's where all the little "whoa-ohs" and "oh-oh-oh-ohs" you hear on my records were born, in the bathroom at Gold Star.

Then, when I finally did go into the studio, I'd hide behind this big music stand while I sang, so Phil and Larry Levine wouldn't see me with my mouth all popped open when I reached for a high note. I'd keep the lyric sheet right in front of my face, and then, after I finished a take, I'd peep out from behind my music stand and look through the window to see how Phil and Larry liked it. If they were looking down and fooling with the knobs, I'd know I had to do it again. But if I saw they were laughing and yelling "All right!" or "Damn, that little girl can really sing!" I'd know we had a take. Since my approach to each song was completely up to me, watching Phil and Larry react afterward was the only real feedback I ever got.

Recording at Gold Star in those days was like one big party. Phil always got the best musicians in town to play at his sessions, guys like Hal Blaine, Nino Tempo, Leon Russell, Barney Kessel, and Glen Campbell. Jack Nitzsche did all of our early arrangements, and the guy was a genius. Then there was Larry Levine, who engineered all our songs. Phil had so many good people working for him that it really was a joy to go into work.

But the biggest fun of all came when it was time to lay down the background vocals, because Phil always invited everyone in the whole studio to join in. If you were standing around and could carry a tune, you were a background singer in Phil's wall of sound. And everybody Phil knew seemed to show up the day we did the backgrounds for "Be My Baby." Darlene Love was there, and we had Fanita James from the Blossoms, Bobby Sheen from Bob B. Soxx and the Blue Jeans, Nino Tempo, Sonny Bono—who was Phil's gofer in those days—and Sonny's girlfriend, who was a gawky teenager named Cher.

I have to be honest—the first time I saw Cher, I thought she was a hooker. It was in a hotel room where I was supposed to meet Phil for a rehearsal. She and Sonny were already in the room sitting at the piano when I walked in. And when I saw this skinny young kid with her long black hair and thick mascara, I just assumed she was a call girl from the hotel. Then Sonny introduced her as his girlfriend, and I was so embarrassed, I just had to laugh. After a few minutes I could tell that she was really just a sweet kid, and we got to be friends.

We would meet in the bathroom at Gold Star to tease our hair. Sitting over the sink, we would share black eyeliner and gossip. We were about the same age, and we both had stars in our eyes, so it was only natural that we would hit it off. I had fun with Darlene and Fanita and the other girls who sang for Phil, but I never felt like I could talk to them the way I did with Cher. I was probably closer to her than to anyone outside of my family in those days. And as time went on, Cher and I began to see that we had a lot more in common than just bangs and makeup.

Sonny always acted extremely jealous of Cher. And when I got out to California, I started to notice that Phil could get pretty possessive of me, too. Neither of them liked for us to go off on our own. But Phil seemed to trust Cher, so she and I spent a lot of time together while Phil and Sonny worked in the studio. We'd go shopping together, or we'd spend the day at the movies. Other days we'd just drive around in Cher's little red MG, looking at all the strange sights of Hollywood.

As soon as we finished "Be My Baby," I flew right back to New York, where the Ronettes were scheduled to start a two-month tour of the East Coast with Joey Dee and the Starliters. One of our first stops was Wildwood, New Jersey. I'll always remember that town, because that was where we heard "Be My Baby" for the first time. It was one of those moments that changes your life forever.

Nedra, Estelle, and I were sleeping late in our motel room on the Saturday morning after our first show in Wildwood. In those days all three Ronettes would share one big bed, and Mom or Aunt Susu would usually sleep in the other one. By the time I woke up that morning, Mom had already gone out to get breakfast, so I walked over and turned the TV on to find "American Bandstand," which we woke up to every Saturday, just like every other teenager in America. You would turn it on even if you were still half-asleep, because you didn't want to miss the latest records.

Even though I was barely awake, I could hear Dick Clark talking about how this next record was guaranteed to be the hit of the century. I couldn't wait to hear what this thing could be. Then I heard "boom-ba-boom-boom"—the drumbeat that starts off "Be My Baby." Even though I was sitting up in bed, I was convinced that I'd fallen back asleep and was only dreaming that Dick Clark was playing our record on "American Bandstand." But if I was dreaming, Estelle and Nedra were having the same dream, because they sprang upright in bed and started staring at the TV, same as me. After that I nearly passed out right there in that motel room.

We sat there for about a minute watching all those happy teenagers dancing to our record. Then Nedra and I ran out to the terrace to tell Joey Dee and the guys, who were all swimming around in the pool.

"Hey, guys!" I yelled. "Get up here. Dick Clark's playing our record!"

It was like we couldn't really believe that this was happening unless we had witnesses.

Joey and the guys ran up the stairs just in time to catch the end of our song. Then they hugged us, and we hugged them. And then we all laughed and sang and enjoyed what it feels like to be on top of the world.

A few minutes later Phil was on the phone. He was as surprised as we were to see the record taking off so fast—or so he said. He told us the Ronettes would have to leave Joey Dee's tour immediately so we could get back to New York to promote the record. Of course, Joey Dee wasn't very happy to hear that. But he didn't want to stand in our way, so he finally did let us out of the tour.

*   *   *

Even after the Ronettes' slump began in 1965, I didn't get too concerned. Phil had just scored the biggest smash of his career with "You've Lost That Lovin' Feeling," by the Righteous Brothers, and he was still as hot as ever. So I figured it was just a matter of time before he turned his attention back to my career.

It wasn't like he could ignore me. I'd practically been living with him since he moved into the mansion on La Collina. Whenever I came out to California, that is. Which actually wasn't that often in 1965, since the Ronettes had personal appearances booked solid throughout the year.

And I was having so much fun onstage with the Ronettes, I didn't have time to worry about our failing recording career. I still had my audience, and I could tell by their applause that they still loved me. Before long, though, I think Phil even grew jealous of them.

We did one of our biggest shows ever in late November, when Phil put us in *The Big T.N.T. Show*, which was a concert he produced in Hollywood that was being filmed for release as a movie. Phil was the orchestra leader for a lineup that included some of the biggest names in rock, including Ray Charles, the Byrds, and the Ike and Tina Turner Revue. Of course, Phil had to be in complete control whenever he produced anything, and this show was no exception.

When the technicians asked us to do some of our act during rehearsal, we ran through our routine just to give the camera guys a basic idea of what we did. We didn't give them a full performance, because we wanted to save that for the show. But Phil was in charge—and he wanted to make sure everyone knew it-so he stopped us in the middle of the rehearsal and started barking out orders at us like we were in the chorus or something.

"Hold it, girls," he commanded. "You're just walking through it. I'd like you to start again, and this time, I want you to do it just like you're going to do it tonight."

That was ridiculous. We'd been doing the same basic routines ever since we started at the Brooklyn Fox, but our act always changed a little bit each night, depending on the audience response. The only thing you could be sure of was that we never ever did exactly the same show twice. But Phil insisted, so we went ahead and played our entire act to this empty theater.

"That wasn't so hard, was it?" he called out after we finished. "Do it *exactly* like that tonight."

That night we did our act the same way we always did it—flat out crazy. I shimmied around the stage and danced wherever the feeling took me. The crowd was up for grabs, but I think it was too much for Phil.

The director and all the cameramen told us how exciting it was, and the other acts all said the nicest stuff. But Phil hated it. He came up to me after the show, steaming mad. "What did you think you were doing out there?" he shouted. I hated it when Phil got like that, but I knew the only thing I could do was humor him until the mood passed.

"What's wrong?" I asked. "Was there something wrong with our routine?"

"It was all wrong," he snapped. "It looked completely different tonight than it did this afternoon."

"But there was no audience then," I explained. "You know I always play the house."

"*Play the house?*" he exclaimed. "You were all over the place. Out of control." That was a big thing with Phil. If I lost control in front of a crowd, he hated it because that meant that I was out of *his* control.

"And on top of everything else, you came in off key!" He could only ever criticize my singing for technical reasons, because he knew I didn't read music, so I couldn't argue. "Don't bother coming to the party after the show," he ordered. "I don't want to see you there!"

I went straight back to my hotel room and cried. I suppose I could've gone to the party anyway, but I never even considered it. I just couldn't go against Phil's wishes in those days. I was like a little Japanese geisha girl walking five paces behind her master. Phil couldn't control what I did once I got out onstage, but that wasn't a problem he had in our personal life.

Of course, he dominated me most of all in the recording studio. After the hamburger incident with Sonny Bono, I knew Phil didn't want me getting too friendly with the other singers and musicians at Gold Star.[4] He never really came out and said so—he didn't have to. He had more charming ways of getting me to do what he wanted.

Once when I was doing backgrounds with a bunch of people at Gold Star, this big fat singer named Olla got me laughing. She was always saying something that cracked me up, and this time I was doubled up with laughter when I happened to catch a peek at Phil, who was smiling at me from behind his glass window in the control room. "Ronnie," he said, waving me into the booth. "Come on in here."

When I got there, Phil pulled up an old wooden stool and motioned for me to sit down on it. Then he turned back to work at the mixing board. "Uh, Phil?" I asked. "What was it you wanted?"

"Nothing, really," he admitted, looking a little embarrassed. "I just felt like I could use some inspiration in here."

It was such a sweet thing to say, and so flattering. Up until then, Phil had always tried to keep up the illusion that our relationship was purely professional. But by inviting me to sit next to him in the control booth, he was admitting to the whole world that I was someone special. I sat straight up on that rickety old stool and felt like a queen.

From then on I always sat in the booth with Phil. He seemed to really enjoy having me in there with him, and it made me feel like a privileged character. Phil would make jokes about whoever happened to be standing on the other side of the glass, and they were especially funny because no one could hear them but me and Larry Levine.

And I also got to watch Phil at work, which was always a thrill. He would sit there in his booth with the speakers blasting so loud I thought he must have been going deaf. But then he would hear something in the mix that no one else could, and he would motion for Larry to stop the tape. One time I saw him point to the end violinist in a row of ten and say, "You. Sounds like you're a little flat. Check your A string." The guy checked his tuning, and Phil was right. It was amazing.

A lot of people have asked me how Phil created his wall of sound, but to understand Phil's sound, you have to understand Phil. The wall of sound was really just a reflection of his own personality, which was very extravagant. When Phil made a record, he might start out with the same basic tracks as everyone else—drums, guitars, bass, and vocals. But then he'd always add in more sounds, because he wanted his records to be as extravagant as he was. He didn't have any use for a record unless it was at least ten times bigger than life. Phil was one guy who believed that *more* is more.

---

4 Ronnie had left to get a hamburger with Sonny Bono during a lull in a recording session without informing Spector. In her absence, Spector proceeded to go into a rage and trash Gold Star Studios.

When he walked into a recording studio, Phil was always looking for a new rule he could break. He wasn't afraid to try anything. I remember there was this little meter on the tape machines that told you how loud the volume was, and it had a needle that would go into the red zone whenever the sound got too loud or distorted. Well, everyone in the record business lived in fear of making that needle go into the red—but not Phil. Sometimes I think he was only really happy when he was in that red zone.

After being in the studio with Phil for a time, it was only natural that you'd get caught up in his madness. Everyone who worked for him did. With Phil as our inspiration, we'd try to push ourselves as hard as he pushed himself. When I'd sing a lyric, I'd close my eyes and try to feel the truest emotion I could find. And I'd keep pushing myself until I got there. Then Phil would add that sound to the sounds of all the other singers, musicians, and engineers. And the result would be a wonderful combination of textures and personalities and genius that people started calling the wall of sound. You can say what you want about Phil Spector, but no one who was there at Gold Star can ever forget the music we made. No one had ever heard anything like it before, and they'll never hear anything like it again.

As much as I loved hanging around the booth with Phil, it wasn't long before I started to miss being out in the studio with the crowd. But the first time I tried to leave the booth and join in on the fun in the studio, Phil made it clear that my place was with him and only him.

"Where are you going, Ronnie?" Phil asked when I got up from my stool.

"I'm just going out to sing a few of these backgrounds with the guys."

"No, no, no," he said. "I don't want you doing that anymore."

"But, Phil," I argued. "Everybody sings backups."

"Not you, Ronnie," he said. "Your voice is too distinctive. It comes right through."

"Well," I suggested, "maybe I could just go 'oooh,' real low." But Phil wouldn't budge. So while everyone else was laughing and joking and smoking cigarettes, I'd sit there watching them in silence from behind my glass wall.

Source: Ronnie Spector with Vince Waldron, *Be My Baby: How I Survived Mascara, Miniskirts, and Madness or My Life as a Fabulous Ronette* (New York: Harmony Books, 1990), pp. 49–55, 104–8.

15

The Beatles, Press Conference, 1964

The Beatles arrived at New York's Kennedy Airport on February 7, 1964, officially sparking the British Invasion that would drastically reshape the face of rock music in the mid-1960s. From their very first steps off the plane, the band found themselves the subjects of intense public scrutiny. While much of their success stemmed from their recordings, it was also the group's charm, wit, and absurdist, self-deprecating humor that endeared the Beatles to the American media. They were the first rock group to use the press conference as their own personal platform, both establishing and playfully mocking their distinctive personas. Historically, Paul was known as the "cute" one, John the "smart" one, George the "quiet" one, and Ringo the "funny" one.

Question: Do any of you have any formal musical training?
John: You're joking.
Question: What do you think of President Johnson?
Paul: Does he buy our records?
Question: What do you think of American girls and American audiences?
John: Marvelous.
Question: Here I am, surrounded by the Beatles, and I don't feel a thing. Fellas, how does it feel to be in the United States?
John: It's great.
Question: What do you like best about our country?
John: You!
Question: I'll take that under advisement. Do you have any plans to meet the Johnson girls?
John: No. We heard they didn't like our concerts.
Question: Are they coming to your performance tonight?
Paul: If they do, we'd really like to meet them.
Question: You and the snow came to Washington today. Which do you think will have the greater impact?
John: The snow will probably last longer.
Question: One final question. Have you ever heard of Walter Cronkite?
Paul: Nope.
John: *NBC News*, is he? Yeah, we know him.
Question: Thanks, fellas. By the way, it's *CBS News*.
George: I know, but I didn't want to say it as we're now on ABC.
Question: This is NBC, believe it or not.
John: And you're Walter?
Question: No, I'm Ed.
John: What's going on around here?
Question: What do you think of your reception in America so far?

John:	It's been great.
Question:	What struck you the most?
John:	You!
Ringo:	We already did that joke when we first came in.
George:	Well, we're doing it again, squire!
Question:	Why do you think you're so popular?
John:	It must be the weather.
Question:	Do you think it's your singing?
Paul:	I doubt it. We don't know which it could be.
Question:	Where'd you get the idea for the haircuts?
John:	Where'd you get the idea for yours?
Paul:	We enjoyed wearing our hair this way, so it's developed this way.
Question:	Well you save on haircutting at least.
Paul:	Roar . . .
John:	I think it costs more to keep it short than long, don't you?
Paul:	Yeah, we're saving our money.
Question:	Are you still number one in Europe?
George:	We're number one in America.
Question:	Where else are you number one then?
John:	Hong Kong and Sweden . . .
Paul:	Australia, Denmark, and Finland.
Question:	And you haven't any idea why?
Ringo:	We just lay down and do it.
John:	In Hong Kong and these other places, suddenly you're number one years after putting out your records. Even here, we've got records we've probably forgotten.
Question:	You call your records "funny records"?
John:	"Funny," yeah, the ones we've forgotten.
George:	It's unusual because they've been out in England for over a year. Like "Please, Please Me" is a big hit over here now, but it's over a year old.
Question:	Do you think they're musical?
John:	Obviously they're musical because it's music, isn't it! We make music. Instruments play music. It's a record.
Question:	What do you call it, rock and roll?
Paul:	We try not to define our music because we get so many wrong classifications off it. We call it music even if you don't.
Question:	With a question mark?
George:	Pardon?
John:	We leave that to the critics.
Question:	Okay, that's it. Have a good time in America.
John:	Thank you. Keep buying them records and look after yourself.

Source: "The Beatles, Press Conference, Washington, DC, February 11, 1964," in Geoffrey Giuliano, ed., *The Lost Beatles Interviews* (New York: Plume, 1994), pp. 12–14.

16

"U.S. Musicians' Union Says, 'Beatles Stay Home'"

VICTOR RIESEL

Because the Beatles have been so thoroughly canonized and celebrated for so long, it is easy to forget that not everyone welcomed their February 1964 arrival onto U.S. shores with open arms. In particular, the American Federation of Musicians (AFM) viewed the Beatles and other British groups quite literally as an invasion that would unfairly disadvantage American musicians and threaten their livelihoods.[1] Acting on this perceived threat, AFM president Herman Kenin (1901–1970) asked the Department of Labor to screen these groups via the Immigration and Naturalization Act, which separated foreign workers into two categories: those who were of "distinguished merit and ability," and thus posed no harm to a general U.S. labor force, and those with "no unique talents," whose entry into the U.S. should be limited or denied. To Kenin, the Beatles and other British rock 'n' roll bands lacked any special cultural merit and clearly fell in the latter category. When newspaper journalist Victor Riesel reported on the conflict in his widely read syndicated column, Beatles fans immediately responded with a flood of petitions and letters (some even addressed to President Johnson) protesting the AFM's decision. The controversy highlighted both the precarious position of musicians as laborers and the tense culture war still brewing over rock 'n' roll. Following this backlash, the Department of Labor relented and allowed the Beatles to return in August 1964 under the unrestricted category of special entertainers, with the agreement that the tour would include U.S. bands and musicians as opening acts.

'Tis the final conflict. Let each stand in his place. At my side is a man of awesome courage, usually a gentle chap, who now is aroused and is rallying some sturdy forces in the U.S. Departments of State, Labor and Justice to stand off another Beatle invasion in May and August—moments for which the Beatlemaniacs have been living.

This fellow is Herman Kenin, successor to James C. Petrillo as president of the American Federation of Musicians (AFM). Kenin just doesn't believe the Beatles are culture. He is not much impressed by "Yeah, Yeah, Yeah . . . I Wanna Hold Your Hand."

---

1 For an excellent overview and analysis of the AFM/Beatles conflict, see Michael James Roberts, *Tell Tchaikovsky the News: Rock 'n' Roll, the Labor Question, and the Musicians' Union, 1942–1968* (Durham: Duke University Press, 2014).

"The Beatles are not immortal to us," Kenin said the other day. "We don't consider them unique. They are musicians and only sing incidentally. We can go to Yonkers or Tennessee and pick up four kids who can do this kind of stuff. Guitars are now in the ascendancy in this country."

"Of course, we have a cultural exchange with other countries, but this is not culture. They are no Rubinsteins or Heifetzes. Artists are welcome. But as for the Beatles, if they do get back into the country, they're going to have to leave their instruments at home, because there are enough musicians in the United States and too many of them are unemployed. They were here before we realized what happened, but it won't happen again."

"They've started an invasion and are taking box offices and audiences away from American entertainers. First came the Beatles. Then the Dave Clark Five, the Swinging Blue Jeans, the Searchers and soon the British will have the rock 'n' roll set sewed up."

Kenin and his colleagues in the musicians federation are incensed. They say that the Britishers can come in only if there is a reciprocal arrangement and American musicians are booked into Britain.

This man-for-man exchange arrangement was made some years ago when Stan Kenton, purveyor of progressive jazz, wanted to swing a tour through England. The London musicians union and the government would have turned him down unless the U.S. took some players from England.

Jimmie Petrillo, who was AFM president then, countered with a proposal that the gates be swung wide open to both countries. The British refused and insisted on a man-for-man swap. The pact was made. Only such artists as Heifetz or Rubinstein were to be allowed free entry.

The agreement was monitored by the Immigration and Naturalization Service and the U.S. Labor Dept. on this side of the Atlantic. All went smoothly until the Beatles swarmed onto the horizon. They claimed they were singers and were in the country before the AFM could protest that they were musicians, and, therefore, should have come under the man-for-man arrangement.

So Kenin wrote to the British Musicians Union. Back came a reply agreeing that the Beatles were primarily musicians.

"We are entirely in sympathy with the view of the AFM that British beat groups should come to the United States only on the basis of reciprocal exchange," wrote Harry Francis, assistant secretary of the British union.

". . . It is true that the members of the Beatles and Dave Clark Five are members of the musicians union. But neither group submitted the contracts for their American visits to us for approval. And you may rely upon it that they will be made sharply aware of our dissatisfaction in the matter. Had we known that they were coming to the U.S. against the wishes of the AFM, they would have been instructed to remain in Britain."

"Having now received your official complaint, we shall arrange to publish a statement in the trade press that in the future British beat groups performing in the U.S. may do so only in reciprocal exchange for the performance of American musicians in Britain."

Having shored up the international front, Kenin turned his justified wrath upon our own government. He protested to the Department of Labor. Secretary Willard Wirtz, to whom the Beatles also came as a distinct shock to a usually well adjusted nervous system, agreed to extend to actors and other entertainers an immigration clearance order which it issues for virtually all other occupations. Under this procedure the department must approve the entry of aliens seeking to work in the United States. Such admission is refused if qualified Americans are available for the work sought by such foreigners.

Thus, the Beatles will need the government's approval for re-admission.

"While this is a difficult responsibility to assume," Wirtz wrote on March 25, "we nevertheless are undertaking, effective April 15, to protect American workers."

Kenin will protest the British invasion unless the English make possible a return flow of U.S. entertainers to London. Since this is not likely, it is just as unlikely that the Beatles will get back here without a fight.

And those who have stood amongst the screamers, the twisters and the jumpers know what a fight it will be. Hell hath no fury like a Beatle-nik spurned.

Source: Victor Riesel, "U.S. Musicians' Union Says, 'Beatles Stay Home'." *Delaware County Daily Times* April 3, 1964, p. 7.

17

"Beatlemania Frightens Child Expert"

DR. BERNARD SAIBEL

From its etymological roots in "madness" and "lunacy" to its more current usage in psychiatry as a hyperactive mental disorder, the word "mania" has long served as a marker for irregular and potentially destructive behavior. Given this history, it should come as little surprise that the arrival of Beatlemania in the United States—punctuated by large demonstrative crowds of hysterically sobbing and screaming teenage girls—aroused the attention of numerous sociologists, pop psychologists, and behavioral specialists.[1] In keeping with this spirit, the *Seattle Daily Times* arranged for its own child expert, Dr. Bernard Saibel (the supervisor of the Washington State Division of Community Services), to attend and report on the Beatles' August 21, 1964 concert at the Seattle Center Coliseum. Saibel's alarmed response, fearful of the sexually charged "orgy" that was unfolding before him, demonstrates the degree to which Beatlemania was indeed perceived as a *mania*, and one that thrust into the media spotlight the moral concerns surrounding teenage female sexuality.

The experience of being with 14,000 teen-agers to see the Beatles is unbelievable and frightening. And, believe me, it is not at all funny, as I first thought when I accepted this assignment.

The hysteria and loss of control go far beyond the impact of the music. Many of those present became frantic, hostile, uncontrolled, screaming, unrecognizable beings. If this is possible—and it is—parents and adults have a lot to account for to allow this to go on.

This is not simply a release, as I at first thought it would be, but a very destructive process in which adults allow the children to be involved—allowing the children a mad, erotic world of their own without the reassuring safeguards of protection from themselves.

The externals are terrifying. Normally recognizable girls behaved as if possessed by some demonic urge, defying in emotional ecstasy the restraints which authorities try to place on them.

The hysteria is from the girls and when you ask them what it is all about, all they can say is: "I love them."

Some, restrained from getting up on the stage after the Beatles left, asked me to touch the drums for them.

---

1 See, for example, A.J.W. Taylor, "Beatlemania—A Study of Adolescent Enthusiasm," *British Journal of Social and Clinical Psychology 5* (September 1966): 81–88. For an insightful analysis of the Beatlemania phenomenon and female sexuality in the 1960s, see Barbara Ehrenreich, Elizabeth Hess, and Gloria Jacobs, "Beatlemania: Girls Just Want to Have Fun," in *The Adoring Audience: Fan Culture and Popular Media*, edited by Lisa A. Lewis (New York: Routledge, 1992), pp. 84–106.

There are a lot of things you can say about why the Beatles attract the teen-age crowd.

The music is loud, primitive, insistent—strongly rhythmic and releases in a disguised way (can it be called sublimation?) the all too tenuously controlled, newly acquired physical impulses of the teen-ager.

Mix this up with the phenomena of mass hypnosis, contagious hysteria and the blissful feeling of being mixed up in an all-embracing, orgiastic experience and every kid can become "Lord of the Flies" or the Beatles.

What is it all about?

Why do the kids scream, faint, gyrate and in general look like a primeval, protoplasmic upheaval and go into ecstatic convulsions when certain identifiable and expected trademarks come forth such as "Oh, yeah!," a twist of the hips or the thrusting out of an electric guitar?

Well, this music (and the bizarre, gnome like, fairy tale characters who play it) belongs to the kids and is their own—different, they think, from anything that belongs to the adult world.

Every time a teen-ager screams over this music he thumbs his nose with impunity and with immunity at an adult or several adults.

Besides, kids, like the other separate and distinct parts of humanity, are competitive. If there is a youngster who can scream loudly, there is one who can scream louder.

If there is one who belongs to the cognoscenti (those in the know), there is one who is more sensitive and more appreciative of this art than any of the others. And to prove it, she faints and all can see how much more affected she is, because she has to be carried out on a stretcher—a martyr, a victim of her capacity for deep understanding and overwhelming emotion.

Regardless of the causes or reasons for the behavior of these youngsters last night, it had the impact of an unholy bedlam, the like of which I have never seen. It caused me to feel that such should not be allowed again, if only for the good of the youngsters.

It was an orgy for teen-agers.

Source: Dr. Bernard Saibel, "Beatlemania Frightens Child Expert," *Seattle Daily Times*, August 22, 1964, p. 1.

18

"Understanding Dylan"

PAUL WILLIAMS

One of the first major rock critics, Paul Williams (1948–2013) launched the influential *Crawdaddy!* magazine in 1966, while still a freshman at Swarthmore College. At the time, serious examinations of rock music were rarely to be found in the popular press. One of Williams's first significant articles, "Understanding Dylan" tackles the subject of rock's most opaque poet, a figure whose complex lyrics virtually begged to be analyzed. What do we gain, Williams asks, from scrutinizing the songs of Bob Dylan (born Robert Zimmerman, 1941), specifically those from his then most recent release, *Blonde on Blonde*? Are we searching for some hidden significance that we can attach to Dylan's biography or some clue to the music's cultural context? Williams's stance is clear throughout. Such undertakings, he argues, are misguided; Dylan's music is an art form that should be experienced, not interpreted. Williams's opinions are radical and debatable, even more so because they echo almost to the word, contentious sentiments that had been bubbling over in the world of art and literary criticism, most notably in philosopher Susan Sontag's provocative 1964 essay "Against Interpretation."[1] By aggressively digging at a text to unearth its meaning, Sontag believed that modern critics were becoming numb to art's more immediate formal properties. What was instead needed, she argued, was an "erotics of art," one that would restore the primacy of art's sensory experience while celebrating its surface transparency. Similarly Williams insists that if we are to "understand" the substance of Dylan's rock 'n' roll poetry, we must approach it on an experiential level.

Perhaps the favorite indoor sport in America today is discussing, worshiping, disparaging, and above all interpreting Bob Dylan. According to legend, young Zimmerman came out of the west, grabbed a guitar, changed his name and decided to be Woody Guthrie. Five years later he had somehow become Elvis Presley (or maybe William Shakespeare); he had sold out, plugged in his feet, and was rumored to live in a state of perpetual high (achieved by smoking rolled-up pages of *Newsweek* magazine). Today, we stand on the eve of his first published book (*Tarantula*) and the morning after his most recent and fully realized LP (*Blonde on Blonde*), and there is but one question remaining to fog our freshly minted minds: what in hell is really going on here?

Who is Bob Dylan, and—this is the question that is most incessantly asked—what is he really trying to say? These are not, as such, answerable questions; but maybe by exploring them we can come to a greater understanding of the man and his songs. It is as an approach to understanding that I offer you this essay.

---

1 Susan Sontag, "Against Interpretation," *Evergreen Review*, 8, no. 34 (December 1964): 76–80, 93; Reprinted in *Against Interpretation and Other Essays*, (New York: Farrar, Straus & Giroux, 1966), pp. 3–14.

Everyone knows that Dylan came east from the North Country in 1960, hung around the Village, and finally got a start as a folksinger. If you're interested in biographical information, I recommend a book with the ridiculous title of *Folk-Rock: The Bob Dylan Story.*[2] The authors' attempts at interpretations of songs are clumsy, but the factual portion of the book is surprisingly reasonable (there is no such word as "accurate"). The book perpetuates a few myths, of course (for instance, the name Dylan actually comes from an uncle of Bob's and *not* from Dylan Thomas); and it has its stylistic stumblings. But for just plain (irrelevant) biographical info, the book is worth your 50 cents.

There are a few things about Dylan's past that *are* relevant to understanding his work (or to not misunderstanding it), however, and these appear to be little known. His roots are deep in country music and blues: he lists Percy Mayfield and Charlie Rich among the musicians he admires most. But he did not start out as a "folksinger," not in the currently accepted sense. From the very beginning his desire was to make it in the field of rock and roll.

In 1960, however, rock and roll was not an open field. The songs were written in one part of town, then sent down to the recording companies in another part of town where house artists recorded them, backed by the usual house bands. A country kid like Dylan didn't stand a chance of getting into rock and roll, and it did not take him long to find that out. The only way he could get anyone to listen to him—and the only way he could keep himself alive—was to start playing the coffeehouses. This got him a recording contract and an interested audience, as well as a reputation as a folksinger, and it was one of the luckiest things that ever happened to him. First of all, it put him under pressure to produce; and nothing better can happen to any young writer. Secondly, it made him discipline his songwriting, and though he may have resented it at the time, it was this forced focusing of his talents that made them emerge. You have to learn some rules before you can break them.

But it was inevitable that "folk music" would only be a temporary harbor. "Everybody knows that I'm not a folk singer," he says; and, call him what you will, there is no question that by the time *Another Side of Bob Dylan* appeared he was no longer thinking his songs in terms of simple guitar accompaniments (to a certain extent, he never had been). He was straining at the bit of folk music's accepted patterns, and fearing, perhaps rightly so, that no one was interested in what he wanted to say any more. But then "Tambourine Man" caught on, and people began responding to him as a man and not as a politician. The light was green: he'd been working very hard on a very important song, and he decided he was going to sing it the way he heard it. That was "Like a Rolling Stone," and its success meant that from now on he could do a song any way he wanted. "I knew how it had to be done," he says; "I went out of my way to get the people to record it with me."

It was a breakthrough. He was into the "rock and roll field" for real now, but of course he is no more a rock and roll singer than a folksinger. He is simply an artist able to create in the medium that for him is most free.

I have gone into this background only because there continues to be so much useless misunderstanding, so much talk about "folk-rock," so much discussion of "the old Dylan" and "the new Dylan." Until you, as a listener, can hear *music* instead of categories, you cannot appreciate what you are hearing. As long as people persist in believing that Dylan would be playing his new songs on a folk guitar instead of with a band, except that recording with a band brings him more money, they will fail to realize that he is a creator, not a puppet, and a creator who has reached musical maturity. Dylan is doing his songs now the way he always wanted to do them. He is a bard who has found his form, no more, no less; and if you're interested in what he's saying, you must listen to him on his own terms.

---

2 Sy and Barbara Ribakove, *Folk-Rock: The Bob Dylan Story* (New York: Dell Publishing Co., 1966).

It is my personal belief that it is not the artist but his work that is important; therefore, I hesitate to go too deeply into the question of *who* Bob Dylan is. Owl and Churchy once had a fantastic fight over whether a certain phrase actually fell from the lips of Mr. Twain, or Mr. Clemens.[3] And someone has pointed out that nobody knows if the *Odyssey* was written by Homer or by another early Greek poet of the same name. Perhaps I don't make myself clear. I only want to point out that if we found out tomorrow that Bob Dylan was a 64-year-old woman who'd changed her sex, and a proven Communist agent, we might be surprised, but the words to "Mr. Tambourine Man" would not change in the slightest. It would still be the same song.

I will say, to dispel any doubts, that Mr. Dylan is not a 64-year-old woman or an agent of anything. I met him in Philadelphia last winter; he is a friendly and straightforward young man, interested in what others are saying and doing, and quite willing to talk openly about himself. He is pleased with his success; he wanted it, he worked for it honestly, and he's achieved it. We talked about the critics, and he says he resents people who don't know what's going on and pretend they do. He named some names; it is my fervid hope that when this article is finished, and read, my name will not be added to the list.

It is difficult to be a critic; people expect you to *explain* things. That's all right if you don't know what's going on ... you can make up almost any clever-sounding explanation, and people will believe you. But if you do understand a poem, or a song, if it is important to you, then chances are you also understand that you're destroying it if you try to translate it into one or two prose sentences in order to tell the guy next door "what it means." If you could say everything that Dylan says in any one of his songs in a sentence or two, then there would have been no point in writing the songs. The sensitive critic must act as a guide, not paraphrasing the songs but trying to show people how to appreciate them.

One problem is that a lot of people don't give a damn about the songs. What interests them is whether Joan Baez is "Queen Jane," or whether or not Dylan dedicated "Tambourine Man" to the local dope peddler. These people, viewed objectively, are a fairly objectionable lot; but the truth is that all of us act like peeping toms now and then. Dylan himself pointed this out in a poem on the back of *Another Side*. He wanders into a mob, watching a man about to jump off the Brooklyn Bridge; "I couldn't stay an' look at him/because I suddenly realized that/deep in my heart/I really wanted/to see him jump." It is a hard thing to admit that we are potential members of the mob; but if you admit it, you can fight it—you can ignore your curiosity about Dylan's personal life and thoughts, and appreciate his generosity in offering you as much as he has by giving you his poems, his songs. In the end you can know Bob Dylan much better than you know your next door neighbor, because of what he shows you in his songs; but first you have to listen to his songs, and stop treating him as though he lived next door.

Another problem, and in a way a much more serious one, is the widespread desire to "find out" what Dylan's trying to say instead of listening to what he is saying. According to him: "I've stopped composing and singing anything that has either a reason to be written or a motive to be sung. . . . The word 'message' strikes me as having a hernia-like sound." But people go right on looking for the "message" in everything Dylan writes, as though he were Aesop telling fables. Not being able to hear something, because you're too busy listening for the message, is a particularly American malady. There's a tragic lack of freedom in being unable to respond to things because you've been trained to await the commercial and conditioned to listen for the bell.

---

3 Owl and Churchy are two characters from the satirical comic strip *Pogo*. Mark Twain was the pen name of Samuel Clemens.

Take a look at a great painting, or a Polaroid snapshot. Does it have a message? A song is a picture. You see it; more accurately, you see it, taste it, feel it . . . Telling a guy to listen to a song is like giving him a dime for the roller coaster. It's an experience. A song is an experience. The guy who writes the song and the guy who sings it each feel something; the idea is to get you to feel the same thing, or something like it. And you can feel it *without knowing what it is*.

For example: you're a sixth grader, and your teacher reads you Robert Frost's "Stopping by the Woods on a Snowy Evening." The poem sounds nice; the words are perhaps mysterious, but still powerful and appealing. You don't know what the poem "means," but you get this feeling; the idea of having "miles to go before I sleep" is a pretty simple one, and it means a lot to you. The poet has reached you; he has successfully passed on the feeling he has, and now you have it too.

Years later you read the poem again, and suddenly it seems crystal clear that the poem is about death, and the desire for it. That never occurred to you as a sixth grader, of course; does that mean you originally misunderstood the poem? Not necessarily. Your teacher could say "We want the peace death offers, but we have responsibilities, we are not free to die"; but it wouldn't give you anything. It's a sentence, a platitude. You don't even believe it unless you already know it's true. What the poet does is something different: walking through the woods, he gets a feeling that is similar to the idea your teacher offered you in a sentence. But he does not want to tell you what he believes; that has nothing to do with you. Instead, he tries to make you feel what he feels, and if he succeeds, it makes no difference whether you understand the feeling or not. It is now a part of your experience. And whether you react to the poem as a twelve-year-old, or an English professor, it is the feeling you get that is important. Understanding is feeling . . . the ability to explain means nothing at all.

The way to "understand" Dylan is to listen to him. Listen carefully; listen to one song at a time, perhaps playing it over and over to let it sink in. Try to see what he's seeing—a song like "Visions of Johanna" or "Sad-Eyed Lady of the Lowlands" (or almost any of his more recent songs) is full of pictures, moods, images: persons, places and things. "Inside the museums," he sings, "infinity goes up on trial." It doesn't *mean* anything; but you know what a museum feels like to you, and you can see the insides of one, the particular way people look at things in a museum, the atmosphere, the sort of things that are found there. And you have your image of a trial, of a courtroom: perhaps you don't try to picture a lazy-eight infinity stepping up to the witness chair, but there's a solemnity about a trial, easily associable with the image of a museum. And see how easily the feeling of infinity slips into your museum picture, endless corridors and hallways and rooms, a certain duskiness, and perhaps the trial to you becomes the displaying of infinity on the very walls of the museum, like the bones of an old fish, or maybe the fact that museums do have things that are old in them ties in somehow . . . there's no *explanation*, because the line (from "Visions of Johanna," by the way) *is* what it is, but certainly the line, the image, can turn into something living inside your mind. You simply have to be receptive . . . and of course it is a prerequisite that you live in a world not too unlike Dylan's, that you be aware of museums and courtrooms in a way not too far different from the way he is, that you be able to appreciate the images by having a similar cultural background. It is not necessary that you understand mid-century America and the world of its youth in order to understand Dylan; but you do have to be a part of those worlds, or the songs will lose all relevance. This is true of most literature, in a way; and of course Dylan has his elements of universality as well as his pictures of the specific.

I *could* explain, I suppose. I could say that "Memphis Blues Again" is about displacement, and tell you why Dylan would think of a senator as "showing everyone his gun." But the truth is, that wouldn't give you anything. If you can't feel it, you can't get anything out of it; you can sneer and say "It's commercialism" or "It's about drugs, and I'm above it," but not only are you dead wrong, you're irrelevant.

In many ways, understanding Dylan has a lot to do with understanding yourself. For example, I can listen to "Sad-Eyed Lady of the Lowlands" and really feel what the song is about, appreciate it; but I have no idea why "a warehouse eyes my Arabian drums" or what precise relevance that has. Yet it does make me feel something; the attempt to communicate is successful, and somehow the refrain "Now a warehouse eyes my Arabian drums" has a very real relevance to me and my understanding of the song. So it isn't fair to ask Dylan what the phrase means, or rather, why it works; the person I really have to ask is the person it works on—me. And *I* don't know why it works—i.e., I can't explain it. This only means I don't understand me; I do understand Dylan— that is, I appreciate the song as fully as I believe is possible. It's the example of the sixth grader and Robert Frost all over again.

If you really want to understand Dylan, there are perhaps a few things you can do. Read the poems on the backs of his records; read his book when it comes out; read the brilliant interview that appeared in last April's *Playboy*.[4] But above all listen to his albums; listen carefully, and openly, and you will see a world unfold before you. And if you can't see his songs by listening to them, then I'm afraid that all the explaining in the world will only sink you that much deeper in your sand trap.

We have established, I hope, that art is not interpreted but experienced (whether or not Dylan's work is art is not a question I'm interested in debating at the moment. I believe it is; if you don't, you probably shouldn't have read this far). With that in mind, let's take a cursory look at *Blonde on Blonde*, an excellent album which everyone with any admiration for the work of Bob Dylan should rush out and buy at once.

Two things stand out: the uniform high quality of the songs (in the past Dylan's LPs have usually, in my opinion, been quite uneven) chosen for this extralong LP; and the wonderful, wonderful accompaniments. Not only is Dylan's present band, including himself on harmonica, easily the best backup band in the country, but they appear able to read his mind. On this album, they almost inevitably do the right thing at the right time; they do perfect justice to each of his songs, and that is by no means a minor accomplishment. *Blonde on Blonde* is in many ways—the quality of the sound, the decisions as to what goes where in what order, the mixing of the tracks, the timing, etc.— one of the best-produced records I've ever heard, and producer Bob Johnston deserves immortality at least. Certainly, Dylan's songs have never been better presented.

And they really are fine songs. It's hard to pick a favorite; I think mine is "Memphis Blues Again," a chain of anecdotes bound together by an evocative chorus ("Oh, Mama, can this really be the end, To be stuck inside of Mobile with the Memphis blues again?"). Dylan relates specific episodes and emotions in his offhand impressionistic manner, somehow making the universal specific and then making it universal again in that oh-so-accurate refrain. The arrangement is truly beautiful; never have I heard the organ played so effectively (Al Kooper, take a bow).

"I Want You" is a delightful song. The melody is attractive and very catchy; Dylan's voice is more versatile than ever; and the more I listen to the musicians backing him up the more impressed I become. They can't be praised enough. The song is lighthearted, but fantastically honest; perhaps what is most striking about it is its inherent innocence. Dylan has a remarkably healthy attitude toward sex, and he makes our society look sick by comparison (it is). Not that he's trying to put down anybody else's values—he simply says what he feels, and he manages to make desire charming

---

4 The *Playboy* interview to which Williams is alluding (and which appeared in the March 1966 issue) is reprinted in *Bob Dylan: The Essential Interviews*, edited by Jonathan Cott (New York: Simon & Schuster, 2017), pp. 99–118. Like many of his interviews from this period, Dylan comes across as a deliberately evasive subject, responding to journalist Nat Hentoff's straightforward queries with nonsensical, absurdist answers.

in doing so. That is so noble an achievement that I can forgive him the pun about the "queen of spades" (besides, the way he says, "I did it . . . because time is on his side" is worth the price of the album).

"Obviously Five Believers" is the only authentic rock and roll song on the record, and it reflects Dylan's admiration of the early rock and rollers. Chuck Berry and Larry Williams are clear influences. "I'd tell you what it means if I just didn't have to try so hard," sings Bob. It's a joyous song; harp, guitar, vocal, and lyrics are all groovy enough to practically unseat Presley retroactively.

"Rainy Day Women #12 & 35" (the uncut original) is brilliant in its simplicity: in a way, it's Dylan's answer to the uptight cats who are searching for messages. This one has a message, and it couldn't be clearer, or more outrageously true. *Time* magazine is just too damn stoned to appreciate it.

I could go on and on, but I'm trying hard not to. The album is notable for its sense of humor ("Leopard Skin Pillbox Hat" and "Pledging My Time" and much else), its pervading, gentle irony (in "4th Time Around," for example), its general lack of bitterness, and above all its fantastic sensitivity ("Sad-Eyed Lady of the Lowlands" should become a classic; and incidentally, whoever decided it would sound best alone on a side, instead of with songs before it and after it, deserves a medal for good taste).

"(Sooner or Later) One of Us Must Know" is another favorite of mine: in its simplicity it packs a punch that a more complex song would often pull. "Visions of Johanna" is rich but carefully subdued ("The country music station plays soft but there's nothing really nothing to turn off" . . . I love that); Dylan's world, which in *Highway 61* seemed to be bubbling over the edges of its cauldron, now seems very much in his control. Helplessness is still the prevalent emotion ("Honey, why are you so hard"), but chaos has been relegated to the periphery. Love (and sex, love's half-sister) are all-important, and love, as everyone knows, has a certain sense of order about it, rhyme if not reason. No one has to ask (I hope) what "I Want You" is about, or "Absolutely Sweet Marie." Or "Just Like a Woman," which I want to cut out of the album and mail to everybody. The songs are still a swirl of imagery, but it is a gentler, less cyclonic swirl; more like autumn leaves. The nightmares are receding.

Blonde on Blonde is a cache of emotion, a well-handled package of excellent music and better poetry, blended and meshed and ready to become a part of your reality. Here is a man who will speak to you, a 1960's bard with electric lyre and color slides, a truthful man with X-ray eyes you can look through if you want. All you have to do is listen.

Source: Paul Williams, "Understanding Dylan," *Crawdaddy!*, August 1966. Reprinted in *Outlaw Blues: A Book of Rock Music* (New York: E.P. Dutton, 1969), pp. 59–69.

19

"Raga Rock"

The Byrds, Press Conference, 1966

In the 1960s rock bands used the press conference not only to showcase their personalities (as we saw with the Beatles in Chapter 15), but also as a strategic opportunity to educate the public and even dictate the very context in which their music would be discussed and received. Such was the case for the Byrds when two of their main members—Roger McGuinn (born 1942) and David Crosby (born 1941)—appeared with publicist Derek Taylor on March 28, 1966 to unveil the band's new single "Eight Miles High." The song was a departure from the Byrds' familiar folk-rock style, drawing instead from the classical Indian music of Ravi Shankar and John Coltrane's improvisatory India-inspired jazz. While McGuinn and Crosby brought a sitar and acoustic guitar with them to demonstrate their combination of eastern and western musical traditions, and provide a platform for how the music should be understood, the press was more eager to discuss the label of "raga rock" that had been circulating around this new crossover phenomenon. Musicians are often wary of embracing such labels, especially ones that hint at gimmickry and cultural mis-appropriation, and McGuinn and Crosby were no exception. Yet, for all their protestations, the Byrds' press conference unwittingly helped to spread the genre, as numerous articles appeared in its wake touting the "raga rock" label.[1] This fascination with the east would become one of the main identifying features of the psychedelic era, culminating with the Beatles' well-publicized 1968 trip to India to visit the Maharishi Mahesh Yogi.

Roger McGuinn: We've been experimenting with Indian music, such that is played in India—the classical music of India. And I have here an instrument called the sitar which is the instrument they play a lot of the classical music of India on, and I am going to demonstrate the sound of it to you. It's made of a gourd and the neck is some kind of rosewood—I think it's rosewood—with ivory inlays, tuned in drone, usually in the key of C or the of D, around there, and the strings are bent to produce a tightening of tone, a tightening of pitch.

(McGuinn plays the sitar, Crosby accompanies on acoustic guitar)

McGuinn: That's the kind of loping style they do it in. They also have very slow ones and ones that are much faster than that. But that's the basic thing. It's in a quarter-tone. They're in different modes of music scales, like the Lydian mode

---

1 The most notable of them was Sally Kempton, "Raga Rock: It's Not Moonlight on the Ganges," *Village Voice*, March 31, 1966, p. 23.

and so on.[2] And they're not in the Mixolydian or the atonal or 12-tonal scale that we have here.

David Crosby: They make up their own scales a lot. And they have different scales for different ragas. And also within a raga they'll have two different scales frequently, one for ascending and one for descending notes. In other words, if you're playing the scale up it might be (sings an ascending scale) and coming down it might be (sings a descending scale), like a different scale, both in the same song. What we've done is not to take this instrument and play it but to listen to the music of it a lot and then come up with an abstraction. This is a tool that we use. It's a small tape recorder, and we run it through an amplifier sometimes and play it back to ourselves. And we listen to tapes of a lot of people. This particular one has got Bach and Ravi Shankar and the Beatles and I think some of the Lovin' Spoonful, but most of it is John Coltrane and Ravi Shankar. I ought to say, while we're at it, something about John Coltrane, because he's a major influence on this record, as well. I don't think anybody's really mentioned that. What we're talking about is all these new influences of sound we are putting into our new record. There are two basic ones: one is Ravi Shankar, very definitely, the instrumental one on the B-side ("Why") is particularly Ravi Shankar, particularly an abstraction of his kind of music. The instrumental on the A-side ("Eight Miles High") is conscious of it but, I think, is closer to an abstraction of a jazz musician named John Coltrane. That's C-o-l-t-r-a-n-e. And we'll play you short bits of both people.

(plays a recording of Ravi Shankar)

Crosby: This is Ravi Shankar at the height of it. That's the end of it. He gets going very fast and starts out very slow in a movement called an "alap." And it's very reflective, and then it builds and builds and builds to an unbelievable climax. They work very tightly with their drummer.

Crosby: This is John Coltrane.

(plays a recording of John Coltrane)

Crosby: You'll notice, in both, a widening of accepted concepts of tone scales. These deal many times in quarter-tone scales or Pentatonic or different ones than are commonly used for jazz or pop music. You'll hear some of that in what we're doing. I don't know—I think really what we ought to do is to play them the record. Have you all heard our new record?

Press: No.

Crosby: I think that would do more about saying what we're trying to do than anything else. If we could arrange to do that . . . Can we arrange to do that?

(plays a recording of "Eight Miles High")

Press: To all of you, why were you thinking that this Hindu raga was a good form to use?

McGuinn: We just like it, you know?

Press: Where did you hear it first?

---

2 Indian scales have structures that can be understood as equivalent to Western European modes. The Kalyan is similar to the Lydian mode.

McGuinn:	I think in the village. Although, we are not using the form, really. We are doing an abstraction of it. We are doing our interpretation of it, rather than the actual form.
Crosby:	The form itself is thousands of years old and very intricate. It's as intricate, and possibly more so, than the western music, but it's not that we are trying to do it. That's not our thing. We are trying to do an abstraction of it. We aren't really *trying* to do it. It just happened to us. We listened to this music a lot and it happens out in what we play. We didn't plan that record that we just played you or the other one. We sit down and play and then the music comes. And this is what came and everyone said. "That's very far out!" So, we'd like to explain it, if anyone wants to know . . .
Press:	It sounds very exciting. I was just interested in how it started . . .
Press:	The large guitar, the sitar, is that applicable for amplification?
Crosby:	Um, I've been informed that there is a company in India that makes an electrified sitar.[3] I'm also advised that a friend of mine is now playing lead electric sitar for Donovan![4] And I know that the Beatles own at least one more. It's a very fascinating instrument and I think we're going to have trouble giving this one back.
Press:	Who do you have to give it back to?
McGuinn:	The rental company!
Crosby:	Hertz Rent-a-Sitar!

*   *   *

Press:	Do you fellows do any of this psychedelic music or do you know anything about it? Can you clarify it a little?
Crosby:	I believe you mean some of the new wave jazz: the Archie Shepp and Ayler people . . . Is that what you're talking about?
Press:	I don't think so!
Crosby:	Um, that's the only . . .
Press:	The Turtles are doing it!
Crosby:	What exactly did you have in mind? Do you know . . .
Derek Taylor:	Could you help us a little? Could you tell us what you mean by psychedelic music?
Press:	Um, very recently, I believe the Turtles have been doing something with combined use of microphones, doing something with microphones along with guitars and producing some sort of sound . . .
Crosby:	I think you've run into another case of someone taking a tag, that's floating around in the semantic air, and sort of dropping it on something neatly, in order to try and package it. Rather than in the genuine meanings of psychedelic awareness: being involved with the music. I'm sure there's a psychedelic awareness involved with its own music—I wouldn't want to say whose—but I doubt it has very much to do with electronic side effects. Those are more "technique" issues.
Press:	Speaking of labels, what do you think of the term "raga-rock" and who came up with it?

---

3 In the United States, the Danelectro company would release the Coral electric sitar the following year, in 1967.

4 Crosby most likely is referring to Shawn Phillips, who played sitar on Donovan's 1966 album, *Sunshine Superman*.

Crosby:	Um, I'm not sure who came up with it, and I hope no one is here who embraces it as a long-term project. I think it's on the same level as "folk-rock," which is also a somewhat limiting label.
McGuinn:	What ever happened to "rockabilly?"
Crosby:	What ever happened to the "ska?" Um, in any case, we wouldn't use that term to describe anything we were doing. We would say that we had listened to Indian music and that it was affecting ours. The music we play is still our music. It is not Indian music. It's "Byrds-rock 'n' roll." And we maintain that.
Press:	You know, if that's the case, why are there all your press releases that have "raga-rock" . . . or on news articles, it says "raga-rock"? Why is that the case?
Crosby:	Well, I'm very surprised if it does, but I'll tell you, we don't like them.
McGuinn:	And it won't be there for long!
Taylor:	And let me tell you, it isn't on any press releases that come from the Byrds. But I think that most people would agree about that: there is a desire outside an area to find a label. It's not a thing that you do yourself. There's a desire for other people to "package," as David said. Certainly, no press release of mine has ever contained the words "raga-rock" or "folk-rock"—except maybe to put it down, to reject it.
Crosby:	There's a real reason that we avoid labels.
Press:	Are you the only people within this area of music at the moment that are doing the Hindu-influence, or are there any others?
Crosby:	No, there are a number of people aware of it. And I think that the Yardbirds' last single definitely had some of that in it.[5] I think they obviously had listened to it. A number of . . .
McGuinn:	The Beatles' "Norwegian Wood" had . . .
Crosby:	The Beatles' "Norwegian Wood" had a sitar in it which was a direct result of Ravi Shankar. I know, personally, for sure. The musician is—that I would like to say again—is the one that has been the most influenced by Shankar and come up with a valid expression of it, is John Coltrane. And to understand that record that we made, you must include him, as well. Would you like to hear the other side? The instrumental on it will show you some of it.

*   *   *

(plays a recording of "Why")

Taylor:	That was called "Why" and it was written by Jim and by David. Have we any more questions? We're not trying to rush you, we're just trying to encourage you . . .
Press:	I've heard someone say, "What's next? Maybe Kabuki-rock?" It kind of strikes me, you're like taking a form which is a thousand—a couple of thousand—years old, like raga, and all of a sudden it gets reduced to rock 'n' roll?
Crosby:	I question the use of the word "reduced." We've been very careful to say "abstracted." We haven't in any form, or in any way, tried to copy or demean the old and very respected form of raga. Nor have we encouraged the use of that term in description of what we're doing. We don't claim that this is a raga. And we would like to make certain that everyone understands that we don't. It is an

---

5 Crosby may be thinking of the Yardbirds' 1965 single "Heart Full of Soul," which was conceived around a sitar melody that Jeff Beck then played on electric guitar for the recording.

abstraction of it. It is the effect of raga on Byrds rock 'n' roll. This is Byrds rock 'n' roll and it will continue to be.

Press: But you're playing straight raga riffs, so to speak?

Crosby: Sometimes, sometimes . . . That's one of the things we do . . .

Press: But why do you think—considering that folksingers and singers in general, people, have been listening to sitar music and Coltrane and this kind of music for ten years—but that it's taken such a long time for it to be assimilated?

McGuinn: Well, the freedom of the pop music business has only begun in the last few years, since the Beatles came out. Now there's a freedom to take these other forms and put them into pop music.

Crosby: I think you'll see a great deal more of it. I know that the instrument, the sitar, is hanging a number of people up. It's one of the instruments we're now using because they can abstract from what they're doing and apply it to what we're doing.

Press: Do the people that buy your records understand what you're trying to do?

Crosby: I think they understand the emotional and telepathic character of the music that we play. Perfectly. And they enjoy it. And they feel it. As to whether they're able to intellectualize it, I sincerely doubt it. But, they do feel what we feel by playing it. And that's the key to it. We feel good playing it, and they feel that.

Press: What about the adults that don't respond to it?

Crosby: The adults that don't respond to it don't respond to our records anyway, I assume!

Press: Have you actually been able to attune your ear to that Hindu quarter-tone scale?

Crosby: It's more a matter of unlearning the preconceptions, than attune to what you're hearing. We're at the point where, right now, we can listen to any scale, I think. I listen to koto music, Malayan music, African music, with all different kinds of scales, and it doesn't bother me at all.

Press: Can you adapt that, feeling-wise, to your own music then? Carrying the nuance of that type scale?

Crosby: I know it'll happen inside my head somewhere. If I listen to it, it'll come out. You know? It's unavoidable. It's what happens.

McGuinn: Allen Ginsberg gave us some songs that he picked up in India, that are Hindu chants . . .

Crosby: Mantras and tantras and yantras . . .

McGuinn: And he gave me about an hour and a half of recorded tape. He was over at the house and we taped it. And the conception in that was that he wanted us to assimilate this in some way—that we've picked up Coltrane and Ravi Shankar and Seeger and Bob Dylan—and he wanted that to come out in our music. He thought that would be a good thing.

Press: What do you tell a young man or woman who wants to learn to play the way you do?

McGuinn & Crosby: Don't quit your day jobs!

Crosby: We really wouldn't tell them that! Encourage them in all possible ways . . .

Press: In other words, and to experiment?

McGuinn: Play in front of people a lot. Perform in front of live audiences as much as possible!

Source: Byrds Press Conference, March 28, 1966. Originally recorded by Don Paulsen of *Hit Parader* magazine. Transcribed and reprinted by Bill Irwin for the liner notes to *The Byrds – Another Dimension*. Sundazed Records, 2005, SEP2 10–168.

20

Motown

"A Whiter Shade of Black"

Jon Landau

Diana Ross and the Supremes, Stevie Wonder, Smokey Robinson and the Miracles—Motown's famed roster virtually defined the height of pop and rock sophistication in the 1960s. Modeling his label's sound on the successful assembly-line production of Detroit's Ford Motor Company, Berry Gordy (born 1929) fashioned a durable hit single formula. The songwriting team of Eddie Holland (born 1939), Lamont Dozier (born 1941), and Brian Holland (born 1941) provided a host of memorable melodies, the Funk Brothers contributed their propulsive rhythm section arrangements, and soulful singers like Levi Stubbs of the Four Tops added their voice and image. The author of "A Whiter Shade of Black," music journalist Jon Landau, would later go on to greater fame in the 1970s as Bruce Springsteen's manager and producer. In this 1967 article, originally published in *Crawdaddy!* magazine, Landau examines the Motown style as a form of musical crossover designed to appeal equally to white and black audiences. Like many other observers, he also contrasts Motown with the more "hard core" sounds of the Stax-Volt label. Landau identifies many of Motown's most characteristic elements, from song forms to details of instrumentation. What he outlines is nothing less than a formula for success, and one whose features have been replicated throughout rock's history, from the 1970s Philadelphia soul explosion to the various hip-hop, dance, and pop production teams that have dominated popular music in the 2000s.

Traditionally there have been three types of Negro musicians in pop music. The first consists of artists who for either aesthetic or financial reasons have chosen to sever their ties with specifically Negro music and instead work in the general field of pop. Richie Havens, as an exponent of the contemporary urban ballad in the Ochs-Dylan-Paxton tradition, and Jimi Hendrix, as an exponent of freaking out, are good examples. The second class consists of performers who are still working in one of the basic Negro musical forms but who seek to alter their approach enough to make it appealing to a large part of the white audience. Motown is the ideal example, but someone like Lou Rawls also falls into this category. Finally there is the hard core: performers who won't or can't assimilate, and therefore just continue to do their thing. If the white audience digs what a performer in this group is doing, it's just gravy; the performer never expected it. This category contains all of the independent R&B labels, most importantly the Stax-Volt group in Memphis, Tennessee.

Obviously the first group identified above is irrelevant in a discussion of Negro music because performers in this group are working in musical idioms which are not distinctively Negro. Motown, as the basic representative of the second group, seeks a white audience but maintains a basically Negro identity, and is a logical starting point for any survey of Negro pop.

Motown is two things above all. It is a place and a form. By the first I mean that it is a community, obviously tightly knit, made up of a group of people all aiming at the same thing. By the second I mean that the music that this community makes is stylized to express precisely what Motown wants it to by use of recurring techniques, patterns, and other devices. In the evolution of Motown the community clearly came first, and a brief look at how Motown began will help us clarify what the Motown form is, and why it takes the form that it does.

When Motown began is not altogether clear. Legend has it that Berry Gordy, Jr., the man who runs the place, quit a job on a Detroit assembly line nine or ten years ago, borrowed some money, and began his rise to success instantly. The history of Motown shows us that it was not all that simple. It is a fact that almost a decade ago Berry Gordy was already in the music business writing for one of the greatest of all Motown performers, although he has never recorded on a Motown label, Jackie Wilson. (Wilson, who was clearly a major influence on Smokey Robinson, has always recorded for Brunswick.) The first records that Gordy produced for his own labels were written by himself, starting around 1960, perhaps earlier. Two of the earliest Motown tunes were Barrett Strong's "Money" and the Contours' "Do You Love Me?" Both of these songs seem remarkably unsophisticated compared to what the typical Motown song-writing team of today throws out, even for flip-side material. Both of these records were in fact indistinguishable from the general R&B of the day. "Do You Love Me?"—the later of the two—even has the old-fashioned twist drumming, a rarity on the oldest of Motown records.

It appears that the first major move Gordy made in his attempt to build Motown was to bring William "Smokey" Robinson into the picture. At first Gordy collaborated with Smokey in writing tunes for Smokey's legendary Miracles. After four or five duds, their joint labors resulted in the spectacular "Shop Around." This was one of the early big ones for the Motown organization and it was not only a financial success but an aesthetic one, with Robinson's faultless lead earmarking the Miracles as something far above the rank and file of R&B vocalists.

Smokey gradually moved up in the organization. But while he was struggling to make a name for the Miracles, other talent was being brought into the picture. Mary Wells, Marvin Gaye, the Marvelettes, Little Stevie Wonder, and the Supremes were all gradually added to the roster. When back-up vocalists were needed for records by big stars, a former Motown secretary named Martha Reeves organized a trio—Martha and the Vandellas. Motown soul records with big booming commercial arrangements were making it into the pop charts. Marvin Gaye put two straight blues, "Wonderful One" and "Can I Get a Witness," right up there, and a little twelve-year-old kid named Stevie Wonder sold a million copies of one of the freakiest Motown records ever, "Fingertips, Pt. II." The community was clearly developing at breakneck speed in the early sixties, but there was still no form. Individual successes were common but they were not based on any specific Motown style. Motown was still just an electric grouping of artists not readily distinguishable from the rest of souldom except by virtue of the fact that they generally did what they did better than anyone else around.

The Motown form came in 1963–64, with the advent of the Supremes. During the pre-Supremes era a Motown vocalist named Eddie Holland had been occasionally releasing singles, mostly poor imitations of Jackie Wilson. Over a period of time he, Brian Holland, and Lamont Dozier formed a song-writing-and-producing team. They had their first significant opportunities to develop their style with Martha and the Vandellas, and they wrote and produced many of the girls' early hits: "Come and Get These Memories," "Quicksand," "Livewire," and "Heatwave."

Apparently the Vandellas could only go so far. Martha has a straight, tough, soul voice and probably was not the right type for the more commercial records being planned. So attention was soon turned to the Supremes. The one advantage Diana Ross had over Martha, on a record, was her cooling sexy voice. This was coupled with the consummated Holland-Dozier-Holland writing-producing concept, and the result, after a few failures, was fantastic financial success. There can be no doubt that "Where Did Our Love Go" and the follow-up, "Baby Love," set the direction for the future of Motown. With these two records, H-D-H and the Supremes had created the Motown definition of success. Each of these records was the product of a carefully thought out, highly distinctive musical form that had been a long time in coming. When the formula paid off, Motown lost no time in refining the form, stylizing it, and imposing it on all of their artists, one way or another.

What then is this Motown style? It is a distinctive approach to all facets of record making, especially rhythm, melody, instrumental sound, and vocal arranging. With regard to rhythm the most important thing is Motown drumming. Up until the time of H-D-H the most common pattern of drumming was for the drummer to hit the snare on the second and fourth beats of every measure. That was changed to the drummer hitting the snare on every beat. While this aspect of the style was not present on the earliest H-D-H productions, with the Vandellas and the Supremes, it soon became a Motown staple to the point where it would be safe to say that seventy-five percent of the records recorded in a Motown studio since "Baby Love" have this style of drumming. In addition, over a period of time production techniques were developed to give added emphasis to the drums, and to give them a distinctive sound. Tambourines were added on some records and in general anything that would deepen or solidify the effect of the beat was thrown in. The Motown beat was to become the key to public identification of the Motown sound.

Motown changed things around melodically as well. Prior to the Supremes there were two basic pop music forms: the blues form and the ballad form. Motown changed all that. Repetition was the new order. "Baby Love" is a circle of repetition. Its form is very close to a-a-a-a. Motown writers were among the first to realize that they were writing for the car radio and they learned early in the game to keep it simple. By and large the songwriting chores were turned over to a select number of teams such as H-D-H or the team of Stevenson-Gaye ("Dancing in the Streets"), all of whom stuck to the basic credo of keeping the melodic structure relatively simple and easy to follow. However, it must be added that within easy-to-follow melodic structures Motown has often produced melodies and chord progressions of surprising sophistication for a pop song.

Perhaps the part of a Motown record that is easiest to recognize is the overall instrumental background. In addition to the distinctive beat, already discussed, Motown has always presented the public with highly regimented, stiff, impersonal back-up bands. Even the solos so common on Motown singles are totally lacking in spontaneity. It's easy to see where the charge of black Muzak comes from. Of course this approach succeeds commercially because it keeps things simple, predictable and danceable, and besides, lots of the basic arrangements are pretty. (Like on "Stop in the Name of Love.")

Equally as important as the instrumental back-up style is the vocal back-up. Here Martha and the Vandellas can take full credit for stylizing the pattern of beginning sentences with high-pitched "Ooh's" and ending them with "di-doo-doo wah's" You can hear them do it perfectly on Marvin Gaye's "Stubborn Kind of Fellow" or throughout their own Dance Party album.

Such is the fourfold path to the Motown sound. However one other thing not strictly a part of the musical form must be mentioned. It is the Motown approach to the lead vocal. I haven't included this as one of the basic characteristics of the Motown sound because I feel there is too great a variation among the Motown lead vocalists and because I don't believe vocals can be stylized in the same way that other aspects of pop music can.

In discussing Motown vocals the first thing to realize is that Berry Gordy, Jr., knows that you can give a singer everything, but if the guy can't sing he won't sell any records. Therefore Motown makes damn sure that everybody who they sign has the basic raw material. Motown takes these vocalists and of course tries to give them a style. But most of the successful Motown artists have retained a strong degree of individual identity.

Within the context of many individual vocal styles, two basic approaches can be identified. One is symbolized by Diana Ross (of the Supremes), one of the most successful vocalists of all time. Diana's approach is to stick closely to the form. She rarely steps out on her own, seldom improvises, and never gets in the way. She restrains herself so as to fit perfectly into the prerecorded instrumental tracks that she dubs her voice into. Consequently she is the least jarring of Motown vocalists, the least disturbing, and the most able to reach a car-radio audience. I wouldn't deny for a second that she has a fantastic voice for what she is doing, that she oozes sex, and that she is a fine vocalist. But she seldom goes beyond what was planned for her by the production team.

The other type of Motown vocalist is seen in Levi Stubbs (lead singer of the Four Tops). His thing is breaking through the barrier that the regimented background sticks him with. All his shouting, his frenzy, his individuality, is something that Motown can't quite control or make predictable. He is an artist who can be told what to say only within certain limitations—once within them he is on his own and there is no telling what he will do. The dichotomy between Levi's style and Diana's is simply this: Diana strives for unity whereas Levi creates conflict. Diana's approach is to roll with the given version of the Motown sound she is to record. She will try to fit snuggly into the overall framework. A very commercial, good record will then be produced, but one without much artistic merit because it contains no tension. It becomes too smooth. The best example of this is Diana's performance on "You Can't Hurry Love." The alternative to this approach is Levi's method of attacking the song, and in the process creating his own dynamic. Levi's style is based on creating tension between the lead vocal and everything else that happens on the record. It is the same dynamic that Stevie Wonder creates when he sings "Uptight," and that David Ruffin creates when he sings "I'm Losing You." When the artist chooses this path the record as a whole improves because the background and the beat no longer have to stand on their own but can act as counterweights to the vocal. And when a record is created in which all the different parts are interacting in this fashion then the listener is suddenly able to appreciate individual excellence on the part of the musicians as well as the vocalists, and you may find yourself digging the fantastic thing the bass is doing on "Bernadette," or the fact that the drummer is socking it to you on "Uptight." This is Motown at its finest.

Having gone this far in identifying a Motown style, it should be noted that things do not remain pat or static within the context of the basic sound. Refinements are constantly taking place and there are always some limited forms of experimentation going on. For example, Smokey's "Tracks of My Tears," one of the classic Motown lyrics, also was notable for the un-Motown-like use it made of the guitars. The Four Tops have been doing songs which have clearly been influenced by the Dylanesque technique of incessant repetition, as Richard Goldstein correctly noted some time ago. However, one thing Motown will never do is go against the grain of its highest value—success. It may dabble here and there in electric variations on its style, but if these variations don't sell records, forget it. Smokey Robinson's activities as songwriter and producer have recently been curtailed, presumably for that reason.

Of course, since the Supremes era began, success has never really been in question at Motown. They have the style and they have the talent, and by God, they sell the records. But success means many things to many people, and here is the rub. The head of the Motown corporation picked up some pretty perverse notions as to what constitutes success, somewhere along the line. It hasn't been enough to just break out of the soul charts and radio stations. It hasn't been enough to outsell the top pop stars in every field. Berry Gordy's idea of success is to be able to put each one of his groups into the big nightclub scene. As I write this the Temptations are at the Copa wowing them with "Swanee," according to the latest issue of *Variety*. As a result of this philosophy Motown has weighed down its artists with absurd album material (Would you believe the Four Tops singing "Strangers in the Night" on their On Broadway album?) and absurd live nightclub acts. There is no sense in laboring the point, because things are going to get worse before they get better. But it should be pointed out that such a policy may put big Motown stars into high-paying clubs but lose them some of their hard-core, record-buying audience in the process.

It has been suggested that Berry Gordy's experience as an auto worker in Detroit before his entrance into the music business has given him too rigid an idea of how to run a record company, and it is certainly true that he likes to run things in assembly-line-like fashion. The Temptations are going to do the Copa bit because that is what Motown stars are expected to do when they reach a certain level of success. And the fact that David Ruffin doesn't sound good singing "The Best Things in Life Are Free" isn't going to keep him from doing it.

This rigidity in management is particularly evident in the Motown album approach. Motown policy here is not hip to the concept being developed by the big pop stars that an album is a whole thing, not just your latest hits and some junk. As a result the best Motown albums are in the "Greatest Hits" series, because such albums at least retain the uniform high quality of Motown singles. They also sell quite well. The best of these is The Temptations' Greatest Hits. Only a few Motown albums outside this series are listenable. Dance Party is certainly one of these, but I don't know how many others could be named. This is a quick-money policy based on the concept that a few hits will sell an album. But as the Doors and the Airplane have recently proven, an album which builds up a reputation of being good unto itself doesn't need big hits on it to sell. Both Surrealistic Pillow and The Doors sold extremely well before any of the album cuts made it as singles. And Sgt. Pepper doesn't have any singles on it at all.

In general, Motown must base its reputation on singles. "Reach Out I'll Be There" is certainly the best record the Four Tops ever made and probably the best record ever produced at Motown. There are simply no flaws. No dumb instrumentals. A beautiful lyric and a very sophisticated chorus. Perfect tension between artist and orchestra. Fantastic use of verbal repetitions in the vocal back-up. It's a record that cuts through, that transcends all the limitations of the recorded rock form. In my opinion if there is any one thing that makes the difference on this record it is the power and absolute conviction of all four vocalists. When Levi sings you know he is not kidding. His voice literally drives that band through the floor of the record . . . And the rest of the Tops push even Levi that one step further with their perfectly timed responses to him, and their "Aahs" at the beginning of each verse.

As manufacturers of single records Motown is unparalleled in both artistic and financial success. From the Supremes on there has always been an abundance of first-rate Motown records. "Shotgun," "Ooh, Baby, Baby," "Heatwave," "Ain't That Peculiar," "Tracks of My Tears," "Baby I Need Your Loving," "Uptight," "Dancing in the Streets": it's positively remarkable what this company has achieved within the limited form they have chosen to produce their music in. And in the last year important steps have been made to broaden that form. Increased virtuosity, particularly of the rhythm instrumentalists, is being featured. The level of songwriting for singles is fantastically high. (Just off the charts: "I Was Made to Love Her," "Ain't No Mountain High Enough," and "More Love.") New production people are being added who are doing good things, like Harvey Faqua.

The night before I started this article I saw Stevie Wonder on Joey Bishop's late-night show. He performed "Alfie," which I think is a decent song, on the harmonica. As they were introducing him I got upset thinking to myself that this was going to be dreadful. Stevie played it beautifully; he really did. And that—right there—showed me the power, the freedom the artist has to transcend the ephemeral, like the particular song he is playing, or the particular band he is working with. And after writing all this if I had to say what makes Motown work, when it does work, I would say it is the combination of the limitations that are imposed on Motown's artists, and their capacity, which manifests itself only occasionally, to shatter them with some little nuance that no one could have predicted. Motown is the transcendence of Levi saying "Just look over your shoulder." And the beautiful thing is that the way Levi says that—that could never be formalized or stylized. The beauty of Motown is that it gives great artists something to work with and against. It gives them salable good songs and a beat and a producer and musicians and supervisors. But it doesn't give its vocalists their voices, their talent, or their soul. When Smokey sings "This is no fiction, this is no act, it's real, it's fact," or when Stevie sings "No one is better than I/ And I know I'm just an average guy," we are no longer listening to a thing called Motown. We are participating in the transcendence of a particular artist, we are drawn into an individual vision of reality. From every aesthetical point of view possible it can truly be said that when these moments occur there is no longer Motown, but only music.

Source: Jon Landau, "A Whiter Shade of Black," *Crawdaddy!*, October 1967. Reprinted in Jonathan Eisen, ed., *The Age of Rock: Sounds of the American Cultural Revolution* (New York: Vintage Books, 1969), pp. 298–306.

21

James Brown
Soul Brother No. 1

FRED WESLEY, JR.

The self-proclaimed "hardest working man in show business," James Brown (1933–2006) had already been a major R&B and soul star for nearly a decade and a half by the time trombonist Fred Wesley, Jr. (born 1943) joined his group in 1968. Wesley was an experienced sideman, having played with Ike and Tina Turner and Hank Ballard. As he reveals in his autobiography, however, nothing could have prepared him for Brown's dynamic stage show and the dictatorial tactics by which he kept his performers within his grip of power. The two passages excerpted here from Wesley's book capture the trombonist's induction into Brown's world, when the singer was at the height of his success in the mid-late 1960s. In Wesley's eyes the musicians deserved the majority of the credit for crafting and perfecting Brown's trademark sound. At the same time he concedes that were it not for Brown's demanding star presence and controlling, manipulative personality, the music would have been far less remarkable. Wesley's initial stay with Brown was relatively short, as he quit in early 1970, following in the footsteps of disgruntled, departed musical director Alfred "Pee Wee" Ellis and countless other former band members. Wesley was soon back with Brown, however, rejoining the band as its musical director in December 1970 and remaining in that position through 1975. During that time Wesley was one of the main architects behind Brown's influential early '70s funk grooves.

Maceo, Pee Wee, and I became and have remained close friends, with Waymon being the connection and catalyst between us.[1] Joe Dupars and St. Clair Pinckney completed the horn section at that time. The other James Brown horn players, who I had known before, Brisco Clark and Mack Johnson, were long gone. For reasons that became clear to me later, there was high turnover in the James Brown horn section. As we sat around between the dressing room and the bus, Waymon, Pee Wee, and the other guys told stories of Brisco's drinking, Mack's insubordination, and other confrontations with the Boss. Jabo, Bernard (who for some reason was known as "Dog" in this band), Junior Gunther, Kenny Hull, and the local stage crew went about setting up the stage.

At about six or seven o'clock, Mr. Brown and an entourage of about four people arrived in what looked to be a rental car. Mr. Brown didn't ride the bus. He would station himself at a central point, in this case Miami, and fly in his private Lear jet back and forth to gigs in the area. Mr. Brown exited the driver's seat, went straight to the stage, and began fooling around with the Hammond B-3 organ that had been the first thing to be set up. He was much shorter than I had imagined him

---

1 Tenor saxophonist Maceo Parker and trumpeter Waymon Reed.

to be from seeing him on stage. Ms. Sanders[2] and the people who were busy on the stage greeted him respectfully. I and the other guys were out of sight on the bus and just kind of observed the arrival.

A beautiful, well-built, light-skinned girl got out of the car and went directly into Mr. Brown's dressing room without saying anything to anyone. The guys told me that she was Marva Whitney, the featured singer on the show, and hinted that she also had a more personal relationship with Mr. Brown. A stockily built guy with what looked like a hairdryer in his hand followed closely behind Ms. Whitney. This, I was told, was Henry Stallings, the hairdresser. Although he sported a nice "do," he looked like anything but a hairdresser. His demeanor also wasn't what you'd expect of a hairdresser. He had the loud, gruff, profane way of speaking you would more likely attribute to a gangster. A big, tall, black, rough-looking dude got out of the car last. He was scuffling with getting the luggage out of the car. This was Baby James, who *was* a gangster. His job was bodyguard, general enforcer, and whatever else Mr. Brown needed done that required brute strength and not a lot of brainpower. Actually, all of the nonmusical employees of the James Brown show sort of fit that description, except for Mr. Bell, the fourth person in the entourage, who was a middle-aged white man who piloted the James Brown Lear Jet.

After an afternoon of meeting people, reacquainting myself with old friends, and generally getting to know my new gig, it was finally time for the show. Unlike the Ike and Tina Turner show and the Hank Ballard show, I didn't go right onstage. I was told that I had to watch, go through a few rehearsals, and be fitted with some uniforms before I could go onstage.

I didn't know what kind of show to expect. I had only seen a small part of the show back in 1962 at the Howard Theater. The Orlando Sports Arena was hardly a theater. This place was more suited for rodeos and stock shows. (There were actually some live animals corralled in the back of the place.) However, the stage was set up with a somewhat elaborate sound system. All of the backline amplifiers were by vox, as were the drums and guitars. In fact, I think the entire sound system was by vox. Conspicuously missing, though, was a monitor system. When I had visited the show in Huntsville, I had seen the four sets of drums onstage, but I still hadn't seen how more than one drummer at a time operated during a show. The multiple-drummer concept was the subject of much discussion and speculation among musicians throughout the world. I was anxious to see firsthand what it was all about.

The horns were positioned on the left of the stage (from the audience's point of view) and in front of the organ. Jabo's drums were positioned upstage, left of center. Clyde's drums were also positioned upstage, but right of center. The bass player—Bernard or Buddy or Dog, whatever you want to call him—was parallel to and between Jabo and Clyde. A little to the right and behind Jabo was Country Kellum on rhythm, and I do mean *rhythm*, guitar. A little to the right and behind Clyde was Jimmy Nolen, the lead guitar player. On an elevated platform, stage left, angled to face center stage, were the three violins, each plugged into their own sound-enhancing amplifier, also by vox. There were two mikes for the horns—one for the saxes and one for the trumpets and trombone. A single mike was at center stage. On a high riser in the center of the stage behind the band was the lone JB Dancer. Although this was a rodeo arena, the James Brown stage had a big-time, professional, showbiz theater look about it.

It was finally show time. The place was packed. There were chairs set up on a portable floor over the ground, which was the real floor of the arena, but most of the crowd was standing all around the arena. The house lights went down and the band took the stage. After an involved musical introduction that included some really hip jazz licks, some funky rhythms, and some real hard

---

2 Gertrude Sanders, Brown's "wardrobe mistress."

bebop-type runs by the horns that melted into a dramatic drumroll, an offstage voice announced, "L-A-DIES AND GENTLEMEN, THE JAMES BROWN ORCHESTRA." Under the direction of Mr. Alfred "Pee Wee" Ellis, the band did a set, about six tunes. The only ones I remember are "Hip Hug-Her," a then-current hit by Booker T. and the MGs, and "Why Am I Treated So Bad," a current hit by the Staple Singers. All the tunes were very interestingly arranged by Pee Wee, immediately convincing me of his musical genius. Maceo and Waymon played most of the solos, with a couple by St. Clair on tenor sax and Pee Wee himself on alto sax.

I was very impressed with the band. Although it wasn't a jazz band, they played jazz very well. It wasn't the Jazztet, but it was far more musical than I had expected. So far, I was happy about being on this gig. The people seemed to be people I could deal with. Some I already liked a lot. And the music seemed to be reasonably challenging. I would be happy if I had to play straight-up blues all night after the band's opening set. I was sure that associating with musicians like Pee Wee and Waymon would make the whole thing worthwhile.

But wait. There was more to come. Suddenly, the stage went black. The band played a grandiose, almost symphonic intro/fanfare type of thing, complete with strings and what I swear sounded like timpani and French horns. When this bodacious introduction decrescendoed, the lights hit center stage and there was James Brown. There he was. Sitting on a stool. Not just an ordinary stool, but a stool of carved, highly polished oak, with a padded leather back, more like a big high chair. He was dressed in a beige, mohair, three-piece suit, with a three-quarter-length coat, a turtleneck shirt, and the baddest burgundy alligator boots I have ever seen. He calmly sang Tony Bennett's "If I Ruled the World." Bear in mind, I'm expecting a screaming and hollering, fast-dancing little sissy to come out and sweat all over the place. Instead, I'm seeing a real cool man, milking one of my favorite ballads dry. The band went out of "If I Ruled the World" into a smooth swing version of Sinatra's "That's Life." The arrangements were absolutely fantastic. Sinatra and Nelson Riddle couldn't have performed the songs any better. I was totally surprised and amazed.

But that's not all. At the end of "That's Life," James Brown pushed the mike forward in a military-rifle-salute type move, accented by a rim shot from Jabo, and the band hit a descending drag triplet riff and went directly into a heartstopping Mobile, Alabama, blues type shuffle. Before I could get straight from the shock, James Brown was deep into "Going to Kansas City." The band was clicking like a funk machine, everything hitting in the right place. Jimmy Nolen, Country, Dog, and—leading the pack—Jabo, doing what nobody in the world can do like him. A hard-driving shuffle. They did several verses and choruses, increasing the intensity of the groove until it spilled over into a vamp that had the rhythm driving wide open, horns screaming in a frenzy, and James Brown, still basically cool, giving us a glimpse of the fury that was to come, with a little mash here and a split there, suddenly leaving the stage as abruptly as he had appeared. Danny Ray, still offstage, promised, "JAMES BROWN WILL BE BACK."

The audience went crazy. I went with them. I don't even remember exactly how it happened, but when I looked up again the lovely Ms. Marva Whitney was onstage singing some song I'd never heard before. It must have been an original. The highlight of her set was a beautiful arrangement of "People." Obviously, the genius of Pee Wee Ellis had struck again.

As she left the stage, the lights went out again, and the spotlight that followed her off followed James Brown back on, as the band hit the intro to "Man's World." This time James was wearing a pantsuit with a formfitting shirt that had bloused sleeves and alternating navy-blue and white pleats. The pants were navy-blue velvet bell-bottoms. This time a pair of navy-blue lizard boots adorned his little fast feet. He was center stage by the time the violins finished their famous run. There was a pause. He sang, in his familiar voice, the familiar line, *"This is a man's world."* The audience and I went berserk again. Even I, a jazz person, was familiar with that hit song. I can't say that I had liked it before. It made so little sense to me. He did the song all the way through. "Man made the car," "Man made money, to buy from other man," and all that. The words were usually silly to me, but seeing it performed, in person, now, was thrilling. He went straight into a ten-minute vamp in which he did a complete production number that included everything from horn "hits"—one, two, three, and four times—to tricks with the mike and drops to his knees, all held together by a steady "motion of the ocean" groove by Jabo and the rhythm section. He finally turned us loose—just before everybody died from ecstasy—and left the stage again. Once again, Danny Ray, offstage, assured us: "JAMES BROWN WILL BE BACK."

The band left the stage, and Danny Ray made himself visible for the first time and made a few announcements about souvenir items on sale in the front of the arena. I had noticed a big fat man set up at a table, selling merchandise. This was the intermission. The band went into the stalls that served as dressing rooms and proceeded to change clothes. The place was littered with clothes bags, hangers, irons, shoes, shoetrees, socks, bow ties, belts, and accessories. After about fifteen minutes of furious activity, the band emerged, dressed in lime-green suits with white satin lapels, bow ties, and patent-leather shoes. The look was absolutely stunning. A startling contrast to the ordinary black tuxedos in which they had opened the show. Each band member looked as if he had just left home in fresh clothes straight out of the laundry. The Army would have been proud of the spit and polish of this band. They stood around, ready, waiting, I guessed, for Mr. Brown to come out of his dressing room.

After a while, Henry Stallings came out of the man's dressing room and in a gruff voice said, *"He's ready."* Everyone moved out immediately and took their positions on stage. I'm standing on the side of the stage now. The band started a quiet, bluesy-jazz vamp that went on until Danny Ray took center stage. The groove was cut off abruptly, and Ray went into his legendary introduction of James Brown. *"The hardest working man in show business," "The man who made 'Try Me,' 'Out Of Sight'. . . ."* Each of his phrases was accented by hits and riffs from the band. He continued: *"The amazing Mr. 'Please, Please, Please' himself . . . JAAAAAAMES BROWN."* With that, James—whom I could see framed in his dressing-room door, prancing and bucking like a race horse in the starting gate—stormed onto the stage and proceeded to do an hour-and-a-half medley of his repertoire. He did songs like "I Got the Feeling," "I Got You," and "I'll Go Crazy," going from tune to tune via clever segues and intros. The groove remained intense, even through all the tempo changes. Most of the things were fast and funky, with the exception of "Try Me" and another long production performance of "Lost Someone."

Mr. Brown was exactly as advertised. His dancing was unbelievable. He did things that seemed impossible for the human body to do. How he could sing with that much energy and dance at the same time was amazing. His rhythm and soulful attitude and demeanor epitomized what black music was all about. The band was now literally a funk machine. Overpowering and relentless. I got the sense that James was plugged into the band, and it was generating energy directly to his body. At times, the band was totally musical, with beautiful chords and melodies mixing with the constant funky grooves. But, at other times, things happened that totally defied musical explanation. There were chords that were just sounds for effect and rhythms that started and ended wherever they started or ended, not in accord with any time signature or form. Through it all, the band was tight, doing all the complicated dance routines and the music at the same time. Everything conspired in exactly the right way to make for an extraordinarily entertaining show that was sometimes directed by Pee Wee, but mostly signaled by the same man who was also doing all the singing and dancing. The sounds, the sights, and the relentlessly intense feeling of that funky groove were completely thrilling and mesmerizing.

By the time the show climaxed with "Please, Please, Please" and the famous act in which James Brown collapses to his knees and is covered sympathetically with a cape by Danny Ray, the audience was completely fucked up, responding to any and everything that James or the band did. After his third drop to his knees and covering by a third, spectacularly designed cape, James Brown left the stage as the band opened up and went all the way crazy. We were all thoroughly entertained, all funked up, wanting more but satisfied, when all of a sudden he was back and giving us what we had forgotten was missing: Mr. Brown's then-current hit, "I Can't Stand Myself." This encore was like a climax on top of an already all-consuming climax. The encore must have lasted another thirty minutes. The crowd—and that included me—was completely satiated. I felt guilty for not having bought a ticket. This was the most completely thrilling, spectacular, hypnotizing, soulful, incredible, unbelievable, entertaining, and satisfying show I had ever seen or heard of.

After the show was over and I had caught my breath, I could barely keep myself from raving to the guys in the band about how thrilled I was with the show. I was very anxious to get onstage and be a part of what had to be the greatest show on earth. It was clear now why they needed another trombone player. All during the show Rasbury[3] was going back and forth between the box office and James's dressing room, and every now and then he would grab his horn, which was a valve trombone, and go onstage for a little while. I didn't miss his part, but it would definitely become a fuller brass sound with me onstage. When they cooled down and changed out of their suits, which were soaking wet with sweat, Waymon and Pee Wee took me to meet "The Man."

We went to the dressing room door and waited and waited until finally Ms. Sanders told us we could come in. As we entered the dressing room, I was amazed that what was probably supposed to be a storeroom had been transformed into a very comfortable dressing room, complete with a rug on the floor, racks of clothes hanging around, shoes lined up in a very orderly manner, an ironing board, a table with a large mirror and make-up on it, and, indeed, a professional looking hairdryer. This room had all the comforts of home. Ms. Sanders even offered us a soda from the cooler that was there.

Mr. Brown was sitting at the table in a robe, rubbing his face with a make-up sponge. He was still dripping sweat from his hair, which Henry was carefully rolling up as Brown talked in his fast, assured way to Rasbury—not leaving any space for Rasbury to get a word in edgewise—about how good the show was and how much the people enjoyed it. Brown seemed amazed and even relieved that the audience had accepted and enjoyed the show as much as they had. This surprised me. At that time, I didn't know if this was a new show that had not been audience tested or if the great James Brown was so insecure that he never took pleasing the audience for granted. I learned later that most true stars are never sure or confident about their performances. Mr. Brown was a glaring example of this insecurity, although he put up a self-confident and cocky, if paper-thin, façade.

After a long time of listening to him rant and rave about how big he was, how well his records were selling, and how much the people loved him, he finally allowed Waymon to say, "Mr. Brown, I'd like you to meet the new trombone player, Fred Wesley." He seemed unimpressed. He didn't turn around from the mirror. Instead, he kept on fussing with his make-up and wiping sweat, then glared at me through the mirror and asked, "Can you dance?" Taken aback, I paused and collected myself, then said, "Yeah." Then I realized that he had probably noticed that I was a little chubby and thought that dancing might be a problem for me. At the same time, I realized that I'd said "Yeah," not "Yes, sir," as everyone else was saying. So I quickly got myself together and started assuring him that dancing was not a problem for me. I said, "Yes, sir, I can dance. I can dance very well." I might have even given him a little step or two. I didn't want anything to keep me from getting this gig. He told me that I was on probation and would be watched and evaluated over the next few days to see if I would fit in. I assured him that I was the right man for the job and that he would not have a problem with me. He still seemed unconvinced but said, "Okay. We'll see."

---

3 Levi Rasbury, trombonist who also doubled as a road manager.

The next few days found me adjusting to the day-to-day routine of the James Brown system. We worked almost every night, making that $225-a-week, work-or-no-work salary, not so great when you considered that the "work-or-no-work" clause was in favor of management. The salary covered anything that came up. Sometimes we did more than one show in the same place, two cities in the same day, recording sessions, and TV shows—all covered by the same weekly salary. I found out that what I had thought was security for a musician was really just a guarantee of cheap labor for James Brown. Most road musicians get paid by the show, making off days detrimental to their income. With bands like Hank Ballard or Bobby Bland or even a jazz group like Art Blakey, a guaranteed weekly salary was a good thing, because you were covered for those off days, and hardly any big stars worked seven days a week, three hundred days a year like James Brown did.

I figured out that James could make anywhere from $350,000 to $500,000 a week, but his payroll remained at about a paltry $6,000 a week. And he acted like he didn't want to give you that. I had to almost beg for a draw during that first week I was out there. It soon became clear that there was no set payday. It was supposed to be Sunday, but it never happened on time. You knew the money was there. You could plainly see bags and even cardboard boxes full of money being loaded into the rented car every night. It was now clear why there was such a high turnover rate in the band.

After my probation period, my salary shot up to $350 a week, so even with paying my own hotel and food out of that, I was able to get enough money home to support my family at least as well as that milkman job would have. Also, although there was a serious discrepancy between the money you were helping to generate and the percentage you were being paid, the salary was still just a little above what you could make in a year with most of the other bands working regularly. Still, like me, most of the guys must have had ulterior motives for staying on the gig; it was clear that none of the James Brown sidemen would ever get rich.

I'm sure that some of the old-timers felt that they were lucky to have a gig on this level and weren't about to take a chance on trying to get another gig even this good somewhere else. Others saw the James Brown show as a stepping-stone to bigger and better things. I'm sure that was the case with guys like Pee Wee and Waymon. And some were there simply because of the glamour and the opportunity to have fun and score exotic and beautiful women, who were always around big-time shows like this.

Whatever their reasons were, Mr. Brown took full advantage of them all and ruled his empire with an iron hand, using all they had to offer for his own benefit, giving back as little as possible in return. He had a knack for knowing how much to take and how much to give to keep his show operating. He knew who he could yell at without getting the hell knocked out of him. He knew how much to pay each individual to keep him hanging on. He also knew who and how to humiliate and insult in order to demonstrate his power and keep everyone on their toes. He would chastise and counsel his employees in front of certain disc jockeys, reporters, and local politicians to make himself look benevolent and merciful, so many people actually thought him to be a leader and father figure. He was a master of manipulation. I more than once saw him talk his musicians into getting into big debt with a house or a car only to fire them, watch them suffer for a while, then hire them back at a lower salary and at his complete mercy. Some of these people actually loved and respected him, no matter how horribly he treated them. It didn't take me long to realize that I was involved with a man unique among performers and among human beings in general. James Brown was a great performer, probably the greatest to ever live, but I had to be careful—this was a man with the power and will and, it seemed, the need to control not only the career but the whole life of every person who worked for him.

It wasn't long before I was onstage, playing and dancing right along with everyone else. I was onstage before my uniforms arrived. I did the gig at the Regal Theater wearing Jimmy Nolen's coat, standing behind the organ speaker to hide my pants. The Regal Theater in Chicago was the site of my first "James Brown Horror Rehearsal." This was a punishment rehearsal. A rehearsal that James called when he felt his grip on somebody or everybody slipping. This type of rehearsal was generally called at the most inopportune time. This particular one was called right after we had done three shows to sold-out Regal Theater audiences. The weather was abominable—there was a Chicago blizzard. Everyone was exhausted. James came out of his dressing room, still in his robe and slippers, and said that we had to get "Please, Please, Please" right. According to him, what we had been doing for weeks was, all of a sudden, all wrong. Of course, that was just his way of keeping us away from what we wanted to be doing after the show. This was the last day of a three-day stint in Chicago, and there was much to be done, like pack after being in the same place for three days. Also, when we stayed in one place for any length of time, many of the guys brought in their wives and loved ones. Brown knew that. He really seemed to hate any distraction or diversion from the show. At the time, I took the rehearsal as his way of letting me know, personally, because I was new, how he could control my life if and when he wanted to. But I now realize that his absolute commitment to the show drove him to want everyone else to have that same commitment.

This type of rehearsal was completely unnecessary musically. "Please, Please, Please" or "Try Me" were always the songs rehearsed because they were the only songs that he could almost make anyone believe he really knew. And it became clear to me right off that he didn't know those two songs either. I know it's hard to believe, but it would have been impossible for James Brown to put his show together without the assistance of someone like Pee Wee, who understood chord changes, time signatures, scales, notes, and basic music theory. Simple things like knowing the key would be a big problem for James. So, when James would mouth out some guitar part, which might or might not have had anything to do with the actual song being played, Jimmy or Country would have to attempt to play it simply because James was still in charge. We all had to pretend that we knew what James was talking about. Nobody ever said, "That's ridiculous" or "You don't know what you're talking about." The whole James Brown Show depended on having someone with musical knowledge remember the show, the individual parts, and the individual songs, then relay these verbally or in print to the other musicians. James Brown could not do it himself. He spoke in grunts, groans, and la-di-das, and he needed musicians to translate that language into music and actual songs in order to create an actual show.

So we just stood and took it while he went through changing little things that didn't need changing, adding things that didn't need adding, going over and over some little phrase and never being satisfied with it. He would tell the horns "It's not ladaladadida, it's ladalada*di*da." We would go ladalada*di*da, and he would say, "No, I said lada*la*dadida." Over and over it continued, until you wanted to just scream. He would get mad and chew out certain individuals (the ones he knew he could get away with chewing out) and do anything else to take up time. After a few hours of this misery or after he finally got tired, he would appear to be pleased and say things like, "Nooooow, we finally got it right. Nooooow, we have an arrangement." The truth of the matter was that nooooow the stuff was so confused that Pee Wee would have to have a real rehearsal to bring the songs back to any semblance of recognizability. That's why, even today, it's hard to recognize some of the songs during the James Brown live performances.

The Chicago rehearsal lasted right up until almost time to get on the bus and go to the next gig. No time to spend with your loved one. Hardly enough time to pack or get some breakfast. Any chance to take care of any business in a large city was gone. All you had time to do now was get on the bus.

Another time in Hollywood, California, at Modern Music Rehearsal Studios, he called one of those rehearsals. Here we are in beautiful Hollywood, full of distractions and diversions, and we have a horror rehearsal. This one was especially memorable because not only did we go through the ladaladadidas and the usual random humiliations, but Brown also created a new and very time-consuming wrinkle. The premise was that if you really knew the show you could recite the song titles really fast. So he had someone write the order of songs down, including the segues, interludes, and introductions. He would then go around the band and have each person recite the order as fast as they could from memory. In the first place, everyone had his own way of remembering the show. I, for one, didn't think of titles. I went more by my part. This is where I play the high B, or this is the song in which I play this rhythm or do this routine, for example. I had many different ways of cueing myself. It was very interesting, the different cues people made for themselves. And the fact is that they all worked, and the show went on. Having to identify each tune by title was automatically confusing and, the real point of the exercise, time-consuming. To an outside observer, it must have been hilarious. Here were people standing around holding instruments and saying rapidly: "There Was a Time Try Me Got the Feeling Cold Sweat Lost Someone Brand New Bag Intro Brand New Bag Please Please Please Can't Stand Myself. . . ."

At first he went around the band in order for a few hours until most everybody got it, but he wasn't satisfied. He then sprang on people at random and actually timed us with a stopwatch, just draaaging the thing out. If you hesitated, you didn't know the show. If you missed something, you didn't know the show. If you didn't do it fast enough, you didn't know the show. We were in agony, but Brown never tired over hours and hours. I've seen people like Ike Turner and Ray Charles try stuff like this, but after a while they would get physically tired and stop. You, me, Ike, Ray, and any other normal human being would eventually grow weary or at least have something else to do. But, in Hollywood, California, James Brown, world-famous entertainer, with all the money in the world, could find nothing better to do than torment his band. I heard him say one time, "That's what makes me *me*."

When you were in the midst of one of those horror rehearsals or recording sessions or self-proclaiming conversations with James Brown, you felt pain, excruciating fatigue, and intense boredom, which led to suppressed anger and hate. I wonder to this day why nobody ever bolted, telling him to his face how ridiculous those rehearsals were and just walking out. And to my knowledge, nobody ever did. I came close many times, but there was always some reason—economic, political, or psychological—that I didn't. Sometimes, oddly, I think that I simply didn't want to risk hurting his feelings. He was so definite in the way he spoke to you that you got the feeling that he really believed the ridiculous stuff he was saying and you didn't want to embarrass him. Also, the few times I did challenge what he had said, he got so loud and so much farther away from reality that I gave up, because I knew he would never admit to seeing my point. It was like being held hostage by real strong, loud, unbeatable ignorance. The kind of ignorance that can make you look crazy if you continue to confront it. To my mind, I am intelligent enough to know that such manipulation and torture is unnecessary to the creation of an act as exciting as the James Brown Show. But, on the real side, there has never been a show that exciting, that tight, that completely entertaining. There also has never been a man so dedicated, so determined, so focused. I reluctantly have to admit that the things he did that seemed so stupid to me were, indeed, what made him *him*, the greatest entertainer in the world. Conversely, the intelligent things that I do are what make me *me*, the greatest sideman in the world.

*   *   *

My first recording session with Mr. Brown was also during that trip to L.A. The whole band was loaded into some station wagons and transported to the vox recording studios somewhere in the Los Angeles area. We set up and Pee Wee proceeded to put together a song—with no written music. He started by giving Clyde a simple drumbeat. Clyde started the beat and held it steady while Pee Wee hummed a bass line to Charles Sherrell, a bass player from Nashville recently hired onto the show. When the bass line had become clear to Charles and locked with the drumbeat, Pee Wee moved to Country, the rhythm guitar player, and began to choose a chord that would fit with the bass notes. A B-flat 9 was finally settled on and a chunky rhythm was matched up with the bass line and the drumbeat. I was, so far, amazed at how this song was coming together. Jimmy Nolen was allowed to find his own thing to fit the developing groove. He came up with sort of a womp-womp sounding, single-string thing that seemed to really pull all of the other parts together. At this point, we, once again, have that washing-machine thang going. That was the best way to describe the various sounds and rhythms, each in its own space, each in its own time, occurring in just the right places, to make for a funky groove. With the rhythm section solidly in place, Pee Wee proceeded to hum out horn parts. We were given some strategic hits with carefully voiced chords and a melodic line that happened whenever it was signaled. Of course, the reeds played a version of the James Brown horns' signature ladidadidat. With this groove firmly in place, Pee Wee started putting together a bridge.

Before he got started on it good, the Boss walked in. Everything went silent. He walked to Pee Wee and said, "Let me hear it." Pee Wee counted it off, and we played what we had been rehearsing for the last two hours. James listened intently, walked over to Clyde and said something to him as we all kept playing. Clyde then started playing a pop-pop every now and then. Brown made similar adjustments to all the parts and, sporting a little grin, started to dance a little bit and kind of winked at us and said "Nooooow *that's* a groove." James and Pee Wee continued to make up a bridge. The whole band did sort of an ensemble stop rhythm on an E-flat major chord, with Jimmy Nolen doing a little doodit solo lick on top. After James was satisfied that everything was in place, he pulled some scraps of paper out of his pocket and started reading what sounded like grunting and groaning, mostly to himself, as the band played on. We had been playing now for about fours hours straight, and I, for one, was getting tired. I mean, how many times can you go da daaaa da dot da dot da da without getting a cramp in your lip? I was young, all right, but I wanted to live to get old.

Just then, Mr. Bobbit, the road manager, and a bunch of people, mostly kids, walked into the studio. We stopped playing, and Mr. Brown went over and greeted them like he had expected them. I had no idea what they had to do with this recording. James was over on one side of the studio, talking and waving his hands with the kids. After this went on for a while, he came back to us and counted the tune off again. When the groove settled, he yelled to the kids, "Say it loud!" The kids responded, "I'm black and I'm proud!" He instructed the kids to say their line on cue and gave us cues to do the bridge and other things. With all the cues and signals in place, we were ready to record. All the time we were getting the groove together, engineers were in and out of the control room, setting mikes, adjusting amplifiers, placing baffles, and the like. They were ready, and we were ready. Mr. Brown was in control now. Pee Wee took his place in the reed section, and James counted it off. The groove was already strong, but when James counted it off and began to dance and direct, it took on a new power. All of a sudden, the fatigue I had been feeling was gone. The kids were doing their chant with a new energy. In fact, the energy level in the whole studio was lifted. James went straight through the whole tune and that was it. After about four hours of preparation, "Say It Loud, I'm Black and I'm Proud" went down in one take.

Source: Fred Wesley, Jr., *Hit Me, Fred! Recollections of a Sideman* (Durham: Duke University Press, 2002), pp. 88–99, 106–7.

22

"Goodbye Surfing Hello God!— The Religious Conversion of Brian Wilson"

JULES SIEGEL

Along with the Beatles, Brian Wilson (born 1942) of the Beach Boys was one of the driving forces behind rock music's mid-1960s transformation from a fad almost exclusively associated with teenagers into a more ambitious medium. Originally known for their surf music style, intricate vocal harmonies, and glorification of the southern California lifestyle, the Beach Boys gained critical acclaim for their lush and lavish studio experimentation on their 1966 album *Pet Sounds*. The follow-up single, "Good Vibrations," was an unprecedented mammoth recording event, one that spanned six months and approximately fifteen separate sessions at four different studios. Wilson eventually was forced to whittle away more than ninety hours of studio tape to arrive at the three-and-a-half-minute finished product, a song which he famously referred to as his "pocket symphony." Jules Siegel's 1967 article describes Wilson's work on his next project, the ill-fated *Smile* (which would lay dormant until Wilson finally completed it in 2004). Siegel portrays a musician struggling with the daunting implications that go with the label of "genius," a word that conjures images of a tortured artist imbued with otherworldly gifts. Siegel's depiction of Wilson certainly fits this bill. The author also paints Wilson as a religious individual, and one who believes in the spiritual power of music. Such portraits were commonplace during the nineteenth century, when critics heralded Romantic era composers for both their genius and the spirituality of their musical creations. To what extent can we reasonably speak of rock music, such as that of the Beach Boys, as part of a spiritual practice, or as fulfilling a spiritual purpose?

It was just another day of greatness at Gold Star Recording Studios on Santa Monica Boulevard in Hollywood. In the morning four long-haired kids had knocked out two hours of sound for a record plugger who was trying to curry favour with a disc jockey friend of theirs in San José. Nobody knew it at that moment, but out of that two hours there were about three minutes that would hit the top of the charts in a few weeks, and the record plugger, the disc jockey and the kids would all be hailed as geniuses, but geniuses with a very small g.

Now, however, in the very same studio, a Genius with a very large capital G was going to produce a hit. There was no doubt it would be a hit because this Genius was Brian Wilson. In four years of recording for Capitol Records, he and his group the Beach Boys had made surfing music a national craze, sold 16 million singles and earned gold records for 10 of their 12 albums.

Not only was Brian going to produce a hit, but also, one gathered, he was going to show everybody in the music business exactly where it was at; and where it was at, it seemed, was that

Brian Wilson was not merely a Genius—which is to say a steady commercial success—but rather, like Bob Dylan and John Lennon, a GENIUS—which is to say a steady commercial success and hip besides.

Until now, though, there were not too many hip people who would have considered Brian Wilson and the Beach Boys hip, even though he had produced one very hip record, *Good Vibrations*, which had sold more than a million copies, and a super-hip album, *Pet Sounds*, which didn't do very well at all—by previous Beach Boy sales standards. Among the hip people he was still on trial, and the question discussed earnestly among the recognized authorities on what is and what is not hip was whether or not Brian Wilson was hip, semi-hip or square.

But walking into the control room with the answers to all questions such as this was Brian Wilson himself, wearing a competition-stripe surfer's T-shirt, tight white duck pants, pale green bowling shoes and a red plastic toy fireman's helmet.

Everybody was wearing identical red plastic toy fireman's helmets. Brian's cousin and production assistant, Steve Korthoff, was wearing one; his wife, Marilyn, and her sister, Diane Rovelle—Brian's secretary—were also wearing them, and so was a once dignified writer from the *Saturday Evening Post* who had been following Brian around for two months trying to figure out whether or not this 24-year-old oversized tribute to Southern California who carried some 250 pounds of baby fat on a 6 foot 4 inch frame, was a genius, Genius or GENIUS, hip, semi-hip or square—concepts the writer himself was just learning to handle.[1]

Out in the studio, the musicians for the session were unpacking their instruments. In sport shirts and slacks, they looked like insurance salesmen and used-car dealers, except for one blonde female percussionist who might have been stamped out by a special machine that supplied plastic mannequin housewives for detergent commercials.

Controlled, a little bored after twenty years or so of nicely paid anonymity, these were the professionals of the popular music business, hired guns who did their job expertly and efficiently and then went home to the suburbs. If you wanted swing, they gave you swing. A little movie-track lushness? Fine, here comes movie-track lushness. Now it's rock & roll? Perfect rock & roll, down the chute.

"Steve," Brian called out, "where are the rest of those fire hats? I want everybody to wear fire hats. We've really got to get into this thing." Out to the Rolls-Royce went Steve and within a few minutes all of the musicians were wearing fire hats, silly grins beginning to crack their professional dignity.

"All right, let's go," said Brian. Then, using a variety of techniques ranging from vocal demonstration to actually playing the instruments, he taught each musician his part. A gigantic fire howled out of the massive studio speakers in a pounding crush of pictorial music that summoned up visions of roaring, windstorm flames, falling timbers, mournful sirens and sweating firemen, building into a peak and crackling off into fading embers as a single drum turned into a collapsing wall and the fire engine cellos dissolved and disappeared.

"When did he write this?" asked an astonished pop music producer who had wandered into the studio. "This is really fantastic! Man, this is unbelievable! How long has he been working on it?"

"About an hour," answered one of Brian's friends.

"I don't believe it. I just can't believe what I'm hearing," said the producer and fell into a stone silence as the fire music began again.

---

1 The *Saturday Evening Post* writer to whom Siegel is referring is himself. The *Post* ultimately rejected his piece, however, and Siegel ended up publishing "Goodbye Surfing" in *Cheetah* magazine.

For the next three hours Brian Wilson recorded and re-recorded, take after take, changing the sound balance, adding echo, experimenting with a sound-effects track of a real fire.

"Let me hear that again." "Drums, I think you're a little slow in that last part. Let's get on it." "That was really good. Now, one more time, the whole thing." "All right, let me hear the cellos alone." "Great. Really great. Now let's *do it!*"

With 23 takes on tape and the entire operation responding to his touch like the black knobs on the control board, sweat glistening down his long, reddish hair on to his freckled face, the control room a litter of dead cigarette butts, Chicken Delight boxes, crumpled napkins, Coke bottles and all the accumulated trash of the physical end of the creative process, Brian stood at the board as the four speakers blasted the music into the room.

For the 24th time, the drums crashed and the sound effects crackle faded and stopped.

"Thank you," said Brian, into the control room mike. "Let me hear that back." Feet shifting, his body still, eyes closed, head moving seal-like to his music, he stood under the speakers and listened. "Let me hear that one more time." Again the fire roared. "Everybody come out and listen to this," Brian said to the musicians. They came into the control room and listened to what they had made.

"What do you think?" Brian asked.

"It's incredible. Incredible," whispered one of the musicians, a man in his fifties, wearing a Hawaiian shirt and iridescent trousers and pointed black Italian shoes. "Absolutely incredible."

"Yeah," said Brian on the way home, an acetate trial copy or "dub" of the tape in his hands, the red plastic fire helmet still on his head. "Yeah, I'm going to call this 'Mrs. O'Leary's Fire' and I think it might just scare a whole lot of people."[2]

As it turns out, however, Brian Wilson's magic fire music is not going to scare anybody—because nobody other than the few people who heard it in the studio will ever get to listen to it. A few days after the record was finished, a building across the street from the studio burned down and, according to Brian, there was also an unusually large number of fires in Los Angeles. Afraid that his music might in fact turn out to be magic fire music, Wilson destroyed the master.

"I don't have to do a big scary fire like that," he later said. "I can do a candle and it's still fire. That would have been a really bad vibration to let out on the world, that Chicago fire. The next one is going to be a candle."

A person who thinks of himself as understanding would probably interpret this episode as an example of perhaps too-excessive artistic perfectionism. One with psychiatric inclinations would hear all this stuff about someone who actually believed music could cause fires and start using words such as neurosis and maybe even psychosis. A true student of spoken hip, however, would say *hang-up*, which covers all of the above.

As far as Brian's pretensions toward hipness are concerned, no label could do him worse harm. In the hip world, there is a widespread idea that really hip people don't have hang-ups, which gives rise to the unspoken rule (unspoken because there is also the widespread idea that really hip people don't make *any* rules) that no one who wants to be thought of as hip ever reveals his hang-ups, except maybe to his guru, and in the strictest of privacy.

In any case, whatever his talent, Brian Wilson's attempt to win a hip following and reputation foundered for many months in an obsessive cycle of creation and destruction that threatened not only his career and his future but also his marriage, his friendships, his relationship with the Beach Boys and, some of his closest friends worried, his mind.

---

2 "Mrs. O'Leary's Fire" appears on Wilson's 2004 version of *Smile* under the name of "Mrs. O'Leary's Cow." The songs take their name from the urban legend that a cow owned by Mrs. O'Leary started the Great Chicago Fire of 1871 by kicking over a lantern in a barn.

For a boy who used to be known in adolescence as a lover of sweets, the whole thing must have begun to taste very sour; yet, this particular phase of Brian's drive toward whatever his goal of supreme success might be began on a rising tide that at first looked as if it would carry him and the Beach Boys beyond the Beatles, who had started just about the same time they did, into the number-one position in the international pop music fame-and-power competition.

"About a year ago I had what I considered a very religious experience," Wilson told Los Angeles writer Tom Nolan in 1966. "I took LSD, a full dose of LSD, and later, another time, I took a smaller dose. And I learned a lot of things, like patience, understanding. I can't teach you or tell you what I learned from taking it, but I consider it a very religious experience."

A short time after his LSD experience, Wilson began work on the record that was to establish him right along with the Beatles as one of the most important innovators in modern popular music. It was called *Good Vibrations*, and it took more than six months, 90 hours of tape and 11 complete versions before a 3-minute 35-second final master tape satisfied him. Among the instruments on *Good Vibrations* was an electronic device called a theremin, which had its debut in the soundtrack of the movie *Spellbound*, back in the '40s. To some people *Good Vibrations* was considerably crazier than Gregory Peck had been in the movie, but to others, Brian Wilson's new record, along with his somewhat earlier release, *Pet Sounds*, marked the beginning of a new era in pop music.

"THEY'VE FOUND THE NEW SOUND AT LAST!" shrieked the headline over a London *Sunday Express* review as "Good Vibrations" hit the English charts at number six and leaped to number one the following week. Within a few weeks, the Beach Boys had pushed the Beatles out of first place in England's *New Musical Express'* annual poll. In America, "Good Vibrations" sold nearly 400,000 copies in four days before reaching number one several weeks later and earning a gold record within another month when it hit the one-million sale mark.

It was an arrival, certainly, but in America, where there is none of the Beach Boys California-mystique that adds a special touch of romance to their records and appearances in Europe and England, the news had not yet really reached all of the people whose opinion can turn popularity into fashionability. With the exception of a professor of show business (right, professor of show business; in California such a thing is not considered unusual) who turned up one night to interview Brian, and a few young writers (such as the *Village Voice*'s Richard Goldstein, Paul Williams of *Crawdaddy!*, and Lawrence Dietz of *New York* magazine), not too many opinion-makers were prepared to accept the Beach Boys into the mainstream of the culture industry.

"Listen man," said San Francisco music critic Ralph Gleason who had only recently graduated from jazz into Bob Dylan and was apparently not yet ready for any more violent twists, "I recognize the LA hype when I hear it. I know all about the Beach Boys and I think I liked them better before, if only for sociological reasons, if you understand what I mean."

"As for the Beach Boys," an editor of the *Post* chided his writer, who had filed the world's longest Western Union telegram of a story filled with unrelieved hero worship of Brian Wilson, "I want you to understand that as an individual you feel that Brian Wilson is the greatest musician of our time, and maybe the greatest human being, but as a reporter you have got to maintain your objectivity."

"They want me to put him down," the writer complained. "That's their idea of objectivity—the put-down."

"It has to do with this idea that it's not hip to be sincere," he continued, "and they really want to be hip. What they don't understand is that last year hip was sardonic—camp, they called it. This year hip is sincere."

"When somebody as corny as Brian Wilson starts singing right out front about God and I start writing it—very *sincerely*, you understand—it puts them very up tight.

"I think it's because it reminds them of all those terribly sincere hymns and sermons they used to have to listen to in church when they were kids in Iowa or Ohio.

"Who knows? Maybe they're right. I mean, who needs all this goddamn intense sincerity all the time?"

What all this meant, of course, was that everybody agreed that Brian Wilson and the Beach Boys were still too square. It would take more than *Good Vibrations* and *Pet Sounds* to erase three-and-a-half years of *Little Deuce Coupe*—a lot more if you counted in those J. C. Penney-style custom-tailored, kandy-striped short shirts they insisted on wearing on stage.

Brian, however, had not yet heard the news, it appeared, and was steadily going about the business of trying to become hip. The Beach Boys, who have toured without him ever since he broke down during one particularly wearing trip, were now in England and Europe, phoning back daily reports of enthusiastic fan hysteria—screaming little girls tearing at their flesh, wild press conferences, private chats with the Rolling Stones. Washed in the heat of a kind of attention they had never received in the United States even at the height of their commercial success, three Beach Boys— Brian's brothers, Dennis and Carl, and his cousin, Mike Love—walked into a London Rolls-Royce showroom and bought four Phantom VII limousines, one for each of them and a fourth for Brian. Al Jardine and Bruce Johnston, the Beach Boys who are not corporate members of the Beach Boys enterprises, sent their best regards and bought themselves some new clothing.

"I think this London thing has really helped," said Brian with satisfaction after he had made the color selection on his $32,000 toy—a ducal-burgundy lacquered status symbol ordinarily reserved for heads of state. "That's just what the boys needed, a little attention to jack up their confidence." Then, learning that he wouldn't be able to have his new car for three months, he went out and bought an interim Rolls-Royce for $20,000 from Mamas and Papas producer, Lou Adler, taking possession of the automobile just in time to meet his group at the airport as they returned home.

"It's a great environment for conducting business," he explained as his friend and former road manager, Terry Sachen, hastily pressed into service as interim chauffeur for the interim Rolls-Royce, informally uniformed in his usual fringed deerskins and moccasins, drove the car through Hollywood to one of Brian's favorite eating places, the Pioneer Chicken drive-in on Sunset Boulevard.

"This car is really out of sight," said Brian, filling up on fried shrimp in the basket. "Next time we go up to Capitol, I'm going to drive up in my Rolls-Royce limo. You've got to do those things with a little style. It's not just an ordinary visit that way—it's an arrival, right? Wow! That's really great—an *arrival*, in my limo. It'll blow their minds!"

Whether or not the interim Rolls-Royce actually ever blew the minds of the hard-nosed executives who run Capitol Records is something to speculate on, but no one in the record industry with a sense of history could have failed to note that this very same limousine had once belonged to John Lennon; and in the closing months of 1966, with the Beach Boys home in Los Angeles, Brian rode the *Good Vibrations* high, driving forward in bursts of enormous energy that seemed destined before long to earn him the throne of the international empire of pop music still ruled by John Lennon and the Beatles.

At the time, it looked as if the Beatles were ready to step down. Their summer concerts in America had been only moderately successful at best, compared to earlier years. There were ten thousand empty seats at Shea Stadium in New York and 11 lonely fans at the airport in Seattle. Mass media, underground press, music-industry trade papers and the fan magazines were filled with fears that the Beatles were finished, that the group was breaking up. Lennon was off acting in a movie; McCartney was walking around London alone, said to be carrying a giant torch for his sometime girl friend Jane Asher; George Harrison was getting deeper and deeper into a mystical Indian thing under the instruction of *sitar*-master Ravi Shankar; and Ringo was collecting material for a Beatles museum.

In Los Angeles, Brian Wilson was riding around in the Rolls-Royce that had once belonged to John Lennon, pouring a deluge of new sounds on to miles of stereo tape in three different recording studios booked day and night for him in month-solid blocks, holding court nightly at his $240,000 Beverly Hills Babylonian-modern home, and, after guests left, sitting at his grand piano until dawn, writing new material.

The work in progress was an album called *Smile*. "I'm writing a teen-age symphony to God," Brian told dinner guests on an October evening. He then played for them the collection of black acetate trial records which lay piled on the floor of his red imitation-velvet wallpapered bedroom with its leopard-print bedspread. In the bathroom, above the wash basin, there was a plastic color picture of Jesus Christ with trick effect eyes that appeared to open and close when you moved your head. Sophisticate newcomers pointed it out to each other and laughed slyly, almost hoping to find a Keane painting among decorations ranging from Lava Lamps to a department-store rack of dozens of dolls, each still in its plastic bubble container, the whole display trembling like a space-age Christmas tree to the music flowing out into the living-room.

Brian shuffled through the acetates, most of which were unlabelled, identifying each by subtle differences in the patterns of the grooves. He had played them so often he knew the special look of each record the way you know the key to your front door by the shape of its teeth. Most were instrumental tracks, cut while the Beach Boys were in Europe, and for these Brian supplied the vocal in a high sound that seemed to come out of his head rather than his throat as he somehow managed to create complicated four and five part harmonies with only his own voice.

"Rock, rock, Plymouth rock roll over," Brian sang. "Bicycle rider, see what you done done to the church of the native American Indian . . . Over and over the crow cries uncover the cornfields . . . Who ran the Iron Horse . . . Out in the farmyard the cook is chopping lumber; out in the barnyard the chickens do their number . . . Bicycle rider see what you done done . . ." A panorama of American history filled the room as the music shifted from theme to theme; the tinkling harpsichord sounds of the bicycle rider pushed sad Indian sounds across the continent; the Iron Horse pounded across the plains in a wide open rolling rhythm that summoned up visions of the old West; civilized chickens bobbed up and down in a tiny ballet of comic barnyard melody; the inexorable bicycle music, cold and charming as an infinitely talented music box, reappeared and faded away.

Like medieval choirboys, the voices of the Beach Boys pealed out in wordless prayer from the last acetate, thirty seconds of chorale that reached upward to the vaulted stone ceilings of an empty cathedral lit by thousands of tiny votive candles melting at last into one small, pure pool that whispered a universal amen in a sigh without words.

Brian's private radio show was finished. In the dining-room a candle-lit table with a dark blue cloth was set for 10 persons. In the kitchen, Marilyn Wilson was trying to get the meal organized and served, aided and hindered by the chattering suggestions of the guests' wives and girlfriends. When everyone was seated and waiting for the food, Brian tapped his knife idly on a white china plate.

"Listen to that," he said. "That's really great!" Everybody listened as Brian played the plate. "Come on, let's get something going here," he ordered. "Michael—do this. David—you do this." A plate-and-spoon musicale began to develop as each guest played a distinctly different technique, rhythm and melody under Brian's enthusiastic direction.

"That's absolutely unbelievable!" said Brian. "Isn't that unbelievable? That's so unbelievable I'm going to put it on the album. Michael, I want you to get a sound system up here tomorrow and I want everyone to be here tomorrow night. We're going to get this on tape."

Brian Wilson's plate-and-spoon musicale never did reach the public, but only because he forgot about it. Other sounds equally strange have found their way on to his records. On *Pet Sounds*, for example, on some tracks there is an odd, soft, hollow percussion effect that most musicians assume is some kind of electronically transmuted drum sound—a conga drum played with a stick perhaps, or an Indian tom-tom. Actually, it's drummer Hal Blaine playing the bottom of a plastic jug that once contained Sparklettes spring water. And, of course, at the end of the record there is the strangely affecting track of a train roaring through a lonely railroad crossing as a bell clangs and Brian's dogs, Banana, a beagle, and Louie, a dark brown Weimaraner, bark after it.

More significant, perhaps, to those who that night heard the original instrumental tracks for both *Smile* and the Beach Boys' new single, "Heroes and Villains," is that entire sequences of extraordinary power and beauty are missing in the finished version of the single, and will undoubtedly be missing as well from *Smile*—victims of Brian's obsessive tinkering and, more importantly, sacrifices to the same strange combination of superstitious fear and God-like conviction of his own power he displayed when he destroyed the fire music.

The night of the dining-table concerto, it was the God-like confidence Brian must have been feeling as he put his guests on his trip, but the fear was soon to take over. At his house that night, he had assembled a new set of players to introduce into his life game, each of whom was to perform a specific role in the grander game he was playing with the world.

Earlier in the summer, Brian had hired Van Dyke Parks, a super-sophisticated young songwriter and composer, to collaborate with him on the lyrics for *Smile*. With Van Dyke working for him, he had a fighting chance against John Lennon, whose literary skill and Liverpudlian wit had been one of the most important factors in making the Beatles the darlings of the hip intelligentsia.

With that flank covered, Brian was ready to deal with some of the other problems of trying to become hip, the most important of which was how was he going to get in touch with some really hip people. In effect, the dinner party at the house was his first hip social event, and the star of the evening, so far as Brian was concerned, was Van Dyke Parks' manager, David Anderle, who showed up with a whole group of very hip people.

Elegant, cool and impossibly cunning, Anderle was an artist who had somehow found himself in the record business as an executive for MGM Records, where he had earned himself a reputation as a genius by purportedly thinking up the million-dollar movie-TV-record offer that briefly lured Bob Dylan to MGM from Columbia until everybody had a change of heart and Dylan decided to go back home to Columbia.

Anderle had skipped back and forth between painting and the record business, with mixed results in both. Right now he was doing a little personal management and thinking about painting a lot. His appeal to Brian was simple: everybody recognized David Anderle as one of the hippest people in Los Angeles. In fact, he was something like the mayor of hipness as far as some people were concerned. And not only that, he was a genius.

Within six weeks, he was working for the Beach Boys; everything that Brian wanted seemed at last to be in reach. Like a magic genie, David Anderle produced miracles for him. A new Beach Boys record company was set up, Brother Records, with David Anderle at its head and, simultaneously, the Beach Boys sued Capitol Records in a move designed to force a renegotiation of their contract with the company.

The house was full of underground press writers; Anderle's friend Michael Vosse was on the Brother Records payroll out scouting TV contracts and performing other odd jobs. Another of Anderle's friends was writing the story on Brian for the *Saturday Evening Post* and a film crew from CBS-TV was up at the house filming for a documentary to be narrated by Leonard Bernstein.[3] The Beach Boys were having meetings once or twice a week with teams of experts, briefing them on corporate policy, drawing complicated chalk patterns as they described the millions of dollars everyone was going to earn out of all this.

---

3 The documentary would broadcast in April 1967 under the title of *Inside Pop: The Rock Revolution*.

As 1967 opened it seemed as though Brian and the Beach Boys were assured of a new world of success; yet something was going wrong. As the corporate activity reached a peak of intensity, Brian was becoming less and less productive and more and more erratic. *Smile*, which was to have been released for the Christmas season, remained unfinished. "Heroes and Villains," which was virtually complete, remained in the can, as Brian kept working out new little pieces and then scrapping them.

Van Dyke Parks had left and come back and would leave again, tired of being constantly dominated by Brian. Marilyn Wilson was having headaches and Dennis Wilson was leaving his wife. Session after session was cancelled. One night a studio full of violinists waited while Brian tried to decide whether or not the vibrations were friendly or hostile. The answer was hostile and the session was cancelled, at a cost of some $3,000. Everything seemed to be going wrong. Even the *Post* story fell through.

Brian seemed to be filled with secret fear. One night at the house, it began to surface. Marilyn sat nervously painting her fingernails as Brian stalked up and down, his face tight and his eyes small and red.

"What's the matter, Brian? You're really strung out," a friend asked.

"Yeah, I'm really strung out. Look, I mean I really feel strange. A really strange thing happened to me tonight. Did you see this picture, *Seconds*?"

"No, but I know what it's about; I read the book."

"Look, come into the kitchen; I really have to talk about this." In the kitchen they sat down in the black and white hounds tooth-check wallpapered dinette area. A striped window shade clashed with the checks and the whole room vibrated like some kind of pop art painting. Ordinarily, Brian wouldn't sit for more than a minute in it, but now he seemed to be unaware of anything except what he wanted to say.

"I walked into that movie," he said in a tense, high-pitched voice, "and the first thing that happened was a voice from the screen said 'Hello, Mr. Wilson.' It completely blew my mind. You've got to admit that's pretty spooky, right?"

"Maybe."

"That's not all. Then the whole thing was there. I mean my whole life. Birth and death and rebirth. The whole thing. Even the beach was in it, a whole thing about the beach. It was my whole life right there on the screen."

"It's just a coincidence, man. What are you getting all excited about?"

"Well, what if it isn't a coincidence? What if it's real? You know there's mind gangsters these days. There could be mind gangsters, couldn't there? I mean, look at Spector, he could be involved in it, couldn't he? He's going into films. How hard would it be for him to set up something like that?"

"Brian, Phil Spector is not about to make a million-dollar movie just to scare you. Come on, stop trying to be so dramatic."

"All right, all right. I was just a little bit nervous about it," Brian said, after some more back and forth about the possibility that Phil Spector, the record producer, had somehow influenced the making of *Seconds* to disturb Brian Wilson's tranquility. "I just had to get it out of my system. You can see where something like that could scare someone, can't you?"

They went into Brian's den, a small room papered in psychedelic orange, blue, yellow and red wall fabric with rounded corners. At the end of the room there was a jukebox filled with Beach Boys singles and Phil Spector hits. Brian punched a button and Spector's *Be My Baby* began to pour out at top volume.

"Spector has always been a big thing with me, you know. I mean I heard that song three and a half years ago and I knew that it was between him and me. I knew exactly where he was at and now

I've gone beyond him. You can understand how that movie might get someone upset under those circumstances, can't you?"

Brian sat down at his desk and began to draw a little diagram on a piece of printed stationery with his name at the top in the kind of large fat script printers of charitable dinner journals use when the customer asks for a hand-lettered look. With a felt-tipped pen, Brian drew a close approximation of a growth curve. "Spector started the whole thing," he said, dividing the curve into periods. "He was the first one to use the studio. But I've gone beyond him now. I'm doing the spiritual sound, a white spiritual sound. Religious music. Did you hear the Beatles album? Religious, right? That's the whole movement. That's where I'm going. It's going to scare a lot of people.

"Yeah," Brian said, hitting his fist on the desk with a large slap that sent the parakeets in a large cage facing him squalling and whistling. "Yeah," he said and smiled for the first time all evening. "That's where I'm going and it's going to scare a lot of people when I get there."

As the year drew deeper into winter, Brian's rate of activity grew more and more frantic, but nothing seemed to be accomplished. He tore the house apart and half redecorated it. One section of the living-room was filled with a full-sized Arabian tent and the dining-room, where the grand piano stood, was filled with sand to a depth of a foot or so and draped with nursery curtains. He had had his windows stained gray and put a sauna bath in the bedroom. He battled with his father and complained that his brothers weren't trying hard enough. He accused Mike Love of making too much money.

One by one, he canceled out the friends he had collected, sometimes for the strangest of reasons. An acquaintance of several months who had become extremely close with Brian showed up at a record session and found a guard barring the door. Michael Vosse came out to explain.

"Hey man, this is really terrible," said Vosse, smiling under a broad-brimmed straw hat. "It's not you, it's your chick. Brian says she's a witch and she's messing with his brain so bad by ESP that he can't work. It's like the Spector thing. You know how he is. Say, I'm really sorry." A couple of months later, Vosse was gone. Then, in the late spring, Anderle left. The game was over.

Several months later, the last move in Brian's attempt to win the hip community was played out. On July 15, the Beach Boys were scheduled to appear at the Monterey International Pop Music Festival, a kind of summit of rock music with the emphasis on love, flowers and youth. Although Brian was a member of the board of this non-profit event, the Beach Boys canceled their commitment to perform. The official reason was that their negotiations with Capitol Records were at a crucial stage and they had to get "Heroes and Villains" out right away. The second official reason was that Carl, who had been arrested for refusing to report for induction into the army (he was later cleared in court), was so upset that he wouldn't be able to sing.

Whatever the merit in these reasons, the real one may have been closer to something another Monterey board member suggested: "Brian was afraid that the hippies from San Francisco would think the Beach Boys were square and boo them."

But maybe Brian was right. "Those candy-striped shirts just wouldn't have made it at Monterey, man," said one person who was there.

Whatever the case, at the end of the summer, *Heroes and Villains* was released in sharply edited form and *Smile* was reported to be on its way. In the meantime, however, the Beatles had released *Sergeant Pepper's Lonely Hearts Club Band* and John Lennon was riding about London in a bright yellow Phantom VII Rolls Royce painted with flowers on the sides and his zodiac symbol on the top. In *Life* magazine, Paul McCartney came out openly for LSD and in the Haight-Ashbury district of San Francisco George Harrison walked through the streets blessing the hippies. Ringo was still collecting material for a Beatles museum. However good *Smile* might turn out to be, it seemed somehow that once more the Beatles had outdistanced the Beach Boys.

Back during that wonderful period in the fall of 1966 when everybody seemed to be his friend and plans were being laid for Brother Records and all kinds of fine things, Brian had gone on a brief visit to Michigan to hear a Beach Boys concert. The evening of his return, each of his friends and important acquaintances received a call asking everyone to please come to the airport to meet Brian, it was very important. When they gathered at the airport, Brian had a photographer on hand to take a series of group pictures. For a long time, a huge mounted blow-up of the best of the photographs hung on the living-room wall, with some thirty people staring out—everyone from Van Dyke Parks and David Anderle to Michael Vosse and Terry Sachen. In the foreground was the *Saturday Evening Post* writer looking sourly out at the world.

The picture is no longer on Brian's wall and most of the people in it are no longer his friends. One by one each of them had either stepped out of the picture or been forced out of it. The whole cycle has returned to its beginning. Brian, who started out in Hawthorne, California, with his two brothers and a cousin, once more has surrounded himself with relatives. The house in Beverly Hills is empty. Brian and Marilyn are living in their new Spanish Mission estate in Bel-Air, cheek by jowl with the Mamas and the Papas' Cass Elliott.

What remains, of course, is *Heroes and Villains*, a record some people think is better than anything the Beatles ever wrote. And there is also a spectacular peak, a song called *Surf's Up* that Brian recorded for the first time in December in Columbia Records' Studio A for a CBS-TV pop music documentary. Earlier in the evening the film crew had covered a Beach Boys vocal session which had gone very badly. Now, at midnight, the Beach Boys had gone home and Brian was sitting in the back of his car, smoking moodily.

In the dark car, he breathed heavily, his hands in his lap, eyes staring nowhere.

"All right," he said at last, "Let's just sit here and see if we can get into something positive, but without any words. Let's just get into something quiet and positive on a nonverbal level." There was a long silence.

"OK, let's go," he said, and then, quickly, he was in the studio rehearsing, spotlighted in the center of the huge dark room, the cameraman moving about him invisibly outside the light.

"Let's do it," he announced, and the tape began to roll. In the control room no one moved. David Oppenheim, the TV producer, fortyish, handsome, usually studiously detached and professional, lay on the floor, hands behind his head, eyes closed. For three minutes and 27 seconds, Wilson played with delicate intensity, speaking moodily through the piano. Then he was finished. Oppenheim, whose last documentary had been a study of Stravinsky, lay motionless.

"That's it," Wilson said as the tape continued to whirl. The mood broke. As if awakening from heavy sleep the people stirred and shook their heads.

"I'd like to hear that," Wilson said. As his music replayed, he sang the lyrics in a high, almost falsetto voice, the cameras on him every second.

"*The diamond necklace played the pawn,*" Wilson sang. "*. . . A blind class aristocracy, back through the opera glass you see the pit and the pendulum drawn.*

"*Columnated ruins domino.*" His voice reached upward; the piano faltered a new set of falling chords.

In a slow series of impressionistic images the song moved to its ending:

I heard the word:
Wonderful thing!
A children's song!" On the last word Brian's voice rose and fell, like the ending of that prayer chorale he had played so many months before.

"That's really special," someone said.

"Special, that's right," said Wilson quietly. "Van Dyke and I really kind of thought we had done something special when we finished that one." He went back into the studio, put on the earphones and sang the song again for his audience in the control room, for the revolving tape recorder and for the cameras which relentlessly followed as he struggled to make manifest what still only existed as a perfect, incommunicable sound in his head.

At home, as the black acetate dub turned on his bedroom hi-fi set, Wilson tried to explain the words.

"It's a man at a concert," he said. "All around him there's the audience, playing their roles, dressed up in fancy clothes, looking through opera glasses, but so far away from the drama, from life—*Back through the opera glass you see the pit and the pendulum drawn.*"

"The music begins to take over. *Columnated ruins domino.* Empires, ideas, lives, institutions—everything has to fall, tumbling like dominoes.

"He begins to awaken to the music; sees the pretentiousness of everything. *The music hall a costly bow.* Then even the music is gone, turned into a trumpeter swan, into what the music really is.

"*Canvas the town and brush the backdrop.* He's off in his vision, on a trip. Reality is gone; he's creating it like a dream. *Dove-nested towers.* Europe, a long time ago. *The laughs come hard in Auld Lang Syne.* The poor people in the cellar taverns, trying to make themselves happy by singing.

"Then there's the parties, the drinking, trying to forget the wars, the battles at sea. *While at port a do or die.* Ships in the harbor, battling it out. A kind of Roman Empire thing.

"*A Choke of grief.* At his own sorrow and the emptiness of his life, because he can't even cry for the suffering in the world, for his own suffering.

"And then, hope. *Surf's up! . . . Come about hard and join the once and often spring you gave.* Go back to the kids, to the beach, to childhood.

"*I heard the word*—of God; *Wonderful thing*—the joy of enlightenment, of seeing God. And what is it? A *children's song!* And then there's the song itself; the song of children; the song of the universe rising and falling in wave after wave, the song of God, hiding His love from us, but always letting us find Him again, like a mother singing to her children."

The record was over. Wilson went into the kitchen and squirted Reddi-Whip direct from the can into his mouth; made himself a chocolate Great Shake, and ate a couple of candy bars.

"Of course that's a very intellectual explanation," he said. "But maybe sometimes you have to do an intellectual thing. If they don't get the words, they'll get the music, because that's where it's really at, in the music. You can get hung up in words, you know. Maybe they work; I don't know." He fidgeted with a telescope.

"This thing is so bad," he complained. "So Mickey Mouse. It just won't work smoothly. I was really freaked out on astronomy when I was a kid. Baseball too. I guess I went through a lot of phases. A lot of changes, too. But you can really get into things through the stars. And swimming. A lot of swimming. It's physical; really Zen, right? The whole spiritual thing is very physical. Swimming really does it sometimes." He sprawled on the couch and continued in a very small voice.

"So that's what I'm doing. Spiritual music."

"Brian," Marilyn called as she came into the room wearing a quilted bathrobe, "do you want me to get you anything, honey? I'm going to sleep."

"No, Mar," he answered, rising to kiss his wife goodnight. "You go on to bed. I want to work for a while."

"C'mon kids," Marilyn yelled to the dogs as she padded off to bed. "Time for bed. Louie! Banana! Come to bed. Goodnight, Brian. Goodnight, everybody."

Wilson paced. He went to the piano and began to play. His guests moved toward the door. From the piano, his feet shuffling in the sand, he called a perfunctory goodbye and continued to play, a melody beginning to take shape. Outside, the piano spoke from the house. Brian Wilson's guests stood for a moment, listening. As they got into their car, the melancholy piano moaned.

"Here's one that's really outasight from the fantabulous Beach Boys!" screamed a local early morning Top-40 DJ from the car radio on the way home, a little hysterical, as usual, his voice drowning out the sobbing introduction to the song.

"We're sending this one out for Bob and Carol in Pomona. They've been going steady now for six months. Happy six months, kids, and dig! *Good Vibrations! The Beach Boys! Outasight!*"

Source: Jules Siegel, "Goodbye Surfing Hello God!—The Religious Conversion of Brian Wilson," *Cheetah*, October 1967, pp. 26–31, 83–87.

23

Rock and the Counterculture

CHESTER ANDERSON

A science fiction novelist and founding member of the Underground Press Syndicate, Chester Anderson (1932–1991) was also an integral presence in the 1960s San Francisco countercultural scene. Anderson's essays appeared in many places, including the *San Francisco Oracle*, whose twelve-issue run from 1966–1968 established the paper as the leading publication of the Haight-Ashbury District (the home of groups like the Jefferson Airplane and the Grateful Dead). The descriptions he sets forth in his "Notes for the New Geology" are a far cry from what rock 'n' roll had signified a mere decade before and hint at a broad generational shift. Anderson evokes a dizzying array of "principles" that situate rock as more than just music; it is a cultural, participatory phenomenon, intimately linked with psychedelic drugs, tribal rituals, and the "aesthetic of discovery." Most of all he sees rock as the greatest realization of Marshall McLuhan's 1960s media age, a synaesthetic technological experience that renders obsolete the "typeheads" (those still rooted in the power of "the word") of an older era.[1] Anderson also evokes what at first glance may seem to be an unusual comparison between rock and Baroque music. Yet as musicologist Richard Middleton has noted, there is a "high syntactic correlation" between rock and Baroque that does not apply as strongly to other historical art music periods.[2] Both use rather formulaic and repetitive harmonic progressions, "strongly marked beats," and fairly limited formal ideas. Procol Harum made this connection explicit in 1967 with their Top 10 hit, "A Whiter Shade of Pale," which derived its harmonic and melodic material from Johann Sebastian Bach's *Cantata BWV 140*, "Sleepers Awake."

I

Rock's the first head music we've had since the end of the baroque.[3] By itself, without the aid of strobe lights, day-glo paints & other sub-imaginative copouts, it engages the entire sensorium, appealing to the intelligence with no interference from the intellect. Extremely typographic people are unable to experience it, which—because TV didn't approach universality till 1950—is why the rock folk are so young, generally. (Most of the astounding exceptions are people, like the poet Walter Lowenfels, who have lived a long time but have not become old.)

---

1 Among Marshall McLuhan's many publications, his most widely read and influential book of the 1960s was *Understanding Media: The Extensions of Man* (New York: McGraw-Hill, 1964.)
2 Richard Middleton, *Studying Popular Music* (Philadelphia: Open University Press, 1990), pp. 30–31.
3 "Head" music was conventional slang for music associated with psychedelic drugs or the psychedelic experience.

II

Some Principles:

- That rock is essentially head (or even psychedelic) music.
- That rock is a legitimate avant garde art form, with deep roots in the music of the past (especially the baroque & before), great vitality, and vast potential for growth & development, adaptation, experiment, etcetera.
- That rock shares most of its formal/structural principles with baroque music (wherein lie its most recent cultural roots), and that it & baroque can be judged by the same broad standards (the governing principles being that of mosaic structure of tonal & textural contrast: tactility, collage).
- That rock is evolving Sturgeonesque *homo gestalt* configurations:[4]
  - the groups themselves, far more intimately interrelated & integrated than any comparable ensembles in the past;
  - super-families, like Kerista & the more informal communal pads;
  - and pre-initiate tribal groups, like the teenyboppers; all in evident & nostalgic response to technological & population pressures.
- That rock is an intensely participational & non-typographic art form, forerunner of something much like McLuhan's covertly projected spherical society.
- That far from being degenerate or decadent, rock is a regenerative & revolutionary art, offering us our first real hope for the future (indeed, for the present) since August 6, 1945; and that its effects on the younger population, especially those effects most deplored by typeheads, have all been essentially good & healthy so far.
- That rock principles are not limited to music, and that much of the shape of the future can be seen in its aspirations today (these being mainly total freedom, total experience, total love, peace & mutual affection).
- That today's teenyboppers will be voting tomorrow and running for office the day after.
- That rock is an intensely synthesizing art, an art of amazing relationships (collage is rock & roll), able to absorb (maybe) all of society into itself as an organizing force, transmuting & reintegrating what it absorbs (as it has so far); and that its practitioners & audience are learning to perceive & manipulate reality in wholly new ways, quite alien to typeheads.
- That rock has reinstated the ancient truth that art is fun.
- That rock is a way of life, international & verging in this decade on universal; and can't be stopped, retarded, put down, muted, modified or successfully controlled by typeheads, whose arguments don't apply & whose machinations don't mesh because they can't perceive (dig) what rock really is & does.
- That rock is a tribal phenomenon, immune to definition & other typographical operations, and constitutes what might be called a 20th century magic.
- That rock seems to have synthesized most of the intellectual & artistic movements of our time & culture, cross-fertilizing them & forcing them rapidly toward fruition & function.
- That rock is a vital agent in breaking down absolute & arbitrary distinctions.
- That any artistic activity not allied to rock is doomed to preciousness & sterility.

---

4 This is a reference to science fiction writer Theodore Sturgeon's 1953 novel *More Than Human*, in which a group of psychically gifted individuals join together their powers to form a single "*homo gestalt*."

- That group participation, total experience & complete involvement are rock's minimal desiderata and those as well of a world that has too many people.
- That rock is creating the social rituals of the future.
- That the medium is indeed the message, & rock knows what that means.
- That no arbitrary limitations of rock are valid (i.e., that a rock symphony or opera, for example, is possible).
- That rock is handmade, and only the fakes are standardized.
- That rock presents an aesthetic of discovery.

III

Marshall McLuhan makes no sense at all, not as I was taught to define *sense* in my inadequately cynical youth. He's plainly no Aquinas. And yet, somehow, he embarrassingly manages to explain to perfection an overwhelming array of things that used to make even less sense than he does and were somewhat threatening as well: things like pop, op & camp (which sounds like a breakfast food); the psychedelic revolution, the pot & acid explosion; the Haight-Ashbury community, and especially what we'll keep on calling Rock & Roll until we can find some name more appropriate for it. (I nominate Head Music, but I don't expect it to catch on.)

Not that McLuhan mentions any of these things. He simply gives the clues. Synthesis and synaesthesia; non-typographic, non-linear, basically mosaic & mythic modes of perception, involvement of the whole sensorium; roles instead of jobs; participation in depth; extended awareness; preoccupation with textures, with tactility, with multisensory experiences—put 'em all together & you have a weekend on Haight Street.

The electronic extension of the central nervous system, the evolutionary storm that's happening right now (which is having, slowly, exactly the same effect on the whole world as acid has had on us) makes everything else make sense; and McLuhan taught us how to see it. He doesn't *have* to make sense.

IV

We're still so hooked on mainly visual perception that the possibilities of our other senses are almost unimaginable. We still interpret highs in visual terms, for instance: though acid is mainly tactile, spatial, visceral & integrative; whilst pot affects mostly hearing & touch. It's all a matter of conditioning: we'll learn.

The things a really imaginative engineer could accomplish by working on our many senses, singly & in orchestrated combinations, are staggering. Imagine: sensory counterpoint—the senses registering contradictory stimuli & the brain having fun trying to integrate them. Imagine *tasting* g minor! The incredible synaesthesiae!

Rock & roll is toying with this notion.

Though we've been brought up to think of music as a purely auditory art, we actually perceive it with the whole body in a complex pattern of sympathetic tensions & interacting stimuli.

Melodies—and especially vocal melodies or tunes in the vocal range—affect the larynx. It follows the tune, subvocalizing. As the line ascends, the larynx tightens, and as the line descends it relaxes, responding sympathetically to the tension of the tones. (The larynx also tightens in response to strong emotion, just before the tears begin.) That's what makes an unexpected high note such an emotional event, because the part of the brain in charge of such things can't tell one kind of tension from another. That's also much of what makes melodies work. Whether you want to or not, you participate.

Meanwhile, low notes—especially on the bass, and most acutely if it's plucked & amplified—are experienced in the abdomen as localized vibrations, an amazingly private sensation impossible to resist. The deeper the note, furthermore, the lower down on the trunk it seems to be felt. A properly organized R&B bass line is experienced as a pattern of incredibly intimate caresses: still more unavoidable participation.

(The same visceral perception yields a sense of musical space.)

A steady bass line in scales induces something like confidence and/or well-being. A jagged, syncopated bass can range you from nervous exhilaration to utter frenzy. (Old Bach knew all about this.) The possibilities are next to endless.

Rhythms, meanwhile, affect the heart, skeletal muscles & motor nerves, and can be used to play games with these pretty much at will. Repeated patterns (ostinati) & drones induce an almost instant light hypnosis (just like grass), locking the mind on the music at hand & intensifying all the other reactions. Long, open chords lower the blood pressure: crisp, repeated chords raise it.

And this is only the beginning, the barest outline of our physical response to music, but data enough for me to make my point. An arranger/composer who knew all this, especially if he had electronic instruments to work with, could play a listener's body like a soft guitar. He could score the listener's body as part of the arrangement, creating an intensity of participation many people don't even achieve in sex. (So far this seems to have happened mainly by accident.) And there's no defense but flight: not even the deaf are completely immune.

Source: Chester Anderson, "Notes for the New Geology," *San Francisco Oracle* I (1967): 2, 23.

24

The FM Revolution

"AM Radio—'Stinking Up the Airways'"

TOM DONAHUE

One of the most crucial transition points in the mid-1960s emergence of rock was the flowering of new, free-form FM radio. AM radio, and its tightly controlled Top 40 singles format, had been the driving force in popular music since the mid-1950s, but as the AM frequencies became increasingly crowded in the early 1960s, the Federal Communications Commission put a halt to AM license applications and began to encourage expansion of the previously underused FM dial. With its possibilities for stereo reception (something missing from the monaural AM), FM offered a natural fit for the high fidelity recordings of the new rock groups. Even more than that, the loose organizational structures of many of the small FM stations offered an opportunity for pioneering disc jockeys like Tom Donahue (1928–1975) to rebel against the market-driven restrictions of Top 40 and instead play the music of their choice. As Donahue explains in his piece for *Rolling Stone*, his approach as program director at KMPX San Francisco was sympathetic to a new generation of musicians like the Beatles and Bob Dylan, for whom the album rather than the single had become a major artistic statement. In addition, free-form became a welcome home to groups like the Grateful Dead, whose songs often far surpassed the three-minute mark favored by Top 40 radio. Donahue's depiction of AM as a "rotting corpse" would indeed turn out to be prophetic, as the success of FM rock rendered AM music stations virtually obsolete by the end of the 1970s. To what extent does the free-form ethos still prevail in radio programming today?

For the past six months KMPX in San Francisco has been conducting a highly successful experiment in a new kind of contemporary music programming. It is a format that embraces the best of today's rock and roll, folk, traditional and city blues, raga, electronic music, and some jazz and classical selections. I believe that music should not be treated as a group of objects to be sorted out like eggs with each category kept rigidly apart from the others, and it is exciting to discover that there is a large audience that shares that premise.

Alan Freed is generally acknowledged to have been the first rock and roll disc jockey. He started in Cleveland, where he was known as Moondog, and later took his show to WINS in New York, where he gained national prominence which was to end in the payola probe of 1960. In the mid-Fifties a number of chain broadcasters initiated what we know today as Top 40 radio programming.

As a rigidly formulated presentation of popular music, it proved extremely successful for a chain of stations in the Midwest owned by Tod Storz, and those in the Midwest and South operated by the Plough Corporation, a Southern pharmaceutical house.

The spectacularly successful concept of Top 40 radio spread quickly from city to city and almost overnight rock and roll music became an industry as record sales boomed. The stations were replete with jingles, sirens and explosions introducing the news and disc jockeys who worked at a frantic pace and never, never lost their jollity. Generally, the stations played about 100 current records, but otherwise the format was almost identical to what is heard today in every city in the nation.

Ten years later, the biggest deterrent to the progress, expansion, and success of contemporary music is that same Top-40 radio.

Once Top-40 stations dominated almost every radio market in the country. Now their audience and their ratings have been on a steady decline for the past three years, during a period of time when the music itself is gaining ever increasing acceptance, as indicated by its sales popularity, the ballroom scenes all over the country, and the fact that rock entertainers are now an integral part of many variety entertainment programs on television.

The music has matured, the audience has matured, but radio has apparently proven to be a retarded child. Where once Top-40 radio reflected the taste of its audience, today it attempts to dictate it, and in the process has alienated its once loyal army of listeners.

There was a period when the so-called rock stations carefully scanned the sales figures from local record stores and made an attempt to play the records the public was buying. This theory in itself was partially invalid, since it was based on the idea that people only wanted to hear what they could buy. What they bought were popular 45's. Three or four months after a record was a hit, they could purchase an LP that contained one or two of the group's hits and ten other songs that had failed to gain public acceptance as singles or had been hastily recorded to fill up an LP.

Then came the Beatles, whose explosive success changed the record scene, the radio scene, and, in many ways, changed the world. At KYA, where I was working at the time, we found ourselves playing six, eight, twelve Beatle cuts out of the fifty or so records we were playing on the air. There was a period of three or four months when the Beatles constituted about 25 per cent of all the music being played on Top-40 radio stations. For the first time, Top-40 stations were playing cuts from LPs.

By the spring of 1965, American groups like the Byrds, following the example of the Beatles, were putting out LPs that were carefully produced from start to finish. Twelve polished cuts—no rejects, no fillers, no junk. The sale of LPs began to rival the sale of singles. When faced with the fact that the Byrds' LP, or the new Bob Dylan album was outselling the single records on their play lists, in most cases Top-40 programmers chose to ignore them rather than attempting to determine cuts to play.

To select cuts from an LP for airing on a Top-40 station meant making independent decisions, reflecting taste and a good ear—attributes that are sadly lacking in most radio programmers and station managements. (Many of the current programmers have risen to their positions through their success in sales rather than their programming or musical background.)

As a result, the bulk of the popular music radio programming in this country today is devoted to absurd jingles that in their content are almost totally divorced from the kind of music the stations are playing, babbling hysterical disc jockeys who are trying to cram into a ten to fifteen second period the inane slogans that the program director has posted on the studio wall.

Somewhere in the dim misty days of yore, some radio statistician decided that regardless of chronological age the average mental age of the audience was twelve-and-a-half, and Top-40 radio aimed its message directly at the lowest common denominator. The disc jockeys have become robots performing their inanities at the direction of programmers who have succeeded in totally squeezing the human element out of their sound, reducing it to a series of blips and bleeps and happy, oh yes, always happy, sounding cretins who are poured from bottles every three hours. They have succeeded in making everyone on the staff sound alike—asinine. This is the much coveted "station sound."

At the same time the station's top brass are telling the advertiser that they have the solid 18–45 year old audience that represents the bulk of the buying public, they incessantly woo a subteen audience and seemingly do everything they can to offend the musical taste and common sense of everyone in their audience over twelve.

Their selection of music is almost invariably determined by what is happening in some other market. They will seldom take a chance on a new record, even when performed by a local group. Their measure is never excellence, but rather acceptance in some other market. Most stations today are playing from a list of approximately thirty records with seven to ten so-called extras.

Each week the stations call a selection of record stores and try to compute a top thirty. Most of them ignore the R&B stores. Few of them make any inquiry at all about LPs. If a record is selling that is more than seven inches in diameter, they don't care about it, don't want to hear it, and most assuredly are not going to play it.

Top-40 radio, as we know it today and have known it for the last ten years, is dead, and its rotting corpse is stinking up the airways.

Source: Tom Donahue, "AM Radio: 'Stinking Up the Airwaves'," *Rolling Stone*, November 23, 1967, pp. 14–15.

25

An Interview with Peter Townshend

JANN WENNER

While 1950s rock 'n' roll drew considerable attention for its visual dimensions, the rock groups such as the Who that emerged in the mid-1960s pushed the style and spectacle associated with the music into uncharted territories. One of the elements of the Who's stage show that first gained the group notoriety was Peter Townshend's (born 1945) ritual smashing of his guitar. In this 1968 interview with *Rolling Stone* editor Jann Wenner, the first one he conducted for his magazine, a typically candid Townshend explains the context of the guitar smashing on a number of levels, ranging from serendipitous discovery to a compensation for his limited guitar skills. In earlier interviews, Townshend had also claimed that his guitar destruction shared an affinity with the "auto-destructive" art of Gustav Metzger, whom he had seen lecture while studying at Ealing Art School in the early 1960s.[1] Regardless of where the inspiration lay, Townshend's actions suggested a cultural shift within rock, as it began to blur the lines between showmanship, avant-garde pop and performance art. In the interview's second half, Townshend addresses the importance of the working-class mod movement to the Who's early success. The mods's self-fashioned rebellious stance marked a dramatic turn from the 1950s, when the popular press routinely characterized rock 'n' roll as a malignant force that had simply descended upon an impressionable and passive young audience. There was rarely any consideration that the audience itself might have a tangible influence on the music or the performers, many of whom were teenagers themselves. The emergence of mod helped shift the dynamics of this relationship, and in the 1970s spurred an intense academic interest in British youth subcultures that remains one of the strongest foundations of popular music studies.

The end of your act goes to "My Generation," like you usually do, and that's where you usually smash your guitar. You didn't tonight—why not?

Well, there is a reason, not really anything that's really worth talking about. But I'll explain the pattern of thought which went into it.

I've obviously broken a lot of guitars, and I've brought eight or nine of that particular guitar I was using tonight and I could very easily have broken it and have plenty more for the future. But I just suddenly decided before I went on that if there was anywhere in the world I should be able to walk off the stage without breaking a guitar if I didn't want to, it would be the Fillmore.

I decided in advance that I didn't want to smash the guitar, so I didn't, not because I liked it or because I've decided I'm going to stop doing it or anything. I just kind of decided about the actual

---

1 See, for example, Miles, "Miles Interviews Pete Townshend," *International Times*, February 13, 1967. Reprinted in *Rock's Backpages* www.rocksbackpages.com.libezproxy2.syr.edu/article.html?ArticleID=14192.

situation; it forced me to see if I could have gotten away with it in advance. And I think that's why "My Generation" was such a down number at the end. I didn't really want to play it, you know, at all. I didn't even want people to expect it to happen, because I just wasn't going to do it.

But Keith still dumped over his drum kit like he usually does.

Yeah, but it was an incredible personal thing with me. I've often gone on the stage and said, "Tonight, I'm not going to smash a guitar and I don't give a shit" - you know what the pressure is on me—whether I feel like doing it musically or whatever, I'm just not going to do it. And I've gone on, and every time I've done it. The actual performance has always been bigger than my own personal patterns of thought.

Tonight, for some reason, I went on and I said, "I'm not going to break it," and I didn't. And I don't know how, I don't really know why I didn't. But I didn't, you know, and it's the first time. I mean, I've said it millions of times before, and nothing has happened.

I imagine it gets to be a drag talking about why you smash your guitar.

No, it doesn't get to be a drag to talk about it. Sometimes it gets a drag to do it. I can explain it, I can justify it and I can enhance it, and I can do a lot of things, dramatize it and literalize it. Basically it's a gesture which happens on the spur of the moment. I think, with guitar smashing, just like the performance itself; it's a performance, it's an act, it's an instant and it really is meaningless.

When did you start smashing guitars?

It happened by complete accident the first time. We were just kicking around in a club which we played every Tuesday, and I was playing the guitar and it hit the ceiling. It broke, and it kind of shocked me 'cause I wasn't ready for it to go. I didn't particularly want it to go, but it went.

And I was expecting an incredible thing, it being so precious to me, and I was expecting everybody to go, "Wow, he's broken his guitar, he's broken his guitar," but nobody did anything, which made me angry in a way and determined to get this precious event noticed by the audience. I proceeded to make a big thing of breaking the guitar. I pounded all over the stage with it, and I threw the bits on the stage, and I picked up my spare guitar and carried on as though I really meant to do it.

Were you happy about it?

Deep inside I was very unhappy because the thing had got broken. It got around, and the next week the people came, and they came up to me and they said, "Oh, we heard all about it, man; it's 'bout time someone gave it to a guitar," and all this kind of stuff. It kind of grew from there; we'd go to another town and people would say, "Oh yeah, we heard that you smashed a guitar." It built and built and built and built and built and built until one day, a very important daily newspaper came to see us and said, "Oh, we hear you're the group that smashes their guitars up. Well, we hope you're going to do it tonight because we're from the *Daily Mail*. If you do, you'll probably make the front pages."

This was only going to be like the second guitar I'd ever broken, seriously. I went to my manager, Kit Lambert, and I said, you know, "Can we afford it, can we afford it, it's for publicity." He said, "Yes, we can afford it, if we can get the *Daily Mail*." I did it, and of course the *Daily Mail* didn't buy the photograph and didn't want to know about the story. After that I was into it up to my neck and have been doing it since.

Was it inevitable that you were going to start smashing guitars?

It was due to happen because I was getting to the point where I'd play and I'd play, and I mean, I still can't play how I'd like to play. *Then* was worse. I couldn't play the guitar; I'd listen to great music, I'd listen to all the people I dug, time and time again. When the Who first started we were playing blues, and I dug the blues and I knew what I was supposed to be playing, but I couldn't play it. I couldn't get it out. I knew what I had to play; it was in my head. I could hear the notes in my head, but I couldn't get them out on the guitar. I knew the music, and I knew the feeling of the thing and the drive and the direction and everything.

It used to frustrate me incredibly. I used to try and make up visually for what I couldn't play as a musician. I used to get into very incredible visual things where in order just to make one chord more lethal, I'd make it a really lethal-looking thing, whereas really, it's just going to be picked normally. I'd hold my arm up in the air and bring it down so it really looked lethal, even if it didn't sound too lethal. Anyway, this got bigger and bigger and bigger and bigger until eventually I was setting myself incredible tasks.

How did this affect your guitar playing?

Instead I said, "All right, you're not capable of doing it musically, you've got to do it visually." I became a huge, visual thing. In fact, I forgot all about the guitar because my visual thing was more about my music than the actual guitar. I got to jump about, and the guitar became unimportant. I banged it and I let it feed back and scraped it and rubbed it up against the microphone, did anything; it wasn't part of my act, even. It didn't deserve any credit or any respect. I used to bang it and hit it against walls and throw it on the floor at the end of the act.

And one day it broke. It just wasn't part of my thing, and ever since them I've never really regarded myself as a guitarist. When people come up to me and say like, "Who's your favorite guitarist?" I say, "I know who my favorite guitarist is, but asking me, as a guitarist, forget it because I don't make guitar-type comments. I don't talk guitar talk, I just throw the thing around." Today still, I'm learning. If I play a solo, it's a game to me because I can't play what I want to play. That's the thing: I can't get it out because I don't practice. When I should be practicing, I'm writing songs, and when I'm writing songs, I should be practicing.

*   *   *

[A] theme, not so dramatically, seems to be repeated in so many songs that you've written and the Who have performed—a young cat, our age, becoming an outcast from a very ordinary sort of circumstance. Not a "Desolation Row" scene, but a very common set of middle-class situations. Why does this repeat itself?

I don't know. I never really thought about that.

There's a boy with pimple problems and a chick with perspiration problems and so on.[2]

Most of these things just come from me. Like this idea I'm talking about right now, comes from me. These things are my ideas, it's probably why they all come out the same; they've all got the same fuckups, I'm sure.

I can't get my family together, you see. My family were musicians. There were essentially middle class, they were musicians, and I spent a lot of time with them when other kids' parents were at work, and I spent a lot of time *away* from them when other kids had parents, you know. That was the only way it came together. They were always out for long periods. But they were always home for long periods, too. They were always very respectable - nobody ever stopped making me play the guitar and nobody ever stopped me smoking pot, although they advised me against it.

They didn't stop me from doing anything that I wanted to do. I had my first fuck in the drawing room of my mother's house. The whole incredible thing about my parents is that I just can't place their effect on me, and yet I know that it's there. I can't say how they affected me. When people find out that my parents are musicians, they ask how it affected me. Fucked if I know; musically, I can't place it, and I can't place it in any other way. But I don't even feel myself aware of a class structure, or an age structure, and yet I perpetually write about age structures and class structures.

---

2 Wenner is referring to the songs "Medac" and "Odorono," respectively, from the Who's 1967 album *The Who Sell Out*.

On the surface I feel much more concerned with racial problems and politics. Inside I'm much more into basic stuff.

You must have thought about where it comes from if it's not your parents. Was it the scene around you when you were young?

One of the things which has impressed me most in life was the Mod movement in England, which was an incredible youthful thing. It was a movement of young people, much bigger than the hippie thing, the underground and all these things. It was an army, a powerful, aggressive army of teenagers with transport. Man, with these scooters and with their own way of dressing. It was acceptable, this was important; their way of dressing was hip, it was fashionable, it was clean and it was groovy. You could be a bank clerk, man, it was acceptable. You got them on your own ground. They thought, "Well, there's a smart young lad." And also you were hip, you didn't get people uptight. That was the good thing about it. To be a mod, you had to have short hair, money enough to buy a real smart suit, good shoes, good shirts; you had to be able to dance like a madman. You had to be in possession of plenty of pills all the time and always be pilled up. You had to have a scooter covered in lamps. You had to have like an army anourak to wear on the scooter. And that was being a mod, and that was the end of the story.

The groups that you liked when you were a mod were the Who. That's the story of why I dig the mods, man, because we were mods and that's how we happened. That's my generation, that's how the song "My Generation" happened, because of the mods. The mods could appreciate the Beatles' taste. They could appreciate their haircuts, their peculiar kinky things that they had going at the time.

What would happen is that the phenomena of the Who could invoke action. The sheer fact that four mods could actually form themselves into a group which sounded quite good, considering that most mods were lower-class garbagemen, you know, with enough money to buy himself Sunday best, you know, their people. Nowadays, okay, there are quite a few mod groups. But mods aren't the kind of people that could play the guitar, and it was just groovy for them to have a group. Our music at the time was representative of what the mods dug, and it was meaningless rubbish.

We used to play, for example, "Heat Wave," a very long version of "Smokestack Lightning," and that song we sang tonight, "Young Man Blues," fairly inconsequential kind of music which they could identify with and perhaps something where you banged your feet on the third beat or clapped your hands on the fifth beat, something so that you get the things to go by. I mean, they used to like all kinds of things. They were mods and we're mods and we dig them. We used to make sure that if there was a riot, a mod-rocker riot, we would begin playing in that area. That was a place called Brighton.

By the sea?

Yes. That's where they used to assemble. We'd always be playing there. And we got associated with the whole thing, and we got into the spirit of the whole thing. And, of course, rock & roll, the words wouldn't even be mentioned; the fact that music would have any part of the movement was terrible. The music would come from the actual drive of the youth combination itself.

You see, as individuals these people were nothing. They were the lower, they were England's lowest common denominators. Not only were they young, they were also lower-class young. They had to submit to the middle class way of dressing and way of speaking and way of acting in order to get the very jobs which kept them alive. They had to do everything in terms of what existed already around them. That made their way of getting something across that much more latently effective, the fact that they were hip and yet still, as far as Granddad was concerned, exactly the same. It made the whole gesture so much more vital. It was incredible. As a force, they were unbelievable. That was the Bulge, that was England's Bulge; all the war babies, all the old soldiers coming back from war and screwing until they were blue in the face—this was the result. Thousands and thousands of kids, too many kids, not enough teachers, not enough parents, not enough pills to go around. Everybody just grooving on being a mod.

How do you think that compares with what's called today the American hippie scene?

I think it compares. I think the hippie thing compares favorably, but it's a different motivation. There are beloved figures. There is pot, there is acid, and there is the Maharishi, there is the Beatles, there is being anti-the-U.S.A., there are a whole lot of red herrings, which aren't what it's all about. What it is all about is *the hippies*, you know, that's what it's all about. The people, the actions, not the events, not the tripping out or the latest fad or the latest record or the latest trip or the latest thing to groove to. The thing is people.

This is what they seem to overlook. You see, this is the thing about the media barrage—you become aware only of the products around you because they're glorified, and so that when somebody gets stoned, what they do is that they don't groove to themselves, really, they just sit around and they dig everything that's around them. They perhaps dig other people. They dig the way the room looks. The way the flowers look, the way the music sounds, the way the group performs, how good the Beatles are. "How nice that is." This is the whole thing: they're far too abject in outlook, they're far too concerned with what is feeding into them and not so much with what they are. This is the difference between the mod thing in England and the hippie thing over here. The hippies are waiting for information, because information is perpetually coming in, and they sit there and wait for it.

This is the incredible thing about the States, man. To get stoned in England is an entirely different trip. I'm not saying that you get stoned and you dig yourself or anything. What you would do is you would get stoned, perhaps you'd walk out and look at a tree or a matchstick or something and come back and have a cup of tea and then go to bed, man. But over here, you just carry on regardless. You to go Orange Julius and you have an Orange Julius, and you watch TV and then you listen to some records, played very, very loud, and you know, it's a whole different pattern, a whole different way.

The acceptance of what one already has is the thing. Whereas the mod thing was the rejection of everything one already had. You didn't want to know about the fucking TV. "Take it away," you know. You didn't want to know about the politicians, you didn't want to know about the war. If there had been a draft, man, they would have just disappeared. If there had been a draft, there wouldn't have been mods, because something like that—the thing was that it was a sterile situation, it was perfect. It was almost too perfect.

Over here it's imperfect, it's not a sterile situation. The group themselves can't become powerful because they can be weakened at so many points. They can be weakened by their education, by their spirituality, by their intelligence, by the sheer fact that Americans are more highly educated. The average American and the average Englishman, and the Englishmen I'm talking about are the people that probably left school when they were fourteen or fifteen. Some of them can't even read or write. But yet they were mods, they were like—you see something nearer, I suppose, in what it's like to be a Hell's Angel, but not as much flash, not as much gimmicking, much less part of a huge machine.

Source: Jann Wenner, "The Rolling Stone Interview: Peter Townshend," *Rolling Stone*, September 14, 1968, pp. 1, 10–15.

26

Gimme Shelter
Woodstock and Altamont

JOEL HAYCOCK

Few events have been more mythologized within rock history than the 1969 Woodstock and Altamont festivals. The former, which took place on Max Yasgur's upstate New York farm between August 15 and 18, and attracted hundreds of thousands of youths and iconic performers such as Jimi Hendrix, has been celebrated as a peaceful, unifying gathering, while the Rolling Stones' hastily arranged Altamont Speedway concert on December 6, with security provided by the Hell's Angels, ended in tragedy with the stabbing to death of Meredith Hunter. Contemporary accounts in the press did much to propagate this contrast, but it is most of all the two documentary movies, 1970's *Woodstock* and *Gimme Shelter*, that have sustained this mythology over time.[1] Joel Haycock's 1971 review of *Gimme Shelter*, published in the scholarly journal *Film Quarterly*, stands as a notable early attempt to interrogate the received meanings of these two festivals and their supposed differences. Haycock pointedly questions not only the sensationalist tendencies of the press, but more specifically the professional ethics of filmmakers such as *Gimme Shelter*'s Charlotte Zwerin (1931–2004), David Maysles (1931–1987) and Albert Maysles (1926–2015) in their attempts to fashion a dramatic narrative out of realistic "direct cinema" footage. The rock documentary has only grown in prominence since these watershed events. Given that we have increasingly relied on such documentaries to communicate rock's meanings and stories in powerful and gripping ways, it is worth considering how Haycock's critique might apply to rock's more recent filmic representations.

The short history of rock 'n' roll festivals is circumscribed by three singular events: the Monterey Festival, the Lake Bethel Festival, and a day-long concert at the Altamont Speedway. Each event's claim to singularity is by this time a matter of commonly received opinion: as our commentators have it, Monterey marked the apotheosis of the San Francisco-based flower culture, the Bethel concert (Woodstock) was the great coming together for, in its advertisement's words, three days of Love, Peace and Music, and Altamont the death of flower-power, the death of Love, the death of Rock, depending on whom you read. How each of these affairs became elevated to the status of a major event, dwarfing even Newport in its heyday, is a question of some interest, especially since both the monied press and the so-called underground press (that press, you will remember, which

---

1 For an excellent critique of the mythology of Altamont, see Joel Selvin, *Altamont: The Rolling Stones, the Hells Angels, and the Inside Story of Rock's Darkest Day* (New York: Dey Street Books, 2017).

grew up in opposition to the established press) subscribe to and share an interest in essentially the same apprehension of all three experiences. The difference between the *Life* magazine extra on Woodstock and *Rolling Stone's* Woodstock issue confines itself to details of taste and description; the broad interpretative outlines are the same, though *Rolling Stone's* hosannas are perhaps a bit more shrill and self-promoting. This confluence of such ostensibly antagonistic perspectives extends to the Altamont concert; from *Newsweek* to the *Berkeley Tribe*, Altamont, in the *Tribe's* words, ". . . like the massacre at Song My, exploded the myth of innocence."

Both the festival at Altamont and the one at Bethel are events identified as places, or, as those not yet embarrassed about the whole charade will tell you, states of mind. The interrelationship between the two events is so directly drawn by so many people that one can't help but nurture some suspicions. The formal integrity seems extravagant—Woodstock's tacky dreams shimmer a little too loudly, while Altamont's function as some sociological reality principle is dramatically too neat. It seems like we've been treated to some show in which one character has been introduced only to be demolished by another's appearance, both acts completed to concerted applause.

After all, what distance could possibly separate two occasions whose circumstances are so similar? In each, hip producers intent on fantastic publicity hurriedly chose an inadequate location, threw up a scaffold, and invited hundreds of thousands of white middle-class kids to enjoy themselves. At Woodstock, the performers received exorbitant salaries, for which the multitude was to pay, but the promoters' hasty greed overstepped the bounds of efficiency, with the result that the fences weren't up at showtime and the music became "free." Altamont's stars—the Stones, the Dead, the Airplane, et al.—performed free, but the Stones' generosity at least was clearly predicated on the bad publicity garnered by their tour's seven-dollar-a-seat demands. Comparing the footage of Altamont in *Gimme Shelter* with that of Bethel in Michael Wadleigh's *Woodstock*, it's hard to see any difference in the crowd's composition or their activities; the former looks like any other mass concert to me, and it's photographed like Woodstock or Monterey for that matter: idyllic scenes with babies or dogs, shots of breasty women, exotic clothing, close-ups of people getting high, a freak-out, a few nude scenes, some unashamed embraces, more drugs, more exotic clothing, another breast, etc. But then there's the Angels, some clubbings, and the death of Meredith Hunter.

Woodstock would hardly seem to deserve its luminous aura. There were beatings; hundreds took bad acid; at one point at least 75,000 people screamed "Jump" to some kid on top of a 300-foot scaffolding; all "natural for a city of 400,000," said the papers. There were deaths at Woodstock also, three of them, but along with two births they were attributed to the "life cycle." A boy without a place to sleep lay down in unknown fields and was run over the next morning by a tractor. Now no camera crew was present then, or when a girl died of a burst appendix before receiving medical attention, just as no photographer recorded the deaths of Mark Feiger and Richard Savlov, two kids killed at Altamont when a driver trying to find the freeway slammed his car into their campsite. No one saw some guy fall into an unlit, unfenced irrigation ditch near the Speedway either; he drowned. And of course for none of these fatalities was there upbeat musical accompaniment, nor were they the subject of Mick Jagger's attentions.

I hope all of this isn't mawkish, but the point is simply that institutional negligence (under which I would classify the callous transgressions of promoters like Michael Lang or Melvin Belli) does not make good copy or flashy movies. When thirty-eight miners suffocate in a mineshaft which doesn't even meet the government's lax specifications, that "tragedy" is accorded the treatment the press gives to earthquakes and other natural disasters, but New York film-makers aren't about to fly down to Kentucky or wherever and compose a film around it. Instead it's the front page one day, then the last bodies are dug up the next day on page seven, and two days later finds a press release on the official enquiry at the bottom of forty-two.

No, when the world goes wrong and we demand that someone pay for it, when *Life* needs a demon for our collective exorcism, we and *Life* look to the powerless (or occasionally to those that have fallen from power, reading that economic demise as testament to some moral failing). Denying one of the central facts of our social life, namely that the most chilling barbarities are fomented in committee, we isolate villains who cooperatively identify themselves by being members of the economic periphery in the first place (non-whites, "criminals," "drug addicts," the "insane," etc.). By assigning responsibility for our own uneasiness to individuals rather than to structures we reassure ourselves that the world has a human face, that if we only could root out the bad guys, vote in our own people (elect a new president), the harmony of our situation could be restored, life would attain once again its manageable shape.

Hence everybody loves murders; they have real human villains, and the good ones have "helpless" victims (women, children, old people), or at least valorous ones (police, prisoners of war). Unsafe assembly lines, malconstructed bleachers, badly made cars can claim lives every day, though we'll hear little about it; but let some psychopath carve up a group of nurses, or someone shoot a cop over in Brighton, and we'll never hear the end of it. Journalism consists in the substitution of an event's dramatic elements for the event itself; newspapers and magazines are drama by other means. Let me entertain you.

Gimme Shelter was directed by Charlotte Zwerin and the Maysles brothers, Albert and David; these last have been two of the most important film-makers to come out of the direct cinema movement. The direct cinematographer is a special kind of film journalist who, rather than creating (or reconstructing) events, attempts to situate himself in the midst of them. Though he cannot transcend his subjective viewpoint, his object is ostensibly an *objet trouvé*, a "real life drama," and the structure of his film is to be determined by the nature of that object in action. Thus Albert says of *Gimme Shelter* that "we structured around what actually turned out to happen"; "what comes out of it is a surprise to us as well."

But *Gimme Shelter*, unlike their earlier *Salesman*, is elaborately contrived, intercutting no less than six numbers (one by Tina Turner) from the Stones' Madison Square Garden concert with short tour episodes, preparations made by Melvin Belli and others for the Altamont concert, two press conferences, the aforementioned crowd scenes, and five numbers from Altamont (one each by the Flying Burrito Brothers and the Jefferson Airplane).[2] We close, to the tune of "Gimme Shelter," with an insipidly lyrical exodus into the rising sun by the Altamont hordes.

Given their direct cinema background the Maysles were undoubtedly uncomfortable with such disjunct segments; there they were with gobs of stage performance footage, an exclusive on Meredith Hunter's murder, and no way to integrate the two. Then someone hit on the bright idea of showing the footage to the Stones, of filming their responses to themselves, to Tina Turner, to the Altamont arrangements, and of course to the stabbing itself. Throughout *Gimme Shelter* the Maysles cut from a filmed event to a shot of that same film running through a viewer, and then cut to one of the Stones' vacant faces—a vacancy, you understand, which is supposed to read as shock, or grief, or incomprehension. When Jagger finally sees the murder footage, the big moment has all the spontaneity and excitement of that astronaut's first words from the moon; stagily concerned, Jagger mumbles, "Can you roll back on that, David."

The device serves two functions. First, it gives *Shelter* an intellectual gloss: Mick or Keith's contemplation suggests the burden of self-consciousness, a filmed discourse on the relation of self

---

2 One of the key figures in the film, Melvin Belli was a noted attorney who represented the Rolling Stones in their last minute negotiations to arrange the concert.

to representation, etc., etc. Naturally this is all glitter; what such a schema really does here is allow the film-makers to cut another slambang rock 'n' roll number in every four or five minutes without risking a stylistic break. That way the sequences of Melvin Belli negotiating for the Stones, virtually the only explanations tendered in the entire film concerning who is responsible for what, are not permitted to drag on at "unnecessary" length, a few shots of Belli in his preposterous office deemed sufficient to reveal all, and then again, it's the Angels who are the pigs, right? But most importantly, the device is real Teen Scene stuff: given the Indo-Chinese War, racism, a murder, or some other tragedy, the big question in all the fans' minds, becomes: How do the Stones react to all this?

Well, not very interestingly, but then what's interesting about the footage in the first place? You learn that Richards identifies with Jagger, that both of them have seen the Beatles' movies and aspire to their brand of self-conscious humor. You see the Stones at work and at play. On stage and off, but the latter sequences are brief, unrevealing, and have sound-overs to help them go down easier. You get two new Stones' songs, one called "Wild Horses," with lines like "Wild horses couldn't drag me away/Wild horses, we'll ride them someday," and the other a derivative "Brown Sugar." And you get lots of live performances, but frankly the cloying, infatuated photography renders even these tedious after three or four songs; the Maysles seemed to have realized this, and *Shelter's* nadir comes when they try to jazz up their presentation of "Love in Vain" with rapturous slow-motion and fancy opticals (an idea handled infinitely better, by the way, in Peter Whitehead's *Tonight Let's All Make Love in London*).

Its practitioners have always claimed that direct cinema's presentation of experience remains faithful to the complexity of experience itself. That faithfulness derives, so the argument runs, from an "innocent" approach to the world, an attempt to capture involuntarily and without predisposition the nature of a chosen subject. Albert denies that he is guilty of any "contrived attempt to take the talent of the Stones and then structure events or a movie around it in some kind of fake way. The life of the tour, which is what the film represents, is a natural happening . . . [the film] raises a lot of questions about what America is all about, but in a way that's not a lecture or anything of that sort."

What's most refreshing about the Maysles' naivete is its sustained self-serving obtuseness. Of course Altamont was a complex event, and it is charitable of the Maysles to help us deal with that complexity by ignoring a number of its main actors, the better to appreciate the intricacies of the remainder, I'm sure. But once you've excised John Jaymes of Young American Enterprises, Sam Cutler, the Dead with their bright ideas, once you've reduced Belli to a harmless comic figure, and the Stones to unwitting spectators of their own spectacle, who's left but the Angels, and what's left but another melodrama, one in which beefy Alfred Jarrys play the villains, and everyone else the innocents?[3] A self-defined outlaw gang, but not the kind of outlaws that sign million-dollar contracts, the Angels are denied appeal. Though Grace Slick says, "People get weird and we need the Angels to keep people in line"; though a member of the Dead says, "Beating on musicians? Doesn't seem right"; though the Stones and their entourage hired the Angels as guards because they were cheap and because they added a little genuine street-fighting class, no tribunal will acquit the Angels on the grounds that they were just following orders (the man charged with Hunter's death *was* acquitted, but for other reasons).

Like the Altamont myth on which it feeds, *Gimme Shelter* is the product of slick, tabloid sensibilities, which is not to say that the filmmakers may not be sincere. But what remonstrance is possible to someone capable of saying, as Albert did, that "I think we would have been disappointed

---

3 John Jaymes of Young American Enterprises was responsible for securing the concert venue; Sam Cutler was the Rolling Stones's road manager.

if everything had stopped just at Madison Square Garden." If not for the Angels, and if not for Meredith Hunter, described to me by David Maysles as being dressed in a "nigger zoot suit, straight out of the nineteen-fifties, you wouldn't believe him if you saw him in a fiction film," the Maysles would have had just another promotional film on their hands. But above all credit is due the American press, without whom the entire shadow-play would not have been possible.

Source: Joel Haycock, "Review: *Gimme Shelter* by David Maysles, Albert Maysles, Charlotte Zwerin," *Film Quarterly* 24, no. 4 (1971), pp. 56–60.

III

THE 1970s

27

"Sweet Baby James"

James Taylor Live

ALFRED ARONOWITZ

Of all the musical developments that marked the transition from the 1960s to a new decade, few were more pronounced than the emergence of the singer-songwriter genre. If the rock group, with its collective membership, had symbolized a certain communal countercultural ideal, then the singer-songwriter as solo artist heralded the arrival of what Tom Wolfe would famously label the "Me Decade." Singer-songwriters such as James Taylor (born 1948) increasingly turned towards their own feelings and inner turmoil for inspiration. Setting their personal experiences directly to song, their music became a form of autobiography. In Taylor's case, his acknowledged bouts with depression and drug dependency formed the basis for his first hit single, "Fire and Rain." *New York Post* music critic Alfred Aronowitz draws attention to these traits in his review of Taylor's breakthrough three-night residency in March 1970 at the renowned Gaslight Café in Greenwich Village. Taylor would ascend to stardom shortly after, eventually landing on the cover of *Time* magazine the following year. Aronowitz mentions that Taylor seems to speak "for his generation." If this is true, what are we to make of Taylor's well-publicized privileged background (as Aronowitz notes, his father was the dean of the University of North Carolina medical school, and Taylor had received treatment for his depression at an exclusive Harvard-based psychiatric institution)? Are such details significant to understanding Taylor's appeal or that of the singer-songwriter genre in general?

Those people spilling off the curb into MacDougal St. last Saturday noon weren't there to watch the eclipse. Not until May 1, 2079, will New York be able to see the moon darken the sun again, but those people standing in MacDougal St. have come to witness an event of obviously greater magnitude. James Taylor was making his only appearance of the year at the Gaslight, and they were waiting to buy tickets.

Who is James Taylor, this young, thin giant with long, dark hair and a wispy beard who walks through the crowds that come to adore him with a half-smile on his lips and distant visions in his eyes like a Jesus in an era when we already have too many, and at the same time one too few? Ask him about himself and he will give you only the barest outlines of a life that was lived for the most part in hurt. You don't talk to Sweet Baby James. You listen to his music.

He tells about himself in the slow, measured phrasing of someone who doesn't want to be misunderstood. His voice is clear crystal. Whatever secrets James Taylor has about himself, he thinks his music is big enough to hide behind. James Taylor steps upon the stage ready to challenge the gods.

Four years ago, he was one of those kid musicians among the hundreds of groups hustling through the Village for any ear that would listen to their own particular cries of prophecy in the wilderness. He belonged to the Flying Machine, a band which is now, as he sings, with sweet dreams in pieces on the ground. When the Flying Machine crashed, so did James.

A couple of years later, he turned up in London and recorded an album for Peter Asher of Apple Records. The album was distributed in this country by Capitol but as Peter says, "I got the feeling Capitol never listened to it." His new album, "Sweet Baby James," is on Warner Brothers and, only a few weeks after its release, James is drawing the kind of crowds you saw standing on the street outside the Gaslight. On Saturday night alone, the club had to turn away 2,000 people, "I can feel it happening," James says. "I'm starting to feel good about it."

The songs that James sings are his own, born out of the torture that twice sent him into mental institutions. His lyrics are, of course, private, personal and mysterious, but at 21, James speaks for his generation with the kind of cool authority that seems destined to elect him one of the spokesmen of his time. Could he be the one, born in Boston and raised in Chapel Hill, the son of the dean of the University of North Carolina Medical School?

He was 17 and in boarding school the first time he committed himself. "I was suicidal," he says. "It was the only place I could go." He committed himself a second time after recording his first album. "It seemed like a good idea at the time," he explains.

You watch him singing on the stage of the Gaslight, sounding exactly as he sounds on his album, and you feel his confidence surrounding you. It's already a little too close in the room and you wonder if you like being crowded by his presence. Sweat from a water pipe collects on the ceiling and begins to drip on him. "My guitar is gently weeping," he says. He sings a Coke commercial and everyone laughs.

"Lord knows you got to take time to think these days," he says. Before he begins to sing again, he tells the audience, "If you feel like singing along, don't." Is James Taylor going to be the next public phenomenon? It's a little early in the cycle for such an event, but that's the league James has applied for. May the Lord have mercy on him.

Source: Alfred Aronowitz, "Sweet Baby James," *New York Post*, March 9, 1970, p. 27.

28

"Cock Rock: Men Always Seem to End Up on Top"

RAT MAGAZINE

The rock world of the late 1960s/early 1970s was a decidedly male-dominated one, where it often seemed as if the aggressive attitudes of groups like the Rolling Stones allowed little agency for women outside the thrill-seeking adventures of groupies.[1] One of the first articles to address the contradictory allure and repulsion of rock music from a woman's perspective, "Cock Rock" originally appeared in the New York-based underground feminist publication *Rat* magazine.[2] The article is cast in a decisively downbeat tone, no doubt influenced by the passing of one of rock's few female icons, Janis Joplin (1943–1970), who had died from a heroin overdose mere days before the essay was published. Like many of the writings in *Rat*, "Cock Rock" appeared without an attributed author, an anonymity that served to reflect the communal solidarity of the women's movement itself. The article was later anthologized, however, under the pseudonym of Susan Hiwatt, a playful allusion to a British line of guitar amplifiers favored by groups like the Who and Pink Floyd.[3]

I. THIS WAS THE WORLD THAT ROCK BUILT

I grew up on Peter Trip, the curly-headed kid in the third row (an AM D.J. in New York City in the late '50s). I spent a lot of time after school following the social life of the kids on *American Bandstand*. Then in high school I spent most of my time in my room with the radio, avoiding family fights. Rock became the thing that helped fill the loneliness and empty spaces in my life. The sound became sort of an alter-world where I daydreamed—a whole vicarious living out of other people's romances and lives. "Sally Go 'round the Roses." "Donna."

In college, rock was one of the things that got me together with other people: hours spent in front of a mirror learning how to dance, going to twist parties—getting freakier—tripping off the whole outlaw thing of "My Generation" and "Satisfaction." I was able to dance rock and talk rock comfortably in a college atmosphere when other things were mystified and intellectualized out of my comprehension and control. You didn't have to have heavy or profound thoughts about rock—you just knew that you dug it.

---

1 For an alternative view of the Rolling Stones, see Karen Durbin, "Can a Feminist Love the World's Greatest Rock and Roll Band," *Ms.*, October 1974, pp. 23–26.

2 *Rat* appeared under various titles throughout its brief publication run, including *Rat Subterranean News* and *Women's LibeRATion*.

3 Susan Hiwatt, "Cock Rock," in Jonathan Eisen, ed., *Twenty-Minute Fandangos and Forever Changes: A Rock Bazaar* (New York: Random House, 1971), 141–47.

A whole sense of people together, behind their own music. It was the only thing we had of our own, where the values weren't set up by the famous wise professors. It was the way not to have to get old and deadened in White America. We wore hip clothes and smoked dope and dropped acid. Going to San Francisco with flowers in our hair.

For a couple of years, when I was with a man, I remember feeling pretty good—lots of people around, a scene I felt I had some control over, getting a lot of mileage off being a groovy couple. For as long as I was his woman, I was protected and being a freak was an up because it made me feel like I had an identity.

When I split from him a whole other trip started. It got harder and harder to be a groovy chick when I had to deal with an endless series of one-night stands and people crashing and always doing the shitwork—thinking and being told that the only reason I wasn't being a freak was because I was too uptight. Going to Woodstock all but bare-breasted somewhere in the middle of all that and thinking I was fucked up for not being able to have more fun than I was having. In a world where the ups were getting fewer and fewer, rock still continued to turn me on.

Then I connected to the women's movement and took a second look at rock.

II. CRASHING: WOMEN IS LOSERS

The Sound of Silence

It took me a whole lot of going to the Fillmore and listening to records and reading *Rolling Stone* before it even registered that what I was seeing and hearing was not all these different groups, but all these different groups of men. And once I noticed that, it was hard not to be constantly noticing: all the names on the albums, all the people doing sound and lights, all the voices on the radio, even the D.J.'s between the songs—they are *all* men. In fact, the only place I could look to see anyone who looked anything like me was in the audience, and even there, there were usually more men than women.

It occurred to me that maybe there were some good reasons, besides inadequacy, that I had never taken all my fantasies about being a rock musician very seriously. I don't think I ever told anyone about them. Because in the female 51 percent of Woodstock Nation that I belong to, there isn't any place to be creative in any way. It's a pretty exclusive world.

There are, of course, exceptions. I remember hearing about some "all-chick" bands on the West Coast, like the Ace of Cups, and I also remember reading about how they were laughed and hooted at with a general "take them off the stage and fuck them" attitude. And how they were given the spot between the up-and-coming group and the big-name group—sort of for comic relief. Or the two women I saw once who played with the Incredible String Band. They both played instruments and looked terrified throughout the entire concert (I kept thinking how brave they were to be there at all). The two men treated them like backdrops. They played back-up and sang harmony, and in fact, they were introduced as Rose and Licorice—no last names. The men thought it was cute that they were there and they had such cute names. No one, either on stage or in the audience, related to them as musicians. But they sure were sweet and pretty.

It blew my mind the first time I heard about a woman playing an electric guitar. Partly because of the whole idea we have that women can't understand anything about electronics (and we're not even supposed to want to), and also because women are supposed to be composed, gentle, play soft songs. A guy once told my sister when she picked up his electric guitar that women were meant to play only folk guitar, like Joan Baez or Judy Collins, that electric guitars were unfeminine. There are other parallel myths that have kept us out of rock: women aren't strong enough to play the drums; women aren't aggressive enough to play good, driving rock.

And then there is the whole other category of exception—the "chick" singer. The one place, besides being a groupie, where the stag club allows women to exist. And women who make it there pretty much have to be incredible to break in, and they are—take, for example, Janis Joplin and Aretha Franklin. It's a lot like the rest of the world where women have to be twice as good just to be acceptable.

Words of Love

Getting all this together in my head about the massive exclusion of women from rock left me with some heavy bad feelings. But still there was all that charged rock energy to dig. But what was that all about, anyway? Stokely Carmichael once said that all through his childhood he went to movies to see westerns and cheered wildly for the cowboys, until one day he realized that being black, he was really an Indian, and all those years he had been rooting for his own destruction. Listening to rock songs became an experience a lot like that for me. Getting turned on to "Under My Thumb," a revenge song filled with hatred for women, made me feel crazy. And it wasn't an isolated musical moment that I could frown about and forget. Because when you get to listening to male rock lyrics, the message to women is devastating. We are cunts—sometimes ridiculous ("Twentieth Century Fox"), sometimes mysterious ("Ruby Tuesday"), sometimes bitchy ("Get a Job") and sometimes just plain cunts ("Wild Thing"). And all that sexual energy that seems to be in the essence of rock is really energy that climaxes in fucking over women—endless lyrics and a sound filled with feeling I thought I was relating to but couldn't relate to, attitudes about women like put-downs, domination, threats, pride, mockery, fucking around and a million different levels of women-hating. For some reason, the Beatles' "rather see you dead, little girl, than see you with another man" pops into my head. But it's a random choice. Admittedly, there are some other kinds of songs—a few with nice feelings, a lot with a cool *macho* stance toward life and a lot with no feelings at all, a realm where, say, the Procol Harum shines pretty well at being insipid or obscure ("A Whiter Shade of Pale"). But to catalog the anti-women songs alone would make up almost a complete history of rock.

This all hit home to me with knock-out force at a recent Stones concert when Mick, prancing about enticingly with whip in hand, suddenly switched gears and went into "Under My Thumb," with an incredible vengeance that upped the energy level and brought the entire audience to its feet, dancing on the chairs. Mass wipeout for women—myself included.

Contrast this with the songs that really do speak to women where our feelings are at, songs that Janis and Aretha sing of their own experience of being women, of pain and humiliation and the love. And it's not all in the lyrics. When Aretha sings the Beatles' "Let It Be," she changes it from a sort of decadent-sounding song to a hymn of hope. A different tone coming from a different place.

The Great Pretenders

The whole star trip in rock is another realm where *macho* reigns supreme. At the center of the rock universe is the star—flooded in light, offset by the light show and the source of incredible volumes of sound. The audience remains totally in darkness: the Stones kept thousands waiting several hours, till nightfall, before they would come on stage at Altamont. The stage is set for the men to parade around acting out violence/sex fantasies, sometimes fucking their guitars and then smashing them, writhing bare-chested with leather fringe flying, while the whole spectacle is enlarged a hundred times on a movie screen behind them. And watching a group like the Mothers of Invention perform is a lesson in totalitarianism—seeing Frank Zappa define sound and silence with a mere gesture of his hand. There is no psychic or visual or auditory space for anyone but the performer. Remember Jesse Colin Young of the Youngbloods turning to his audience with disdain and saying, "the least you could do is clap along"? First you force the audience into passivity and then you imply that they are fucked up for not moving.

Smile On Your Brother

Something else about the audience. Even after I realized women were barred from any active participation in rock music, it took me a while to see that we weren't even considered a real part of the listening audience. At first I thought I was being paranoid, but then I heard so many musicians address the audience as if it were all male: "I know you all want to find a good woman," "When you take your ol' lady home tonight . . ." "This is what you do with a no-good woman," etc., etc. It was clear that the concerts were directed only to men and the women were not considered people, but more on the level of exotic domestic animals that come with their masters or come to find masters. Only men are assumed smart enough to understand the intricacies of the music. Frank Zappa laid it out when he said that men come to hear the music and chicks come for sex thrills. Dig it!

It was a real shock to put this all together and realize rock music itself—all the way from performing artist to listener—refuses to allow any valid place for women. And yet I know there would never be rock festivals and concerts if women weren't there—even though we have nothing to do with the music. Somehow we're very necessary to rock culture.

Women are required at rock events to pay homage to the rock world—a world made up of thousands of men, usually found in groups of fours and fives. Homage paid by offering sexual accessibility, orgiastic applause, group worship, gang bangs at Altamont. The whole rock scene (as opposed to rock music) depends on our being there. Women are necessary at these places of worship so that, in between the sets, the real audience (men) can be assured of getting that woman they're supposed to like. Well, it's not enough just to be a plain old cunt. We have to be beautiful and even that's not enough: we've got to be groovy, you know, not uptight, not demanding, not jealous or clinging or strong or smart or anything but loving in a way that never cuts back on a man's freedom. And so women remain the last legitimate form of property that the brothers can share in a communal world. Can't have a tribal gathering without music and dope and beautiful groovy chicks.

For the musicians themselves there is their own special property—groupies. As one groupie put it: "Being a groupie is a fulltime gig. Sort of like being a musician. You have two or three girl friends you hang out with, and you stay as high and as intellectually enlightened as a group of musicians. You've got to if you're going to have anything to offer. You are a non-profit call girl, geisha, friend, housekeeper—whatever the musician needs."

This total disregard and disrespect for women is constant in the rock world and has no exceptions. Not even Janis Joplin, the all-time queen of rock. She made her pain evident in all her blues—that's what made them real. And the male rock world made her pay for that vulnerability in countless ways. Since women don't get to play the instruments, it means they're always on stage with nothing to relate to but the microphone, and nothing between them and the audience but their own bodies. So it is not surprising that Janis became an incredible sex object and was related to as a cunt with an outasight voice. Almost everyone even vaguely connected to rock heard malicious stories about how easy she was to fuck. This became part of her legend, and no level of stardom could protect her because when you get down to it, she was just a woman.

And Who Could Be Fooling Me?

And who ever thought this was all the brothers were offering us when they rapped about the revolution? Why do we stick with it? Women identified with youth culture as the only alternative to our parents' uptight and unhappy way of life. We linked up with rock and never said how it fucked us over. Partly this was because we had no sense of being women together with other women. Partly because it was impossible to think of ourselves as performing as exhibitionists in *macho* sex roles, so we didn't wonder why there weren't more of us on stage. Partly because we identified with the men and not other women when we heard lyrics that put women down. And a lot because we have been completely cut off from perceiving what and who really are on our side and what and who don't want to see us as whole people.

In a world of men, Janis sang our stories. When she died, one of the few ties that I still had left with rock snapped. It can't be that women are a people without a culture.

Source: "Cock Rock: Men Always Seem to End Up On Top," *Rat*, October 15–November 18, 1970, pp. 16–17, 26.

29

Carly Simon on Music and the Women's Movement

LORAINE ALTERMAN

One of the most significant developments of the early 1970s singer-songwriter movement was the creative and expressive space that it opened for female artists such as Carole King, Joni Mitchell, Carly Simon and many others. The emergence of these musicians ran parallel with the powerful rise of Women's Liberation, which had thrust the Equal Rights Amendment squarely into the national headlines, and many music critics and writers were quick to note the connection.[1] One of the most prominent female music writers of the time, Loraine Alterman tackles the subject directly in her interview with Simon (born 1945), which is excerpted here from a forum with two other artists that appeared as part of a mammoth 35 page "Women in Music" special report in the music industry trade publication *Record World*.[2] In her introduction to the interview Alterman holds up Simon and the others as models of "the independent role women are assuming in society" and explains her interest in how these women are "providing a new point of view about relationships between men and women." While Simon acknowledges the impact of Women's Liberation, she is somewhat hesitant to situate her music or songwriting approach as part of the movement. What are we to make of this reluctance? How would you compare it with the attitudes of contemporary female musicians towards feminism?

Record World: In what way do your own songs or the songs you select reflect your experiences as a woman?

Carly Simon: I don't think of myself as being a woman. I mean that's not what hits me first. The fact that I am a woman, of course, is reflected in the songs but I don't think that that comes first. That's why a song like "You're So Vain" is not necessarily sung at a man and not really pointed at a man or a woman. In fact, that song is as much about myself as it is about anybody else. Now there's this whole business about androgyny—male characteristics in female characteristics. I feel that in a lot of very basic ways, in fact in the most basic ways, there are probably more similarities between men and women than there are dissimilarities. I try to

---

1 See, for example, Lynn Van Matre, "Singing Songwriters: 1971 is Woman's World," *Chicago Tribune*, July 4, 1971, Section Five, p. 4 and Ellen Sander, "Rock and Roll Woman," *Crawdaddy*, April 2, 1972, pp. 25–30.

2 The two other artists that Alterman interviewed were Dory Previn and Mary Travers (of Peter, Paul and Mary).

de-condition myself all the time to being what is thought of as a woman. In my early songs I was thinking much more about what it was to be a woman and to not be able to call up a man, to have to be the one to be sought after and not the seeker. That's not nearly so much in my songs now.

RW: Has the Women's Liberation Movement affected your songwriting or choice of material?

Simon: Again, I don't do it on a conscious level. It comes out of my being a person because I am a woman and there's a lot of subconscious and unconscious material. I think, for instance, the Helen Reddy song, "I Am Woman," was a conscious attempt to make women and men realize that women weren't going to be put down any longer. I didn't happen to like the song particularly because it just came on too strong. There was nothing delicate about it. It was like she was out to do a certain thing and it was just over-stating the fact.

I don't sit down and think well, I want to get the world roused up about this or that. Anyway, I don't write songs for the public, I write them for myself. I write them out of little ideas that come into my head during the day. For example, I started to write a song about being a little girl and standing in the doorway and listening to my parents and their friends' conversation and thinking as a child, "How safe they are, how sure of themselves the grownups are and how when I get to be their age I'll be sure of myself too." But really, it's the penny candy syndrome. You think I just can't wait until I have enough money to get 100 sticks of penny candy and then when you are able to afford it, it makes you fat or it puts cholesterol in your blood or you don't want it any more. It's just that whole thing about growing up and being grown up myself. Just the other night a little girl was standing in the door and looking with such awe at me for being one of the grownups.

I was sitting there thinking, "I feel so uncomfortable, so shy and unsure of myself." And all the songs kind of come out of an experience and I don't consciously want to put a message across. If it happens, it happens. I guess there are some people who sit down and say, "All right, I want to write a hit single, what's a big item at the moment?", but I've never worked like that.

I'm aware of the influence of women's liberation sinking in by osmosis but it hasn't had an overt effect on me . . . You can't avoid the media and I certainly listen to what other people are singing and I'm very interested to read what women are writing about. I read recently a book called "Women and Madness" by Phyllis Chessler. It's a really, really heavy book. It talks about men who force women into roles which they don't know how to extricate themselves from which leads to depression or anxiety or some form of neurosis. That leads them into therapy, often with a male psychiatrist who perpetuates the whole syndrome of male–female role playing . . .

I've never felt that because I was a woman I was less capable. The major difference that I've felt in relation to men since the movement started, I guess, is that I really don't have the tools to be as out front, as aggressive as I'd like to be. Men grow up with tools that kind of teach them to succeed in a certain manner by being aggressive and going after what they want. Women are taught the tools to be feminine and recessive in a way.

RW: In your work do you consider the problems of men as well as women in relation to liberation from traditional role playing?

Simon: As I said in the beginning, my awareness isn't singled out in the category of what the problems are with women. It's with what the problems are to be a person and the sex roles somehow fit into that category, but I don't think really distinctly about them. Jacob Brackman wrote the lyrics of "That's The Way I've Always Heard It Should Be" out of a conversation we had had about it. But, the same thing in a way was happening to him. He was going through a period in his life where, when his girlfriend moved in with him, he had the same fear that he would no longer be him first, by himself and that this woman was going to come in and was going to live in his roots and that her things would gather among his things.

RW: Have you had any formal involvement with the women's cause?

Simon: No, because it's always helped me to get together with my women friends and talk about common problems. And I've always somehow been able to fortify myself and my conviction about what it is that I want as a woman by talking to other women who seem to have the same problems . . . I've always felt a kind of comradery with women that I don't with men. I feel a different type of comradery with men.

RW: In your career have you ever felt discriminated against in any way because you are a woman?

Simon: I don't like being made a sex object. I don't like it when I'm asked to pose for a picture in a sexy way. I guess that is a certain form of discrimination that you are a more salable commodity because you're a sexual woman. If I were short, fat and bow-legged, I probably wouldn't be as successful as I am, which is not to say that I'm a raving beauty, but the people on the selling end have tried to make a lot out of my sex appeal for some reason. I don't think it's bad to have sex appeal and if I have it, I'm really happy about it.

             I think men are probably being discriminated against in the same ways. Certain men who are sexy will have an easier time of it in show business so that's really not being discriminated against. It's being made into a sex object. Every time I think of whether I'm being discriminated against, I think of men and the fact that they are too. . . .

             In fact, I've felt special in the business because I am a woman. It's strange but I've been coddled and taken care of in a way that I probably wouldn't have if I were a man. I've never gotten paid less because I was a woman.

RW: Do you detect any changes in the attitudes of men in the music business towards women?

Simon: I hear a lot of stories about women being exploited and about men in the business just thinking that women are kind of the brainless vocalists who get up in front of the mike and "just sing the song, honey, we'll do the rest." This certainly does happen. I've heard stories of women getting rotten deals, but then again I hear stories about men too. I mean men are really awful to other men. One of the questions that Phyllis Chessler points out in "Women And Madness" is that if women do win the fight, if it is a fight, and become the leaders of our society, will they be fair? Won't they go overboard just as much and oppress men. So it certainly is true that men are the leaders of our society and that there are more men politicians and executives than women politicians and executives but I would be curious to see what would happen if women took control.

Source: Loraine Alterman, "*Record World* Forum: Three Artists on the New Consciousness," *Record World,* May 19, 1973, Section II, pp. 4, 5, 18, 20, 24, 32, 33.

30

"How to be a Rock Critic"

LESTER BANGS

Nearly a decade after the rock press had first taken shape via the pages of *Crawdaddy!, Rolling Stone*, and other magazines, the mid-'70s "rock critic" had become a recognized music industry career occupation, an alluring bohemian profession for scores of young music fans. Among the many influential critics of the era, Lester Bangs (1948–1982) stands out as arguably the most notorious and revered of them all. While Bangs's tastes in music could be eclectic, he is especially remembered for championing the "authentic" rock primitivism of then unfashionable styles like heavy metal and punk. Fired from *Rolling Stone* in 1973 for "being disrespectful to musicians," Bangs joined the staff of the irreverent Detroit-based rock magazine *Creem*, where for many years he served as both a writer and editor. Bangs's writings are instantly recognizable, steeped in the subjective style of New Journalists like Tom Wolfe and Hunter S. Thompson, yet mixed with equal doses of his own unique cynical attitude, corrosive wit and expressive insights. For many, this intense, self-reflexive approach signified an unparalleled level of integrity in rock journalism. Offered in the form of a humorous MadLib, "How to be a Rock Critic" is typical of Bangs's famed off-the-cuff "first draft" style.

Lately I've noticed a new wrinkle on the American landscape: it seems as if there's a whole generation of kids, each one younger than the last, all of whom live, breathe and dream of but one desire: "I want to be a rock critic when I grow up!"

If that sounds condescending let it be known that I was once just like them; the only difference was that when I held such aspirations, the field was relatively uncluttered—it was practically nothing to barge right in and commence the slaughter—whereas now, of course, it's so glutted that the last thing anybody should ever consider doing is entering this racket. In the first place, it doesn't pay much and doesn't lead anywhere in particular, so no matter how successful you are at it, you'll eventually have to decide what you're going to do with your life anyway. In the second place, it's basically just a racket in the first place, and not a particularly glorious one at that.

It almost certainly won't get you laid. (Rock critics are beginning to get groupies of a sort now, but most of them are the younger, aspiring rock critics—like the kind on Shakin' Street—of one sex or another.) It won't make you rich: the highest-paying magazine in the rock press still only pays thirty bucks a review, and most of the other magazines fall way below that. So you'll never be able to make a living off of it. Nobody will come up to you in the street and say, "Hey, I recognize you! You're Jon Landau! Man, that last review was really far out!" A lot of people, in fact, will hate you and think you're a pompous asshole just for expressing your opinions, and tell you so to your face.

On the other side of the slug, though, are the benefits. Which are okay, if you don't get taken in by them. The first big one is that if you stay at this stuff long enough you'll start to get free records in the mail, and if you persevere even longer you may wind up on the promotional mailing lists of every company in the nation, which will not only save you a lot of money on payday and ensure that you'll get to hear everything and anything you want, but help to pay the rent on occasion when you sell the albums spilling into your bathroom to local used records stores, at prices ranging from $.05 to over a dollar apiece. Plus on Christmas you don't have to buy anybody any presents if you don't want to: just give your mother the new Barbra Streisand album Columbia sent you because Barbra's trying to relate, your big sister one of the three copies of the new Carole King that you got in the mail, your little sister that Osmonds double live LP you never even opened because you're too hip . . . all down the line, leaving you with enough money saved to stay fucked up on good whiskey over the holidays this year.

Another fringe benefit which will sooner or later accrue if you hew steadily on this jive ass scrawl, is that you will be invited to press parties for the opening of new acts in town. It helps to live in places like L.A. and New York, because they have more of them there; I know some people, in fact, who have almost literally kept themselves from starving for months at a time by eating dinner at a different press party every night. (I know other people who have made entire careers out of attending these things, but that's a different story.) The food's usually pretty good to magnificent, unless it's some bluejeaned folkie and the company's trying to be with-it by serving organic slop unfit for the innards of a sow; even in such an extreme case as that, though, you can content yourself with sopping up the booze, which is plentiful and usually of high quality. So even if you live at home or haven't had any trouble lately keeping the wolf from the door, you can get drunk free a lot and that's always a pleasure, even if you do usually have to sit through some shit like John Prine or Osibisa just for a few glasses of gin. Sure you're prostituting yourself in a way, but so are they, and what are most modern business, social or sexual relationships if not a process of symbiotic exploitation? It's the same tub of shit no matter where it perches, so you might as well kick back and enjoy yourself while you can.

The next big step up after press parties is that you'll start receiving invitations to concerts, events and record company conventions in distant cities. Free vacations! The record companies will pay your plane fare, put you up in a swank hotel with room service (usually), and wine and dine you like mad for the duration of your stay, all just because they want you to write about some act they're trying to break. This is where things get a little cooler and less of a hustle, because once you've had enough stuff published that they're willing to drop a few hundred smackeroos to get you to do a story on somebody in their stable, you can pretty much pick and choose who you want to write about. Well, not totally, but everybody finds their own level, and it finds them. Like if you're a redhot flaming-eared heavy metal fanatic, they'll call you up one day and offer to fly you to Chicago or New York to see, oh, the Stooges, maybe. Or at least Jukin' Bone.

The final benefit (and for some people, the biggest) is that during most of these stages and at an increasingly casual level as time goes on, you'll get to hobnob with the Stars. Backstage at concerts, in the dressing room drinking their wine, rapping casually with the famous, the talented, the rich and the beautiful. Most of 'em are just jerks like everybody else, and you probably won't really get to meet any real Biggies very often since the record companies don't need publicity on them so why should they inflict you on 'em, but you will become friends with a lot of Stars of the Future. Or at least also-rans.

Okay, so that's the rosy vista. I painted it for true, and if you want it, it's yours, becuz after almost five years in this racket I finally decided I'm gonna break down and tell the whole world how to break in. I could get a lotta dough for this if I wanted to—some of us have talked for years about starting a Famous Rock Critics' School—but fuck it, I'm too lazy to take the time to set up some shit like that, and besides it's about time everybody got wind of the True Fax of Rock 'n' Roll Criticism. Listen well, and decide for yourself whether you wanna bother with it.

The first thing to understand and bear in mind at all times is that the whole thing is just a big ruse from the word go, it don't mean shit except exploitatively and in the zealotic terms of wanting to inflict your tastes on other people. Most people start writing record reviews because they want other people to like the same kind of stuff they do, and there's nothing wrong with that, it's a very honest impulse. I used to be a Jehovah's Witness when I was a kid so I had it in my blood already, a head start. But don't worry. All you gotta do is just keep bashin' away, and sooner or later people will start saying things to you like "How do you fit the Kinks into your overall aesthetic perspective?"

Well they won't really talk that jiveass, but damn close if you travel in the right (or wrong, as the case may be) circles. Because that old saw is true: most rock critics are pompous assholes. Maybe most critics are pompous assholes, but rock critics are especially—because they're working in virgin territory, where there's absolutely no recognized, generally agreed on authority or standards. Nor should there be. Anything goes, so fake 'em out every chance you get. Rock 'n' roll's basically just a bunch of garbage in the first place, it's noise, it's here today and gone tomorrow, so the only thing that can possibly trip you up is if you begin to reflect that if the music's that trivial, can you imagine how trivial what you're doing is?

Which actually is a good attitude to operate from, because it helps keep the pomposity factor in check. Half the rock critics in the country, no, 90% of the rock critics in the world have some grand theory they're trying to lay on each other and everybody else, which they insist explains everything in musical history and ties up all the loose ends. Every last one of 'em has a different theory and every last one of the theories is total bullshit, but you might as well have one as part of your baggage if you're going to pass. Try this: ALL ROCK 'N' ROLL CULTURES PLAGIARIZE EACH OTHER. THAT IS INHERENT IN THEIR NATURE. SO MAYBE, SINCE WHAT ROCK 'N' ROLL'S ALL ABOUT IS PLAGIARISM ANYWAY, THE MOST OUT-AND-OUT PLAGIARISTS, THE IMITATORS OF THE PRIME MOVING GENIUSES, ARE GREATER AND MORE VALID THAN THOSE GENIUSES! JUST CHECK THIS OUT: THE ROLLING STONES ARE BETTER THAN CHUCK BERRY! THE SHADOWS OF KNIGHT WERE BETTER THAN THE YARDBIRDS! P.F. SLOAN'S FIRST ALBUM WAS A MASTERPIECE, WAY BETTER THAN BLONDE ON BLONDE (I know one prominent rock critic in Texas who actually believes this; he's a real reactionary, but so are most of 'em!)!

Pretty pompous, huh? Well, that just happens to be one of my basic theories, although I don't really believe all the stuff I said in there (not that that makes a diddley damn bit of difference), and you can have it if you want it to bend or mutate as you please. Or come up with your own crock of shit; anyway, it's good to have one for those late-nite furious discussions leading absolutely nowhere. See, the whole thing's just a big waste of time, but the trappings can be fun and you always liked to whack off anyway. Like, look, you can impress people you wanna fuck by saying impressive things like "John Stewart Mill couldn't write rock 'n' roll, but Dylan could have written 'An Essay On Human Understanding'. Only he would have called it 'Like a Rolling Stone!'" (Dave Marsh of *Creem* magazine actually said that to me, and everybody else who lived with us, and everybody he talked to on the phone for the next month, once.) Just imagine laying that on some fine little honey—she'd flip out! She'd think you were a genius! Either that or a pompous asshole. But in this business, like any other, you win some and you lose some. Persevere, kid.

Where were we? Ah yes, you should also know that most of your colleagues are some of the biggest neurotics in the country, so you might as well get used right now to the way they're gonna be writing you five and ten page single spaced inflammatory letters reviling you for knocking some group that they have proved is the next Stones. It's all very incestuous, like this great big sickoid club full of people who were probably usually the funny looking kid in class, with the acne and the big horn rims, all introverted, and just sat home every night through high school and played his records while the other kids yukked and balled it up. Tough luck, genius is pain. Or frustrated popstars, all rock critics are frustrated popstars and you should see 'em singing to themselves when nobody else is around. Boy, do they get corny! Melodramatic? Whooo!! Some of them actually go so far as to invest their entire life savings in trendy popstar wardrobes, and others are so mono-maniacal as to go beyond that to the actual steps of forming a band of their own.[1] And you can rest assured that all of them write songs, and have constant daytime and nightdaze fantasies of big contracts with ESP-Disk at least.

Speaking of investing your life savings, another good way of letting on to everybody on the block that you're a rock critic is to go out and waste a lot of money buying old albums in bargain bins. They have these turd-dumps in most drugstores or supermarkets, full of last year's crap and older stuff at prices ranging from as low as a quarter all the way up to $2.50 and more. If you patronize these scumholes regularly, you will soon begin to build a Definitive Rock 'n' Roll Albums Collection, which is of course a must for anybody who's into this way of life really seriously. The object is simple: you gotta have EVERYTHING, no matter how arcane or shitty it is, because it all fits into the grand bulwark of Rock. So just go out there and throw all your money away, it's a good investment. You'll be filling your room with mung, but so what: how many other people do you know who have the Battered Ornaments album? Right. They don't know what they're missing.

I know one rock critic who actually drew out his life's savings and drove from St. Louis, where he lived, to New York and back, by way of Chicago, Detroit and New Jersey, AND STOPPED AT EVERY BARGAIN BIN ALONG THE WAY. That was the entire purpose of the trip, to visit bargain bins. Now this guy is obviously a real doofus and totally out of his mind, but you can see where this business can lead you if you're lucky and apply yourself: *down blind alleys.*

Speaking of this same doofus reminds me of another riff that is essential to have if you're gonna be a hotshit rock critic. You gotta find some band somewhere that's maybe even got two or three albums out and might even be halfway good, but the important thing is the more arcane it is the better, it's gotta be something that absolutely nobody in the world but you and two other people (the group's manager and one member's mother) knows or cares about, and what you wanna do is TALK ABOUT THIS BUNCH OF OBSCURE NONENTITIES AND THEIR RECORD(S) LIKE THEY'RE THE HOTTEST THING IN THE HISTORY OF MUSIC! You gotta build 'em up real big, they're your babies, only you alone can perceive their true greatness, so you gotta go around telling everybody that they're better than the Rolling Stones, they beat the Beatles black and blue, they murtelyze the Dead, they're the most significant and profound musical force in the world. And someday their true greatness will be recognized and you will be vindicated as a seer far ahead of your time.

Sometimes this scheme can really pay off, like if you happen to pick a Captain Beefheart or Velvet Underground way before they get widely known, although they're not really eligible because this group has gotta be so obscure that they can put out all kindsa albums and nobody pays any attention to 'em but you, they're just off mouldering in a cutout rack somewhere if not for your devoted efforts.

Doofus (of the preceding paragraph) came up with a lulu in this department, couple of 'em in fact: All he ever talks about is Amon Düül II, Bang and Budgie. Ever heard of any of 'em? That's what I thought. And you probably never will except if he's around to pester you about them. Amon Düül II are this psychedelic experimental avant-garde chance music free jazz electronic synthesizer space rock group from Germany. They got all kinds of albums out over there, there's even two groups with the same name, Amon Düül I and Amon Düül II, but they only got three albums out here and hardly anybody ever heard of 'em, although a whole shitload of people sure will if Doofus keeps up his one-man propaganda campaign on their behalf! They happen to be real good, but

---

1 Bangs would form his own band three years later in 1977.

that's beside the point. And Bang and Budgie, his other two pet monomanias, are a couple of Black Sabbath imitations, one from Florida and one from England, one pretty good and one not so hot. So he and this other critic from Texas (also previously mentioned) send big long hate letters back and forth to each other telling each other what morons they are, because the Texan don't like Budgie or something like that. Get the idea?

Also I turned Doofus onto Can, another German psychedelic schnozz-ball that has lotsa 17-minute electroraga jams, and he listens to one side of their album one time and sez to me: "Don't you think Can are better than the Stooges?" See what I mean? When all week he's been asking me things like "Don't you think Amon Düül II are the greatest group in history?" and "Don't you think *Dance of the Lemmings* (one of their albums, featuring such standards as "Dehypnotized Toothpaste," "Landing in a Ditch" and "A Short Stop at the Transylvanian Brain Surgery") is the greatest album of all time?" and I keep saying no, but he won't take no for an answer, he's a man with a Plan! A crusader on behalf of Neglected Genius. So you see the key: *persistence*. Make a total nuisance of yourself, and people will begin to take you seriously. Or at least stop regarding you as not there. And if he wants to continue on this obscuro roller-coaster ride, there are zillions of German bands: take Guru Guru or Floh de Cologne, for example—these qualify as two of the finest choices in the Arcane Masterpiece department in history, indeed they do, because both are imports and you can't even find a single Floh de Cologne or Guru Guru album anywhere in the United States except by ordering it special from Germany! *Nobody* knows what it sounds like so they gotta listen to Doofus. So as you can see Doofus copped himself a real hot item, but chances like that come only once in a lifetime.

That pretty much takes care of the qualifications. Like what you see? Wanna give it a try? Well, get ready, because the big time is just around the corner. The only thing left to mention before you embark on your career as a rock critic is that talent has absolutely nothing to do with it, so don't worry if you don't know how to write. Don't even worry if you can't put a simple declarative sentence together. Don't worry if you can only sign your name with an X. Anybody can do this shit, all it takes is a high level of unconsciousness (and you just got done reading an unconsciousness expanding session) and some ability to sling bullshit around. Also the bullshit is readymade, you don't even have to think it up, all you gotta do is invest in a slingshot. All the word-type stuff you need has already been written anyway, it's in old yellow issues of *Shakin' Street*, *Rolling Stone*, *Creem* and all the rest; just sit around reading and rereading the damn things all day and pretty soon you'll have whole paragraphs of old record reviews memorized, which is not only a good way to impress people at parties and girls you're trying to pick up with your erudition, but allows you to plagiarize at will. And don't worry about getting caught, because nobody in this business has any memory and besides they're all plagiarists too and besides that all record reviews read the same. I learned to write 'em outta *Down Beat*, and it's the same shit in *Rolling Stone*; it's the same shit all over. Just stir and rearrange it every once in awhile. Take one riff and staple it to another; and if you get tired of thinking about how you're a rock critic, remember William Burroughs and the cutup methods and think about being avant-garde. I do it all the time.

Okay, now it's time for you to write YOUR VERY FIRST ORIGINAL RECORD REVIEW. It's easy, all you gotta do is point. First, pick a title for the album:

A. *Oranges in Exile*
B. *Outer City Blues & Heavy Dues*
C. *Cajun Sitar Dance Party*
D. *Hungry Children of Babylon*
E. *Eat Your Coldcream*

Got it? Okay, the next part's just as easy. Just fill in the blanks: This latest offering from _____

    A. Harmonica Dan and His Red Light District
    B. The Armored Highchair
    C. Ducks in Winter
    D. The Four Fat Guys
    E. Arturo de Cordova

is _____

    A. a clear consolidation of the artistic moves first tentatively ventured in his/her/their/its last album.
    B. a real letdown after the masterpiece album and single that carried us all the way through the summer and warmed us over in the fall.
    C. important only insofar as it will delineate the contours of the current malaise for future rock historians, if there are any with all the pollution around now.
    D. definitely the album of the year.
    E. a heap of pig shit.

(How you doin' so far? See how easy it is!) Onward! Choose one of the following for the next sentence: _____

    A. In dealing with such a record, the time has come at last to talk about the responsibilities, if any, which any artist making rock 'n' roll bears to his audience, and specifically how those responsibilities relate to the political situation which we, all of us, and perforce rock 'n' roll, are compelled to come to terms with by dint of living in the United States of America today.
    B. I don't really think these guys/this dude/the chick in question/a singing dog can defend musical output which has proven increasingly shoddy by referring to such old handles as "personal expression," "experimentalism," "a new kind of artistic freedom," or any other such lame copout.
    C. It's such a thrill that this album finally came, that I am finally actually holding it in my hands, looking at the fantastically beautiful M. C. Escher drawing on the cover whilst trembling all over to the incredible strains of the music on the record from inside it which even now are wafting from the old Victrola, that I really don't know if I am going to come or cry.
    D. It's so goddam fucking boring to have to open all these pieces of shit every day, you waste your time, you break your fingernails, half the time it's just a repeat of an album that came yesterday, that I can hardly bring myself to slit open the shrinkwrap once I get 'em outta the cardboard (which piles up in a big mess all over the house after it gets dragged outta the corner by all my asshole friends!), and I really can just barely stand to put the goddam things on the turntable after that. I wish it would break anyway so I wouldn't have to listen to 'em anymore. (Good one, huh, more than one sentence in this one!) But anyway, I put this piece of shit on just like all the others except the ones I never get around to, and right now I'm listening to it and you know what? I was right. It is a piece of shit!
    E. I don't remember how I got here, whose house this is or where this typewriter came from, but anyway this new album is by the greatest fucking rock 'n' roll band in the whole wide world/most talented, sensitive balladeer of his generation whom many of us are already calling

the New Dylan/sweetest songbird this side of the Thames has saved my life again just like all the others did, so I don't even care where I am, I don't care if I got rolled last night, I don't care if this place gets busted right now, I don't care if the world comes to an end because the cosmic message of truth and unity which this music is bringing to me has made me feel complete for the first time since 1968.

(Well, that wasn't hard at all, was it? A whole paragraph written already! But this is no place to stop: the most fun's yet to come. Tally ho!)

The first song on side one _____

    A. "Catalina Sky"
    B. "Death Rays in Your Eyes"
    C. "I Wish I Was a Rusty Nail"
    D. "Lady of Whitewater"
    E. "Nixon Eats"

(choose again) _____

    A. is a rousingly high spirited opener in march tempo.
    B. starts things off at an extremely high energy level.
    C. sets the pace and mood of the album most atmospherically.
    D. won't win any Grammies this year.
    E. reminds me of my Grandmother puking up her sherry into the bathtub the night we had fish that had gone bad for dinner when I was three years old.

The first thing you notice is _____

    A. the vicious, slashing guitar solo.
    B. the deep, throbbing bass lines.
    C. how mellowly the sensitive, almost painfully fragile vocal is integrated with the mesmerizing Spanish chords from those four fine hollow-body Gibson guitars.
    D. the cymbals aren't miked right.
    E. that the entire mix is a washout and this album has what is probably the worst production of the year.

The full impact of what's going on in this cut may not reach you the first time, but if you keep listening a couple of times a day for a week or two, especially through headphones, it will come to you in a final flash of revelation that _____

    A. you were wasting your time.
    B. you are listening to a masterpiece of rock which so far transcends "rock" as we have known it that most people probably won't recognize its true worth for at least ten years.
    C. the instruments are out of tune.
    D. you should have bought the Band instead.
    E. you're deaf in one ear.

Cut two is _____

    A. a nice change of pace
    B. more of the same phlegm
    C. a definite picker-upper
    D. interesting, at least
    E. insulting to the human ear (my dog didn't like it either)

by virtue of the fact that _____

    A. it was produced by Phil Spector's cousin from Jersey.
    B. it's only two seconds long.
    C. the lyrics say more, and more concisely, about what we have done to our natural environment than anything else written in the past decade.
    D. Bobby Keyes, Jim Price and Boots Randolph sit in for a real old time "blowing session."
    E. I spilled Gallo Port in the grooves and it made it sound better.

In spite of that, I feel that the true significance of its rather dense and muted lyrics can only be apprehended by _____

    A. the purchase of a hearing aid.
    B. reading the sheet enclosed with the record.
    C. going back and listening to "Memphis Blues Again," *then* come back to this and see if it doesn't blow you out the door!
    D. taking a course in German.
    E. throwing the incoherent piece of pig shit in the trash and going out for a beer, where something good is probably on the jukebox.

(Time for paragraph three already! Smooth sailing, bunky! You're almost there.) This record has inspired such _____

    A. ambivalent feelings
    B. helpless adoration
    C. bile and venom
    D. total indifference
    E. a powerful thirst

in me that I can't bring myself to describe the rest of the cuts. Track by track reviews are a bore anyway, and the album only costs $4.97 at the right stores, so go down and get it and find out for yourself whether you'll like it or not. Who am I, who is any critic or any other sentient being on the face of the earth, to tell you what a piece of music sounds like? Only your ears can hear it as only your ears can hear it. Am I right or am I wrong? Of course I am. I do know that I will

_____

    A. go on listening to this album till I drop dead of cancer.
    B. walk out into the backyard and toss this offense unto mine eyes into the incinerator soon as I finish typing this spew.

C. never forget the wonderful chance I've had here in the pages of *Fusion* to share this very special record, and my own deepest dredged sentiments about it, with you, who whether you know it or not are a very special person whom I love without qualification even if we've never seen each other, I don't even know your name, and am so righteous that I don't even care if you look like a sow.

D. break this elpee over the head of the very next Jesus Freak or Hare Krishna creep I see in the street, just for thrills!

E. go to sleep now and awaken upon a new morning in which I may be able to appreciate this unabridged poetic outpouring with fresh ears.

So before I sign my name at the bottom of this page and pick up the check from the cheap kikes that run this rag who will never pay me anyway, I would like to leave you with one thought:

_____

A. Today is the first day of the rest of your life.

B. There are many here among us who feel that life is but a joke.

C. The red man lost this land to you and me.

D. Rock 'n' roll is dead. Long live rock 'n' roll.

E. Since these assholes that're stupid enough to print this stuff don't pay me anything, why don't you? I've probably turned you on to a lot of good records over the years, and what do I get out of it? Nothing but a lot of grief! A lot of abuse from cretins who can't understand that rock 'n' roll IS the Revolution! A lot of cheap bloodsuckers like hellhounds on my trail! I got "Yer Blues"! I've paid my body and soul! So send me some $$$, goddammit, or I'll never write a word again as long as I live!

Your faithful correspondent, _____

You did it! You really did it! There, you see, that wasn't so hard, was it? Now YOU TOO are an officially ordained and fully qualified rock critic, with publication under your belt and everything. Just cut out the review, if you're finished filling in all the blanks, and send it to the rock magazine of your choice with a stamped, self-addressed envelope! If they send it back, send it to another one! Be persistent! Be a "go getter"! Do you think Jon Landau ever let rejection slips get him down? No! And if you send it to all the rock mags in America, one of them is bound to print it sooner or later because most of them will print the worst off the wall shit in the world if they think it'll make 'em avant-garde! You could send 'em the instruction booklet on how to repair your lawn mower, just write the name of a current popular album by a famous artist at the top of the cover, sign your name at the bottom of the last page, and they'll print it! They'll think you're a genius!

And you are! And when all the money you asked for in this review starts pouring in from your fans, you'll be rich! David Geffen will invite you out to his house in the Catskills for the weekend! Miles Davis will step aside when you walk down the street! Seals of Seals & Crofts will tip his hat to you and sing "Bah'aii!" as you walk down the street! David Peel will write songs about you! So will John Lennon! So will everybody! Andy Warhol will put you in his movies! You'll tour with David Bowie, Leon Russell and Atomic Rooster, reading your most famous reviews to vast arenas full of rabid fans! You'll be an international celebrity and die at 33![2] You made the grade! You are

---

2 Bangs himself would eventually die at the age of 33 from a drug overdose.

now a rock critic, and by tomorrow you will be one of the most important critics in America! You'll make *Esquire*'s Heavy Hundred in 1974!

Congratulations, and welcome to the club!

Your pal,
R. J. Gleason[3]

Source: Lester Bangs, "How to be a Rock Critic: A Megatonic Journey with Lester Bangs," *Shakin' Street Gazette*, October 10, 1974. Reprinted in Jim DeRogatis, *Let It Blurt: The Life & Times of Lester Bangs, America's Greatest Rock Critic* (New York: Broadway Books, 2000), pp. 247–60.

---

3 One of the foremost jazz and rock critics of the 1960s, Gleason was also a cofounder of *Rolling Stone*, the magazine that had fired Bangs back in 1973.

31

"Reggae
The Steady Rock of Black Jamaica"

ANDREW KOPKIND

Reggae artists enjoyed a smattering of popularity outside of Jamaica throughout the late 1960s and early 1970s, but it was not until 1972 and the release of the film *The Harder They Come* and its accompanying soundtrack that the music seemed primed to cross over into the American market. A number of articles on reggae appeared in the film's wake, among them Andrew Kopkind's report for the radical Berkeley-based magazine *Ramparts*. Given the publication's leanings, it should come as little surprise that Kopkind highlights reggae's revolutionary role in the Jamaican political landscape and its significance as the voice of Jamaica's oppressed people. The article also draws attention to reggae's distinctive rhythmic grooves, what singer Jimmy Cliff (born 1948) calls a type of "rock turned over." Taking stock both of reggae's musical and cultural allure, Kopkind expresses his misgivings about its possible exploitation as the "next big thing," a forecast that would be realized over the course of the next three years with Bob Marley's rise as reggae's first international star.

The bleached white tourists at the Holiday Inn Reef Club, the Banana Boat and the Jamaica Hilton still request "Day-O" and gasp with the joy of recognition when a crooner starts "I Left a Little Girl in Kingston Town." And at the $12-a-head beach parties the Jamaica Tourist Board throws for the swinging set, short-haired frat boys still shove their giggling girlfriends under the limbo stick in time to the latest 1957 Belafonte hits. In the same vein but on the other hand, heavy American freaks under the palms at Negril keep the natives at bay with blasts of strong *ganja* and hard rock from hidden hi-fi's. But the time-encapsulated world of winter-week visitors to the Caribbean sands is particularly absurd in Jamaica this year, because an entirely new style of popular culture—soon to be mass-marketed in North America—is growing in native groves alongside the stands of tourists. The new form (new to us up North) is called reggae: at bottom a percussive beat and a melodic line of music, but by extension a social and artistic movement that expresses the special Jamaican mood of suffering, blackness and heavenly peace.

Reggae sounds have been drifting into the U.S. off and on for several years, and the music is well-known in Britain with its large West Indian communities. Desmond Dekker's "The Israelites" was a kinky hit of sorts; Paul Simon's "Mother and Child Reunion" presented Jamaican reggae overlaid with L.A. kitsch; and Johnny Nash made it biggest last year with a reggae single, "I Can See Clearly Now." But the industry called all that "novelty." Now, the Anglo-American music moguls are hyping reggae into a commercial craze, and their rock stars are flying off to Kingston to record personal versions. The Rolling Stones have already been and gone (Mick Jagger hired a reggae band to play at his wedding); Cat Stevens came soon thereafter; the Jefferson Airplane went down to check it out; Roberta Flack is reported en route. J. Geils recorded a reggae number safely in white America, while Paul McCartney did it in England. Jimmy Cliff, the first Jamaican multi-media reggae star (Johnny Nash comes from Texas), has been signed by Warner Brothers Records for an upcoming album, and his Jamaican-made film, "The Harder They Come," is seeking provincial bookings after its *succes d'estime* in New York.

"We took the *ts-ts-ts*—the syncopation—out of jazz," Cliff explained, by way of a definition and a history of reggae, when we talked not long ago in a Warner Brothers office in New York. "The guitar rhythm is out of calypso, the percussion part of it is Latin and West African. The drumming is like the reverse of rock, it's rock turned over: rock drumming is off the beat, reggae drumming is right on the beat—and the bass goes in between." However obscure that exegesis may be, the sound is obvious after the first hearing. It is danceable and whistleable like the best old rhythm & blues before rock ran it into the ground.

In its purely musical form, reggae (also called rock steady) is an outgrowth of ska, a Jamaican style popular in the early '60s. For years before that, Jamaicans had fed on American R&B records; when the rock-and-roll boom slowed R&B exports, Jamaicans began going it alone. Ska put a West Indian flavor into black North American Music. Later—in the mid-'60s—reggae developed as a Caribbean counterpart of soul, with more than a few echoes of fundamentalist church gospel singing and African chants. You can hear a kind of unself-conscious reggae flowing from any church in Jamaica every Sunday: as you can hear pre-commercial soul in any rural black church in America.

But the content of reggae music—lyrically and melodically—is strikingly different from most North American black pop music today, even though the forms have resulted from the cross-pollenization of all the same Afro-American strains. Reggae lyrics are rarely macho and violent in the manner of Shaft or Super Fly; rather, they say something about the pain of the world and the hope for a sunnier future—sentiments that sound naive and perhaps primitive to cool Americans, but replicate exactly the visual tones of Jamaican shantytown poverty against the agonizing beauty of the Caribbean sea-sky.

"Sixty percent of reggae is the frustration of oppressed people," Jimmy Cliff said with the calm and kindly honesty that softens the hard edge of Jamaicans' anger—in person and in music. "They're just fighting to get out from under that heavy weight. They know that pie-in-the-sky is a fake. But still, 40 percent of it is fantasy. The music is happy; we sing a happy melody, but it's sad underneath. You can sing a happy song and underneath you're really hungry. The Prime Minister once said that if you want to know what's going on in Jamaica, look at what's on the charts, listen to the words of the songs."

In fact, the Jamaican Prime Minister, Michael Manley, is said to prefer European classical music to reggae, but his advice is sound enough. His political party, the reformist Peoples National Party, upset the decade-long rule of the Jamaica Labour Party last year by riding an insurgent campaign style off which reggae and "The Harder They Come" seemed to be in the cultural vanguard. The conservative Labour Party Government closed down the movie set several times during production because of the insurrectionist attitudes the film was bound to convey to Jamaicans (although it seems somewhat less revolutionary in the U.S.; politics rarely survives a sea journey). Cliff plays a country boy who comes to Kingston to make it as a pop singer, suffers humiliation from a music industry boss, a horny, authoritarian clergyman, and a mocha middleclass lady (played by Prime Minister Manley's wife), and drifts into the *ganja* trade. He almost gets to the top smuggling dope to the U.S. market, but he falls hard in the end—a political conclusion, written into the script, with which Cliff disagrees. All this after offing a spectacular array of uniformed and civilian pigs, with the universal approval of the island populace, on-screen and off.

The movie scored an historic success in Jamaica, and its implicit political messages, Cliff said, contributed to the PNP's electoral victory: an ambiguous outcome, he thought, because "if the

Jamaica Labour Party had been returned, there would have been a revolution." There are no significant whites in "The Harder They Come," no long shots of manicured beaches and planted palms. It was made in a Jamaica that tourists simply do not see. "It is not," Jimmy Cliff said emphatically, "a tourism promotion film." By its concentration on black and poor Jamaicans, the movie takes some kind of a stand against the pervasive Anglo-American penetration of the island— even, contradictorily, while the imperial entertainment industry is making plans for the biggest cultural rip-off since Calypso.

Reggae is the only "fresh" music around today, as Jimmy Cliff claims, and more than that it's the only true *popular*—that is to say, people's—music capable of commercial success. Reggae is still close to spontaneous folk forms, a professionalized version of common rhythms and harmonies that you can hear in the beeping of automobile horns and the cry of fruit vendors. Jamaican kids tap distinctive reggae rhythms when they idly and unconsciously hit a stick against a rock in play.

North American "folk" is mostly intellectualized and commercialized; rock is degenerating into rococo repetitions of itself; and Lenox Avenue soul is on a sex-'n-violence trip that destroys itself and its cultural context. The David Bowie-Lou Reed gender-fuck idea, which was so promising in its beginning (see RAMPARTS, March 1973) is already being blown by hype into fatuous fraudulence.

That leaves reggae as the next exploitable number. The music industry is looking for a really big gimmick "like Presley or the Beatles," an RCA publicity person said the other day. It's doubtful that reggae could fill the bill: it is too fragile, too vulnerable, too honest to withstand the massive assaults on its authenticity that the collective corporate shuck would mount. Jimmy Cliff may translate some of his Jamaican success into American—although few other artists from Kingston will be so lucky— but he'd better watch out for the American music monster. Naturally, he is optimistic. "We've been kicked and licked and repressed," he said at the end of our talk, in a line which is equally honest as his song lyric and a political philosophy, "and we'll stand the test."

Source: Andrew Kopkind, "Reggae: The Steady Rock of Black Jamaica," *Ramparts*, June 1973, pp. 50–51.

32

"Roots and Rock
The Marley Enigma"

Linton Kwesi Johnson

Jamaican born poet and activist Linton Kwesi Johnson (born 1952) first rose to prominence during the 1970s in England, where his politically charged writings and reggae dub poetry performances earned him great critical acclaim. In the decades since, he has remained one of the most visible social commentators and compelling voices for black British culture. In his 1975 essay "Roots and Rock," which originally appeared in the London-based journal *Race Today*, Johnson addresses Bob Marley's rise to fame and his crowning within the American and British music press as the "new king of rock." Marley (1945–1981), and his group the Wailers, were pivotal in bringing reggae to a larger international audience. As Johnson points out, much of Marley's success hinged upon the generalized appeal of his Rastafarian lifestyle, and a rebellious image that seemed to fit seamlessly within rock's prescribed set of heroic values. Johnson has provided *The Rock History Reader* with his own introduction (in italics below), which further places the article in its proper historical context.

I wrote "Roots and Rock: The Marley Enigma" as a fan of the Wailers, after the group had broken up, and Bob Marley was declared the new "King of rock" following the release of "Natty Dread." In 1975 when I wrote the article, I was a young consumer, collector and student of reggae music. The departure of Peter Tosh and Bunny Wailer from the Wailers and the appropriation of Bob Marley as the new hero of rock music felt like a double blow. It led me to consider the commodification and commercialisation of the music. Today I recognise the genius of Bob Marley and the enormous contribution he has made to popular culture the world over. © Linton Kwesi Johnson, June 2006.

So Bob Marley has made it and the Wailers too, what's left of them—after eleven years of musical devotion and changing emotions. The 'little brown man' from down a St. Ann is now a big big man, albeit a musical one. Now everyone is singing Marley's song—even Johnny Nash, once called 'the king of reggae' by the white music culture—vultures. The rock critics of Europe and North America now hail Bob Marley the new king of rock and protest, the new King Emperor Haile I/King Selassie I/King of kings. They speak of the new Hendrix, the new Dylan, the musical messiah of the rockers, the hippies, the beatniks, the trendies and the drop outs. But the 'I yah' man knows that:

> *The rise of the 'rasta rebel from Trench Town'*
> *who likes to wear a frown*
> *is not fulfilment of prophecy,*
> *but the realisation of a commercial dream*
> *a capitalist scheme.*

To be sure, the coming of the new musical messiah had been long awaited in Europe and North America, since the departure of Hendrix, who could not stand the 'purple haze'. Dylan, the lyrical propagandist of the campus revolutionaries, seems to have died with the 'hippies' and their sit-in revolution. There was a vacuum of vogue until

> *Marley let riddim drop*
> *and it was not*
> *or rather, it was not until*
> *the capitalists sighted the gap*
> *Sought and found*
> *The right man with the right sound*
> *who was not black but brown.*

Truly, it was a capitalist affair. What a sensation, Bob Marley, the talk of the musical nations/ The standing ovations/The long citations. The man behind it all? Chris Blackwell, descendant of slave masters and owner of Island records, continuing the tradition of his white ancestors. Blackwell puts his vision of Marley for capital thus: 'I think that generally rock music has become a bit stale and I think Bob's music has an energy and a fresh feel to it.' Indeed.

The energy of which Blackwell speaks, is the dynamism of the culture of the urban unemployed, the sufferers, the oppressed of Jamaica. The 'fresh feel' is the soul and rock elements which have been incorporated into the music of the Wailers. But this alone with Marley's lyrical excellence could not spell success. The commodity is not complete and it is commodities that the capitalist deals in, not music per se. There had to be an angle, an image. And what better image than that of the Rasta rebel (the long haired rasta rebel).

From the very beginning, it could be seen, Marley was destined for fame; destined to become the chosen one. For it is a unique set of experiences and circumstances that has shaped Marley's music, the son of an Afro-Jamaican woman and an Englishman. His experiences are rooted within the sufferers of Jamaica. He celebrated the rudi 'rebellion' of the 60's and defended 'rudi' in tunes like, 'Let Them Go'. Living in America for a while, Marley was very much influenced by American rhythm and blues and soul music. By 1969 'reggae' had superseded 'rock steady' and ska as the new musical mode of Jamaica. Bob and the Wailers came back on the scene after a short impasse as the new 'soul rebels'. 'I am a rebel/soul rebel', sang Marley, 'I am a capturer soul adventurer' in Temptations style. By this time Marley's lyrical excellence had been acknowledged by the sufferers in the ghettoes, at least. His persecution by babylon lent a new style of rhetoric to his lyricism; this was the rhetoric not of protest but of defiance and rebellion. And the language was that of Rastafarai.

This is the image that is used to sell Marley, the image of the rasta rebel, and god only knows the eroticism and romanticism that this image invokes in the mind of his white fans. And this is where the ironies multiply. The 'image' is derived from rastafarianism and rebellion, which are rooted in the historical experience of the oppressed of Jamaica. It then becomes an instrument of capital to sell Marley and his music, thereby negating the power which is the cultural manifestation of this historical experience. So though Marley is singing about 'roots' and 'natty', his fans know not. Neither do they understand the meaning or the feeling of dread. And there is really no dread in Marley's music. The dread has been replaced by the howling rock guitar and the funky rhythm and what we get is the enigma of 'roots' and rock.

Source: Linton Kwesi Johnson, "Roots and Rock: the Marley Enigma," *Race Today* 7, no. 10 (October 1975), pp. 237–38.

33

Dub and the "Sound of Surprise"

Richard Williams

During the 1970s, *Melody Maker*, along with the *New Musical Express* and *Sounds*, was one of Britain's three main rock-oriented weekly music magazines. Addressing a mainstream audience, rock critic Richard Williams presents an overview in this 1976 article of one of reggae's most influential offshoots: dub. As he describes, the placement of dub remixes on the B-sides of reggae singles allowed producers like Lee "Scratch" Perry (born Rainford Hugh Perry, 1936) and King Tubby (Osbourne Ruddock, 1941–1989) to assert themselves through the mixing board as active "composers," reimagining a familiar song in a new, surprising way. Williams proposes that dub may also be understood as an "aesthetic," one that could have a broader application and influence the direction of future musical styles. Since its emergence in the 1970s, dub has indeed expanded well beyond its specific associations with reggae music. It has become, in short, a familiar technique, where one isolates vocals and instrumental layers in the mix, shifting them in and out of the texture, or even "shrouding them in echo." Nowhere is dub's legacy outside of reggae more apparent than in hip-hop and electronic dance music, where producers have completely absorbed the essence of dub's studio manipulations and tricks.

How can I persuade you not to laugh when I say that the technique of dub may well be the most interesting new abstract concept to appear in modern music since Ornette Coleman undermined the dictatorship of Western harmony almost two decades ago?

First, I'm assuming that you're aware of dub's existence. For those who unaccountably aren't, the briefest of rundowns: It's what you find on the flip side of most reggae singles, where the producer has taken the A-side and fed it through various equalisation facilities (sound-modification devices) available on his mixing board.

Vocals and instruments appear and disappear with what at first seems a bewildering anarchy, often shrouded in echo or distorted beyond recognition.

It's completely bizarre, and yet among Jamaicans the dub records are usually more popular than the straight versions of the same tunes. It's not abnormal for several dubs of the same basic track to appear, and prerelease dub albums sell at enormous prices in considerable quantities.

What I want to discuss, however, is not necessarily dub in its present application, interesting though that may be.

It strikes me that there are possibilities inherent in this aberrant form which could perhaps resonate through other musics in the years to come; this may seem wild prophesy, but it could change the nature of some areas, and the nature of the ways in which we both play and apprehend music.

THE ROOTS OF DUB

Dub had its beginning in the mid-sixties, when Jamaican disc jockeys first started making funny noises through their microphones in time to the records they played; this eventually found its way onto the records themselves. A primitive and popular example would be Prince Buster's hit "Al Capone," where a voice provides a curious and persistent quasi-percussive accompaniment.

A few years later, gathering courage, jocks like U-Roy started making up impromptu verse on top of the records, and when this too was reproduced in the studio, the original singer's voice was frequently faded in and out around the overdubbed chanting (or "toasting," as it became known).

The next step was to muck around with the sound of the instruments themselves, and with the whole arrangement of the track.

Producers like Lee Perry (the rawest), King Tubby (the most innovatory), and Jack Ruby (the most sophisticated) vied with each other to create the most eccentrically ear-bending effects.

A couple of years ago dub had become so popular that an album called "King Tubby Meets the Upsetter" (a kind of "battle of the boards" between Tubby and Perry) bore, on the rear of its sleeve, large pictures of the mixing consoles used by the two protagonists. Not a human in sight.

Currently, and perhaps most interesting of all, certain reggae bands are beginning to duplicate dub in live performance.

As yet they haven't managed to reproduce the full panoply of bass and drum techniques, but the use of heavy sporadic echo on lead instruments like harmonica and guitar is being featured.

THE AESTHETICS OF DUB

One's overriding impression, on initial exposure to dub at the high volume for which it is intended, is that this is the nearest aural equivalent to a drug experience, in the sense that reality (the original material) is being manipulated and distorted.

I have no doubt that this was an important motivation in dub's development, whether consciously or otherwise. That's quite interesting but ultimately insignificant when compared with its other and more sophisticated effects on the listener.

Because it's most often applied to an already-familiar song or rhythm track, dub has a uniquely poignant quality: memories are revived, but rather than being simply duplicated (as when we hear a "golden oldie" from our youth on the radio) they are given subtle twists. Memory is teased rather than dragged up, and is thereby heightened.

It is, above all, the supreme sound of surprise, whether that of an anguished, Echoplexed scream, or a rimshot mechanically flared into a facsimile of thunder, or a steady bass riff suddenly and mysteriously disappearing in the middle of a bar (with an effect like that of stepping into an empty lift shaft).[1]

Ideally, therefore, no dub performance should be heard more than once.

Its evanescence and randomness make it perhaps the most existential of musics, and its most stunning implication comes with the realisation that no dub track is ever "correct" or "finished": it can always be done again a thousand different ways, each one as "correct" as any other.

For the nonaligned (i.e., non–West Indian) listener to cope with this, some values must be adjusted in order to accept and enjoy the constant sense of shock it provides when the hands of a Lee Perry or a Tappa Zukie are at the controls. Once assimilated, though, it can have the invigorating effect of the best so-called Free Music.

---

1 The Echoplex was an electronic device that created a tape delay.

Does it, can it, have a wider implication? I think so, and we may already be on the road. Two examples:

(1) When Roxy Music was formed, it was Brian Eno's function—him again!—firstly to introduce relevant sound effects (the standard and expected sirens, bleeps, whooshes, and so on), and secondarily to modify the form and content of what the musicians onstage were playing. (In the early days, Eno's synthesizer and tape machines were positioned at the mixing desk.)

A couple of weeks ago Phil Manzanera was quoted in this paper as saying that, then, he was never sure how his guitar would sound once Eno had finished interfering with its output.

As Roxy Music became more conventional, stripping away one by one the original experimental factors in a curious instance of success actually inhibiting exploration, Eno became more of a "player" in his own right and less of a modifier . . . and then he left. A missed opportunity.

(2) Late last year one of the young groups currently fashionable on the punk rock scene recorded a song which purposely employed elements of dub: repeat-echo on harmonica, delay and superimposition of rhythm guitars, and the occasional tweak on the lead vocal.

Although it has yet to be released, the track was a complete artistic success: the tension which resulted from these devices was wholly congruous, thoroughly in keeping with the spirit and atmosphere of such music.

Looking elsewhere, one can spot other signs. Ever since "What's Going On," Marvin Gaye has been developing a kind of sound-stratification which allows for a certain randomness within the overall texture.

This is slightly misleading, because Gaye's records (I'm thinking particularly of "Let's Get It On" and "I Want You") must be the result of many hours of forethought and care and patience, all of which would appear to be inimical to the crucial spontaneity of dub.

Miles Davis's last release, the in-concert "Agharta," displayed an almost dublike nonchalance and disregard of "planning," but here the difference is that all the musicians are left to their own devices, unhindered.

I have sometimes felt, too, that the loud and apparently arbitrary synthesizer interjections which Joe Zawinul is prone to perpetrate during Weather Report concerts (but not their records) have something of the spirit of King Tubby—although that is perhaps being too lenient.

THE POLITICS OF DUB

In its present "natural" state, dub has no inbuilt politics; were it to be utilised by nonreggae musicians, though, these would arise and create controversy, for one of its major principles is the denial of the right of the musician to control completely his own output.

While advocating its study and wider use, I am not of course suggesting that it would benefit everyone. Only a fool would maintain that the formal purity of a Joni Mitchell or the majestic poise of a John Coltrane could be improved by meddling.

But, in the hands of adventurous groups and composers, it could be a fascinating tool. It seems to me to be a gripping and revolutionary idea that an outside agency—in other words, the man at the mixing desk—could control the actual content of a live performance, choosing exactly what he wanted to be heard, so that while (say) a bassist might be playing throughout a piece, only an unpredetermined proportion of his contribution would be heard. And he'd be as surprised as anybody by what did (and what didn't) come out.

Rather than the performers serving as an interface between composer and audience, therefore, the composer himself would assume that function, standing very relevantly between the players and the listeners.

(Another precedent comes to mind: anyone who's seen Gil Evans conducting an orchestra will know the way he seems to draw out punctuations and colours at will.)

At the lesser end of the scale, dub offers a range of new playing and recording gimmicks which could be plagiarised and thereby enliven all kinds of styles, from Chinn-and-Chapman to Anthony Braxton. At the limit of its potential, it proposes nothing less than a new kind of composing.

Source: Richard Williams, "The Sound of Surprise," *Melody Maker,* August 21, 1976, p. 21.

34

Reflections on Progressive Rock

BILL BRUFORD

Bill Bruford (born 1949) was one of the most respected drummers of the British progressive rock era. He began in 1968 as one of the original members of Yes, and over the course of the 1970s played with other similar-minded groups such as Genesis, UK and, most significantly, King Crimson, a group he would rejoin for a second stint in the early 1980s, and, for a third time in the mid 1990s. In this excerpt from his 2009 autobiography, Bruford examines the backgrounds and creative intentions of the British musicians and bands that comprised the 1970s British progressive rock movement. As he explains, these groups very much reflected their uniquely British social and cultural context. While they reached a large audience in the United States, they were often met by hostile rock critics quick to skewer the movement's seemingly pretentious musical ambitions.[1] Bruford's account of the era is eloquent, critical, self-reflective, and better researched than the typical rock musician's autobiography. He even includes academic-styled endnotes that cite such important musicological studies as Edward Macan's *Rocking the Classics: English Progressive Rock and the Counterculture* and Allan F. Moore's *Rock: The Primary Text*. Bruford, who has since gone on to earn a PhD in music in 2016, approaches the subject with a seriousness and thoughtfulness that in many ways reflects the depth and complexity of the progressive rock movement itself.

Without The Beatles, or someone else who had done what The Beatles did, it is fair to assume that there would have been no progressive rock. The music emerged out of the psychedelic and pastoral folk styles of the late 60s and had a golden age from the early to mid 70s. Psychedelic bands such as Pink Floyd, The Moody Blues, Procol Harum, and The Nice, themselves all in transition, laid the foundations between 1966 and 1970. The release of King Crimson's album *In The Court Of The Crimson King* in 1969 signalled the emergence of the mature progressive rock style that reached its commercial and artistic zenith between 1970 and 1975 in the music of such bands as Jethro Tull, Yes, Genesis, ELP, Gentle Giant, Van der Graaf Generator, and Curved Air.

Demographically, progressive rock was a music from south-east England, overwhelmingly made by nice middle-class English boys like me. The musicians' backgrounds were strictly white-collar, and their parents were often downright distinguished. Never working-class, it was rather the vital expression of a bohemian, middle-class intelligentsia.

Art schools, colleges, and universities contributed mightily, but if you want to understand why the style grew and flourished in England rather than the USA, look no further than that powerful cultural agent, the Anglican Church. Many of the primary participants were initially moved by

---

1 For an examination of progressive rock's critical reception in the 1970s, see John J. Sheinbaum's "Progressive Rock and the Inversion of Musical Values," in Kevin Holm-Hudson, ed., *Progressive Rock Reconsidered* (New York: Routledge, 2002), pp. 21–42.

church attendance as youths: John Wetton of King Crimson; Peter Gabriel of Genesis; Chris Squire of Yes; Peter Hammill of Van der Graaf; all had formative experiences in the music of the church. Many of the bands had Hammond organists who were often church or college trained. Soft Machine's Mike Ratledge, Rick Wakeman, and one of the few foreign musicians, the Swiss keyboard player Patrick Moraz, all trained at or played in church.

Like many other musical advances, prog was accompanied by, or mediated through, or initiated by one or several parallel technological developments. The long-player vinyl record was ripe and ready to host the long song form of the progressives. Multi-track stereo recording encouraged increased production values. Both these were introduced into an era of rapidly rising living standards in the developed West, with more and more hi-fi systems being sold to an ever expanding middle-class to while away its new-found leisure hours. The technological wind was set fair for we progressives.

Added to this was a confidence in things English and an increasing advocacy of the romantic and pastoral, representing the softer or more feminine side of progressive rock. Following American group The Band's well publicised back-to-the-roots experiment, in which they communally reintroduced themselves to the American folk heritage by actually leading a more rural existence, British bands adopted this practical extension of pastoralism and decamped in their droves in order to, in the parlance of the day, 'get it together in the country'.

Gentle Giant put down roots in a farm near Portsmouth; Genesis decamped to Dorking, safely away from London. The band I was in moved lock stock and barrel to a farm in South Molton, Devon, to write and rehearse our breakthrough record *The Yes Album*, and the farm remains to this day the property of my friend, guitarist Steve Howe, who is probably there as I write. Song titles became self-consciously British—such as 'Grantchester Meadows' by Pink Floyd—and tended to involve things like tea parties. Peter Gabriel and Genesis sang about lawnmowers in 'I Know What I Like (In Your Wardrobe)', and we exhorted our singers to sing in English, not American.

The contrast between technical and pastoral, present and past, male and female produced a tension in the music that was ideally suited to the long songs. Typically, a blistering intro of some sort would give way to a rather fey, dreamy vocal delivery over some twinkling backing. This would wind its often tortured way through a number of extensions, second subjects, and codicils before a return, probably in a different metre or with a different orchestration, of the overtly masculine bravura main theme.

On the one hand there was a highly competitive arms race whereby every band wanted a newer, bigger PA, better lights, louder amps, the latest mark of Hammond organ, and if the other lot had just recorded with a symphony orchestra, then we had better do that too. Newer instruments meant a better sound; additional classical musicians meant bigger voicings, a bigger sound.

On the other hand there lay the remains of a Romantic pastoralism of the die-hard hippies, where all was softness and light, where the feminine was equated with the 'natural', where if Traffic had gone to a farm in the country to write an album then so did you. This was well illustrated by The Incredible String Band, a two-men two-women group that had scored hugely at the Newport Folk Festival and whose third album, *The Hangman's Beautiful Daughter*, rode high on the British charts.

The Holy Grail of all this seemed to be the production of a unified art work in which music, visual motifs, and verbal expression are inextricably linked to produce a single coherent artistic vision. This was not a new idea. The term Gesamtkunstwerk, or 'unified art work', was used to indicate the same thing in connection with the 19th-century composer Richard Wagner. This idea, implicitly or explicitly, seemed to be what the progressives were after. It embodied the counter-cultural ideal of protesting the soulless bureaucracy that was squeezing any trace of spiritual life out of Western culture, while simultaneously suggesting an ideal society in which technology and nature, past and future, matriarchal and patriarchal social values could be harmoniously interwoven. If the Gesamtkunstwerk was a real or imaginary goal, how close did we progressive rockers come?

The band I had helped to form, Yes, had come from early Beatles covers to the fragility of the earth on *Fragile* (1971) to *Close To The Edge* (1972), loosely based on Herman Hesse's *Siddhartha*, and to 1974's huge *Tales From Topographic Oceans*, structured around the teachings of Paramhansa Yogananda in his *Autobiography Of A Yogi*. The band seemed about ready to explode with the 'Gates Of Delirium', said to be loosely based on Tolstoy's *War And Peace*.

Now, I like a good meaty theme as much as the next man, but this was getting ridiculous. I'd got off the bus by this point, constitutionally unable to cope with any more of this, and perhaps in sympathy with the growing undercurrent that inevitably was gathering strength in opposition to the prevailing cosmic climate. After an opening bout with the Mighty Crim, it was therefore ironic to find myself back in the cosmic swirl with Genesis, playing 'Supper's Ready'.[2] This was a psychedelic recounting of the New Testament's *Book Of Revelation* that presents the New Jerusalem as the model of the perfect, fulfilled society, only won, of course, after an epic struggle between Good and Evil.

If the progressives approached the Wagnerian concept of the Gesamtkunstwerk at all, it was only intuitively and obliquely. Certainly no one sat around at rehearsals and suggested we alter things so that they would better fit the shape of the Gesamtkunstwerk. Like most musicians, the plan was to get started and keep going, to survive failure, and then—much harder—to survive success. With critical hindsight, it may be apparent that there was a remarkable drift in the musical, visual, and verbal (but, notably, no dance) aspects to a unified theme or art work, but generally the chief protagonists didn't know where we were going with this—we were only able to look back on where we had been.

I think we were pleasantly surprised although hard-pressed to explain why this particularly British music found such a welcoming audience in the USA. From roughly 1966 to 1971, the musicians and audience were essentially similar in age and class-origins: the solidly middle-class socio-economic background ensured both parties were singing from the same high-cultural song sheet. By 1972, most of the major players that had broken in the States were touring in stadiums to the accompaniment of astonishing record sales, and the music had grown from a sub-cultural to a mainstream style.

The music flourished particularly in the Northeast and Midwest, both regions with a strong WASP population. The young white audience found a resonance in the nationalism of the music and a kind of surrogate ethnic identity at a time when the question of what it meant to be a white person in America was coming under scrutiny. In the Southeast, however, with its strong indigenous culture of roots and country music, progressive rock fared much less well.

The AOR radio format (album-oriented rock, or adult-oriented rock) that many FM stations adopted in the early to mid 70s replaced the freeform 'underground' FM stations with a solid diet of progressive, metal, hard rock, and singer-songwriters, ensuring that the stadiums were filled when the bands came to town. The groups usually ploughed back the enormous gross receipts from these concerts into their evermore-elaborate stage shows, each act vying to outdo the other. The rooms got bigger, the music got slower, the better to translate in a hockey arena (Pink Floyd's fastest tempo was about the speed of a medium-slow jazz ballad), and the visuals became ever more expensive and stunning. And the audiences kept coming, at least for a while.

---

2 The "Mighty Crim" is King Crimson. Bruford joined them in 1972 directly after leaving Yes, and played with them through 1974 before the group disbanded. Bruford later joined Genesis for six months on their 1976 tour.

Critically, progressive rock was more or less loathed as much then as it is today, but that, of course, says as much about the critics as it does about the genre itself. Lester Bangs, classically portrayed by director Cameron Crowe in the movie *Almost Famous*, said of ELP: 'These guys amount to war criminals.'[1] To many critics, especially at the leading American magazines *Rolling Stone* and *Creem*, progressive rock's aesthetic stance was anathema, nothing short of heresy. They resented the insinuation that the progressives' appropriation of the classical tradition expanded the frontiers of popular music or enabled kids to listen to music with more 'quality'. This attitude seemed like a betrayal and smelled of elitism.

Even the style's heavy reliance on instrumental music was looked on with great suspicion. Robert Christgau spoke condescendingly of my band-mate Robert Fripp's 'rare if impractical gift for instrumental composition in a rock context'.[2] In general, the neo-Marxist critics—Bangs, Marsh, Christgau, and the rest—were deeply suspicious in three main areas: the lack of a political stance within the music; its over-reliance on high culture; and its commercial success. In the critical court of law, the progressive rockers were guilty on all three counts.[3]

Chipping away at the foundations, the critics would eventually cause enough damage to bring the ever-inflating edifice crashing to the ground. Their view was not seriously challenged until Allan F. Moore's book *Rock: The Primary Text* of 1992, and it would seem we are only just now arriving at a place where we can view the cultural history of the 70s from a clearer, more objective standpoint.[4]

As with psychedelia and the Summer Of Love, I remained disinterested through most of this. More by accident than design, progressive rock was the musical milieu in which I had to work, impress, survive. The usual immediate short-term considerations pressed hard as they were always to press: how do I stay relevant and stay in business, and who should I be doing these things with? Lofty considerations as to the music's value in the longer term were for the armchair pundit and for another day.

NOTES

[1] Lester Bangs *Energy Atrocities* quoted in Edward Macan *Rocking the Classics: English Progressive Rock and the Counterculture* (Oxford University Press 1997).
[2] Robert Christgau *Christgau's Record Guide: The 80s* p. 232 (Pantheon 1990).
[3] Edward Macan *Rocking the Classics: English Progressive Rock and the Counterculture* (Oxford University Press 1997) and Paul Stump *The Music's All That Matters: A History of Progressive Rock* (Quartet 1997) informed much of the analysis of progressive rock here.
[4] Allan F. Moore *Rock: The Primary Text—Devloping A Musicology of Rock* (Open University Press 1992).

Source: Bill Bruford, *Bill Bruford: The Autobiography* (London: Jawbone Press, 2009), pp. 114–20.

35

"Disco! Disco! Disco?
Four Critics Address the Musical Question"

The disco explosion that swept through the recording industry in 1978 was a true musical and cultural phenomenon symbolized by the unprecedented success of the *Saturday Night Fever* soundtrack, an album whose international sales of 30 million copies made it the best-selling record in history at that time. Disco's popularity ensured that it was instantly polarizing, especially to numerous rock fans who saw disco's orchestrated and synthesized style of dance music as the antithesis to rock music's 'naturalized' mode of authentic expression. The four music critics assembled to discuss disco's "musical question" by the Chicago-based "independent socialist newspaper" *In These Times* highlight the tensions surrounding the movement, from its unabashed commercialism to its roots in urban gay audiences. Not long after this article was published, the vilification of disco reached an apex in July 1979 when Chicago rock radio DJ Steve Dahl organized a "Disco Demolition Night" at Comiskey Park as part of a between-game exhibition stunt for a White Sox baseball doubleheader. With nearly 50,000 frenzied fans looking on, Dahl exploded a pile of disco records, inciting the crowd to swarm the field to thundering chants of "disco sucks." Decades later, disco has assumed a more privileged place in popular music history. The notorious exploits of nightclubs like Studio 54 have passed into myth as one of the last bastions of pre-AIDS-awareness hedonistic abandon and disco has been reevaluated as a pivotal moment in both the history of electronic dance music and the emergence of a significant gay presence in American culture.[1]

1. BY BRUCE DANCIS[2]

"Disco," like "rock," is too large a type of popular music to characterize easily with one pithy phrase. The best disco—songs by Sister Sledge, Gloria Gaynor and the Atlantic Starrs—strikes me as being as good as the best current soul music. Similarly, the worst disco—Madleen Kane and the tackily discofied versions of "Tuxedo Junction" and "McArthur Park"—equals or sinks beneath the most mindless rock.

But disco bears two additional burdens that weigh down much of the genre. Dominated by producers much more than rock, disco too often reflects business or commercial viability over artistic vitality. Although imaginative auteurist producers have always existed in rock music, for the most part producers reign when musicians have least to say.

---

1 See for example, Tim Lawrence, *Love Saves the Day: A History of American Dance Music Culture, 1970–1979* (Durham: Duke University Press, 2004) and Alice Echols, *Hot Stuff: Disco and the Remaking of American Culture* (New York: W.W. Norton, 2010).

2 Dancis is the only one of the four critics whose affiliations are not listed in the article. At the time, he was the main contributing music critic to *In These Times*.

Disco also suffers from its predominant function as a dance music. The insistent beat, which is never allowed to vary, constrains even the most boisterous group. A good example is Atlantic Starr's "(Let's) Rock 'n' Roll," on their *Straight to the Point* album (A&M Records). Excellent vocals and a solid band seem to be chained awkwardly, struggling to break out of the rigid rhythm. In addition, for dancing purposes disco songs tend to be extremely long—eight to ten minute album cuts are the norm. In the history of rock music, *no one*, with the exception of Bob Dylan, has been able to sustain excitement and tension beyond 2–4 minutes. To me, this says more about the vitality of concentrated power than it does about any death of creativity.

Much of the across the board dismissal of disco borders on homophobia and racism, the product of insecure and defensive rock fans flailing away at this strange beast that suddenly came to dominate the singles charts. (Why people are so freaked out is a surprise to me; since the British invasion of the mid '60s, the Top 40 has seldom reflected the most compelling trends.)

Still, there is something sleazy about the ease, no, the desire of many disco stars to toady up to the worst creeps in the music industry. The day that Graham Parker appears in a suit and tie on the cover of *Fortune*—as the Bee Gees did in the April 23 issue is the day this rockophile hangs up his headset.

2. BY ABE PECK

Besides the sheer exuberance of freaking, spanking, rocking or simply stomping out, what interests me most about disco music is its current universality. Disco music includes both the fiery rhythms of Parliament-Funkadelic, Instant Funk—you get the idea—*and* the icily technocratic music of *Midnight Express*, which won an Oscar for producer Giorgio Moroder, even though nobody can name a musician who played on the album. It includes calculated excursions of the Rolling Stones and Rod Stewart, *and* the hilariously crass attempts best exemplified by the late Percy Faith, who gave the world the disco version of "Hava Nagila."

The clubs have the same range: from the Snub Sado-Masochism of New York's Studio 54 to the funky ambience of the haunts where the next new dance will be born. And who goes? Blacks and whites, gays and straights, sybaritic boogie children snorting coke off glass table tops and working-class Tony Maneros feverishly transcend the daily grind out there on the Saturday Night dance floor.[3]

Disco seems to bridge the cusp between the American Way and the Great Outside. Visit a disco on, say, the island of Jamaica. One minute a local reggae song explodes out of a bank of Stateside speakers, and the Visitors from the North left foot the oddly syncopated reggae movements the locals have down pat. Then the music smoothly segues into some stateside disco tune, and the dancing assumes equal axes, natives and visitors checking each other out for new moves.

Even in the U.S. of A., "mainstream" and "outside" coexist in a way they never did even during the supposedly egalitarian heyday of rock 'n' roll. The Village People's disco jingles appeal both to those who think "Y.M.C.A." is the most wholesome song since the Mormon Tabernacle Choir's last release and those who wink knowingly at its gay appeal. Black artists conquer the pop charts in a way they never did even during the height of rhythm and blues.

But any music that satisfies so broadly runs the risk of ultimate superficiality. Like rock before it, disco has moved from the outside to pop cult status to its current mass culture position. It's already an $8 billion business, and the truly giant record companies, Columbia and Warner Brothers, have just gone disco to retain control of the grooves.

---

3 Tony Manero is the lead character played by John Travolta in *Saturday Night Fever*.

It's apt that one current funk/disco group is called Mass Production; the minimal music that is much of disco offers only so many variations on a theme. Many black musicians complain they've had to jump on the disco bandwagon or be trampled by it. Many whites hope that New Wave or some other music will reassert rock—which wouldn't hurt disco creatively (every "Miss You" has been countered by a score of misses), but would sap its music-industry bankroll.

What does the next flash of the strobe augur? Before we know it, we could be saying, "Forget disco, here's the Next Big Thing."

But that's what they said would happen last year.

> **Abe Peck, Chicago _Sun-Times_ feature writer, wrote the Village People cover story for _Rolling Stone_'s recent disco issue.**

3. BY TOM SMUCKER

It's a little late to debate the merits of disco music as if it were something that we could think out of existence if we want to. Particularly in the pages of a paper like _In These Times_, which expresses an interest in where the American public is at, not just where it should be at. Because disco has become one of _the_ dominant forms of American and trans-Atlantic pop music.

Nevertheless, let me list what I think are some of disco's selling points, reasons besides its incredible popularity that should make it interesting to readers of _ITT_.

First: disco is the first pop music in a long while with a multiracial appeal. Elvis may have topped the pop, country, and black charts when he started, but that was 25 years ago. Since then there's been borrowing between black and white music, and some crossing-over of performers from one audience to another, but the lines of racial segregation could always be drawn. Disco, however, is sung, produced, danced and listened to by whites and blacks (as well as Latins, but that's a more complicated case).

There is, naturally, disco music that appeals more to one audience or another, and none of this signals the end of racism. But disco has created a common cultural ground for whoever wants to use it, even if just to throw a successful dance party or disco fund-raiser for black and white friends or fellow workers—something that would have been hard with the segregated music of five years ago.

Second: disco is the first pop music with an openly gay component. It originated in the urban gay subculture and the trendsetters and taste-makers of disco continue to be gay. This doesn't end sexual repression, but it does mean that an interesting, even encouraging space exists that includes both straight and gay.

Finally: disco, like punk rock, encourages energetic public action, unlike the music of the laid-back singer songwriters who dominated the early and mid-'70s. For every beautiful people gossip column gold mine like Studio 54, we should keep in mind the hundreds of discos and disco parties where the rest of us escape our work-a-day lives. Whether this leads to stupor or euphoria is still an open question, but it beats nodding off in private. A culture that tries for some sort of public ecstasy, if only on Saturday night, is at least aroused enough to respond to alienation in a group. That's a first step.

There's a connection, largely ignored, between the return to dance and the return to mass public demonstrations. People have energy again. No matter how tentative that connection is, one would guess that populist left-wingers would try to make it as strong as possible, the way the anti-war movement tried to connect to rock'n'roll.

Yet many leftists feel free to dismiss disco as "mindless," or "watered down," or "plastic," and leave it at that, using the same narrow minds their leftist parents used to dismiss swing music and their leftist older siblings used to dismiss rock'n'roll.

It's just pop music and there's no reason to feel obligated to enjoy disco if you don't. But any political person should be interested in the space and energy it creates.

**Tom Smucker writes on popular music for the *Village Voice*
and a variety of other publications.**

4. BY GEORGIA CHRISTGAU

Disco never needed me. Since its earliest—say the Trammps' "Where the Happy People Go," it celebrated itself, its fans, its milieu. It could be superficial ("More, More, More") or up-front ("Push, Push in the Bush"); either way, it lacked subtlety, and didn't take well to the page. Since it happened "underground"—gay bars, black and Latin communities—I and most of my peers had little experience with it. Then the Bee Gees wrote a monster hit for a white, or white enough, working-class hero in *Saturday Night Fever*, and disco became a phenomenon. And here we are, writing about it after it had already parodied itself with The Village People.

Anti-disco rock'n'rollers never needed me, either. They come complete with their own spectrum, from the bleeders at punk clubs to the fans of platinum-sellers like Bob Seger who sings, "Don't take me to no disco," to cheers from people who've never been inside one, either.

Three progressive FM rock stations in New York run anti-disco campaigns. It's not hard to do—radio is already segregated black from white. At a sellout show of Twisted Sister, a local group with a white following, a banner displayed from the balcony read, "We hate disco because it sucks." This isn't opinion, it's willful ignorance, racism feeding on paranoia: where will rock'n'rollers go now that "boogie" has become "boogie down"?

If the Beatles turned on the world to Chuck Berry, the Bee Gees are inspired by the Stylistics, or at least revive the memory of Smokey Robinson. Disco carries on a tradition in American music of integration, a synthesis of sharing as well as antagonism. People my age, white and black, can swoon to Sam and Dave or the Righteous Brothers, but some of them haven't made the disco connection. Polyester suits, strobe lights and mirrored floors threaten the flannel and jeans lifestyle. One powerful image cancels out the other; much money has been invested promoting the disco way of life, money that must see a return.

Me, I try to ignore the promo-hype. I enjoy disco without going to Studio 54, and have never purchased a whistle or sniffed amyl nitrate. I listen to enough disco to stay interested in its history. 1974's "Rock Your Baby" sounds like a garage band compared to 1978's "Supernature." Partial to southern rhythm and blues, I dance to Candi Staton, KC and the Sunshine Band, and Betty Wright—who've all had huge disco "crossover" hits. A sucker for extremes, I'm taken with Grace Jones, and fascinated by disco deejays, new superstars who know how to make the music never stop. For dancing, I rely on some version of the L.A. Hustle a friend from Detroit learned on vacation in Miami, which still holds up on the floor after five years. Do I really love disco? No, But when Blondie hits big with "Once had a love, it was a gas/Soon turned out to be a pain in the ass," I celebrate disco, too. It's the same old song.

Georgia Christgau writes on music for the *Village Voice* and other publications.

Source: Bruce Dancis, Abe Peck, Tom Smucker, and Georgia Christgau, "Disco! Disco! Disco?: Four Critics Address the Musical Question," *In These Times*, June 6–12, 1979, pp. 20–21.

36

"Why Don't We Call It Punk?"

LEGS MCNEIL AND GILLIAN MCCAIN

"Lurid, insolent, disorderly, funny, sometimes gross, sometimes mean and occasionally touching"—in the words of its *New York Times* review, Legs McNeil's and Gillian McCain's punk rock history *Please Kill Me* is a book utterly befitting of the musical phenomenon it seeks to describe. Published in 1996, twenty years after New York punk icons the Ramones released their groundbreaking self-titled debut album, *Please Kill Me* was one of the first oral histories of American punk rock drawn from the scene's participants.[1] Like any oral history or filmed documentary, the editors chose to stitch together a story from a variety of different sources, including original testimonies and previously published materials. The narrative sketched out in the passage below centers on the formation of *Punk* magazine, and comes primarily from one of its founders, Legs (Eddie) McNeil (born 1956), and contributing writer, Mary Harron (born 1953).[2] Along the way appearances from the four original Ramones (Joey, Johnny, Dee Dee, and Tommy), an inadvertent cameo from former Velvet Underground front man Lou Reed (1942–2013), and the storied Bowery Avenue club CBGB's provide the appropriate local New York City color.[3]

Leee Childers: The first time I went to CBGB's was with Wayne County. There were six people in the audience. We ate the chili, which, years later, Bebe Buell was horrified to learn. She said, "You ate the chili? Stiv told me the Dead Boys used to go back in the kitchen and jerk off in it."

I said to her, "So what? I've had worse in my mouth."

So the first time I went to CBGB's, we ate chili, which tasted horrible. The whole place stunk of urine. The whole place smelled like a bathroom. And there were literally six people in the audience and then the Ramones went onstage, and I went, "Oh . . . my . . . God!"

And I knew it, in a minute. The first song. The first song. I knew that I was home and happy and secure and free and rock & roll. I knew it from that first song the first time I went to see them. I was the one who called Lisa Robinson and said, "You won't

---

1 Other notable oral histories of punk have included John Lydon, *Rotten: No Irish, No Blacks, No Dogs* (New York: Picador Press, 1994), Marc Spitz and Brendan Mullen, *We Got the Neutron Bomb: The Untold Story of L.A. Punk* (New York: Three Rivers Press, 2001), and John Robb, *Punk Rock: An Oral History* (Oakland, CA: PM 2012).

2 Harron has since gone on to an acclaimed directing career with such films as *I Shot Andy Warhol* and *American Psycho*.

3 The full name is CBGB's OMFUG (Country Bluegrass Blues & Other Music for Uplifting Gormandizers).

believe what's going on!" and she said, "Oh, what are you talking about? Oh, the Bowery, ugggghhhhh!!!"

I said, "Just come."

Danny Fields: I was editing *16* magazine and writing a column in the *SoHo Weekly News*, and I was always gushing about the wonderfulness of Television and how exciting their performances were.

I rarely wrote about the Ramones. I hadn't seen them, I didn't know who they were. I was always writing about Television and Patti Smith. They came first, chronologically, of that bunch. And Johnny Ramone would say to Tommy, "You're supposed to be in charge of publicity. Why doesn't Danny Fields write about us?"

I could just hear it happening. I wasn't there, but I can just imagine the conversations. So Tommy would call me at *16* magazine and say, "Please, why don't you ever write about us?" I always had the feeling that someone was prodding in the background, like he better deliver on this or else. And the Ramones were doing the same thing to Lisa Robinson as they were doing to me. That's when Lisa and I decided to divide up. There was some other band who was harassing both of us at that time and we decided to kill two birds in one night. I would go see the other band and Lisa would see the Ramones. I don't remember the other band, they must have left me cold. The next day Lisa called me up all excited about the Ramones, saying, "Oh, you'll love them. They do songs one minute long and it's very fast and it's all over in less than a quarter of an hour. And it's everything you like and you'll love it. And it's just the funniest thing I've ever seen."

And she was right. I went down to see them at CBGB's, and I got this seat up front with no problems. In those days I don't think anybody packed it in. And they came on and I fell in love with them. I just thought they were doing everything right. They were the perfect band. They were fast and I liked fast. Beethoven quartets are supposed to be slow. Rock & roll is supposed to be fast. I loved it.

I introduced myself to them afterwards and I said, "I love you so much, I'll be your manager."

And they said, "Oh good, we need a new drum set. Do you have money?" I said I was going down to see my mother in Miami. When I got to Miami, I asked my mother for three thousand dollars and she gave it to me. That's how I started managing the Ramones. I bought myself into being their manager.

Legs McNeil: When I was eighteen, I was living in New York, working at some hippie film commune on Fourteenth Street, making this horrible movie about a stupid advertising executive who takes acid and drops out and becomes sexually, emotionally, and spiritually liberated. It was just crap.

This was 1975, and the idea of taking acid and dropping out was just so lame—like ten years too late. And the hippie film commune was just as lame. I hated hippies.

Anyway, summer came, and I went back to Cheshire, Connecticut, where I grew up, and made this Three Stooges comedy—sixteen millimeter, black and white film—with two high school friends of mine, John Holmstrom and Ged Dunn.

John Holmstrom was a cartoonist, and Ged Dunn was a business guy, so at the end of the summer we decided we were going to work together. We had all worked together before when we were in high school—Holmstrom had put together this theater group called the Apocalypse Players, which was Eugène Ionesco meets Alice Cooper. We even had the police close down one of our shows when I missed throwing a pie and hit somebody in the audience.

But when John and Ged and I regrouped, it was kind of undetermined just what we were going to do—films, comics, some sort of media thing.

Then one day we were riding in the car, and John said, "I think we should start a magazine."

All summer we had been listening to this album *Go Girl Crazy* by this unknown group called the Dictators, and it changed our lives. We'd just get drunk every night and lip-sync to it. Holmstrom had found the record. He was the one who really followed rock & roll. He was the one who turned Ged and I on to the Velvet Underground, Iggy and the Stooges, and the New York Dolls. Up until then I just listened to Chuck Berry and the first two Beatles records, and Alice Cooper.

But I hated most rock & roll, because it was about lame hippie stuff, and there really wasn't anyone describing our lives—which was McDonald's, beer, and TV reruns. Then John found the Dictators, and we all got excited that something was happening.

But I didn't understand why Holmstrom wanted to start a magazine. I thought it was a stupid idea.

John said, "But if we have a magazine, people will think we're cool and stuff and want to hang out with us."

I didn't get it. Then he said, "If we had a magazine, we could drink for free. People will give us free drinks."

That got me. I said, "Okay, then let's do it."

Holmstrom wanted the magazine to be a combination of everything we were into—television reruns, drinking beer, getting laid, cheeseburgers, comics, grade-B movies, and this weird rock & roll that nobody but us seemed to like: the Velvets, the Stooges, the New York Dolls, and now the Dictators.

So John said he wanted to call our magazine *Teenage News*, after an unreleased New York Dolls song. I thought it was a stupid title, so I told him that. And he said, "Well, what do you think we should call it?"

I saw the magazine Holmstrom wanted to start as a Dictators album come to life. On the inside sleeve of the record was a picture of the Dictators hanging out in a White Castle hamburger stand and they were dressed in black leather jackets. Even though we didn't have black leather jackets, the picture seemed to describe us perfectly—wise guys. So I thought the magazine should be for other fuck-ups like us. Kids who grew up believing only in the Three Stooges. Kids that had parties when their parents were away and destroyed the house. You know, kids that stole cars and had fun.

So I said, "Why don't we call it *Punk*?"

The word "punk" seemed to sum up the thread that connected everything we liked—drunk, obnoxious, smart but not pretentious, absurd, funny, ironic, and things that appealed to the darker side.

So John Holmstrom said, "Okay. Well, I'm gonna be the editor." Ged said, "I'm gonna be the publisher." They both looked at me and said, "What are you gonna do?" I said, "I don't know." I had no skills.

Then Holmstrom said, "You can be the resident punk!" And they both started laughing hysterically. Ged and John were both like four years older than me. And I think half the reason they hung out with me was because I was always getting drunk and into trouble and Holmstrom found it constantly amusing. So it was decided I would be a living cartoon character, like Alfred E. Neuman was to *Mad* magazine. And Holmstrom changed my name from Eddie to Legs.

It's funny, but we had no idea if anybody besides the Dictators were out there. We had no idea about CBGB's and what was going on, but I don't think we cared. We just liked the idea of *Punk* magazine. And that was all that really mattered.

Mary Harron: I met Legs when I was working as the cook for Total Impact, the hippie film commune on Fourteenth Street. Legs came in and was the only one who said this movie sucks and these people are crazy. So I asked him what he was doing. Legs said he was just doing some part-time work on the movie, and he asked me what I did. I said I wanted to be a writer and he said, "We're starting a magazine. It's called *Punk*."

I thought, What a brilliant title! I don't know why it seemed so brilliant, because this was before there was punk, but it was obviously so ironic.

I mean there was something in it, you know, because if somebody said that they're starting a magazine, you think, Oh, a literary magazine. But *Punk*, it was so funny, bratty—it was so unexpected—and I thought, Well, that's really great. So I said, "Oh, I'll write for you," even though I didn't know what it was about.

A few nights later I was in the kitchen of the horrible film commune, I was washing the floor, being a Cinderella, and doing the dishes. Legs and John came in and said they were going to go to CBGB's and I thought, Okay.

We all went to CBGB's to hear the Ramones and that was the night everything happened.

Legs McNeil: We talked our way into CBGB's, and then we were walking down the length of the bar, when I saw this guy with really short hair and sunglasses sitting at a table and I recognized him as Lou Reed. Holmstrom had been playing Lou Reed's *Metal Machine Music* for weeks. That was Lou's two-album set of nothing but feedback. It was awful, just noise, which Holmstrom loved and proclaimed the ultimate punk album. We were always having big fights about John playing the record: "Come on, take off that shit!" That's how I knew who Lou Reed was.

So when I spotted Lou at the table, I went up to Holmstrom and said, "Hey, there's that guy you're always talking about. Maybe we should interview him too?" I was thinking, you know, as long as we were there. So I went up to Lou and I said, "Hey, we're gonna interview you for our magazine!" You know like, "Aren't you thrilled?" I had no idea of what we were doing. Then Holmstrom said to Lou, "Yeah, we'll even put you on the cover!" Lou just turned around, real deadpan, and said, "Oh, your circulation must be fabulous."

Mary Harron: I was horrified when Legs and John went up to Lou Reed and told him they wanted to interview him. I thought, Oh my god, what are they doing?

Because Lou was a famous person and I thought, Oh that's so rude. What do they think is going to happen?

I think I was in awe of Lou much more than John or Legs were. I knew quite a lot about Andy Warhol, because I'd had a complete Warhol obsession, and I was a fan of the Velvet Underground. So I was cringing.

Legs McNeil: Just as we were talking to Lou Reed the Ramones hit the stage and it was an amazing sight. Four really pissed-off guys in black leather jackets. It was like the Gestapo had just walked into the room. These guys were definitely not hippies.

Then they counted off a song—"ONE, TWO, THREE, FOUR!"—and we were hit with this blast of noise, you physically recoiled from the shock of it, like this huge wind, and before I could even get into it, they stopped.

Apparently they were all playing a different song. The Ramones had a mini-fight onstage. They were just so thoroughly disgusted with each other that they threw down their guitars and stomped off the stage.

It was amazing. It was like actually seeing something come together. Lou Reed was sitting at the table laughing.

Joey Ramone: That was the first night we met Lou Reed. Lou kept telling Johnny Ramone that he wasn't playing the right kind of guitar, that he should play a different kind of guitar. It didn't go over so favorably with Johnny. I mean when John found his guitar he didn't have much money—he bought his guitar for fifty dollars. And Johnny liked the idea of the Mosrite because nobody else used a Mosrite—so this would be his sort of trademark. So Johnny thought Lou was a real jerk.

Legs McNeil: Then the Ramones came back, counted off again, and played the best eighteen minutes of rock & roll that I had ever heard. You could hear the Chuck Berry in it, which was all I listened to, that and the Beatles second album with all the Chuck Berry covers on it. When the Ramones came offstage we interviewed them, and they were like us. They talked about comic books and sixties bubble-gum music and were really deadpan and sarcastic.

I really thought I was at the Cavern Club in 1963 and we had just met the Beatles. Only it wasn't a fantasy, it wasn't the Beatles, it was *our* band—the Ramones. But we couldn't hang out with them that long, because we had to go interview Lou Reed, who was old, and snotty, and like someone's cranky old drunken father.

Mary Harron: We all went off to the Locale and none of us had any money and we couldn't order food. I remember Lou Reed ordered a cheeseburger because I was so hungry. Lou was with Rachel, who was the first transvestite I'd ever met. Very beautiful, but frightening. But I mean definitely a guy: Rachel had stubble.

Legs and John were chatting with Lou so I sat next to Rachel, and I asked her what her name was—him, what his name was—and he said, "Rachel."

I thought, Right. That kind of shut me up for a bit. I think I actually sort of tried to make conversation with him, but Rachel wasn't talkative. I think that was the sum total of our conversation.

I was quite startled because of the way Legs and John would ask the questions. It was quite amateurish. They would ask, "What kind of hamburgers do you like?" Like student journalism, and I thought, Oh god, who are these guys? What are they doing? What are you asking these stupid questions for?

Then Lou Reed started showing some of his famous nastiness. He was mean to Legs. Very mean. And I was very upset by that, actually. I thought he was quite devastating really. But Legs and John didn't seem to mind.

But the night was very exciting, you know—seeing the Ramones, meeting Lou Reed ... I remember thinking, Oh my god, wait till I tell people back home I've met Lou Reed! That was really going through my head—Wait until I tell people ...

But then, somehow, because of Lou lashing out or getting bored or whatever, it had ended on this rather sour note. Lou started getting so hostile. I can't remember why. He got very mad at Legs, he just hated him.

But when we got out in the street, John Holmstrom was jumping around being ecstatic and I was thinking, I don't really understand this. Why he's so happy?

I couldn't understand why he was so excited, ecstatic. Because what did we get? Lou Reed being rude to us really.

Legs McNeil: Holmstrom kept jumping up and down, saying, "We got Lou Reed for the cover! We got Lou Reed for the cover!" I didn't know what he was so excited about. I just said, "Yeah, but did you see that chick he was with?"

Mary Harron: When I finished writing the Ramones article it was late and I still had no money, so I walked that night all the way across town to deliver the article to the "Punk Dump," the *Punk* magazine office on Tenth Avenue. It must have been ten avenues—you know, one side of the city to the other.

It was *Taxi Driver* time, you know, steam coming out of the manholes. It was really a beautiful kind of weird New York night—and the Punk Dump was an incredible place. It looked like something out of *Batman*. It was a storefront under the train tracks on Tenth Avenue with the windows painted black—like a cave. So I found the door and the light was on and John Holmstrom was there at his desk, his glasses on, and he was doing the artwork for the cover, for the Lou Reed interview—the first issue of *Punk*.

He showed it to me, and it was a *cartoon*! I read the Lou Reed interview quickly, and I could see that everything that was humiliating, embarrassing, and stupid had been turned to an advantage. And that's when I knew that *Punk* was going to work.

Legs McNeil: The next thing we did was go out and plaster the city with these little posters that said, "WATCH OUT! PUNK IS COMING!" Everyone who saw them said, "Punk? What's punk?" John and I were laughing. We were like, "Ohhh, you'll find out."

Debbie Harry: John Holmstrom and his living cartoon creature, Legs McNeil, were two maniacs running around town putting up signs that said, "Punk is coming! Punk is coming!" We thought, Here comes another shitty group with an even shittier name.

James Grauerholz: I was living at the Bunker, John Giorno's loft at 222 Bowery, which became William Burroughs' home in New York City. I'd had an affair with William, and when that ended I started working for him. But at that time William was not as well known. I mean, he was the world-famous William Burroughs, but only a tiny minority knew anything about who that was. William was kind of considered to be a little bit of a has-been in some ways. He was revered, but his works had gone out of print. So I began to see myself as the impresario of William and we began to see ourselves as kind of a symbiotic partnership.

In late 1975, I used to go to Phoebe's a lot. Phoebe's was the off-off-Broadway theater hangout, a restaurant up the street from the Bunker. Phoebe's was a real mainstay. So on my little route from the Bunker to Phoebe's, I would pass these street poles, right outside my house, with posters glued up: "PUNK IS COMING!"

And I loved it, from the first moment I saw that sign I thought, punk is coming! I thought, What is this gonna be? A band or what?

But "punk!"—I loved it, because it meant to me a derisory word for a young, no-count piece a shit. And then from Burrough's *Junky*—you know, there's that great scene where William and Roy, the sailor, are rolling the lushes in the subway and there's two young punks. They cross over and they give Roy a lot of shit and Roy says, "Fucking punks think it's a joke. They won't think it's so funny when they're doing five twenty-nine on the island." You know, five months and twenty-nine days.

"Fucking punks think it's a joke."

So I knew that punk was a direct descendant of William Burroughs' life and work. And I said, "We've gotta put these two things together for the benefit of all parties." And that's what I did.

William Burroughs: I always thought a punk was someone who took it up the ass.

Source: Legs McNeil and Gillian McCain, *Please Kill Me: The Uncensored Oral History of Punk* (New York: Grove/Atlantic, 1996), pp. 201–8.

37

The Subculture of British Punk

Dick Hebdige

The academic study of popular music took a quantum leap in the mid-1970s thanks to the influential research emanating from the University of Birmingham Centre for Contemporary Cultural Studies (CCCS). Turning their gaze toward Britain's diverse youth groups, CCCS sociologists like Dick Hebdige attempted to unravel the layered meanings of the teddy boys, mods, skinheads, rastafarians, rude boys, and other subcultures, framing them as "resistant" social formations. Pitted against the dominant, or "parent," culture's ordered "systems of beliefs" and "use of objects and material life," the subculture was seen to fashion their own set of values, so as to "significantly differentiate them from the wider culture."[1] One of the first book-length studies to put these theories to test, Hebdige's 1979 *Subculture: The Meaning of Style* takes as its subject a broad cross section of British subcultures. Much of his attention, however, is devoted to the appearance of punk in 1976. In regard to this "spectacular subculture," Hebdige asks what types of meaning we can glean from a style that deliberately seems to signify disorder. To this end he introduces the concept of *bricolage*, taken from the writings of anthropologist Claude Levi-Strauss, while borrowing liberally from other intellectual traditions as well. While *Subculture*'s scholarly tone would have a profound impact on the rise of academic-based popular music studies, it also received favorable publicity and reviews in the mainstream rock music press as well. As such, it was a landmark book that signified an important crossover moment in the study of popular music.

April 3, 1989, Marrakech

The chic thing is to dress in expensive tailor-made rags and all the queens are camping about in wild-boy drag. There are Bowery suits that appear to be stained with urine and vomit which on closer inspection turn out to be intricate embroideries of fine gold thread. There are clochard suits of the finest linen, shabby gentility suits . . . felt hats seasoned by old junkies . . . loud cheap pimp suits that turn out to be not so cheap, the loudness is a subtle harmony of colours only the very best Poor Boy shops can turn out. . . . It is the double take and many carry it much further to as many as six takes (William Burroughs, 1969).

---

1 John Clarke, Stuart Hall, Tony Jefferson, and Brian Roberts, "Subcultures, Cultures and Class: A Theoretical Overview," *Resistance Through Rituals: Youth Subcultures in Post-War Britain*, edited by Stuart Hall and Tony Jefferson (London: Hutchinson, 1976), pp. 10, 14.

HOLIDAY IN THE SUN: MISTER ROTTEN MAKES THE GRADE

The British summer of 1976 was extraordinarily hot and dry: there were no recorded precedents. From May through to August, London parched and sweltered under luminous skies and the inevitable fog of exhaust fumes. Initially hailed as a Godsend, and a national 'tonic' in the press and television (was Britain's 'curse' finally broken?) the sun provided seasonal relief from the dreary cycle of doom-laden headlines which had dominated the front pages of the tabloids throughout the winter. Nature performed its statutory ideological function and 'stood in' for all the other 'bad news', provided tangible proof of 'improvement' and pushed aside the strikes and the dissension. With predictable regularity, 'bright young things' were shown flouncing along Oxford Street in harem bags and beach shorts, bikini tops and polaroids in that last uplifting item for the *News at Ten*. The sun served as a 'cheeky' postscript to the crisis: a lighthearted addendum filled with tropical promise. The crisis, too, could have its holiday. But as the weeks and months passed and the heatwave continued, the old mythology of doom and disaster was reasserted with a vengeance. The 'miracle' rapidly became a commonplace, an everyday affair, until one morning in mid-July it was suddenly re-christened a 'freak disorder': a dreadful, last, unlooked-for factor in Britain's decline.

The heatwave was officially declared a drought in August, water was rationed, crops were failing, and Hyde Park's grass burned into a delicate shade of raw sienna. The end was at hand and Last Days imagery began to figure once more in the press. Economic categories, cultural and natural phenomena were confounded with more than customary abandon until the drought took on an almost metaphysical significance. A Minister for Drought was appointed, Nature had now been officially declared 'unnatural', and all the age-old inferences were drawn with an obligatory modicum of irony to keep within the bounds of common sense. In late August, two events of completely different mythical stature coincided to confirm the worst forebodings: it was demonstrated that the excessive heat was threatening the very structure of the nation's houses (cracking the foundations) and the Notting Hill Carnival, traditionally a paradigm of racial harmony, exploded into violence. The Caribbean festival, with all its Cook's Tours connotations of happy, dancing coloured folk, of jaunty bright calypsos and exotic costumes, was suddenly, unaccountably, transformed into a menacing congregation of angry black youths and embattled police. Hordes of young black Britons did the Soweto dash across the nation's television screens and conjured up fearful images of other Negroes, other confrontations, other 'long, hot summers'. The humble dustbin lid, the staple of every steel band, the symbol of the 'carnival spirit', of Negro ingenuity and the resilience of ghetto culture, took on an altogether more ominous significance when used by white-faced policemen as a desperate shield against an angry rain of bricks.

It was during this strange apocalyptic summer that punk made its sensational debut in the music press.[1] In London, especially in the south west and more specifically in the vicinity of the King's Road, a new style was being generated combining elements drawn from a whole range of heterogeneous youth styles. In fact punk claimed a dubious parentage. Strands from David Bowie and glitter-rock were woven together with elements from American proto-punk (the Ramones, the Heartbreakers, Iggy Pop, Richard Hell), from that faction within London pub-rock (the 101-ers, the Gorillas, etc.) inspired by the mod subculture of the 60s, from the Canvey Island 40s revival and the Southend r & b bands (Dr Feelgood, Lew Lewis, etc.), from northern soul and from reggae.

Not surprisingly, the resulting mix was somewhat unstable: all these elements constantly threatened to separate and return to their original sources. Glam rock contributed narcissism, nihilism and gender confusion. American punk offered a minimalist aesthetic (e.g., the Ramones' 'Pinhead' or Crime's 'I Stupid'), the cult of the Street and a penchant for self-laceration. Northern Soul (a genuinely secret subculture of working-class youngsters dedicated to acrobatic dancing and fast American soul of the 60s, which centres on clubs like the Wigan Casino) brought its subterranean tradition of fast, jerky rhythms, solo dance styles and amphetamines; reggae its exotic and dangerous aura of forbidden identity, its conscience, its dread and its cool. Native rhythm 'n' blues reinforced the brashness and the speed of Northern Soul, took rock back to the basics and contributed a highly developed iconoclasm, a thoroughly British persona and an extremely selective appropriation of the rock 'n' roll heritage.

This unlikely alliance of diverse and superficially incompatible musical traditions, mysteriously accomplished under punk, found ratification in an equally eclectic clothing style which reproduced the same kind of cacophony on the visual level. The whole ensemble, literally safety-pinned together, became the celebrated and highly photogenic phenomenon known as punk which throughout 1977 provided the tabloids with a fund of predictably sensational copy and the quality press with a welcome catalogue of beautifully broken codes. Punk reproduced the entire sartorial history of post-war working-class youth cultures in 'cut up' form, combining elements which had originally belonged to completely different epochs. There was a chaos of quiffs and leather jackets, brothel creepers and winkle pickers, plimsolls and paka macs, moddy crops and skinhead strides, drainpipes and vivid socks, bum freezers and bovver boots—all kept 'in place' and 'out of time' by the spectacular adhesives: the safety pins and plastic clothes pegs, the bondage straps and bits of string which attracted so much horrified and fascinated attention. Punk is therefore a singularly appropriate point of departure for a study of this kind because punk style contained distorted reflections of all the major post-war subcultures.

STYLE AS INTENTIONAL COMMUNICATION

> I speak through my clothes. (Eco, 1973)

The cycle leading from opposition to defusion, from resistance to incorporation encloses each successive subculture. We have seen how the media and the market fit into this cycle. We must now turn to the subculture itself to consider exactly how and what subcultural style communicates. Two questions must be asked which together present us with something of a paradox: how does a subculture make sense to its members? How is it made to signify disorder? To answer these questions we must define the meaning of style more precisely.

In 'The Rhetoric of the Image', Roland Barthes contrasts the 'intentional' advertising image with the apparently 'innocent' news photograph. Both are complex articulations of specific codes and practices, but the news photo appears more 'natural' and transparent than the advertisement. He writes—'the signification of the image is certainly intentional . . . the advertising image is clear, or at least emphatic'. Barthes' distinction can be used analogously to point up the difference between subcultural and 'normal' styles. The subcultural stylistic ensembles—those emphatic combinations of dress, dance, argot, music, etc.—bear approximately the same relation to the more conventional formulae ('normal' suits and ties, casual wear, twin-sets, etc.) that the advertising image bears to the less consciously constructed news photograph.

Of course, signification need not be intentional, as semioticians have repeatedly pointed out. Umberto Eco writes 'not only the expressly intended communicative object . . . but every object may be viewed . . . as a sign' (Eco, 1973). For instance, the conventional outfits worn by the average man and woman in the street are chosen within the constraints of finance, 'taste', preference, etc. and these choices are undoubtedly significant. Each ensemble has its place in an internal system of differences—the conventional modes of sartorial discourse—which fit a corresponding set of socially prescribed roles and options.[2] These choices contain a whole range of messages which are transmitted through the finely graded distinctions of a number of interlocking sets—class and status, self-image and attractiveness, etc. Ultimately, if nothing else, they are expressive of 'normality' as opposed to 'deviance' (i.e., they are distinguished by their relative invisibility, their appropriateness, their 'naturalness'). However, the intentional communication is of a different order. It stands apart—a visible construction, a loaded choice. It directs attention to itself; it gives itself to be read.

This is what distinguishes the visual ensembles of spectacular subcultures from those favoured in the surrounding culture(s). They are *obviously* fabricated (even the mods, precariously placed between the worlds of the straight and the deviant, finally declared themselves different when they gathered in groups outside dance halls and on sea fronts). They *display* their own codes (e.g., the punk's ripped T-shirt) or at least demonstrate that codes are there to be used and abused (e.g., they have been thought about rather than thrown together). In this they go against the grain of a mainstream culture whose principal defining characteristic, according to Barthes, is a tendency to masquerade as nature, to substitute 'normalized' for historical forms, to translate the reality of the world into an image of the world which in turn presents itself as if composed according to 'the evident laws of the natural order' (Barthes, 1972).

As we have seen, it is in this sense that subcultures can be said to transgress the laws of 'man's second nature'.[3] By repositioning and recontextualizing commodities, by subverting their conventional uses and inventing new ones, the subcultural stylist gives the lie to what Althusser has called the 'false obviousness of everyday practice' (Althusser and Balibar, 1968), and opens up the world of objects to new and covertly oppositional readings. The communication of a significant *difference*, then (and the parallel communication of a group *identity*), is the 'point' behind the style of all spectacular subcultures. It is the superordinate term under which all the other significations are marshalled, the message through which all the other messages speak. Once we have granted this initial difference a primary determination over the whole sequence of stylistic generation and diffusion, we can go back to examine the internal structure of individual subcultures. To return to our earlier analogy: if the spectacular subculture is an intentional communication, if it is, to borrow a term from linguistics, 'motivated', what precisely is being communicated and advertised?

STYLE AS *BRICOLAGE*

> It is conventional to call 'monster' any blending of dissonant elements. . . . I call 'monster' every original, inexhaustible beauty. (Alfred Jarry)

The subcultures with which we have been dealing share a common feature apart from the fact that they are all predominantly working class. They are, as we have seen, cultures of conspicuous consumption—even when, as with the skinheads and the punks, certain types of consumption are conspicuously refused—and it is through the distinctive rituals of consumption, through style, that the subculture at once reveals its 'secret' identity and communicates its forbidden meanings. It is basically the way in which commodities are *used* in subculture which mark the subculture off from more orthodox cultural formations.

Discoveries made in the field of anthropology are helpful here. In particular, the concept of *bricolage* can be used to explain how subcultural styles are constructed. In *The Savage Mind* Levi-Strauss shows how the magical modes utilized by primitive peoples (superstition, sorcery, myth) can be seen as implicitly coherent, though explicitly bewildering, systems of connection between things which perfectly equip their users to 'think' their own world. These magical systems of connection have a common feature: they are capable of infinite extension because basic elements can be used in a variety of improvised combinations to generate new meanings within them. *Bricolage* has thus been described as a 'science of the concrete' in a recent definition which clarifies the original anthropological meaning of the term:

[Bricolage] refers to the means by which the non-literate, non-technical mind of so-called 'primitive' man responds to the world around him. The process involves a 'science of the concrete' (as opposed to our 'civilised' science of the 'abstract') which far from lacking logic, in fact carefully and precisely orders, classifies and arranges into structures the *minutiae* of the physical world in all their profusion by means of a 'logic' which is not our own. The structures, 'improvised' or made up (these are rough translations of the process of *bricoler*) as *ad hoc* responses to an environment, then serve to establish homologies and analogies between the ordering of nature and that of society, and so satisfactorily 'explain' the world and make it able to be lived in. (Hawkes, 1977)

The implications of the structured improvisations of *bricolage* for a theory of spectacular subculture as a system of communication have already been explored. For instance, John Clarke has stressed the way in which prominent forms of discourse (particularly fashion) are radically adapted, subverted and extended by the subcultural *bricoleur*:

Together, object and meaning constitute a sign, and within any one culture, such signs are assembled, repeatedly, into characteristic forms of discourse. However, when the bricoleur relocates the significant object in a different position within that discourse, using the same overall repertoire of signs, or when that object is placed within a different total ensemble, a new discourse is constituted, a different message conveyed. (Clarke, 1976)

In this way the teddy boy's theft and transformation of the Edwardian style revived in the early 1950s by Savile Row for wealthy young men about town can be construed as an act of *bricolage*. Similarly, the mods could be said to be functioning as *bricoleurs* when they appropriated another range of commodities by placing them in a symbolic ensemble which served to erase or subvert their original straight meanings. Thus pills medically prescribed for the treatment of neuroses were used as ends-in-themselves, and the motor scooter, originally an ultra-respectable means of transport, was turned into a menacing symbol of group solidarity. In the same improvisatory manner, metal combs, honed to a razor-like sharpness, turned narcissism into an offensive weapon. Union jacks were emblazoned on the backs of grubby parka anoraks or cut up and converted into smartly tailored jackets. More subtly, the conventional insignia of the business world—the suit, collar and tie, short hair, etc.—were stripped of their original connotations—efficiency, ambition, compliance with authority—and transformed into 'empty' fetishes, objects to be desired, fondled and valued in their own right.

At the risk of sounding melodramatic, we could use Umberto Eco's phrase 'semiotic guerilla warfare' (Eco, 1972) to describe these subversive practices. The war may be conducted at a level beneath the consciousness of the individual members of a spectacular subculture (though the subculture is still, at another level, an intentional communication) but with the emergence of such a group, 'war—and it is Surrealism's war—is declared on a world of surfaces' (Annette Michelson, quoted Lippard, 1970).

The radical aesthetic practices of Dada and Surrealism—dream work, collage, 'ready mades', etc.—are certainly relevant here. They are the classic modes of 'anarchic' discourse.[4] Breton's manifestos (1924 and 1929) established the basic premise of surrealism: that a new 'surreality' would emerge through the subversion of common sense, the collapse of prevalent logical categories and oppositions (e.g., dream/reality, work/play) and the celebration of the abnormal and the forbidden. This was to be achieved principally through a 'juxtaposition of two more or less distant realities' (Reverdy, 1918) exemplified for Breton in Lautréamont's bizarre phrase: 'Beautiful like the chance meeting of an umbrella and a sewing machine on a dissecting table' (Lautréamont, 1970).

In *The Crisis of the Object*, Breton further theorized this 'collage aesthetic', arguing rather optimistically that an assault on the syntax of everyday life which dictates the ways in which the most mundane objects are used, would instigate

> . . . a *total revolution of the object*: acting to divert the object from its ends by coupling it to a new name and signing it. . . . Perturbation and deformation are in demand here for their own sakes. . . . Objects thus reassembled have in common the fact that they derive from and yet succeed in differing from the objects which surround us, by simple *change of role*. (Breton, 1936)

Max Ernst (1948) puts the same point more cryptically: 'He who says collage says the irrational'.

Obviously, these practices have their corollary in *bricolage*. The subcultural *bricoleur*, like the 'author' of a surrealist collage, typically 'juxtaposes two apparently incompatible realities (i.e., "flag": "jacket"; "hole": "teeshirt"; "comb: weapon") on an apparently unsuitable scale . . . and . . . it is there that the explosive junction occurs' (Ernst, 1948). Punk exemplifies most clearly the subcultural uses of these anarchic modes. It too attempted through 'perturbation and deformation' to disrupt and reorganize meaning. It, too, sought the 'explosive junction'. But what, if anything, were these subversive practices being used to signify? How do we 'read' them? By singling out punk for special attention, we can look more closely at some of the problems raised in a reading of style.

STYLE IN REVOLT: REVOLTING STYLE

> Nothing was holy to us. Our movement was neither mystical, communistic nor anarchistic. All of these movements had some sort of programme, but ours was completely nihilistic. We spat on everything, including ourselves. Our symbol was nothingness, a vacuum, a void. (George Grosz on Dada)

> We're so pretty, oh so pretty . . . vac-unt. (The Sex Pistols)

Although it was often directly offensive (T-shirts covered in swear words) and threatening (terrorist/ guerilla outfits) punk style was defined principally through the violence of its 'cut ups'. Like Duchamp's 'ready mades'—manufactured objects which qualified as art because he chose to call them such, the most unremarkable and inappropriate items—a pin, a plastic clothes peg, a television component, a razor blade, a tampon—could be brought within the province of punk (un)fashion. Anything within or without reason could be turned into part of what Vivien Westwood called 'confrontation dressing' so long as the rupture between 'natural' and constructed context was clearly visible (i.e., the rule would seem to be: if the cap doesn't fit, wear it).

Objects borrowed from the most sordid of contexts found a place in the punks' ensembles: lavatory chains were draped in graceful arcs across chests encased in plastic bin-liners. Safety pins were taken out of their domestic 'utility' context and worn as gruesome ornaments through the cheek, ear or lip. 'Cheap' trashy fabrics (PVC, plastic, lurex, etc.) in vulgar designs (e.g., mock leopard skin) and 'nasty' colours, long discarded by the quality end of the fashion industry as obsolete kitsch, were salvaged by the punks and turned into garments (fly boy drainpipes, 'common' miniskirts) which offered self-conscious commentaries on the notions of modernity and taste. Conventional ideas of prettiness were jettisoned along with the traditional feminine lore of cosmetics. Contrary to the advice of every woman's magazine, make-up for both boys and girls was worn to be seen. Faces became abstract portraits: sharply observed and meticulously executed studies in alienation. Hair was obviously dyed (hay yellow, jet black, or bright orange with tufts of green or bleached in question marks), and T-shirts and trousers told the story of their own construction with multiple zips and outside seams clearly displayed. Similarly, fragments of school uniform (white bri-nylon shirts, school ties) were symbolically defiled (the shirts covered in graffiti, or fake blood; the ties left undone) and juxtaposed against leather drains or shocking pink mohair tops. The perverse and the abnormal were valued intrinsically. In particular, the illicit iconography of sexual fetishism was used to predictable effect. Rapist masks and rubber wear, leather bodices and fishnet stockings, implausibly pointed stiletto heeled shoes, the whole paraphernalia of bondage—the belts, straps and chains—were exhumed from the boudoir, closet and the pornographic film and placed on the street where they retained their forbidden connotations. Some young punks even donned the dirty raincoat—that most prosaic symbol of sexual 'kinkiness'—and hence expressed their deviance in suitably proletarian terms.

NOTES

[1] Although groups like London SS had prepared the way for punk throughout 1975, it wasn't until the appearance of the Sex Pistols that punk began to emerge as a recognizable style. The first review of the group which, for the press at least, always embodied the essence of punk, appeared in the *New Musical Express*, February 21, 1976. The most carefully documented moment of this early period was the Sex Pistols' performance at the Nashville in West Kensington in April, during which Johnny Rotten allegedly left the stage in order to help a supporter involved in a fight. However, it wasn't until the summer of 1976 that punk rock began to attract critical attention, and we can date the beginning of the moral panic to September 1976, when a girl was partially blinded by a flying beer glass during the two-day punk festival at the 100 Club in Soho.

[2] Although structuralists would agree with John Mepham (1974) that 'social life is structured like a language', there is also a more mainstream tradition of research into social encounters, role-play, etc. which proves overwhelmingly that social interaction (at least in middle-class white America!) is quite firmly governed by a rigid set of rules, codes and conventions (see in particular Goffman, 1971 and 1972).

[3] Hall (1977) states: '... culture is the accumulated growth of man's power over nature, materialised in the instruments and practice of labour and in the medium of signs, thought, knowledge and language through which it is passed on from generation to generation as man's "second nature"'.

[4] The terms 'anarchic' and 'discourse' might seem contradictory: discourse suggests structure. Nonetheless, surrealist aesthetics are now so familiar (though advertising, etc.) as to form the kind of unity (of themes, codes, effects) implied by the term 'discourse'.

BIBLIOGRAPHY

Althusser, L. and Balibar, E. (1968), *Reading Capital*, New Left Books.

Barthes, R. (1972), *Mythologies*, Paladin.

Breton, A. (1924), 'The First Surrealist Manifesto', in R. Seaver and H. Lane (eds.), *Manifestos of Surrealism*, University of Michigan Press, 1972.

———. (1929), 'The Second Surrealist Manifesto', in R. Seaver and H. Lane (eds.), *Manifestos of Surrealism*, University of Michigan Press, 1972.

———. (1936), 'Crisis of the Object', in L. Lippard (ed.), *Surrealists on Art*, Spectrum, 1970.

Burroughs, W. (1969), *The Wild Boys*, Caldar & Boyers.

Clarke, J. (1976), 'Style' in S. Hall, *et al.* (eds.), *Resistance Through Rituals*, Hutchinson.

Eco, U. (1972), 'Towards a Semiotic Enquiry into the Television Message', *W.P.C.S. 3*, University of Birmingham.

———. (1973), 'Social Life as a Sign System', in D. Robey (ed.) *Structuralism: The Wolfson College Lectures 1972*, Cape.

Ernst, M. (1948), *Beyond Painting and Other Writings by the Artist and His Friends*, ed. B. Karpel, Sculz.

Goffman, E. (1971), *The Presentation of Self in Everday Life*, Penguin.

———. (1972), *Relations in Public*, Penguin.

Hall, S. (1977), 'Culture, the Media and the "Ideological Effect"', in J. Curran *et al.* (eds), *Mass Communication and Society*, Arnold.

Hawkes, T. (1977), *Structuralism and Semiotics*, Methuen.

Lautréamont, Comte de (1970), *Chants de Maldoror*, Alison & Busby.
Levi-Strauss, C. (1966), *The Savage Mind*, Weidenfeld & Nicolson.
Lippard, L. (ed.) (1970), *Surrealists on Art*, Spectrum.
Mepham, J. (1974), 'The Theory of Ideology in "Capital"', *W.P.C.S.*, no. 6, University of Birmingham.
Reverdy, P. (1918), *Nord-Sud*.

Source: Dick Hebdige, *Subculture: The Meaning of Style* (New York: Methuen, 1979), pp. 23–26, 100–108.

38

"The Confessions of a Gay Rocker"

ADAM BLOCK

Since its very beginnings rock music has been extolled for its liberating and empowering qualities. It has provided a space wherein performers and fans have explored identities and played with societal conventions of gender and sexuality. In the early 1970s, for example, musicians from David Bowie and Lou Reed to the New York Dolls delved into androgyny and role-playing, sparking the glitter and glam rock movement. Yet as music critic Adam Block (1951–2008) points out in his essay written for gay lifestyles magazine *The Advocate*, rock musicians have rarely embraced an openly homosexual, public identity. Block's essay is essentially a travelogue examining the relationship between rock and gay identity, taking the reader through rock's first quarter century, stopping at the point in the early 1980s where MTV was beginning to introduce American audiences to a new wave of British musicians such as Soft Cell and Pete Shelley. Had Block written his article a year or two later he might have mentioned Culture Club's cross-dressing Boy George or Frankie Goes to Hollywood's gay anthem "Relax." Still, even considering these examples, and the many more that have followed, it is worth reiterating Block's comments and complaints even today, many decades later. To what extent has rock served as an expressive medium for gay performers? And in what ways has rock spoken to gay audiences?

JOHNNY ARE YOU QUEER?

In 1971 I was a teen-ager struggling with coming out. The scary part wasn't my family, and shucks, I knew I liked boys. The scary part was my music. "You can't be a homo," I kept thinking, "Homos don't like rock 'n' roll."

How was a kid raised on The Rolling Stones, The Animals and The Who supposed to relate to a world where the reigning deities seemed to be Judy Garland and Barbra Streisand, where polite conversation required a fascination with the minutiae of show tunes and opera? I figured you could always spot a homo by his record collection, and mine was a disgrace.

I had this nightmare: I would bring a male date home, and the mischievous tough would crouch on his haunches and flip casually through my LPs. Then he would cock his head suspiciously and demand, "You slumming or something, bub? I *know* you ain't gay. You don't even have a copy of *Stoney End.*"[1] Irrefutable.

Rock was more than the soundtrack of my youth. It was a shared secret language that linked me to every other fan. It was unnerving and invigorating: the sound of lust and revolt, passion and humor—a public triumph over my private fears and aspirations. The problem was that rock, for all its daring celebrations, stopped short at the ultimate taboo: Boys don't kiss boys. That had me spooked . . .

---

1 He is referring to Barbra Streisand's 1971 album release, *Stoney End*.

If homos didn't like rock, I couldn't swear that the feeling wasn't mutual. The only performers my friends agreed were fruits were Liberace and Wayne Newton. Hardly inspirational role models.

Despite my panic, I took the plunge. At first it looked as if none of this was a very big deal. The post-Stonewall baby boom hitting the bars in San Francisco in '71 didn't seem to know or care whether we were taken for hippies or homos. Our only demand of the music was that it be danceable, and from Loggins and Messina to "Brown Sugar," from Janis Joplin to "Shaft's Theme," that covered a lot of territory.

There *seemed* to be plenty of gay rockers out there, but you could look in vain for an openly gay rock star. Rock was still a part of mainstream culture: a place, as Vito Russo said of the movies, "where one learned to pass for straight, where one learned the boundaries of what America would accept as normal." The next year, I was in London and thinking about the ways that rock and gay lib touched each other, when those boundaries began to stretch to the breaking point.

MY OBSESSION, YOUR OBSESSION: WALKIN' IT LIKE YOU TALK IT

In the summer of '72 the British press was full of David Bowie, an admitted bisexual who was releasing his *Ziggy Stardust* LP and inspiring young boys to pile on the make-up and glitter. I read an account of a 16-year-old who said he felt strange getting a hard-on while he watched Mick Jagger perform. That made me grin.

"I think that teen-ager's hard-on says more about rock as gay lib than Bowie's notoriety," I told a fellow writer. "Bowie may be claiming the form, but a hard-on, that's *function*."

In fact, both said a lot. If the Gay Revolution never took hold in rock, that said as much about gay lib as it did about music. Rock's strongest appeals have always been more implied than overt: sly promises in a shared, secret language—ambiguous in the same way that sexual ambivalence can be. Forthright celebrations and denunciations were folkie tools that often preached to the converted. Rock was more shadowy and subversive; the walk often was the talk.

The fact is that to this day I can't think of one rock artist who has been gay and proud, erotic and liberating—seizing the airwaves and giving the boys boners. Many who claim to be bi or straight have touched on the subject in exciting ways, but the fear and resentment of gays and gay impulses run deep, and hip rock is no exception. I began to look for music that expressed those fears and even dismantled them. Rock was built by voices that wreaked havoc with a nation's notion of deviance and decency. I watched to see the impulses of rock cross paths with the fact of being gay.

IT'S THE SINGER, NOT THE SONG

That same summer of '72, Little Richard appeared at a rock revival show at Wembley Stadium. Mascaraed to the tits, under a lacquered bouffant, the self-proclaimed Georgia Peach was grotesque and a little magnificent. Though he was acting like an outrageous queen in the '70s, Little Richard had been an apparition in a zoot suit in '55—the man was beyond camp, beyond macho—he was rock 'n' roll.

Greil Marcus has written, "He disrupted an era, broke rules, created a form. Little Richard gave shape to a vitality that wailed silently in each of us until he found a voice for it. . . . I can only marvel at his arrogance, his humor, his delight: Delivering a new vision of America with music, and more people than anyone can count are still trying to live in it."

Arrogance, humor and delight have always been our most effective weapons against despair and censure. Little Richard danced over the abyss and that will stand.

Some racy novelty numbers featured gay players in the '30s and '40s (collected on Stash Records' *AC/DC Blues*), but gays were invisible in the rock and pop of the '50s and early '60s. Gays could stake a claim only on the unconscious camp of the girls and girl groups: Lesley Gore's "It's My Party and I'll Cry If I Want To," covered by a coolly fey Brian Ferry in '74; The Angels' "My Boyfriend's Back," recently released with a lisp by the Bee Jays; or The Crystals' "He's a Rebel," which would reemerge in '81 as an obscure gay novelty, "He's a Rabbi," by David Roter.

These camp readings were subversions of the aggressively heterosexual fantasies of the time: acts of comic revenge (enacted well after the fact) that inserted a gay presence into a territory that had carefully excluded us. Gays had to reinvent the songs if they were going to find a place in them. That began to change as the shock troops started arriving from the United Kingdom.

THE BRITISH INVASION

A decade after Little Richard burst upon the scene, a major rock band, The Rolling Stones, appeared in drag on a record sleeve. Camp and drag were comic traditions in England, but the rockers were willing to make them threatening.

Ray Davies, the ever fey and tough leader of The Kinks (get it?) was regularly limp-wristed and loony. His early ballad "See My Friends," sounded to some like a subtle homo lament, but it was *mighty* subtle and was never a hit. In 1970, however, he scaled the Top 10 with his music-hall celebration of an innocent seduced by a transvestite.[2] It was the first gay rock song; the first time I'd ever heard us perverts mentioned, let alone celebrated, on the radio.

Some of the gay input was coming from bands' managers. British critic Simon Frith writes, "The sharp, college-educated music pushers were, unusually often, homosexuals; their stars were given a surly, sensual, leather-boy appeal." None more so than The Rolling Stones.

Mick Jagger invented himself in a way that embodied contradictions: the middle-class student of economics playing leather tough; a white Brit singing black American music, a heterosexual who liked to flirt with boys. He made those juxtapositions exciting and liberating.

The Stones' gay manager, Andrew Loog Oldham, pushed the bad-boy image, fueled by sexual ambiguity. Oldham wrote a song (with guitarist Keith Richards) called "I'd Much Rather Be with the Boys," which was a bit much even for the danger boys. It was eventually released in '75 on *Metamorphosis*.

Jagger outdistanced even Oldham with his 1971 song "Cocksucker Blues," in which he crowed, "I need to get my cock sucked. I need to get my ass fucked." It is probably the greatest gay rocksong ever recorded, but you're not liable to hear it. It was written to be unreleasable, in order to settle a contractual obligation to a party whom Jagger had no intention of helping. Jagger's song spotlighted the phobia that he knew would prevent either release or success for the cut.

Brian Epstein, who discovered, groomed and managed The Beatles, was a middle-class homo. The band knew his predilections. When he mentioned to the lads that he was writing an auto-biography and asked if they had any suggestions for a title, John Lennon cracked laconically, "Yeah, how about *Queer Jew*?"

Epstein, closeted and unhappy, never mentioned his sexual bent in the memoir. A few years later he was dead from an overdose of sleeping pills. It's a shame that Epstein never lived to see the post-Stonewall era, when all those Beatle fans began to come out and demand a bit more breathing space.

In 1965 Tom Robinson was a schoolboy going quietly to pieces over his infatuation with another lad. He heard The Beatles on the radio sing: "Everywhere people stare,/Each and every day./I can see them laugh at me,/and I hear them say, 'Hey,/you've got to hide your love away.'" The song

---

2 The song described here is "Lola."

seemed to be addressed to him, just one more proof to Robinson that he was losing it. Years later he would learn that Lennon had written the song after a vacation in Spain with Epstein, and that Lennon considered it his first "serious piece of songwriting." Maybe Lennon had been singing Epstein's song, reaching out a hand to a gay friend. At the time it was only a glimmer to Robinson, who was institutionalized after he fell apart. Ten years later he would remember the incident, when he made a bid to be the first openly gay rock star.

In '67 some gays were finding a glimmer of recognition in The Rolling Stones' "Sitting on a Fence." Jagger sang: "Since I was very young I've been very hard to please./And I don't know wrong from right./But there is one thing I could never understand:/Some of the sick things that a girl does to a man./So, I'm just sitting on a fence." You could decide for yourself whether the fence-sitter was a bisexual or just a misogynist refusing to plunge in to marriage. But the Stones looked to be forever plunging.

The Stones aren't a gay group, but they have played with the fear and allure of faggotry with more wit and panache than anyone else in rock. Jagger's marriage of camp to macho expressed an ambivalence that wasn't willing to choose one over the other. Nevertheless, Jagger never exposed any male liaisons. He got married and had a kid.

For that matter, so did David Bowie. But Bowie *admitted* to sleeping with boys. In '72 he seemed poised to do the unthinkable—to bring rock and gay lib together. Bowie brought Lou Reed over to England to produce an LP for him and Reed promptly announced that he too was gay, though he too would later marry—twice.

The fact is that Bowie's sexuality has always been as cool and costume-like as the rest of his act. I saw him in his glitter heyday, when he was flirting with his lead guitarist and giving the instrument head. I saw the master of masks perform Brel's "My Death" in Dietrich drag, but as Bowie's ambitions grew, the gay trappings would fall steadily away.

GLITTER IN THE U.S.A.

I was back in the states by '73, primed to watch glitter-rock sweep the continent. Lou Reed scored with "Take a Walk on the Wild Side," and suddenly there were addicts, transvestites and hustlers lounging in the Top 20. Ziggy Stardust toured, while critics raved about the outrageous androgyny of the New York Dolls. Fourteen-year-old boys were filching their mommies' mascara as Bowie sang, "Rebel, rebel how could they know? Hot tramp, I love you so."

If gay lib and rock had seemed poised for an alliance in those heady days (gay libbers even asked Bowie to write them an anthem), well, the moment passed. It wasn't just that glitter-rock failed to penetrate the heartland, or that what did get through was more costume than conviction. The rub was that gays weren't dancing to "Rebel, Rebel," which peaked at #64 in the pop charts, but to "Don't Rock the Boat" by The Hues Corporation, which hit #1. While Bowie had been busy making waves, gays were nailing down a luxury suite on the ark.

In the first flush of Bowie's success American record companies rushed out to sign their own house homos. There was Jobriath (the American Bowie), Sylvester (as black glitter-rocker) and Steven Grossman (the gay James Taylor). All came out of the closet and headed straight for the bargain bins.

As gay glitter was consumed in its own glare, I was unnerved by this rear-flank attack. Gays, blacks and Latins hadn't tried to attack the mainstream—they were building a scene on the fringes: a place to meet and dance. Disco side stepped the world of rock prophets and celebrities. The artists were faceless, the stars were on the dance floor. Why worry about when the first rock star would come out on the radio? Boys were kissing boys in the clubs.

SECRET STRATEGIES

By 1975 I was feeling a bit schizophrenic. By day I was writing about rock, but at night the clubs were locked down by that divinely enforced rhythm track that even a spastic on two quaaludes could follow. Disco seemed like some secret gas—turn the stuff on and suddenly you were in a queer bar. I never brought it home. If my heart was in rock, well, at least my crotch was in the discos.

Pop music came on aggressively straight, but I was learning that that image masked significant gay input. I found that being gay was giving me the leap on pop culture. The catch was that you'd almost have to be in the know already to see how gays were making stars.

Because gays were outsiders, they could sidle up to a risky talent, inspire it, celebrate it and let it roll on out to the suburbs. The trick seemed to be that America loved the gay spirit of outrageousness for its entertainment value, as long as the sex part didn't intrude. Boys still didn't kiss boys.

—HERE IS YOUR THROAT BACK, THANKS FOR THE LOAN—BOB DYLAN

Three voices I'd first encountered as gay cult figures went national in '75. I had first heard Labelle in Paris in '72, where gay discos spun "Moonflower" with a vengeance.[3] In '75, the group swept to the #1 spot in the U.S. pop charts with "Lady Marmalade" and a glitter-disco stageshow.

In '75 Patti Smith released her debut LP, *Horses*, which opened with her lesbo-erotic version of "Gloria" and featured the explicit, poetic rape of schoolboy Johnny up against a gym locker, by a pretty tough. Smith became the bohemian darling of the rock press, and broke the pop Top 50.

Meanwhile, gay discos were alive with a Euro-import single by an unknown named Donna Summer. By the time "Love to Love You, Baby," was beginning its climb towards #2 in the pop charts, Summer had already been crowned as gay royalty: the Queen of Disco.

It wasn't just happenstance that these "gay discoveries" were all women. That was the tradition. Gay men could identify with the raptures women were allowed to indulge. The women could even impersonate and give voice to male fantasies, while remaining straight themselves. Even "liberated gays," who seemed uncomfortable with men singing openly to other men, offered scant encouragement to male artists who might be so inclined.

Labelle, Smith and Summer were early signals of two scenes developing on the margins, punk and disco. Gays were midwives to both. Each promised to lend us some visibility and maybe free some people from their soul-sucking fear of homosexuality. What I *hadn't* counted on was the punk and disco scenes developing into opposing armed camps.

DISCO DETENTE

By 1976, there seemed to be nothing *but* disco in gay bars, and I found that more than a little irritating. The ugly thing about disco was that it seemed to announce and enforce an overwhelming conformity. I'd always thought that the liberating secret of coming out was, "Hey, it's OK to be different": it hadn't occurred to me that homos might create a society as intolerant as the one they had escaped from.

Put simply, gays discovered disco while they were discovering one another. People came out to that split 4/4 beat in unprecedented numbers. The rhythm was reassuring, indomitable and danceable. After all the agony and hurt, all disco insisted on was seamless celebration.

---

3 Block most likely means Labelle's version of Cat Stevens's "Moonshadow."

Disco boasted an upfront gay star in Sylvester, who scaled the charts with "You Make Me Feel" six years after he had flopped as a glitter-rock wonder. Syl didn't get invited on by Merv and Johnny to talk about being gay, although he never concealed his homosexuality. Nevertheless, his songs made little direct reference to the subject.

If disco had any allegiance to gay liberation, you'd hardly have known it from the lyrics, unless you would settle for: "If it feels good, do it." Tell it to a fag-basher. I didn't hate disco, but it did set me to wondering if maybe I'd been right—that homos really *didn't* like rock 'n' roll.

Critic Ellen Willis wrote, "The difference was that rock and roll as a musical language was always on some level about rebellion, freedom, and the expression of emotion, while disco was about cooling out as you move up, about stylizing and containing emotion."

Disco did in fact represent a kind of rebellion. But if punk was out to rip off the emperor's clothes, disco intended to outdress the mother. Both wanted to subvert the social order; it was just that disco intended to beat society at its own game: flaunting the rewards that ads had always promised as the hallmarks of success (luxury, beauty, sex), while refusing to pay the price of abandoning faggotry. The fruits of capitalism and celebrity were celebrating and adorning the fruits themselves. As William Burroughs puts it, "Money is what the other guy has got."

PUNK IT UP

While disco was busily announcing a society of "insiders" appropriating the emblems of success, the punk scene emerged as a society of "outsiders" attacking those emblems. Disco perverted legitimacy. Punk made perversity legitimate. Homos who had grown up in the '60s flocked to both scenes. But if disco was upwardly mobile and coolly hedonistic, punk was downwardly mobile and aggressively nihilistic. Though both developed in alternative "fringe" music scenes, they came to view each other as the enemy. The diverse motley of homos that I had met in the bars in the early '70s were facing off against one another five years later. And a lot of the punks were as insufferably insular as their disco counterparts.

In 1978 Andrew Kopkind reported, "No one hates punk worse than a gay disco purist, and no one has more venom for disco than a gay punk."

When I had to pick a side, it was with the underdog punks who insisted that music could still be a scary brand of fun. Gay punks were rejecting both the mainstream rock and mainstream gay scenes. They were creating an arena that welcomed sexual ambiguity, revolt. They were also a declaration against mainstream gay stereotypes.

The Ramones, the original intentional cartoon of a three-chord garage band, kicked things off with "53rd & 3rd," the account of a gay hustler turned fag-basher. A Frenchman, Plastique Bertrand, had a hit with a punk-novelty number called "Ca Plane pour moi," Freely mistranslated by a Brit who called himself Elton Motello, it became "Jet Boy, Jet Girl," a savagely playful bit of homoerotica that made Bowie's "Rebel, Rebel" sound touchingly chaste. The maniacal British band 999 roared in with a tune that insisted, "Let's face it—the boy can't make it with girls."

None of these songs were hits, and only "Jet Boy, Jet Girl" even gained much notoriety, but they spotlight an aggressive brand of honesty that was missing from both mainstream rock and disco. It was a message even more clearly stated in the rage, music and humors than in the lyrics.

The scene was a haven for the musically and socially disenfranchised. Many of the band managers, club owners, D.J.'s and critics who helped create this alternate scene were gay. But it only produced one openly gay artist who made that fact unavoidable in his music.

Tom Robinson emerged in '78, when his embittered anthem "Sing If You're Glad to be Gay" became a surprise hit in the United Kingdom. Touring the United States during the height of

Briggs & Anita Fever,[4] he got a lot of interest from the press, but even in San Francisco he failed to draw crowds. Neither gays nor rockers turned out in force. Robinson was more earnest folkie than erotic rocker, and you couldn't dance disco to the anthems.

After a second LP, his band broke up, and Robinson cut a single with his own money—all proceeds to go to London's Gay Switchboard. Robinson even tried disco. Elton John wrote the music, a weak retread of "Philadelphia Freedom," and Robinson sang to a hot boy: "You know I hate to be salacious,/But it's hard to fight the feeling./Lechery can be such fun," while black girls chanted, "Sexist, Sexist." Who'd ever heard of a *rocker* worrying that horniness might not be politically correct? Let alone a disco queen? The noble failure nearly bankrupted the singer.

A subsequent band, Sector 27, put the politics on a back burner but failed to find an audience. He is currently working up material with his original guitarist. "Whenever I get depressed about the career," Robinson told me. "I can think about the letters I got—like the one from this kid in Ohio who was literally at the point of suicide when he heard "Glad to Be Gay" on the radio. Saving a life, that's something."

THE PATRICIA NELL WARREN OF POP?

In the late '70s songs written by and for straights, but specifically about homos, began to show up in mainstream pop. Rod Stewart's "Ballad of Georgie" arrived seven years after "Lola" broke the Top 10.

The most forthright and tender of the lot wasn't even written by a man. It wasn't rock or new wave. It wasn't even disco—just a waltz with a piano accompaniment. In the last verse she sang about two boys, "holding each other as young lovers do. To me they will always remain: untamed, unchained and unblamed. The altar boy and the thief,/grabbing themselves some relief."

"The Altar Boy and the Thief" was on an LP, released in '77, called *Blowin' Away*. It was intended as a big commercial bid for Joan Baez. Unfortunately it didn't sell. God knows what the "Kumbayah" crowd would make of it. I guess it was inevitable that a woman would be the one to write it, but it still astonished me.

I GIVE IT A 90. IT'S GOT A GOOD BEAT. I CAN'T DANCE TO IT

By the end of the decade, new wave and disco were occupying the same chart in Billboard. It was called the Disco Chart, but they might as well have labeled it the Gay Page because the queer bars were calling the shots in dance music. New-wave artists had kicked a hole in the bell jar of disco and staked a claim on the dance floor, and if many disco purists were as ferociously defensive as ever, and if lots of gay new-wavers still claimed that their knees locked when a disco tune came on, well there were artists breaking through in both camps. Prince, Grace Jones, The Go Gos, The Jacksons, Soft Cell and Pete Shelley were all showing up on any play-list that wasn't hermetically sealed in '81. If categories weren't exactly exploding, there was some hope that they could soon become too hopelessly confused to prove useful to anyone.

RADIO REVELATION AND TEEN-AGE PANIC

It was one of those hazy days late last summer, and I was propped up on my tar-and-pebbled San Francisco roof, feeling as Mediterranean as the circumstances allowed. The radio was tuned to KUSF.

---

4 Conservative California legislator John Briggs had launched an initiative to ban gays and lesbians from teaching in public schools; Florida-based celebrity Anita Bryant created the "Save Our Children" campaign to contest Dade County's newly passed gay rights ordinance.

They were playing the latest new wave and I wasn't really listening. A bright girl-group came on. They were singing about high-school heartbreak.

"When you asked for a date, I thought that you were straight. Johnny are you queer?" the girl demanded. I squinted at the radio, unbelieving. I hiked the volume. Then I laughed out loud.

The song was talking in the gum-chewing cadences of suburban teens, and it was admitting, plaintively and playfully, that homos in the high schools were confusing their girlfriends.

"Johnny Are You Queer," is a novelty—one silly, shocking bolt from the blue. But I hope that song reaches some kid off in Dubuque, feeling scared and baffled as he cranks up AC/DC and Van Halen on his radio and I hope it makes *him* grin. Because the song is also an anomaly. In 1982, rock and gay lib still rarely join forces on public airwaves. Ten years ago there weren't *any* high-school homos in rock, and I was the kid by the radio.

I'VE GOT SILENCE ON MY RADIO

The final irony may be that in the last decade rock has lost much of its significance as a shared voice, its power to define a passionate conspiracy among its young listeners. Today's teens seem more excited by a new video game than a new LP, and the current crop of stadium supergroups look to be competing with the ersatz firepower of the Asteroids Experience. Maybe I should be hoping for a gay Space Invaders, instead of a homo Springsteen.

Besides, the whole notion of a homo Springsteen sometimes seems hopelessly at odds with both gay and rock traditions. Both cultures favor innuendo—the suggestive attitude or lyric that makes the listener a conspirator in determining meaning. For gays, the choice has been camp over candor; for rockers, sly sexy promises over overt declaration.

Ambiguity forces the listener to think twice, to consider the alternatives.

Two current artists are combining these traditions in a way that just may disarm their mutual distrust. Soft Cell, a male duo who sound fabulously queer, scored with the song "Tainted Love"; and Pete Shelley (who casually admitted his bisexuality a couple of years back when he was with The Buzzcocks) beat all odds with the astonishing gay-inflected "Homosapien." Neither song became a radio hit, but they came close.

So with the kids becoming video zombies, and many gays and straights being shell-shocked after a decade of fashion wars, we may finally find a voice. It may not be bellowing the truth—just taking it for granted with arrogance, wit and delight. Turn it up.

Source: Adam Block, "The Confessions of a Gay Rocker," *The Advocate*, April 15, 1982, pp. 43–47.

IV

THE 1980s

39

Punk Goes Hardcore

Jack Rabid

Information about independent and local punk rock bands and culture circulated in the late 1970s via networks well off the radar of the mainstream music industry. One of the most important forms of punk journalism emerged in the shape of numerous fanzines written and produced by young, devoted fans. Punk fanzines were essentially small, self-published magazines, which were often printed as Xerox copies and distributed either for free or sold with a nominal cover charge. Musician and punk fan Jack Rabid started the *Big Takeover* (named after a Bad Brains song) in June 1980 as a modest two-page New York City publication. Since then it has grown into an internationally renowned biannual magazine totaling roughly 150 pages in length. In this excerpt from an issue celebrating the magazine's twentieth anniversary, Rabid takes a retrospective look at *Big Takeover* nos. 4 & 5 from 1981. The original fanzine text is presented in italics. Rabid's commentary, as well as reminiscences from former New York punk fan Geoff Hutchinson, is presented in plain type. Rabid details the emerging early '80s "hardcore punk" scene—a louder/faster version of the older punk sound, complete with a new type of slam dancing—as it developed on the West Coast and illustrates the glaring differences between punk in New York and Los Angeles.

THE BIG TAKEOVER, ISSUE FOUR, FEBRUARY 1981—JACK RABID

The first concert I saw out in L.A. was **Black Flag**[1] *at the Starwood. This band really deals in distortion. Their concerts are all potential riots. They are very imposing looking.* **Greg** *(guitar),* **Chuck** *(bass),* **Robo** *(drums), and* **Dez** *(vocals, succeeding* **Keith Morris** *and* **Ron Reyes**) *played all the songs off their two EPs. Their best song is 'Depression,' which can be found on* Decline of the Western Civilization, *a live compilation LP just released.*[2] *Next I saw* **The Circle Jerks**. *They're the best band in California as of now, which is amazing considering they just started less than a year ago. Their 14-song LP* Group Sex, *out this week, takes 15 minutes to play, but it's 15 minutes of superb, lightning-quick rock. (If you thought no one was as fast as The Bad Brains, check out "Red Tape" and "What's Your Problem.") I think they might even be better than* **The Dead Kennedys** *(see their "California Über Alles" single) and* **The Germs**, *whose singer,* **Darby Crash**, *just committed suicide last month. I saw many lesser known bands—***Gears**, **China White**, **Fear**, **Adolescents**, **UXA**, *etc.—all very exciting. It's super to see so many loud, fast bands in one city/area. Punk dead, indeed!*

The night before I returned home, I went to the Polish Hall to see Mad Society, The Runs, The Hits, and The Assassins. Upon arrival, I saw 1000 kids (!) milling about outside unable to get in

---

1 As is the *Big Takeover*'s custom, the editor, Jack Rabid, places all references to band and artist names in bold type.
2 Rabid is referring to *The Decline of Western Civilization*, the soundtrack to the 1981 L.A. punk documentary.

because it was already filled. Every color of hair, all dressed to kill. It was almost frightening. Black Flag made a surprise appearance to open the show at 9PM, but there were still more kids outside than in. Back outside, I was talking to my friend, photographer Glen Friedman from New York [he of the My Rules punk books since], when I saw a bunch of youths smashing the back windows. They would not be denied. Hundreds hurled themselves into the room through the broken glass. I re-entered the front just as the LAPD riot squad poured through the back entrance, clubs raised. This is when the violence really started, as the police began to club the kids. There was a stampede out the front to rival the Who concert, but I got out to see angered kids throwing chairs, stones, bottles, and bricks at the hall.[3] Within minutes, the place was surrounded by maybe 200 police cars, with a helicopter overhead lighting the area. I thought I was safe where I was: two blocks away, but I was wrong. The riot squad stormed around the corner, and one of the police brought his club crashing down on my head. I hit the ground and he started to kick me, a savage look on his face as he repeatedly screamed, 'Get out of here!' I took his advice.

Saturday, January 31, I went to Washington, D.C. to see an incredible Bad Brains/Stimulators gig at the 9:30 Club. Washington is a very California-type scene. There are many similarities in attitude and dress, as well as musical taste. I have never seen so many young punks in one place on the East Coast before. I felt that these kids also had been studying California audiences. With the first notes of 'Run, Run, Run,' these kids went wild, slamming into each other like L.A. They even hop onto the stage to dive bomb back in the crowd, like out there. At times, there were eight or ten people on the stage, leaping over one another and singer Patrick. I talked to as many people as I could. All told me that there are few things worth seeing in D.C., so when something like this happens they come from all over the region. The Bad Brains are the leading band, but new bands like S.O.A. and Minor Threat are emerging. The Bad Brains' show was exciting as only they can be. H.R., Darryl, Dr. Know, and Earl are really loved by the fans. They turned over the house for a second show with these two bands, which I was told is an unusual occurrence for D.C. Even the DJ was good (a first). He must have played six songs from Stiff Little Fingers' Inflammable Material *LP.*

Geoff Hutchinson, 2000

"In the summer of 1977 I had a camp counselor who was also a DJ at a college radio station. He was a bit aloof, and quite cool. At the end of the summer I asked him to name me one band that he thought was the best thing going, he said **Talking Heads**. As soon as I got home I bought *Talking Heads '77*. This was the start. Two months later my brother got a new stereo for his birthday, with a receiver. We soon discovered WFMU college radio of Upsala college in N.J.; we heard **Television**, **Patti Smith**, **Sex Pistols**, everything! Our lives were transformed. At that time you either liked **Led Zeppelin**, **Grateful Dead**, **Jethro Tull**, **Yes** or **E.L.P.** And your friends were the same as you."

"My friends and I liked **David Bowie**, that made us freaks! Kids yelled 'freaks!' at us in the halls of our high school."

"We suffered for our taste, but we really didn't care, we didn't like those dumb jocks anyway. The first show we saw was (except for Bowie), Patti Smith. I remember the power, it was scary to me. The intensity, the chords, Patti did a few monologues, she suggested getting really high, and then reading the book of *Revelations*! I tried it. It's very trippy."

"Soon after that we discovered the New York scene. The group that you always wanted to see was **Johnny Thunders' Heartbreakers**. There was such drama! You waited for hours for them to

---

3 There had been a stampede at the Who's December 3, 1979, concert at Cincinnati's Riverfront Stadium that resulted in eleven deaths.

get sufficiently high to get on-stage, and then it finally happened. It always started with this recording of bombs, and third Reich speeches and marching troops (*see the band's* Live at Max's *LP, though that's just an excerpt—Rabid*). We instantly tossed the tables of Max's to the sides, and began pogoing. The energy was ecstatic. A bunch of freaks dancing. For me, a kid from the lily white suburb of Summit NJ, this was paradise. There were gays, blacks, transsexuals, artists, everyone all dancing together. It was real freedom."

"In those days there were so few people interested in this new music, that when you saw someone dressed like you, you had an instant friend. We made lots of new friends that way. Riding the train in to New York, if you saw others dressed like you, you knew you could talk to them. That's how small the scene was. You knew you had a friend by sight, and we made lots of friends that way."

This egalitarian system lasted only for a few years, however. The dance at that time was the pogo, which was supposedly created by **Sid Vicious** (*still unsubstantiated, but very possibly true—ed.*). This dance was, as I viewed the scene, an all-inclusive dance. There was no skill, no violence. If you fell, everyone was there to help you up, and back in. Everyone could participate, and that was what it was about. Later, when slam dancing came about, people who didn't want to risk injury, especially girls, couldn't dance anymore. That to me was a death."

"As punk became more popular, non-freaks came into the scene. The Mudd Club was born. The Mudd Club was the first 'punk' club to have a red velvet rope at the door. Before the Mudd Club, if you knew about the event, then that was enough, you were cool enough to get in. I remember trying to see a show there, and not being let in by some self important asshole, who made some judgment about maybe my 'coolness' or something. I felt then that the truth had gone out of the scene."

"There are always people out here who are interested in creating a real reality, there was once a collective group called punks who had a dream together of creating a new society, but as things get popular, they get absorbed, or stolen by the general media. Things that are pure like that was, last only for a short time. I still look for them . . ."

Jack Rabid, 2000

[Issue No. 4 of the *Big Takeover*] contains the first small seeds of my disillusionment with the punk scene I'd been so excited about, seeds that would grow into an embittered divorce from it in less than two years. Los Angeles was my first glimpse of the future doom of a scene that had spawned so many tantalizing offshoots in a million different directions, from The Cramps and Suicide to Talking Heads to Ramones.

It is perhaps important to note that the New York scene I had literally grown up in was a smaller one and an older one. We as teens were *encouraged* to come up to the higher intellectual and creative level of veteran scene members in their 20s and 30s, and that was part of the excitement. (We in turn gave our teenage zeal and burgeoning knowledge and record collections.) The Stimulators, Mad, and Bad Brains shows had drawn 100–300 people at small clubs like Max's, Tier 3, CBGB, One Under, Botony, and Hurrah, while the newer young bands like our Even Worse, The Offals, Nastyfacts, and later The False Prophets drew maybe 40–50 friends.[4] The local bands we were following were lucky to even have a single out. There were no labels for them, and the local buzz and bigger label attention had long since passed punk bands–even the *New York Rocker* and *Trouser Press* didn't cover them.

---

4 Even Worse was a punk band that Rabid had started shortly before he began his fanzine.

So to see audiences in L.A. in the thousands, all kids even younger than I, was bewildering, to say the least. True, it was also enticing to see hot local punk rock bands of little renown drawing *huge crowds*–it was like some kind of alternative universe! (Even famous first-wave punk bands had played to small crowds prior to this, as noted in recent excellent books such as *Please Kill Me*, *From the Velvets to the Voidoids*, and *Make the Music Go Bang!*)

But at the same time, the violence, immaturity, and mob-mentality of the L.A. scene disgusted me. The riots, club and hall-destruction, and thuggish police beatings at the Whiskey Black Flag/ D.O.A. show, and at Baces Hall and Vex had been chronicled throughout 1980 in *Damage*.[5] Meanwhile, our contingent in New York were unable to understand how that could happen, since the New York cops never took any notice of us, and we never broke anything of note or caused any mayhem worthy of arrest. When I saw the incessant fights, slam-dancing, and wanton destruction of the venues for myself, and got beaten indiscriminately by the government's brightest crisis team to boot, it was more of an eye-opener than I had bargained for.

I remember driving back by myself to Santa Barbara that night in my parents' little Chevette, my head bleeding all over the seats, being as much revolted by the punks' blockheaded conduct (no wonder no clubs would let punk groups play there any more, as the Germs' manager lamented in the *Decline* movie—their "fans" were breaking every window, urinal, or chair they could smash), as I was over the brownshirt tactics of a helmeted police force with shields beating the hell out of skinny, unarmed 16-year-olds, *and really getting off on it*. My ribs ached from the boot-kicking, my head was woozy from the blow to the back of the head, and the shirt I had used as a towel was as much crimson as much as white.

Seeing me hurt, my usually punk-despising parents actually felt sympathy for me. The next day, the two-paragraph story in the *L.A. Times* said something like, "Five Officers Hurt in Punk Riot." Looking at the bloody shirt, I remember thinking, "Nice job of reporting, that" and even my folks had to allow from my eye-witness accounts the *Times's* story was a gross distortion.

The next day, I was on a plane home, thinking, "It's a good thing this stuff only happens in California, we have a much better scene back East!" It was like I was returning from barbarity to civilization, as strange as that sounds in reference to mean-streets-era New York. Yet only three weeks later I would discover, via that trip to D.C., that the L.A. scene *had* crossed the continent. Inaugural Dischord band Teen Idols had gone to L.A., seen the slam dancing and stage diving, and brought it back to D.C. with them. I had met Henry Rollins and Ian MacKaye at a Sham 69 show at Hurrah in December 1979, and had thought them as being just like me–part of the united U.S. punk scene. So it felt only natural to pass on news of their newer, as yet unrecorded bands, S.O.A. and Minor Threat in issue four. And though the 9:30 show *was* a blast, again, it seemed bizarre that they could get 300 *kids*, with nary a hint of post-college adults, for a show. Again, I was glad that our scene was more diverse and older. Even at 18, I knew I wanted to go to the next level, to the next course, not wallow in what I'd already passed through.

But this diversity and maturity connected to underground punk scenes was not to last, as becomes more plain in subsequent issues. The D.C. kids and the soon-to-be-touring L.A. bands would change punk to hardcore and then to thrash; would scare away all the open-minded older folks with more varied interests who had also supported punk; would soon even scare away punk fans like me, and would finally pave the way for a scene that resembled the worst aspects of junior high school, in place of the post-grad art school madness and sexual/creative smorgasbord it had once been.

---

5 *Damage* was a San Francisco-based punk fanzine.

I saw the fetid future coming for the first time at the Whiskey, at the Starwood, at Polish Hall, and at 9:30, though I'd somehow thought it would never come to roost in my town. Fortunately, there were at least two years left before the rot would set in completely and altogether engulf this great scene. I was still taking pride in the frowning stares I got from the passengers on the Greyhound from Easton to D.C. and back–a miserable journey otherwise. It was nice, then, to think you could really shake someone up by daring to dress as you pleased, and I thought it was wonderful to surprise people who'd made up their minds, by being well-spoken. It added to my later sorrow in seeing something noble become a self-parodying mirror of the media's image of it.

In any case, this somewhat emotional issue four also marked the first grain of an editorial comment in *BT*. On the next issue I would feel compelled to break into the first actual editorial. From now on, as thorns began appearing among the roses, I would find myself driven to address these issues as well as the music that still inspired the publication.

Donald typed up issue four and printed it in on yellow paper, and I signed it, as I had the previous two issues. It seemed like a good arrangement, but it wasn't to last. All I was doing after writing the issues was taking the copies wherever I went, to clubs and stores, leaving little stacks of them on the jukebox at Max's or at 99 Records, and giving them to folks I knew. It was a lot easier than the weeks of distribution efforts these days! Come to think of it, it takes a little longer than one day to write the mag these days now, too.

THE BIG TAKEOVER, ISSUE FIVE, MARCH 1981

*Sat. March 14, was the New York debut of **Black Flag**, at Peppermint Lounge. Seeing them here was considerably different than seeing them at the Starwood or the Polish Hall in L.A. They were much looser here. **Mission of Burma** from Boston opened, the less said of them the better (a great band that played like shit! . . . expected more). [Note: they played 1000 times better at subsequent New York shows, removed from the hardcore context, blowing everyone away.] Black Flag came out and started with "Damaged." But first they spent a long time tuning. They made a lot of noise with their big amps, and they played loud and trebly.*

*There were a lot of people at the **Black Flag** show from Washington, D.C. there, many I recognized from the **Bad Brains/Stimulators** show at the 9:30 Club in January. I must admit I was a little upset at their attempts to turn the dance floor into the mess that it is in L.A. C'mon fellas, this was the Peppermint Lounge, not Hollywood, and the so-called "hippies" (basically anyone who wasn't dancing, and a few who were) did not get in your way. It seems to me pretty ridiculous that people should be attacked for the crime of dancing with the wrong outfit or haircut, and moreover, people have the right to stand off to the side and just watch if they so choose, and to go out of your way to bother them is a stupid, macho, phony trip. Dancing in front of the stage where I could watch the singer, **Dez**, I was and am more interested in seeing the band than in seeing how many people I could annoy, injure, etc. I enjoyed the band and I hope they come back soon, but I hate to see this kind of fake toughness going on. As one person stated, 'If you're so tough, go take on a Hell's Angel, their hair is longer than yours.' If you guys insist on this bullshit attitude then we may as well forget all the positive aspects of our scene and chuck the whole thing out the window. And may a "hippie" beat the living shit out of you.*

Jack Rabid, 2000

Well, there you have it, the very first *Big Takeover* editorial! A one-paragraph rant. I've always been happy in retrospect that it was on the malignant evil of slam dancing, and was penned only two days after its first sighting in New York. I'm proud of being on record as despising this squalid practice right from the first moment it raised its foul head here, and recognizing from the first its potential to destroy a vibrant underground music scene just beginning to get a national footing.

To this day, nothing has done more to hurt the spread and growth of underground music of any real aggression. Idiotic slam-dancing turns off people who 1) have brains, 2) are over the age of 19, 3) just want to see a band and dance and have fun, as we had for years at "punk" shows before then, and 4) are women or smaller men who want to stand anywhere near a stage. (I might add that all-male shows are pathetic and unappealing. Going to punk gigs since 1983 has ever felt like a testosterone-addled circus.) It's a loathsome, immature, inconsiderate, gig-ruining anti-sport that is grievously still with us 19 years later; though thankfully it's *finally* much in decline in nightclubs (though still in full force at giant shows for macho jocks and angry suburban kids).

Thus, March 14, 1981 was the day the once valiant punk rock scene of New York City was infected with a fatal virus. It was initially an annoying trifle, but over those next two years the disease grew and punk went from a profound inspiration to a childish exercise not worth defending. There were (and still are) great bands that were worth getting excited about. And as fans and as a magazine, we have always tried to separate great bands from the dull-witted supporters they've drawn. But something that was once so "unhealthily fresh" (to borrow a Howard Devoto phrase) was now worse than a seventh grade fist-fight where everyone surrounds the combatants and yells "fight, fight!" instead of breaking it up. The music and its message disappeared that day in the melees in front of Black Flag . . . It became just background music to the fracas.

This was also the first incidence of large numbers of "skinheads" (most from D.C.) at a New York gig. Until then, most punks in the East had hair of varying length. There was no uniformity in dress, hairstyles, or tastes. This also vanished. Though not all members of the human race with extreme crew cuts in punk rock garb were or are dolts, it's a prejudice that's been hard to shake since. To think that it was the D.C. skinheads, some of whom would go on to underground fame and to repudiate such inherently gangish, violent behavior who were going out of their way to slam into anyone that didn't fit their purist punk rock parameters. Talk about your "Star-Belly Sneetches."

Not surprisingly, the dance floor at this show was ugly: Dozens of "long-hair" (ha!) New Yorkers who'd never heard of West Coast slam-dancing were quite surprised to have people viciously hurtling into them out of nowhere. The New Yorkers responded with angry fists, so fights broke out all over the dance floor of the Pep. It was something out of The Ruts' "Staring at the Rude Boys." Going home covered in bruises (even though I'd retreated to the balcony after a few songs), I remember being more upset than I had even three months before when I'd been clubbed by the L.A. SWAT team. This was home, not some foreign war theater.

As slamming was to catch on (particularly after Fear played *Saturday Night Live* seven months later, with these same D.C. kids slamming their sad brains out), and a new breed of much younger kids made it a staple, it was sad to see an entire cluster of 20 and 30-year-olds *vanish* from punk rock shows, making subsequent punk gigs seem even more like a high school field trip for the worst elements of the school. And with this aging-down came the inevitable dumbing down. I am glad I spotted it right from the first, and said so in print.

A cultural force that surrounded the most feral rock 'n' roll in history was now in the process of being lost, after a nice six-year run, 1976–1982. The music has survived since, but only barely.

Source: Jack Rabid, "The Big Takeover: The Punk Rock Years, 1980–81," *The Big Takeover,* no. 47 (2000), pp. 53–55, 164.

40

College Rock

"Left of the Dial"

GINA ARNOLD

R.E.M., The Replacements, Camper Van Beethoven: by the end of the 1980s it was not uncommon to find alternative bands like these lumped together under the generic label of "college rock." As one can surmise from the following excerpts from Gina Arnold's book *Route 666*, this association reflected not only the popularity of these bands among college-aged audiences, but also the crucial exposure they had received from college radio airplay. Arnold, a prominent rock critic and academic whose work has appeared everywhere from the *Los Angeles Times* to *Rolling Stone*, approaches the topic from a personal perspective, beginning her narrative as a teenager listening to KSAN-FM, San Francisco's legendary, progressive station. KSAN, however, would eventually be swallowed up by Metromedia Inc., an act which prompts Arnold to symbolically pass the "progressive" torch along to the numerous college stations that since the late 1970s have represented one of the last bastions of free-form radio. Arnold portrays college radio as a social setting populated by outcasts and adventurous souls, unrestricted by formatting concerns and rigid playlists. Reflecting on her own experiences as a DJ during the 1980s, she describes the typical college station record library as a vast reservoir filled with the latest American underground bands, all of them connected in some way to a thriving network of regional scenes spread across the entire country.

Once upon a time, radio was a sound salvation. It played all the time, in the kitchen, in the bedroom, on the pool deck, in the car. The tinny pop chug-a-lug wired the air around it with bright-minded echoes of retro romance and fakey fun, filling up the empty blue space that envelops all suburbia with the simplest of all possible remedies for boredom: a beat. You had your little radio on all the time, night and day, and it brought you something rich and nimble: dumb ideas and wacky fantasies, pretty pieces of movable furniture for your headroom, private and possibly ridiculous visions of a lovesexy life. I even used to like the way songs were repeated over and over all week long in high rotation: they changed so gradually, like the seasons, till suddenly, months later, you noticed you never heard your favorite anymore. Oh, when television was static and unreal and movies so hard to belong to, there was always the radio to light up your inner life. Inside its plastic confines, song followed sweet song, day in and day out. You turned each other on.

But one day the radio died. Disco killed it. In Frederic Dannen's book *Hitmen*, he describes the complex record company machinations that led to a monetarily based system of radio formatting so constipated and corrupt that any new record of merit or imagination without a large budget behind it would have no way of being played.

Add to that the mechanization that developed in the late seventies and early eighties: autoprogramming, which eliminated the fine art of disc jockeying. Then there was a simultaneously disturbing rise of personality radio, plus the demographic polarization of the charts into the separate worlds of Black (Urban), AOR (Album-Oriented Rock, or seemingly, Always on the Radio), and CHR (Contemporary Hit Radio). Rock 'n' roll radio was ruined. To quote Abba, who shut down around the same time, no more carefree laughter. Silence ever after.

Throughout the seventies my brother and sister and I listened to two stations: KFRC-AM, the trashy top-forty station that was the only one we could get in our mother's dumb Barracuda, and KSAN-FM, the ground-breaking free-form AOR station that had, once upon a time, led American radio out of a thicket of quick hits and, in 1977, jerked our attention toward punk rock.

We loved KSAN so much. Its deejays (Bonnie Simmons, Tony Kilbert, Beverly Wilshire), its music (from Bruce Springsteen to Bob Marley to the Clash to the Talking Heads), its spirit, its live broadcasts from the Savoy Tivoli and Winterland, and its unspoken conviction that rock 'n' roll music still had meaning in this world, in spite of the marketplace. It was the soundtrack to San Francisco: to Armistead Maupin's *Tales of the City*, which we read serialized in the *Chron* every morning, to the free Pearl Harbor and Tubes shows we'd periodically see at Embarcadero Center, to tooling up Columbus Avenue after an afternoon spent browsing at Tower Records on Bay.

Always, my favorite deejay—my whole family's favorite deejay—was Richard Gossett. Vocally, he was almost a stereotype of the laid-back FM deejay made fun of on "Saturday Night Live" and the movie *FM*: a low, even boy's voice, muttering into the night. He was funny, in a dry sort of way, and often sounded stoned (or so my brother, who knew about such things, postulated gleefully). But what I liked best about Richard was his music. It was on his show—weeknights, six to ten—that I first heard Elvis Costello, the Jam, the Police, Television, Talking Heads, and the Clash. He played a lot of Michael Jackson, Graham Parker, and Toots and the Maytals. And there was a long time when his favorite song was "You're the One That I Want," by John Travolta and Olivia Newton-John. He used to segue it into "Rockaway Beach" by the Ramones all the time, thus unwittingly teaching me everything I needed to know about the magic art of radio programming. Rule number one: there are no real borders between genres and artists, only pretend ones, born of stupid snobbery and fashion. Rule number two: act on that principle alone, and you'll be all right.

When I went away to college in Los Angeles, I used to irritate my entire dorm by talking incessantly about how great KSAN was: how much better was its musical taste, how superior were its deejays, how much more fun it was to listen to in general than the bland white sound of L.A.'s monster rock stations. I couldn't walk into a room that had KMET or KLOS on its dial (inevitably playing tracks from Supertramp's *Breakfast in America*, an LP I can't hear without thinking of that time) without starting in on my long sad story: KSAN this, KSAN that, and how in San Francisco the Ramones play for free in Embarcadero Center . . . information to which everyone at UCLA's unanimous response was, *So?*

But by the time I came home, KSAN sounded different from what I remembered: more staid, less adventuresome, filled with a new, oppressive atmosphere that permeated its offices and came right through the receiver. It seemed that while I'd been away, they'd been sold to an entertainment conglomerate, Metromedia, Inc., which had instituted a number of changes, including a stiff playlist. Rumor had it that Richard Gossett was fired for not adhering to it: one day, in defiance of it, he played the Clash's "Complete Control," and that was the end of that. (If this rumor's not true, please don't ever tell me.) You know, it's right what they say about how you can't go home again.

KSAN struggled on as a corporate giant for a couple of years before turning into a country-and-western station. Richard Gossett got various shifts in one or two other places, but wound up getting a job at the Anchor Steam Brewery. And instead of sticking to the stiff new formats that were emanating from the corporate ogre, I, like so many other people in those fateful years, turned to the left of the dial.

College radio stations had, of course, always existed in some form or another—as a training ground for electrical engineers and as an extracurricular activity for campus-bound newsies, sportifs, and queers. By the mid-seventies, following the trend of the post-hippie music world, many such stations boasted late-night radio shows hosted by collegiate music fiends who delighted in playing the longest tracks off albums by obscure British art bands: Pink Floyd, Gentle Giant, Caravan. But when mainstream radio lost its grip on music, then the long-dormant airwaves of the college radio stations (reserved for years for *um*-ridden play-by-plays of intercollegiate football games) at schools ranging from the University of Texas and the University of Kansas to Upsala College in Orange, New Jersey, and to the University of San Francisco and U.C. Berkeley, where I was, began simultaneously to create new music programs that dealt more competently with the rest of radio's insufficiencies.

And suddenly—not gradually at all, but quite suddenly—those stations became an invaluable American network, linking the nascent punk rockers of each city to one another, and providing all the bands within a community with a way in which to prosper. Years later, while dining at an industry conclave with R.E.M. and a bunch of record company VIPs, Peter Buck asked the collected party how many had worked in college radio. Every single person present at the table—twenty-five or so, ranging from journalists and mainstream deejays to industry execs, record store clerks, and musicians, including a couple of Buck's own friends—raised a hand.

In some ways, the story of college radio has been like a fairy tale come true—or, at the very least, a made-for-TV movie: the geekiest, most unpopular nerds at the college decide to barricade themselves into a closet and start a gonzo radio station, alienating their more popular peers and professors by blaring out noisome, underproduced garage rock featuring the F word and worse. But the radio station struggles on, the geeks grow up and prosper, and *voilà!*, the records they've been playing—by U2, the Cure, R.E.M.—go platinum! The deejays get hired to positions of influence by major record companies! The airwaves have been won back by the righteous, and rock 'n' roll will rule again.

Oddly enough, that's almost exactly how it happened. For a while there in the early eighties, college radio really was our sound salvation. It, after all, still played free-form radio, nipping expertly from James Brown to James Chance, from Fairport Convention to the Slits, soundtracking not just the hits of the moment but the history of rock, giving it some context, teaching its listeners its secrets, creating an interior world of newfound glamour and romance and escape. And they provided an outlet for all the record nerds and frustrated musicians to meet each other, enabling them to form a community of misfits, maybe twenty people per town, generally just enough people to tempt bands to the area, to play whichever VFW hall or old-man bar was willing to allow them on the premises. And lastly, the stations, such as they were, became the inevitable conduit for all the independently released records to be given their due. They played the unheard music.

The college radio effect happened at the same time in obscure tiny towns all over America—at Oberlin in Ohio, at Florida State, at Evergreen in Olympia, Washington . . . anyplace where there was a bunch of bored and frustrated white kids with large record collections, and one kid in particular with the will to make things happen. But Boston was the city where this all happened in the most concentrated manner, and where the significance of college radio began to take on a larger meaning. Thanks to a predominance of colleges—some, like Harvard and MIT, containing far more than their share of record geeks and electrical whizzes—plus a proximity to New York City, it became a hotbed of punk rock early on. As early as 1976, WTBS (later called WMBR) at MIT had begun running the first punk rock show in America. And then, not surprisingly, since Boston is a city overrun with hypercompetitive overachieving white kids, Harvard's college station, WHRB, followed suit. Pretty soon, every significant college station in Boston—Harvard, MIT, Emerson, and Boston College—had its own resident punk rock show.

Scott Becker was a freshman at Tufts University in Boston when he tuned in to "Shakin' Street," the late-night proto-punk program on Harvard's WHRB, in 1977.[1] "I remember I heard the New York Dolls, and then the Ramones, for the very first time on the radio, and it shocked the hell out of me. That guy got the Pistols' import 45's first of everybody. Shortly after that, Oedipus, who back then had pink hair and a 45 adaptor tattooed on his shoulder, started doing a punk rock show on MIT's station, and pretty soon, every college in Boston had a punk rock show on their station.

"Before that, when I was in high school in Connecticut in the mid-seventies, the AOR station seemed so hip," recalls Becker. "But then suddenly it started to dawn on me that it wasn't that hip at all. It was punk rock that did it. It was just clear that there was the whole new scene and all these new labels and exciting new records, and commercial radio just rejected it, totally."

Becker describes himself as a high school recluse. "I just loved radio, way more than TV. I don't know what other kids did after school, maybe played football or smoked pot, but I ran home and listened to the radio for hours and hours and hours." When he applied to Tufts, one of his main concerns was the on-campus station, WMFO. But as a freshman, he found himself too shy to volunteer. "I went to a couple station meetings, but everybody knew each other and I was too out of it."

Happily, as a sophomore, his next-door neighbors were involved. By the end of the year, he was music director and, he recalls laughingly, part of an embattled cabal, immediately tied up in a serious intrigue. His first priority at the station was to emphasize and add records such as those from the nearby Rounder Records label—a specialty label featuring bluegrass, blues, and a new record by George Thorogood and the Destroyers—to the playlist. "We were ten watts, no guidance, no faculty advisor, no money, and no one got paid, and whenever we asked the student council for money, they'd go, 'Well, don't you get free records?' For us to just be on the air was really an accomplishment. We went from trying to imitate an AOR station to making our own."

Tufts's station wasn't as punked out as larger Boston college stations (though, Becker recalls, there was a gradual shift: "'Less Dead—more Ultravox' was our rallying cry"). Instead, its main concern, Becker recalls, was remaining free-form. "That didn't mean a person could play anything they wanted," he notes, "it meant playing a broad mix of different kinds of music. That was the ongoing philosophical debate of the era. We'd get into these big arguments with the student body 'cause they thought the music we played was weird. There was always a lot of politicking and intrigue around the station management. Someone was always trying to boot the general manager and put someone else in his place. But our main point of argument was specialty programming. We had an all-Portuguese hour, which served a really large local Portuguese-speaking community, and the student body was always going, 'But no one here speaks Portuguese!' And we had an R & B show that was real alien to white middle-class kids, that played the worst kind of disco and 'quiet storm' stuff."

These kinds of debates are still going on at college stations around the country, though in these trying times, merely getting funding for something as anachronistic as radio is difficult enough without adding in the trials of keeping programming consistent.

*   *   *

By the time I started working at a college radio station in late 1983, R.E.M. had two and a half records out, the EP *Chronic Town* and two LPs, *Murmur* and *Reckoning*, on the independent label IRS. Me, I'd just crawled back from college, having just spent every penny I ever managed to scrape together on bumming around Europe, and now I had to live in my old bedroom and be persecuted

---

1 Becker would go on to publish the influential alternative music magazine *Option* from 1985 to 1998.

by the specter of adulthood and feel incredibly embarrassed and inadequate because I did not have a life. (This is my mom: "Honey, have you ever considered technical writing? My friend's daughter has a degree in English from Stanford and she's making thirty grand at Apple!") Instead of something proper like that, I had a stupid job stage-managing *Peter Pan* at the local children's theater, putting on the Indians' makeup and making all the Lost Boys hush.

So just for fun, I volunteered at the college radio station, putting together their little program guide, and deejaying four-hour fill-in shifts beginning at midnight. But I was never a very good deejay. I was almost entirely ignorant of everything between the Buzzcocks and Howard Jones. I could play the Ruts, but Wire had passed me by. It was only newfound love of R.E.M. that made it all right that I didn't know any songs by Freur, that I didn't understand why people thought the Birthday Party were a good band, that I had never heard of the Minutemen. The only thing I knew about was circa 1978 punk rock—The Clash, the Jam, the Ramones, and the Undertones—plus a little Elvis Costello, the Pretenders, Television, and T Heads, stuff like that. I wasn't adventurous enough with the new stuff, plus I hated the sound of my own voice, I'd be OK for an hour or two, playing my favorites by Gang of Four and XTC, but the last ninety minutes would be sheer hell, searching among the C library, pulling out "Burning for You" by Blue Oyster Cult or something by Stiff Little Fingers, Then I'd get pretty darn slipshod, hurling the headphones down on old album covers, or throwing the longest song I knew, "Marquee Moon" by Television, on the turntable in order to finish up some novel or the new *Rolling Stone*.

That's what I was doing the day I had my great Amerindie revelation; hunching up on the deejay stool, monitor on loud, headphones off, seven or so minutes into the great masterpiece by Television. I was reading *Record* when I came across a quote from Peter Buck in an article about R.E.M. that completely turned around my way of thinking about rock. He said: "I guarantee that I have more records from 1983 in my collection than any other year. I mostly buy independent records by American bands, and there's a lot of good ones. All over the country we go, and every town has at least one really top-notch group. Maybe they're too uncompromising or maybe they're all not pretty boys, or maybe they're just weird. From Los Angeles, which has a million good bands now—Dream Syndicate, Rain Parade, Black Flag, Channel 3, Minutemen—to the Replacements and Hüsker Dü from Minneapolis, Charlie Burton and the Cutouts from Nebraska, Charlie Pickett and the Eggs from Ft. Lauderdale, Jason and the Scorchers from Nashville, there are good bands all over America doing exciting things, and no one really hears them."[2]

Well, there I was, surrounded by all the records he mentioned. What would you have done? I leapt off my stool and shoved aside my boring old punk rock picks—a song by X Ray Spex, the new one by the Smiths ("Jeane"). I scrabbled frantically among the vinyl. Headphones on, I carefully re-cued. And the next minute I was on the air, reading the above-mentioned paragraph aloud, before bopping the button, before turning up the news. *Don't know what to do when pink turns to blue . . .*"

That winter Hüsker Dü played a benefit for the station in the cafeteria, and before I knew what had happened, I'd suddenly become an Amerindie devotee, shunning all things British, dreaming of a world full of kudzu and mimosa and people who shopped at the Piggly Wiggly. Then suddenly it was spring, and me and my friend Francesca, renamed Jane from Occupied Europe and Divine Discontent, began hosting an early-morning show once a week that was entirely devoted to the American underground. Midwest and South, the Northeast and Texas, portions of the country we'd never thought about in our California cloud, took on all this significance in our poor little geographically deprived brains. No longer did we long to go to Paris or Tahiti; instead we pined

---

2 The quote is from Anthony Decurtis, "An Open Party: R.E.M.'s Hip American Dream," *Record*, June 1984, p. 62.

for Athens and Minneapolis and Boston, creating in our minds' eyes a new America where every small town contained exactly four cool people and one large garage. Elvis Costello went by the wayside in our fury to follow Buck's advice. We played everything he'd told us to and then some, ranging from across the map of the United States with exactly the same results he'd foretold. From Boston, Mission of Burma and the Lyres and the Neats. From the New York/New Jersey area, the Feelies and the Bongos and the Individuals and the Dbs. From Ohio, Pere Ubu and Human Switchboard. The Violent Femmes, from Milwaukee, Wisconsin. The Windbreakers, from Mississippi. Defenestration and the Embarrassment, both from Lawrence, Kansas. We played the Woods and Let's Active and the Dbs and the Young Fresh Fellows, the Wipers and the Fastbacks and the Pontiac Brothers and more. We played Savage Republic and Redd Kross and the Meat Puppets, Camper Van Beethoven and 10,000 Maniacs, TSOL, Minor Threat, Black Flag, Soul Asylum. We played everything that came our way as long as it was American, and Buck was right: it was all really, really good.

And so, girls and boys alike, from coast to coast, we were spoken to not by the band's members, but by its music, heard live, heard not in our brains but deep down in our souls. Listening to R.E.M. was like watching the landscape flicker by on a train from the inside, not the sexual rock'n'roll churning of Aerosmith, Jeff Beck, and Muddy Water's "Train Keep A Rolling,"[3] but the prismatic impressionism of "Driver 8" and everything that came before it: Television, the Velvet Underground, Tom Petty, the Byrds. "Come on aboard, I promise you, we won't hurt the horse," sang Stipe on a B side called "Bandwagon," and that welcoming gesture, that basic ethic of hospitality was what really distinguished R.E.M. from both its predecessors and its peers. Throughout the early eighties, other alternatively oriented artists talked incessantly about avoiding the bandwagon: busting trends, keeping clean, not selling out and just generally being hipper than the masses. R.E.M. just invited everyone to come along for the ride.

Source: Gina Arnold, *Route 666: On the Road to Nirvana* (New York: St. Martin's Press, 1993), pp. 21–25, 61–63.

---

3 Arnold most likely has in mind Tiny Bradshaw's version of "Train Kept A Rollin," covered most notably by the Yardbirds and Aerosmith.

41

"Roll Over Guitar Heroes; Synthesizers Are Here"

JON YOUNG

A paradigm, as philosopher and popular music studies scholar Theodore Gracyk explains, is "an exemplary case or body of work around which a community organizes its practices and beliefs."[1] In the case of rock music, paradigms can emerge through specific artists (the Beatles), recordings (the Ramones' first album), or even entire genres or styles (disco). At the time of its greatest popularity in the early 1980s, few paradigms rivaled the growing use of synthesizers associated with the rise of important new wave groups like Depeche Mode and Soft Cell, both of whom had jettisoned guitars and drums entirely in favor of the new technology. Exploring the attitudes and aesthetics of the new synthesizer bands, Jon Young's article for *Trouser Press*—one of the only magazines of the era with a specific new wave orientation—provides a thorough overview of the newly emerging style. As Young points out, synthesizers had already been established in the 1970s through such virtuoso progressive rock keyboardists as Keith Emerson and Rick Wakeman. The new generation of musicians that Young profiles, however, had generally renounced the "synthesizer solo" as an outmoded venue of expression, turning instead for inspiration to punk's DIY ethos and the more minimal sounds of creative experimentation of groups like Kraftwerk. Like many paradigms, the prominence of synthesizers in rock began to wane by the beginning of the 1990s, only to appear once more in the 2000s as various groups looked back to the 1980s as a point of musical inspiration.

Not a day goes by when you don't press a button, whether it's for a cup of coffee or to turn on the stereo or video. People are so surrounded now by electronics, of course there's electronic music.

—**David Ball of Soft Cell**

When Devo first sputtered onto the scene in 1978 they were fond of announcing in interviews that eventually they would give up guitars and switch over to synthesizers exclusively. Devo's provocative, revolutionary idea, however, was already accepted in England: the Human League, Gary Numan, Orchestral Manoeuvres in the Dark and other daring souls had begun mounting projects that would disregard the guitar's long dominance in rock in favor of a box of wires that made strange sounds.

---

1 Theodore Gracyk, *I Wanna Be Me: Rock Music and the Politics of Identity* (Philadelphia: Temple University Press, 2001), p. 69.

Of course, the synthesizer wasn't invented in 1978 to amuse Gary Numan. Throughout the '70s the instrument slowly infiltrated pop music as knowledge of its unique qualities spread. Such major creative forces as Todd Rundgren, Stevie Wonder and Brian Eno (with and without Roxy Music) successfully integrated synth into their songs and encouraged others to do the same—and Kraftwerk's whimsical robotics and Tangerine Dream's ethereal oozings were available long before the emergence of Britain's latest chart sensations.

But today everyone from Abba to Public Image Ltd. uses synthesizers as a matter of course. So what actually did change?

One very significant thing. Pure, unadulterated synthesizer sound now appears on (more or less) conventional pop tunes. The instrument doesn't call attention to itself, as it had with Kraftwerk and their ilk; machine and song now meet on equal terms. In Britain, at least, the public has signaled its approval. Current UK charts are studded with synthesizer bands like Soft Cell, Human League and Orchestral Manoeuvres in the Dark, as well as groups heavily dependent on the instrument, such as Ultravox (the link between Roxy Music and Gary Numan).

What is a synthesizer, anyway? Guitars, drums and so forth are easy to comprehend, but these newfangled contraptions seem forbiddingly alien. Never fear. Scott Simon of Our Daughter's Wedding, a New York City trio that is one of the American alternatives to UK synth bands, offers a layman's explanation of how the thing works.

"The sound of a synth comes from a noise generator, which is an oscillator that puts out a signal with a wave shape. That's sent via circuit boards through filters that change the wave shape and pitch of the initial signal. *That* goes into a triggering system—the keyboard. A few different things happen to the signal as it goes through the process. What makes a synth complicated is what happens between the oscillator and keyboard."

Those options, Simon goes on to explain, include being able to store exact sounds in the synth's memory bank (a dead giveaway that computers are involved), the ability to change the shape or pitch of a note, and flexibility in setting the decay, or rate at which a note drops off. The sequencer, beloved to Who fans after *Who's Next*, "stores notes and puts them out the same way they're put in. You can alter their shape and speed at which they're sent back out, but the notes will always be in the order you put them in."

OK? Technology buffs will find more sophisticated insights into the workings of this modern electronic wonder in next month's TP.[2]

Daniel Miller is regarded as an elder statesman of the British synth-pop scene. In 1978 he inaugurated his Mute Records with a single by the Normal ("TVOD"/"Warm Leatherette"), which was actually Miller working alone. He went on to release an album of novelty synthesizer tunes as the Silicon Teens, and in 1981 signed and produced Depeche Mode, now a major UK chart success. He spoke to TP while in New York to mix sound on Depeche Mode's US tour.

Miller's involvement with the instrument is typical of current synthesizer musicians. "I was a fan of German bands [Can, Faust, Neu, Tangerine Dream] in the early '70s and I thought a lot about the possibilities of electronic music for someone like me, who's not a very good musician but likes playing music. I used to play guitar in really bad groups when I was at school. It was frustrating— I knew what I wanted to play but I practiced and still couldn't." Instead Miller saved up his money and purchased a synthesizer and tape recorder around the time the punk movement exploded.

Others experienced similar dissatisfaction. Scott Ryser of San Francisco's Units recalls, "I'd played in rock bands before and I got really sick of the people, of the whole scene." Vocalist Keith

---

2 Dominic Milano, "Man Meets Machine: The Whys and Wherefores of Synthesizers," *Trouser Press*, June 1982, pp. 31–33.

Silva of Our Daughter's Wedding was bored with stereotypic new wave bands when he took up the synth. Andy McCluskey of Orchestral Manoeuvres remembers that he and Paul Humphreys simply tired of writing parts for guitars and drums in their Liverpool band: "We wanted to do our songs exactly how we wanted to do them—just myself, Paul and a tape recorder."

Punk galvanized these malcontents. Anyone who suffered through the long reign of flashy progressive bands like Yes or Emerson, Lake and Palmer may find the connection between oft-overused synthesizers and punk's refreshing simplicity hard to grasp. However, David Ball of Soft Cell feels that "synthesizer bands now have got a lot to thank the punk bands of '77 for. The punk thing gave anybody a chance to get up and do it. It didn't matter how well you played as long as it was fast and energetic and exciting."

"I was very interested in punk as it was nonelitist," Daniel Miller says. "It started me doing my own things. I heard a link between the Ramones and Kraftwerk. If you analyze the music they're quite similar."

OMD's Andy McCluskey makes the connection more explicit. "In some ways it's quite strange that synthesizers were so hated in the punk era. They're the ideal punk instrument if you believe in the ethic of 'anybody can do it.' Someone who's been playing synth for 10 minutes can easily sound as good as someone who's been playing for years, provided the ideas are there.

"I think a lot of English bands would say one reason they use synths is because they're easy to play."

You'll get no argument on that count from the overly modest youths in Depeche Mode. Andy Fletcher looks back on their early days two years ago and remarks, "We couldn't play hardly at all then; we can't play very well now." Not that they undervalue their work. Singer Dave Gahan notes, "In pop music nowadays you don't need technical ability, you need ideas and the ability to write songs. That's the main thing."

Easy access to synthesizers has given them a bad image as a stale, monotonous instrument. Since practically anybody can play one, a lot of dullards have gotten involved. Andy Fletcher observes that "because you can get such good sounds on the synth you can get away with murder. You can have an awful song and make it sound quite good. Quite a lot of bands do that."

Some "sophisticated" musicians also don't understand how their own equipment works. "We're not Kraftwerk," Andy Fletcher says, acknowledging the obvious. "Kraftwerk built their own computers and keyboards." Dave Gahan adds, "If someone gave us a computer and said, 'Use that,' we wouldn't know what to do with it."

Andy McCluskey laughs at the situation. "We and a lot of other bands who use synths have this technological image that few bands actually deserve. For Kraftwerk, it's a total ideology; it's the way they work. The fact that they use synths is important to them. But as for a lot of new English bands—we don't understand how the hell the things work! Paul [Humphreys] did study electronics, so he knew the principles behind it, but I had to learn by hit and miss."

Those not deterred (or bothered) by electronic complexity find other attractions in addition to the synthesizer's pleasing sound and ready availability. Small, cheap synthesizers used by a beginning band are invariably more mobile than the guitars and cumbersome amplifiers necessary for even the most rudimentary rock bands. (A synthesizer can be plugged directly into the house p.a.) Our Daughter's Wedding boasts that at first their synths were carry-on luggage on airplanes.

Depeche Mode's Dave Gahan says the logistics of getting to London gigs from their home town of Basildon 25 miles away was a determining factor in their switch from guitars to synths. Andy Fletcher adds "Until about six months ago we used to go to and from gigs by train. The audience would see us play and they'd see us on the train afterward with our instruments!"

The band also raves about how easy it is to conduct a pre-show soundcheck. Once Depeche Mode's three players tune their instruments to a synthetic drum tape it's all systems go. Andy Fletcher says the process usually takes no more than an hour. By comparison, he notes, "When we supported Ultravox at the Rainbow, they were soundchecking for about five hours."

"I couldn't stand being in that sort of group." Soft Cell's David Ball cringes at the thought of playing in a "traditional" rock band. The instrumental half of Soft Cell (Marc Almond furnishes vocals) usually needs no more than an hour to get ready for a show.

Both Depeche Mode and Our Daughter's Wedding held early practice sessions in small suburban bedrooms. Since they didn't need amps, it was a simple matter to plug headphones directly into the synth and commence creating. (And no nasty noises to annoy Mom!) By the same token, Depeche Mode doesn't even use the big room in a recording studio; the band just plugs directly into the control room console. How's that for simple?

All well and good, you say, but what about the sound of synthesizers? Anyone who's been exposed to Gary Numan's whiny drone [*Singing or playing?—Ed.*] for more than three minutes may well conclude the synthesizer is an evil menace to rock, designed to eviscerate all feeling.

Rachel Webber, who shares the Units' synthesizer duties with Scott Ryser, probably speaks for the wary American public when she voices reservations about the current crop of British synth bands. "In general—'cause I like Orchestral Manoeuvres—those bands can get pretty similar. I don't like the Gary Numan type of scene."

Scott Ryser adds, "It doesn't seem like there's much depth to it. I like it for dancing, but it's hard to take very seriously."

Webber feels a lot of groups "just get a basic sound they know will work. Those cute little squiggles do work, as far as what people like, but it's not very challenging."

Don't blame the poor old inanimate synthesizer for appearing on a lot of boring records. Blame the musicians. Layne Rico of Our Daughter's Wedding observes, "A lot of people are against synthesizers and say, 'All you have to do is press a button'—which in a way is quite true. It's all down to how each individual plays the instrument."

Bandmate Keith Silva adds, "Some people use only what's easy to get out of it, but if you search there's a lot you can do."

The "new romantic" movement, with its watery dress-up ideology and simplistic dance motifs, has probably done a lot recently to give synths a bad name. Tedious stuff is being ground out with the aid of synthesizers—but what else is new? There are plenty of mediocre guitarists too.

Andy McCluskey recognizes the dangers. "Over the last 20 years or so kids who've wanted to be musicians have decided, 'I've gotta be a guitar player. I wanna be an axe hero.' They'd adopted what were new ways of playing at the time, but because they were copying they'd just start adopting clichés.

"In the last 10 years it seems like there have been very few new methods of playing guitar. Everybody's just trotting out the same old clichés, pulling the same faces, striking the same old rock 'n' roll poses.

"The synthesizer now has a history and there are already clichéd ways of playing it. You can sound like Gary Numan on a Polymoog. You can do lead solos like Billy Currie on an ARP Odyssey—that wailing, no-melody type of riffing. There are popular guidelines for playing synthesizer laid down by people who were around before.

"Recently I talked to a young guy from Liverpool who played us a demo. I asked him why it was so unmelodic and discordant; he refused to play melodies. He said, 'The trouble is, every time you play a melody on synthesizer you sound like Orchestral Manoeuvres!'"

McCluskey laughs, no doubt thankful he got there first.

Despite his reservations, McCluskey does not share Rachel Webber's skepticism about the current wave of English synth-pop groups. He sees great diversity among the bands, and frowns on efforts to lump them all together because of their choice of weapon.

"People from outside Britain see all bands that play synthesizer as part and parcel of the same movement or ideology, which is far from the truth. The music we and other bands make, and the reasons behind the making of the music, are actually quite different from each other.

"A few examples: That Human League plays synthesizers is almost unimportant. It's pop music for the '80s. The lyrical content is very traditional: 'I love you and you love me' or 'I love you and you don't love me.' When we write a love song it tends to be more offbeat. Depeche Mode is a very young thing, the sound of young boys. The lyrical content of Heaven 17 is fairly radical."

Some synth bands try to minimize the mechanical aspect of their electronic instruments. Keith Silva says that Our Daughter's Wedding avoids sequencers whenever possible. "To me it makes the music a little too sterile. I prefer the actual physical attack of playing a note yourself. I think the feeling actually changes when you use sequencers."

The rhythm section in a synth group tends to be its weakest component. Those tinny, ticking rhythm boxes used to sound pretty feeble coming out of Lowery organs; their descendants don't fare much better trying to drive a loud battalion of synths. Depeche Mode deals with the problem by taping all their percussion one element at a time. The sight of a big Teac reel-to-reel machine onstage where a drummer should be comes as a shock, but the output is, Dave Gahan says, "really clear and punchy." The band's tape consists of a bass drum sound from Daniel Miller's old ARP, the snare drum sound of a rhythm machine, and various sequencer bits.

On their five-song EP, *Digital Cowboy*, Our Daughter's Wedding used ace drummer Simon Phillips instead of a rhythm box. Onstage Layne Rico augments the mechanical beat with a Synare synth, which can produce either percussive or melodic tones.[3] The Units recently enlisted a percussionist and a drummer. On *Architecture & Morality* Orchestral Manoeuvres combine acoustic and synthetic drums for a hybrid sound.

Soft Cell and producer Mike Thorne concocted an intriguing approach for *Non-Stop Erotic Cabaret*. As David Ball reveals, "We took the output of an electronic snare and put it through a little speaker, which we laid face down on top of a snare drum; then we miked that up. So we were getting a real snare sound, but it was triggered by a drum machine. I think it gives a slightly richer sound."

There's no reason for any two synthesizer bands to sound alike if they've got talent and aren't too rigid in their outlook. Paul Humphreys believes synths are "*the* most versatile instrument—but there are things you can't do on a synthesizer, like get the power and rawness of strumming a guitar." That's why *Architecture & Morality* features OMD's first use of guitar, as well as horns, piano and saxes.

"Very often the mainstay of a song is not synthesizers but sound ideas in general," Andy McCluskey observes. OMD's recent single "Joan of Arc" employs a glockenspiel "which gives it springiness, and I did two different vocal takes. One has all these little voices—I'm trying to follow a synthesizer I'd set on D. On the other one I sing high-pitched, almost falsetto harmonies."

"Souvenir" resulted from equally ingenious procedures. Humphreys took tapes of an eight-member church choir singing scales and made up the tape loops that give the song its wobbly, shifting quality.

In other words, smile when you call Orchestral Manoeuvres a synth band. "They're not our number one priority," McCluskey states. "We're not on some electronic crusade; we're not interested in the synthesizer as an image. We have a load of them onstage because that's what we play. We just use them as a means to an end."

A close look reveals that, in one sense, most of these bands aren't all that different from traditional rock groups. Our Daughter's Wedding, the Units and Depeche Mode all dole out responsibilities

---

3 The Synare was an electronic drum that consisted of synthesizer pads one played with sticks.

for melody, bass and percussion to different members, just like the good old days. In most cases the material could be rearranged to accommodate implements of yore like guitars and drums. Our Daughter's Wedding recalls Sparks. Orchestral Manoeuvres sometimes suggests a smarter Beach Boys. Soft Cell's massive UK smash "Tainted Love" was originally an obscure '60s soul recording by Gloria Jones.

"We've just worked up a James Brown tune ['It's a Man's, Man's, Man's World'], so I guess a guitar band could work one of ours up," the Units' Ryser says. (He originally wanted the Units to be "real brash and hard, the Iggy Pop of synthesizers.") David Ball would like to hear an orchestra tackle one of Soft Cell's songs.

Keith Silva even goes so far as to label Our Daughter's Wedding a rock band: "We're all keyboards but we still feel we're a rock band. It takes people a while to figure out, 'Hey, these guys just play good music and it rocks.'" Layne Rico adds that "'Lawnchairs' or 'Target for Life' could be done by Van Halen or any other band. It's just music."

If you were looking forward to a bloody shoot-out in the charts between guitars and synths, forget it. "There's room for everything," David Ball remarks. "Synthesizers are just another option. If people want to play guitars, that's great. You should be able to play any instrument you like."

Rachel Webber says, "There's supposed to be this big rivalry between synthesizers and guitars, which I think is pretty weird. I don't think people are sick of guitars, I just think they're looking for something different. If anything, guitars have gotten stronger."

The search for alternative means of expression may eventually lure synth bands into trying out guitars. Depeche Mode has already considered such a move.

"I think the guitar is a beautiful instrument," Layne Rico of Our Daughter's Wedding says. "When everybody thinks we're going too electronic, we might do a big circle and come onstage with guitars."

Made possible by the onward march of science, synthesizers and synthesizer bands will continue to change with the technology. Layne Rico is anxiously awaiting a set of hexagonal electronic drums. "They're made of the same material as football players' helmets. Playing them is like hitting a drumstick against a barstool. These drums are only about two inches deep; they look like hexagonal pie pans. We'll finally be able to break away from the rhythm machines a bit."

On a less sophisticated front, basic synthesizers have dropped in price so much that anyone with $200 can become at least a fledgling artiste.

Soon a generation that grew up on Gary Numan and the Human League, rather than the Stones and Led Zeppelin, will be ready to enter the musical job market. Andy Fletcher knows seven- and eight-year-olds who can play melodic lines on the synth; tomorrow's musicians will test the instrument's capabilities without treating it as a futuristic aberration. Sooner or later a bona fide synthesizer genius steeped in the early electronic bands may come along and revolutionize the field, just as Jimi Hendrix absorbed the blues and early rock guitar styles before emerging as staggeringly original.

David Ball has no doubts that synthesizers have arrived. "When electric guitars were first used I'm sure people were saying, 'Do you really think this is gonna last?' Electric guitars have been with us for years now, and I think it will be the same with synths. People have accepted it as a conventional instrument rather than a freak of science."

"I think synthesizers are here to stay," Daniel Miller sums up, "regardless of what they're playing now. A lot of things I thought were gonna happen a few years ago have happened.

"England has a basis for synthesizer music. I don't think it's a fad, because it's lasted. Since Gary Numan there's always been synthesizer music in the English charts. It's gone through all the different fashions and it's still there.

"The synthesizer's such a flexible instrument. You can play anything on it. It's not a kind of music; it's a way of making music."

Synthesizers now have the potential to become the next classic rock 'n' roll instrument. Keep your ears open. Who knows—in a few years the sequel to this piece may even star you!

Source: Jon Young, "Roll Over Guitar Heroes; Synthesizers Are Here," *Trouser Press*, May 1982, pp. 22–27.

42

"MTV Ruled the World"

The Early Years of Music Video

GREG PRATO

On August 1, 1981, when the cable network MTV—Music Television—aired its first broadcast in select U.S. markets, cable television was for many homes a luxury item. Radio remained the most crucial medium in "breaking a hit" and the music video was still a relatively unknown quantity. Within two years, however, MTV and cable had expanded nationally and become a driving force within the industry, helping to make stars of those artists who could adapt to and take advantage of the new medium. Like any station, MTV, which was initially modelled on an Album-Oriented-Rock (AOR) radio format style, thrived because it was able to create a specific identity—but one that was also embroiled in controversy. The following excerpts from Greg Prato's oral history of MTV's early years reveal some of the struggles and tense debates that arose regarding the network's programming decisions and its video content. Would MTV, as an overwhelmingly white rock station, play the videos of black pop stars such as Michael Jackson (1958–2009)? Were women to be relegated to the roles of sex objects, most noticeably in the videos for popular heavy metal "hair bands"? Drawing on a variety of perspectives and conflicting accounts, ranging from video directors, MTV video jockeys (VJs), and MTV CEO Bob Pittman to the musicians themselves, Prato's interviews capture both the seismic impact that MTV had during the 1980s and the contested historical terrain it inhabits to this day.

Some Struggle in the Age of Video

Ann Wilson [Heart singer]:   Suddenly, you had to be able to do some minimal amount of acting, and you had to be able to take direction from a "visual director." Some people just were a little bit too . . . some of the southern rock bands, you saw them once, and said, "Oh, OK. I can go see them live, and that's who they are." Suddenly, there was a whole new role put upon you that I think some people couldn't handle. I keep alluding to the silent pictures and the talkies. Some of the big silent screen actors couldn't make the break because their voices weren't cool enough. Some of the bands couldn't make the jump because they didn't have enough creativity and wonder in their look or in their ability to act or translate the song visually.

Geddy Lee [Rush singer/bassist]:   It suddenly shifted everybody's thinking, because bands that were not image-oriented—in a way, that was us—suddenly had to start thinking about doing a visual presentation. And I think, for some people, it came naturally. Obviously, the pop stars were more used to that, because it was "face first" for those bands and those singers, anyway. But we were a band that didn't think of ourselves in terms of anything other than guys that liked to play.

Joe Elliott [Def Leppard singer]:   It also wrecked a few careers, too. If you were one of them bands that had that horrible, balding bass player with a mustache, that was "career gone," because now, they knew what you looked like. It really was much more beneficial to Duran Duran than, say, Uriah Heep.

Frank Stallone [Solo artist/singer]:   It wasn't even about the music anymore. It was like, Christopher Cross came out with one of the best break-out solo albums I'd ever heard [*Christopher Cross*]. But then all of a sudden when they saw him—and he looked like this truck driver—it killed him. I mean, I saw him at the Roxy. This guy had a beautiful voice, and you're figuring this really cool-looking guy will come out, looking like Charlie Sexton. And he came out looking like Bluto. I felt really bad for him because he was really good. So he was definitely not "MTV friendly."

Daryl Hall [Hall & Oates singer/keyboardist]:   There's the anecdote that I find offensive, but they always said that Christopher Cross was too ugly to be a rock star. Which I think is a terrible thing . . . but I think there might be a little truth in that kind of thing.

John Oates [Hall & Oates singer/guitarist]:   I think some were better looking than others. After all, it is a visual medium.

Roger Powell [Todd Rundgren/Utopia keyboardist]:   Some of those guys were just butt ugly. [Laughs] From the 40th row, it's OK, but once you start really *seeing* people . . . it's kind of an odd comment, but whatever, God bless 'em all.

Eric Bloom [Blue Öyster Cult singer/guitarist]:   You might have a handsome lead singer that would carry the whole thing because he's hot. [Laughs] Maybe the music isn't so good, but he is, or she is. There's that phenomena that you would never know from the airplay, but now you see who's singing. And vice versa. I can think of a few acts that were just not particularly photogenic.

Rik Emmett [Triumph singer/guitarist]:   I don't think it's any mystery that there are some people that the closer the camera gets, the more it loves them. That's why there's movie stars and people in daytime soaps, because they're beautiful people, and the closer the camera gets, you go, "Oh my God, her skin is flawless," or "Oh my God, look at how big and beautiful her eyes are," or "Oh my God, look at that guy . . . does he have a flaw anywhere?"

Mickey Thomas [Jefferson Starship singer]:   You mean, aside from the fact that we were just so damned good looking? [Laughs] I don't know. Looks is part of it. I think we had a pretty interesting looking band for the time. I mean, shit, *we had Grace Slick*. [Laughs] And then the fact, too, that most of us in the band were open to expanding our horizons visually and theatrically. I've always been interested in movies and incorporating other forms of art into the music. Paul Kantner was not afraid of that. Craig Chaquiço was very much into it. Grace of course. So we were not afraid to take risks and some chances and not afraid to fall on your face and make a fool of yourself if you look stupid.

Fee Waybill [The Tubes singer]:   A lot of those bands—Grateful Dead and stuff—they didn't even look up when they played. They were playing in Levi's. They had their head down and half the time their back to the audience. They just didn't translate to TV. Whereas we—that was our whole deal. We were all about TV and doing a big theatrical presentation, and we're very gregarious kind of guys and really put it out there. A lot of people weren't.

Dave Marsh [music journalist]:   I think the prog bands had more trouble, because first of all, the prog bands didn't have concise songs. And secondly, they didn't have poppy songs. They tended to be more morose. It wasn't something that MTV was terribly good at displaying. No great loss.

*   *   *

Black Artists and MTV

Chuck D [Public Enemy rapper]:   They tried to run away from black music as fast as possible. The only thing black on MTV at that time was JJ Jackson, who was a VJ. They even said no to Michael Jackson.

Bob Giraldi [Video director: Michael Jackson's "Beat It"]:   I don't know if I'd say there weren't that many [black artists played on MTV]. There weren't *any*. No matter what you're being told by anybody, it was a racist station. A different point of view, they had a different philosophy, it was being played and marketed to white teenagers in the suburbs, and there was no place in their mind for what was pop-soul, music. And Michael [Jackson], as always, bridged the gap. Made the change. Led the way.

Steve Barron [Video director" Michael Jackson's "Beat It"]:   There was a weird moment where MTV saw the video ["Billie Jean"], and they said, "It's not really our demographic." And the head of CBS, Walter Yetnikoff, just went nuts. He said, "You're kidding me? This is a fantastic pop song and a really striking video, and you're MTV." They felt their audience was very "Midwest"—from what I remember—and that this would be not their demographic. And there was a couple of weeks where they weren't going to play it. Of course, the irony that turned that all around is Michael Jackson became the driving force behind MTV for many years. But there was a moment where there was a clash of demographics.

Alan Hunter [MTV VJ]:   I remember hearing the news that Michael Jackson had this video, "Billie Jean," that was just blowing everybody away. We got the tape of it down at the studio. I think Mark and I were watching it as soon as it came to MTV. There was some debate early on I remember. The debate was still raging whether or not we were going to show it. But it didn't last long. There was not a whole long hand-wringing over that one. It was, "You know what? We've got to show this. *It's too extraordinary.*" The video was unbelievably great. It was Michael Jackson, it's a great song, [and] it just made sense. So it wasn't a painful decision on anybody's part. I remember being very excited. Mark and I were talking about how cool this was, how much it was going to change things and open up the doors. Everybody had that feeling. It was the first big premiere of its kind. That was another first for MTV, to premiere a video like that. The kind of promotion we put behind it weeks in advance. We'd get memos. "You've got to say this; you've got to do every break." After, we thought the doors were wide open.

Bob Giraldi: I met with Bob [Pittman], and we had plenty of arguments. I think that history shows that they made a choice, and they were pressured to change the choice. And that was the right thing to do. Nobody bought as many records as they did *Thriller*. You can talk all you want about white bands, but it was the black artists that were selling most at that time. History was changed, and history was made. There's nobody to point fingers at. It's just the way it happened. And it was the right thing. It wasn't like it was a mistake, and history went with it. It was the right thing. Lionel came out with *Can't Slow Down*, Stevie Wonder had his, Ray Charles had his, Diana Ross had hers. Everybody had their moment. It was the time in history when the music business was the most glorious.

Bob Pittman [MTV CEO]:   It started with Rick James. We had a review committee, and he didn't pass it for "Super Freak," which, by the way, today would be extraordinarily tame. So it didn't pass, and we wouldn't play it. He got in the press and said, "They're not playing any black artists." Which, of course, wasn't true. We *were* playing black artists. But just like white artists, there were a whole lot of black artists that didn't have videos, and there were a whole lot of white artists that didn't have videos. But the charge stuck. At first, our reaction was, "Of course, everybody will look at the channel and know that's not true." But they didn't look at the channel. They just wrote it. And this thing built up some momentum.

Les Garland [MTV executive]:   I took it quite personally—specifically, Mr. Rick James. He was the guy that I had the biggest problem with. He flat-out used my name one day. The guy had never even met me and accused me of being a racist. *I lost my mind.* And for people who knew me, knew that was absolutely not true. And then, finally, the confrontation with him came. It was a bit of a face-off, and I said, "Look, you don't even know me. You need to make some calls before you go around making statements about people." I was pissed. About a week later, he called and asked if he could come down and see me. He did and said, "Garland, I owe you an apology." I accepted it, we hugged, and became friends. I knew him—not a dear buddy, not a guy I hung out with—but we made our way through that. That guy made a mistake making statements like that, and he stood up like a man and admitted it. It got personal. The Michael Jackson story that flies around—that never happened. There were people of color on MTV. There just wasn't much selection of music videos coming from the music companies.

Bob Pittman: It's probably the reason Michael Jackson got so much attention. We started going out to black artists and saying proactively, "You've got to produce a video." Tina Turner was really big for us and Michael Jackson. And, actually, Quincy Jones is my son's godfather, as a result of Quincy and I becoming great friends through that process, because I began spending a lot of time with Quincy, saying, "Look, we've got to get this done. We've got to get Michael on the air." And, of course, they had "Billie Jean" and "Beat It," which were great videos.

Les Garland: It's become a part of Internet folklore, I guess. By the way, one of the guys that fuels it is one of my dear friends, Mr. Walter Yetnikoff. Walter Yetnikoff was the head of CBS back in the day, the most powerful music company in the world. And they had Michael Jackson. The story somehow got told that we said no to Michael Jackson. That MTV said, "No, we were not going to play the Michael Jackson video." Which couldn't have been further from the truth. I was the first person at MTV to see it, and I'll never forget putting it in my 3/4-inch machine, hitting the start button, hearing the bass beat to "Billie Jean" start up, and going, "Holy shit . . . *are you kidding me?!*" I called everybody in and said, "You've got to see this. This is the best video of its time!" Pittman was on the west coast. I phoned him and said, "Bob, wait until you see 'Billie Jean.' It's going to blow your mind." We put it on mid-week. It wasn't even a Tuesday add. But, somehow, this whole story erupted that we denied it, we weren't going to play it, and there were threats made by CBS that, if we didn't play it, they were going to pull all their music videos. This story just started gathering steam. Why? I don't know. Publicity? I don't know. I've got my theories. But it never happened, and I've dispelled this hundreds of times. It just never happened like that.

Gerald Casale [Devo bassist]:   It was absolutely true. Those stories are true. When MTV tries to refute the way that went down . . . no, it's absolutely the way it went down. Walter

Yetnikoff basically forced the situation, forced them to play Michael Jackson, by holding some other stuff over their heads, since they had such a huge label with other artists. MTV was never hip. They were always the last to the table on anything. But, of course, when you control that media like that, you rewrite history. You get credit where credit wasn't due.

Verdine White [Earth, Wind & Fire bassist]:   It was true. I think with MTV at the time, because the program dynamically wanted to appeal to rock audiences, I don't think we really saw a lot of African American videos until BET did hip-hop and things like that. And I think Walter Yetnikoff at the time really put his foot down on MTV to even play Michael Jackson, because at first, I'm not sure if MTV was going to play him. Because the first ads on MTV was "I want my MTV!" and the ads were the Police and more the pop groups, not the African American groups.

Dave Marsh: They didn't play black artists until they were coerced into it by Walter Yetnikoff is exactly what happened. Pittman may deny it—he did at the time—but the fact is that Walter threatened to pull all the rest of the CBS videos if Michael's *Thriller* record didn't get played. That was it. Typically, there was resistance, and then when they finally broke the resistance—I can't tell you how much I love this—it became one of the biggest videos they ever would have, because it was the "Billie Jean" video. And to reject the "Billie Jean" video—which is what they were rejecting—they must have seen it.

Because the performer was black, that isn't even a close call about whether it's Ku Klux Klan-level racism. There was no other reason ever advanced why they didn't play that video, except the race of the artist. I mean, maybe they used some codified lip service about musical genre or something. And I don't think they even did that. I just think they said, "We don't play black records." And, of course, the same thing went down with hip-hop. That was the next thing that got banned. And when they finally broke their own ban on it, it became the driving force of a whole sub-generation . . . I don't know if it was a whole generation, but several years worth of MTV viewers were lured there more by hip-hop than anything else.

*   *   *

John Oates: I think the parallel was it was very similar to radio. It was segregated the way radio programming was segregated. You had FM-kind of rock stations playing basically white rock music. And then you had top 40 stations, and then you had R&B stations and urban stations. They weren't called "urban" in those days; they were called "R&B" or "soul." And you had stations that only played disco. You remember "disco wars" and all that crap that was going on? I think that MTV followed that pattern. They viewed themselves as a niche for rock and pop music. Whether they were racially biased or not, I kind of doubt. I think they just saw it as that was the most viable way of getting on TV and having the major labels jump on board.

Daryl Hall: This all came out of the radio format, and I think MTV thought of themselves at that time as a visual arm of radio—pop radio, rock radio, whatever you want to call it. Which was to some degree still . . . I won't say completely segregated, but it was. It's hard to remember what it was like and how "weird" we were in those days, because we had hits on black radio *and* white radio. There weren't that many people like that. So I think they tended to format themselves in that direction, the way radio was formatting themselves in those days. It was wrong, but it's what it was. I remember championing people. I remember bringing August Darnell of Kid Creole and the Coconuts on the show to be a guest VJ with me, because I knew he was a great musician, and I wanted to introduce him to the MTV audience. I did my little part to try and desegregate MTV in the very early days. And, eventually, they saw the light, of course.

George Thorogood [Solo artist, singer/guitarist]:   They played the black artists that were available. Mostly, of older black artists, artists that were already established. Smokey Robinson. That's all there was. And the movement of the era of Michael Jackson had yet to come. The era of Prince had yet to come. I think those two artists, more than anything, were foremost in breaking contemporary black music at that time. If you look at MTV, it's been around since 1981, so if Michael Jackson or Prince got in there in '85, that's relatively new. It wasn't like they were passed over. It's just that they weren't emerging yet. But once they did, they were on there. You saw them.

Les Garland: The racism bullshit—I'm so over talking about it. We've talked about it until we're blue, y'know? It didn't exist. It was nonexistent. It was trumped up in the press. It was trumped up by other people making statements. It starts with who's making the music videos, and I remind everybody, the number of videos being submitted to us by the music company side by artists of color were very, very minimal. As much as we encouraged making music videos for all their artists. We had visions of launching other channels one day. Maybe it would be urban-based. Maybe it would be country. We were smart enough to know that we had to land our audience first, and either grow that audience or launch other channels and acquire new audiences. We weren't stupid people. We were award-winning radio programmers, who were artists with a bit of a scientific mind. Because I understood the science of ratings and television and appealing to people. Because I had gone through all that, and I had learned all that in my radio years. It's science meets art, but let's let art outweigh the science just enough. And you've got that "artistic/creative edge," if you will. MTV was that. It never had anything to do with the color of people's skin. To think that people said these things about us was a very painful time.

Alan Hunter: JJ Jackson—the one black guy in the troupe here—was a great defender, although in an interview, Mark Goodman was interviewing David Bowie one time, and David leveled Mark and said, "Why don't you play any black artists?" And JJ, I remember him saying [he] wished that he could have had a conversation with David to set him straight somewhat. We *were* playing black artists. There was Garland Jeffreys, Gary U.S. Bonds, Joan Armatrading, but they played more mainstream rock 'n' roll. Michael Jackson represented the "pop world," and that just wasn't in the parameters. There was certainly no overt racism about the thing. It was just what their idea of the music that we were going to play was. But Michael was definitely a turning point. Did that mean that we were going to be playing R&B? Were we going to be playing Lionel Richie? It opened up everything at that point, which, of course, was great. That was what MTV was all about, this total mishmash of heavy metal up against Howard Jones up against the Commodores up against Sting. It was all over the place, and that's what people liked about it.

Nina Blackwood [MTV VJ]:   Bottom line—if you go back and you listen to rock radio at that exact period of time, you are not going to hear a lot of black artists. And initially, MTV started—as hard as it is to believe now—its initial intention was as an AOR music channel. More rock 'n' roll. So it was not a case of the color of your skin or racism. It was the genre of music. If there was some behind-the-scenes racism going on, I was not aware of that, because we did have Garland Jeffreys, Phil Lynott, Joan Armatrading, Jon Butcher Axis. I used to feel that I don't need to sit here naming the black artists that we play, because I never felt it was a racist thing at all. I mean, we had JJ for crying out loud. *Come on!* And then, when the whole Michael Jackson thing . . . again, I was not in on the acquisition meetings. I have read several books that are supposedly in-depth about what was going on behind-the-scenes, and it was "Billie Jean" that they didn't want to play. I don't know if that was racist motivation behind that, but that was just plain stupid, because the song was great. For whatever reason they were reluctant to play that was just plain dumb, because the song itself was a genre that crossed over pop and rock. It was so tremendous a piece of music that it could be played on any channel. I mean, I'm sure if Jimi Hendrix had a video in 1981, we would have been playing it.

*   *   *

Portrayal of Women in Music Video

Dave Marsh: People talk moralistically about hip-hop and metal in terms of their exploitation of women. Well, who encouraged them more than anybody else to do it? Not radio. Not really the record companies. The encouraging factor was MTV, and they never get put on the hook for that. Or at least not very often. There's a difference between "Roxanne Roxanne" and what came later. MTV didn't have nothing to do with "Roxanne Roxanne." That was an empowered woman there.

Debora Iyall [Romeo Void singer]:   A lot of the videos that came on probably post-when we got started, especially once the more mainstream artists were making videos, then the women were just like "props." Totally. *Well-dressed* props. But when it first started out, there was, in my mind, a lot of creativity about women being artists. In "Video Killed the Radio Star," the girl was an individual personality. She wasn't dressing herself to be a sex object. And Bow Wow Wow was like that, and Altered Images were on real early, and Joan Jett and "I Love Rock n' Roll." Before there was more of the pop music or mainstream rock on it, it was "showing the new way." You can be a musician and be yourself. And not a commodity so much, but as an artist statement.

Ann Wilson: They were portrayed as sex kittens or dragon ladies, but always from an extremely hyper-sexualized standpoint. That seemed to be the only arena that was open to women on MTV, then and now. It was kind of like that old Marilyn Monroe movie, where she gets stuck in the porthole. She's stuck because her hips are too big to get out, so she has to stay in this tight little place. She has to stay there, flop around, and look gorgeous.

Martha Davis [The Motels singer]:   The whole "women" issue is interesting, because I'm a child that grew up in Berkeley, California, and saw the whole '60s thing, watching women fighting for their rights. And then, all of a sudden, it's back to a *Girls Gone Wild* kind of situation. Especially with the big hair bands, there was definitely the gratuitous sex, which hasn't gone away since. I guess maybe gratuitous sex is here to stay. I have no idea. I think it's all everybody's comfort level. It doesn't bother me . . . but it's not something that I would do. I don't know if it's "forward" anything, but it's rock music. It's about sex, basically. So I think it's all good.

Dave Marsh: Women didn't exist. "Girls" existed, to start with. I mean, maybe there would be a mom once in a while or an older school teacher. There weren't any "women." It was basically a world of teenaged sluts. The Whitesnake videos, the ZZ Top videos, Duran Duran videos. There was a cluster of them. There were bands that prospered on the basis of doing sort of sub-*Penthouse* video shoots. And the problem with it wasn't that young women were being "sexualized." Young women do a fine job of sexualizing themselves, or even that they were being stereotyped. The problem was that it was so one-sided. Very few female artists, for instance. And absolutely no female perspective, unless you count Nina and Martha . . . and that would be ridiculous.[1]

* * *

Joe Elliott: Probably like they were portrayed before the suffragette movement. I mean, you look at the "Photograph" video, and it's one of the many examples where there are hot chicks caged up with torn clothes on. [Laughs] It was before the full-PC thing kicked in. So, it wasn't exploitive in the sense of . . . look, we didn't shove them in there against their will. They willingly took the money to be paid to do it. And it wasn't prostitution. It was role-playing. It was tragically sad by today's standards. But you see, it's such a macho-fucking-business. Let's think about it—throughout the whole MTV thing, other than Pat Benatar, I'm scratching my head to think of another female that was actually . . . Janet Jackson came much later. I never saw that much of Joan Jett. I mean, she was great, but I didn't see her videos as much as I saw Billy Idol's, you know what I mean?

Pete Angelus [Video director]:   That was a very sexual time, really. Listen, I know that there were a lot of videos that portrayed women in a very negative light, but not any more so than how some of the women are portrayed in rap videos to this day. I remember when we did "Hot for Teacher," getting a phone call that some organization—I can't remember what it was—but females were appalled, disgusted, insulted by the fact that these "teachers" were dancing on desk tops and that the classroom had been turned into a strip club. But listen, this is meant to be humorous. We are certainly not trying to degrade that woman in that role. Those were attractive women. I can't speak for all young men, but I can tell you that I personally had a lot of those fantasies when I was in school. I didn't think it was such a far stretch, and it certainly wasn't done with the intention of being insulting, by any means. It was speaking more towards those kids' fantasies and thoughts.

I can understand why some people got upset, but here's the bottom line. People are always upset about *something*, no matter how you handle it. At the time, I remember there was a lot of media about how those women were portrayed in "Hot for Teacher," but in reality, it just garnered more attention to the band and to the video. I've seen some things on MTV where I was like, "Wow, that's going pretty far with that woman there." And is it necessary? Probably not. I mean, basically, *she's fucking the television.* Is that good for younger people to see? Maybe, maybe not. I don't know. I'm not sure exactly what the message is of all these asses in the camera, but apparently, these people are trying to send a message . . . and I'm not going to spend a lot of time trying to figure out what it is. MTV was an art-form. It was a blank canvas, and some of it was handled well. And some of it, the paintings just weren't that attractive.

Michael Sadler [Saga singer]:   Generally, they were portrayed—especially in Whitesnake videos or Ratt or Cinderella or Poison, that whole genre—as "the groupie," as the subservient fan that would do anything for the band. And, generally, that was the case. Maybe art imitating life, I don't know. But I know that that was the lifestyle with those kinds of bands, the "hair bands" of the time. But they were portrayed as a lot of them . . . unfortunately, that was not that fictitious. That was pretty much what was happening at the backstage doors and hotel rooms.

---

1 Martha refers to Martha Quinn, one of the five MTV video jockeys.

Mark Weiss [Rock photographer]:   I think they were the way it should be in rock 'n' roll—girls with big boobs and scantily dressed and sex. To me, that's the way they were designed for in the '80s. I mean, the '70s, there was the groupies, and in the '80s, there were the bimbos. Everyone used to hang out with the rock stars, and you took it to the max. I used to pull girls out of the crowd all the time and photograph them—naked, half-naked. I'd say, "Do you want to take a picture with the band?" And they'd take their top off and have their backs to the camera, whatever.

John Doe [X singer/bassist]:   It was just as revolting as it is now. But that was why the hair bands succeeded and punk rock bands didn't, because they were willing to play that game. They were willing to play that card, and not be mentally challenging. And that played into MTV. Pretty antifeminist point of view. The kind of rap artists and urban artists, that came later . . . maybe not. I don't remember Grandmaster Flash and the Furious Five videos. I do remember Kurtis Blow, but that was kind of shots of the street, as far as I remember.

Jello Biafra [Dead Kennedys singer]:   I think it was a deliberate throwback. I mean, how many of those videos were ever directed by women? It's the same old Hollywood we've had for decades, where generation after generation or hypertalented female actresses can't get a job because of the way they look. Remember, Jane Fonda was ordered to get a bunch of her teeth pulled, because Hollywood didn't think her face was skinny enough, and she resisted. I mean, that still goes on, only we have boob jobs, nose jobs, and thanks in part to "eMpTyV" and *American Idol*, now we have aspiring L.A. chicks getting boob jobs from their parents as a high school graduation present.

I have very, very deep objections to this whole way the "fashion police" beat up on people—both guys, but especially, young girls. Where no matter how smart, creative, or interesting you are, what you really have to worry about is you're too fat, or you don't look enough like Britney Spears, or your friends might not like you, or somebody might think you're weird, and, "Oh my God, you're an ugly duckling unless it's the *90210* world or *Dawson's Creek* for you." Both of which I think were pitched at MTV viewers, and the influence crept in on those, too. Granted, I did watch the "prom" episode of *90210* with a room full of drag queens all in prom dresses once. I thought that was pretty amusing.

The pin-up girls of the '40s and '50s could never get jobs in Hollywood today, because they're not emaciated enough. "We want a bulimic body with a great big boob job on top, or you don't get on camera. Because the only roles we're going to bother writing for you in our stupid movies and our stupid TV shows . . . the guys can play *characters*, but you're going to play *the girl*." And there are a few over the years that have been able to break out of that, but considering how few of them have been able to establish themselves, a la Meryl Streep, Julia Roberts, Rosie O'Donnell, or Sarah Silverman, versus how many guys can break out of that, it's still "Exhibit A" on how far we have to go in the way that women are treated not only in culture but also in daily life. A friend of mine who worked in that scene in L.A. had a great term for what they do with women in a lot of videos. She called them "wiggle girls."

Joe Elliott: But with the women thing, I don't think there was ever a sexist stance. I just don't think that generally that many women got into it. I wish the Runaways would have started seven or eight years later. I would have loved to have seen them do a video for "Queens of Noise" or "Cherry Bomb."

Lita Ford [Solo artist, singer/guitarist]:   I had to change lyrics. I had to change a few things—clothes. Especially being a woman, women can be extremely sexual . . . as well as a man.

But for some reason, they have to pick on the women. I did get some attitude from the record company. "Lita, don't wear so much make-up," and "Maybe you should cover yourself up a little bit," or "Don't wear black nail polish." I was always being told what to do and what not to do. I never listened to any of them. I just went ahead and did what I wanted to do. If they wanted to sign somebody like Britney Spears, then they should have signed Britney Spears if they didn't like me. But I didn't want to change. I wanted to be different. I wanted to be one of the first to do what I do. Being a female guitarist, the sexuality thing is part of the act. Sex attracts. And that's what I wanted to get across. It wasn't the fact that I was just trying to be a sex symbol or anything. I was just trying to sell records.

Kmart, Target, Wal-Mart, all those kind of stores refused to put *Out for Blood* in their stores because of the guitar being broken in half, with the guts hanging out and stuff. I was wearing a g-string. I don't remember what I wore in the video . . . I personally think it's decent. Women wear a lot less these days than they did back then, and that was an issue, because of the things that I was wearing . . . or not wearing. I remember having to do re-do the album cover, so I didn't look so "undressed," and holding the guitar in front of my crotch, so you didn't see the g-string so much. Just stuff like that I had to deal with. I went ahead and did a lot of it anyway. How many times are they going to tell you, "No, no, no"? Because each time they do, it costs them a ton of money. So I just tried to stick to "Lita." That's who I am, and that's who I wanted to portray. I didn't want to put on some pink dress or whatever. It really was an issue, and I had to fight it.

Source: Greg Prato, *MTV Ruled the World: The Early Years of Music Video* (lulu.com, 2010), pp. 67–69, 153–57, 158–60, 349–50, 352–55.

43

"Molly Hatchet
Celebrity Rate-A-Record"

HIT PARADER MAGAZINE

For decades music magazines from *Down Beat* to *Melody Maker* took the "celebrity record review" as an opportunity to offer its readership a more personal glimpse into the worlds of their favorite artists. Cast as critics, musicians could reinforce the taste hierarchies of the genre(s) to which they most closely belonged, or they could use the review platform to reveal an unexpected depth and breadth in their listening habits. Invited by the heavy metal/hard rock magazine *Hit Parader* in the summer of 1983 to review the latest batch of 7-inch vinyl singles (45s), vocalist Danny Joe Brown (1951–2005) and lead guitarist Dave Hlubek (1951–2017) of the southern rock band Molly Hatchet accomplish a little of both. As their brutally blunt comments make clear (it is difficult to imagine such a review being published today), a genre like southern rock or heavy metal is defined as much by exclusion as it is by inclusion. Taken as a whole, the range of music they encounter serves as a reminder that at any given moment rock can consist of an astonishingly diverse array of styles.

We gave Molly Hatchet's Dave Hlubek and Danny Joe Brown a stack of recent 45s and asked them to give us their first impressions. The pair pulled no punches when it came to analyzing the product.

I Eat Cannibals, **Total Coelo**

Dave Hlubek: (looking at the picture sleeve) Is she squatting to take a leak?
Danny Joe Brown: Let's hear ZZ Top. Fuck this cannibal shit.
DH: They look like real pros. There's Kansas' fiddle player. Is he squatting on it too? And they say our careers are in trouble! Duane Allman is going to rise from his grave and slap these bitches. (Breaks the record.)

Electric Avenue, **Eddy Grant**

DH: It's a poor copy of Men At Work, those faggots from Australia. Rate-A-Record? A one.
DJB: A six on a scale of 100.

Living On The Ceiling, **Blancmange**

DH: They get a zero for originality. It's all the same. They all should make one big group; they're already using the same band and changing the names. These fuckers are stupid.
DJB: Wait a minute, I was getting into the lyrics. "I'm so tall, I'm so tall." That's fucking happening for tall people.

DH: Well then let's do a cover version for our next album. I'm thinking about all the good musicians out of work. I wouldn't even shit on this stuff. It really sucks. That's like puke on a record. (Breaks the record.)

Body Talk, **Kix**

DH: This is it, I like this song. It sounds like a speeded-up version of (I Am) Iron Man. That's the only part I like, the part "body talk," where it sounds like a heavy metal rubber duck. I can't break this one.

Gimme All Your Lovin', **ZZ Top**

DH: (cranks it very loud) I heard it a lot on the radio. I made sure it got a lot of radio— I paid the station managers.

DJB: Sounds like a real drum already.

DH: Drums by Mattel. Look at these three guys and call them faggots and they'll kick your ass. They are the most powerful three-piece band ever. I've been called narrow-minded, and that's one of the lighter comments, Great record. This is mine (puts it under his coat).

Windows, **Missing Persons**

DH: (breaks it) Oh, I was supposed to listen to it first.

Photograph, **Def Leppard**

DJB: Def is smoking. Let's hear that. They've done better.

DH: So Def Leppard did a cop on Boston's sound. You would think that Tom Scholz produced it because they've taken that sound. It's Boston for sure.

DJB: We're Skynyrd clones, so they've got to be something.

DH: This song deserves to be in the top 10. It worked for Boston for two years. Maybe we sound like the wrong people. I like this song. No wonder it's a hit.

Little Red Corvette, **Prince**

DH: That sound reminds me of Bette Davis Eyes. I knew somebody else would use it. If it was titled differently and the lyrics were different, I'd like the song. The music is different. I kind of like this. (Danny Joe Brown gets up to turn off the record.) Danny doesn't like it. How can I tell? Something about the record flying through the air.

DJB: When that guy grows up, he'll be Michael Jackson.

Mr. Soul, **Neil Young**

DH: That's not the Mr. Soul I knew.

DJB: This is great—I love this. I dig the shit out of this.

DH: We used to do this song. We wanted to record it because we all love Buffalo Springfield. I'm used to hearing the up tempo version. This is so much slower. Wait, this is his disco beat. I like it better the other way.

Saturday At Midnight, **Cheap Trick**

DH: That's Cheap Trick. They sold out. How do you top the Beatles? Frankly, I'm disappointed with Cheap Trick. We toured with them several times; we watched Bun E. Carlos get laid in Amsterdam. But c'mon Rick, Robin, get wise.

DJB:	What a waste of talent.
DH:	This is what happens when you do it yourself.

This Is For Real, **Aretha Franklin**

DH:	It's Aretha. I love Aretha. As always, the champagne lady still serves champagne. This is timeless. She doesn't care about the trends. She's been there and will always be there. This is music. She gets an A+ on this.
DJB:	I'd like to hear her and Lionel Richie together.
DH:	That would be smoking.

Never Say Goodbye, **Yoko Ono**

DH:	If she sounds as good as on the *White Album*, it should smoke. It sounds like an Uncle Ben's commercial. You notice her voice on the beginning of the record? That's her whining. She doesn't have an ounce of talent.

Put Angels Around You, **Maggie Bell and Bobby Whitlock**

DH:	Bobby Whitlock . . . tried to steal my bass player and drummer.
DJB:	He's trying to sound like Michael McDonald and it's not working.
DH:	It's coming out like a drunk Joe Cocker and it's not happening. Bobby Whitlock doesn't know where he wants to go musically.

Source: "Celebrity Rate-A-Record: Molly Hatchet," *Hit Parader*, September 1983, p. 23.

44

The Parents Music Resource Center

Statement before Congress

Susan Baker and Tipper Gore

Few events involving rock music in the 1980s generated more media attention than the September 1985 congressional hearings instigated by the Parents Music Resource Center (PMRC). Led by Susan Baker (wife of Treasury Secretary James Baker) and Tipper Gore (wife of Tennessee senator Al Gore)—and accordingly dubbed the "Washington Wives" by the press—the PMRC convinced the Senate to hear testimony on the questionable content and escalating influence of contemporary rock music and MTV videos. As Baker and Gore insisted, the organization's intent was solely to make information available for parents and consumers concerned about the contents of the records that their children were purchasing. While they initially sought a rating system similar to the Motion Picture Association of America's guidelines for films, the PMRC eventually prevailed on a more general scale when it convinced the recording industry to implement the "parental advisory—explicit content" sticker. In the Senate testimony excerpted here, Baker and Gore justify the rationale for the parental advisory label, and with the aid of Jeff Ling, a Fairfax, Virginia youth pastor, cite numerous musical examples (the majority of them drawn from heavy metal) meant to demonstrate the extremities of rock's explicit sexual content and graphic violence. The PMRC hearings revisited age-old debates over the relationship between music and society. Does rock music perpetuate America's most troublesome social ills or, as its advocates claim, is it simply 'entertainment'? And where should the responsibility for society's troubles ultimately lie? The PMRC's testimony was followed by three respondents—Frank Zappa, John Denver, and Dee Snider—all of whom felt that the organization had forced their ideological interpretations on the music, and was wading into the dangerous waters of censorship. Do you agree with their assessment?

As one might expect with a document such as this Senate hearing, the translation from oral testimony to printed matter resulted in many inaccuracies. These are most noticeable in the misspelling of artist names (Billie Holiday, Ozzy Osbourne, Mercyful Fate, and Metallica among them) and record labels (Elektra, Capitol), and slight discrepancies in song titles (e.g. "Give Me More" as opposed to "Gimme More"). These are relatively minor and remain uncorrected in the text. There are other instances, however, where the errors are more substantial or significant, and these are addressed in the accompanying footnotes.

Mrs. BAKER. Thank you very much, Mr. Chairman. We would like to thank you and the committee for the opportunity to testify before you.

The CHAIRMAN. Could you please speak directly into the microphone, thank you.

Mrs. BAKER. Before I begin, I would like to introduce the president of the PMRC, Pam Howar, and our treasurer, Sally Nevius.

The Parents Music Resource Center was organized in May of this year by mothers of young children who are very concerned by the growing trend in music toward lyrics that are sexually explicit, excessively violent, or glorify the use of drugs and alcohol.

Our primary purpose is to educate and inform parents about this alarming trend as well as to ask the industry to exercise self-restraint.

It is no secret that today's rock music is a very important part of adolescence and teenagers' lives. It always has been, and we don't question their right to have their own music. We think that is important. They use it to identify and give expression to their feelings, their problems, their joys, sorrows, loves, and values. It wakes them up in the morning and it is in the background as they get dressed for school. It is played on the bus. It is listened to in the cafeteria during lunch. It is played as they do their homework. They even watch it on MTV now. It is danced to at parties, and puts them to sleep at night.

Because anything that we are exposed to that much has some influence on us, we believe that the music industry has a special responsibility as the message of songs goes from the suggestive to the blatantly explicit.

As Ellen Goodman stated in a recent column, rock ratings:

> The outrageous edge of rock and roll has shifted its focus from Elvis's pelvis to the saw protruding from Blackie Lawless's codpiece on a WASP album. Rock lyrics have turned from "I can't get no satisfaction" to "I am going to force you at gunpoint to eat me alive."[1]

The material we are concerned about cannot be compared with Louie Louie, Cole Porter, Billie Holliday, et cetera. Cole Porter's "the birds do it, the bees do it," can hardly be compared with WASP, "I f-u-c-k like a beast." There is a new element of vulgarity and violence toward women that is unprecedented.

While a few outrageous recordings have always existed in the past, the proliferation of songs glorifying rape, sadomasochism, incest, the occult, and suicide by a growing number of bands illustrates this escalating trend that is alarming.

Some have suggested that the records in question are only a minute element in this music. However, these records are not few, and have sold millions of copies, like Prince's "Darling Nikki," about masturbation, sold over 10 million copies. Judas Priest, the one about forced oral sex at gunpoint, has sold over 2 million copies. Quiet Riot, "Metal Health," has songs about explicit sex, over 5 million copies. Motley Crue, "Shout at the Devil," which contains violence and brutality to women, over 2 million copies.

Some say there is no cause for concern. We believe there is. Teen pregnancies and teenage suicide rates are at epidemic proportions today. The Noedecker Report states that in the United States of America we have the highest teen pregnancy rate of any developed country: 96 out of 1,000 teenage girls become pregnant.

Rape is up 7 percent in the latest statistics, and the suicide rates of youth between 16 and 24 has gone up 300 percent in the last three decades while the adult level has remained the same.

There certainly are many causes for these ills in our society, but it is our contention that the pervasive messages aimed at children which promote and glorify suicide, rape, sadomasochism, and so on, have to be numbered among the contributing factors.

---

1 The quote comes from Ellen Goodman, "Rock Ratings," *The Washington Post*, September 14, 1985, p. A19.

Some rock artists actually seem to encourage teen suicide. Ozzie Osbourne sings "Suicide Solution." Blue Oyster Cult sings "Don't Fear the Reaper." AC/DC sings "Shoot to Thrill." Just last week in Centerpoint, a small Texas town, a young man took his life while listening to the music of AC/DC. He was not the first.

Now that more and more elementary school children are becoming consumers of rock music, we think it is imperative to discuss this question. What can be done to help parents who want to protect their children from these messages if they want to?

Today parents have no way of knowing the content of music products that their children are buying. While some album covers are sexually explicit or depict violence, many others give no clue as to the content. One of the top 10 today is Morris Day and the Time, "Jungle Love." If you go to buy the album "Ice Cream Castles" to get "Jungle Love," you also get, "If the Kid Can't Make You Come, Nobody Can," a sexually explicit song.

The pleasant cover picture of the members of the band gives no hint that it contains material that is not appropriate for young consumers.

Our children are faced with so many choices today. What is available to them through the media is historically unique. The Robert Johnson study on teen environment states that young people themselves often feel that they have: One, too many choices to make: two, too few structured means for arriving at decisions: and three, too little help to get there.

We believe something can be done, and Tipper Gore will discuss the possible solution. Thank you.

Mrs. GORE. Thank you, Mr. Chairman.

We are asking the recording industry to voluntarily assist parents who are concerned by placing a warning label on music products inappropriate for younger children due to explicit sexual or violent lyrics.

The Parents Music Resource Center originally proposed a categorical rating system for explicit material. After many discussions with the record industry, we recognize some of the logistical and economic problems, and have adjusted our original suggestions accordingly. We now propose one generic warning label to inform consumers in the marketplace about lyric content. The labels would apply to all music.

We have asked the record companies to voluntarily label their own products and assume responsibility for making those judgments. We ask the record industry to appoint a one-time panel to recommend a uniform set of criteria which could serve as a policy guide for the individual companies. Those individual recording companies would then in good faith agree to adhere to this standard, and make decisions internally about which records should be labeled according to the industry criteria.

We have also asked that lyrics for labeled music products be available to the consumer before purchase in the marketplace. Now, it is important to clearly state what our proposal is not.

A voluntary labeling is not censorship. Censorship implies restricting access or suppressing content. This proposal does neither. Moreover, it involves no Government action. Voluntary labeling in no way infringes upon first amendment rights. Labeling is little more than truth in packaging, by now, a time honored principle in our free enterprise system, and without labeling, parental guidance is virtually impossible.

Most importantly, the committee should understand the Parents Music Resource Center is not advocating any Federal intervention or legislation whatsoever. The excesses that we are discussing were allowed to develop in the marketplace, and we believe the solutions to these excesses should come from the industry who has allowed them to develop and not from the Government.

The issue here is larger than violent and sexually explicit lyrics. It is one of ideas and ideal freedoms and responsibility in our society. Clearly, there is a tension here, and in a free society there always will be. We are simply asking that these corporate and artistic rights be exercised with responsibility, with sensitivity, and some measure of self-restraint, especially since young minds are at stake. We are talking about preteenagers and young teenagers having access to this material. That is our point of departure and our concern.

Now, Mr. Chairman, one point we have already made, that the material that has caused the concern is new and different. It is not just a continuation of controversies of past generations. To illustrate this point, we would like to show a slide presentation, and to this end I turn the microphone over to Jeff Ling, who is a consultant to our group, and he will show you some of the material that we are talking about.

Thank you.

Mr. LING. Mr. Chairman, if we could have the lights turned down.

[Slides were then shown.]

Mr. LING. Mr. Chairman and distinguished members of the committee, thank you for allowing me to speak to you today. The purpose of this presentation is to acquaint you with the type of material that is in question.

I will be covering the themes of violence and sexuality. Bear in mind that what you are about to see and hear is a small sample of the abundant material available today. Today the element of violent, brutal erotica has exploded in rock music in an unprecedented way. Many albums today include songs that encourage suicide, violent revenge, sexual violence, and violence just for violence's sake.

This is Steve Boucher. Steve died while listening to AC/DC's "Shoot to Thrill." Steve fired his father's gun into his mouth.

A few days ago I was speaking in San Antonio. The day before I arrived, they buried a young high school student. This young man had taken his tape deck to the football field.

He hung himself while listening to AC/DC's "Shoot to Thrill." Suicide has become epidemic in our country among teenagers.

Some 6,000 will take their lives this year. Many of these young people find encouragement from some rock stars who present death as a positive, almost attractive alternative.

The album I am holding up in front of you is by the band Metalica. It is on Electra Asylum records. A song on this album is called "Faith in Black."[2] It says the following. "I have lost the will to live. Simply nothing more to give. There is nothing more for me. I need the end to set me free."

Consider the self-destructive violence that is encouraged in their song "Whiplash." "Bang your head against the stage like you never have before. Make it rain, make it bleed, make it really sore . . ."

Ozzie Osbourne on his first solo album, shown here, sings a song called "Suicide Solution." Ozzie insists that he in no way encourages suicidal behavior in young people, and yet he appears in photographs such as these in periodicals that are geared toward the young teenage audience.

For those of you who cannot make that out because of the lights, it is a picture of Ozzie with a gun barrel stuck into his mouth.

This is the cover of Twisted Sister's high selling LP for Atlantic Records called "Stay Hungry." An example of Twisted Sister's appeal to young people is evident in the back to school contest being run by MTV. First prize is a get together with Twisted Sister. The first prize is a meeting with Twisted Sister.

The hit song from the album, "We're Not Going to Take It," was released as a video, which you saw just a moment ago, a video in which the band members proceed to beat up daddy, who will not let them rock. Their first album, which has been rereleased by Atlantic Records, is called "Under the Blade."

---

2 The correct song title is "Fade to Black."

The title song includes words like "Your hands are tied, your legs are strapped, you are going under the blade." In lyrics from the song "Shoot them Down," the band sings, "They think we are fools who want to make their own rules. It only gets us madder . . . Shoot them down with a fucking gun."

This is the cover of AC/DC's brand new album for Atlantic Records, "Fly on the Wall."

One of the songs from the album "Back in Business" was released as a single for airplay and included the words, "Don't you struggle or try to bite. You want some trouble. I am the king of vice. I am a wrecking ball. I am a stinging knife . . . Steal your money. Going to take your life."

Of course, AC/DC is no stranger to violent material. Their song "Squealer" contained the following. "She said she had never been balled before, and I don't think she'll ball no more. Fixed her good."

One of their fans I know you are aware of is the accused Night Stalker.[3]

Judas Priest sings of violent rape in their song "Eat Me Alive" from their Columbia Records released "Defenders of the Faith." "Squealing in passion as the rod of steel injects. Gut wrenching frenzy that deranges every joint. I am going to force you at gunpoint to eat me alive."

The band Great White in their album "On Their Knees"[4] sings these words "Knocking down your door, going to pull you to the floor . . . going to drive my love inside you, going to nail your ass to the floor."

This is Motley Crue. Their albums for Electra Asylum sell millions, and they are one of the top 10 grossing concert bands this year. Their albums include songs like "Bastard." "Out goes the light. In goes my knife. Pull out his life. Consider that bastard dead."

"Live Wire." "I will either break her face or take down her legs. Get my ways at will. Go for the throat and never let loose. Going in for the kill."

And "Too Young to Fall in Love." "Not a woman, but a whore. I can taste the hate. Well, now I am killing you. Watch your face turning blue."

This is the cover of the new album by the band Abattoir.

The title song is about a homocidal maniac, and notice on the cover the arms of the man wrapped around the woman. In one hand is a long knife. The other hand holds a hook being pressed against the woman's breast.

This is the cover of an album entitled "Rise of the Mutants" by the band Impaler.

Notice the man with the bloody meat in his mouth and hand. He is kneeling over the bloody arm of a woman.

The back cover shows a woman with a bloody face at the feet of the drummer.

While both of these albums were released on independent labels as opposed to major labels, they are reviewed and featured in teen rock magazines and are available in local record stores.

This band, WASP, recently signed a $1.5 million contract with Capital Records. This is their first release. The capital item is entitled "The Torture Never Stops." Violence permeates the album as well as their stage show, which has included chopping up and throwing raw meat into the audience.

Drinking blood from a skull.

And until recently the simulated rape and murder of a half-nude woman.

This single is available in record stores across the country. The cover features the cod piece that lead singer Blackie Lawless wears on stage. In this picture, there is blood dripping down his stomach, hands, and off of the blade between his legs. The song that accompanies this photo is "Fuck Like a Beast."

---

3 Mass-murderer Richard Ramirez, a.k.a. the "Night Stalker," had been brought into custody roughly three weeks before the PMRC's senate testimony.
4 The correct title is "On Your Knees"

This band, Piledriver, fuses together the elements of sexual violence and occult in the song "Lust."[5] I forgot. It is right here in front of me. The song is called "Lust." The lyrics say, "Hell on fire. Lust, desire. The devil wants to stick you. The devil wants to lick you. He wants your body. He wants your spirit . . . Sex with Satan. Sex with Satan."

While we will not consider the subject in depth at this time, it should be noted that occultic themes, primarily Satanism, is prevalent among such bands as Slayer, Venom, and Merciful Fate, one of whose albums is shown in this picture.

Let us move on to sexuality, a theme which has been part of rock music since its beginning. Today's rock artists are describing sexual activity and practice in terms more graphic than ever before. Many of you are aware of Purple Rain, the multimillion seller by Prince. Much has been said about the song "Darling Nikki" from the album. "I met a girl named Nikki. I guess you could say she was a sex fiend. I met her in a hotel lobby masturbating with magazines."

Another album by Prince called "Dirty Mind" presents a positive attitude toward the subject of incest.

These lyrics are from the song called "Sister." "I was only 16, but I guess that is no excuse. My sister was 32, and kind of alone. My sister never made love to anyone but me. Incest is everything it's said to be."

This is the cover of the album "Stakk Attakk" by the band Wrath Child. The back cover of this album, which is available to young children in record stores, included this photo of a nude woman on the back of the album. Songs include "Sweet Surrender." "I lick my lips and make advances. You lay on down and let me in. But you can't fight. You've got no choice. I will take you down and rub my cream in."

Another song on an earlier album called "Cock Rock Shock" said the words "We are going to fuck you" and "Oh, you fucking little bitch."

This is Motley Crue's album, "Shout at the Devil," double platinum. The song on the album we are concerned with here is "Ten Seconds to Love." "Touch my gun, but don't pull my trigger. Shine my pistol some more. Here I come . . ."

The band KISS, popular with young people, "At All Times," their brand new album,[6] was released just yesterday, includes songs such as "Fits Like a Glove."[7] "Ain't a cardinal sin, baby. Let me in. Girl, I am going to treat you right. Well, goodness sakes, my snake's alive, and it is ready to bite . . ."

And the song, "Give Me More." "Hot blood, need your love. Hard as rock, can't get enough . . . Make you sweat, make you moan. Come on, lick my candy cane."

This is Betsy. She is the lead singer of a band called Bitch. The album is called "Be My Slave." It is available in record stores. One of the songs is called "Give Me a Kiss." "The way you grab me makes my knees shake. The way you pull my arms makes my body quake . . . Come on and slap me in the face, and I will get down on my knees and move you like this."

And the song "Leatherbound." "The whip is my toy. Handcuffs are your joy. You hold me down, and I am screaming for more . . ."

The Rolling Stones on their album "Under Cover" also sang of sadomasochistic activities in the song "Tie You Up." "The pain of love, you dream of it, passion it. You even get a rise from it. Feel the hot come dripping on your thigh from it . . ."

---

5 The correct song title is "Sex with Satan."
6 The album that KISS had just released is entitled *Asylum*, not *At All Times*.
7 "Fits Like a Glove" and "Gimme More" both come from the group's 1983 release, *Lick It Up*.

Even the Jacksons' mainstream pop music today, their song, "Torture," was released as a video, and was shown on national TV. That video included pictures of women dressed in leather bondage, masks, with whips in their hands, in chains, and wrapped up in handcuffs.

Some artists take their pornograph rock to the stage. This is a picture of Wendy O'Williams in concert. Concerts that young adolescents can attend.

[End of slide presentation.]

Mr. LING. HOW bad can it get? The list is endless. This album was released just recently by a band called the Mentors. It was released in an album with the label Enigma Records, which also launched Motley Crue's career. The album includes songs like "Four-F Club," "Find Her, Feel Her, Fuck Her, and Forget Her,"[8] "Free Fix for a Fuck,"[9] "Clap Queen," "My Erection is Over," and the song "Golden Showers," which says these words, "Listen, you little slut, do as you are told, come with daddy for me to pour the gold . . . Bend up and smell my anal vapor. Your face is my toilet paper. On your face I leave a shit tower. Golden showers." Mr. Chairman, that concludes my remarks. I thank you.

Source: Hearing Before the Senate Committee on Commerce, Science, and Transportation, *Contents of Music and the Lyrics of Records*, 99th Congress, First Session, September 19, 1985, pp. 10–16.

---

8 This is not a song title, but rather the refrain from the song "Four-F-Club."
9 The correct song title is just "Free Fix."

45

Heavy Metal and The Highbrow/ Lowbrow Divide

Robert Walser

Robert Walser, Professor of Musicology at Case Western Reserve University, was one of the first academic scholars to attempt a serious and sympathetic analysis of the much-maligned genre of heavy metal in his landmark study *Running with the Devil: Power, Gender, and Madness in Heavy Metal* (Hanover: Wesleyan University Press, 1993). The essay reprinted here draws on material from his book, and was originally presented as part of a 1992 American Studies conference at Princeton University. At the time, few could have imagined two more polar opposites than the supposedly brutish power of "lowbrow" heavy metal and the sophisticated taste of "highbrow" classical music. But Walser complicates this assumed division, showing how heavy metal guitarists from Ritchie Blackmore (born 1945) to Eddie Van Halen (born 1955) have long "experimented with the musical materials of eighteenth- and nineteenth-century European composers," to the point where classical conventions are an essential component of the heavy metal style. Walser carefully demonstrates how classical's symbolic values and theoretical musical language has become imbued in heavy metal through such pedagogical forces as the widely influential magazine, *Guitar for the Practicing Musician*. Long after its commercial peak of the 1980s, heavy metal continues to thrive as a popular international style. To what degree does classical music figure into today's heavy metal?

In his recent book on the emergence of cultural hierarchy in the United States, Lawrence Levine reminds us that when we use the terms "highbrow" and "lowbrow," we pay homage to the racist pseudoscience of phrenology.[1] Nineteenth-century phrenologists correlated moral and intellectual characteristics with brain size and skull shape, creating a hierarchy that conveniently placed themselves, white men, at the top. Subsequently, as "highbrow," "lowbrow" and "middlebrow" came into common usage to designate the relative worth of people and cultural activities, the social category of class was also mapped onto this hierarchy, and working-class culture acquired the aura of primitivity that nineteenth-century writers had projected onto non-white races. Levine's book is a valuable reminder that types such as "highbrow" and "lowbrow," or "classical" and "popular," do not simply reflect internal properties of texts or practices, but are, rather, invented categories that do cultural work. Like phrenology, cultural hierarchy functioned to naturalize social and cultural inequalities and deny the creative capacities of whole groups of people.

But Levine's topic does not belong to the nineteenth century alone; whether or not the same labels are used (and they often are), such essentializing categories are still at work at the end of the twentieth century, and they retain the power to affect millions of lives. People are constantly being typed by their cultural allegiances, respected or dismissed because of the music they like. Moreover, we internalize these categories; when I interviewed heavy metal fans, I found that while some of them regarded heavy metal music as the most important thing in their lives, they nonetheless completely accepted the conventional wisdom that classical music is categorically superior to any popular music. Many other people are similarly led to believe in their own inferiority because of the stories that are told about their culture. No one ever actually explains why classical music is better than all other musics, because no one ever has to explain; cultural hierarchy functions to naturalize social hierarchies through the circular reinscription of prestige—foreclosing dialogue, analysis and argument. Music historians are still writing textbooks of "Twentieth-Century Music" that omit popular musics entirely, without even explaining their exclusion of most of the music that people have actually heard and cared about during the last hundred years.[2]

But not everyone abides by the rules of cultural hierarchy. In the liner notes for his 1988 album, *Odyssey*, heavy metal guitarist Yngwie J. Malmsteen claimed a musical genealogy that confounds the stability of conventional categorizations of music into classical and popular spheres. In his list of acknowledgments, along with the usual cast of agents and producers, suppliers of musical equipment, relatives and friends, Malmsteen expressed gratitude to J. S. Bach, Nicolo Paganini, Antonio Vivaldi, Ludwig van Beethoven, Jimi Hendrix and Ritchie Blackmore.[3] From the very beginnings of heavy metal in the late 1960s, guitar players had experimented with the musical materials of eighteenth- and nineteenth-century European composers. But the trend came to full fruition around the time of Malmsteen's debut in the early 1980s; a writer for the leading professional guitar magazine says flatly that the single most important development in rock guitar in the 1980s was "the turn to classical music for inspiration and form."[4]

Throughout heavy metal's history, its most influential musicians have been guitar players who have also studied some aspects of that assemblage of disparate musical styles known in the twentieth century as "classical music." Their appropriation and adaptation of classical models sparked the development of a new kind of guitar virtuosity, changes in the harmonic and melodic language of heavy metal, and new modes of musical pedagogy and analysis. Of course, the history of American popular music is replete with examples of appropriation "from below"—popular adaptations of classical music. But the classical influence on heavy metal marks a merger of what are generally regarded as the most and least prestigious musical discourses of our time. This influence thus seems an unlikely one, yet metal musicians and fans have found discursive fusions of rock and classical musics useful, invigorating and compelling. Moreover, the meeting took place on the terms established by heavy metal musicians, at their instigation. That is, their fusions were not motivated by the desire for "legitimacy" in classical terms; rather, they have participated in a process of cultural reformulation and recontextualization that has produced new meanings. To those blinkered by the assumptions of cultural hierarchy, such reformulations are impossible to trace or understand because they step outside the dominant logic of cultural production.

Heavy metal appropriations of classical music are in fact very specific and consistent: Bach not Mozart, Paganini rather than Liszt, Vivaldi and Albinoni instead of Telemann or Monteverdi. This selectivity is remarkable at a time when the historical and semiotic specificity of classical music, on its own turf, has all but vanished, when the classical canon is defined and marketed as a reliable set of equally great and ineffable collectibles. By finding new uses for old music, recycling the rhetoric of Bach and Vivaldi for their own purposes, metal musicians have reopened issues of signification in classical music. Their appropriation suggests that, despite the homogenization of that music in the literatures of "music appreciation" and commercial promotion, many listeners perceive and respond to differences, to the musical specificity that reflects historical and social specificity. Thus the reasons behind heavy metal's classical turn reveal a great deal not only about heavy metal, but also about classical music. We must ask: if we don't understand his influence on the music of Ozzy Osbourne or Bon Jovi, do we really understand *Bach* as well as we thought we did?

*   *   *

Many rock guitarists have drawn upon classical techniques and procedures in their music; among the most important were Ritchie Blackmore in the late 1960s and 1970s, and Eddie Van Halen in the late 1970s and 1980s. Both had early classical training which familiarized them with that music; later, like most heavy metal guitarists, they turned to methodical study, emulation and adaptation. Blackmore took harmonic progressions, phrase patterns and figuration from Baroque models such as Vivaldi. As Blackmore himself has pointed out in numerous interviews, these classical features show up in many of the songs he recorded with Deep Purple: "For example, the chord progression in the "Highway Star" solo on *Machine Head* . . . is a Bach progression." And the solo is "just arpeggios based on Bach."[5]

Eddie Van Halen revolutionized rock guitar with his unprecedented virtuosity and the "tapping" technique he popularized in "Eruption" (1978), which demonstrated the possibility of playing speedy arpeggios on the guitar. Van Halen also participated in the technological developments that helped make Baroque models newly relevant to heavy metal guitar players.[6] The electrification of the guitar, begun in the 1920s, and subsequent developments in equipment and playing techniques, particularly the production of sophisticated distortion circuitry in the 1960s, acquired for the guitar the capabilities of the premier virtuosic instruments of the seventeenth and eighteenth centuries: the power and speed of the organ, the flexibility and nuance of the violin. Increases in sustain and volume made possible the conceptual and technical shifts that led players to explore Baroque models.

Two guitarists of the 1980s, Randy Rhoads and Yngwie Malmsteen, brought heavy metal neoclassicism to fruition and inspired a legion of imitators. Like Edward Van Halen, Rhoads grew up in a musical household; he enrolled as a student at his mother's music school at the age of six, studying guitar, piano and music theory, and a few years later began classical guitar lessons, which he would continue throughout his career. In 1980, he landed the guitar chair in a new band fronted by ex-Black Sabbath vocalist Ozzy Osbourne; during his brief tenure with Osbourne's band (ending with his death at age twenty-five in a plane crash), Rhoads became famous as the first guitar player of the 1980s to expand the classical influence, further adapting and integrating a harmonic and melodic vocabulary derived from classical music. Among his early musical influences, Rhoads cited the dark moods and drama of Alice Cooper, Ritchie Blackmore's fusion of rock and classical music, Van Halen's tapping technique, and his favorite classical composers, Vivaldi and Pachelbel.[7]

Rhoads's and Osbourne's "Mr. Crowley" (1981) begins with synthesized organ, playing a cyclical harmonic progression modelled on Vivaldi. The minor mode, the ominous organ and the fateful cyclicism, culminating in a suspension, are used to set up an affect of mystery and doom, supporting the mocking treatment of English satanist Aleister Crowley in the lyrics.[8] The progression that underpins Rhoads's "outro" (closing) solo at the end of the song is a straightforward Vivaldian circle of fifths progression: Dm | Gm7 | C | F | Bb | Em7b5 | Asus4 | A. Until classically influenced heavy metal, such cyclical progressions were unusual in rock music, which had been fundamentally blues-based. The classical influence contributed to a greater reliance on the power of harmonic progression to organize desire and narrative, as well as the turn toward virtuosic soloing. Rhoads's solo on the live recording of "Suicide Solution" (1981) makes even more extensive use of Baroque rhetoric, including diminished chords, trills, sliding chromatic figures, a gigue and a tapped section that focuses attention on the drama of harmonic progression.[9] Like the tapping in Van Halen's "Eruption," such figuration leads the listener along an aural adventure, as the guitarist continually sets up implied harmonic goals and then achieves, modifies, extends or subverts them.

Not only the classical materials in his music, but also Rhoads's study of academic music theory influenced many guitarists in the early 1980s. Throughout the decade, years after his death, Rhoads's picture appeared on the covers of guitar magazines, advertising articles that discussed his practicing and teaching methods and analyzed his music. The inner sleeve of the *Tribute* album (1987) reproduces a few pages from Rhoads's personal guitar notebook, showing his systematic exploration of classical music theory. One sheet is titled "Key of C#"; on it, for each of the seven modes based on C# (Ionian, Dorian, Phrygian, and so on), Rhoads wrote out the diatonic chords for each scale degree, followed by secondary and substitute seventh chords. On another page, he composed exercises based on arpeggiated seventh and ninth chords.

Rhoads's interest in music theory was symptomatic of the increasing classical influence on heavy metal, but his success also helped promote classical study among metal guitarists. Winner of *Guitar Player's* "Best New Talent" Award in 1981, Rhoads brought to heavy metal guitar a new model of virtuosity which depended on patterns of discipline and consistency derived from classical models. Besides his classical allusions, and his methods of study and teaching, Rhoads's skill at double-tracking solos (recording them exactly the same way more than once, so that they could be layered on the record to add a sense of depth and space) was extremely influential on subsequent production techniques.[10] Rhoads's accomplishments also contributed to the growing tendency among guitarists to regard their virtuosic solos in terms of a division of labor long accepted in classical music, as opportunities for thoughtful composition and skillful execution, rather than spontaneous improvisation.

Classically influenced players such as Van Halen and Rhoads helped precipitate a shift among guitar players towards a new model of professional excellence, with theory, analysis, pedagogy and technical rigor acquiring new importance. *Guitar for the Practicing Musician*, now the most widely read guitarists' magazine, began publication in 1983, attracting readers with transcriptions and analyses of guitar-based popular music. Its professional guitarist-transcribers developed a sophisticated set of special notations for representing the nuances of performance, rather like the elaborate ornament tables of Baroque music. Their transcriptions are usually accompanied by various kinds of analysis, such as modal (for example, "The next section alternates between the modalities of Eb Lydian and F Mixolydian. . . ."), stylistic (relating new pieces to the history of discursive options available to guitar players) and technical (detailing the techniques used in particular performances).

Swedish guitar virtuoso Yngwie J. Malmsteen continued many of the trends explored by Blackmore, Van Halen, and Rhoads, and took some of them to unprecedented extremes. Malmsteen was exposed to classical music from the age of five; his mother wanted him to be a musician, and made sure he received classical training on several instruments. Yet he claims to have hated music until television brought him a pair of musical epiphanies that, taken together, started him on the path to becoming the most influential rock guitarist since Van Halen. "On the 18th of September, 1970, I saw a show on television with Jimi Hendrix, and I said, 'Wow!' I took the guitar off the wall, and I haven't stopped since."[11] Malmsteen's first exciting encounter with classical music—his exposure to the music of Paganini, the nineteenth-century violin virtuoso—also took place through the mediation of television.[12] Thus the mass mediation of classical music makes it available in contexts that cannot be conventionally policed, for uses that cannot be predicted.

Upon the release of his U.S. debut album in 1984, which won him *Guitar Player's* "Best New Talent" award that year and "Best Rock Guitarist" in 1985, Malmsteen quickly gained a reputation as the foremost of metal's neoclassicists. He adapted classical music with more thoroughness and intensity than any previous guitarist, and he expanded the melodic and harmonic language of metal while setting even higher standards of virtuosic precision. Not only do Malmsteen's solos recreate the rhetoric of his virtuosic heroes, Bach and Paganini, but he introduced further harmonic resources and advanced techniques such as sweep-picking, achieving the best impression yet of the nuance and agility of a virtuoso violinist. Moreover, as I will show below, Malmsteen embraced the ideological premises of classical music more openly than anyone before.

Guitar for the Practicing Musician published a detailed analysis of Malmsteen's "Black Star," from his first U.S. album, *Yngwie J. Malmsteen's Rising Force* (1984). Such analytical pieces are intended as guides to the music of important guitarists, facilitating the study and emulation practiced by the magazine's readers. The following excerpts from Wolf Marshall's commentary can serve both as a summary of some technical features of Malmsteen's music and as a sample of the critical discourse of the writers who theorize and analyze heavy metal in professional guitarists' magazines:

> "Black Star" shows off the many facets of Yngwie's singular style. Whether he is playing subdued acoustic guitar or blazing pyrotechnics, he is unmistakably Yngwie—the newest and perhaps the most striking proponent of the Teutonic-Slavic *Weltsmerz* (as in Bach/Beethoven/Brahms Germanic brooding minor modality) School of Heavy Rock. . . . The opening guitar piece is a classical prelude (as one might expect) to the larger work. It is vaguely reminiscent of Bach's *Bourree* in Em, with its 3/4 rhythm and use of secondary dominant chords. . . . The passage at the close of the guitar's exposition is similar to the effect . . . [of the] spiccato ("bouncing bow") classical violin technique. It is the first of many references to classical violin mannerisms. . . . This is a diminished chord sequence, based on the classical relationship of C diminished: C D♯ F♯ A (chord) to B major in a Harmonic minor mode: E F♯ G A B C D♯. . . . The feeling of this is like some of Paganini's violin passages. . . . While these speedy arpeggio flurries are somewhat reminiscent of Blackmore's frenzied wide raking, they are actually quite measured and exact and require a tremendous amount of hand shifting and stretching as well as precision to accomplish. The concept is more related to virtuoso violin etudes than standard guitar vocabulary. . . . Notice the use of Harmonic minor (Mixolydian mode) in the B major sections and the Baroque Concerto Grosso (Handel/Bach/Vivaldi) style running bass line counterpoint as well.[13]

Marshall's analysis is quite musicological in tone and content; he deliberately compares Malmsteen's recorded performance to classical techniques, contextualizes it through style analysis, and translates certain features into the technical vocabulary of music theory. The style analysis situates "Black Star" with respect to two musical traditions: classical music (Bach, Paganini, Beethoven and so on) and rock guitar (Blackmore). Marshall simultaneously presents a detailed description of the music and links it to the classical tradition by employing the language of academic music theory: chords, modes, counterpoint, form. As rock guitarists have become increasingly interested in studying the history and theory of classical music, Marshall can safely assume that his audience is able to follow such analysis.[14]

Moreover, Marshall's analysis shows that metal guitarists and their pedagogues have not only adopted the trappings of academic discourse about music, but they have also internalized many of the values that underpin that discourse. Even as he carefully contextualizes Malmsteen's music, Marshall insists on its originality and uniqueness ("Yngwie's singular style," "unmistakably Yngwie"). The commentary emphasizes Malmsteen's precision of execution as well ("measured and exact," "tremendous . . . precision"). Most tellingly, Marshall implicitly accepts the categories and conceptions of academic music analysis, along with its terms. For apart from the comment about "arpeggio flurries," Marshall deals exclusively with pitch and form, the traditional concerns of musicological analysis. And just as the discipline of musicology has drawn fire from within and without for ignoring or marginalizing musical rhythm, timbre, gesture, rhetoric and other possible categories of analysis, metal guitarists' own theorists and pedagogues could be criticized for the same restricted analytical vision.[15]

If they are to become effective musicians, metal guitarists must in fact learn to maneuver within musical parameters beyond pitch and form, just as their counterparts within conservatories and music schools must learn much that is not written down. In the academy, such learning is referred to as "musicality," and it is often the focal point of a mystification that covers up classical music's reliance on oral traditions. In both classical music and heavy metal, virtually the same aspects of music are far less theorized, codified and written; music students must learn by listening, emulating and watching the rhythm and gesture of bodily motion. Theorists of metal, like their academic counterparts, rarely deal with musical rhetoric and social meanings; one analysis of Van Halen's "Eruption" merely named the modes employed (E phrygian, A and E aeolian) and summed up with the blandness of a music appreciation text: "a well-balanced, thought-out guitar solo, which features a variety of techniques."[16]

Yngwie Malmsteen exemplifies the wholesale importation of classical music into heavy metal—the adoption of not only classical musical style and vocabulary, models of virtuosic rhetoric and modes of practice, pedagogy and analysis, but also the social values that underpin these activities. These values are a modern mixture of those that accompanied music-making of the seventeenth, eighteenth and nineteenth centuries, fused with the priorities of modernism. Along with virtuosity, the reigning values of metal guitar include a valorization of balance, planning and originality, a conservatory-style fetishization of technique and sometimes even a reactionary philosophy of culture—Malmsteen bemoans the lack of musicianship in today's popular music, and looks back on the "good old days" of the seventeenth century, when, he imagines, standards were much higher.[17] Malmsteen is particularly noted for his elitism, another value he derives from contemporary classical music, and which he justifies by emphasizing his connections with its greater prestige. In interviews, he constantly insists on his own genius, his links to the geniuses of the classical past, and his distance from virtually all contemporary popular musicians, whose music he regards as simple, trite and inept. Because he aspires to the universal status often claimed for classical music, he denounces the genre he is usually thought to inhabit, insisting "I do *not* play heavy metal!"[18]

While he has been known to claim that, as a genius, he never had to practice, Malmsteen also presents himself as one who has suffered for his art. A joint interview with bassist Billy Sheehan preserves an account of his early devotion to music, and its costs:

Yngwie: I was extremely self-critical. I was possessed. For many years I wouldn't do anything else but play the guitar.

Billy: I missed a lot of my youth. I missed the whole girl trip. I didn't start driving until I was 25.

Yngwie: I also sacrificed a lot of the social thing. I didn't care about my peers. To me, nothing else was even close in importance.

Such statements undoubtedly reflect the tendency toward self-aggrandizement and self-pity that have made Malmsteen unloved by his peers in the guitar world. But they also further reflect his virtually total acceptance of the model of music-making promulgated in classical music. Malmsteen, along with many other musicians, sees a need for music to "evolve" toward greater complexity and "sophistication." The pursuit of virtuosic technique usually requires many thousands of hours of patient, private repetition of exercises. To this end, many young players pursue a fanatical practice regime, a pursuit of individual excellence that often leaves little room for communal experiences of music-making, just as is the case in the training of classical musicians.[19]

The extreme extension of this set of ideological values is the complete withdrawal of the musician from his or her public, in pursuit of complexity and private meanings. This strategy, which had earlier been championed by academic composers such as Milton Babbitt, can now be recognized in some virtuosic guitar players. Steve Vai boasts of his most recent album:

What I did with *Passion and Warfare* is the ultimate statement: I *locked* myself into a room and said, "To hell with everything—I'm doing this and it's a complete expression of what I am.

I'm not concerned about singles, I'm not concerned about megaplatinum success, I'm not concerned about record companies." It was a real special time. All too often kids and musicians and artists just have to conform to make a living. I'm one of the lucky few and believe me, I don't take it for granted.[20]

Vai is trying to claim "authenticity" here, trying to prove his autonomy as an artist who is free of the influences of the very social context that makes his artistic statements possible and meaningful. When he goes on to describe his fasting, his visions, his bleeding on the guitar—and his compositional process of painstaking and technologically sophisticated multitrack recording—he presents himself as an updated, self-torturing, Romantic artist, reaching beyond the known world for inspiration. This individualism and self-centeredness unites classical music and heavy metal, and stands in stark contrast to many other kinds of music. For example, a bit later in the same issue of *Musician*, B. B. King says,

What I'm trying to get over to you is this: . . . when I'm on the stage, I am *trying* to entertain. I'm *not* just trying to amuse B. B. King. I'm trying to entertain the people that came to see me. . . . I think that's one of the things that's kind of kept me out here, trying to keep *pleasing* the audience. I think that's one of the mistakes that's happened in music as a whole: A lot of people forget that they got an audience.[21]

Malmsteen's work has convinced some that the classical influence is played out, even as it has been the leading inspiration for the eager experimentation of the avant-garde. He has helped turn many players to a fruitful engagement with the classical tradition, even as he has helped lead them toward the impoverishing regimes of practice and analysis that now dominate that tradition. Malmsteen's abrasive elitism contrasts with his attempt to forge links with the musical past and reinvigorate reified discourses for mass audiences. The new meritocracy of guitar technique he helped to create both encourages the fetishization of individual virtuosity and opens doors for female and African-American musicians, such as Jennifer Batten and Vernon Reid.[22] His music brings to light contradictions that add to our understanding of both heavy metal and classical music.

For heavy metal and classical music exist in the same social context: they are subject to similar structures of marketing and mediation, and they "belong to" and serve the needs of competing social groups whose power is linked to the prestige of their culture. The immense social and cultural distance that is normally assumed to separate classical music and heavy metal is in fact not a gap of musicality, but a more complex one constructed in the interests of cultural hierarchy. Since heavy metal and classical music are markers of social difference and enactments of social experience, their intersection affects the complex relations among those who depend on these musics to legitimate their values. Their discursive fusion provokes insights about the social interests that are powerfully served by invisible patterns of sound.

Heavy metal guitarists, like all other innovative musicians, create new sounds by drawing on the power of the old, and by fusing together their semiotic resources into compelling new combinations. They recognize affinities between their work and the tonal sequences of Vivaldi, the melodic imagination of Bach, the virtuosity of Liszt and Paganini. Metal musicians have revitalized eighteenth- and nineteenth-century music for their mass audience, in a striking demonstration of the ingenuity of popular culture. Although their audience's ability to decode such musical referents owes much to the effects of the ongoing appropriations of classical music by TV and movie composers, heavy metal musicians have accomplished their own adaptation of what has become the somber music of America's aristocracy, reworking it to speak for a different group's claims to power and artistry.

Metal musicians have appropriated the more prestigious discourses of classical music and reworked them into noisy articulations of pride, fear, longing, alienation, aggression and community. Their adaptations of classical music, while they might be seen as travesties by modern devotees of that music, are close in spirit to the eclectic fusions of J. S. Bach and other idols of that tradition. Metal appropriations are rarely parody or pastiche; they are usually a reanimation, a reclamation of signs that can be turned to new uses. Unlike art rock, the point is typically not to refer to a prestigious discourse and thus to bask in reflected glory. Rather, metal musicians adapt classical signs for their own purposes, to signify to their audience, to have real meanings in the present. This is the sort of process to which the linguistic philosopher V. N. Volosinov referred when he wrote that the sign can become an arena of class struggle; Volosinov and the rest of the Bakhtin circle were interested in how signs not only reflect the interests of the social groups that use them, but are also "refracted" when the same signs are used by different groups to different ends.[23] Thus heavy metal musicians and "legitimate" musicians use Bach in drastically different ways.

Like classical musicians, heavy metal musicians draw upon the resources of the past that have been made available to them through mass mediation and their own historical study. But it is precisely such predations that the musical academy is supposed to prevent. Bach's contemporary meanings are produced jointly by musicologists, critics and the marketing departments of record companies and symphony orchestras, and the interpretation of Bach they construct has little to do with the dramatic, noisy meanings found by metal musicians and fans, and everything to do with aesthetics, order, hierarchy and cultural hegemony. The classical music world polices contemporary readings of the "masterworks"; the adaptations of Randy Rhoads and Bon Jovi are ignored, while the acceptability of Stokowski's orchestral transcriptions is debated. Malmsteen's inauthentic performances fall outside the permissable ideological boundaries that manage to contain Maurice André and Glenn Gould. The drive to enforce preferred ideological meanings is, as both Bakhtin and Volosinov put it, "nondialogic." It is oppressive, authoritative and absolute.

> The very same thing that makes the ideological sign vital and mutable is also, however, that which makes it a refracting and distorting medium. The ruling class strives to impart a supraclass, eternal character to the ideological sign, to extinguish or drive inward the struggle between social value judgements which occurs in it, to make the sign uniaccentual.[24]

The social function of distinctions such as "highbrow" and "lowbrow" is precisely to stabilize signs, prop up automatic dismissals, and quash dialogue and debate. But since cultural hegemony is never absolute, appropriations such as those by heavy metal musicians constantly appear on the field of social contestation we call "popular culture."[25] Such disruptions are rarely even acknowledged by academics. In the histories they write and the syllabi they teach, most musicologists continue to define "music" implicitly in terms of the European concert tradition, ignoring non-Western and popular musics, and treating contemporary academic composers such as Milton Babbitt as the heirs to the canon of great classical "masters."

But Babbitt's claim to inherit the mantle of Bach is perhaps more tenuous than that of Randy Rhoads, and not only because Bach and Rhoads utilize, to some extent, a common musical vocabulary. The institutional environment within which Babbitt has worked (and which he helped create and vigorously championed) rewards abstract complexity and often regards listeners and their reactions with indifference or hostility; both Bach and Rhoads composed and performed for particular audiences, gauging their success by their rhetorical effectiveness. Babbitt's music demonstrates his braininess; Bach's and Rhoads's offer powerful, nuanced experiences of trans-cendence and communality. Despite their important differences, Bach and Rhoads have in common their love of virtuosic rhetoric and their willingness to seek to move people, to deploy shared musical codes of signification, to work in musical discourses that are widely intelligible, however complex.

In a recent journalistic defense of cultural hierarchy, Edward Rothstein begins by granting most of the usual objections to it—he admits that both high and low can be good or bad, simple or complex; that particular works of art cannot be considered innately high or low because they move up and down the ladder of cultural prestige as time passes; and that cultural categories are thus neither stable nor self-evident. In the end, though, Rothstein simply insists that the high/low distinction is necessary, falling back on some familiar mystical dogma about autonomy and timelessness, and implying that attacks on cultural hierarchy are attacks on culture. The idea seems to be that the worthy have high culture and the unworthy have popular culture and perhaps a bit of "music appreciation" to let them know what they're missing, a view I would characterize as "voodoo aesthetics" (after George Bush's derisive label for Reagan's trickle-down defense of economic hierarchy). Rothstein concludes by noting that classical composers have appropriated features of popular music, but seems unaware that the reverse has occured incessantly throughout the history of the split; he asserts that "while the high provides tools and perspectives which can comprehend the low, the low is powerless to comprehend the high."[26] Such a leap of faith, such imperial confidence, is prerequisite to voodoo aesthetics.

Rothstein's argument is of the sort that is common among those who know the fenced-in terrain of the so-called "high" much better than the vast, diverse spaces of the "low," for it depends upon denying the creative agency of those who inhabit the latter realm. Like musical phrenologists, critics such as Rothstein work to naturalize a hierarchy that privileges themselves and the culture they care about at the expense of everyone else. But heavy metal guitarists' creative appropriations of classical music rebut such attempts to ground cultural hierarchy in the inherent features of texts or practices. Metal musicians erupted across the Great Divide between "serious" and "popular" music, between "art" and "entertainment," and found that the gap was not as wide as we have been led to believe. As Christopher Small put it,

> The barrier between classical and vernacular music is opaque only when viewed from the point of view of the dominant group; when viewed from the other side it is often transparent, and to the vernacular musician there are not two musics but only one. . . . Bach and Beethoven and other "great composers" are not dead heroes but colleagues, ancestor figures even, who are alive in the present.[27]

Heavy metal musicians' appropriations of classical music help us to see "high culture" and "low culture" as categories that are socially constructed and maintained. Like "highbrow" and "lowbrow," the deployment of such terms benefits certain individuals and groups at the expense of others, and their power depends chiefly upon intimidation. By engaging directly with seventeenth-, eighteenth-, and nineteenth-century composers and performers, by claiming them as heroes and forebears despite contemporary boundaries that would keep them separate, and by mastering and recontextualizing the rhetoric and theoretical apparatus of "high" music, heavy metal musicians have accomplished a critical juxtaposition that undermines the apparent necessity and naturalness of cultural hierarchy. The specific meanings of metal's appropriations in their new contexts are of great importance, of course. But for cultural criticism, perhaps the most salient legacy of the classical influence on heavy metal is the fact that these musicians have "comprehended the high" without accepting its limitations, defying the division that has been such a crucial determinant of musical life in the twentieth century.

NOTES

[1] Lawrence W. Levine, *Highbrow/Lowbrow: The Emergence of Cultural Hierarchy in America* (Cambridge: Harvard University Press, 1988), pp. 221–23. Theories of brows "scientifically" mapped onto the human body the more general concept of "high" and "low" culture, which had been most powerfully theorized earlier in the nineteenth century by German cultural nationalists. Sanna Pedersen has examined the extent to which the emergence of "autonomous" German instrumental music depended on the creation of a demonized other; see her "Enlightened and Romantic German Music Criticism, 1800–1850," Ph.D. dissertation, University of Pennsylvania, forthcoming.

[2] See, for example, Robert P. Morgan, *Twentieth-Century Music: A History of Musical Style in Modern Europe and America* (New York: Norton, 1991); Robert P. Morgan, ed., *Anthology of Twentieth-Century Music* (New York: W. W. Norton, 1992); Glenn Watkins, *Soundings: Music in the Twentieth Century* (New York: Schirmer Books, 1988); and Bryan R. Simms, *Music of the Twentieth Century: Style and Structure* (New York: Schirmer Books, 1986). Of course, there is nothing wrong with writing about some kinds of music and not others; my point is that to use the grand title "Twentieth-Century Music" for a specialized repertoire is to make an implicit ideological argument that these authors neither admit nor defend.

[3] Malmsteen's first U.S. album, *Yngwie J. Malmsteen's Rising Force* (1984), had offered "special thanks" to Bach and Paganini

[4] John Stix, "Yngwie Malmsteen and Billy Sheehan: Summit Meeting at Chops City," *Guitar for the Practicing Musician* (March 1986), p. 59. To be sure, heavy metal, like all forms of rock music, owes its biggest debt to African-American blues. The harmonic progressions, vocal lines and guitar improvisations of metal all rely heavily on the pentatonic scales derived from blues music. The moans and screams of metal guitar playing, now performed with whammy bars and overdriven amplifiers, derive from the bottleneck playing of the Delta blues musicians, and ultimately from earlier African-American vocal styles. Many heavy metal musicians have testified that they learned to play by imitating urban blues guitarists such as B. B. King, Buddy Guy, and Muddy Waters, and those who did not study the blues directly learned it secondhand, from the British cover versions by Eric Clapton and Jimmy Page, or from the most conspicuous link between heavy metal and black blues and R & B, Jimi Hendrix. Glenn Tipton, guitarist with Judas Priest, offers a demonstration of the blues origins of heavy metal licks in J. D. Considine, "Purity and Power," *Musician* (September 1984), pp. 46–50.

[5] Martin K. Webb, "Ritchie Blackmore with Deep Purple," in *Masters of Heavy Metal*, Jas Obrecht, ed., (New York: Quill, 1984), p. 54; and Steve Rosen, "Blackmore's Rainbow," in *Masters of Heavy Metal*, p. 62. Webb apparently misunderstood Blackmore's explanation, for what I have rendered as an ellipsis he transcribed as "Bm to a D$$ to a C to a G," a harmonic progression which is neither characteristic of Bach nor to be found anywhere in "Highway Star." Blackmore was probably referring to the progression that underpins the latter part of his solo, Dm | G | C | A. "Highway Star" was recorded in 1971 and released in 1972 on the album *Machine Head*.

[6] This is described, among other places, in Jas Obrecht, "Van Halen Comes of Age," in *Masters of Heavy Metal*, Jas Obrecht, ed., (New York: Quill, 1984), p. 156.

[7] See Wolf Marshall, "Randy Rhoads: A Musical Appreciation," *Guitar for the Practicing Musician* (June 1985), p. 57.

[8] At the Princeton conference, I performed excerpts of Rhoads's solos on electric guitar, analyzing as I went. Since the printed format prevents me from using sounds and audience reactions as evidence for my arguments, my concern in this paper is more with the cultural significance of metal musicians' activities as appropriators rather than with the musical meanings of the resulting texts. For more on the latter, as well as theoretical discussions of how to ground musical analyses of affect, see my *Running with the Devil: Power, Gender, and Madness in Heavy Metal Music* (Hanover, NH: Wesleyan University Press, 1993); see also Susan McClary, *Feminine Endings: Music, Gender, and Sexuality* (Minneapolis: University of Minnesota Press, 1991), especially chaps. one and seven.

[9] By "Baroque rhetoric," I mean the kind of transgressive virtuosity to be found in, for example, the cadenza of Bach's Brandenburg Concerto No. 5, or his E minor Partita. See Susan McClary's analysis of this Brandenburg in "The Blasphemy of Talking Politics During Bach Year," in *Music and Society: The Politics of Composition, Performance, and Reception*, Richard Leppert and Susan McClary, eds., (Cambridge: Cambridge University Press, 1987), pp. 13–62. The live recording of "Suicide Solution" appears on *Ozzy Osbourne/Randy Rhoads, Tribute* (CBS, 1987 [recorded in 1981]). For a fuller discussion of the song, see my *Running with the Devil*, chap. 5.

[10] See Wolf Marshall, "Randy Rhoads," *Guitar for the Practicing Musician* (April 1986), p. 51.

[11] Matt Resnicoff, "Flash of Two Worlds," *Musician* (September 1990), p. 76.

[12] Joe Lalaina, "Yngwie, the One and Only," *Guitar School* (September 1989), p. 15

[13] Wolf Marshall, "Performance Notes: Black Star," *Guitar for the Practicing Musician Collector's Yearbook* (Winter 1990), pp. 26–27.

[14] In fact, in my experience, many metal guitarists (most of whom, like Bach and Mozart, never attended college) have a much better grasp of harmonic theory and modal analysis than most university graduate students in music.

[15] Compare Janet Levy's cautious but valuable exposé of the values implicit in the writings of academic musicologists, "Covert and Casual Values in Recent Writings About Music," *Journal of Musicology* 6:1 (Winter 1987), pp. 3–27.

[16] Andy Aledort, "Performance Notes," *Guitar for the Practicing Musician Collector's Yearbook* (Winter 1990), p. 6.

[17] John Stix, "Yngwie Malmsteen and Billy Sheehan," p. 59. On the other side of his lineage, Malmsteen cites early Deep Purple as another moment of high musicianship (p. 64).

[18] Fabio Testa, "Yngwie Malmsteen: In Search of a New Kingdom," *The Best of Metal Mania #2* (1987), p. 35.

[19] Guitar players who are members of bands, however, are usually the leading composers of their groups, and the collaborative experience of working out songs and arrangements in a rock band is a type of musical creativity seldom enjoyed by classical musicians.

[20] Matt Resnicoff, "The Latest Temptation of Steve Vai," *Musician* (September 1990), p. 60. Compare Milton Babbitt's "Who Cares If You Listen?" *High Fidelity* (February 1958), pp. 38–40, 126–127.

[21] *Musician* (September 1990), p. 112.

[22] Jennifer Batten, who has toured with Michael Jackson and others, is also a columnist for *Guitar for the Practicing Musician*. Vernon Reid, of Living Colour, has been featured on the cover and in the analyses of the same magazine.

[23] V. N. Volosinov, *Marxism and the Philosophy of Language* (Cambridge, MA: Harvard University Press, 1986). Some authorities believe that this work was actually written by M. M. Bakhtin.

[24] Volosinov, *Marxism and the Philosophy of Language*, p. 23. See also M. M. Bakhtin, *The Dialogic Imagination: Four Essays* (Austin: University of Texas Press, 1981), and Speech Genres and Other Late Essays (Austin: University of Texas Press, 1986).

[25] See Stuart Hall, "Notes on Deconstructing 'The Popular,'" in *People's History and Socialist Theory*, Raphael Samuel, ed., (London: Routledge and Kegan Paul, 1981), pp. 227–240.

[26] Edward Rothstein, "Mr. Berry, Say Hello to Ludwig," *New York Times* (April 5, 1992), p. H31.

[27] Christopher Small, *Music of the Common Tongue: Survival and Celebration in Afro-American Music* (New York: Riverrun, 1987), p. 126.

Source: Robert Walser, "Highbrow, Lowbrow, Voodoo Aesthetics," in Andrew Ross and Tricia Rose, eds., *Microphone Fiends: Youth Music and Youth Culture* (New York: Routledge, 1994), pp. 235–49.

46

"The Real Thing—Bruce Springsteen"

Simon Frith

Few writers since the 1970s have helped bridge the gap between journalistic rock criticism and academic popular music scholarship more than Simon Frith. A longtime contributor to such publications as the *Village Voice* and *London Times*, he also is the author of such pioneering studies as *The Sociology of Rock* (London: Constable, 1978) and *Performing Rites: On the Value of Popular Music* (Cambridge: Harvard University Press, 1996). During the 1980s, Frith, like many others, was intrigued by the overwhelming popularity of Bruce Springsteen (born 1949), whose two mid-decade releases, *Born in the U.S.A.* and *Bruce Springsteen & the E Street Band Live 1975–85* combined to sell nearly 30 million records in the United States alone. As Frith points out, much of Springsteen's success can be attributed to the authenticity of his strong "populist anti-capitalism" image, which while carefully constructed, nonetheless expresses something tangible for his large fan base. Yet, according to Frith, this presents an inherent contradiction: Springsteen's appeal is that he appears to be so singularly "real," but this is also precisely why he is one of rock's best-selling commodities. And as a commodity Springsteen cannot dictate what his music means to his audiences. As a case in point, Springsteen's "Born in the U.S.A.," a bitterly ironic portrait of a rejected, disillusioned Vietnam veteran and a strident critique of the American dream, earned "The Boss" a Top 10 single. Yet much of its success hinged on its misperception as a patriotic anthem, an appropriated soundtrack that helped bolster Ronald Reagan's 1984 presidential campaign.

INTRODUCTION

My guess is that by Christmas 1986 Bruce Springsteen was making more money per day than any other pop star—more than Madonna, more than Phil Collins or Mark Knopfler, more than Paul McCartney even; *Time* calculated that he had earned $7.5 million in the first *week* of his *Live* LP release. This five-record boxed set went straight to the top of the American LP sales charts (it reputedly sold a million copies on its first day, grossing $50 million 'out of the gate') and stayed there throughout the Christmas season. It was the nation's best-seller in November and December, when more records are sold than in all the other months of the year put together. Even in Britain, where the winter charts are dominated by TV-advertised anthologies, the Springsteen set at £25 brought in more money than the tight-margin single-album compilations. (And CBS reckon they get 42% of their annual sales at Christmas time.) Walking through London from Tottenham Court Road down Oxford Street to Piccadilly in early December, passing the three symbols of corporate rock—the Virgin, HMV and Tower superstores—each claiming to be the biggest record shop in the world, I could only see Springsteen boxes, piled high by the cash desks, the *safest* stock of the season.

Sales success at this level—those boxes were piled up in Sydney and Toronto too, in shop aisles in Sweden and Denmark, West Germany, Holland and Japan—has a disruptive effect on the rest of the rock process. American television news showed trucks arriving at New York's record stores from the CBS warehouses—they were immediately surrounded by queues too, and so, in the USA, Springsteen was sold off the back of vans, frantically, like a sudden supply of Levis in the USSR. Within hours of its release, the Springsteen box was jamming up CBS's works. In America the company announced that nothing from its back catalogue would be available for four months, because all spare capacity had been commandeered for Springsteen (and even then the compact disc version of the box was soon sold out—not enough, only 300,000, had been manufactured). In Europe the company devoted one of its three pressing plants exclusively to the box. Springsteen dominated the market by being the only CBS product readily available.

Whatever the final sales figures turn out to be (and after Christmas the returns of the boxes from the retailers to CBS were as startling as the original sales), it is already obvious that *Bruce Springsteen and the E Street Band Live* is a phenomenal record, a money-making achievement to be discussed on the same scale as *Saturday Night Fever* or Michael Jackson's *Thriller*. Remember, too, that a live record is cheaper to produce than a new studio sound (and Springsteen has already been well rewarded for these songs from the sales of previous discs and the proceeds of sell-out tours). Nor did CBS need the expensive trappings or promo videos and press and TV advertising to make this record sell. Because the Springsteen box was an event in itself (the only pop precedent I can think of is the Beatles' 1968 *White Album*), it generated its own publicity as 'news'—radio stations competed to play the most tracks for the longest times, shops competed to give Bruce the most window space, newspapers competed in speculations about how much money he was really making. The Springsteen box became, in other words, that ultimate object of capitalist fantasy, a commodity which sold more and more because it had sold so well already, a product which had to be *owned* (rather than necessarily used).

In the end, though, what is peculiar about the Springsteen story is not its marks of a brilliant commercial campaign, but their invisibility. Other superstars put out live sets for Christmas (Queen, for example) and the critics sneer at their opportunism; other stars resell their old hits (Bryan Ferry, for example) and their fans worry about their lack of current inspiration. And in these sorry tales of greed and pride it is Bruce Springsteen more often than not who is the measure of musical integrity, the model of a rock performer who cannot be discussed in terms of financial calculation. In short, the most successful pop commodity of the moment, the Springsteen Live Set, stands for the principle that music should not be a commodity; it is his very disdain for success that makes Springsteen so successful. It is as if his presence on every fashionable turntable, tape deck and disc machine, his box on every up-market living-room floor, are what enables an aging, affluent rock generation to feel in touch with its 'roots'. And what matters in this post-modern era is not whether Bruce Springsteen *is* the real thing, but how he sustains the belief that there are somehow, somewhere, real things to be.

FALSE

Consider the following:

Bruce Springsteen Is a Millionaire Who Dresses as a Worker

Worn jeans, singlets, a head band to keep his hair from his eyes—these are working clothes and it is an important part of Springsteen's appeal that we do see him, as an entertainer, working for his living. His popularity is based on his live shows and, more particularly, on their spectacular energy: Springsteen works *hard*, and his exhaustion—on our behalf—is visible. He makes music physically, as a *manual* worker. His clothes are straightforwardly practical, sensible (like sports people's clothes)—comfortable jeans (worn in) for easy movement, a singlet to let the sweat flow free, the mechanic's cloth to wipe his brow.

But there is more to these clothes than this. *Springsteen wears work clothes even when he is not working.* His off-stage image, his LP sleeves and interview poses, even the candid 'off duty' paparazzi shots, involve the same down-to-earth practicality (the only time Springsteen was seen to dress up 'in private' was for his wedding). Springsteen doesn't wear the clothes appropriate to his real economic status and resources (as compared with other pop stars), but neither does he dress up for special occasions like real workers do—he's never seen flashily attired for a sharp night out. It's as if he can't be seen to be excessive or indulgent except on our behalf, as a performer for an audience. For him there is no division between work and play, between the ordinary and the extraordinary. Because the constructed 'Springsteen', the star, is presented plain, there can never be a suggestion that this is just an act (as Elvis was an act, as Madonna is). There are no other Springsteens, whether more real or more artificial, to be seen.

Springsteen Is Employer-as-Employee

It has always surprised me that he should be nicknamed 'The Boss', but the implication is that this is an affectionate label, a brotherly way in which the E Street Band honour his sheer drive. In fact 'boss' is an accurate description of their economic relationship—Springsteen *employs* his band; he has the recording contracts, controls the LP and concert material, writes the songs and chooses the oldies. And whatever his musicians' contributions to his success (fulsomely recognized), he gets the composing/performing royalties, could, in principle, sack people, and, like any other good employer, rewards his team with generous bonuses after each sell-out show or disc. And, of course, he employs a stage crew too, and a manager, a publicist, a secretary/assistant; he has an annual turnover now of millions. He may express the feelings of 'little' men and women buffeted by distant company boards but he is himself a corporation.

Springsteen Is a 37-year-old Teenager

He is 20 years into a hugely successful career, he's a professional, a married man old enough to be the father of adolescent children of his own, but he still presents himself as a young man, waiting to see what life will bring, made tense by clashes with adult authority. He introduces his songs with memories—his life as a boy, arguments with his father (his mother is rarely mentioned)—but as a performer he is clearly *present* in these emotions. Springsteen doesn't regret or vilify his past; as a grown man he's still living it.

Springsteen Is a Shy Exhibitionist

He is, indeed, one of the sexiest performers rock and roll has ever had—there's a good part of his concert audience who simply fancy him, can't take their eyes off his body, and he's mesmerising on stage because of the confidence with which he displays himself. But, for all this, his persona is still that of a nervy, gauche youth on an early date.

Springsteen Is Superstar-as-Friend

He comes into our lives as a recording star, a radio sound, a video presence and, these days, as an item of magazine gossip. Even in his live shows he seems more accessible in the close-ups on the mammoth screens around the stage than as the 'real' dim figure in the distance. And yet he is still the rock performer whose act most convincingly creates (and depends on) a sense of community.

Springsteen's Most Successful 'Record' Is 'Live'.

What the boxed set is meant to do is reproduce a concert, an *event*, and if for other artists five records would be excessive, for Springsteen it is a further sign of his album's truth-to-life—it lasts about the same length of time as a show. There's an interesting question of trust raised here. I don't doubt that these performances were once live, that the applause did happen, but this is nevertheless a false event, a concert put together from different shows (and alternative mixes), edited and balanced to sound like a live LP (which has quite different aural conventions than an actual show). Springsteen fans know that, of course. The pleasure of this set is not that it takes us back to somewhere we've been, but that it lays out something ideal. It describes what we *mean* by 'Springsteen live', and what makes him 'real' in this context is not his transparency, the idea that he is who he pretends to be, but his art, his ability to articulate the right *idea* of reality.

TRUE

The recurring term used in discussions of Springsteen, by fans, by critics, by fans-as-critics is 'authenticity'. What is meant by this is not that Springsteen is authentic in a direct way—is simply expressing himself—but that he represents 'authenticity'. This is why he has become so important: he stands for the core values of rock and roll even as those values become harder and harder to sustain. At a time when rock is the soundtrack for TV commercials, when tours depend on sponsorship deals, when video promotion has blurred the line between music-making and music-selling, Springsteen suggests that, despite everything, it still gives people a way to define themselves against corporate logic, a language in which everyday hopes and fears can be expressed.

If Bruce Springsteen didn't exist, American rock critics would have had to invent him. In a sense, they did, whether directly (Jon Landau, *Rolling Stone*'s most significant critical theorist in the late sixties, is now his manager) or indirectly (Dave Marsh, Springsteen's official biographer, is the most passionate and widely read rock critic of the eighties). There are, indeed, few American rock critics who haven't celebrated Springsteen, but their task has been less to explain him to his potential fans, to sustain the momentum that carried him from cult to mass stardom, than to explain him to himself. They've placed him, that is, in a particular reading of rock history, not as the 'new Dylan' (his original sales label) but as the 'voice of the people'. His task is to carry the baton passed on from Woody Guthrie, and the purpose of his carefully placed oldies (Guthrie's 'This Land Is Your Land', Presley and Berry hits, British beat classics, Edwin Starr's 'War') isn't just to situate him as a fellow fan but also to identify him with a particular musical project. Springsteen himself claims on stage to represent an authentic popular tradition (as against the spurious commercial sentiments of an Irving Berlin).

To be so 'authentic' involves a number of moves. Firstly, authenticity must be defined against artifice; the terms only make sense in opposition to each other. This is the importance of Springsteen's image—to represent the 'raw' as against the 'cooked'. His plain stage appearance, his dressing down, has to be understood with reference to showbiz dressing up, to the elaborate spectacle of cabaret pop and soul (and routine stadium rock and roll)—Springsteen is real *by contrast*. In lyrical terms too he is plain-speaking; his songwriting craft is marked not by 'poetic' or obscure or personal language, as in the singer/songwriter tradition following Dylan, folk-rock (and his own early material), but by the vivid images and metaphors he builds from common words.

What's at stake here is not authenticity of experience, but authenticity of feeling; what matters is not whether Springsteen has been through these things himself (boredom, aggression, ecstasy, despair) but that he knows how they work. The point of his autobiographical anecdotes is not to reveal himself but to root his music in material conditions. Like artists in other media (fiction, film)

Springsteen is concerned to give emotions (the essential data of rock and roll) a narrative setting, to situate them in time and place, to relate them to the situations they explain or confuse. He's not interested in abstract emotions, in vague sensation or even in moralizing. He is, to put it simply, a story-teller, and in straining to make his stories credible he uses classic techniques. Reality is registered by conventions first formulated by the nineteenth-century naturalists—a refusal to sentimentalize social conditions, a compulsion to sentimentalize human nature. Springsteen's songs (like Zola's fictions) are almost exclusively concerned with the working-class, with the effects of poverty and uncertainty, the consequences of weakness and crime; they trawl through the murky reality of the American dream; they contrast utopian impulses with people's lack of opportunity to do much more than get by; they find in sex the only opportunity for passion (and betrayal). Springsteen's protagonists, victims and criminals, defeated and enraged, are treated tenderly, their hopes honoured, their failure determined by circumstance.

It is his realism that makes Springsteen's populism politically ambiguous. His message is certainly anti-capitalist, or, at least, critical of the effects of capitalism—as both citizen and star Springsteen has refused to submit to market forces, has shown consistent and generous support for the system's losers, for striking trade unionists and the unemployed, for battered wives and children. But, at the same time, his focus on individuals' fate, the very power with which he describes the dreams they can't realize (but which he has) offers an opening for his appropriation, appropriation not just by politicians like Reagan but, more importantly, by hucksters and advertisers, who use him to sell their goods as some sort of *solution* to the problem he outlines. This is the paradox of mass-marketed populism: Springsteen's songs suggests there is something missing in our lives, the CBS message is that we can fill the gap *with a Bruce Springsteen record*. And for all Springsteen's support of current causes, what comes from his music is a whiff of nostalgia and an air of fatalism. His stories describe hopes-about-to-be-dashed, convey a sense of time passing beyond our control, suggest that our dreams can only be dreams. The formal conservatism of the music reinforces the emotional conservation of the lyrics. This is the way the world is, he sings, and nothing really changes.

But there's another way of describing Springsteen's realism. It means celebrating the ordinary not the special. Again the point is not that Springsteen is ordinary or even pretends to be, but that he honours ordinariness, making something intense out of experiences that are usually seen as mundane. It has always been pop's function to transform the banal, but this purpose was to some extent undermined by the rise of rock in the sixties, with its claims to art and poetry, its cult-building, its heavy metal mysticism. Springsteen himself started out with a couple of wordy, worthy LPs, but since then he has been in important ways committed to common sense. Springsteen's greatest skill is his ability to dramatize everyday events—even his stage act is a pub rock show writ large. The E Street Band, high-class professionals, play with a sort of amateurish enthusiasm, an affection for each other which is in sharp contrast to the bohemian contempt for their work (and their audience) which has been a strand of 'arty' rock shows since the Rolling Stones and the Doors. Springsteen's musicians stand for every bar and garage group that ever got together in fond hope of stardom.

His sense of the commonplace also explains Springsteen's physical appeal. His sexuality is not displayed as something remarkable, a kind of power, but is coded into his 'natural' movements, determined by what he has to do to sing and play. His body becomes 'sexy'—a source of excitement and anxiety—in its routine activity; his appeal is not defined in terms of glamour or fantasy. The basic sign of Springsteen's authenticity, to put it another way, is his sweat, his display of *energy*. His body is not posed, an object of consumption, but active, an object of exhaustion. When the E Street Band gather at the end of a show for the final bow, arms around each other's shoulders, drained and relieved, the sporting analogy is clear: this is a team which has won its latest bout. What matters is that every such bout is seen to be real, that there are no backing tapes, no 'fake' instruments, that the musicians really have played until they can play no more. There is a moment in every Springsteen show I've seen when Clarence Clemons takes centre-stage. For that moment he is the real star—he's bigger than Springsteen, louder, more richly dressed. And he's the saxophonist, giving us the clearest account all evening of the relationship between human effort and human music.

To be authentic and to sound authentic is in the rock context the same thing. Music can not *be* true or false, it can only refer to *conventions* of truth and falsity. Consider the following.

Thundering drums in Springsteen's songs give his stories their sense of unstoppable momentum, they map out the spaces within which things happen. This equation of time and space is the secret of great rock and roll and Springsteen uses other classic devices to achieve it—a piano/organ combination, for example (as used by The Band and many soul groups), so that melodic-descriptive and rhythmic-atmospheric sounds are continually swapped about.

The E Street Band makes music as a group, but a group in which we can hear every instrumentalist. Our attention is drawn, that is, not to a finished sound but to music-in-the-making. This is partly done by the refusal to make any instrument the 'lead' (which is why Nils Lofgren, a 'lead' guitarist, sounded out of place in the last E Street touring band). And partly by a specific musical busy-ness—the group is 'tight', everyone is aiming for the same rhythmic end, but 'loose', each player makes their own decision as to how to get there (which is one reason why electronic instruments would not fit—they're too smooth, too determined). All Springsteen's musicians, even the added back-up singers and percussionists, have individual voices; it would be unthinkable for him to appear with, say, an anonymous string section.

The textures and, more significantly, the melodic structures of Springsteen's music make self-conscious reference to rock and roll itself, to its conventional line-up, its cliched chord changes, its time-honoured ways of registering joys and sadness. Springsteen himself is a rock and roll star, not a crooner or singer/songwriter. His voice *strains* to be heard, he has to shout against the instruments that both support and compete with him. However many times he's rehearsed his lines they always sound as if they're being forged on the spot.

Many of Springsteen's most anthemic songs have no addresses (no 'you') but (like many Beatles songs) concern a third person (tales told about someone else) or involve an 'I' brooding aloud, explaining his situation impersonally, in a kind of individualised epic. Listening to such epics is a public activity (rather than a private fantasy), which is why Springsteen concerts still feel like collective occasions.

CONCLUSION

In one of his monologues Springsteen remembers that his parents were never very keen on his musical ambitions—they wanted him to train for something safe, like law or accountancy: 'they wanted me to get a little something for myself; what they did not understand was that I wanted *everything!*'

This is a line that could only be delivered by an American, and to explain Springsteen's importance and success we have to go back to the problem he is really facing: the fate of the individual artist under capitalism. In Europe, the artistic critique of the commercialization of everything has generally been conducted in terms of Romanticism, in a state of Bohemian disgust with the masses and the bourgeoisie alike, in the name of the superiority of the *avant-garde*. In the USA there's a populist anti-capitalism available, a tradition of the artist as the common man (rarely woman), pitching rural truth against urban deceit, pioneer values against bureaucratic routines. This tradition (Mark Twain to Woody Guthrie, Kerouac to Credence Clearwater Revival) lies behind Springsteen's message and his image. It's this tradition that enables him to take such well-worn iconography as the road, the river, rock and roll itself, as a mark of sincerity. No British musician, not even someone with such a profound love of American musical forms as Elvis Costello, could deal with these themes without some sense of irony.

Still, Springsteen's populism can appeal to everyone's experience of capitalism. He makes music out of desire aroused and desire thwarted, he offers a sense of personal worth that is not determined by either market forces (and wealth) or aesthetic standards (and cultural capital). It is the USA's particular account of equality that allows him to transcend the differences in class and status which remain ingrained in European culture. The problem is that the line between democratic populism (the argument that all people's experiences and emotions are equally important, equally worthy to be dramatized and made into art) and market populism (the argument that the consumer is always right, that the market defines cultural value) is very thin. Those piles of Bruce Springsteen boxes in European department stores seem less a tribute to rock authenticity than to corporate might.

'We are the world!' sang USA For Africa, and what was intended as a statement of global community came across as a threat of global domination. 'Born in the USA!' sang Bruce Springsteen on his last great tour, with the Stars and Stripes fluttering over the stage, and what was meant as an opposition anthem to the Reaganite colonization of the American dream was taken by large sections of his American audiences as pat patriotism (in Europe the flag had to come down). Springsteen is, whether he or we like it or not, an American artist—his 'community' will always have the Stars and Stripes fluttering over it. But then rock and roll is American music, and Springsteen's *Live 1975–1985* is a monument. Like all monuments it celebrates (and mourns) the dead, in this case the idea of authenticity itself.

Source: Simon Frith, "The Real Thing—Bruce Springsteen," *Musica E Dossier*, 1987. Reprinted in *Music for Pleasure: Essays in the Sociology of Pop* (New York: Routledge, 1988), pp. 94–101.

47

Hip Hop Nation

GREG TATE

Originally published as the lead essay in a special *Village Voice* feature devoted to the "Hip Hop Nation," Greg Tate's 1988 article "It's Like This Y'all" provides a window into a style of music that at that time was enjoying its first true taste of commercial success. Throughout the 1980s, rap music had been bubbling under as an exciting urban underground phenomenon. But by 1986 and 1987, breakthrough albums from Run D.M.C., L.L. Cool J, and others had made it clear that hip hop was crossing over into a much larger fan base. Addressing hip hop's African American culture as a whole, Tate provides a brief overview of its various dimensions—from graffiti and break dancing to DJ scratching and rapping—while also defending the music from its various critics. His writing style suits the subject, as he mirrors rap's rich wealth of allusions, slang, and playfully combative, boastful verse. Tate places the music within the roots of its urban environment; for example, recalling a conversation between two early 1980s downtown New York icons, graffiti/visual artist Rammellzee (1960–2010) and East Village artist and critic Nicolas Moufarrege (1947–1985). Most of all, he situates hip hop within a long musical lineage stretching from the blues and jazz to funk and fusion. Nowhere, however, does he mention rock music. Which begs the question: exactly how *does* hip hop relate to rock?

Where will rap end up? Where most postmodern American products end up: highly packaged, regulated, distributed, circulated and consumed. Upper-middle-class white students at Yale consume a lot of Run-D.M.C.

—**Cornell West**

Fuck hiphop. I don't define that shit. I define this, man: It's music. Let's not call it hiphop no more, Fred. We ain't writing graffiti on walls, we're trying to get paid.

—**L.L. Cool J**

Radio stations I question their blackness/They call themselves black/But we'll see if they play this.

—**Public Enemy, "Bring the Noise"**

We begin this benediction by sending out a message of love to the ancestors Kool Herc, Taki 183, and the Nigger Twins.

We know from her secretary that the Billie Holiday first wore gardenias to mask a bald spot made by an overzealous hot comb. Tell us, old muse, about the beauties bred from black disgrace. Had there never been discos, B-boys might have never become so engaged in class struggle, fashion rebels risen up to defy the Saturday night dress code, economically shamed into aggression. But hiphop in its manifold forms—rapping, scratch DJing, break dancing, graffiti—also emerges, in the twilight of '70s gang warfare, as a nonfratricidal channel for the B-boy's competitive, creative, and martial urges. All the aforementioned expressions flowered, like swing-era saxophone playing, *specifically*, in the hothouse of the cutting contest.[1]

Hiphop is the most modern example, after capoeira and basketball, of African culture's bent towards aesthetic combat—what the graffiti movement itself long ago defined as "style wars." We are reminded of an exchange between Rammellzee and Nicolas A. Moufarrege.

Moufarrege: Do you call your work total realism. Is this poster total realism? [Note: the images in Rammellzee's drawings do not resemble what is habitually referred to in art as realism; the drawing is cartoon, comic strip, pop, and science fiction related.]

Rammellzee: There's about 50,000 kids walking out the street who look just like that: Pumas, bell-bottom jeans—they have their pants hanging off their ass showing their underwear—shades and doo-rags.

What are doo rags? . . . You say that this is real and that Picasso is abstract?

Yes. . . . The human body is abstracted; why do you want to abstract it even further? . . . Man, on the street they'll burn it, they'll break it down. They'll say what is this shit? Are we your future too? No!

The battle flows in two directions—against the technique of rival virtuosos and against the city. The city fathers strike back, like that's their job. Ghetto blasters and bombed trains, might, as Jean Baudrillard proclaims, territorialize the urban bush, but they also invoke noise ordinances, razored barbed wire, and the patrolling of train yards by guard dogs. Rammellzee speaks of this as a war of symbols, but the execution of Michael Stewart was no symbolic gesture.[2] His death was status quo: another marginal man pushed into the marginality of the grave by the powerful for crimes surreal or imagined. Were Goetz's victims B-fashion victims too?[3] Do clothes make the man a target?

When the black-on-black crime that occurs before, during, and after (often blocks away) rap concerts is reported as "rap violence," the aging pontificators forget that hiphop is the flipside of being young, black, and urban-situated: the fun side, the funkyfresh side. Take out rap and one could go dying for a belly laugh in modern black pop. If drum sound is this music's heartthrob, humor is its blood vessels. The urge to snap, crack, jone, boast, toast, to stay forever anal, adolescent, and absurdist—to talk much, shit, in other words, and create new *slanguage* in the process—is what keeps the oral tradition's chuckle juices flowing through the rap pipeline. (If we have to, we can invoke holy tradition: the preacher goes "Huh!," James Brown goes "Unnhh!," George Clinton goes "Ho!," Bob Marley goes "Oh-oh-wo-oh-oh," and the DJs scratch their ecstatic ejaculations.)

Rap keeps alive the lineage of juke-joint jive novelty records that began with the first recorded black music—so-called classic blues. Here, too, we're talking your citified country Negro's mongrel sound, part jazz, part coonfoolery, part bawdy response to the man-woman question. Black vaudeville tent-show entertainment was best put to wax by heavy-duty womanists Ma Rainey and Bessie Smith. Bringing us to the position of the sistuhs in rap. No, Stokely, not prone, but coming into their own, going beyond the first flurry of lubricated lip answer records to go stone careerist. Roxanne Shanté's jockin' *and* clockin'.

The minds behind the music's muscle are its DJs and producers—Russell Simmons, Eric B., Larry Smith, Teddy Riley, Rick Rubin, Dennis Bell, Hank Shocklee, Hurby Azor, Mantronik, Marley Marl, Terminator X. We continually marvel at this fraternal order of rhythm tacticians, this

---

1 In jazz, the phrase "cutting contest" describes a competitive duel between two musicians, one of whom figuratively "cuts" off the other's head.

2 Stewart was a train graffiti "tagger" who had been beaten to death in 1983 by the New York City Transit police.

3 Tate is alluding to the subway vigilante Bernard Goetz, who in 1984 had shot and wounded four black youths on a New York City train.

consortium of beat boppers, mega-mix researchers, sound-collage technicians, and rare-groove clerics. They think about electronic percussion orchestrally—voicings and shit—like any jazz drummer worth his African roots. We understand that analogies between hip-hop and jazz rankle the jazz police who believe harmonic improvisation on Western concert instruments is the measure of black genius. Partly because the beat-boppers' axes (save the wheels of steel) originate in the digital age—drum machines, sequencers, and samplers—the ears of the jazz police fly off the handle.

The suckers have yet to figure out the prototype—Miles Davis's 1972 *On the Corner*—so we can't expect them to listen to Eric B. & Rakim as Wynton Marsalis listens to Ornette Coleman, for his finesse with rhythmic changes. And it goes without saying that New Music America-type festivals don't consider these percussive melodists composers.[4] Probably because the beatboppers audience dances to the music.

The coordinated chaos of hiphop's dance component holds clues to the origin of the universe. You want to understand why the subatomic realm is so full of strange behavior? Look to the body language of the black teens. Their culturally acquired fluidity are new dance forms waiting to happen. Who can lament break dancing's faddish decline knowing such energy is never destroyed but transformed, in this case, into the Wopp, the Snake, the Cabbage Patch, and other spasms yet to be named.

For some, hiphop will always be "that chain-snatching music." We are reminded of a buppie party in Brooklyn where the hostess denied a request for Run-D.M.C. "This isn't a Run-D.M.C. kind of party." A Doritos and disco dipshit party is what it was. What can we expect from Philistines? Hiphop, Russell Simmons informs us, is an artform. To which we add, it's the *only* avant-garde around, still delivering the shock of the new (over recycled James Brown compost modernism like a bitch), and it's got a shockable bourgeoisie, to boot. Hiphop is not just Def Jam shipping platinum, but the attraction/repulsion of commodification to the black working class and po'-ass class. The music that makes like a saccharine pop ditty with a dopebeat today could be the soundtrack to a Five Per Cent Nation jihad tomorrow. Hiphop might be bought and sold like gold, but the miners of its rich ore still represent a sleeping-giant constituency. Hiphop locates their market potential and their potential militancy.

Public Enemy pointman Chuckie D wants to raise consciousness though his manifesto serves dreamers and schemers alike: "This jam may hit or miss the charts/But the style gets wild as state of the art/Dazzling in science/Bold in nerve/But giving my house what it deserves." Later for the revolution. For the here and now, hiphop's stance of populist-futurism is progressive enough. Is there any creative endeavor outside of recombinant gene technology whose shape to come is more unpredictable? Latter-day prophets predicting hiphop's imminent demise have already becomes extinct. Afrika Bambaataa sez rap will be around as long as people keep talking. You think we're gonna let 'em shut us up now? Sheee.

Source: Greg Tate, "It's Like This Y'all," *Village Voice*, January 19, 1988, pp. 21–22.

---

4 The New Music America Festival was a yearly event devoted to contemporary art music composers.

48

"Madonna—Finally, a Real Feminist"

CAMILLE PAGLIA

Along with Michael Jackson, Madonna (born Madonna Louise Ciccone, 1958) established herself over the course of the 1980s as one of MTV's most dazzlingly innovative and risk-taking video stars. From the Marilyn Monroe homage of "Material Girl" (1985) and peep show eroticism of "Open Your Heart" (1986) to the daring religious and racial iconography of "Like a Prayer" (1989), Madonna constantly reinvented her glamorous image while wading into socially taboo waters. The controversy surrounding the singer reached a climax in the fall of 1990 with the release of the sexually suggestive "Justify My Love," the first Madonna video that MTV refused to air. On December 3, 1990, ABC's *Nightline* showed the unedited video for the first time, and spotlighted the singer in an interview. Madonna's appearance on *Nightline* generated a flurry of responses, among them Camille Paglia's editorial for the *New York Times*. Paglia (born 1947), an outspoken cultural critic and University Professor of Humanities and Media Studies at the University of the Arts in Philadelphia, whose own controversial book *Sexual Personae: Art & Decadence from Nefertiti to Emily Dickinson* (New Haven: Yale University Press, 1990) had just been released, uses "Justify My Love" as an opportunity to proclaim Madonna's significant role in a new era of American feminism. Madonna's forays into issues of gender, sexuality, and identity would attract the interest of many other academics throughout the early 1990s, even leading to an *Inside Edition* exposé on "Madonna scholars."

Madonna, don't preach.

Defending her controversial new video "Justify My Love" on "Nightline" last week, Madonna stumbled, rambled and ended up seeming far less intelligent than she really is.

Madonna, 'fess up.

The video is pornographic. It's decadent. And it's fabulous. MTV was right to ban it, a corporate resolve long overdue. Parents cannot possibly control television, with its titanic omnipresence.

Prodded by correspondent Forrest Sawyer for evidence of her responsibility as an artist, Madonna hotly proclaimed her love of children, her social activism and her condom endorsements. Wrong answer. As Baudelaire and Oscar Wilde knew, neither art nor the artist has a moral responsibility to liberal social causes.

"Justify My Love" is truly avant-garde, at a time when that word has lost its meaning in the flabby art world. It represents a sophisticated European sexuality of a kind we have not seen since the great foreign films of the 1950's and 1960's. But it does not belong on a mainstream music channel watched around the clock by children.

On "Nightline," Madonna bizarrely called the video a "celebration of sex." She imagined happy educational scenes where curious children would ask their parents about the video. Oh, sure!

Picture it: "Mommy, please tell me about the tired, tied-up man in the leather harness and the mean, bare-chested lady in the Nazi cap." O.K., dear, right after the milk and cookies.

Mr. Sawyer asked for Madonna's reaction to feminist charges that, in the neck manacle and floor-crawling of an earlier video, "Express Yourself," she condoned the "degradation" and "humiliation" of women. Madonna waffled: "But I chained myself! I'm in charge." Well, no, Madonna the producer may have chosen the chain, but Madonna the sexual persona in the video is alternately a cross-dressing dominatrix and a slave of male desire.

But who cares what the feminists say anyhow? They have been outrageously negative about Madonna from the start. In 1985, *Ms.* magazine pointedly feted quirky, cuddly singer Cyndi Lauper as its woman of the year. Great judgment: gimmicky Lauper went nowhere, while Madonna grew, flourished, metamorphosed and became an international star of staggering dimensions. She is also a shrewd business tycoon, a modern woman of all-around talent.

Madonna is the true feminist. She exposes the puritanism and suffocating ideology of American feminism, which is stuck in an adolescent whining mode. Madonna has taught young women to be fully female and sexual while still exercising total control over their lives. She shows girls how to be attractive, sensual, energetic, ambitious, aggressive and funny—all at the same time.

American feminism has a man problem. The beaming Betty Crockers, hangdog dowdies and parochial prudes who call themselves feminists want men to be like women. They fear and despise the masculine. The academic feminists think their nerdy bookworm husbands are the ideal model of human manhood.

But Madonna loves real men. She sees the beauty of masculinity, in all its rough vigor and sweaty athletic perfection. She also admires the men who are actually like women: transsexuals and flamboyant drag queens, the heroes of the 1969 Stonewall rebellion, which started the gay liberation movement.

"Justify My Love" is an eerie, sultry tableau of jaded androgynous creatures, trapped in a decadent sexual underground. Its hypnotic images are drawn from such sado-masochistic films as Liliana Cazani's "The Night Porter" and Luchino Visconti's "The Damned." It's the perverse and knowing world of the photographers Helmut Newton and Robert Mapplethorpe.

Contemporary American feminism, which began by rejecting Freud because of his alleged sexism, has shut itself off from his ideas of ambiguity, contradiction, conflict, ambivalence. Its simplistic psychology is illustrated by the new cliché of the date-rape furor: "'No' always means 'no'." Will we ever graduate from the Girl Scouts? "No" has always been, and always will be, part of the dangerous, alluring courtship ritual of sex and seduction, observable even in the animal kingdom.

Madonna has a far profounder vision of sex than do the feminists. She sees both the animality and the artifice. Changing her costume style and hair color virtually every month, Madonna embodies the eternal values of beauty and pleasure. Feminism says, "No more masks." Madonna says we are nothing but masks.

Through her enormous impact on young women around the world, Madonna is the future of feminism.

Source: Camille Paglia, "Madonna—Finally, a Real Feminist," *New York Times*, December 14, 1990, p. A39.

49

"Can Madonna Justify Madonna?"

Barbara Grizzuti Harrison

For all the controversy that Madonna generated herself, what was perhaps more remarkable was the way in which the discourse *surrounding* her served to spark debates over the "true" meanings of feminism. Were Madonna's actions empowering or were they demeaning? Was she resisting patriarchal conventions or simply reinscribing them? In her editorial for *Mademoiselle* magazine, Barbara Grizzuti Harrison (1934–2002) responds to Camille Paglia's essay from the previous chapter, as well as Caryn James's feminist reading of Madonna from the *New York Times*.[1] Harrison, a highly regarded author and one of the first contributors to *Ms.* magazine, addresses Paglia's claims from the perspective of someone who had been heavily involved with the formative years of the women's movement in the 1960s and 1970s.

Is Madonna a feminist? Gimme a break. Do pigs fly?

There was a time that I didn't know the difference between Madonna and Cyndi Lauper. (I have these problems; it was a long time before I was absolutely sure which were flora and which were fauna.) Then, suddenly, I was reading and hearing about Madonna all over the place; and since I don't live in a cave, I'd seen her videos. It interested me to see how someone who was decidedly not beautiful could nonetheless manage, for seconds at a time, to project beauty. I thought it was a neat trick. Certainly a marketable trick. I thought: She's a sly one (I never for a moment thought: She's quite a feminist); and that was that . . .

Well, not *quite* that. I find Joan Rivers awfully persuasive (I can *so* tell the difference between her and Phyllis Diller); and when I heard Rivers' amusing speculation, on her TV talk show, that Madonna had a problem with body hair, I was no longer able to think of Madonna as a person who could project beauty, even for a few seconds. (I'm Italian, too; I know all about dark fuzz on the upper lip.)

The next thing I knew, magazine editors were standing in line to ask me to interview Madonna. Why? I said. Because, they (invariably) said, she invents herself and keeps on inventing herself. What does that mean, exactly? I said. Does it mean hiding behind flamboyant disguises? Coloring and recoloring your hair? (Have you noticed that you can't stop dark roots from showing on television? Pity.) And why is this inventing/reinventing business thought to be a good thing—as opposed, for example, to constancy? It had me beat.

Then along came someone called Camille Paglia to explain to me, in the *New York Times*, the significance of Madonna's chameleonlike antics. She was a Real Feminist, *the* True Feminist, wrote

---

1 Caryn James, "Beneath All That Black Lace Beats the Heart of a Bimbo . . . and a Feminist," *New York Times*, December 16, 1990, H38,44.

Paglia, unlike all the other feminists who claimed to be feminists. Gosh. I never knew that all of us who call ourselves feminists have so much in common that it's possible for us to stand on one side of an ideological fault line, on the other side of which stands . . . *Madonna?* At first I thought it was a joke. (Paglia is the author of a book called *Sexual Personae: Art and Decadence From Nefertiti to Emily Dickinson;* at first I thought *that* was a joke, too; alas, it is not.)

Paglia rested much of her case for Madonna's feminism on her latest video, *Justify My Love*—which, as you of course already know, was banned by MTV on the grounds that it was too sexually explicit; and, as you also know, became a hit, in part because people always long to see what they are not permitted to see. If nobody had told me. I would have thought *Justify My Love* was a home movie. It's dumb. Like there's this parodic boneless male dancer—he looks like Gumby in silhouette—and he keeps popping up in the bedroom where Madonna lets her boyfriend—who wears more lipstick than she does—do lascivious things to her black underwear (she's in it). It's also decadent, druggy (well, everyone *tilts;* it looks like either everyone is stoned or Madonna needs a new camera for Christmas), and seems to include a lot of people in drag.

Madonna calls this "art." I heard her say so on *Nightline:* "Well, no, you know, with the wave of censorship being, you know—and the conservatism that is, you know, sort of sweeping over the nation. . . . It is my artistic expression . . . we're dealing with sexual fannies [sic]—fantasies, and being truthful and honest with our partner you know." In the video, she has a lot more than one partner; there are flash-cut references to multiple partners, voyeurism, leather, sadomasochism, dominance-submission, Nazi paraphernalia and Christ on the cross, an image Madonna evidently finds very turn-on-y. She also grabs her crotch a lot (she's always grabbing *something*—her breasts, her neck . . .). This, too, is supposed to be feminist: *Michael Jackson did it and so can she, ha ha ha, nyah, nyah, nyah.*

And what is the "feminist" message of a previous video, *Open Your Heart*, wherein Madonna sets up shop as a peepshow dancer? I hated that video like poison, not least because a little boy was in it—he played a would-be customer—and at the end he and a saucy Madonna skipped off into the sunset together, just two kids at play. . . . This is where sentiment becomes bilge, and this is where that which is silly becomes that which is dangerous.

In *Express Yourself*, another one of Madonna's works of so-called art, she is seen chained to a bed and crawling under a table—putrid images, you must admit. So here's what Madonna said on *Nightline:* "Okay, I have chained myself, though, okay? No—there wasn't a man that put that chain on me. . . . I was chained to my desires. [Come again? I thought it was a bed] . . . I'm in charge, okay. Degradation is when somebody else is making you do something against your wishes, okay?"

It really is not okay. Okay? It makes me inexpressibly weary to have to say the obvious—that the very worst degradation is that which we inflict upon ourselves. It won't do to say *I chose it, so it's okay.* What about self-laceration? Self-flagellation? Self-destruction? Whatever Madonna the producer may have chosen, Madonna the performer comes across as a dementedly cheerful masochist.

Nonetheless, Paglia says Madonna "has taught young women to be fully female and sexual while still exercising total control over their lives." The *Times's* Caryn James adds her voice: To Madonna, "feminism means the freedom to be sexy as well as sexual, to be in control of one's image as well as one's life. . . . Madonna [suggests] mastery of one's fate." But who in this green wide world has total control over her life? Beyond a certain point, mastery of one's fate is illusory. We *act* as if we have free will—that is what it means to be human; but we know that life acts upon us just as we act upon it.

Madonna has minor talent and major marketing skill. In her works the line between person and image has become hopelessly blurred, as has the line between responsibility and manipulation (both go by the name of *control*). Yes, an image can be manipulated; no, a life cannot be and *should* not be. We don't produce our lives as if they were videos; the script is not a one-woman exercise.

Madonna, her fan Paglia says, "embodies the eternal values of beauty and pleasure." Whereas traditional, no-fun-at-all feminists want to put an end to masks. "Madonna says we are nothing but masks." I find this scary beyond belief. Not the beauty-and-pleasure part; let's hear it for beauty and pleasure! Who's against it? Not I. The masks. In the '50s, when women wore the same push-up bras and high, high heels that Madonna postures in today, rebels against conformity spoke one word: *authenticity*. They knew that to wear a mask is an act of extreme defensiveness or aggression. What it is *not* is an act of existential courage.

As long as Madonna wears masks—and confuses the person with the image—there *is* no real person there (and no real risk). That's why, after a while, Madonna-adulation is dopey . . . as in "Madonna loves real men" (Paglia). Yeah? Like Warren Beatty, he who is evidently incapable of commitment? Or, as in (James); "Her lyrics . . . are a feminist anthem. 'Don't settle for second best, baby,' she sings. . . . 'You deserve the best in life . . .'" Oh, dear. That's as profound as a greeting card. Are we so starved for heroines that we have to make Madonna into one? We deserve better.

Source: Barbara Grizzuti Harrison, "Can Madonna Justify Madonna?," *Mademoiselle*, June 1991, pp. 80–82.

V

THE 1990s

50

Is As Nasty As They Wanna Be *Obscene?*

Judge Jose Gonzalez and Kathleen M. Sullivan

In 1990, 2 Live Crew's battles with the Florida judicial system brought the Miami-based rap group to national prominence as they faced prosecution on the grounds of obscenity for their album *As Nasty As They Wanna Be*. This was not the first time that musicians had been brought to trial on such charges. Four years earlier Jello Biafra, lead singer of hardcore punk band the Dead Kennedys and owner of the independent Alternative Tentacles record label, had been charged with distributing "harmful matter to minors," on the basis of a graphic poster included with the band's *Frankenchrist* album. *As Nasty As They Wanna Be*, however, moved the battle over obscenity to completely different grounds as the rappers were indicted solely for their music. The trial drew extensive commentary, including a special feature that appeared in *Reconstruction*, a Harvard-based journal devoted to issues of African American culture. Reprinted here from *Reconstruction* are two items: Judge Jose Gonzalez's ruling on the case and a response from Kathleen M. Sullivan, a professor of Constitutional Law. Both of their comments revolve around the three-pronged criteria for obscenity outlined in the 1973 *Miller v. California* ruling, a case that had involved the mass distribution of graphically illustrated advertisements for sex books. In his statement, Judge Gonzalez refutes the trial testimony of Carlton Long, a Columbia University political science professor who defended the band's music as part of such longstanding black cultural traditions as boasting and parody.[1] 2 Live Crew's music, Gonzalez declares, is inarguably obscene. Sullivan responds by questioning the very logic of *Miller v. California* itself. In the end, 2 Live Crew was vindicated when nearly a year and a half after their conviction, the U.S. Court of Appeals reversed the Gonzalez ruling. The Supreme Court upheld the decision, refusing to hear any further appeals.

SKYYWALKER RECORDS INC. V. NICHOLAS NAVARRO (SHERRIF, BROWARD COUNTY, FLORIDA) UNITED STATES DISTRICT COURT, S.D. FLORIDA, JUNE 6, 1990

Judge Jose Gonzalez

This is a case between two ancient enemies: Anything Goes and Enough Already.

Justice Oliver Wendell Holmes, Jr. observed that the First Amendment is not absolute and that it does not permit one to yell "Fire" in a crowded theater. Today, this court decides whether the First Amendment absolutely permits one to yell another "F" word anywhere in the community when combined with graphic sexual descriptions.

---

1 An even more prominent scholar, Henry Louis Gates, Jr., took up the group's cause as well, in a *New York Times* editorial. See Gates Jr., "2 Live Crew Decoded: Rap Music Group's Use of Street Language in Context of Afro-American Cultural Heritage Analyzed," *New York Times*, 19 June 1990, op-ed., A23.

Obscenity and the First Amendment

The First Amendment to the United States Constitution provides that "Congress shall make no law . . . abridging the freedom of speech."

The First Amendment is one of our most sacred liberties since freedom of thought and speech are the key to the preservation of all other rights. Free speech plays a critical role in furthering self-government, in encouraging individual self-realization, and fostering society's search for truth via exposure to a marketplace of ideas."

To protect that sacred right, the judiciary carefully scrutinizes government regulation to determine if such regulation impermissibly infringes upon it. When legislative or executive action is directed at the content of one's speech, it will pass judicial review only upon a showing that the action is designed to further a compelling governmental interest by narrowly drawn means necessary to achieve the end.

Obscene speech has no protection under the First Amendment. The rationale is simple: the message conveyed by obscene speech is of such slight social value that it is always outweighed by the compelling interests of society as manifested in the laws enacted by its elected representatives. Sex has been called "a great and mysterious motive force in human life." Because of its power, both federal and state governments have chosen to regulate its abuse. The Florida Legislature enacted a statutory scheme [that] criminalizes the distribution, sale, or production of any obscene thing including a "recording" which can be "transmuted into auditory . . . representations."

An argument underlying the plaintiffs' position is that obscenity or non-obscenity of any material should not be a concern of the criminal law, but rather should be left to the free market of ideas. Let each individual member of the public decide whether they wish to buy the material. This is the argument of those absolutists who believe all speech, regardless of its content, is protected by the First Amendment. Such individuals label all regulation of speech as "censorship" and "paternalism."

The absolutists and other members of the party of Anything Goes should address their petitions to the Florida Legislature, not to this court. If they are sincere let them say what they actually mean— Let's Legalize Obscenity! It is much easier to criticize the law, however, that it is to work to repeal it.

In an era where the law and society are rightfully concerned with the rights of minorities, it should not be overlooked nor forgotten that majorities also have rights.

Men and women in good faith may agree or disagree as to whether obscenity should be prohibited. They can argue that the obscenity statutes should or should not be repealed. In the meantime, however, the law must be obeyed and the Sheriff has a duty to enforce it.

The *Miller v. California* Test

In deciding whether a specific work is or is not obscene the court must apply the controlling test enunciated [by the Supreme Court] in *Miller v. California*. To be obscene, there must be proof of all three of the following factors: (1) the average person, applying contemporary community standards would find the that the work, taken as a whole appeals to the prurient interest, (2) measured by contemporary community standards, the work depicts or describes in a patently offensive way, sexual conduct, specifically defined by the applicable state law, and (3) the work, taken as a whole, lacks serious literary, artistic, political, or scientific value.

The Relevant Community

This court finds that in assessing whether this work is obscene, the relevant community is the area of Palm Beach, Broward, and Dade Counties. [T]his area is remarkable for its diversity. The three counties are a mecca for both the very young and the very old. Because of the beaches and the moderate year-round climate, this area includes young persons establishing homes and older residents retiring to enjoy life under the sun. There are both families and single individuals residing in the communities. Generally, the counties are heterogeneous in terms of religion, class, race, and gender.

The Average Person Standard

The next inquiry is more difficult because this court must determine what are the standards for determining prurient interest and patent offensiveness in Palm Beach, Dade, and Broward Counties.

This court finds that the relevant community standard reflects a more tolerant view of obscene speech than would other communities within the state. This finding of fact is based upon this court's personal knowledge of the community. The undersigned judge has resided in Broward County since 1958. As a practicing attorney, state prosecutor, state circuit judge, and currently, a federal district judge, the undersigned has traveled and worked in Dade, Broward, and Palm Beach. As a member of the community, he has a personal knowledge of this area's demographics, culture, economics, and politics. He has attended public functions and events in all three counties and is aware of the community's concerns as reported in the media and by word of mouth. In almost fourteen years as a state circuit judge, the undersigned gained personal knowledge of the nature of obscenity in the community while viewing dozens, if not hundreds of allegedly obscene film and other publications seized by law enforcement.

The *Miller* Test: Prurient Interest

This court finds, as a matter of fact, that the recording "As Nasty As They Wanna Be" appeals to the prurient interest. The Supreme Court has defined prurient as "material having a tendency to excite lustful thoughts." Appeals only to "normal, healthy sexual desire" are not adequate to meet the test. The material must exhibit a "shameful or morbid interest in nudity, sex, or secretion."

"Nasty" appeals to the prurient interest for several reasons. First, its lyrics and the titles of its songs are replete with references to female and male genitalia, human sexual excretion, oral-anal contact, fellatio, group sex, specific sexual positions, sado-masochism, the turgid state of the male sexual organ, masturbation, cunnilingus, sexual intercourse, and the sounds of moaning.

Furthermore, the frequency and graphic description of the sexual lyrics evinces a clear intention to lure hearers into this activity. The depictions of ultimate sexual acts are so vivid that they are hard to distinguish from seeing the same conduct described in the words of a book, or in pictures in periodicals or films.

It is also noteworthy that the material here is music. 2 Live Crew itself testified that the "Nasty" recording was made to be listened and danced to. The evident goal of this particular recording is to reproduce the sexual act though musical lyrics. It is an appeal directed to "dirty" thoughts and the loins, not to the intellect and the mind.

The Second *Miller* Test: Patently Offensive

The court also finds that the second element of the *Miller* test is satisfied in that the "Nasty" recording is patently offensive. The recording depicts sexual conduct in graphic detail. The specificity of the descriptions makes the audio message analogous to a camera with a zoom lens, focusing on the sights and sounds of various ultimate sex acts.

While the above facts are sufficient to support a finding that this material is patently offensive, there are additional considerations that support such a finding. First, the "Nasty" lyrics contain what are commonly known as "dirty words" and depictions of female abuse and violence. Secondly, the material here is music which can certainly be more intrusive to the unwilling listener than other forms of communication. Unlike a videotape, a book, or periodical, music must be played to be experienced. A person can sit in public and look at an obscene magazine without unduly intruding upon another's privacy; but, even according to the plaintiffs' testimony, music is made to be played and listened to. A person laying on a public beach, sitting in a public park, walking down the street, or sitting in his automobile waiting for the light to change is, in a sense, a captive audience. While the law does require citizens to avert their ears when speech is merely offensive, they do not have an obligation to buy and use ear plugs in public if the state legislature has chosen to protect them from obscenity.

The Third *Miller* Test: Social Value

The final factor under *Miller* is whether the "Nasty" recording, taken as a whole, lacks serious literary, artistic, political, or scientific value. This factor is not measured by community standards. The proper inquiry is whether a reasonable person would find serious social value in the material at issue. The plaintiffs correctly note that the value of a work can pass muster under *Miller* if it has serious merit, measured objectively, even if a majority of the community would not agree.

As a preliminary matter, it is again important to note what this case is not about. Neither the "Rap" or "Hip-Hop" musical genres are on trial. The narrow issue before this court is whether the recording entitled "As Nasty As They Wanna Be" is legally obscene. This is also not a case about whether the group 2 Live Crew or any of its other music is obscene.

This court must examine the "Nasty" recording for its content; the inquiry is objective, not ad hominem.

Finally, this court's role is not to serve as a censor or an art and music critic. If the "Nasty" recording has serious literary, artistic, political, or scientific value, it is irrelevant that the work is not stylish, tasteful, or even popular.

The plaintiffs themselves testified that neither their music nor their lyrics were created to convey a political message. The only witness testifying at trial that there was political content in the "Nasty" recording was Carlton Long, who was qualified as an expert on the culture of black Americans. This witness first stated that their recording was political because the 2 Live Crew, as a group of black Americans, used this medium to express themselves. While it is doubtless true that "Nasty" is a product of the group's background, including their heritage as black Americans, this fact does not convert whatever they say, or sing, into political speech. Professor Long also testified that the following passages from the recording contained political content: a four sentence phrase in the song "Dirty Nursery Rhymes" about Abraham Lincoln, the word "man" in the Georgie Porgie portion of the same song, and the use of the device of "boasting" to stress one's manhood. Even giving these isolated lyrics the meaning attributed by the expert, they are not sufficient in number of significance to give the "Nasty" recording, as a whole, any serious political value.

In terms of science, Professor Long also suggested that there is cultural content in 2 Live Crew's recording which rises to the level of serious sociological value. According to this witness, white Americans "hear" the "Nasty" recording in a different way than black Americans because of their different frames of references. Long identifies three cultural devices evident in the work here: "call and response," "doing the dozens," and "boasting." The court finds none of these arguments persuasive.

The only examples of "call and response" in the "Nasty" recording are portions where males and females yell, in repetitive verse, "Tastes Great—Less Filling" and, in another song, assail campus Greek-letter groups. The phrases alone have no significant artistic merit nor are they examples of black American culture. In the case of "Tastes Great—Less Filling," this is merely a phrase lifted from a beer commercial.

The device of "doing the dozens" is a word game composed of a series of insults escalating in their satirical content. The "boasting" device is a way for persons to overstate their virtues such as sexual prowess. While this court does not doubt that both "boasting" and "doing the dozens" are found in the culture of black Americans, these devices are also found in other cultures. "Doing the dozens" is commonly seen in adolescents, especially boys, of all races. "Boasting" seems to be part of the universal human condition.

Professor Long also cited several different examples of literary devices such as rhyme and allusion which appear in "Nasty," and points to the song title "Dick Almighty" as an example of the literary device of personification. This, of course, is nonsense regardless of the expert's credentials. "A quotation from Voltaire in the fly leaf of a book," noted the Supreme Court in *Miller*, "will not constitutionally redeem an otherwise obscene publication."

Initially, it would appear very difficult to find a musical work obscene. As noted by the American Civil Liberties union, the meaning of music is subjective and subject only to the limits of the listener's imagination. Music nevertheless is not exempt from a state's obscenity statutes. Musical works are obscene if they meet the *Miller* test. Certainly it would be possible to compose an obscene oratorio or opera and it has probably been done.

Obscenity? Yes!

The recording "As Nasty As They Wanna Be," taken as a whole, is legally obscene.

* * *

2 LIVE CREW AND THE CULTURAL CONTRADICTIONS OF *MILLER*

Kathleen M. Sullivan

Miller v. California, decided in 1973, is the Supreme Court's last effort to draw a line between obscenity and protected speech. *Miller* denies First Amendment protection to a work that appeals to the "prurient interest," depicts sex in a "patently offensive" way, and lacks "serious" artistic or other value. Prurience and offensiveness are to be judged by the compass of the "average person applying contemporary community standards," while artistic value is to be assessed not by the local average but rather by the universal "reasonable" person. *Miller* was meant to build a categorical wall separating art from pornography, permitting hard-core material to be suppressed without throwing Joyce or Lawrence out with the bathwater.

But lately the art-porn boundary is breaking down. Obscenity law has come out of the porn shop and into the record store and the art museum. Federal Judge Jose Gonzalez made history when he declared 2 Live Crew's rap music obscene in *Skyywalker Records*. Never before had a record album been held to flunk the *Miller* test. Elsewhere too, obscenity law is overstepping its old Skid Row boundaries. In another legal first, officials of a Cincinnati art museum have been charged criminally for exhibiting Robert Mapplethorpe's graphic photographs of homoerotic scenes and naked children. And efforts continue in Congress to legislate content restrictions on the National Endowment for the Arts that would bar public support for supposedly obscene art.

Against these imperial tendencies of the anti-obscenity movement, *Miller* is proving weak constraint. That is no surprise, for *Miller* sets forth an extraordinarily incoherent standard—as the 2 Live Crew case illustrates.

The first two parts of the *Miller* test pose a psychological contradiction. By requiring an obscene work to have *both* prurient appeal *and* patent offensiveness, *Miller* requires the audience, in vernacular terms, to be simultaneously turned on and grossed out. How can both conditions be satisfied at once?

There are two possible solutions. The first is to posit that every individual—even the average person applying contemporary community standards—has both a base and a noble side, or at least an id and a superego. An obscene work stimulates bodily sexual arousal that the higher faculties recognize as base. In other words, obscenity initially bypasses the brain and heads straight for the groin, but the brain quickly recognizes what has happened and overrides arousal with shame. This is the psychological dynamic the Supreme Court suggests when it seeks to define "prurient" interest in sex as "shameful or morbid" rather than "normal and healthy."

Judge Gonzalez's opinion, however, illustrates the problems with this approach. Human response to speech cannot be so readily subdivided into the high and the low, the cognitive and the physiological. Other areas of First Amendment law have long acknowledged that speech strikes chords both above and below the neck. The Supreme Court, for example, protected a person's right to wear a jacket emblazoned with the slogan "Fuck the Draft" on the ground that "words are often chosen as much for their emotive as their cognitive force." Great political speeches target both hearts and minds, prompting tears as well as thoughts. True, *Miller* tries to draw the line a little lower than the neck. But it is a psychological throwback to pretend that "the loins" any more than the heart are completely unconnected to "the intellect and the mind," as Judge Gonzalez, faithful to *Miller*, tries to do.

There is an additional problem with resolving the seeming contradiction in the first two parts of the *Miller* standard by assigning prurience to the id and offensiveness to the superego. What self-respecting decisionmaker wants to admit to being aroused by materials that are patently offensive? If shame is the name of the game, human instinct is to deny being turned on in the first place. Sure enough, Judge Gonzalez's opinion gingerly sidesteps just this point: it finds the "prurient interest" test satisfied *despite* evidence that, in the judge's words, "the Nasty recording did not actually physically excite anyone who heard it and indeed, caused boredom after repeated play." If that is the case, why ban it?

These problems suggest turning to a second, alternative method for finding prurient interest and patent offensiveness at the same time: subdivide the community rather than the individual psyche, and find the work sexually arousing to one subcommunity while patently offensive to others. This has the virtue of sparing the average decisionmaker the embarrassment of admitting any personal arousal. Not surprisingly, this is the escape hatch used by the Supreme Court to permit suppression of homoerotic, sadomasochistic, or other "deviant" pornography—deem it someone else's turn-on, but offensive to the community at large. And this may be the truest account of what is really going on in the 2 Live Crew case: the dominant culture is reining in a black male youth subculture whose portrait of its own sexuality offends those outside it.

The minute the case is described this way, however, its offense to free speech principles is made obvious. The Supreme Court has always disavowed that obscenity law has anything to do with suppressing the message or viewpoint conveyed—the cardinal sin forbidden by the First Amendment. Indeed, the Court has struck down state efforts to regulate sexually explicit speech whenever they could be characterized as viewpoint-discriminatory. The Court has invalidated, for example, right-wing efforts to suppress porn on the ground that it celebrates hedonistic promiscuity over monogamous marriage, and left-wing efforts to suppress porn on the ground that it constructs and reinforces unjust sexual hierarchy by eroticizing the domination of women by men.

Although Judge Gonzalez avoids any overt characterization of the case along these lines, distaste for 2 Live Crew's misogyny and sexual narcissism lurks as a subtext just beneath the surface of the opinion. It is not the judge's fault that he cannot be more direct. First Amendment law requires him to launder popular judgments of disapproval into judicial findings of low value.

Enter the third part of *Miller*—the "serious artistic value" test—which plays out in the 2 Live Crew case as farce. In an age where university literature departments teach "trash-lit" courses and where Madonna is a leading subject for doctoral dissertations, surely the "serious/non-serious" boundary in art is at risk. Indeed, as a recent *Yale Law Journal* note argues, it is a boundary that postmodern aesthetics deliberately challenges. Nonetheless, the 2 Live Crew case suggests that the third part of the *Miller* test remains useful for at least one purpose: as a source of employment for academics willing to testify about such matters as the role of personification in "Dick Almighty." But it does nothing to reduce the tautological character of the decision. In the end, the late Justice Potter Stewart was right when he said that he couldn't define obscenity but that he knew it when he saw it: whether *Miller* switches a case onto the track of art or porn depends ultimately on a subjective hunch.

The 2 Live Crew decision should not survive appeal. You cannot take sex out of rock-and-roll or rhythm-and-blues. True, the quality of the mixture spans a wide range. 2 Live Crew's sexual lyrics are crude, vulgar, and blunt. They cannot hold a candle to the infinitely more clever double-entendre and subtle innuendo of earlier and greater sexually suggestive songs—there are no metaphorical "jellyrolls" or "handymen" in need of decoding in 2 Live Crew. But which is more "obscene"—sexual lyrics that are coded or blunt? No court should even start down the road toward an answer.

Source: Skyywalker Records Inc. v. Nicholas Navarro (Sherrif, Broward County, Florida) United States District Court, S.D. Florida, June 6, 1990, and Kathleen M. Sullivan, "2 Live Crew and the Cultural Contradictions of *Miller*," *Reconstruction* 1, no. 2 (1990), pp. 16–20.

51

"Public Enemy's Bomb Squad"

Tom Moon

As we have seen in descriptions of such artists as Phil Spector and Brian Wilson, producers often obsess over the details of sound that comprise the musical "mix." In this respect, Hank Shocklee, the head of New York rap group Public Enemy's influential Bomb Squad production team, fits squarely into the history of rock's most musically innovative personalities. Hip-hop producers like Shocklee (born James Henry Boxley III, 1967), however, broke with one of rock's most staunch traditions, substituting live musicians with backing tracks concocted out of samples. Consequently many critics and rock fans during the late '80s treated them more as plagiarists than composers. Shocklee convincingly dismisses such claims, explaining how the Bomb Squad (comprised of Shocklee, his brother Keith, Carl Ryder, and Eric Sadler) takes a songwriting approach to Public Enemy's music. As he shows, the Bomb Squad arranges their dense collage of layered samples with particular care and craft, and an awareness of earlier production techniques, such as those used by Motown. By deliberately highlighting elements of harmonic tension, placing samples slightly out of rhythm, and utilizing the potential of abrasive noise and dissonance, Shocklee's structures complement the political lyrics of Public Enemy's main rappers, Chuck D and Flavor Flav, in powerful ways.[1]

Hank Shocklee's favorite word is "situation." As in "master of the recording studio situation." As in a man who enjoys problem solving. With his assertive, assaultive productions for Public Enemy and remixes for Ziggy Marley, Ralph Tresvant and others, Shocklee has become the sonic saint of hip-hop, the producer with the sound—that thickly layered noise-manipulation thing that defies transcription—most often imitated. He understands that situation: The eyes of the hip-hop world are on him. Everybody is going after his favorite samples. Everybody wants those same beats. Rather than keep his secrets secret, he's started SOUL (Sound of Urban Listeners) Records, and embarked on an ambitious roster of production projects (Son of Bazerk, the Young Black Teenagers, etc.).

When he talks about building a rap track, Shocklee gives credit to the other members of the Bomb Squad—his brother Keith, Carl Ryder and Eric Sadler. The group, which he describes as a band, has won critical praise; nonetheless, Shocklee's still sore about critics' distinction between trained musicians and so-called rap hacks. "People say we just copy, we can't make our own music," Shocklee says, lounging on the couch in the A room at Manhattan's Soundtrack Studios, where he's in the middle of mixing the frenetic Son of Bazerk record. "Let's be realistic here. There are only

---

1 For a particularly compelling musical analysis of Public Enemy's 1990 single "Fight the Power," see musicologist Robert Walser's "Rhythm, Rhyme, and Rhetoric in the Music of Public Enemy," *Ethnomusicology* 39, no. 2 (Spring/Summer 1995): 193–217.

so many chords you can come up with. Everybody's copying variations anyway. The difference is we're taking it from the record and manipulating it into something else. That's another type of musicianship. It would take less time to bring a band in and have them play this live than it does manipulating it our way, but what fun would that be?" he says, reaching over the console to punch buttons that isolate percussion tracks in his dense schemata. (Shocklee builds rap songs using as many as 48 tracks—far more than most rap producers.)

In fact, much of the Bomb Squad work is not very much fun. It's not a sweatshop, but it's close: The group cranks out beats and rhythm patterns and loops every day, whether there's a project or not. "It's not like an artist who leaves the piano if nothing's happening. We'll do something—a beat, some samples—and file it away. Then when we're thinking about a track, we'll call it up and try it out."

The business of building the tracks begins at "Demo World," the Squad's production studio in Hempstead, Long Island. "That's where we have our records and our sound libraries. We each have our specialties: My brother is amazing with computers, so he's always got sounds, and he knows records like an encyclopedia. Eric, I consider him a programming wizard. He knows drum machines backwards and forwards. They're like the builders and I'm the architect. I'm thinking about arrangements—putting in the chorus at times you don't really expect a chorus, coming up with that extra little interruption." Shocklee has become an executive architect now. Public Enemy's *Apocalypse '91: The Empire Strikes Black* credits him as executive producer, which means, Shocklee says, that he's "in and out, not as much hands-on, but not like a record company guy handling paperwork."

Assembling beats and loops from any number of sources, the Bomb Squad drafts a blueprint which is then used to match the sound with the message. "If the title of the album is *AmeriKKKa's Most Wanted*," Shocklee says, "your beat better sound like the most wanted, you know?[2] We look at that phrase and we've got darkness in our minds—rough streets, gloomy, hard, these are the things you have to put on tape. So once we get the outline, we think about trying to complement the vocal situation by making the backing tracks as aggressive as possible. Whatever you bring up as a sample, whatever beat you work with, has to be an exclamation point to the situation."

Shocklee can't stress this enough: "Music is a mood situation. As the Bomb Squad, we score to personalities. Nobody goes in and says, 'We're going to make the deffest record.' You know how you feel that day. Then you listen and say, this sounds like such-and-such emotion."

When they start really examining how the content fits the music, the Squad usually starts arguing. "It gets down to the very specifics of perception," Shocklee says, diving back onto the couch. "Here you've got a click on the one. Here you've got a snare drum that you want to put on the one with the click, right? How it's perceived depends on how it hits the one. For example, you rush something—a couple of seconds before the one—and there's a mood of emergency. Of uneasiness. On a lot of the early records we rushed the samples a bit. So you're constantly going, 'Why is this pushing me?' Now, if you bring it back a little bit, you're laying back. That's a whole other mood. You haven't changed the situation—you've still got a click and you've still got a snare, but now the perception is changed. That's the thing people feel. A loop is purposefully placed a little bit off, a little ajar, so that when it comes around again, it's like a wooosh against the snare.

"We fight to figure it out. Somebody'll say, 'I don't want this snare on the one, because instead of being laid-back it has the feeling of not doing anything.' That's what pop records do to you—it doesn't make you feel one way or the other. You went in the same way you come out. That's what we don't want. We want records that reach and transcend."

---

2 The Bomb Squad had provided the production for *AmeriKKKa's Most Wanted*, the debut solo album from former N.W.A. rapper Ice Cube.

To get those records, the Bomb Squad has to do some fancy drum-machine footwork. Facing the limitations of the metrically rigid machines, Shocklee and Sadler work to create rhythm programs that swing—not the ricky-ticky new-jack style, but a deep and buoyant groove that automatically induces motion. It is a point of pride: "You'll hear three different kick drums, three snares, three hi-hats, and each has its own time frequency. This is because you've got to recreate all kinds of stuff. You've got to simulate that laziness—when the drummer hits the snare and gets a repeating note because he didn't lift the stick up. Also, a drummer's stick doesn't hit the skin in the same place all the time, but that happens with a machine. That right there adds the funk: We've got to take these machines and recreate mistakes on purpose."

Harmonic dissonances (listen to Public Enemy's "Bring the Noise") meet with the same debate. "Eric sings on key," Shocklee says, "while I'm like, fuck the key. I'm looking for a mood, a feeling. So some things are purposely out of key. Like Son of Bazerk, it's an R&B band, their stuff is in key. But I believe in complements, and Bazerk, he's meaner than anybody I've ever heard on wax. I work with him by having what's behind him in key, otherwise you lose Bazerk. If I put things in key behind Chuck D, you lose Chuck, because his vocal is smooth. So you have to put it against abrasion."

Today is a rare day in the studio: Shocklee usually observes a no-visitors policy. "If everybody is not focused on the same situation," says Hank, "we're not going to meet our goal. So I'm the leader, and I don't settle. There are no split decisions in music, no ties. It's either the right way or the wrong way. If somebody's walking around with that 'I don't give a fuck, let's just do this' attitude, that will come through. One negative can destroy the whole situation. People react to that, they know when it's not feeling good."

Once enough of the grooves and adornments are in place, the Bomb Squad leaves Demo World, transporting the not-so-basic tracks and programs to one of the large facilities in Manhattan (very occasionally, L.A.) for final touches and all-important mixing sessions.

The mix is everything. It doesn't matter how many cool sounds and structural surprises Shocklee and his crew put into the track—if the mix ain't happening, the magic's lost. So the Bomb Squad spends most of its time tweaking sounds, checking balances, carefully adjusting the dense collage so that every element comes through. Here, too, Shocklee has a renegade outlook. Operating on the assumption that most people don't sit in front of two speakers to listen to music, Shocklee puts his mixes through unusual tests. "Sometimes you hear three or four loops on the same track, all happening at different places with different levels and EQ settings. If one little thing is out of balance, everything is wack. That's why I'm here doing this now. There are certain things we want to cut through the track and other things we want in there, but not cutting through. For example, that string line we just heard, that little loop—if you have that too loud, you become too aware of it. It's got to be at a level where you still hear the line but you don't hear that it's repeating. We don't want it flat, like those old Motown songs, but if it's too high it's going to take away from the kick drum and everything else. So it's delicate. Sometimes we open up tracks to get more hiss. Hiss acts as glue—it fills in cracks and crevices so you get this constant wooooooffff. So you play around with everything, get to where you can hear it and what it's doing, and pretty soon the whole track is breathing.

"That's why I sit on the couch. Because music has to hit you. I don't want to hear it up close. I'll go listen in the hallway and decide whether the mix was pulling me in. I want to make records so that when a car is driving by and you hear the thing blaring, you could tell it was my record. Most of the time you just hear it as blaring. I want mine to be so distinct you want to stop and ask the guy, 'What was *that*?'"

Source: Tom Moon, "Public Enemy's Bomb Squad: Hank Shocklee Explodes in Your Ear," *Musician*, October 1991, pp. 69–72, 76.

52

"The Death of Sampling?"

Mark Kemp

By the early 1990s, hip-hop had become a major commercial force, and its producers were finally receiving recognition for their intricate use of samples. Given rap's increasing visibility, however, it was inevitable that hip-hop artists would eventually find the legality of their sampling practices questioned in a court of law. In December 1991, Judge Kevin Thomas Duffy ruled that rapper Biz Markie's song "Alone Again" was in copyright violation of the song it had sampled, Gilbert O'Sullivan's 1972 hit "Alone Again (Naturally)." Duffy's decision was forceful, but also vague; he did not state what amount of sampling *would* be permissible. As such, the ruling created a culture of fear within the music industry. It seemed implicit that any and all samples, regardless of their length, would require clearance. Mark Kemp's article for *Option* magazine captures in illuminating detail the debates that emerged in the wake of the Biz Markie case. Years later, many of the concerns that Kemp raises have come to be realized. On the one hand, since the early '90s most major hip-hop artists have taken a financially efficient approach to sampling, severely limiting their borrowing to only one or two prominently placed, and repeated, samples per song. On the other hand, many rap producers have worked around copyright restrictions by using obscure sources, or by deliberately altering samples to the point where the original is no longer recognizable. Whether or not the "Biz Markie case 'stole the soul' from rap music," as copyright expert and Fair Use advocate Siva Vaidhyanathan has maintained, is debatable. But its impact is impossible to ignore.[1]

When a New York judge quoted the Bible in his decision to grant a temporary injunction barring further sales of Biz Markie's album *I Need a Haircut* last December, it sent a shock wave through the music industry.

"Thou shalt not steal" were the first words of Judge Kevin Thomas Duffy's ruling.

It was a reaction to Markie's use of a loop from the 1972 Gilbert O'Sullivan hit "Alone Again (Naturally)" in his rap song simply entitled "Alone Again." The Markie case marks the first time sampling has ever gone before a judge—earlier cases were settled out of court—and Duffy's words were chillingly clear and simple: if you're going to sample from another artist's work, you'd better get permission.

The ruling has caused a minor panic among some record companies. Top brass immediately sent down memos to the effect that all digital samples on all new albums would have to be cleared before release. But some artists who use digital samples in their work say such a requirement would be virtually impossible to comply with; and as a legal precedent, it stands to threaten the creative process of contemporary pop music altogether.

---

1 Siva Vaidhyanathan, *Copyrights and Copywrongs: The Rise of Intellectual Property and How it Threatens Creativity* (New York: New York University Press, 2001), p. 144.

"It's going to affect *everyone's* process," says Hank Shocklee of Public Enemy's production team, the Bomb Squad. "A whole chain of events will start happening: people are going to be trying like crazy to find all their sources, and records won't come out on time. It's impossible to keep up with every snippet of sound you use."

Shocklee should know. Unlike Biz Markie's song, in which a large portion of O'Sullivan's tune was sampled and looped throughout, the Bomb Squad's sound collages involve a veritable soup of samples. "You know how some people say. The Bomb Squad uses all these samples and I can't tell where they come from?'" Shocklee asks. "Well, *we* can't tell where they come from either. You change the sound, you alter them, and then you plug them into your mix; six months down the road, after you've been working with all these different samples, you have no idea where every one of them came from."

Los Angeles attorney Evan Cohen sees things differently. In 1989, Cohen represented Mark Volman and Howard Kaylan of the '60s pop group the Turtles in a landmark lawsuit against rappers De La Soul, who had used a sample of the Turtles' 1969 hit "You Showed Me" in their own "Transmitting Live From Mars" (the case was settled out of court). Cohen suggests that Judge Duffy's decision in the Biz Markie case is a milestone for copyright holders. "It should provide the final removal of doubt as to whether the Fair Use Doctrine applies to digital sampling," he says.

Cohen's reference is to the Fair Use Doctrine of 1972, an amendment to the copyright law which allows for various exceptions to the law, including appropriation of copyrighted materials for social comment, education, and other such purposes. Some observers, such as De La Soul's attorney Ken Anderson, feel that Fair Use should apply to certain instances of digital sampling. However, Cohen sees the judge's decision as definitive: "The judge in New York says sampling is stealing if one doesn't ask permission beforehand."

Anderson dismisses his colleague's observation, calling it premature. "The Biz Markie case doesn't even *refer* to Fair Use," Anderson says. "There has not yet been a case which analyzes the copyright issues relative to sampling. We're still waiting for that."

Since it made its way into popular music in the mid-'80s, digital sampling has been a highly charged issue of ownership, often pitting young, black, inner-city experimental hip-hop musicians against older, baby-boomer pop stars of the '60s and '70s. The Turtles, perhaps, were the symbolically perfect '60s group to sue for copyright infringement. They created perfectly happy melodies in a pure-pop structure. Side-by-side, the Turtles and De La Soul represented the past and future of pop music. "We weren't wanting to prohibit them from moving in a creative way," says Turtle Mark Volman. "No one I know wants to stop them from being creative, but at the same time you have to deal with legalities.

"It's important that artists receive their fair share and what's due. If someone's using music that's already been created and spent for, then they should pay for it. It was only a matter of time before the courts would say that.

"When Bob Dylan wrote that the times are a changing, hey, they still are," Volman adds. "Music is changing, too. Rock'n'roll takes on so many different ways, and rap is one of them."

Certainly, times have changed since popular groups penned simple verse-chorus-verse songs; with the advent of samplers and other technological advances, even the most mainstream popular music has become a more experimental medium. It's now common practice to incorporate snippets of prerecorded material into songs. But hip-hop has never been the only music built around electronic samples. In the early '80s, avant-garde musicians were playing around with sampling machines at about the same time, and since then all kinds of music, from R&B and dance music to heavy metal and alternative rock, have begun using samples.

But Judge Duffy's decision stands to put a damper on such experimentation. After the decision was handed down, record companies immediately instituted their new tougher policies. "It's much more stringent now than it had been," says Warner publicity head Bob Merlis. "We took a lot of stuff on faith before, but now we're demanding proof that these things are being cleared." Merlis admits that such policies "are going to slow things down." Lillian Matulic of Priority, N.W.A's label, agrees, saying, "We were issued a memo saying they have to clear all samples before we release anything." A spokesman for De La Soul's record company Tommy Boy, who agreed to talk on condition of anonymity, says it was the process of clearing all samples that caused the year-long delay of that group's second album, *De La Soul Is Dead.* "Here, we wait until *everything* is cleared— every drum beat, however small it is." he says. "It's like, why play around, right? The De La Soul vs. the Turtles situation really wised us up."

On the surface, this sort of caution may seem obvious: if you take from Gilbert O'Sullivan, you should get Gilbert O'Sullivan's permission. But there's a tremendous gray area in sampling. Markie's case indicated a clear breakdown in communication, and his attorney's argument that it's a common practice to go ahead and use non-cleared samples was not a real argument at all. Further evidence that Markie had sought O'Sullivan's permission beforehand, was denied it, and then released the song anyway, seemed to make the case clear-cut. After all, when MC Hammer released "U Can't Touch This," whose main hook was Rick James' 1981 hit "Super Freak," he had obtained James' permission, and even worked out a deal that gave James co-credit—and ultimately, big royalties.

The danger in Judge Duffy's decision is that sampling is still not a cut-and-dry issue. Duffy, who was so oblivious to pop music that he had to be told what the term "R&B" means, didn't address the more complex and subtle uses of sampling. As Anderson points out, sampling "is not the kind of thing that lends itself to the statement, 'Thou shalt not steal.' It's a little more sophisticated than that." Still, Anderson plays down the significance of the Markie case. "I don't think it has any legal impact at all because it doesn't analyze the copyright issues of whether sampling constitutes infringement."

"What this case *doesn't* answer are those borderline cases," says entertainment attorney Richard P. Dieguez, who distinguishes between what he terms *de minimis* sampling—a short horn blast, a James Brown scream, a kick or snare drum—from what he refers to in plainer English as "the primary hook of an actual master recording." For instance, Dieguez says, "if you deleted the sample from the Biz Markie song, you wouldn't have anything left but Biz kind of talking to himself. That's an obvious case. On the other hand, if you deleted any of the samples in a Public Enemy record, you'd still have a composition. I couldn't imagine anyone getting nailed for taking a snare. The difficulty is the stuff in the middle."

"Right now," says Dieguez, "there's no precedent. Some people want to believe that there's a set number of bars that's allowable, but that's just not true. It doesn't matter how many bars of a song are taken; it's an ad hoc judgment. No one can come up with a blanket rule."

"It's impossible," says Hank Shocklee of the possibility that he would have to account for all the sounds on a Public Enemy record. "I look at rap culture—and R&B culture, too—as becoming more of a scavenger culture," he says. "After a while, you start mixing it all together, mixing all the colors together, and you lose the source. I think that's what's *good* about it, the way it evolves into something else. I *like* that aspect of it."

Accordingly, Shocklee doesn't consider the Markie case a sampling issue, per se. "Biz did a cover of a song," he says. "People confuse that issue. A sample's when you take a snippet. Biz didn't just sample it, he took a hunk of it." Shocklee ultimately blames higher-ups for allowing the song to get out without clearance in the first place. "It goes to show how little record executives know about the music they put out. It shows that either they don't care about the music or that they don't know about it. And now that the Biz Markie song got past them, they're trying to cover their tails. Now, you're going to be asked to account for every snippet, and that's just not possible."

"I totally disagree," says DJ Daddy-O of Stetsasonic. "That's just a bunch of bullshit." Daddy-O has put his own group on hold for the moment because he has become a producer very much in demand lately, working on various hip-hop and R&B records, including Queen Latifah, as well as remixes for rock bands, such as Sonic Youth and the B-52s. Daddy-O feels the Biz Markie case should make DJs more responsible, that it should encourage those who sample to go beyond the mere looping of familiar songs. "Every DJ in the world knows what records he uses." Daddy-O says. "So for Hank to sit there and say, 'Six months down the road, when I'm working with the Bomb Squad, I don't know what I use,' that's bullshit. You're making records, you have to be responsible for where your material comes from."

But there's a distinction between Shocklee's technique and the approach taken by those who merely loop songs. And Daddy-O is somewhat sensitive to this. "I actually kind of understand what he's saying, though, because Public Enemy's music works in a different way, sort of like a painting," Daddy-O says. "What happens in the mix is the same thing that happens with paint—after a while some of the stuff starts blending together in the background, creating a foundation. So it's hard to tell what's there. It's like when you blend green with yellow: you get something very different. That's what happens in a PE mix. But I think people should still be aware of where their stuff is coming from.

"In fact, we as rap artists have got to start getting beyond what we've done in the past," he adds. "We need to think about making classic records, like all the classic rock and R&B records of the past. We need to be making records that people are happy with and not saying, 'Oh, all they're doing is stealing samples.' Look at what's happening in rock. Today, with the technology we have, you don't *need* guitars to make music. Yet look at what happened with the Nirvana record. And there's no reason that record should *not* have gotten as far as it did. It's a great record. Everything about it is right—it's got the melodies and it's got the power. It's just right. And it's regular old guitar rock. That's the level that our music should be going, and that's what we should be striving for.

"The Biz Markie situation was a stupid move," Daddy-O continues, "but everything happens for a reason. I think in a way it's good, because now it's going to make people start looking towards the future, looking towards that next level."

Source: Mark Kemp, "The Death of Sampling?," *Option*, March/April 1992, pp. 17–20.

53

"Kurt Cobain and the Politics of Damage"

Sarah Ferguson

When college rock favorites Nirvana and their front man Kurt Cobain (1967–1994) were thrust into the spotlight in 1991 on the strength of their major label debut *Nevermind*, the media quickly heralded them as the forerunners of a new alternative rock movement. While alternative came to encompass a number of styles—everything from Nine Inch Nails' industrial rock to Teenage Fanclub's power pop—its most popular manifestation was undoubtedly that of grunge. As a label, the term "grunge" seemed to fit perfectly the dirty, distorted guitars, metallic riffs, and hoarse, shouted vocals of groups like Pearl Jam, Mudhoney, and others. More than that, though, grunge became attached to a regional scene (Seattle), a fashion style, and, as Sarah Ferguson points out in her article for the *Utne Reader*, an attitude of alienation and victimization, crystallized in songs like "Smells Like Teen Spirit" and "Jeremy" and mirrored in the music's audience. Ferguson questions the reasons and social significance behind grunge's "politics of damage." If grunge is to be taken seriously as an authentic expression of the times, she argues, then it needs to be considered along lines of race, class, gender, and the place of youth within the American family.

I came face to face with the essence of grunge culture last summer, when I was out in Seattle interviewing street punks. I was hanging out with a runaway vegan anarchist named Jackie and his street friend Anthony when we decided to go party with their friends from the band Suffocated. We took a shortcut to their house on the outskirts of the U district, tramping through the woods and under the bridge where the "trolls" (street kids) slept when they didn't have a squat to crash, then circling around the back of Safeway to scavenge for moldy sandwiches in the Dumpster.

Suffocated's lead guitarist received us nonchalantly, nodding at the 40-ouncers we'd picked up with Jackie and Anthony's panhandled change. Anthony said he wanted to try out his new piercing needle and disappeared into the bathroom upstairs. He said he wanted to pierce his scrotum, said he liked the experience of pain.

So Jackie and I sat there in the living room, watching the band members scarf down lines of speed and bong hits amid a blistering blur of crustcore and metal. At the end of the tape, the guitarist dug out a new one. "Mind if we listen to Nirvana?" he asked, almost apologetically, like he was 'fessing to being a Bon Jovi fan. "Sure," Jackie shrugged, but I just smiled. These were Kurt Cobain's people, the forgotten white trash he celebrated. If I'd asked them up front, they would have said they hated Nirvana for the same sellout reasons that Cobain hated himself. Yet even among this jaded crowd, Cobain's anguished wail offered a refuge of authentic despair.

Courtney Love said, "Every kid in America who's been abused loves Kurt Cobain's music." In fact, Nirvana made abuse his generation's defining metaphor. The hit "Smells Like Teen Spirit" was an anthem of powerless rage and betrayal. It was a resounding fuck you to the boomers and all the false expectations they saddled us with about rock 'n' roll revolution. And it made psychological damage—with all its concurrent themes of child abuse, drug addiction, suicide, and neglect—a basis for social identity.

Like Pearl Jam's "Jeremy," which tells the story of an alienated kid who blows his head off in school, Nirvana's "Teen Spirit," and indeed all of grunge culture, is rooted in the feeling of damage. Coming out of the get-ahead '80s, it's easy to understand the appeal. Being damaged is a hedge against the illusory promises of consumer culture. For grunge's primary audience, white male teens, damage offers a defense against the claims of gangsta rappers and punk rock feminists. It's a great equalizer at a time when multiculturalism seems to have devolved into competing schools of victimization. Grunge appeals to white kids because it tells them that they're not responsible for the evils of racism and injustices, that they are victims too.

The empowered feeling you get from listening to these songs lies in unearthing that essential nugget of shame. It's like going to a 12-step meeting. You stand up, announce the wrongs done to you as a child, your response (drugs, suicide attempts). Simply identifying and acknowledging your damage is empowering, because society seems to deny you the right to feel damaged.

What's frustrating is how the politics of the music remains so acutely personal. When the Sex Pistols screamed "No Future," they were condemning a society that gave young people no hope, no prospects for change. Yet underlying that nihilistic message was a vital rage at all the politicians and people in power who, they felt, had restricted their prospects. In other words, punk knew who the enemy was.

By contrast, grunge music seems more muddled. It's as if kids don't know who to blame: their parents, the media, the schools—or themselves. Even Cobain doubted the privilege of his despair. "I'm a product of a spoiled America," he once said. "Think of how much worse my family life could be if I grew up in a depression or something. There are so many worse things than a divorce. I've just been brooding and bellyaching about something I couldn't have, which is a family, a solid family unit, for too long."

In fact, the dissolution of the American family has exerted a tremendous torque on the members of Cobain's generation. And while they may not be growing up in the midst of the Great Depression, with the official unemployment rate for young people hovering at 13.2 percent, kids have reason to complain. The dwindling timber economy of Cobain's hometown, Aberdeen, Washington, was certainly no picnic. Yet Cobain and his fellow grunge balladeers never really aspire to protest, preferring to remain mired in their own sense of inadequacy. The inverted pose of the music mirrors the incoherence of the left and the replacement of class politics with self-help politics. In the absence of a viable counterculture, it's no wonder young people don't know who to blame.

Indeed, grunge expresses this generation's almost willful refusal to reach for larger truths. Instead, it engages in a kind of mournful nostalgia for a childhood without violation. Grunge sees the lie of consumer culture but still yearns for the manufactured suburban bliss of *Leave It to Beaver* and *Mayberry R.F.D.* (two of Cobain's favorite shows). It's an odd yet poignant stance, given rock's traditional aversion to the constraints of the nuclear family. "Daddy didn't give attention / To the fact that mommy didn't care," Eddie Vedder anguishes. Grunge is music for kids who grew up too fast. They keep reaching back for a childhood denied.

The contrast between Cobain's self-deprecation and his fans' adulation was jarring when I saw Nirvana play New York's Coliseum during their last concert tour. As the roadies wheeled out the hermaphroditic figurines and fiberglass trees for the *In Utero* stage set, I was struck by the band's unwillingness to indulge the audience's yearning for spectacle. Despite the corporate veneer of a big band setup, these hulking plastic dummies with their exposed innards had a kind of malevolent camp, like a twisted take on the witch's forest on *H.R. Pufnstuff.*

The crowd let out a dull roar as Dave Grohl's rapid-fire drumroll launched the band into the opening chords of "Breed." But Cobain steadfastly refused to play the role of a revered rock star, insulting his fans with sloppy chords and (apparently) drug-addled stupor. The overwhelmingly white, overwhelmingly male, overwhelmingly suburban crowd didn't seem to care. They sang along blithely to "Polly," a song about a girl being molested, and pogoed to "Rape Me," Cobain's angst-filled response to commercial fame.

The saddest moment came when the band played "Dumb": "I think I'm dumb, or maybe just happy. Think I'm just happy . . ." Cobain droned, underscoring the terribleness of not knowing the difference. The crowd stilled, grew listless, then restless, but Cobain kept intoning, "I think I'm dumb, I think I'm dumb." And for the first time it wasn't his audience's stupidity that he was railing at but his own, the horror of finding out that this was all his art could attract—people who stare back sheepishly, or worse, reverently, at your rage. He'd succeeded beyond his wildest dreams of combining punk and pop and created a Frankenstein that by its success seems to invalidate the thrust of its rebellion. You could hear him wanting to scoop it down the garbage disposal, nuke it in the microwave, except he couldn't. It just kept mutating into some yet more profitable venture.

What Cobain's suicide in April and the whole trajectory of his band's success prove is the inability of youth to own their own rebellion. The loop taken by a new musical style from the underground to the mainstream is now so compressed that there's no moment of freedom and chaos when a counterculture can take root. Even anti-corporatism can be rerouted into a marketing ploy. MTV makes fun of itself in order to ingratiate itself with its audience, but it's still one big extended commercial.

"There is no youth culture. It's like we've been robbed of culture," a street punk named Bones told me last summer as we were hopping freight trains through the South. A skinny 19-year-old with droopy brown eyes, he had covered his body with a latticework of tattoos tracing the different stages of his youth: skinhead, heroin addict, born-again Christian, skatepunk, acidhead, sous-chef. His latest "tat" was an almost photographic image of an Iraqi woman weeping over a skull.

Yet what struck me most was the battered *Sesame Street* Ernie doll that he'd sewn on the top of his backpack. It was meant to be goofy. But a flea-ridden high school dropout on food stamps tramping through train yards with this remnant of his childhood was a little like thrusting a stuffed animal into a propeller blade.

Nirvana's formula of Beatle-esque pop juxtaposed with bursts of harsh heavy metal captures the same dissonance. It recapitulates the violation of childhood innocence, the ultimate betrayal kids see in commercial culture, which promised *Brady Bunch* lives and gave them single-parent homes. The fact that this generation bought the *Brady Bunch* myth in the first place is testament to the totalitarian nature of commodity culture. Their dreams and desires have been manufactured and controlled at such an early age, they lack a clear sense of authentic experience. Perhaps that's why the theme of child abuse is so engaging. It's a visceral pain that adults produce but don't control.

And it's an accusation. In kids' eyes, it's the adults of America who are truly damaged. Their children are just collateral damage.

Source: Sarah Ferguson, "The Comfort of Being Sad: Kurt Cobain and the Politics of Damage," *Utne Reader*, July/August 1994, pp. 60–62.

54

"The Problem with Music"

STEVE ALBINI

Renowned post-punk producer/engineer and musician Steve Albini (born 1962) issued the following eye-opening polemic against the mainstream recording industry at a time in the early 1990s when many major labels were aggressively courting underground bands in the hopes of discovering the next Nirvana. Albini strips away the illusory trappings of financial fame to reveal the industry's devious machinations. As he explains, inexperienced bands often unwittingly assume the expenses of studio time, big name producers, and other numerous perks, while relinquishing the majority of their profits. And in the end these bands generally sacrifice much of their creative control as well. Albini's diatribe ultimately underscores the extent to which notions of "authenticity," in all its various guises (whether it's one's 'punk' credentials or the vintage instruments they play) circulate within the rock industry. The article's acerbic prose is typical of Albini's writings and interviews, and is equally matched by the music he has released with such abrasive bands as Big Black, Rapeman, and Shellac. Albini is equally well known for his extensive engineering credentials, a point he deliberately drives home during a lengthy detour in the middle of the article. All told, Albini has produced and recorded literally hundreds of independent bands, as well as major artists ranging from PJ Harvey and Nirvana to Jimmy Page and Robert Plant.

Whenever I talk to a band who are about to sign with a major label, I always end up thinking of them in a particular context. I imagine a trench, about four feet wide and five feet deep, maybe sixty yards long, filled with runny, decaying shit. I imagine these people, some of them good friends, some of them barely acquaintances, at one end of this trench. I also imagine a faceless industry lackey at the other end, holding a fountain pen and a contract waiting to be signed.

Nobody can see what's printed on the contract. It's too far away, and besides, the shit stench is making everybody's eyes water. The lackey shouts to everybody that the first one to swim the trench gets to sign the contract. Everybody dives in the trench and they struggle furiously to get to the other end. Two people arrive simultaneously and begin wrestling furiously, clawing each other and dunking each other under the shit. Eventually, one of them capitulates, and there's only one contestant left. He reaches for the pen, but the Lackey says, "Actually, I think you need a little more development. Swim it again, please. Backstroke."

And he does, of course.

A&R SCOUTS

Every major label involved in the hunt for new bands now has on staff a high-profile point man, an "A&R" rep who can present a comfortable face to any prospective band. The initials stand for "Artist and Repertoire," because historically, the A&R staff would select artists to record music that they had also selected, out of an available pool of each. This is still the case, though not openly.

These guys are universally young (about the same age as the bands being wooed), and nowadays they always have some obvious underground rock credibility flag they can wave. Lyle Preslar, former guitarist for Minor Threat, is one of them. Terry Tolkin, former NY independent booking agent and assistant manager at Touch and Go is one of them. Al Smith, former soundman at CBGB is one of them. Mike Gitter, former editor of *XXX* fanzine and contributor to *Rip*, *Kerrang* and other lowbrow rags is one of them. Many of the annoying turds who used to staff college radio stations are in their ranks as well.

There are several reasons A&R scouts are always young. The explanation usually copped-to is that the scout will be "hip" to the current musical "scene." A more important reason is that the bands will intuitively trust someone they think is a peer, and who speaks fondly of the same formative rock and roll experiences.

The A&R person is the first person to make contact with the band, and as such is the first person to promise them the moon. Who better to promise them the moon than an idealistic young turk who expects to be calling the shots in a few years, and who has had no previous experience with a big record company. Hell, he's as naïve as the band he's duping. When he tells them no one will interfere in their creative process, he probably even believes it.

When he sits down with the band for the first time, over a plate of angel hair pasta, he can tell them with all sincerity that when they sign with company X, they're really signing with *him*, and he's on their side. Remember that great gig I saw you at in '85? Didn't we have a blast?

By now all rock bands are wise enough to be suspicious of music industry scum. There is a pervasive caricature in popular culture of a portly, middle-aged ex-hipster talking a mile-a-minute, using outdated jargon and calling everybody "baby." After meeting "their" A&R guy, the band will say to themselves and everyone else, "He's not like a record company guy at all! He's like one of us." And they will be right. That's one of the reasons he was hired.

These A&R guys are not allowed to write contracts. What they do is present the band with a letter of intent, or "deal memo," which loosely states some terms, and affirms that the band will sign with the label once a contract has been agreed on.

The spookiest thing about this harmless sounding little "memo," is that it is, for all legal purposes, a binding document. That is, once the band signs it, they are under obligation to conclude a deal with the label. If the label presents them with a contract that the band doesn't want to sign, all the label has to do is wait. There are a hundred other bands willing to sign the exact same contract, so the label is in a position of strength.

These letters never have any term of expiry, so the band remains bound by the deal memo until a contract is signed, no matter how long that takes. The band cannot sign to another label or even put out its own material unless they are released from their agreement, which never happens. Make no mistake about it: once a band has signed a letter of intent, they will either eventually sign a contract that suits the label or they will be destroyed.

One of my favorite bands was held hostage for the better part of two years by a slick young "He's not like a label guy at all," A&R rep, on the basis of such a deal memo. He had failed to come through on any of his promises (something he did with similar effect to another well-known band), and so the band wanted out. Another label expressed interest, but when the A&R man was asked to release the band, he said he would need money or points, or possibly both, before he would consider it.[1]

---

1 "Points" is industry lingo for the "percentage points" of retail profits that producers, labels, managers, and others can claim from the band . . . e.g. 10 percent = 10 points.

The new label was afraid the price would be too dear, and they said no thanks. On the cusp of making their signature album, an excellent band, humiliated, broke up from the stress and the many months of inactivity.

WHAT I HATE ABOUT RECORDING

1. Producers and engineers who use meaningless words to make their clients think they know what's going on. Words like "Punchy," "Warm," "Groove," "Vibe," "Feel." Especially "Punchy" and "Warm." Every time I hear those words, I want to throttle somebody.

2. Producers who aren't also engineers, and as such, don't have the slightest fucking idea what they're doing in a studio, besides talking all the time. Historically, the progression of effort required to become a producer went like this: Go to college, get an EE degree. Get a job as an assistant at a studio. Eventually become a second engineer. Learn the job and become an engineer. Do that for a few years, then you can try your hand at producing. Now, all that's required to be a full-fledged "producer" is the gall it takes to claim to be one.

   Calling people like Don Fleming, Al Jourgensen, Lee Ranaldo or Jerry Harrison "producers" in the traditional sense is akin to calling Bernie a "shortstop" because he watched the whole playoffs this year.

   The term has taken on pejorative qualities in some circles. Engineers tell jokes about producers the way people back in Montana tell jokes about North Dakotans. (How many producers does it take to change a light bulb?—Hmmm. I don't know. What do *you* think? Why did the producer cross the road?—Because that's the way the Beatles did it, man.) That's why few self-respecting engineers will allow themselves to be called "producers."

   The minimum skills required to do an adequate job recording an album are:
   - Working knowledge of all the microphones at hand and their properties and uses. I mean something beyond knowing that you can drop an SM57 without breaking it.
   - Experience with every piece of equipment which might be of use and every function it may provide. This means more than knowing what echo sounds like. Which equalizer has the least phase shift in neighbor bands? Which console has more headroom? Which mastering deck has the cleanest output electronics?
   - Experience with the style of music at hand, to know when obvious blunders are occurring.
   - Ability to tune and maintain all the required instruments and electronics, so as to insure that everything is in proper working order. This means more than plugging a guitar into a tuner. How should the drums be tuned to simulate a rising note on the decay? A falling note? A consonant note? Can a bassoon play a concert E-flat in key with a piano tuned to a reference A of 440 Hz? What percentage of varispeed is necessary to make a whole-tone pitch change? What degree of overbias gives you the most headroom at 10 kHz? What reference fluxivity gives you the lowest self-noise from biased, unrecorded tape? Which tape manufacturer closes every year in July, causing shortages of tape globally? What can be done for a shedding master tape? A sticky one?
   - Knowledge of electronic circuits to an extent that will allow selection of appropriate signal paths. This means more than knowing the difference between a delay line and an equalizer. Which has more headroom, a discrete class A microphone preamp with a transformer output or a differential circuit built with monolithics? Where is the best place in an unbalanced line to attenuate the signal? If you short the cold leg of a differential input to ground, what happens to the signal level? Which gain control device has the least distortion, a VCA, a printed plastic pot, a photoresistor or a wire-wound stepped attenuator?

Will putting an unbalanced line on a half-normalled jack unbalance the normal signal path? Will a transformer splitter load the input to a device parallel to it? Which will have less RF noise, a shielded unbalanced line or a balanced line with a floated shield?

- An aesthetic that is well-rooted and compatible with the music, and
- The good taste to know when to exercise it.

3. Trendy electronics and other flashy shit that nobody really needs. Five years ago, everything everywhere was being done with discrete samples. No actual drumming allowed on most records. Samples only. The next trend was Pultec Equalizers. Everything had to be run through Pultec EQs.

Then vintage microphones were all the rage (but only Neumanns, the most annoyingly *whiny* microphone line ever made). The current trendy thing is *compression*. Compression by the ton, especially if it comes from a *tube* limiter. Wow. It doesn't matter how awful the recording is, as long as it goes through a tube limiter, somebody will claim it sounds "warm," or maybe even "punchy." They might even compare it to the Beatles. I want to find the guy that invented compression and tear his liver out. I hate it. It makes everything sound like a beer commercial.

4. DAT machines. They sound like shit and every crappy studio has one now because they're so cheap. Because the crappy engineers that inhabit crappy studios are too thick to learn how to align and maintain analog mastering decks, they're all using DAT machines exclusively. DAT tapes deteriorate over time, and when they do, the information on them is lost forever. I have personally seen tapes go irretrievably bad in less than a month. Using them for final masters is almost fraudulently irresponsible.

Tape machines ought to be big and cumbersome and difficult to use, if only to keep the riff-raff out. DAT machines make it possible for morons to make a living, and do damage to the music we all have to listen to.

5. Trying to sound like the Beatles. Every record I hear these days has incredibly loud, compressed vocals, and a quiet little murmur of a rock band in the background. The excuse given by producers for inflicting such an imbalance on a rock band is that it makes the record sound more like the Beatles. Yeah, right. Fuck's sake, Thurston Moore is not Paul McCartney, and nobody on earth, not with unlimited time and resources, could make the Smashing Pumpkins sound like the Beatles. Trying just makes them seem even dumber. Why can't people try to sound like the Smashchords or Metal Urbain or Third World War for a change?

THERE'S THIS BAND

There's this band. They're pretty ordinary, but they're also pretty good, so they've attracted some attention. They're signed to a moderate-sized "independent" label owned by a distribution company, and they have another two albums owed to the label.

They're a little ambitious. They'd like to get signed by a major label so they can have some security—you know, get some good equipment, tour in a proper tour bus—nothing fancy, just a little reward for all the hard work.

To that end, they got a manager. He knows some of the label guys, and he can shop their next project to all the right people. He takes his cut, sure, but it's only 15%, and if he can get them signed then it's money well spent. Anyway, it doesn't cost them anything if it doesn't work. 15% of nothing isn't much!

One day an A&R scout calls them, says he's "been following them for a while now," and when their manager mentioned them to him, it just "clicked." Would they like to meet with him about the possibility of working out a deal with his label? Wow. Big Break time.

They meet the guy, and y'know what—he's not what they expected from a label guy. He's young and dresses pretty much like the band does. He knows all their favorite bands. He's like one of them. He tells them he wants to go to bat for them, to try to get them everything they want. He says anything is possible with the right attitude. They conclude the evening by taking home a copy of a deal memo they wrote out and signed on the spot.

The A&R guy was full of great ideas, even talked about using a name producer. Butch Vig is out of the question—he wants 100 g's and three points, but they can get Don Fleming for $30,000 plus three points. Even that's a little steep, so maybe they'll go with that guy who used to be in David Letterman's band. He only wants three points. Or they can have just anybody record it (like Wharton Tiers, maybe—cost you 5 or 10 grand) and have Andy Wallace remix it for 4 grand a track plus 2 points. It was a lot to think about.

Well, they like this guy and they trust him. Besides, they already signed the deal memo. He must have been serious about wanting them to sign. They break the news to their current label, and the label manager says he wants them to succeed, so they have his blessing. He will need to be compensated, of course, for the remaining albums left on their contract, but he'll work it out with the label himself. Sub Pop made millions from selling off Nirvana, and Twin Tone hasn't done bad either: 50 grand for the Babes and 60 grand for the Poster Children—without having to sell a single additional record.[2] It'll be something modest. The new label doesn't mind, so long as it's recoupable out of royalties.

Well, they get the final contract, and it's not quite what they expected. They figure it's better to be safe than sorry and they turn it over to a lawyer—one who says he's experienced in entertainment law—and he hammers out a few bugs. They're still not sure about it, but the lawyer says he's seen a lot of contracts, and theirs is pretty good. They'll be getting a great royalty: 13% (less a 10% packaging deduction). Wasn't it Buffalo Tom that were only getting 12% less 10? Whatever.

The old label only wants 50 grand, and no points. Hell, Sub Pop got 3 points when they let Nirvana go. They're signed for four years, with options on each year, for a total of over a million dollars! That's a lot of money in any man's English. The first year's advance alone is $250,000. Just think about it, a quarter-million, just for being in a rock band!

Their manager thinks it's a great deal, especially the large advance. Besides, he knows a publishing company that will take the band on if they get signed, and even give them an advance of twenty grand, so they'll be making that money too. The manager says publishing is pretty mysterious, and nobody really knows where all the money comes from, but the lawyer can look that contract over too. Hell, it's free money.

Their booking agent is excited about the band signing to a major. He says they can maybe average $1,000 or $2,000 a night from now on. That's enough to justify a five-week tour, and with tour support, they can use a proper crew, buy some good equipment and even get a tour bus! Buses are pretty expensive, but if you figure in the price of a hotel room for everybody in the band and crew, they're actually about the same cost. Some bands (like Therapy? and Sloan and Stereolab) use buses on their tours even when they're getting paid only a couple hundred bucks a night, and this tour should earn at least a grand or two every night. It'll be worth it. The band will be more comfortable and will play better.

The agent says a band on a major label can get a merchandising company to pay them an advance on t-shirt sales! Ridiculous! There's a gold mine here! The lawyer should look over the merchandising contract, just to be safe.

---

2 The "Babes" are Babes In Toyland, a Minneapolis band who had begun on Twin Tone records before signing with Warner Brothers.

They get drunk at the signing party. Polaroids are taken and everybody looks thrilled. The label picked them up in a limo.

They decided to go with the producer who used to be in Letterman's band. He had these technicians come in and tune the drums for them and tweak their amps and guitars. He had a guy bring in a slew of expensive old "vintage" microphones. Boy, were they "warm." He even had a guy come in and check the phase of all the equipment in the control room! Boy, was he professional. He used a bunch of equipment on them and by the end of it, they all agreed that it sounded very "punchy," yet "warm."

All that hard work paid off. With the help of a video, the album went like hotcakes! They sold a quarter million copies!

Here is the math that will explain just how fucked they are:

These figures are representative of amounts that appear in record contracts daily. There's no need to skew the figures to make the scenario look bad, since real-life examples more than abound. Income is underlined, expenses are not.

> Advance: <u>$250,000</u>
> Manager's cut: $37,500
> Legal fees: $10,000
>
> Recording budget: $150,000
>   Producer's advance: $50,000
>   Studio fee: $52,500
>   Drum, Amp, Mic and Phase "Doctors": $3,000
>   Recording tape: $8,000
>   Equipment rental: $5,000
>   Cartage and Transportation: $5,000
>   Lodgings while in studio: $10,000
>   Catering: $3,000
>   Mastering: $10,000
>   Tape copies, reference CDs, shipping tapes, misc. expenses: $2,000
>
> Video budget: $30,000
>   Cameras: $8,000
>   Crew: $5,000
>   Processing and transfers: $3,000
>   Offline: $2,000
>   Online editing: $3,000
>   Catering: $1,000
>   Stage and construction: $3,000
>   Copies, couriers, transportation: $2,000
>   Director's fee: $3,000
>
> Album artwork: $5,000
> Promotional photo shoot and duplication: $2,000
>
> Band fund: $15,000
>   New fancy professional drum kit: $5,000
>   New fancy professional guitars (2): $3,000

New fancy professional guitar amp rigs (2): $4,000
New fancy potato-shaped bass guitar: $1,000
New fancy rack of lights bass amp: $1,000
Rehearsal space rental: $500
Big blowout party for their friends: $500

Tour expense (5 weeks): $50,875
    Bus: $25,000
    Crew (3): $7,500
    Food and per diems: $7,875
    Fuel: $3,000
    Consumable supplies: $3,500
    Wardrobe: $1,000
    Promotion: $3,000

Tour gross income: <u>$50,000</u>
    Agent's cut: $7,500
    Manager's cut: $7,500

Merchandising advance: <u>$20,000</u>
    Manager's cut: $3,000
    Lawyer's fee: $1,000

Publishing advance: <u>$20,000</u>
    Manager's cut: $3,000
    Lawyer's fee: $1,000

Record sales: 250,000 × $12 = $3,000,000 gross retail revenue
Royalty (13% of 90% of retail): <u>$351,000</u>
    Less advance: $250,000
    Producer's points: (3% less $50,000 advance) $40,000
    Promotional budget: $25,000
    Recoupable buyout from previous label: $50,000
Net royalty: (<u>−$14,000</u>)

Record company income:
Record wholesale price $6.50 × 250,000 = $1,625,000 gross income
Artist royalties: $351,000
Deficit from royalties: $14,000
Manufacturing, packaging and distribution @ $2.20 per record: $550,000
Gross profit: $710,000

The Balance Sheet

This is how much each player got paid at the end of the game.

Record company: $710,000
Producer: $90,000

Manager: $51,000
Studio: $52,500
Previous label: $50,000
Agent: $7,500
Lawyer: $12,000
Band member net income each: $4,031.25

The band is now 1/4 of the way through its contract, has made the music industry more than 3 million dollars richer, but is in the hole $14,000 on royalties. The band members have each earned about 1/3 as much as they would working at a 7-Eleven, but they got to ride in a tour bus for a month.

The next album will be about the same, except that the record company will insist they spend more time and money on it. Since the previous one never "recouped," the band will have no leverage, and will oblige.

The next tour will be about the same, except the merchandising advance will have already been paid, and the band, strangely enough, won't have earned any royalties from their t-shirts yet. Maybe the t-shirt guys have figured out how to count money like record company guys.

Some of your friends are probably already this fucked.

Source: Steve Albini, "The Problem with Music," *The Baffler,* no. 5, 1993, pp. 31–38. Reprinted in Thomas Frank and Matt Weiland, eds., *Commodify Your Dissent: Salvos from The Baffler* (New York: Norton, 1997), pp. 164–76.

55

"Feminism Amplified"

KIM FRANCE

The role of "women in rock" has long been a topic of serious contention for feminist critics. Writing in 1970, Patricia Kennealy-Morrison lamented the limited "male-specified" stereotypes assigned to female musicians. Folk singers and singer-songwriters aside, she argued that women were expected either to be a distant and brittle "ice princess" along the lines of Grace Slick or assume the passionate, sexy "down-home ball" stance of a Janis Joplin.[1] In the years that followed, punk, new wave, and indie introduced spaces where women could expand and move beyond these roles. But it was specifically the rise of 1990s alternative rock that finally pushed images of aggressive, confrontational female musicians fully into the mainstream. In 1993 Liz Phair's *Exile in Guyville* became the first album in almost two decades by a female artist to top the *Village Voice*'s prestigious "Pazz & Jop" poll, a feat which was duplicated in 1994 by Hole (and their front woman Courtney Love), and in 1995 by PJ Harvey. By the mid-90s, the notion of a strong, independent female rock musician no longer seemed an anomaly. Rock critic Kim France's 1996 article surveys the situation at that time, examining from a feminist perspective the conflicting opinions surrounding the liberating rise of these female performers. Her discussion begins with Alanis Morissette's *Jagged Little Pill*, which along with Shania Twain's *Come On Over* and Whitney Houston's soundtrack to *The Bodyguard* would eventually rank as one of the three best-selling albums of the decade—all by women. Near the article's end, however, France wonders if women have made any real progress. Indeed to what extent *have* feminist attitudes gained a hold or transformed rock since the 1990s?

If the true test of social change is whether it's reflected in the marketplace, then this year's Grammy Awards were pretty compelling proof that feminism—at least a certain kind of feminism—is not dead at all. There was Mariah Carey—the type of standard-issue cream puff most commonly rewarded at this type of event—looking increasingly miffed as 21-year-old Alanis Morissette bounded onstage to receive five awards. Morissette's debut album, *Jagged Little Pill*, has spent almost a year on the *Billboard* charts. Her breakout single, "You Oughta Know," is a growly diatribe notable largely for stalkerlike lyrics that detail how she will make an ex-boyfriend pay for his betrayal. She is a woman who clearly has some issues with men, and she is beloved across the land.

Morissette's got little credibility with critics, who point out that she got her start as a fluffy, Debbie Gibson-style singer in her native Canada; that *Jagged Little Pill* was produced by cheesemeister Glen Ballard (whose résumé also includes such ultracommercial acts as Paula Abdul and Wilson Phillips); that she represents little more than a corporate expropriation of the kind of female-rage music that had been all but ignored by the music industry and the public for years. Whatever her

---

1 Patricia Kennealy-Morrison, "Rock Around the Cock," in Evelyn McDonnell and Ann Powers, eds., *Rock She Wrote: Women Write about Rock, Pop, and Rap* (New York: Delta, 1995), pp. 357–63.

musical pedigree, Morissette has inarguably marked the arrival to the mass-market of an entirely new female-rocker persona. A woman moving so far beyond delicate, weepy declarations of loss and longing to express explicit rage in the context of a sexual relationship does not, traditionally, a Top 40 single make. Susan Faludi has often pointed out that while our culture admires the angry young man, who is perceived as heroic and sexy, it can't find anything but scorn for the angry young woman, who is seen as emasculating and bitter. That is, unless she is the kind of angry woman who, à la Camille Paglia, reserves her contempt for other women. Says Andrea Juno, editor of the forth-coming anthology *Angry Women in Rock:* "In the back of women's heads, they were gonna be delibidinized: You're unsexy, you won't be loved, and you won't get screwed."

But with the unrepentantly unscrewed Morissette of "You Oughta Know," a whole new palette of female emotions hitherto confined to college and alternative audiences has become acceptable—even admirable—to the lowest-common-denominator record buyers whose tastes are reflected by the Grammys and the *Billboard* charts. The Morissette persona harks back to *Fatal Attraction*, says Nina Gordon of the female-fronted band Veruca Salt, but with a difference: "Nobody identified with the Glenn Close character—she was clearly the villain—whereas people are like, 'You go girl!' to Alanis."

This does not mean that women everywhere can dance a happy jig to the end of the anti-feminist backlash. "But I think it probably reflects some growth in the consciousness of the audience, which translates into sales," says Mercury Records president and CEO Danny Goldberg, whose own label has done brisk business this year with the bluesy folk-rocker Joan Osborne. "There's no question that record companies, like any other business, are driven by business." Shirley Manson, lead singer of the band Garbage, puts it a bit more bluntly. "Alanis," she says, "has wiped the floor with the music industry, and I think that's phenomenally exciting. Because I know now that there's hundreds of A&R men running around trying to find the next Alanis."

There have been certain moments in the past few decades when rebellion has been expressed most acutely through popular music, when artists have provided more complicated, pointed answers to what's going on in the culture than self-styled thinkers. You don't "read" pop music the way you read *The Beauty Myth*, of course, but Liz Phair—by design and by example—happens to be a much more interesting feminist thinker than, say, Rebecca Walker. So it makes a lot of sense that the generation that came of age in the shadow of feminism—that both reaped its rewards and paid for its shortcomings—is using rock as a vehicle to make some powerful and nuanced statements about gender.

I was born in 1964, which is long enough ago for me to have formed a vague firsthand impression of suburban, middle-class seventies feminism. I remember consciousness-raising groups, and the few daring wives in the neighborhood who insisted on being called *Ms.* I remember a book that my mother's friend had given her husband as a joke: The title was *What I Understand About Women*, and all the pages were blank. What *I* didn't understand about women—who as far as I could tell spent their days playing tennis and carpooling—was what they needed liberation from, except possibly boredom.

I was way too young to get it, of course, and by the time I got to my lefty college, I was reading the Robin Morgan anthology *Sisterhood Is Powerful* and going to Take Back the Night marches. But after graduation, I dropped any pretense of being part of a movement. I went to a Women's Action Committee meeting once but was bored and annoyed by the main order of business, which was agreeing on the design of the T-shirt that the group would wear to the big pro-choice march on Washington. Outside of the collegiate petri dish, Big-F Feminism was revealed to be a pallid little affair, like American communism in the forties, that had little direct relevance to life as it is actually lived.

I didn't realize it at the time, but a lot of what I—and other young lapsed feminists—thought and felt was reflected in the complexity and contradictions of pop music. And after a while I understood that it didn't matter that my generation had no Gloria Steinems, Germaine Greers, or even Nancy Fridays or Erica Jongs. Because we have the Breeders, PJ Harvey, Liz Phair, Morissette, Courtney Love, Veruca Salt, Joan Osborne, Elastica, Tori Amos, and Tracy Bonham.

If these women constitute a movement, it's a helter-skelter one. The Breeders are pool-playing, beer-drinking tough chicks, and they make music that rocks in a hard and murky way and top it off with pretty harmonies. Courtney Love is all about anger, excess, obsession, confession, and great melodies. Polly Jean Harvey is restrained, theatrical, a diva. All of them are dealing with issues that feminism has traditionally claimed but without trafficking in constricting, sexless Women's Studies 101 dogma (and anyone who's ever puzzled over why the talent booked at pro-choice rallies is so consistently lame can attest to the necessity for that). Eschewing the usual angry platitudes, they give full symphonic vent to the particular pleasures and terrors of being female. This is very good news indeed to those of us who love Liz Phair's frisky, do-me lyrics and *still* think date-rape apologist Katie Roiphe is full of it.[2]

"The future of rock belongs to women," Kurt Cobain predicted in 1994, and it is partly due to him that this is turning out to be true. He not only redefined the genre but also provided an updated guy-in-rock prototype. First of all, he wasn't a goon: He was inward, vulnerable—he sometimes wore dresses!—and he didn't seem to be in it for the money or the fame. And instead of dating models, Cobain married Courtney, showing himself to be the kind of man whose idea of masculinity involved loving a strong, opinionated woman, and carrying their baby in a Snugli.

"People like Kurt Cobain, Eddie Vedder, Michael Stipe, and Billy Corgan are very, very different as symbols of maleness for adolescents than Axl Rose or Steven Tyler and some of the other more muscle-bound, macho figures that immediately preceded them," says Danny Goldberg, who was a close friend of Cobain's. "And I think that created a sort of consciousness on the part of the audience. Kurt was very outspoken about the need for women to be respected, and he was passionate in his belief in Courtney. I think what happened in male rock and roll five years earlier broke up the macho hegemony over the rock part of the culture and gave the oxygen for some of the women to find an audience."

Nirvana also fired the final shot at that lumbering beast known as classic rock. No longer were radio listeners exclusively showered with music by way-past-their-prime peacocks like the Rolling Stones and Rod Stewart: Stations that shifted to modern-rock playlists were freed up to play bands like the Breeders or Hole—along with the now inevitable Soundgarden and Stone Temple Pilots—without worrying quite so much that listeners would switch stations once they heard female vocals. "Radio had always been a little afraid of that before," says Joan Osborne. "You know, they would play one Melissa Etheridge song in a four-hour slot and think that that was all they could do. Audiences I don't think ever really cared that much about those kind of distinctions. They just want something good. But it took a while for the programmers and people like that to catch up to that idea."

Furthermore, girls who loved music but had been too intimidated to pick up instruments—having somehow internalized the information that one had to possess some special boy gene in order to get behind a drum set—were inspired by Nirvana's punk-rock do-it-yourself ethos. "People who couldn't play anyway—boys—were doing it, and once that opened up, there was no reason not to be a girl and do it," says Phair, whose career started after a tape of songs she'd recorded in her

---

2 Ropie's controversial book *The Morning After: Sex, Fear and Feminism* (Boston: Little Brown and Co., 1993), which accused women of embracing a culture of victimization, had stirred tense debates among feminists.

bedroom scored her a record deal. The band Veruca Salt, which is fronted by Gordon and Louise Post, inspired a major-label bidding war in 1994 when the single "Seether"—from a cheaply produced album on a tiny Chicago label—started getting radio play and heavy MTV rotation. They eventually signed with Geffen, which re-released the album and sold 700,000 copies. "It is much less expensive to make a record than do anything else in the media, other than fanzines, but that doesn't have the potential to plug into the mainstream culture the way a record can," says Goldberg. "It's not a moral thing, it's not an aesthetic thing, it's just an economic reality that that doorway exists in music. The nature of the medium is less top-down, it's more decentralized, it's more a vehicle for personal visions, and one of these visions has been women."

> When we first started getting written about, people kept saying we were 'angry post-feminists,' and we were like, 'Hmm . . . I guess, whatever.' It was like, 'Oh, thank you for reducing me to a little pat phrase that really means nothing to me.'
>
> **—Nina Gordon of Veruca Salt**

A few years ago, I met some rock-critic friends for dinner before going to see a show at Irving Plaza. It was around the time PJ Harvey—who is sort of the Maria Callas of rock—released her first record, and we were talking about a profile in which she'd said she didn't consider herself a feminist. As it happened, I had interviewed Miss America just that afternoon for a piece I was writing about how the pageant was trying to update its image, and we agreed that it is a strange world we live in, where Miss America will say she's a feminist and PJ Harvey won't.

Actually, though, it's not so ironic. Increasingly, feminism itself has become a meaningless term: You're now a victim feminist, a do-me feminist, a womanist. Then there are people like Miss America and swimsuit models who fashion themselves as feminists as a defense mechanism because the alternative would be too hard to countenance. Who can blame PJ Harvey for not wanting to sign herself up for that team?

Rock succeeds where textbook feminism has stalled for a variety of reasons. A huge question that sixties feminism failed to answer had to do with sex: Could a healthy heterosexual libido be reconciled with good movement politics? Were we tools of the patriarchy just because we enjoyed renting the occasional porno movie with our boyfriends? Or if we read *Vogue* and profoundly believed in the magic of Maybelline? The Big Thinkers famously recused themselves from such mundanities.

In the meantime, rock started providing ad hoc, provisional answers. The medium permitted contradiction; you could change your mind without having to justify it. And the more you broke the rules, the more likely you'd be rewarded. New images of strength and sexuality emerged out of the pop-cultural ooze. There was leather-clad, eyelinered Chrissie Hynde of the Pretenders, who beginning in the eighties projected a tough, almost-but-not-quite-bulletproof cool. "The thing I found so fascinating about Chrissie Hynde when I was growing up was that I found her incredibly sexy but she also embodied what I found attractive about men," says Shirley Manson of Garbage. "She wasn't wearing pretty skirts and being a victim and talking about love. She was standing at that microphone with her legs spread, she was playing her guitar, and she was the coolest sight I'd ever seen in my life. It was the first time I really connected with a woman like that."

Exene Cervenka of the Los Angeles band X made it cool to be a punk chick; Cyndi Lauper made it okay to be a goofy party girl. And Madonna made it okay to be entirely about sex and still be in control. Though the brazen, brassiere-by-Gaultier look she presented ten years ago looks quaint by today's standards, and her appeal never had much to do with her musicianship or songwriting abilities, it is amazing how many young rock women today proudly cite her as a role model.

The change Madonna wrought has been most visible on MTV. For the network's first decade, the women shown in videos tended to be either big-hair pop goddesses like Taylor Dayne, or heavy-metal video extras, or Apollonia humping Prince's thigh, or the zombie-ish Robert Palmer girls. "There are these sort of low moments—and there are plenty of them, believe me—at MTV," says Judy McGrath, the network's president and one of the handful of genuinely powerful women in an industry that is still largely run by men. She recalls a 1988 staff meeting during which a video for the song "Wild Thing"—in which Sam Kinison mud-wrestled a bikini-clad Jessica Hahn—was screened. "The level of despair on the faces of the women was beyond description," she says. "We haven't gotten a video in the door in years that made you feel that way.

"There's a certain exhilaration now, even from the guys here, about all these women," McGrath continues. "There's a guy in the music-programming department who is like, you know, he's Mr. Rock. And he always says, 'This rocks!' And if you go into his office, he has a nine-foot picture of PJ Harvey plastered to his wall. I've seen a change in that regard. It isn't like the Steven Tyler Hall of Fame in here anymore."

McGrath believes that the fact that so many of these artists are giving voice to so many different perspectives on the female experience—and not doing it under the banner of revolution—is precisely why fans are so attracted to it. "I think this is a watershed moment," she says. "When I was growing up, I knew the difference between Betty Friedan and Gloria Steinem and so on, and you had to line up in one of those camps or you weren't, you know, in the game. And now I think there are so many voices."

If a woman is acting dolled up and sexy in a video these days, chances are it's her own. But even when she's not dolled up and sexy, it's likely that she will be singing about sex in a way women have never sung about sex before. In one song, Elastica's Justine Frischmann, sounding very male, bemoans the guy who can't get it up when she's in the mood. Shirley Manson of Garbage vamped around the stage last month at Roseland with a pink feather puff attached to the mike stand at precisely crotch level. Tori Amos is famous for straddling the piano bench suggestively while she plays.

Not everyone is hailing this as tremendous social progress. "There was some article in one of the British magazines about one of our shows saying that we set feminism back ten years, because Louise [Post] applied lipstick onstage," says Veruca Salt's Gordon. "And I remember thinking, 'Who is this woman?'—it was a woman who wrote the article—'Who is this woman who thinks it's important to point that out?'"

She was probably a woman very much like Exene Cervenka, who doesn't understand why PJ Harvey performs in evening gowns, or why Liz Phair poses for pictures wearing nothing but a slip dress. "I kind of call it 'Rod Stewart Feminism,'" she says. "It's kind of the same mentality, which is if it's okay for guys to do it, it's okay for girls to do it. Tori Amos straddling a piano bench—is that empowering women or is that *Penthouse*-ing women? I don't know."

It's debatable whether men see this sexuality as edifying rather than merely hot. Writing about Maureen Dowd in *The New Yorker* a few weeks ago, James Wolcott bemoaned "one of the odd aftereffects of feminism . . . that it seems to have softened and juvenilized so much of women's journalistic swagger." He went on to cite other areas where he perceived the phenomenon to be occurring: "In pop music, a kooky singer-songwriter chick seems to surface every six months to be photographed barefoot for *Spin*." Wolcott, presumably, would prefer they pose in sackcloth and ashes or, alternatively, in nothing at all. Would that clear up the confusion?

Of course, women have been all over *Spin* recently, generally shod. Only one of the *Spin* cover girls, Tori Amos, could be considered kooky—she named her most recent album after the goddess of creation and destruction and has said she was a Viking in another life. But she has also never shied away from hard topics, writing smart, cant-free songs that deal with rape and the church's oppression of women. "Tori's no one to be messed or trifled with," says Phair, whose music could not possibly be more different from hers. "She's a goddess."

Amos is a minister's daughter; she's got a song, "Icicle," about being upstairs in her bedroom masturbating while the rest of the family is in the living room praying. The struggle to be at home with her sexuality has been too hard-won for her to care what anyone thinks about it. "Somebody made this really funny comment about me that I just giggled over: 'You can't fight the patriarchy in a tube top,'" she says. "So I went, 'Okay, so why don't I wait for that writer to fax me on what I should wear to fight the patriarchy?' To me, when you cut yourself off—mentally, emotionally, or physically—then you've just been dominated by somebody else's thought."

Joan Osborne, 33, is one of the few female rockers who go out of their way to call themselves feminists. She aligns herself with mainstream feminist causes like NARAL, and performed on *Saturday Night Live* in a CHOICE T-shirt. She's the most middle-of-the-road, VH-1–friendly artist of the group, and the sexuality she projects onstage and in videos is subdued. "Feminism as I always understood it—and I was somebody who read a lot of Germaine Greer and stuff like that—part of the manifesto was to find a way for women to reclaim their own sexuality, to not only be the object of male desire but discover what their own desire was about, and claim that for themselves," she says. "And of course, an ingredient of rock has always been this sexual display, and women have been more and more finding out a way that they can do that. Instead of just being the chick in the spandex with the teased-up hair that all the guys want to screw, it's more like, 'Yeah, this is how I'm going to project my sexuality, and these are my desires.'"

It's amazing how threatening that can still be to men. Liz Phair's first album was a godsend to female fans because it communicated so explicitly the ambivalent knot of feelings that coexist with sexual desire. That this clean-scrubbed college graduate from Winnetka could think as dirty as any man floored a lot of people. "I heard a lot of men saying that they were listening to my album because someone told them they should, then one day they suddenly heard the words and it flipped them out," says Phair. "They all expressed this powerful feeling of being both fired at and caught, like, for being what they are. And the women were like, 'Well, I heard the words from the beginning, and they made perfect sense to me.'" She says she was shocked that men were shocked. "For me what it highlighted was how very rarely they had felt that before. Because there wasn't anything that damning. And it just made me realize that women hadn't nailed them before."

Part of Liz Phair's appeal is how heady her lyrics are. She and many of the other women in rock right now are quite self-evidently overqualified for the job intellectually—though alternative rock these days seems increasingly to be performed by and for slumming grad students—and their songs have a truth-telling complexity and confidence that was hardly available on vinyl twenty years ago. Joni Mitchell was wonderful, but she has comparatively little to say to the proverbial just-dumped 16-year-old that Liz Phair cannot say better. Today's teenage girls simply have it over their elders in the tell-it-sister department. "I didn't have high self-esteem when I was a teenager," Morissette told the *New York Times*. "I used to think I was alone in that. Oh, man, I wish I had me to listen to when I was 14."

One of the best things about going to see PJ Harvey or Hole or Elastica or Veruca Salt is witnessing the hordes of teenage girls who force their way into the mosh pit. The fact that they're not climbing on their boyfriend's shoulders and whipping off their halter tops—but rocking out to a woman wailing on her guitar—changes everything. "It's like having someone in a movie that you can follow," says Phair. "It's like having a character you can live through. And for so long, they didn't. You go to a rock show because you want the guy to stare at you. You want to be noticed and singled out as an object. And this time, they are watching someone and pretending they are *her*. And that's a very good experience, I think, for the self-esteem of the young American girl."

Those looking for role models, however, will be as disappointed as basketball fans who wish Dennis Rodman would stop showing his butt to the kids. But since when have pop musicians had to be role models? (At precisely the same moment as women and rap stars started selling records, it would appear.) The personal has always made for better rock music than the straight-forwardly political has, and that's a lesson these artists have taken to heart. "I don't want to be anyone's revolutionary," says Liz Phair. "I don't want to lead a movement. I mean, it turns me off so much. I never saw music as a way—and a lot of people do, especially riot grrrls—to make change happen. I never, ever saw it that way. I still don't. Anyone with any kind of sensitivity beyond their general age group knows you can't tidy life up like that."

No one is less tidy than Courtney Love. Experiencing Love, onstage or on CD, in the gossip pages or on the Internet (where, most recently, she has bitterly railed against Morissette), one can't help but notice that the line between her art and her life is hopelessly blurred. The raw, exposed manner in which she makes her music and conducts her affairs has made her the most loved/loathed figure in rock today. "I'm a huge admirer of Courtney Love," says Garbage's Manson. "She's vulnerable and I warm to that. She's incredibly intelligent and incredibly articulate and she's not afraid to open her mouth up and attack anybody and anything. She's neither black nor white and that's why, I think, she irritates a lot of people, but that's what I find endearing about her."

Cervenka, predictably, is not as impressed. "People who are pathologically insane don't interest me," she says. "Courtney has nothing to do with reality as far as I'm concerned. You've got to talk about people who are sober, who can raise their children, and who are not involved in all kinds of scandalous tabloid-style gimmicks in order to become famous."

Still, as wild as she's been, Courtney certainly hasn't done anything that would have raised eyebrows backstage at a Led Zeppelin show, and *those* guys just got inducted into the Rock and Roll Hall of Fame. Plus, she's a whole lot more interesting than Robert Plant. Love is a walking Rorschach test. Either a liberating angel or the Yoko Ono of alternative rock, she has quite improbably become an embodiment of all that is interesting, exciting, and depressing about being a young woman now. (Teenage boys in online chat groups, grossed out by her schizo aggressiveness and anti-pinup mien, often suggest that she has no right to be alive.)

Love is obviously well aware of her role. She has said that she was moved to name her band Hole by a line from Euripides' *Medea:* "There's a hole that pierces right through me." She once told a writer from *Spin* the band's name also refers to something her mother, a hippie feminist of the *Our Bodies, Ourselves* era, used to say: "You can't walk around with a big hole inside yourself."

Things are never that simple in Love-land. The song "Asking For It" was inspired, she told an interviewer, by the experience of stage-diving into the crowd at a show: "Suddenly, it was like my dress was being torn off me, my underwear was being torn off me, people were putting their fingers inside of me and grabbing my breasts really hard." The worst thing, she went on, was seeing a photograph of herself later "and I had a big smile on my face like I was pretending it wasn't happening. I can't compare it to rape because it isn't the same. But in a way it was. I was raped by an audience—figuratively, literally, and yet, was I asking for it?" The song is a more nuanced treatment than any ten essays about date rape of the way women can feel torn between the desire to be driven by their sexuality and the horror that the desire might ultimately degrade or even destroy them.

Love has also taken prototypically male gestures, transformed them into female ones, and made them powerful again and new. When a male artist, for instance, props his leg up on a monitor and launches into a guitar solo these days, he looks stupid—like he's playing in a Foghat cover band at some Bleecker Street tourist club. But when Love, wearing torn stockings, props a stiletto-heeled leg up on a monitor, the entire gesture changes—it is undeniably theatrical and brazen, but it's certainly interesting.

I share this theory of mine with Phair, who wonders whether I'm not getting a little carried away. "There is something that is rock itself, and it is an attitude that is genderless, and it is what is appealing about rock," she says. When Courtney does that thing with the monitor, she continues, "that's her just being infected with this thing called Rock. But probably I'm wrong, and she actually watched a million guys do that, sticking your foot up there, and she is saying, 'Fuck you, I'm the front guy; deal with my frontalness.'"

Phair pauses, then sighs. "I'm wondering, would Courtney Love really think about doing that gesture, or is it just like a way to really, you know, crunch into her guitar? . . . I'll bet she's just like, 'Why shouldn't I be right up at the edge of the stage?' She's just free in her mind. It's not so much that she has something. It's that she doesn't have something, which is the fear that traditionally keeps women in their place."

It's tempting, sometimes, to think that women are being allowed this moment only because we have seen every conceivable rock pose many times over from men, and the one thing that really feels fresh right now is a chick jabbing her stiletto heel into a monitor. And for all of their bravado, none of the artists I spoke to felt like a fundamental transformation had occurred; they thought the odds were about even that next year the charts will be ruled by guys again. "The industry still views bands fronted by women as novelties," says Nina Gordon. "It seems like to me that right now women are entitled to just one shining moment."

But Cervenka, the progressive-rock darling of 1982, was by far the most cold-eyed. "There's always some woman who is the new angry young woman," she said. "It was me, and it was someone else, and it was someone else. But as far as selling millions and millions of records, to me that's no validation whatsoever. It means nothing. If it means anything to me, it means it's *not* okay to be an angry young woman—it's cute to be an angry young woman; it's trendy to be an angry young woman." But is Love-ism really just the flavor of the month?

"I want to be the girl with the most cake," she sings on "Doll Parts." Women love that line; it's all about authorizing desire, and about winning, which remain as tricky as ever for a woman. And when I start thinking that *Ms.* magazine–era feminism has nothing to do with my life, I think about another person who wanted to be the girl with the most cake—Sylvia Plath's Esther, in *The Bell Jar.* There's that passage where she sees all of her options—wife and mother, famous writer, magazine editor—as figs on a tree. But she can choose only one, and she can't make up her mind, and the figs all wither and die.

Women, of course, have it better than they did when Plath wrote that book in 1963, but how much has really changed? You could argue that our culture still isn't rewarding women who try to stake out new territory. But Courtney Love is an object lesson in the punishments and rewards that come to a woman who tries. "Courtney's got the kind of ambition most people would associate with a male rock star," says Justine Frischmann. "One thing you have to admire her for is that she refuses—just refuses—to be overlooked in any way."

Source: Kim France, "Feminism Amplified," *New York,* June 3, 1996, pp. 34–41.

56

"Rock Aesthetics and Musics of the World"

MOTTI REGEV

From its very beginnings rock 'n' roll has been perceived as a distinctly American (and soon thereafter, Anglo-American) cultural product. At the same time, rock has circulated for decades around the world, where its presence has been felt as an influence on local music-making practices. While one could certainly see this spread of rock as yet another example of American cultural imperialism, Motti Regev argues against such a reading.[1] Regev, a sociologist at the Open University of Israel, instead emphasizes the way in which an international "rock aesthetic" has emerged, granting its participants a certain symbolic freedom. Drawing on the sociological studies of Pierre Bourdieu and Scott Lash, Regev suggests that those who take part in rock music making are figuratively "thrown" into two fields. From a spatial standpoint, they are members of a "local field," wherein they grasp some relationship to a larger national identity. At the same time, they are operating within the general "field of popular music," wherein rock has been accorded a privileged status of authenticity and innovation. "Thrown" into these fields, local musicians find a certain agency through rock's authenticity, one that allows them to explore the boundaries of national identity. In the following excerpt from Regev's article, he outlines three different ways in which the "rock aesthetic" is articulated in the local field: Anglo-American pop/rock as such, "imitation," and hybridity.

The uses and appropriations of rock by musicians and audiences around the world are far from homogeneous. The various styles could be easily described as completely different in pure musical terms. The point in discussing them together is, first, the relative sameness of meaning which is attributed to them, in the practices of listening or discursively and, second, the fact that they can all be shown to be influenced by and incorporate elements of the rock aesthetic.

The sameness of meaning is basically one: rock music is used to declare a 'new'—modern, contemporary, young, often critical-oppositional—sense of local identity, as opposed to older, traditional, conservative forms of that identity. The music patterns, however, differ in the extent to which rock music is used as-it-is, or subjected to appropriations, articulations and selective practices that produce hybridity. Each one of these patterns represents a slightly different strategy for legitimizing rock within the local culture. Accordingly, I have divided these patterns into three main categories: Anglo-American pop/rock as such; 'imitation' of foreign styles; and hybrids. Each is discussed below, with some examples. They are presented here as analytic 'ideal types'—in practice, they might be hard to distinguish.

---

1 On this debate, see Dave Laing, "The Music Industry and 'Cultural Imperialism' Thesis," *Media, Culture and Society* 8 (1986): 331–41.

ANGLO-AMERICAN POP/ROCK AS SUCH

Using Anglo-American rock itself as a cultural resource for constructing local identity is typically based on a logic which demands 'freedom of taste'. The interest in rock, and the desire to have (imported) records available or to have local concerts by Anglo-American rock stars—when denied—are formulated in terms of 'opening' the local culture to a modern, even liberating cultural form. This happens not only in the most obvious places and times like East Europe in the 1960s, but later on in industrial societies as well. Thus in Bulgaria, during the 1960s, British rock 'was seen not only as good music but also as a sort of symbol of freedom, of a liberated individuality and independent stand' (Levy, 1992: 211). Even in Italy, as late as 1982, concerts by the Rolling Stones had:

> provoked a bitter row between the leading political parties . . . accusing rock of being the transmitter of disorder, corruption, violence and drugs . . . [but the audience in these concerts responded with] . . . wonderful scenes in which joints and tricolors were juxtaposed for the first time ever, without incident and with a perfect sense of harmony. 'Viva l'Italia, viva rock'n'roll!'—a combination of slogans which was much more than the masses . . . could ever have expected (Fiori, 1984: 261–2).

These are two examples to which others could easily be added. The point is that within conservative contexts or totalitarian regimes, attempts to prevent or just control the dissemination of Anglo-American rock, invoke the use of this music as a means to construct a local sense of autonomous identity.

Obviously, Anglo-American rock does not become, in the process, 'local authentic' music. It remains 'foreign' music. But it does become part and parcel of a generation's collective memory, of its different local/national sense of identity as opposed to that of an older generation (see Lou Reed's interview with Václav Havel, about the role of 1960s rock in general and that of the Velvet Underground in particular in Czech politics; Reed, 1991: 145–62). And in that regard, Anglo-American pop/rock does become an integral part of local/national cultures around the world, at least for some sectors within them.

'IMITATION'

The inverted commas indicate that although local, non-Anglo-American styles of punk, metal, rap, progressive or other sub-styles of rock can be understood as sheer imitations of the originals, they can also be interpreted as hybrids, be it only for their use of a language other than English. The main difference between this pattern of using rock music and listening to Anglo-American rock as such is the relative ease with which claims for legitimacy (within the local/national context) or interpretations of the music as 'locally authentic' can be made.

The turning point for the emergence of such claims is when local rock musicians move from 'covering', in English, hits by famous Anglo-American musicians, and from performing straight translations or other local-language versions of such songs, to producing original rock music. Indeed, beginning in the early 1960s, probably thousands of rock groups from Spain to Japan, from Scandinavia to South Africa and Latin America, have been performing rock hits. Starting with songs made famous by Elvis Presley, the Kinks or Otis Redding, later on some groups were performing music by Led Zeppelin or Pink Floyd. Gaining sufficient competence in the rock habitus, groups from non-English-speaking countries occasionally found success with an international hit in English (e.g., Spain's Los Bravos with 'Black is Black' in 1966, or Holland's Shocking Blue with 'Venus' in 1970).

But as much as these groups represent vivid local rock scenes, they do not supply the basis for legitimacy claims. Such claims emerge as rock groups start to produce original music, in a local language, even as they stick to Anglo-American rock sub-styles. One way of doing that is by appropriating styles associated mostly with African-Americans, for strengthening local ethnic or regional identity. Thus one strain of Italian hip hop has been used to distinguish Southern Italian identity, invoking in the process a supposed mythical affinity with Africa (whose northern shores are not too far away) and finding roots of rap in traditional folk music (Mitchell, 1995).

More typical is the attribution of 'artistic authenticity' to local versions of rock, and the emergence of a bohemian-oppositional 'counter-culture' which considers itself to be an avant-garde of the national or local conservative culture. This has been the case particularly under totalitarian regimes, where the local rock scene declared itself to be a site for the preservation of national artistic freedom. Producing original music, including lyrics in the local language, supports such claims and helps in making them into a cultural reality—despite the music itself being an 'imitation' of Anglo-American rock sub-styles.

Such is the case of Russian rock, which emerged during the Soviet regime in the 1970s and 1980s. Listening to historical recordings or even more recent records by leading Russian rock groups—Mashina Vremeni, Aqvarium, Alica, Kino, Aukzion and others—one gets to hear variations of hard rock or heavy metal. Indeed, as Kushman (1995: 53) points out, well into the 1980s 'Russian musicians continued to draw on those forms of rock music which were made available to them and to imitate and reproduce what they heard'. *Russification* of the music took place mostly through lyrics and singing, interpreting them as sung poetry. Regarding themselves as inheritors and carriers of a Russian tradition of poetry, Russian rock musicians perceive their art as a form of contemporary poetry. As Yuri, a prominent Russian rock musician who, according to Kushman (1995: 70) has been alternately referred to as 'a Russian Bruce Springsteen' and 'a second [Vladimir] Vysotsky' puts it:

> The main thing is that before . . . the poets like Bella Akhmadulina, Okudzhava, Voznesenskii read poems and drew huge audiences. Now poetry has sunk into rock-and-roll. Real poetry lives in rock-and-roll. In Russia that's for sure. Especially in the '80s, because the official youth poetry was not poetry at all. But the best, the finest poetry was in rock-and-roll music. That is, the best, the purest, most sincere of everything went into rock-and-roll in the '80s (quoted in Kushman, 1995: 105).

Another example is Argentinean rock. Its leading musicians—Charly García, Luis Alberto Spinetta, David Lebon (and their groups Sui Géneris, Almendra, Seru Girán), León Gieco, Fito Páez and others—since the mid-1970s have been sounding, more often than not, like Spanish versions of hard rock, progressive rock and singer/songwriters. During the 1976 to 1983 military dictatorship, the core of Argentinean rock music—as the *rock nacional* movement—became a focus of opposition to the regime. It:

> played an extremely important part in the socialization and re-socialization of broad sectors of Argentinean youth during the military period, restoring truthful communication regarding the real country. . . . The highly oppositional content of the songs, the frankly critical attitude of the audiences, and the gathering together in public places to express opposition to the military regime . . . [created] popular and communal channels of participation. . . . (Vila, 1987: 147–8).

Thus, although not sounding 'genuinely Argentinean' (except for the lyrics), *rock nacional* gained, in the eyes of its members, something which has been inscribed in its name: national legitimacy, Argentinean-ness. That this trait has been of primary importance to rock fans, can be learnt from this prominent Argentinean rock commentator, who insists that:

> The pioneers of [our] native rock did not step down here from a flying saucer, they emerged from the grain of the people, like the folklorists and the tango-ists before them. Our rock is already part of the Argentinean musical tradition, despite those who view it solely as 'foreign penetration'. The [acoustic] guitar and the bandoneon were also imported to these pampas and it occurs to nobody to consider them aliens (Grinberg, 1993: 18; my translation).

Indeed, later on, as Argentinean rock became the herald of a much larger phenomenon of *rock en español* in Latin America and Spain, defense of rock in general and in other national contexts grew broader (De Garay Sanchez, 1993).

Although in a better position to claim national legitimacy than Anglo-American rock as such, rock musicians and audiences practicing the 'imitation' pattern in various countries, are often forced to justify the 'local authentic' quality of their music. One way of doing this is by elaborating a specific genre of rock as a 'national' one—like the emphasis on local progressive rock in some European countries during the 1970s. The point I want to stress here is the spontaneous commitment to such justifications. As much as musicians and fans believe in the general artistic qualities of rock, they are also strongly committed to localizing rock, to produce its meaning as national music.

HYBRIDITY

Very different, in this regard, is the position of music scenes in which rock elements are selectively adapted and mixed with traditional-local styles to produce hybrids. Practitioners of such hybrid musics sometimes do not even have to claim their 'local authenticity'. It is inscribed in the essence of the sonic texture and affective impact of their music to begin with. These are typically the 'rock' sub-styles that garner the most enthusiastic response within the Western, Anglo-American rock establishment—probably because of their readily perceived 'exoticism', 'otherness' and 'authenticity'—and which are collectively labeled 'world music' (together with non-rock styles, see Mitchell, 1993).

Many of the contemporary 'world music' rock styles that found sympathetic audiences in Western countries are African—and they barely need introduction. Senegalese *mbalax*, South African *mbaqanga*, Nigerian *juju*, Ghanaian *highlife*, Zairean *soukous*, Zimbabwean *chimurenga* and *jit* are the most prominent. While some of these hybrids embody early influences of Western music, dating back to the 19th century (Collins and Richards, 1989), most of them took a turn into rock aesthetic during the 1970s—or indeed came into their own being in the wake of rock's presence in their countries. Musicians in these genres incorporate not only typical rock instrumentation (electric guitars, bass and organs, synthesizers, drumkits), but most often also rock sound texture like fuzz, distortion, shouting, etc. Mixing these with traditional instruments, vocal styles and 'ethnic' rhythms, they create musics that sound as much 'rock' as planted in the local culture.

Thus *soukous* (probably the most widespread style in Africa), after being consolidated by Franco and Tabu Ley as a relatively 'sweet' and polished electric mixture of rumba and Zairean elements, became much rockier during the 1970s with the group Zaiko Langa Langa:

> They were wild. It was like the Sex Pistols coming on to the scene. They twisted everything around . . . Zaiko were uncompromising. They challenged the old established musical norms of Zaire, and the youth followed (Mwana Musa, Sierra-Leonean musician, quoted in Stapelton and May, 1990: 173).

The group 'blew a rude, rough-house blast of folk rhythms, hard snare drums, wild guitars and rough vocals' (Stapelton and May, 1990: 174). In a similar manner, the Zimbabwean group the Bhundu Boys followed Thomas Mapfumo's already rocky hybrid of traditional music (which he called *chimurenga*) with a rockier style called *jit*.

Another example of hybridity can be found in (former) Yugoslavia, and in particular in the music of the group Bijelo Dugme, led by Goran Bregovic. Blending Balkan touches of melody, female harmonies and poetic imagery with dramatic metallic-distorted electric guitars, and soaring vocals commenting on Yugoslav social reality, during the 1970s and 1980s Bijelo Dugme produced rock anthems that made them the most popular and acclaimed group of the country. Bregovic (born in Bosnia to a Serb mother and a Croat father), insisting on his general Yugoslav identity and taking Anglo-American rock as his artistic reference point, demonstrates clearly the dual character of 'ethnic rock':

> Our big advantage is that we are really Yugoslav. There is a Yugoslav character to our music. But by the same virtue, our music is a little bit too rude and too primitive for the outside world. So you can say we are a rock 'n' roll band, but we are popular in the way that a country and western band would be in the United States. . . . For me, the future of rock music, not just in Yugoslavia but in the world, is ethnic music. Some really fine rock records in the last few years are really close to ethnic music, like Paul Simon, like Peter Gabriel, like U2. They all draw upon ethnic elements. I am doing this too, and I have been doing this from the beginning. After all, there is no point just copying American rock 'n' roll (Goran Bregovic, in 1989, quoted in Ramet, 1994: 133–9).

One last example of hybridity is Algerian *(pop-)rai*. It emerged in the 1970s, when synthesizers, drum-machines and electric guitars, as well as rock rhythmic and melodic elements had been added to the traditional instruments and rhythms of *rai*. The leading musicians—Chaba Zahouania, Chaba Fadela, Cheb Sahraoui, Cheb Mami and Cheb Khaled (chabas and chebs are general appellations for youth)—became, with their sound and often erotic-hedonistic lyrics, national exponents for young people who 'challenged official puritanism and patriarchal authority . . . [and] who were chafing at traditional social constraint' (Gross et al., 1994: 7).

Nevertheless, *rai* signifies the ethnic-national identity as well, as is evident from its use (together with Arab *rap*) by Franco-Maghrebis (Algerians, Moroccans, Tunisians) 'to carve a space for themselves in France . . . [and] identify simultaneously with French and Arab cultures' (Gross et al., 1994: 25).

This last function exemplifies the use of rock hybrids among contemporary diaspora communities. There, the rock aesthetic becomes a tool for constructing an identity and claiming legitimacy in the 'host' culture as well. Thus, the emergence of *bhangra-rock* within the British-Asian community expresses claims for contemporary British as well as South-Asian identity (Banerji, 1988).

The list of local rock hybrids, as well as of 'imitations', which are used as tools to construct contemporary local identities, is far from exhausted—more could be added. And in a sense this is only part of the story of 'rock in the world'. The rest of it has to do with the fact that musicians and others within the Western, Anglo-American rock establishment, upon 'discovering' rock hybrids from various countries, import them and make them yet another 'scene' within rock culture. Perceived as another frontier of 'authenticity' (Garofalo, 1992) or artistic innovation, some of these styles are incorporated into the work of major musicians, and then distributed to additional parts of the world and influence them. Reggae, which emerged as a Jamaican hybrid of rock, and then influenced musicians all over the world, is the prime example. Another practice which should be noted in this regard is the mixing of sampled 'ethnic' musics with electronic, mostly dance-rhythms, which is done by Western musicians and then distributed to the whole world.

BIBLIOGRAPHY

Banerji, Sabita (1988) 'Ghazals to Bhangra in Great Britain', *Popular Music* 7: 207–14.
Collins, John and Paul Richards (1989) 'Popular Music in West Africa', pp. 12–46 in Simon Frith (ed.) *World Music, Politics and Social Change.* Manchester: Manchester University Press.
De Garay Sanchez, Adrián (1993) *El Rock También es Cultura.* Mexico: Universidad Iberoamericana.
Fiori, Umberto (1984) 'Rock Music and Politics in Italy', *Popular Music* 4: 261–78.
Garofalo, Reebee (ed.) (1992) *Rockin' the Boat.* Boston, MA: South End Press.
Grinberg, Miguel (1993) *Como Vino la Mano.* Buenos Aires: Distal.
Gross, Joan, David McMurray and Ted Swedenburg (1994) 'Arab Noise and Ramadan Nights; Rai, Rap, and Franco-Maghrebi Identity', *Diaspora* 3: 3–39.
Kushman, Thomas (1995) *Notes from the Underground: Rock Music Counterculture in Russia.* Albany: State University of New York Press.
Levy, Claire (1992) 'The Influence of British Rock in Bulgaria', *Popular Music* 11: 209–12.
Mitchell, Tony (1993) 'World Music and the Popular Music Industry', *Ethnomusicology* 37: 309–38.
———. (1995) 'Question of Style: Notes on Italian Hip Hop', *Popular Music* 14: 333–48.
Ramet, Sabrina Petra (ed.) (1994) *Rocking the State: Rock and Politics in Eastern Europe and Russia.* Boulder, CO: Westview Press.
Reed, Lou (1991) *Between Thought and Expression.* New York: Hyperion.
Stapelton, Chris and Chris May (1990) *African Rock: The Pop Music of the Continent.* New York: Obelisk/Dutton.
Vila, Pablo (1987) 'Rock Nacional and Dictatorship in Argentina', *Popular Music* 6: 129–48.

Source: Motti Regev, "Rock Aesthetics and Musics of the World," *Theory, Culture and Society*, 14, no. 3 (1997), pp. 131–36.

57

"Electronic Eden"
Techno Goes Mainstream

KAREN SCHOEMER

When British electronic dance music (EDM) groups like the Chemical Brothers and Underworld began attracting attention in America throughout 1996 and 1997, the press was quick to herald the arrival of a new "techno" or "electronica" movement, one that in the wake of alternative rock's decline might prove to be 'the next big thing'. For all the anticipation, however, many questioned whether EDM, with its lengthy, primarily instrumental song forms and relatively anonymous DJs, could succeed with American rock audiences. Thus, it is unsurprising that *Newsweek*'s "Electronic Eden" feature begins by focusing not on the music or its makers, but on the more immediately arresting (and easily sensationalized) images of techno's young fans and their vibrant, drug-fueled nightlife scene. If the author presents this portrait as the music's authentic face, then the rest of the article takes a decidedly jaded tone, convinced that techo's concessions to the mainstream will smooth out its gritty underground presence, and throw the focus instead on the more marketable rock-like sounds of groups like the Prodigy. As the article correctly forecasts, the Prodigy did indeed manage to cross over to a large audience, their 1997 album *The Fat of the Land* debuting at the top of the Billboard charts. But by the turn of the millennium, as the Prodigy and other artists failed to sustain their initial sales promise, the industry's enthusiasm for the movement began to wane. EDM, however, would eventually enjoy a resurgence in the early 2010s, this time fueled by the popularization of styles like dubstep. To what extent, if any, has rock influenced or figured into this latest wave of EDM?

Natania, 18, looks like a young, technofied Annette Funicello. She has lovely, pale skin and wide-set eyes that scrunch a bit, even when she's not smiling. Her dark hair is pulled back retro style into a wide headband, and she wears sleek black pants and a gray zip-up sweater. There's something innocent about her, but she's a long way from "Beach Blanket Bingo." Every Monday night, Natania goes to Koncrete Jungle, a dance party on New York's Lower East Side that plays a hip, relatively new offshoot of dance music known as drum & bass—or, in a more general way, techno, a blanket term that describes music made on computers and electronic gadgets instead of conventional instruments, and performed by deejays instead of old-fashioned bands. Inside, bright lights flash in blinding whites and blues. A deejay plays records made up of breathlessly fast, staccato beats and hazy keyboard swirls. A couple of kids break-dance in the center of the floor, but most sit nervously around the fringes. It's barely midnight; the drugs haven't kicked in yet.

Natania heads downstairs to the club's basement. Here, a different deejay plays harder, funkier beats with a lightly psychedelic overlay of sampled effects and vocal phrases. She huddles and laughs with her friends Cecil, a lanky 22-year-old with stumpy dreadlocks, and Mark, a slight, 17-year-old drug dealer. They slip into an empty coatroom where a dozen or so other kids stand on chairs, dangle off empty racks and groove to the music. Cecil lights a joint. Mark disappears into a corner, dispensing $20 hits of liquid PCP. The beats grow louder and more insistent, and the guys on the chairs chant "Brooklyn! Brooklyn!," pounding up and down with the rhythm. One guy starts punching and karate-kicking the wall, and his foot comes within inches of Natania's head. She ducks toward the door. "Too much PCP," she whispers. "He doesn't feel anything."

The scene at Koncrete Jungle may seem alien to outsiders. But if the music business has its way, techno culture will be coming to your neighborhood soon. And by the time it arrives, rest assured that most of the danger will have been wiped from it. Shrewd music-business minds will strip it of its seedy drug roots, add catchy pop choruses and package it neatly for mass consumption. Droney, eight-minute dance-floor opuses will be edited into radio-friendly nibblets. Deejays who once preferred to stay anonymous will emerge with MTV-ready haircuts. And a complex, rebellious, often nihilistic scene will be jimmied and goosed into shelves in Sam Goodys everywhere. "It's an underground scene—it's not meant to be exposed," Natania says, yelling over the booming beats. "Society doesn't necessarily agree with our lifestyles. Only a certain crowd can handle it."

Techno isn't really new: it's been brewing in America for four or five years in underground dives, warehouse parties, big-city discos and all-night outdoor raves. It's been evolving even longer in Europe, where British acts like the Prodigy and the Chemical Brothers have scored No. 1 hits. And though the most popular acts are British, the music actually got its start in the early '80s in Detroit and Chicago, where pioneer deejays like Juan Atkins and Blake Baxter reinvented disco and soul with a high-tech, minimalist vocabulary.

Nowadays techno includes a dizzying array of subgenres: the dainty stoner grooves of drum & bass, the gnarled-out psychedelia of acid house, the blissed-out luxury of ambient. And though drugs can be a part of the scene, they're not always part of the scene. "You don't need to take drugs to get the music," says Jim Fouratt, a vice president at Mercury Records. "It's dance music, which is very communal. I like that sense of seduction—that collective ecstasy, which now has a manufactured name."

Promoter Gerry Gerrard will help techno go legit this summer with a package tour booked into 5,000- to 10,000-seat arenas. "Avant-garde kids of any scene always have their own drugs," he says. "I'm 46, and I started with the Stones and the Beatles in the West End of London, and drugs were everywhere. Once these things surface, [the drug scene] gets shut down."

Until fairly recently, the mainstream U.S. record industry left the techno world to its own devices. But now, after a year of flat sales and poor showings by big rock acts like Pearl Jam and Hootie & the Blowfish, executives are desperate for a new big thing. Genres like alternative, gangsta rap and country, which drove the industry for much of the '90s, have lost commercial momentum amid a glut of identical-sounding bands. "There's a real staleness with rock music in general," says Steve Levy of Moonshine, an independent techno label. "It's been beaten to death by the major labels. The alternative rock that came out in '90, '91 was turned into formula, and eventually kids saw through it."

Techno, in all its varied forms, is being touted as a cure. Artists and executives who scuttled to the alternative-rock bandwagon five years ago are now stampeding to techno. That's not necessarily a bad thing: MTV's trippy new show "Amp," which features electronic artists like Aphex Twin, Coldcut and Alex Reece, is the most mesmerizing thing on the channel. Alternative radio stations are shaking up their playlists with rock-edged techno groups like the Prodigy and the Chemical Brothers. And David Bowie, who's blurred the line between rock and dance music for years, does it exceptionally well on his new album "Earthling," a barrage of drum & bass rhythms, droning guitars and trademark oddities. "I was listening to early drum & bass in '93," Bowie says.

"There was incredible work going down: M-Beat, General Levy, the JB. It was deep London, strictly black and incredibly radical and aggressive. That's what I've tried to bring to my album."

Bowie is doing what most industry executives agree has to be done for techno to succeed on a mainstream level: he's combining it with pop, giving it a human face and a recognizable structure. For fans of conventional pop, most electronic music is a stretch. It's amorphous and fluid, with simple rhythmic phrases often repeated to trancelike effect for minutes on end. It's decorated with bleeps, swooshes and other noises out of a computer's innards that often bear little resemblance to "proper" sounds like guitar chords and snare drums. And it frequently lacks the vocals, melodies and linear narratives that form the backbone of pop. Techno fans find this sonic abandon liberating. "We have the ability to take every sound and make it absolutely perfect: sculpt it and design it until the artist is totally happy," says Todd Mueller, producer of MTV's "Amp."

The industry would like to sculpt something a little more mundane. One of its hopefuls is the Chemical Brothers, two low-key British deejays who sample and loop very live-sounding distorted guitars and drumbeats. Tom Rowlands and Ed Simons enlisted Noel Gallagher of Oasis for a guest vocal on "Setting Sun," a Beatlesque techno-romp with an in-your-face, rocklike slam. "We made a name for ourselves deejaying in London," says Simons. "It was a mad scene, really crazy. People were tight as sardines, but jumping up and down the whole time. The ceiling was low and they'd come back with grazed knuckles."

The group Underworld offers a techno-pop hybrid of driving syncopated rhythms, live guitar and occasional vocals. Their demure, luscious "Born Slippy" was a standout on the "Trainspotting" soundtrack, and they're currently in the midst of a major-label bidding war. Guitarist Karl Hyde was drawn to the scene because "there wasn't this bunch of egos onstage that you were coming along to praise," he says. "The deejay responds to the audience. There's no hero." But that lack of identification can be an obstacle. Orbital writes wispy melodic riffs with throbbing electronic pulses, and the shy, unassuming brothers Paul and Phil Hartnoll admit their clinical technician image isn't much of a grabber. "None of us is David Bowie," says Paul. "It makes it hard for the marketing departments. I wouldn't want to do their job."

If techno artists really are to sweep the U.S. mainstream, a nifty haircut will have to lead them. And that haircut belongs to Keith Flint of the Prodigy. Already a pop phenomenon in England, the Prodigy have all the prerequisites for palatability: grinding guitars, a jabbing beat, a snarling lead singer and a live show that offers lots of rocklike moving around. Flint's bright-colored devil tufts and menacing attitude provide an excuse for what the industry so desperately needs: hype. "Really, the energy is parallel to that of Nirvana," raves Marco Collins of KNDD-FM in Seattle. Madonna's label, Maverick, recently beat out 20 other companies to license the band from its indie label, Mute; a new album is due in May. "I think the album will debut in the Billboard top 10," says Mute's Mark Fotiadis. "And I wouldn't be surprised if it sold between 1 and 3 million."

The sad thing is, of all the techno acts coming to your neighborhood, the Prodigy is probably the least interesting. They lack the tortured boy-genius aspect of Aphex Twin's Richard D. James, who creates quirky sonic pictures as fresh as dreams peeled out of his head. They lack the jaunty humor of the Chemical Brothers and the limpid expressionism of Orbital. When the Prodigy hits America, audiences will see the strangely disemboweled remnants of an astonishingly diverse and eccentric movement, with the nuances removed and the danger made cartoonish. And that's a shame. Not everyone needs to experience the harsh extremes of Natania and her friends at Koncrete Jungle, but that primal disobedience needs to remain in the music's memory.

Source: Karen Schoemer, "Electronic Eden," *Newsweek*, February 10, 1997, pp. 60–63.

58

Nü Metal and Woodstock '99

BARRY WALTERS

As rock entered its fourth decade in the mid-90s, the celebration and canonization of its now lengthy history escalated on numerous fronts. The Rock and Roll Hall of Fame and Museum opened its doors in 1995, new glossy British magazines such as *Mojo* (1993) and *Uncut* (1997) devoted extensive coverage to "classic" rock history, and a nonstop parade of CD reissues and box sets united listeners across generations. Given this climate, it was perhaps to be expected that the collective memory of one of rock's most enduring symbols, Woodstock, should entice promoters to restage the festival on its 25th anniversary in 1994 and then again in 1999. Woodstock '99, however, differed dramatically from its famous forebear. Tickets for the three-day event cost $150 and rock's strong capitalist allure attracted festival vendors selling overpriced bottled water. Most of all, Woodstock's historic message of communal harmony was lost on a young audience clamoring for angry, aggressive music. By the festival's end, destructive riots and reports of rape and sexual assault had cast a dark shadow over the event. As journalist Barry Walters writes in his Woodstock review, at the center of the maelstrom lay the music of headlining acts like Limp Bizkit, Korn, and Kid Rock. Mixing together elements of grunge, rap, and a resuscitated heavy metal style, these groups were generally lumped together under the label of "nü metal." Given the attitudes towards women that seemed to surface at the festival, it is worth asking how far rock had progressed (or regressed) in the three decades since feminists lamented the oppressive nature of "cock rock."

Just as history has looked back on the original Woodstock with grainy footage of body-painted hippies, Woodstock '99 will undoubtedly be remembered by the bonfires that raged out of control as concertgoers rioted and looted. But the more pervasive recurring image in the 65 hours of pay-per-view coverage was of shirtless young women floating above a sea of male bodies, waiflike teens struggling to maintain strained smiles for the camera as they swatted away unwanted hands.

Singer Sheryl Crow described Woodstock '99 as "the most disconcerting audience and worst performing experience I've ever had." Crow, who also performed at the 1994 Woodstock festival, said that this year's event was different. "This year was much more focused on young, white, male America—an aggressive, macho energy full of discontentment, and I think that's where rock is about right now.

"These people were so full of rage and totally unappreciative of the music, kids raised without any pride in themselves. I'm still really [angry] about the event and regret being a part of it," she said.

What was it about this year's Woodstock that created such tension?

Although each day started with veterans and unknowns, acts that have had hits or may someday have hits, each night climaxed with performances by bands that are happening right now—Korn,

Limp Bizkit, Rage Against the Machine, Metallica and Red Hot Chili Peppers. All are exclusively male, excessively loud, defined by a diffuse wrath against anything resembling authority, and driven more by rhythm and fury than melody. In other words, they're classic rock groups.

Which means boy rock groups. Right now, the music industry is running scared from the future. The rise of the Internet, the threat of unprofitable music duplication via digital downloads, the predicted demise of the conventional record store, and the commonplace buying and selling of record labels by multinationals have fostered a panicked corporate mentality that frowns on artistic development and looks for quick hits. The promised electronica revolution didn't instantly happen, so American music bizzers have fallen back on what they know—teeny-bop pop and boy rock.

Although reigning sugar harmony kings the Backstreet Boys, their solo female counterpart Britney Spears and Latin heartthrob Ricky Martin will most likely score the year's best-selling albums, the teen-pop backlash began soon after these acts topped the charts. The typical male rock fan *hates* this stuff with a vehemence that hasn't been seen since the "disco sucks" days of Donna Summer and the Village People, and although the music industry is much more attentive to female and African American audiences than it's ever been, its primary allegiance will always be to college-age white boys.

And rap-influenced hard rock is what college-age white boys like these days.

This is not necessarily a bad thing. When the last technological media upheaval occurred—at the beginning of the '80s with MTV—rock and black pop were seen as mutually intolerant opposites. Eager to shake off its recent disco past, black popular music was either smoothing out in the easy-listening balladry of Kool & the Gang, or roughing up in the form of rap, a sound ignored by major record companies in its crucial developmental years. Despite the fact that plenty of New Wave acts drew on disco and reggae rhythms, black pop was shut out of the rock world, and it took performers on the charismatic level of Michael Jackson and Tina Turner to break down the color barrier of MTV and rock-leaning radio.

Not since rock-and-roll's infancy have white musicians drawn so explicitly and so consciously on contemporary black sounds. And unlike the '50s Pat Boone fan who could fall in love with sanitized renditions of R&B hits and remain unaware of their black origins, today's Korn, Limp Bizkit and Kid Rock fan knows that his heroes are paying tribute to the rhythms and attitudes of hip-hop poets from Run-D.M.C. to Snoop Dogg. Many of the same kids sending Limp Bizkit to the top of the charts have also made possible the mainstream success of such ghetto-centric talents as Jay-Z and the Wu-Tang Clan. Today's typical white male rocker is somewhat supportive of R&B acts like TLC, Ginuwine or Lauryn Hill.

This is progress.

The flip side of rock's current openness to African American culture is that black pop's most positive elements are not always what's most successfully crossing over. Woodstock '99 favorites Limp Bizkit, Kid Rock and Insane Clown Posse all mimic the misogyny that hard-core hip-hop seems incapable of shaking off, and although their more introspective compatriots in Korn and Rage Against the Machine address topics like gay-bashing and modern-day imperialism, their delivery is often so ham-fisted that any thoughtful intent is lost on the kids who need to hear it most.

It was telling that the final words of Rage Against the Machine's Saturday night set—an anti-war chant of "[Expletive] you, I won't do what you tell me"—was appropriated the next night by arsonists and looters facing off with police.

While pop celebrates girl power, rock is once again all about boy power. The inroads made by grunge guy softies wary of thuggish heavy metal and female renegades from Liz Phair to Bjork seem lost to fashion. While VH1 honors the women of rock, hoisting Aretha Franklin and Tina Turner to the top of its honors list, MTV negotiates the divided desires of its young audience by pumping up the rap-rock bad boys so that college-age males don't turn the channel at the mere sight of their younger sisters' goody-goody favorites.[1]

The problem with this strategy is that it leaves out much of the most innovative, soul-searching, potentially lasting music happening right now, and that lack was reflected in Woodstock '99. Not every female musician is busy with Lilith Fair right now, and although Sleater-Kinney, Drain S.T.H. or even Courtney Love and Missy Elliott don't sell the same numbers as Korn and Limp Bizkit, their presence certainly could've helped defuse the male rage that characterized much of the festival.

Although Crow only had Jewel and Alanis Morissette for female company on Woodstock '99's vast three-day lineup, she feels the bill's gender demographics—which included mellow afternoon performances by such summer festival senior standbys as Los Lobos, Bruce Hornsby and George Clinton—were irrelevant: It was the festival's pervasive bullying tone culminating in several rapes that allegedly took place in the mosh pits and on the campgrounds that mattered.

During Crow's set, males in the audience repeatedly asked her to take off her shirt. "At first, I thought it was in fun," says Crow. "But then I saw all these young women who had their tops off being disrespected by the guys, and everyone's bad behavior was exacerbated by the constant presence of the pay-per-view cameras. There is absolutely no justification for rape. None. But I think girls were taking their tops off and the guys were groping them just so they could get on TV."

Crow's sentiments are echoed by Brian "Dexter" Holland of the Southern California punk band Offspring, who was one of two rockers who tried to curb his fans' cop-a-feel free-for-all. (The other was repentant bad boy bassist Flea of the Red Hot Chili Peppers.)

"I stopped our show and reminded the crowd that girls should not have to fear being assaulted just because they are girls," Holland says. "We hate to see anyone bullied, guys or girls. It is not what live music is about. But then you look around at the TV cameras and all they are focusing on is girls with their tops off. So more girls take their tops off. No problem, right? Except then there are girls who don't want to take off their tops and they start getting ridiculed."

A smaller point: At a time when much of rock and pop's creativity is coming from overseas, the fact that few non-North American performers were featured on the main stage is inexcusable. The late-night programming of electronica acts Moby and Fatboy Slim meant no pay-per-view coverage, and techno's Chemical Brothers—the one major act that managed to plug into the original Woodstock's euphoric togetherness—had to go up against Metallica.

"I played in the rave tent late at night to about 40,000 to 50,000 people, and the crowd was very good-natured, gregarious, fun-loving. I personally had a great performance experience, even if $5,000 worth of my T-shirts went up in flames Sunday night," says Moby.

"But the rest of what I witnessed at Woodstock had a frat party vibe that was totally oppressive. Now I personally like testosterone-driven rock—I've played it myself. Yet it's got to be balanced by something else, and that something else was hardly there. Instead they had one aggressive band after the other because aggressive bands are selling records right now," Moby says. "But I don't think the outcome should've surprised anyone."

Source: Barry Walters, "The Arson is Blowin' in the Wind: Why Woodstock '99 Devolved into a Frat-Style Free-For-All," *The Washington Post*, August 8, 1999, p. G1.

---

1 Following the conclusion of Woodstock '99 the VH1 network ran a five-part series counting down the "100 Greatest Women of Rock and Roll" between July 26 and August 1, 1999.

59

Indie Pop Goes Twee

Joey Sweeney

In theory, "indie" is one of the easiest words in the rock lexicon to define. The term is simply short for "independent" record labels. Yet beyond this initial designation, indie opens onto an entire realm of attitudes, audience formations, and musical genres—all of them set in some way against the mainstream of musical values. Joey Sweeney's *Salon.com* review of the Expo 2000 Athens, a five-day festival hosted by the local-based Georgia label, Kindercore Records (one of the most prominent American indie labels of the late '90s) offers a unique window into the indie pop world. Sweeney, a music critic and indie musician himself, bases his description of Kindercore and their roster of artists on the style of "twee," a subgenre that at the time enjoyed one of the indie underground's most devoted fan followings. Sweeney draws attention to the distance separating twee from rock 'n' roll's rebellious pose. And indeed, comparing Sweeney's account of the Expo with Barry Walters' review of Woodstock '99's "frat-style free-for-all" (in Chapter 58), it is hard to imagine a sharper contrast at the turn of the millennium than between indie pop and nü metal audiences.

If you're not of a certain age or social subset—as director Hal Hartley once put it, "white, middle-class, college-educated" and on and on—you might not know a thing about this thing called twee. And if you're not obsessed by music, obscurantist, willfully infantile and smitten with all things Japanese, you probably don't even care.

But this loose subculture lives among you, in English-speaking countries and abroad (especially in Spain and Japan). Twee music and the twee lifestyle—such as there is one—are a refutation of all that we know about rock 'n' roll. For twee kids, who use the term with equal parts reverie, disdain and cheek, the subculture doesn't really have anything to do with actually, you know, rebelling or anything. Twee kids listen to an emasculated version of rock 'n' roll. They don't care much for sex or drugs. They favor puppy love over scary sex, prefer Japanese candy over beer and pot and like looking at postcards instead of going out into an intimidating, rainy world.

They clad themselves in tight T-shirts with "Brady Bunch" stripes and mix-and-match corduroy. They wear unfortunate bedhead hairstyles and thick glasses rescued, almost always, from the bottom of a cardboard box at the local Lenscrafters.

Twee kids are a lot like the punk rockers before them, but you could say that twee, since its erstwhile inception in the '80s, has always rebelled against punk. Back then, cornerstone twee acts like the Smiths and Marine Girls (an outfit featuring Tracey Thorn, who went on to become the singer in Everything But the Girl) eschewed the gutteral reactionism of punk in favor of the sweetness and light (and yes, craft) of naive '60s pop groups such as the Mamas and the Papas or the Association. At the same time, twee cops several of punk's do-it-yourself moves: There are twee magazines, twee all-ages shows, twee record labels and twee local music scenes filled with bands that can't really play their instruments—or at the very least, bands that aspire to radically unlearn what has gone immediately before them.

And in that radical unlearning, that nostalgia for the great pop eras of the past, there's the one major and defining difference between punk and twee: Twee kids love Mom and Dad. In fact, if they could, they'd stay with them forever. I've seen several twee shows at family homes. Twee kids, instead of defining themselves against their parents, embrace a Jonathan Richman worldview: The Old World was better; love was pure and, more than that, less confusing.

Today, Belle and Sebastian, the dainty Scottish pop band, are the Beatles of twee, and their influence looms large over just about every group in the subgenre.

The Kindercore record label is the biggest purveyor of twee music and happiness in the United States. First an Athens, Ga., label, then a New York one and then very shortly thereafter based in Athens again, Kindercore enjoys a generous patronage through a manufacturing deal with California's Emperor Norton label and, as a result, has put out more high-quality twee product, pound for pound, than probably any of its competitors worldwide: March Records, Siesta (based in Spain), Matinee and a handful of others.

And there's apparently an audience for it, although it's hard to tell unless you do the books for an independent record store. Besides Belle and Sebastian, whose last record debuted in the '80s on the Billboard chart, no twee band moves the number of records it would take to, say, be even mildly attractive to a major label. But if you put all the bands into a genre, they can earn a small pile of cash for a little record store, just as punk bands do by hobbling along on word of mouth. In terms of whether twee bands and labels register on SoundScan, the service that tracks record sales, well, they don't. Moneywise, it isn't very much. But then again, the rock underground has rarely made millions for anyone until it ceased being underground.

And that's exactly why Kindercore was able to pull off Expo 2000 Athens, a five-day celebration of the label's take on twee. With 50 releases in all, Kindercore is big enough to have something like this and know that people will come to it, but still small enough to know that it'll know most of the folks who do.

That's because Kindercore, like so many of its successful punk and twee predecessors, keeps close tabs on fans. The Kindercore expo, with its $30 passes, was as much about thanking those 300 or so fans as it was about celebrating its own achievements (neither of the label's co-heads is even close to being out of the 20s) and showing off some new signings. All told, 30 bands played over the five nights, all but one of which were held at Athens' legendary 40 Watt Club—the same club (although now in a different location) where bands like R.E.M., Pylon and the B-52's put Athens on the map more than 15 years ago. Of the 30 bands, roughly half hailed from or had significant ties to Athens. That made the Athens of Expo 2000 a rare sight in rock 'n' roll: a faded boomtown booming once again. The coffee shop a few doors down from the 40 Watt bore a handwritten sign, knowingly saying, "Welcome Indie Rockers!"

The four nights of music I attended revealed a group of awkward, beat-phobic kids getting turned on to what most of us in the world of pop music have known for a while: Dance music is really fun! They also demonstrated a label on the cusp of growing out of its Garanimals, and bittersweetly relishing every minute of it. Because as much as Kindercore's pop jones invites dinky, jangly twee bands, it was only a matter of time before the label invited in featherweight pop as a whole. And from the crowd, it looked like Kindercore at long last was stretching out its hands and accepting what it for so long had hinted at: a genuine love for pop in all its forms.

The 40 Watt looks like a lot of rock clubs in the South. It's a big, airy dive (way bigger than the dives you have to patronize to see rock bands in the North) that's part converted auto garage, part church basement—and thanks to a tenuous tiki, Christmas lights and disco-ball décor—part *M*A*S*H* canteen. Budweiser and Shiner are only two bucks a bottle, and the bartenders look like

Wilco: rock-scene lifers, and damn proud of it. It doesn't sound like much, but if your town doesn't have at least one place like this, you should probably move.

Pulling into Athens late, I caught the tail end of Wednesday night's Expo acts, including Japancakes, a local five-piece that is currently doing for the lap steel what Stereolab did for the Moog a few years back. Japancakes are one of the more hypnotic, sublime and even mature acts on the Kindercore label, which might explain why they pulled in a way smaller crowd than they deserved. As the band ran through a handful of the eight-minute epics that make up their *I Can See Dallas* LP and *Down the Elements* EP, a large video display at stage left revealed loops of silhouetted trees and telephone wires, shot from below at dusk in a passing automobile.

They were pretty good, but for my money, they didn't even touch the 8-Track Gorilla.

Simply put, the 8-Track Gorilla is just that: some guy in a gorilla suit with an old portable eight-track player around his neck, singing along in a deadpan Ben Stein voice over whatever tape happens to be catching his fancy at the moment. On this particular night, that meant some old Kinks stuff (including, appropriately enough, "Ape Man"), a rousing rendition of the Stones' "Happy" and a sexy duet of some "Pina Colada Song"-esque '70s tune with a saucy blond Goth chick that veered from strangely tender to nearly queasy making. The 8-Track Gorilla was not so much a proper Kindercore act as a joke that seems to have mutated far beyond whatever stoned fantasy provoked him into existence in the first place. Audience reactions to the guy—whose set ran a full 40 minutes, just like the sets of the rest of the Kindercore artists—vacillated wildly, but to me, watching a guy in a gorilla suit sing along with Keith Richards after being in a car for 13 hours seemed just about right.

I loved it, couldn't get enough of the guy—I mean, Gorilla. And I wasn't alone. All week, my traveling companion, Martin, would wander around the 40 Watt Club, secretly staring at the hands of men to see if they revealed the 8-Track Gorilla's telltale black nail polish. It became something of a collective obsession for the both of us. Which, I suppose, is why we went down to Athens in the first place.

TWISTING, IN THE WIND, BY THE POOL

Sooner or later, even Martin and I knew that as our snickering about the man in the ape suit fell away we were going to have to socialize with our own kind. For once in our lives, we were in a town overrun with indie, a town where, at least for this week, striped T-shirts flew like freak flags and the stars in the sky from any direction spelled twee. For maybe the first time ever, soaked in the mid-August heat, there was a confederacy of twee. It was nerve-racking even just walking down the street and seeing people who looked just like me.

So imagine our surprise on Thursday afternoon when we went to take a dip in the hotel's pool and found, to our mutual shock, titillation and dismay, some kind of twee pool party. This made sense when you thought about it; unlike South by Southwest or the CMJ music conference, the Expo held no daytime events. Where else were we going to go during the day? Still, this was alarming. One, twee kids have little, tiny bodies well into their 20s and carry for them a kind of skinny shame usually reserved for anorexics, which makes it hard to catch any sun at all. Two, to venture into the pool, which would mean at least in part removing the two layers of coverup clothing just about all of us wore, you had to strip quickly and quietly down to your swimsuit and get into the pool in deep enough water before anyone noticed you. This was all but impossible.

Instead, most of us just sat by the pool, inspecting the badges on each other's backpacks, pretending to read and simultaneously praying for and dreading the moment when we'd all finally introduce ourselves on this, the first day of indie-pop summer camp.

THE RUSHMORE PLAYERS, A.K.A. OF MONTREAL

On most nights of the Expo, a band called Of Montreal appeared onstage as either themselves or as the backing band for another project on an average of twice a night. We saw principal members of the Athens group participating in sets by the Marshmallow Coast, Summer Hymns and the Great Lakes—as well as during their own set, which bridged the gap between *Magical Mystery Tour*-era Beatles and dadaist high school theater. The band is part of the second wave of groups in the Elephant 6 collective of neo-retro pop bands. Engineered by the Apples in Stereo, the Olivia Tremor Control and Neutral Milk Hotel, the E6 collective is split mostly between Denver and Athens and is to indie pop today what Death Row was to hip-hop in the mid-'90s.

The omnipresent Of Montreal were both a blessing, when they worked and the bands they helped came off as something more than the total of their influences, and a curse, when it just seemed that Of Montreal's loopiness was getting spread thin. But either way, the Of Montreal bands seemed to be the most succinct statement of the brand of fresh-faced (if only marginally inventive) guitar pop Kindercore has been going after. In stark relief to the willfully juvenile stuff the label has been passing off for a few years with bands like Masters of the Hemisphere and Kincaid—the former of which, for instance, has offered a free comic book with its new album, a concept piece that seems like a direct lift of the Jim Henson show *Fraggle Rock*—Of Montreal delivered that kind of exuberance without any of the cringe-worthy infantilism that makes this kind of thing so hard to take for so many people. What's more telling about the level of craft in Of Montreal's flights of fancy is that, note for note, the music sounds even more youthful than that of their contemporaries, "Partridge Family" tambourines, junior-high nasal vocals and all. And yet, it doesn't grate; during their set, even the old farts in the crowd like me had to pogo just a little. I mean, these days, how many chances do you get?

And if the new signings are any indication, the label seems to be getting better and better. Norway's Kings of Convenience took the stage like a Euro Smothers Brothers, punctuating quiet, winsome tunes in the manner of Simon and Garfunkel or Nick Drake with a snappy stage presence that suggested, for the first time on the Expo stage, that here was a pair of guys actually interested in craft. Another new signing that debuted on Saturday night was San Francisco's Call and Response (C.A.R.), which invoked the Jackson 5 and the Mamas and the Papas way more than, say, early twee prototype groups like Heavenly or Beat Happening. Self-assured, sassy and with the chops and harmonies to match, Call and Response turned the earnest, honest approach Kindercore has been hammering away at for years into something that was heartbreaking, uplifting and pretty all at once: pure pop for now people.

BUT DOES TWEE KNOW HOW TO PARTY?

On any given night of the Expo shows, in my immediate surroundings I would see at least two girl flutists, two people curled up on any of the 40 Watt's gross couches, obsessively, manically "journaling," and one table full of people playing Mad Libs.

This does not a party make, and even though reports of kids filing into the bathrooms to vomit after drinking too many Red Bull energy drinks shot through with vodka were many, the Expo kids seemed seriously laid-back, verging on what I saw in some eyes as downright despondency. This fell in line with the collective message I was getting after seeing so many of the Kindercore bands: Kindercore records are the records Belle and Sebastian fans are listening to when they're not listening to Belle and Sebastian.

But how much of this is a pose? It seemed as if any chance the kids got to rage, they took it on, no questions asked. I saw it during Of Montreal's raucous (if cute) set, during the Four Corners' big-rock pastiche and even—although I could be reading too much into this—during what I saw as the 8-Track Gorilla's glorious (and apt) rewrite of rock history. Something in twee bubbles under, and that something is the sex and freedom of rock that twee so coyly tries to repress.

So on Friday night, when attention turned to Kindercore's two new groups—groups that you could actually dance to—it wasn't hard to imagine a block-rockin' beat falling in the forest. I imagined twee kids like the guy one of my friends called Badge Museum—with his perfectly symmetrical display of buttons bearing the logos of his favorite bands—politely acting as though they couldn't hear the beat. But it was just the opposite. The five-piece guitar-house band called VHS or Beta took the stage in blue plastic suits, staring indie pop in the face while brandishing a vocoder and electronic drums—the kind the guy in New Order used to play. A quiet descended over the crowd and people started to nod at first. Within a few minutes I swear I could see feet moving and one massive thought bubble hovering over the crowd: "Oh, we get it. And, just between us, we are so very glad to finally get it."

A dance party sponsored by Electronic Watusi Boogaloo, an Amsterdam breakbeat label, opened up a few doors down an hour or so later. The Expo crowd all but ran into the warehouse space. A wall broke and twee went dance; Kindercore turned a corner and you could feel the kids turning with it.

THE MADDENING CROWD

So far, Kindercore has been able to sell a fairly idiosyncratic vision of what it considers valuable music. And to move along in this strange epoch of the music industry, the label has been pretty adept at consistently refining what it is and what it is not.

As noble as those efforts are, in the meantime it is stuck with a lot of deadwood, bands lacking the same kind of inspiration. Unfortunately, just about all of them played at Expo 2000, right alongside the bands that could help the label make something of lasting importance for people who don't work at record stores or at college radio stations.

But while those bands allowed the Expo to be a more complete event, by the last night my head began to hurt. When that headache split open and I had left the club, a fairly obvious realization hit me: There is nothing that I've heard on the Kindercore label that has made much of an effort to touch me on an emotional level. For as nakedly ambitious as the label is, it still adheres pretty rigorously to the tenets of twee: that nothing should make you cry unless it is in the name of sheer sentimentality, and furthermore, in no circumstances does the music want to make you do what rock 'n' roll is supposed to want you to do: to fight or fuck.

Kindercore is a label with plenty of Herman's Hermits and no Rolling Stones. But it's trying.

HOW TO MAKE FRIENDS AND CONFOUND PEOPLE: BOY-BAND REVISIONISM

In all of this, if you didn't care about the music; if you thought these pasty white kids and their bullshit bands were repellent; if you didn't see the sense in all the hoo-ha about what a genius Brian Wilson was and saw no need for so much inept tribute laid at his feet, here and now in the summer of 2000; if, not to put too fine a point on it, you were a bartender at the 40 Watt Club and just wanted to make your money and go home, thank you; and if you were not really looking for entertainment, you had to hand it to Kindercore for at least one thing: When it invited anyone in the whole pop world who wanted to have a look-see into its home and head, it had the balls on the biggest night of its shindig to pull a total goof on itself.

Especially for the Expo, Kindercore constructed its own stable of boy bands. Not some retro goofiness like the Wonders in the Tom Hanks movie *That Thing You Do!* but the real, sweaty, icky, present-day faux-sexy thing. Adding to a world of Backstreet Boys and 'N Syncs, Kindercore presented on Friday night From U 2 S (pronounced "from you to us") and N2 Her (pronounced, uh, "into her"). It was one of the most hilarious things I've ever seen in my life.

Starting out by clearing the stage and setting up a movie screen to show a "Making the Band"/"Behind the Music"-styled mockumentary on how the groups came into existence, label co-head Ryan Lewis approached the mike to introduce the proceedings as if they were yet another band on the label. "Well, we know a lot of people have been dying to see these guys, so without further ado . . ."

And that quickly, the Spinal Tap of boy bands took the stage: There was a clean-cut one, a dirty one, a half-naked one, a tiny one. And they had dance routines! Like so much teen pop, the music tracks accompanying the boy bands were a weird mix of Celica-thumping Miami bass and synth-driven, up-tempo trip-hop—until you realized that the songs they were singing were misappropriated indie anthems: Unrest's "Make-Out Club," for From U 2 S, and for N 2 Her, Pavement's "Summer Babe," with sections of Stephen Malkmus' deadpan lyrics recast into a Jay-Z-esque rhyme.

Everything Kindercore wanted to or could have said about itself got said on Friday night: that it was above all, like the Immediate label that put out fresh, sunshiny pop in the '60s, simply "happy to be a part of the industry of human happiness," and that, once in a while, sweating the details pays off.

Source: Joey Sweeney, "We're the Younger Generation," *Salon.com*, August 31, 2000, http://archive. salon.com/ent/music/feature/2000/08/31/kindercore/

60

"So You Wanna Fake Being an Indie Rock Expert?"

SoYouWanna.Com

The anonymous internet essay "So You Wanna Fake Being an Indie Rock Expert?" bears the stamp of its late 1990s origins, an era that saw the rise in popularity of easily digestible reference tomes like the *For Dummies* series and illustrated comic book paperbacks like *Philosophy for Beginners*. Like those types of guides, "So You Wanna" begins with the assumption that the topic at hand is laden with enough complexities that essentially it must be translated into a more accessible language for a lay audience. "Indie rock" indeed has long been a notoriously difficult term to define, especially in terms of a specific musical style. The article steers the discussion away from this angle, however, focusing instead on one of indie's most distinctive features: its prominent connoisseur audience. Connoisseurship traditionally is measured in terms of knowledge and taste, and as the article shows "indie rock" comes with its own rules for how this can be mastered. Crucially, it is not the knowledge itself that makes one an expert, but rather how one wields this vast storehouse of information that separates the suave hipster from the socially ill-equipped nerd and transparent poseur.[1] Is the article's outline and advice convincing? Could you imagine how similar instructional guides for other popular music styles might read?

You're sick of digesting mainstream, overproduced drivel from the likes of MTV and the local "be-caller-100" pop station. You'd like to be edgier and more "underground"—or at least you'd like to pretend you're both those things. The only trouble is, you don't know where to begin. Being in-the-know about independent rock music—a.k.a. "indie rock"—can seem like an overwhelming task. Indie fans often come across as if they belong to some sort of secret society, frowning upon all those poor, ignorant souls who just don't "get it" when it comes to music. Lies. We're here to tell you that you too can be a hipster. By learning the basics of what the indie phenomenon is all about, you should be well on your way to passing yourself off as a die-hard fan.

By the way, we should probably warn you that we're assuming you have at least some musical savvy. We're about to make lots of references to bands, albums and record labels that aren't exactly household names. So if obscurity scares you, save yourself the trouble and click here.[2]

---

1 For an excellent analysis of these connoisseur stereotypes, see Will Straw, "Sizing Up Record Collections: Gender and Connoisseurship in Record Collections," in Sheila Whiteley, ed., *Sexing the Groove: Popular Music and Gender* (New York: Routledge Press, 1997), pp. 3–16.

2 In the original web version, "click here" was a hyperlink that took the viewer to a fan page for the teen pop group, Backstreet Boys.

1. Look the part

To begin a sham indie rock education, you might be tempted to think you should go buy some indie rock records. Don't be a fool. There are several personal actions you must undertake before bothering with the music itself. After all, part of being an indie rock expert is having the image that goes along with it.

- The first thing you should do is alter your bathing habits. By no means does that mean you should develop a complete disregard for hygiene, but you might want to cut back on the frequency with which you wash your hair. The "bedhead" look is too obvious, but a modified bedhead with a greasy sheen to it will have you blending right in with the crowd at the indie rock show.
- Next, think about your shirtwear. An old undersized T-shirt is a safe bet, but it should be some vibrant color—green, orange, and yellow are all good choices—never white or black. White is gauche, and black is too glamorous, too L.A. Generally speaking, the shirt should look like something you would find at a thrift store, but it shouldn't look like you bought it at a thrift store.
- Got a nice car? Good. Lose it. If you want to be indie rock you can't drive a car that has fewer than 100,000 miles on the odometer and had an original sticker price of more than $20K. As a rule, money is antithetical to indie rock. Unless you are Matt Groening, it's hard to make piles of cash when you are a clever cynic (as most indie rockers like to think of themselves).

2. Know some of the history

Now that you're dressed for the occasion, you next need to immerse yourself in all that is indie rock. Here is a brief history of the subject, which, fortunately for you young wannabes, is summarized here in ultra-abridged form.

The '60s

Were it to exist, The Indie Rock for Dummies book might put the roots of the indie rock tree in the Velvet Underground, a band that hit the scene during the mid-to-late '60s. As the rest of the world was into peace, love, and really good hallucinogenics, the Velvet Underground was taking the rock rulebook, tearing out the pages, and using them to wipe their butts. Their music kinda sounded like rock, but incorporated elements of social realism and the beginnings of punk and new wave. In short, the Velvet Underground was way ahead of its time.

The '70s

After the VU, the deconstructive proposition born in the bowels on New York's Bowery, quickly took the form of punk. Punk became somewhat successful/mainstream, so it had to die. That left a bunch of post-punk bands, many of whom (Elvis Costello, Talking Heads, the Pretenders) started getting airplay, and also became successful and (even worse) old. Post-punk bottomed out when the Clash made Combat Rock, a radio-friendly album that included such commercially viable songs as "Rock the Casbah" and "Should I Stay or Should I Go."

The '80s

Sometime in the late '80s, the moniker of underground tunes changed from "punk" to "college music." This was not because only people in college listened to it, but also because the only people who played it were deejays at college radio stations. Anybody with a radio was free to listen, but not very many people did . . . until people realized that despite the weird names of some of these bands, they weren't scary like punks. In fact, a lot of college music was just pop music. R.E.M., U2, Camper Van Beethoven—they were college bands and they were harmless.

As many of those bands became popular, the powers-that-be at the college radio stations became a little bitter that "their bands" were taken away and given to the masses. They reacted by going a little harder and a little darker (a la Nirvana). That's when college music started to become known as "alternative." Again, the general idea was that it was an alternative to say, Tiffany or Bon Jovi or what you might hear on the radio (notice the pattern?).

The '90s

In the early '90s, Nirvana released Nevermind. As a result, alternative launched its own radio format, and paradoxically became mainstream. So the bands who were still an alternative to something that was getting airplay became (drum roll, please) "indie rock."

3. Become familiar with current indie rock bands and labels

So what makes something indie rock? Good question. Unfortunately, there is no clear set of criteria that you can apply to make that determination; it is easier to define indie rock by what it isn't. It isn't successful, it isn't glamorous, it isn't sexy, it isn't insipid, and it isn't likely to get you laid. Nonetheless, getting to the point where you can identify those negative predications is going to take a little work. You might actually have to read a book or some magazines to get a sufficient feel for what qualifies as indie in order to pull this off.

Whatever you do, don't read Rolling Stone. Rolling Stone is for housewives and teenage girls. In Rolling Stone you can read about Puff Daddy and Lilith Fair. That's the kind of fodder that feeds indie rock disdain. Spin—it's for poseurs. You might be best off flipping through a copy of Alternative Press. But don't buy it off the newsstand. Paying retail is not at all indie rock.

Familiarize yourself with the names of the indie record labels because seven times out of ten, if it's on an indie label, it's indie rock. Remember this name: Matador Records. Once cooler than Steve McQueen, Matador is now the Warner or Sony of indie rock, as its staff numbers about 30 people and its roster includes about 40 bands. Hardly small. In fact a few of their most popular artists (e.g., Liz Phair, The Jon Spencer Blues Explosion) have distribution deals with Capitol Records.

You know the drill: because Matador has become moderately successful, in many respects it's yesterday's news. So now, even if you've never listened to the Jon Spencer Blues Explosion (a.k.a. JSBX), you can act like you think they are passé because you know that they're on Matador. In fact if you've ever been around a music snob, you probably already know the phrase, "Yeah, their old stuff is better." It's a cliché, but in the case of JSBX, it's true. If you want to talk about them, limit the conversation to either their Extra Width or Orange albums, both of which, incidentally, are truly worth owning if you actually like indie rock. But if you do actually like indie rock, you probably own them already.

Other labels you should familiarize yourself with include:

- Merge
- Kill Rock Stars
- Lookout
- Evil Teen
- Amphetamine Reptile
- Alternative Tentacles

- Shimmy Disc
- K Records
- Bong Load
- Touch and Go
- 4AD
- spinART
- Thrill Jockey
- The belated Trance Syndicate

And if you see anything on C/Z Records in the used bin, you might be wise to jump on it or at least read the name of the band on the CD so it will be familiar in conversation. Bloodshot is certainly indie but it ain't rock, but even if twang ain't your thang, you should still have respect for the label's adherence to general indie principles.

Unlike most major labels, which are as likely to sign a rapper as a teen boy band, indie labels are kind of like brands, meaning that they generally stay stylistically consistent. This is especially true when the label is young and small. For example, most of the early Seattle grunge bands were playing under the Sub Pop label long before David Geffen showed up in the Pacific Northwest with a checkbook and started playing Who Wants to Be a Millionaire? with a bunch of depressed kids in flannel shirts. It's not so much the case anymore, but once upon a time, you knew that if you bought a band on the Sub Pop label, you wouldn't need a volume knob. (Oh, and as a brief aside: do not wax nostalgic for the pre-Nirvana Sub Pop days yet. It's still too early for that. You can, however, still be bummed out about what Island Records and Casey Kasem did to SST Records as a result of the Negativland/U2 incident.)[3] The point is: if you can identify the sound of one band on the label, there's a better than even-money chance you'll be in the ballpark with the others.

4. Learn to talk the talk

If you look cool enough, eventually someone is going to talk to you and expect you to talk back; and if you open your mouth and say something like, "David Cassidy is really cool," you are liable to get the foo kicked out of you. And that would be really embarrassing because the indie rock world is populated largely by wussies.

So start somewhere safe: Sonic Youth. You cannot go wrong if you like Sonic Youth. Everybody in indie rock likes Sonic Youth, and those who don't are afraid to admit it. So you can talk all night long about what a genius frontman-guitarist Thurston Moore is, and nobody will ever think you are an idiot or don't know what you are talking about.

Once you've worn out all possible conversation topics regarding Sonic Youth, try these tips:

- Know that the coolest indie rock band is someone nobody has heard of and is on a label that doesn't even exist yet. That's just the way it works. Of course you can't talk exclusively about bands nobody else knows anything about, and if you go to their shows, no one else will be there.
- Don't invent bands. If you make up a name, you will give yourself away. You might think, "How can that be?" Again, that's just the way it works. So no cheating.

---

3 The SST group Negativland released an EP in 1991 that featured U2's name on the cover, and a song that combined a parody of the group's "I Still Haven't found What I'm Looking For" with samples of the disc jockey Casey Kasem angrily disparaging U2 during a rehearsal of his American Top 40 radio show. U2's label, Island Records, quickly brought a lawsuit against Negativland and SST.

Depth, not breadth

If you want to look like you know what you are talking about, depth is more important than breadth. And you just need to be deep in one or two places. That is where something like the Trouser Press Guide might come in handy.[4] It's cross-referenced so you can peruse through it and easily pick up information on bands related by history and specifically find out what other bands the members might have been in. That way, when you speak, you transcend simple knowledge by appearing to having a sense of history when you really don't.

For instance, you look up Built to Spill because you've read about them in some indie 'zine. You see that there is this other band cross-listed with Built to Spill called Stuntman. That's a bonus because Stuntman is still pretty obscure. Where you really rack up the points is by pointing out that both those bands arose out of Treepeople. You couldn't pick Treepeople out of a lineup, but you've just linked three cool bands from Idaho. That's right, Idaho. Who the heck is going to doubt your authority after that?

OK, so let's throw an example at you now: you read about Galaxy 500 and the two bands it spawned-Luna, and Damon and Naomi. Then, when you're at the indie rock show, you say:

"Yeah, DEAN WAREHAM is such a LOU REED and VELVET UNDERGROUND disciple. But it's funny because GALAXY 500 was more about the drone, but LUNA has more of the pop-strum feel of Loaded. So he's covered the gamut of LOU's influence in his career. I don't like DAMON AND NAOMI, though. They are way too Lo-Fi (Pause). You know, I saw LUNA open for VU in Prague back in the early '90s on their European reunion tour."

Translation:

- First, as in the previous example, you linked two good indie bands (Luna, and Damon and Naomi) to their parent band (Galaxy 500).
- You referenced them back to Lou Reed and the Velvet Underground. That means you were paying attention in the history section of this article, and acknowledged the importance of VU enough to integrate them into your thoughts on indie rock.
- You recognized the differences between Dean Wareham when he fronted Luna from when he fronted Galaxy 500, and you threw in another VU reference—this time to Loaded.
- You were careful not to do too much work for your interlocutor. You left him/her an opening to say something like. "Yeah, but Loaded wasn't really a VU record, because John Cale had already left the band by then." You are on fire. If this is a member of the opposite sex that you are talking to, you probably just got yourself a date if you want it.
- You dissed Damon and Naomi. Good. Don't be afraid to not like someone. But not only did you dis them, you also referenced an indie sub-genre (lo-fi) in your dismissal, and you did it without hesitation. Perfect.
- You were not done, though. You go for legendary status. You were at arguably THE coolest show of the '90s. You not only knew about that tour, but you were there. Note: if you are currently under 26 years old and you reached for that last one, you blew it. You weren't in Europe when you were 18. You were clearly trying to look cooler than you were. No bigger sin in indie city.

---

4 The encyclopedic *Trouser Press Record Guide* first appeared in 1983 as a spin-off of *Trouser Press*, one of the few American magazines at the time that was devoted to punk and new wave music. The fifth and final edition, *The Trouser Press Guide to '90s Rock*, was published in 1997.

5. Complete the ruse

You've got the basics down, now you need to fill in some of the gaps. Remember, you don't need to fill in all of them . . . you don't want to actually BE an indie rock expert because that's a lifetime of work, and you've got better things to do. You just need to fill in enough of the holes to keep people from prying further to see how many are actually there.

So here's what ya gotta do:

- Familiarize yourself with The Elephant 6 Collective of the Olivia Tremor Control, Apples in Stereo, and Neutral Milk Hotel. This is a group of bands who have taken up where the Stones' Their Satanic Majesties Request and the Beatles' Revolver left off. The Beatles and the Stones? That may sound mainstream, but these guys do retro psych-pop in a way that nobody with a Britney Spears CD would ever want to sit through.
- Know about Minneapolis in the heyday of the '80s, when the Replacements, Hüsker Dü, and Soul Asylum (they used to be cool) were the underground holy trinity of rock. Drop mentions of the Replacements whenever possible. Oh, and also mention Peter Jesperson, even if you have no idea who he is. It doesn't matter. Just say something like, "Yeah, I hear Jesperson's got something new going on," then just bluff your way from there.
- Finally it will be advantageous to pick one favorite band that just never broke despite their genius, someone like, say, Spoon. Do you own both Spoon records as well as the Soft Effects EP? Probably not because they are not easy to find, but if someone sees you in a record store (and it damn well better be an indie record store), that's what you tell them you are looking for. As for what you buy at the record store—CD or vinyl—you are free to go either way without really affecting your indie cred (that's indie-speak for credibility).
- If you really want to do the extra credit work, pick a foreign country and school yourself in some of its bands. For instance, you can pick Japan and drop names like Lolita No. 18, Zoobombs, Melt Banana, Cornelius, Buffalo Daughter, Guitar Wolf, and Husking Bee. You should actually listen to one or two of them. That way you can make a judgment like, "You know, the Japanese bands are finally starting to move away from simple imitation of American music and are now starting to incorporate elements that are wholly original." But don't say that. That's our line.
- One last minefield you need to navigate is what happens when an indie band jumps to a major label. No matter how cool a band is, this is bound to happen. Sometimes it doesn't mean much, and other times it is the end of the band. Again, Sonic Youth were cool even on DGC, but the Goo Goo Dolls, who did about the coolest Prince cover ever ("I Could Never Take the Place of Your Man"), became something else when they went to a major label. Showing anything but disdain for that bunch of milksops will get you cast out east of indie Eden. Then there are cases like Dinosaur Jr.—Green Mind, good; but anything after Where You Been, bad. There is no science here; and without a good knowledge of the bands you are only likely to get into trouble.

Source: "So You Wanna Fake Being an Indie Rock Expert?" *SoYouWanna.com*, date unknown, https://web.archive.org/web/20001119135300/http://www.soyouwanna.com:80/site/syws/indierock/ indierock.html.

VI

THE 2000s

61

Metallica vs. Napster

LARS ULRICH

The rise in peer-to-peer (P2P) file sharing, of consumers freely sending digital MP3 audio files to one another, threw the recording industry into a panic at the close of the century. The industry had dealt with similar crises before, most noticeably in the early 1980s, when the threat of blank cassette sales and illicit duplication prompted the memorable slogan, "home taping is killing music." Such concerns seemed relatively minor, however, when compared with the emergence of the online service Napster, and its rapidly expanding millions of users. And this time, it was not just the Recording Industry Association of America (RIAA) that sought legal recourse, but some music artists as well. When the heavy metal group Metallica learned in early 2000 that a demo of their song "I Disappear," set to appear on the *Mission Impossible II* soundtrack, had been leaked on Napster, they followed the RIAA's lead and filed a lawsuit for copyright infringement. Soon after, in a dramatic gesture, drummer Lars Ulrich (born 1963) engineered a press conference at Napster's main office, where he handed them thirteen boxes containing the names of more 335,000 users who had illegally shared Metallica's music, and demanded that they be removed from the service. Two months later, a Senate Judiciary Committee invited Ulrich to appear as part of a hearing on Internet music services. Ulrich's statement, included here in its entirety, not only expresses Metallica's own individual concerns over the control of intellectual property, but also implies the tragic effects that music theft will have upon the recording industry's many anonymous everyday employees.[1] In another strategic move, Ulrich seeks to counter the prevailing media image of Napster as a rebellious grassroots tech uprising, and instead emphasizes the organization's own desires to protect their copyrighted interests. Ulrich's stance, while certainly rational in its tone, ultimately earned Metallica a wave of negative publicity, for he unwittingly demonized consumers while failing to grasp the complexities of file sharing. Some Metallica fans, for example, were encouraged to buy CDs or attend concerts *because* they had first heard a free audio file. While the industry would eventually win its case against Napster, it proved to be a hollow victory. As physical sales of CDs declined at a staggering rate throughout the 2000s, the industry struggled to contain the inevitable spread of digital downloading. In this light, the industry's refusal to embrace Napster's potential was increasingly portrayed as a devastating, if not fatal, missed opportunity.

Mr. Chairman, Senator Leahy, Members of the Committee, my name is Lars Ulrich. I was born in Denmark. In 1980, as a teenager, my parents and I came to America. I started a band named *Metallica* in 1981 with my best friend James Hetfield. By 1983 we had released our first record, and by 1985 we were no longer living below the poverty line. Since then, we've been very fortunate to

---

1 The Motion Picture Association of America (MPAA) employed a similar tactic in 2003, when they produced a series of anti-piracy spots delivered by stunt men and set painters, whose blue-collar livelihoods were meant to create a more emotional and sympathetic appeal.

achieve a great level of success in the music business throughout the world. It's the classic American dream come true. I'm very honored to be here in this country, and to appear in front of the Senate Judiciary Committee today.

Earlier this year, while completing work on a song for the movie Mission Impossible II, we were startled to hear reports that a work-in-progress version was already being played on some U.S. radio stations. We traced the source of this leak to a corporation called Napster. Additionally, we learned that all of our previously recorded copyrighted songs were, via Napster, available for anyone around the world to download from the Internet in a digital format known as MP3. As you are probably aware, we became the first artists to sue Napster, and have been quite vocal about it as well. That's undoubtedly why you invited me to this hearing.

We have many issues with Napster. First and foremost: Napster hijacked our music without asking. They never sought our permission—our catalog of music simply became available as free downloads on the Napster system.

I don't have a problem with any artist voluntarily distributing his or her songs through any means the artist elects— at no cost to the consumer, if that's what the artist wants. But just like a carpenter who crafts a table gets to decide whether to keep it, sell it or give it away, shouldn't we have the same options? My band authored the music which is Napster's lifeblood. We should decide what happens to it, not Napster— a company with no rights in our recordings, which never invested a penny in Metallica's music or had anything to do with its creation. The choice has been taken away from us.

What about the users of Napster, the music consumers? It's like each of them won one of those contests where you get turned loose in a store for five minutes and get to keep everything you can load into your shopping cart. With Napster, though, there's no time limit and everyone's a winner— except the artist. Every song by every artist is available for download at no cost and, of course, with no payment to the artist, the songwriter or the copyright holder.

If you're not fortunate enough to own a computer, there's only one way to assemble a music collection the equivalent of a Napster user's: theft. Walk into a record store, grab what you want and walk out. The difference is that the familiar phrase a computer user hears, "File's done" is replaced by another familiar phrase: "You're under arrest."

Since what I do is make music, let's talk about the recording artist for a moment. When Metallica makes an album we spend many months and many hundreds of thousands of our own dollars writing and recording. We also contribute our inspiration and perspiration. It's what we do for a living. Even though we're passionate about it, it's our job.

We typically employ a record producer, recording engineers, programmers, assistants and, occasionally, other musicians. We rent time for months at recording studios, which are owned by small businessmen who have risked their own capital to buy, maintain and constantly upgrade very expensive equipment and facilities. Our record releases are supported by hundreds of record company employees and provide programming for numerous radio and television stations. Add it all up and you have an industry with many jobs— very few glamorous ones like ours— and a greater number of demanding ones that cover all levels of the pay scale for wages which support families and contribute to our economy.

Remember too, that my band, Metallica, is fortunate enough to make a great living from what it does. Most artists are barely earning a decent wage and need every source of revenue available to scrape by. Also keep in mind that the primary source of income for most songwriters is from the sale of records. Every time a Napster enthusiast downloads a song, it takes money from the pockets of all these members of the creative community.

It's clear, then, that if music is free for downloading, the music industry is not viable; all the jobs I just talked about will be lost and the diverse voices of the artists will disappear. The argument I hear a lot, that "music should be free" must then mean that musicians should work for free. Nobody else works for free. Why should musicians?

In economic terms, music is referred to as intellectual property, as are films, television programs, books, computer software, video games and the like. As a nation, the U.S. has excelled in the creation of intellectual property, and collectively, it is this country's most valuable export.

The backbone for the success of our intellectual property business is the protection that Congress has provided with the copyright statutes. No information-based industry can thrive without this protection. Our current political dialog about trade with China is focused on how we must get that country to respect and enforce copyrights. How can we continue to take that position if we let our own copyright laws wither in the face of technology?

Make no mistake, *Metallica* is not anti-technology. When we made our first album, the majority of sales were in the vinyl record format. By the late 1980's, cassette sales accounted for over 50% of the market. Now, the compact disc dominates. If the next format is a form of digital downloading from the Internet with distribution and manufacturing savings passed on to the American consumer, then, of course, we will embrace that format too.

But how can we embrace a new format and sell our music for a fair price when someone, with a few lines of code, and no investment costs, creative input or marketing expenses, simply gives it away? How does this square with the level playing field of the capitalist system? In Napster's brave new world, what free-market economy models support our ability to compete? The touted "new paradigm" that the Internet gurus tell us we Luddites must adopt sounds to me like old-fashioned trafficking in stolen goods.

We have to find a way to welcome the technological advances and cost savings of the Internet while not destroying the artistic diversity and the international success that has made our intellectual property industries the greatest in the world. Allowing our copyright protections to deteriorate is, in my view, bad policy, both economically and artistically.

To underscore what I've spoken about today, I'd like to read from the "Terms of Use" section of the Napster Internet web site. When you use Napster you are basically agreeing to a contract that includes the following terms:

"This web site or any portion of this web site may not be reproduced, duplicated, copied, sold, resold, or otherwise exploited for any commercial purpose that is not expressly permitted by Napster."

"All Napster web site design, text, graphics, the selection and arrangement thereof, and all Napster software are Copyright© 1999–2000 Napster Inc. All rights reserved Napster Inc." "Napster, the logo and all other trademarks, service marks and trade names of Napster appearing on this web site are owned by Napster."

"Napster's trademarks, logos, service marks, and trade names may not be used in connection with any product or service that is not Napster's."

Napster itself wants— and surely deserves— copyright and trademark protection. *Metallica* and other creators of music and intellectual property want, deserve and have a right to that same protection.

In closing, I'd like to read to you from the last paragraph of a *New York Times* column by Edward Rothstein: "Information doesn't want to be free; only the transmission of information wants to be free. Information, like culture, is the result of a labor and devotion, investment and risk; it has a value. And nothing will lead to a more deafening cultural silence than ignoring that value and celebrating [companies like] Napster running amok."

Mr. Chairman, Senator Leahy and Members of the Committee, the title of today's hearing asks the question, "The Future of the Internet: Is there an Upside to Downloading"? My answer is yes. However, as I hope my remarks have made clear, this can only occur when artists' choices are respected and their creative efforts protected. Thank you.

Source: Lars Ulrich, Testimony before the Committee on the Judiciary, United States Senate, *Music on the Internet: Is There an Upside to Downloading,* 106th Congress, Second Session, July 11, 2000, http://ftp.resource.org/gpo.gov/hearings/106s/74728.txt

62

"Mother, Should I Build a Wall?"

Radiohead Face the Challenges of New Rock

Douglas Wolk

Radiohead's *OK Computer* (1997) was one of the most critically acclaimed releases of the decade; an album whose ambitious conceptual approach garnered glowing comparisons to the earlier art rock of groups like Pink Floyd. Their heavily anticipated 2000 follow-up *Kid A* saw the band pursue more experimental electronic music influences, a decision that drew sharply divided critical responses.[1] Music critic Douglas Wolk's review of Radiohead's October 11, 2000 show at New York's Roseland Ballroom, their first in the United States in support of *Kid A*, considers the band at this crucial juncture in their career, acknowledging both their rock legacy (the article's title references a song from Pink Floyd's *The Wall*) and their new electronic direction. Wolk considers not only how Radiohead navigates these competing musical interests and tensions in a live setting, but also extends his review into a lengthier examination of the new maze-like, fan-curated online milieu in which the band and their music had become embedded. As Wolk observes, for a band like Radiohead averse to rock's promotional demands, it is easy to "disappear" inside this new, heavily mediated environment. Wolk concludes, however, by posing an intriguing query: for a band so adamantly resistant to rock's commercialism and branding, does that very stance effectively not provide Radiohead with their most powerful brand identity (i.e.—the 'anti-brand' band)?

In the Flesh

The audience at Radiohead's Roseland Ballroom show look like the only 3,000 people in New York who've found the golden tickets to paradise. They're crying in anticipation, screaming with joy and bathing in a warm, ecstatic glow, even if scalpers charged them hundreds of dollars for the privilege.

They've paid to be in the presence of Radiohead's aura as much as to see the performance. And why shouldn't they? Radiohead is arguably the most exciting rock band in the world right now, the group whose next move matters more than their last one. And part of the thrill is that their show, one of only three in the U.S. last year, is not a rote greatest-hits set: A lot of what the band will play isn't even on their new album, *Kid A* (Capitol). The bandmembers skip most of their best-known songs, they don't indulge in stage gimmickry, and they don't ask anyone to sing along (though the

---

1 For good summaries of *Kid A*'s polarizing critical reception, see Marianne Letts, *Radiohead and the Resistant Concept Album: How to Disappear Completely* (Bloomington & Indianapolis: Indiana University Press, 2010) and Marvin Lin, *Kid A* (New York: Continuum, 2011).

"rain down" bit of "Paranoid Android" turns into a roar from the audience anyway). We're gratified, because they're not trying too hard to please us.

Still, you can see a change come over the whole band's body language as they switch between new material and old, between more traditionally structured rock songs and the songs that haunt rock's abandoned house. When the group members reach back for old nuggets like "Just" or "The Bends," they're incandescent and physical, lunging into every chord, looking as if they're remembering a skill they'd put aside; when they try "Everything In Its Right Place" or the brand new, groove-based encore "I Might Be Wrong," they barely move, and seem to be concentrating very hard on losing themselves inside the song. Yorke recently said in an interview that he's contemplated changing Radiohead's name, and at the Roseland show, that choice suddenly made sense. But if it's tough to be the most exciting band in the world, imagine being the *two* most exciting bands in the world.

You Gotta Be Crazy, You Gotta Have a Real Need

If you want to shield your eyes from the Radiohead halo and actually interview the mystical wizards behind the curtain, keep in mind that there are plenty of guards at the gate. These days, here's what you do: First, apply for a username and a password from one of their publicists. If you're approved, you go to a special Web site (www.spinwithagrin.co.uk), log in with the password, and type your question in. Your query is forwarded to the publicist, who determines if it's interesting enough for the band to answer; if it passes *that* test, it's re-forwarded to Radiohead, who respond to it (if they feel like it, maybe, eventually), and post both the question and answer on the site, whereupon every Radiohead fan site on the planet links to it.

Transmitting a question is like an act of supplication to the Oracle at Delphi: Sacrifice the calf wrong, and you'll get a curt, sarcastic comeback. Sometimes a bandmember writes something meaningful, and signs it ("JG" is guitarist Jonny Greenwood, "Dr. Tchock" and its variants are singer/guitarist Thom Yorke); sometimes you just get an uncredited torrent of sub-Joycean misspellings and self-contradicting thoughts. But no one gets to see the Wizard—not directly, at any rate.

Don't Leave Me Now

Is it weird for Radiohead to perform old songs from when their creative process was very different and their heads were in a very different place—and have they ever wanted to ditch them altogether? We asked the Oracle, and the answer came:

> I think it's basically unhealthy to disown music that you've done in the past. So long as you're not attached to it and realize it comes from where you were, then it's okay. And that now you have moved on elsewhere, playing a song in a concert in front of people is a way of reclaiming it back. If we could not play any of our old stuff, I don't think we would, simply. It fucks with the flow of writing and making music to try too hard to distance yourself from certain things you do. But then crowd-pleasing doesn't exactly come natural to us so, sometimes when you play it doesn't mean anything, sometimes you remember something in it that you thought you forgot, which is great. In a way it's whatever the audience gives back to you.

"Crowd-pleasing" is a central problem of Radiohead's career—they've never, *ever* been comfortable with it. At this point, if people expect Radiohead to do something, that makes them pretty much incapable of doing it; *Kid A* and what comes after it are Radiohead inventing workarounds to avoid rock normalcy.

The two-year record/tour cycle is unfathomably depressing to them, so we can expect album number five shortly; the original plan was that it would be more of the dozens of songs from the epic *Kid A* sessions, but the latest word is that at least some of it will be newer. The interview process bugs them, so we get Spin With A Grin. They had one fairly straightforward old-style Radiohead song going into *Kid A*—"Knives Out," a recent live staple—and they spent more than a year, off and on, trying to get the recording right (and haven't released it yet).

And then there's the matter of touring the way rock bands are "supposed" to, and what's supposed to happen when they're onstage, which may be why their 2001 tour is rumored to be up in the air. It's part of their appeal that they never do the obvious thing. And when not doing the obvious thing becomes what they're expected to do—well, that's where they hit a wall of their own devising.

Waiting for the Worms

That's not to say that Radiohead is afflicted with creative stagnation. Just the opposite, actually; snap open the CD tray of *Kid A*, and you'll find an extra, hidden booklet, with fragments of lyrics from material they left off the album. Nonetheless, *Kid A*'s tune "How To Disappear Completely" could be about their songs—especially songs that have been eagerly anticipated but haven't yet shown up on record. "Lift," "Follow Me Around" and "True Love Waits," among others, have surfaced in the band's live repertoire, been tossed around as possible album tracks or singles, and then vanished before a recording ever appeared.[2] There's a song called "Cuttooth" that guitarist Ed O'Brien's online diaries suggested was a highlight of the *Kid A* sessions, an extended three-chord juggernaut. One of the best Radiohead fan sites is named after it. Nobody beyond Radiohead's inner circle has ever even heard it.[3]

So what's the story with the disappearing material? Is it that certain songs, even some of their best, resist recording? We asked the Oracle:

> If you got to the unofficial sites, you'll see there are lists of songs that have never made it right to tape. We're trying to work from the basis that it doesn't matter how it is done technically in the studio, that is one workspace, and playing it in front of people is another. It's a case of rewriting things. Some of it works, some of it doesn't. The most important thing is not feeling in any way restricted. Sometimes what sounds good live cannot be translated like that. It sounds dull and lifeless. But so what? It's in a different place. We try hard not to have a problem with it. Missing songs find their way back eventually.—Tchocky (Keen aren't I?)

Welcome to the Machine

Oh, yes, the unofficial sites—ground zero for Radiohead's fanbase, and for the PR coups that helped drive *Kid A* to No. 1. In the old way of thinking, if you're a fan of a band, its direct involvement with your life stops at discrete, "official" activities: buying the album, going to see them play,

---

2 "True Love Waits" was eventually recorded as a studio track for the 2016 album *A Moon Shaped Pool* and "Lift" was included the following year on the anniversary compilation *OK Computer OKNOTOK 1997 2017*. "Follow Me Around" has yet to appear in a studio format.
3 "Cuttooth" would be released later in 2001 as a track on the band's "Knives Out" single.

maybe getting a T-shirt. But we are not in that world anymore; we are in a world with unstoppable information flow, and the old paradigm no longer pertains.

Radiohead's brilliant move is blurring the "official"/"unofficial" line, so that they can draw their listeners more deeply into their world. Instead of updates on current band news, Radiohead.com points to fans' volunteer sites like the excellent Greenplastic.com and Ateaseweb.com; Radiohead.com itself is mostly a deep, dense, marvelously complicated piece of art designed by Stanley Donwood, who plays Hipgnosis to their Pink Floyd. (Earlier versions of it have been archived by fans; there are links at www.radiohead.com/waitingroom.html.) The band's marketers programmed an "iBlip"— a mini-site with links to multimedia goodies—for *Kid A*, available to anyone who wanted to stick a link to it on the Web; they streamed the entire album over the Web weeks before its release. The band has even been making noise about considering an electronic subscription model for their new music, so it could come out as they finish it in a way that hasn't been possible since the fall of the non-album single.

The band knows that any song they perform in public will immediately circulate to all of their serious fans. They *depend* on that. *Kid A* proper is so carefully engineered, so rich in sonic detail, that a pirated MP3 is simply not an adequate substitute, and the fan sites are windows to their work in progress. At Roseland, Yorke dedicated the new "Pyramid Song" to "everyone who's already heard it on Napster." But how do they feel about the fact that when they change a song before they release it officially, the previous draft is already documented?

Speak, great Oracle:

> It doesn't matter at all. I always get worried when a song gets set in a certain way. Because to me that can just end up being habit forming, you loose [sic] where it's coming from and you get bored, so much so that we used to tape everything we played and listen to it and analyze it to make sure we hadn't missed anything. Then [we] remembered, actually, the good stuff sticks.

A Lead Role in a Cage

The dilemma that the members of Radiohead are facing as musicians right now is another facet of the crowd-pleasing problem: how to express their new music, constructed out of sound manipulations in the gravity-free world of ProTools, in the language of the stage. Radiohead's first couple of albums essentially documented material from live performances, very often road-tested before it was recorded—the demi-hit "My Iron Lung" (1994) was mostly a live recording, in fact.

OK Computer (1997) split the difference, a studio creation that doubled as arena-rock; if "Climbing Up The Walls" sounded half obliterated by a malicious subroutine, "Lucky" spawned a hundred thousand air-guitarists, and "Paranoid Android" became the junior axeman's math-rock drill of choice.

Kid A's songs, though, sound like they were devised in the studio; their essence is far from the muscle and riffage that earned Radiohead their live rep. In order to perform the new songs (and they've played them all onstage, aside from the ineffable textural doodle "Treefingers"), the band can either translate them into the fingers-and-instruments idiom, and risk losing the compositions' power and meaning, or be faithful to the recordings, and risk becoming slaves to a tape.

What Shall We Do to Fill the Empty Spaces?

At their Roseland show, the band has a few solutions worked out for translating the new material. During "The National Anthem," it brings on a massive horn section that stokes the recording's gluey free Dixieland into a four-alarm blaze; "Optimistic" 's loop becomes a continuous rumbling tattoo from drummer Phil Selway, finally exploding from the cymbals in its final minute. On the other hand, "Idioteque," which relies very heavily on a pre-programmed, Autechre-inspired beat on the album, springs out of the same can onstage. And as charismatic as Yorke is, contorting himself around his mic stand and chattering "ice age coming, ice age coming," the performance is obviously borrowed from the record's vernacular. Ditto for "Motion Picture Soundtrack," whose live incarnation was once a perfectly heartbreaking acoustic piece; the recording's faux-celestial strings and harps trickle out of the speakers at the Roseland, though they're nowhere to be seen on stage.

How does Radiohead decide when to paraphrase their records with their instruments and when to resort to prerecorded sounds? Can I get an Oracle to testify?

> We never use anything prerecorded. It's off a sequencer. It's pre-programmed but then Jonny pulls the wires out and flicks switches. How do we decide? I don't know it's all new at the moment to us.—Tchcok [sic]

Which explains nothing at all, except that they're as confused as we are.

By the Way, Which One's Pink?

The punch line is that, despite Radiohead's all-permeating abhorrence of the ultimate rock-band banality, the consumerist machine—it turns up in everything from their packaging to their advocacy of Naomi Klein's anti-branding book, *No Logo*, to the "non-branded environment" of their European tour last summer—they've got a more finely honed brand identity than any other band of the moment. The collection of *The Bends* and *OK Computer* videos is called *Seven Television Commercials*, which is a good joke, but the short "blips" they made in lieu of videos for *Kid A* genuinely are commercials: They promise an esthetic experience, where a video delivers one. The design collective that makes Radiohead T-shirts, W.A.S.T.E., is every bit as much a clothing imprint as, say, Triple 5 Soul. Radiohead even has its own icon: the little "blinkybear," the critter that resembles a cross between the Ween logo and the Grateful Dead logo. Is it a coincidence that both of those bands also empower their fans to do their marketing work for them?

Still, this kind of questioning only comes up because there's a stratospheric standard for Radiohead right now. The *Kid A* backlash started appearing a couple of weeks after its initial, rhapsodic reception. How great is the album, really? The answer is that it's so great there's a backlash. You can love Radiohead or you can hate them, but if you care enough to have heard their new incarnation, you care enough to have staked out a strong opinion on it; that's always a good sign.

And look where the strongest opinions are coming from: the members of Radiohead are fighting hard to not be like anybody else which is the mark of real artists and innovators. They're refusing the obligation we in the press pin on them to be fascinating individuals on cue, which is fair (much as we hate to admit it). But they're also fighting to be unlike what they used to be. They're struggling so hard that they're building the inveterate rebel's wall around themselves—of perfectionism, isolation, self-doubt, suspicion of anything that seems like compromise. The only backlash they have to worry about is the one from themselves.

Source: Douglas Wolk, "Mother, Should I Build a Wall? Now that Radiohead has taken Rock to New Planes, They Face a Bigger Challenge: Taking it to the Stage," *CMJ New Music Monthly*, February 2001, pp. 44–48.

63

"My Week on the Avril Lavigne E-Team"

CHRIS DAHLEN

From the late 1990s through the early 2000s, teen pop was one of the most pervasive of popular music genres. Following the groundbreaking success of Britney Spears and Christina Aguilera, the industry welcomed a wave of young female artists, ranging from the R&B pop sounds of Pink and Nelly Furtado to the more rock-oriented styles of Michelle Branch and Avril Lavigne. In his 2002 article "My Week on the Avril Lavigne E-Team," music critic Chris Dahlen examines the rapid rise up the charts of the 17-year-old Lavigne (born 1984), whose debut *Let Go* would finish as the third best-selling album of the year. Joining the Avril Lavigne "E-Team" under an assumed identity, Dahlen offers a revealing glimpse into what it means to be a pop music fan in an era of message boards, chat rooms, online communities, and interactive television programs like MTV's video countdown show *Total Request Live* (TRL), which aired between 1998 and 2008. In the process, he raises intriguing questions about the mechanisms of the industry's star-making machinery and the measurement of popularity in the Internet age. As a side note, it is worth pointing out that Dahlen's article, which originally appeared on the influential Web magazine *Pitchfork Media*, is itself indicative of rock music's move toward an increasingly online discourse.

I saw a lot of girls at my bachelor party in Montréal, but the one I was sober enough to remember was Avril Lavigne. We were watching Canadian cable in our hotel room, polishing off a case of Molsons before we went out for lunch, and as we flipped through the music stations we stumbled across Avril Lavigne's "Complicated." None of us knew who she was, and most of the guys didn't care, but I made us stop and watch.

At first glance, Avril's just another cute teen-pop star. But rather than dancing in choreographed formation with gay New Yorkers, she whizzes around on a skateboard; she's a female pop singer, but she plays with a rock band, cops a wholesome mid-80s punk look, and acts like a tomboy. She probably hangs with the outsiders at school—the kids who smoke weed, hate football and try to read Camus. No, her music isn't great, and no, she's not as punk as her record label claims. But she's spunky, sharp, and comes off as a real teen instead of a creepy blow-up doll. If I could go to school with these girls—and don't think I don't dream about it—Britney Spears is the girl I'd ogle, but Lavigne's the one I'd knock myself out to impress.

One day I was skimming through her website (because, um, I'm a rock critic, and I have to keep up on this stuff) and I found a weird ad: "Join the official Avril eTeam!" Lavigne's handlers have hired a company called the Hype Council to start a grassroots marketing effort: they're getting fans to sign up and spread the word about Avril, online. It's the same concept as a street team, where a label gets kids to blanket the city with posters and bumper stickers to promote a show or a record release. Street teams are a time-honored way to get free labor out of dedicated fans. But eTeams are more efficient, more powerful—and just as cheap.

But exactly how does it work? What's in it for us? A free t-shirt? Concert tix? Maybe, dare I dream, a chance to meet Avril? It had to be checked out.

MY LIFE AS A TEENAGE GIRL

I knew I couldn't go into this thing as a grizzled 28-year-old music snob. So step one was to create a cover for myself: I became Kate Thompson, born on July 4th, 1984, and currently living in Allston, Massachusetts (a.k.a. "Rock City!!"). All I know about being a girl is what I've learned from Judy Blume novels and the WB, but I figured I could bluff it well enough to get in the door. I set up a fake e-mail address in Kate's name and then sent in my application for TeamAVRIL.

While I waited to hear back, I also got a copy of her album, *Let Go*, and listened to it a few times. Listening as a teenage girl and not as a critic, I've got to say, it's not bad—half heartfelt angst, half high-energy spaz pop. The songs come off as honest, genuine teenage mood swings, from the crashing guitars and angst-drenched cries of "Losing Grip" to whimsical and hyper-poppy tracks like her latest hit, "Sk8er Boi." Expect to see the lyrics from "Anything but Ordinary" scribbled all over yearbooks across America's junior high schools: "To walk within the lines would make my life so boring!!/I want to know that I have been to the extreme . . . I'd rather be anything but ordinary." Lavigne's voice is pretty strong, too, as she started out singing country music, where weak pipes will get you nowhere. (But don't tell anyone about the country connection—if the kids find out, it'll be worse than if she had VD.)

And now it's my job to help push her record as far up the charts as it'll go.

MICHELLE BRANCH, YOU WANNABE, YOU'RE GOING DOWN

Within days I got—that is, Kate Thompson got—marching orders from TeamAVRIL, in a four-page long e-mail from someone named "Wag."

Wag runs TeamAVRIL on behalf of the Hype Council, and at last count, she's in charge of over 60,000 rabid Avril fans. I couldn't find a biography or a profile of her (if Wag is even a woman), but I would guess that she's an early-to-mid-twentysomething with dotcom marketing experience who was once: 1) a camp counselor; 2) on the prom committee; or 3) the plane crash survivor who ate everyone else.

Wag's there to keep the kids in line with a friendly but firm hand, encouraging us to finish our tasks and helping us through the frequent site outages and relaunches that plague the TeamAVRIL site. Every week, Wag sends us the latest news on Avril, and then gives us a list of ways to help her. From the first update, it didn't look like Lavigne needed much help: *Let Go* went double platinum the last week of August and hit #3 on the *Billboard* 200 (behind the Dixie Chicks and Eminem). The video for "Sk8er Boi" hit full rotation on MTV and made #1 on "Total Request Live," that critical gauge of teen pop fame. And best of all, as Wag wrote: "Avril won the VMA [Video Music Award] for Best New Artist!!! What an absolutely COOOOOOL night that was!"

But as Wag reminded us, "the competition wants #1. Let's heat it up!!!" And it's true: as big as Avril gets, a dozen other wannabes vie for her spot—for example, porcelain doll Michelle Branch, who, like Avril, claims she writes her own songs and never uses a stylist. Branch won MTV's 2002 Viewer's Choice and her song "Goodbye to You" is climbing the charts. Wag didn't need to spell it out: we had to put that bitch down.

So how do you help Avril? TeamAVRIL focuses on three kinds of targets: online polls, message boards, and "Total Request Live." The polls are the easiest. Many pop websites run some kind of survey where you vote for your favorite new artist; Wag has listed them all, and told us to hit them early and often. The most critical is CosmoGIRL.com's, where we're voting for nothing less than the CosmoGIRL of the Year. If Avril wins, you'll see her raccoon-eyed, necktie-sporting Canadian visage on the cover of the November issue.

I had to register on the CosmoGIRL site to vote, which means CosmoGIRL gets my (fake) registration and demographics info. But at least they send me helpful make-up and fashion tips. They've narrowed the poll options to Sarah Michelle Gellar, Gwen Stefani, Katie Holmes, Shirley Manson, and our girl Avril. Now, you may think CosmoGIRL would only give one vote to each registered visitor. Instead, they encourage you to vote up to one hundred times a day. So naturally, that's how many times I voted. I thought about tossing a couple votes to Gellar because I dig "Buffy," but she's been phoning it in for the past couple of years. In the end, all my votes went to Avril.

The next task is to look for message boards and chat rooms and barrage them with Avril propaganda. In case you're not familiar with these forums, the basic idea is that anyone in the world can go to a website with a message board or a chat room, and just start typing. For example, you may create a subject titled, "Avril RAWKS," and post a few comments about why. Then a dozen other people will come in and post messages saying, "Avril SUX." Then you write back telling them to blow themselves. This can go on for days.

There are many message boards that focus on music, and all of them, from the poppiest to the snobbiest, have at least a couple threads about Avril. Most of them are negative, taking her to task for not being "real" and not being "punk." Cocky teenagers with hit singles have to expect some amount of flak, but Avril inspires profound hatred. On the "Total Request Live" boards, punkdrummergirl15 writes: "I would love to wack her in the head with a tennis racket (the one she should be holding!) she is a freaking yuppie wannabe!!" Or from RapSmirk: "Avril Lavigne looks worse than an adult diaper with semen in it."

As an upstanding member of the team, I just kept posting back, trying to turn the tide. "She's not trying to be anything! She does what she wants—she doesn't sing songs about being a punk, she sings about being alone, or depressed, about being lonely but not wanting to act just like everyone else in her class . . ." I ended each post with, "AVRIL RAWKS! Nobody's gonna talk trash about my girl!"

THE MOST IMPORTANT FORUM IN POP—AND IT'S RUN BY IDIOTS

At the end of the week I sent in a detailed two-page status report. And then I waited, until this Monday, when I got another update and found out how we were doing. *Let Go* still holds the #3 spot on the *Billboard* 200—no movement there, but at least it hasn't slipped. Nothing much else had changed. But there was one way I could watch our progress: sit through "Total Request Live" and see if Avril's video stayed at #1.

From what I can tell, "Total Request Live" is the most important forum in teen music. It's a daily show that broadcasts live right after school, from 3:30 to 4:30. They rank and play the top ten videos of the day, ostensibly chosen by you the viewer, who can call in or vote online for your favorite music. In the days of street teams, labels encouraged the fans to call radio stations and request songs. But TeamAVRIL doesn't even bother mentioning the radio: it's too local, and no station can touch "TRL"'s influence. In addition, radio stations barely take requests, while "TRL" claims to work strictly from your votes. Granted, you only get 60 videos to choose from, but if you want to write in a vote for some weirdo indie band, there's a form for that, too.

Usually, Carson Daly hosts "TRL," but today the second stringers were in charge: up in the studio was Quddus, a bland guy who kept saying "bro" and "man" to remind us that he's black, and working the crowds on the street was a featureless twig named Hilarie. These dopes made Daly look like Cronkite.

I waded through eight crappy videos before it came down to Eminem and Avril fighting for the top spot. And Avril won! Eminem got the #2 spot with that whiny song about how his mom didn't love him as a child. Listen, Em, you goddamn bleached weasel, I've got problems, too—I don't need to hear about yours. "Sk8er Boi" topped the charts once again and we got to watch the video, where Avril flies around on a dirt bike, hangs with her band, and runs around with that silly necktie she's always wearing. I clapped and cheered. Maybe it was my 500 votes that put her over the top! Every little bit helps.

IT'S ONLY CHILD LABOR IF YOU PAY THEM

Now, this is all pretty exciting, until you look at the big picture.

What do the members of TeamAVRIL get for all their hard work and trouble? Nothing. That's right, nothing. Not even a t-shirt. At best, you're entered in a contest to *win* a t-shirt, or an autographed CD. The hardest working team member, out of all 60,000, wins an autographed guitar. But the rest of us don't get shit—not a discount, not advance orders on tickets, nothing.

The site does promise 'exclusive content' that only TeamAVRIL members can see. This might be cool for the dedicated fans that typically sign up for this kind of stuff, but when I joined, nothing was up there but a clip from the song "My World" (which is already on the album) and a personal message of thanks from Avril: "Thank you for all of your e-mails and calls to 'TRL' and [Canadian music channel] 'MuchMusic' which helped me get to #1 on both, which in turn increased record sales . . ." Wow, that came from the heart.

The only real perk is that as soon as you're accepted as a member of TeamAVRIL, you get access to their 'backstage area', where you can check your TeamAVRIL e-mail (yourname@teamavril.com— prestigious!), or access the message board. This message board seems to be the only one in the world where nobody makes fun of Avril, thereby making it some kind of refuge.

I had a blast hanging around the board. You probably want me to quote some of the funny things I read, in some kind of "16-year-old Avril Lavigne fans say the darndest things!" expose. But I won't, mainly because I wasn't any smarter or cooler at their age. Besides, apart from some arguments over whether Avril *really* plays guitar or whether she's *really* punk, it was a pretty average board. It has male and female fans, from their pre-teens to early twenties. Kids wrote in to complain about the first day of school, or make plans to meet after Avril concerts; they talked about music and posted links to their home pages.

And even though I could rant about how TeamAVRIL is scamming us, I'm willing to bet that most of the thousands of TeamAVRIL members just signed up to hang out and use the board. After all, if everyone followed orders, Avril would have 60,000 votes on the RollingStone.com "Who's Gonna Win the Pop Pack Race?" poll; instead, she got a mere 4,000, putting her far behind Anastacia and Dropline. Maybe TeamANASTACIA hands out free shirts.

CONCLUSION: WHAT A SCAM

A lot of energy gets wasted on this. It's free labor, with kids like me as the suckers who click these stupid polls and chat up Avril. And it's even worse because the company's not just after your time: they want to use you as marketing data. Even the members who do nothing have handed the Hype Council their names, ages and addresses. It never hurts to have 60,000 people come to you with their personal information, so whether or not TeamAVRIL makes a difference, the Hype Council and the record company still win.

But if the fans like Avril that much, more power to them: you can't really choose the music you like. Heck, I'll admit even I've got a soft spot for Avril after doing so much work for her. Maybe it's true what they say about missionaries: if nothing else, you end up converting yourself.

Source: Chris Dahlen, "My Week on the Avril Lavigne E-Team," *Pitchforkmedia.com*, September 12, 2002, www.pitchforkmedia.com/watw/02-09/avril.shtml.

64

"In Defense of Post-Grunge Music"

SASHA GEFFEN

In the early 2000s no style of rock music met with more critical disdain than the "post-grunge" bands that followed in the wake of '90s alternative rock icons such as Nirvana and Pearl Jam. The most successful of these groups, Nickelback, would become the best-selling rock band of the 2000s, and not coincidentally find itself routinely placed atop various lists of the world's "worst" or "most hated" bands.[1] Looking back on the post-grunge era a decade later in 2012, music critic Sasha Geffen offers a defense of the oft-maligned genre. Much like Richard Dyer's classic 1979 essay, "In Defense of Disco," Geffen approaches the music from her own personal perspective as part of a marginalized audience.[2] Where Dyer frames disco within the aesthetics of gay experience, Geffen gives voice to the many pre-teen and teenage girls who like herself once found a resonance in post-grunge's emotional palette. Given the long-entrenched biases of both gender and age that have shaped the rock canon for many decades now, Geffen's fresh alternative viewpoint urges us to consider with more nuance how and why we have been so eager to dismiss certain kinds of rock music such as post-grunge. What other kinds of rock music might benefit from similar re-examinations?

I don't have to wonder what kind of person owns a Nickelback CD because I was one. Not a standard-issue American release, either—a double album imported from Japan. There was some kind of hologram on the cover. It never got much play next to the Coldplay and U2 I was spinning, but what's weird is that my dad bought me the record. This is a guy who bases a large part of his identity on his taste in music. He owns more than 10,000 LPs. When our basement flooded, the insurance agent who surveyed our house accused him of running an underground record store because of the sheer number of records that got ruined. He's the closest real-world analogue to John Cusack's character in *High Fidelity*, and he's never shy to call contemporary rock boring and derivative. He would happily rip apart The White Stripes or The Strokes after a single chord progression, yet he bought me a Nickelback CD after hearing "How You Remind Me" on the radio every time he drove me to middle school.

---

1 For an extensive analysis of the critical animus surrounding Nickelback, see Salli Anttonen, " 'Hypocritical Bullshit Performed through Gritted Teeth': Authenticity Discourses in Nickelback's Album Reviews in Finnish Media," *Metal Music Studies*, 2, no. 1 (2016): 39–56.
2 Richard Dyer, "In Defense of Disco," in Simon Frith and Andrew Goodwin, eds., *On Record: Rock, Pop, & the Written Word* (New York: Pantheon, 1990), pp. 410–18.

Despite its canned affect and scuffed-up bombast, I liked "How You Remind Me" when I first heard it at 12. It hit me in a lonely place; I had just transitioned from a tiny, urban elementary school to a middle school in the suburbs. I had no idea how to engage with my surroundings. Suddenly, I was at a school big enough to harbor cliques. I'd never really had to stake a claim for myself in a social environment before. It was middle school and I was awkward. And, while I couldn't literally relate to most of the lyrics in "How You Remind Me"—substance abuse and dysfunctional relationships were demons I had yet to meet—the song's core loneliness resonated. "This is how you remind me of what I really am." I was stuck in a place where no one seemed to be like me, and all I wanted was to find a fundamental sameness in someone else.

I don't know if there's ever been another band maligned the way Nickelback has been maligned. They emerged as part of a moment in popular music that still functions as the perfect locus of hate for people who consider their taste to be good. Just last month, *L.A. Weekly* ran a listicle called "The 10 Worst Post-Grunge Bands."[3] Nickelback topped the thing. Of course they did. In April 2012, Chuck Klosterman went on a double-dare of music journalism and saw Creed and Nickelback on the same night, like a Greek hero sneaking into Hades.

"Over the past 20 years, there have been five bands totally acceptable to hate reflexively (and by 'totally acceptable,' I mean that the casual hater wouldn't even have to provide a justification— he or she could just openly hate them and no one would question why)," Klosterman writes.[4] He's right on all five (Bush, Hootie and the Blowfish, Limp Bizkit, Nickelback, and Creed) but I don't think the list stops there. That apparently self-explanatory loathing is focused on a whole moment, a period of time around the turn of the millennium when post-grunge kept topping the alternative charts and people who felt they knew better than the masses kept hating it with every fiber.

That moment seemed to last five years, from 1998 to 2003, when bands like Fuel, Puddle of Mudd, Lifehouse, The Calling, 3 Doors Down, Staind, and Hoobastank saw singles flicker up to the top of Billboard's Modern Rock Tracks chart. Many scored hits over on the Hot 100, too. These songs were ubiquitous, and many were so fundamentally similar to one another that they felt like one song played over and over again for five years straight. As soon as you were done with "Higher," it crept back into your car stereo as "Blurry."

Still, the lingering, unanimous aversion seems strange. Homogeneity itself isn't usually enough to provoke the hatred that the post-grunge moment still inspires, a moment that Chris Molanphy calls "possibly the most loathed period for music of the last half-century."[5] Kids who grew up in the '90s now look back glowingly on the glut of dance-pop that populated the same radio stations, and same-y soft rock bands like the Goo Goo Dolls, Third Eye Blind, and Matchbox 20 always brought on giddy waves of nostalgia at the college parties I attended. But everyone still talks about Nickelback like they were part of a scourge we were lucky to survive.

I connected to Puddle of Mudd too, a band that nearly beat out Nickelback to become the bottom-barrel offender of the post-grunge moment. "Blurry" started getting airplay in 2001, the same year as "How You Remind Me." I was in seventh grade then. "Everything's so blurry/ and everyone's so fake/ and everybody's empty/ and everything is so messed up." It was like an echo of my inner monologue. One way to defend yourself against the feeling that you don't exist is to turn

---

3 In the online publication this title links to the article: Adam Steininger, "The 10 Worst Post-Grunge Bands," *LA Weekly*, August 23, 2013, www.laweekly.com/music/the-10-worst-post-grunge-bands-4169278.

4 Here the article links to Chuck Klosterman, "A Night with the World's Most Hated Bands," *Grantland*, April 24, 2012, http://grantland.com/features/taking-concert-doubleheader-creed-nickelback-world-most-hated-bands/.

5 In the online publication, the article links to Chris Molanphy, "Radio-Friendly Unit Shifters: 25 Years of Billboard's Alternative Music Chart," *Pitchfork*, September 9, 2013, https://pitchfork.com/features/article/9214-radio-friendly-unit-shifters-25-years-of-billboards-alternative-music-chart/.

the tables and insist to yourself that you're the only one who's real. I think a lot of girls in seventh grade think up the same stuff. Puddle of Mudd nailed it. The song was a comfort. I wasn't the only person who felt the entire world around me was lonely and hollow. Some scruffy guy from Kansas City was there with me.

I hadn't yet heard of Nirvana, but their legacy was all around me. Kurt Cobain's death left an aesthetic void in alternative music that labels jumped to fill. The novelty of grunge had worn off by 1998, but its pull hadn't. In the shadow of Nirvana's fame, major labels mass-produced an alt-rock that gestured toward grunge, but lacked its rawness and nuance. These bands pissed off people with taste by dressing up in Nirvana's gruffness, while hollowing out their strangeness. Post-grunge was a surge of vanilla pop hits costumed in flannel and shaggy hair.

In his recap of the Modern Rock chart's history, Molanphy names Fuel and Puddle of Mudd as part of post-grunge's "amelodic grunting" faction. But songs like "Blurry" and "Shimmer" rely more on vocal melody than most Nirvana cuts. The vocals on "Shimmer" dart up and down the C scale while constantly modulating their syllabic density, a strategy that cuts closer to "Save Tonight" than "Smells Like Teen Spirit." In 2003, Staind released a string of singles that were easily mocked for their melodrama, or "self-righteous self-pity," as Molanphy puts it, but succeeded on the grace of their melodies. These bands hid pop songs in an aesthetic derived from *Bleach*, an album that privileged texture and energy over melody. Grunge may have fused stoner rock and punk into something that sounded like primal grunts at first listen, but post-grunge had melody. It had the same kind of melody as the bubblegum pop it followed up the charts. It was melodic pop engineered to sound like amelodic grunting.

The post-grunge moment suffered from an overpopulation of solid pop songwriters who got shoehorned into trendy, corny production choices. The formula was reliable: Most of the period's biggest hits began with a guitar arpeggio. Sometimes two guitars, an electric and an acoustic, would harmonize with each other. There were ham-fisted crashes of distorted power chords. There were drum fills that put Phil Collins to shame. Thanks to "Dumb," there were cellos. Lifehouse even sprinkled in some flutes. These memes coagulated into the perfect object of hate for music snobs. They were constant, they were everywhere, they were easy to peg as bad.

But another rift separates grunge from post-grunge. The lyrics changed. On a textual level, frontmen like Cobain and Chris Cornell opted to perform the roles of storyteller, soothsayer, and occasional comedian in lieu of strictly confessional songwriter. Grunge's heavy hitters stayed oblique on paper, outlining emotional states with loose, tangled metaphors ("Black Hole Sun," "Heart-Shaped Box") or detached third-person narratives ("Jeremy," "Daughter"—Pearl Jam was especially comfortable in this mode). Even Nirvana's first person list poem "Pennyroyal Tea" condensed its ennui into the consumables that soothed it. Cobain never sang bluntly about desire, or self-loathing, or pain. He sang about their mundane indicators. He balanced raw feeling with deadpan humor: "I tried hard to have a father/ but instead I had a dad."

Post-grunge plunged directly into the "I." There is no mystery in the lyrical narratives of Fuel, and Staind, and Lifehouse. There's only longing in its plainest terms. Most of the hits call after a prospective or past companion in the first person. There's a lot of talk about distance. "It's too far away for me to hold," sings Fuel's Brett Scallions on "Shimmer." "There's oceans in between us/ but that's not very far," Puddle of Mudd's Wes Scantlin agrees. The Calling's "Wherever You Will Go," 3 Doors Down's "Here Without You," and Audioslave's "Like A Stone" are all sung to someone from an imagined or metaphorical afterlife. Even Lifehouse's hopeful "Breathing" imagines a longing at the edge of death: "I want nothing more than to sit outside heaven's door/ and listen to you breathing."

Meanwhile, Staind and Nickelback shouted out from a personal hell, lamenting relationships ruined by substance abuse. On 2003's "It's Been Awhile," Aaron Lewis confesses, "It's been awhile since I wasn't addicted." Chad Kroeger used "How You Remind Me" to admit that he'd "been down to the bottom of every bottle." "It's Been Awhile" adopts a passive aggressive tone ("It's been awhile since I've gone and fucked things up/ just like I always do"), but "How You Remind Me" approaches apology: "It must have been so bad/ 'cause living with me must have damn near killed you." Alice in Chains' *Dirt* illustrated the throes of heroin abuse with "Junkhead" and "God Smack," but Layne Staley defended his addiction like it was a natural reaction to enlightenment: "If you let yourself go and opened your mind/ I'll bet you'd be doing like me/ and it ain't so bad." Grunge's frontmen posed with their addictions; post-grunge's songwriters sought redemption for them.

These were all songs made by tough-looking men with long hair and tattoos, ostensibly intended for an audience that was at least half male, but their lyrics echoed the confessional alt-rock made by women songwriters a few years before. Alanis Morissette rarely sang in anything but the first and second person; there was nothing oblique about her 1995 chart-topping barb "You Oughta Know," just good old-fashioned anger aimed at a very specific "you." No Doubt released "Don't Speak" in the same year, and in 1997 Sarah McLachlan looked back at her own ruined relationship with "Adia." Morissette, McLachlan, and Gwen Stefani eschewed grunge's vagueness in their songwriting. They weren't trying to be enigmatic. They sang songs to people with whom they shared emotional experiences, to express anger, or ask forgiveness, or simply to cauterize severed ties. Their alt-rock was personal, and they crystallized the songwriting strategy that would form the emotional core of the post-grunge moment.

But post-grunge didn't just share DNA with songs made by women. It fit the mold of songs made for women, too—or more specifically, songs made for teenage and pre-teen girls. At the same time that alt-rock was recuperating from the death of grunge, mainstream charts started seeing an eruption of perfectly candied boy band hits. Throughout the mid-'90s, Backstreet Boys, 98 Degrees, and 'N Sync soundtracked my childhood and millions of others. In 1999, Backstreet Boys achieved international superstardom with the single "I Want It That Way" off their now 13-times platinum record *Millennium*: the first CD I ever bought for myself.

Listening to "I Want It That Way" now, I notice fundamental similarities to the post-grunge with which it shared airplay. Like "Blurry." "Hanging By A Moment," "It's Been Awhile," and pretty much every song by Creed, "I Want It That Way" opens with a fingerpicked guitar riff. Lyrically, it focuses on a longing for a distant someone. It's full of regret for a relationship tarnished by misunderstanding. It's a dead ringer for "Blurry." "We are two worlds apart" could easily be swapped out for "there's oceans in between us" in the magnetic poetry kit of '90s lyrics. "No matter the distance, I want you to know/ that deep down inside of me/ you are my fire." "This is how you remind me/ of what I really am."

Post-grunge led me from Top 40 airwaves to Nirvana, to Soundgarden, to Alice in Chains, and to Pearl Jam, but it hooked me because it was music I already knew dressed up tough. It adopted the emotional themes and lyrical strategies of music that 12-year-old girls tend to gravitate to, and it pointed to a history of music considered sacrosanct by male critics and fans in their 20s. No wonder the post-grunge moment pissed off so many angry dudes. These bands took songs that wore signs of femininity and closed them tight inside hypermasculine shells. If there's one thing angry dudes can't stand, it's gender scraping against gender.

The genre repeated itself ad nauseum, and plenty of its affect feels contrived. But, it rings with me because it posits a masculinity that's content to state its intentions and let the object of its affection make her decision. "Even if you don't want to speak tonight/ that's alright, alright with me," sings Jason Wade on "Breathing." On "Like A Stone," Cornell promises "in your house/ I long to be/ room by room/ patiently/ I'll wait for you there." These aren't love songs about imposing your will on somebody else, about "winning" anybody. They're passive displays of affection. Maybe that's what prompted one reviewer, on one of those early-aughts websites with black backgrounds whose gimmick was making brutal fun of everything, to call Audioslave's debut "cock rock for pussies." Audioslave made their share of weak production choices—the rhythm section on "Like A Stone" sounds like they'd be more comfortable in a classic hip-hop outfit—but did we have to drag everybody's genitals into it?

I can make fun of "It's Been Awhile" with the rest of them—these dudes tended to sing like they were dredging mud up from the back of their throats, I'll admit—but I can't rag on Staind's "Zoe Jane." This is a ballad from Aaron Lewis to his daughter about how he wants to be a better father, how he wants a better life for her than the one he had. "I want to hold you/ protect you from all of the things I've already endured." This is dad rock in the purest sense. He sings it like he means it, like it's the only thing he means.

Even "Blurry" and "Shimmer" feel warm when I listen to them now. There's a comfort in hearing corporate alt-rock with a little more lyrical nuance than, say, Imagine Dragons, a little less mismatched aggression than AWOLNATION. Sometimes turning on alternative radio these days feels like getting hit in the face. There's a comfort in hearing Nickelback from when they meant something to me, when Kroeger still sounded like he was apologizing for mistreating women instead of indulging in full-blown misogyny. There's a comfort in hearing songs written during a time when you could miss someone completely, when you couldn't check up on their online presence, when it was still possible to have no idea where someone was or what they were doing.

This feeling is at least part nostalgia; after all, I seem to have no trouble getting behind hate for the folk rock and brostep poles that are churning out the Nickelbacks of today. I'm not above reflexive disdain for music beloved by people who hear something different than I do. But, post-grunge was my hinge into alternative as it existed before the term got swallowed up by the mainstream. I'm not mad that it got me there. I was on the inside of that hatefest. Maybe it's awful, but if it's an awful that works for sad girls in seventh grade, it's an awful I'll own.

Source: Sasha Geffen, "In Defense of Post-Grunge Music." *Consequence of Sound*, October 7, 2013, consequenceofsound.net/aux-out/in-defense-of-post-grunge-music/.

65

Defining Emo

Urban Dictionary

When emo, an "emotional" or "emotive" underground punk-oriented style dating back to the mid-1980s, erupted into the mainstream in the early 2000s via popular releases from artists like Dashboard Confessional and My Chemical Romance, the genre generated more intense debate, and attracted more scorn, than arguably any other rock music of the decade. Those who attacked emo generally took aim at the culture surrounding the music, specifically the stereotypes of "melodramatic" male fans and their cross-gender fashion and appearance, elements that amplified the unease that American society (and especially rock's teenage audience) has traditionally felt in dealing with expressions of emotional masculinity. In an earlier era, the fan discourse around such a contested genre might have unfolded in the letters section of some rock magazine like *Creem*, but by the 2000s much of that discussion had migrated to the internet, where message boards and websites provided a faster, looser and more freely flowing forum for the exchange of opinions. The emo definitions that comprise this chapter come from one of the more heavily trafficked user-generated content (UGC) websites of the 2000s, the slang reference *Urban Dictionary*. All of the website's entries follow a prescribed format: the user (identified on the site by a pseudonym) provides a definition, and then in italics gives an example of the word in context. While the *Urban Dictionary* users take a variety of stances towards emo, most agree that the label is problematic. As one user mentions, what music does *not* have an emotional basis; could we not consider nearly *any* musical artist or endeavor to be emo? If that is the case, then why exactly *are* we inclined to hear some rock music as more emotional than others? What are the stylistic elements, expressive gestures and cultural codes that ensured that certain artists, bands and their fans would be lumped together under the emo label?

Emo

Genre of softcore punk music that integrates unenthusiastic melodramatic 17 year olds who dont smile, high pitched overwrought lyrics and inaudible guitar rifts with tight wool sweaters, tighter jeans, itchy scarfs (even in the summer), ripped chucks with favorite bands signature, black square rimmed glasses, and ebony greasy unwashed hair that is required to cover at least 3/5 ths of the face at an angle.

::sniff sniff:: "The Demise of the Siberian Traintracks of Our Rusty Forgotten Unblemished Love" sounds like it would make a great emo band name. ::cry::

by **7ThisIsWudie7** Jun 8, 2003

* * *

Like a Goth, only much less dark and much more Harry Potter.

My life sucks, I want to cry.

by **Lockesly** Apr 6, 2004

* * *

Punk music on estrogen. Often acoustic guitar with soft, high male vocals that dwell exessively on the singer's feelings, especially melancholy remembrances of past relationships/mistakes in life. A form of music that diverged from punk in the '80s, the name "emo" is derived from the emotive style of the lyrics and music. This genre has lately been marketed heavily by the music industry to teenagers with bands such as Dashboard Confessional and Taking Back Sunday, and has seen much commercial and mainstream success. The music has also spawned a subculture which conforms to certain conventions in dress such as tight sweatshirts, tight band T-shirts and horn-rim glasses. Adherents profess to exessively melancholy temperments. Males that adhere to the emo subculture are sometimes confused with metrosexuals; indeed the line between the two is somwhat blurred, though both groups claim to be intouch with their emotional side. The ephemeral and hackneyed nature of emo songwriting suggests that its audience will be restricted largely to teenagers. the genre suffers from a lack of credibility outside the aforementioned demographic group, much like current Nu Metal bands.

girlfriend: C'mon, lets have sex.
boyfriend: I'm too sad to have sex.
girlfriend: I'm sad too; lets have sex and cry.
boyfriend: I'm already crying.

by **Pureblarney** Jul 30, 2004

* * *

Emo is genre of hardcore punk music started in the mid eighties by a band called Rites Of Spring. Their lead singer had been a big fan of the band Minor Threat, and after their breakup, had decided to start his own band. It was similar in the musical sense, however the lyrics were different. Instead of spitting about politics and anti-capitalist themes, the lyrics were more personal, and hateful towards themselves. This new music managed to drive away many old punk fans, and attract many new ones.

The DC emo scene exploded and became excessively popular amongst the underground. However, it fizzled out almost as fast as it had begun.

In the early 90's, two new bands, Sunny Day Real Estate and Jawbreaker, started the new wave of emo music. SDRE started the "post indie emo" genre. Bands that can be categorized under this genre could be Texas Is The Reason, Taking Back Sunday, Mineral and other music following those lines, that are often confused for emo.

Jawbreaker were the new wave of emo revival, although still remotley underground, the music continues to be popular with the people who can search it out.

Thanks to MTV, the perception of what real emo is has been completely changed and most people do not understand what it is, automatically assuming that DASHBOARD CONFESSIONAL or anyone else with an acoustic singing about breakup is emo. Emo isn't pussy music, it's heartfelt, and hardcore at the same time. An angry emotional release of self loathing and self depreciation.

The style of music that band played was pretty similar to the emo stuff that Rites did.

by **Maya** Feb 14, 2005

* * *

"Emo" is not short for "Emotional." "Emo" does not mean Taking Back Sunday and Dashboard Confessional, despite what MTV has lead you to believe in the last few years. "Emo" is not sidebangs, tight pants, and male vocalists who sing like little girls about their failed relationships. "Emo" is not the use of diluted, meaningless metaphors and similes such as "My arms are like pinecones," and most definitely is not the rampant use of words such as "autumn," "heart," "knife," "bleeding," "leaves," and "razorblade."

I just thought I'd clear that up after all of these "definitions" in which I have encountered an unbelievable amount of people who try to pass off their blatantly false pretenses as fact, and are slowly infecting others with their high-horse, holier-than-thou bullshit. Because honestly, with your ridiculous definitions, Beethoven, George Gershwin, and Britney Spears are/was "emo bands."

Now, onto the real definition.

In the early 90s there was a movement in the hardcore genre that came to be known as "Emotive Hardcore," spearheaded by Rites Of Spring. Harder-core-than-thou kids, who swore by Dischord Records a la Minor Threat, actually coined the term "Emo" as something of a put-down for the kids who really liked Rites Of Spring, Indian Summer and this new wave of "Emotive" Hardcore bands. That's right, "Emo" was once not something kids called themselves. The field exploded outwards from there—Level-Plane Records has always been the most famous Emo label. Acts like Yaphet Kotto, I Hate Myself, Saetia, Hot Cross, A Day In Black And White, Funeral Diner, I Would Set Myself On Fire For You, You And I, and hosts of others came in the next decade. Most emo bands have since broken up, but there's still the occasional hold-out (again, the majority of Level-Plane Records' roster has been a procession of emo acts). Like most DIY hardcore/punk of the time, a majority found its way onto vinyl and not much else. Some people consider bands like Fugazi, and later Sunny Day Real Estate, a progression of emo, but personally, I don't quite follow that philosophy.

Often, more recently, this gets intertwined with post-hardcore, and understandably so—that's nothing to make an issue of, since well shit, at least it's close.

Since the late 90s, though, bands have been emerging in the vein of Taking Back Sunday, Dashboard Confessional, and the thousands of their clones. As far as I can tell, some lazy journalist somewhere, writing an article about them, decided "Well, fuck, no one knows what emo is anyways, so I'll call these bands 'emo'—sounds more appealing than bubblegum pop rock . . ." and the spiral continued downwards into the current amalgomation of bands MTV has told everyone is "emo."

Somehow, people decided that "emo" meant "emotional," which is obviously bullshit, as 99% of bands make music to illicit emotion, which would make "emotional" a completely all-encompassing genre from classical to opera to pop to rap.

Hope that helps.

Taking Back Sunday, Senses Fail, and My Chemical Romance falls under the "horrible pop rock" genre, not the emo genre.
Rites of Spring is emo.

by **Chelsea** Mar 2, 2005

* * *

(adjective) attention seeking pseudo-depressive individuals (usually middle-class teenage boys) who cry about how they can't get laid, and hate their parents. Usually self-indulgent losers who mistake artless public descriptions of their "emotional depth" and "suffering" for genuine sophistication. If they really are that miserable, they could try listening to The Smiths. At least they were witty.

"I'm not talking to you—you're not emo enough!" (I've actually overheard someone saying this).

by **Joemanji** Apr 4, 2006

*   *   *

a musical genre/ scene that has almost 1000 definitions in urban dictionary most of which are making fun of it

im gonna add another definition for emo cuz 1000 isnt enough

by **burgerking2** Jun 25, 2006

*   *   *

Something that all stereotypes agree on they hate.

Metalheads, preps, jocks, punk rockers and goths all put aside their differences and agree on one thing: they hate emos.

by **andrea-** Jul 3, 2006

*   *   *

A stupid trend. Followers of this trend, often referred to as emo kids, think they are "alternative" (how is that possible when MTV stirred it all up?), when infact they are just as much sheeps as the preps. All emo kids look the same. They share the exact same values. They listen to the same horrible bands. Is that to be an individual? Is that unique? No. Most don't even know the origins of emo. Many of them claim they are "non-conformists". These days, "non-conformist" has lost its true meaning and is just another synonym for poser. How does supporting major clothing lines such as Hot Topic make you a non-conformist? You are the antithesis of that. Wake up. The emo trend is like hair-metal; in a few years you'll burn all pictures of yourself, being so ashamed that you had such an ugly haircut.

The third-wave emo movement is a testimony on how MTV (Manipulating Teenage Views) is able to pick up just about anything and mold it into a trend in order to make money, even if this results in mindless teenagers who can't think for themselves and destroying what's left of the real music scenes.

by **andrea 91** Jul 10, 2006

*   *   *

Attention whores. Kids and young adults who really don't have any actual problems, and instead decide to use their creativity, or lack thereof, to craft false problems.

Emo kids are mostly seen with acoustic guitars and My Chemical Romance attire, as well as black hair that simply screams "kick me in the balls as hard as you can".

High-pitch nasally voice can often be heard uttering the words "You just don't understand", followed by the sound of slamming door, then muffled whimpering as the individual proceeds to scratch their wrist, hoping you'll take notice of their weak and futile efforts to portray suicide and/or self-mutilation.

But most notably, Emos keep records of their so-called "problems" in diaries. These records mostly include pointless whiny rants:

"Dear Diary, those stupid jocks at school think I'm gay. Why can't they understand that heterosexual boys like me just like to kiss other heterosexual boys once in a while. They're so mean, and it depresses me . . . They say I'm Emo, even though I'm just misunderstood."

sniff *scratch*

"They just don't understand"

"And Karen dumped me today. She says I'm the perfect guy, and that I'm always there for her, just like when her Chimichangas were too cold, and she ended up cutting her wrist out of shear depression. She says it's not me, it's her. She says I'm too good for her. I love her so much . . . I think I'll express my undying love for her by throwing my pillows and crying . . . and perhaps I'll write a love song and sing it off-key . . ."

sniff

by **2phast** Jul 18, 2006

*   *   *

The word that holds the record for the most definitions at urbandictionary.com at 1,181.

Come on. Cheer up, emo kid.

by **Marshall Rousso** Sep 20, 2006

*   *   *

The other 1200 definitions explain the term itself and its origins better than I can here, but it is important to note that the music and accompanying culture currently labeled "emo" by the press and popular media (as well as by the kids themselves) is essentially the same music and culture we all would have simply referred to as "alternative" a decade ago, and which has been shoveled into the media-created pigeonhole formerly occupied by the (arguably artificial) subgenre of "alternative" music known as "grunge" back in the '90s.

My sister's boyfriend swears he's too emo to watch MTV, but I know he got his Vans at the mall.

by **Panic! In My Pants** Jan 27, 2007

Source: "Emo," *Urban Dictionary* www.urbandictionary.com/define.php?term=Emo%20

66

"Even Heavy-Metal Fans Complain that Today's Music Is Too Loud!!!"

Evan Smith

Loudness has long been an idealized sonic quality of rock recordings. As the Rolling Stones implored on the record jacket of 1969's *Let It Bleed*: "This Record Should be Played Loud." While loudness in the rhetoric of rock is generally associated with an aesthetic of the sublime—of one that overwhelms a listener with awe-inspiring power—its prevalence has also created an environment where record labels and their artists have striven to be louder than their competitors. As this competition waged throughout the 1990s and early 2000s, recording engineers increasingly employed digital means to create a hyper-compressed, or "hot" sound designed to give the artists an edge on FM rock radio. As Evan Smith details in his article for the *Wall Street Journal*, this instigated a "loudness war" that reached a tipping point with the 2008 release of Metallica's *Death Magnetic*, an album whose lack of dynamic range, and resultant distortion and digital clipping, represented to many fans, audiophiles, and even the engineers themselves, the worst of this tendency toward increased loudness.[1] In the years since, the loudness war has been a subject of intense debate not just for new releases, but especially for those remastered reissues that have arguably compromised the original recordings by attempting to match the sonic standards of newer, louder rock bands. As the article mentions, the loudness war was partially enmeshed in arguments that prized the authenticity of analog recording and vinyl that had gone missing in the move toward digital technology and compact discs. Given the steady decline of CD sales in recent years, and the diminished importance of FM rock radio, it is worth considering to what extent the loudness war remains an issue. How does the sound of *Death Magnetic* and other loud recordings from the mid-2000s compare with more recent rock music?

Can a Metallica Album Be Too Loud?

The very thought might seem heretical to fans of the legendary metal band, which has been splitting eardrums with unrivaled power since the early 1980s.

---

1 For a good summary of the "loudness war" in the 2000s, see Greg Milner, *Perfecting Sound Forever: An Aural History of Recorded Music* (New York: Faber and Faber, 2009). On the longer historical meanings of the "loudness war," see Kyle Devine, "Imperfect Sound Forever: Loudness Wars, Listening Formations and the History of Sound Reproduction," *Popular Music*, 32, no. 2 (2013), pp. 159–76.

But even though Metallica's ninth studio release, "Death Magnetic," is No. 1 on the album chart, with 827,000 copies sold in two weeks, some fans are bitterly disappointed: not by the songs or the performance, but the volume. It's so loud, they say, you can't hear the details of the music.

"Death Magnetic" is a flashpoint in a long-running music-industry fight. Over the years, rock and pop artists have increasingly sought to make their recordings sound louder to stand out on the radio, jukeboxes and, especially, iPods.

But audiophiles, recording professionals and some ordinary fans say the extra sonic wallop comes at a steep price. To make recorded music seem louder, engineers must reduce the "dynamic range," minimizing the difference between the soft and loud parts and creating a tidal wave of aural blandness.

"When there's no quiet, there can be no loud," said Matt Mayfield, a Minnesota electronic-music teacher, in a YouTube video that sketched out the battle lines of the loudness war.[2] A recording's dynamic range can be measured by calculating the variation between its average sound level and its maximum, and can be visually expressed through wave forms. Louder recordings, with higher average sound levels, leave less room for such variation than quieter ones.

Some fans are complaining that "Death Magnetic" has a thin, brittle sound that's the result of the band's attempts in the studio to make it as loud as possible. "Sonically it is barely listenable," reads one fan's online critique. Thousands have signed an online petition urging the band to re-mix the album and release it again.

Metallica and the album's producer, Rick Rubin, declined to comment. Cliff Burnstein, Metallica's co-manager, says the complainers are a tiny minority. He says 98% of listeners are "overwhelmingly positive," adding: "There's something exciting about the sound of this record that people are responding to."

But the critics have inadvertently recruited a key witness: Ted Jensen, the album's "mastering engineer," the person responsible for the sonic tweaks that translate music made in a studio into a product for mass duplication and playback by consumers. Responding to a Metallica fan's email about loudness, Mr. Jensen sent a sympathetic reply that concluded: "Believe me, I'm not proud to be associated with this one." The fan posted the message on a Metallica bulletin board and it quickly drew attention.

Mr. Jensen regrets his choice of words but not the sentiment. "I'm not sure I would have said quite the same thing if I was posting it to the bulletin board," he says. But "it's certainly the way I feel about it."

The battle has roots in the era before compact discs. With vinyl records, "it was impossible to make loud past a certain point," says Bob Ludwig, a veteran mastering engineer. But digital technology made it possible to squeeze all of the sound into a narrow, high-volume range. In addition, music now is often optimized for play on the relatively low-fidelity earbuds for iPods, reducing incentives to offer a broad dynamic range.

The loudness war began heating up around the time CDs gained popularity, in the early 1980s. Guns N' Roses' "Appetite for Destruction" upped the ante in 1987, as did Metallica's 1991 "Black Album" and then the Red Hot Chili Peppers' "Californication" in 1999.

Music released today typically has a dynamic range only a fourth to an eighth as wide as that of the 1990s. That means if you play a newly released CD right after one that's 15 years old, leaving the volume knob untouched, the new one is likely to sound four to eight times as loud. Many who've

---

2 Matt Mayfield, "The Loudness War," *YouTube*, uploaded by Matt Mayfield Music, October 7, 2006, www.youtube. com/watch?v=3Gmex_4hreQ.

followed the controversy say "Death Magnetic" has one of the narrowest dynamic ranges ever on an album.

Sound engineers say artists who insist on loudness paradoxically give people less to hear, because they end up wiping away nuances and details. Everything from a gently strummed guitar to a pounding snare drum is equally loud, leading to what some call "ear fatigue." If the listener turns down the volume knob, the music loses even more of its punch.

But many musicians, producers and record-company executives "think that having a louder record is going to translate into greater sales," says Chris Athens, Mr. Jensen's business partner and a fellow engineer. "Nobody really wants to have a record that's not as loud as everybody else's" in an iTunes playlist, he adds.

Mastering engineers are caught in the crossfire. "I've had lots of people—I mean lots and lots of people—try and push a record to a place I thought it didn't belong," Mr. Athens says. "We try to deliver something that mitigates the damage the client wants. I drag my feet and give them something a little louder and a little louder."

Albums by some of the biggest names in rock, including the most recent by U2, Bruce Springsteen and Paul McCartney, have drawn flak. Bloggers last year singled out Mr. Ludwig, the veteran engineer, for the sound on Mr. Springsteen's "Magic," which some thought was tinny and loud.

Mr. Ludwig wouldn't discuss the instructions he was given, but said, "Bruce doesn't let anything out unless it's exactly the way he wants it to be." Mr. Springsteen and his manager, Jon Landau, declined through a spokeswoman to comment.

As for the deafening "Death Magnetic," it struck one fan as fitting for these tumultuous times, thanks to songs like "Broken, Beat and Scarred" and "All Nightmare Long," says Metallica's co-manager, Mr. Burnstein. He says an investment banker emailed to say that "the album and its song titles have just become the soundtrack of Wall Street for fall 2008."

Source: Evan Smith, "Even Heavy-Metal Fans Complain that Today's Music Is Too Loud!!!," *The Wall Street Journal*, September 25, 2008, www.wsj.com/news/articles/SB122228767729272339.

67

The Whiteness of Indie and the "Myth of Vampire Weekend"

PAUL LESTER

When we last encountered indie music at the end of the 1990s (in Chapters 59 and 60), it was a decidedly underground movement existing on the margins of the mainstream. Over the course of the 2000s, however, indie became one of rock's most prominent genres as groups such as Bright Eyes, the Shins, Arcade Fire and Vampire Weekend all landed releases in the *Billboard* Top 10 album chart, a previously unheard-of feat for such small-scale artists. With this new visibility came an increased scrutiny of the culture surrounding indie, specifically what many perceived to be its overwhelming whiteness—an association made clear by indie music's inclusion in the 2008 satirical book *Stuff White People Like*.[1] The connection between indie music and whiteness takes center stage in Paul Lester's profile of Vampire Weekend, and their second album *Contra*, for British newspaper *The Guardian*. As Lester's conversation with the group's front man Ezra Koenig (born 1984), makes clear, the definition of whiteness is difficult to pin down. Is it simply a matter of race or ethnicity? If so, then how can a group like Vampire Weekend, with both Jewish and Persian members, simply be considered white? Or do we define whiteness by such things as class, economic status, and appearance, as seen in the band's Ivy League Columbia University pedigree and "preppy" fashion? Is the band's musical cultivation of Afropop and other styles a refusal to conform to any monolithic understanding of rock, or, as their critics maintain, is this very eclecticism only made possible through the band's aura of educated white privilege? Given the recent appearance of articles such as "The Unbearable Whiteness of Indie," it is clear these issues remain a central point of contention within indie music.[2]

Vampire Weekend are being mobbed in California. By teenage girls. In a skate park normally frequented by crystal meth addicts. What makes this so unexpected is that Vampire Weekend are not a band you would associate with California, teenage girls, skate parks or crystal meth. In fact, they stand for a completely opposite set of values: as cerebral New Yorkers, as rejecters of rock cliché, as combiners of bright pop melodies and African rhythms, as writers of songs exploring ideas about architecture and grammar, class difference and social status.

---

1 Christian Lander, *Stuff White People Like: A Definitive Guide to the Unique Taste of Millions* (New York: Random House, 2008), pp. 49–50.
2 Sarah Sahim, "The Unbearable Whiteness of Indie," *Pitchfork*, March 25, 2015, https://pitchfork.com/thepitch/710-the-unbearable-whiteness-of-indie/.

The band have just played a gig showcasing tracks from their imminent second album, *Contra*, on a chilly evening in a town called Lake Elsinore, about an hour and a half outside LA. Instead of retreating to the hut that serves as their dressing room, they have chosen to spend 45 minutes in the freezing cold signing autographs for fans.

"Oh my god, sign my shoe!" pleads one girl, removing a white Converse All-Star and handing it to bassist Chris Baio with a pen. The group's other Chris – drummer Chris Tomson, wearing a sensible red cardigan – scrawls on a crumpled dollar bill. Keyboard player Rostam Batmanglij is being asked to make his mark on a mobile phone. Meanwhile, over at a makeshift merchandise stand, band T-shirts are selling fast to fans requiring a larger canvas for their Vampire Weekend signatures.

One eager young female has rather more ambitious, intimate designs: can she get a photo of singer-guitarist Ezra Koenig planting a kiss on her lips? He politely declines, giving her a big, brotherly hug instead. "I don't want to get into trouble with my girlfriend," he explains with a slightly nervous smile.

The small yet fervent crowd comprises a range of indie types, from the smartly collegiate to emo kids and punks with more radical clothes and hair. But no one hides their excitement at the band's decision to unveil their new songs in this featureless suburb as part of a mini-tour of the less trodden parts of California. It is treated like a visitation from four young gods.

"Look at Ezra's pockets," gasps one girl when she sees Koenig re-emerge from the hut wearing a coat. She whispers conspiratorially to a friend: "They're huge! I bet he has snacks in there for when he's hungry." Earlier, when I asked a couple of girls during the gig why they liked the band so much, their answer was simple. "Because they're so clever," said one. "And we love their lyrics," added the other. What, I asked, did they imagine those songs were about? "We have no idea," they replied, and carried on bopping along to the music.

The band's genius is to make even their most cryptic songs utterly infectious. On their 2008 debut album – which sold half a million copies in the US, went gold in Britain, and arguably made it possible in 2009 for the likes of Dirty Projectors (with whom Koenig toured in the early days), Grizzly Bear and Animal Collective to enjoy their most successful year to date – serious subjects were placed in perky, sunny contexts, so it didn't matter whether or not you "got" them.

The problem for some listeners came when they did pay close attention: were the songs meant to be critiquing or celebrating middle-class liberal values? The use of African and West Indian music idioms by these self-styled exponents of "Upper West Side Soweto" further complicated the issue, even as the tunes came bubbling out of student halls and shop PAs: here were songs about colonialism and privilege buoyed along by rhythms and melodies taken from the colonised and underprivileged. It was to Vampire Weekend's credit that they didn't so much hide their affluent credentials as wear them on their Ralph Lauren shirt sleeves. They came not to perpetuate the myth of the rock'n'roll rebel – "a withered archetype", as Tomson puts it – but to bury it to a soundtrack of Congolese soukous music while modelling finest preppy wear.

"The way I look at it is: it's my God-given right to wear a cricket sweater just as it is my right to wear a [Ralph Lauren] Polo shirt," asserts Koenig at a Chinese restaurant the day after the skate-park siege and an hour before another out-of-town gig, this one mercifully indoors. "And part of why I'm so into these clothes is that they are more complicated than people think – Ralph Lauren was the son of Russian Jewish immigrants who grew up in the Bronx not far from where my dad grew up."

For Koenig it's "a joke" to see himself and the band endlessly paraded as sons and heirs of outrageous good fortune. "My dad grew up in a working-class Jewish neighbourhood," he says, "and I got a scholarship from my dad's union to go to college. I went there to get an education, not as an extension of privilege." Tomson, joining our table, says he grew up on a farm in New Jersey, while Batmanglij's parents were forced to flee Iran in 1979, and Baio is of Italian stock – his dad, a child actor, was Davy Jones's understudy in a stage version of *Oliver!* and appeared in an episode of The Monkees television series.

Koenig, however, is generous in understanding how the band have come to be perceived in the way they have. "Because we favour certain ways of dressing and don't shy away from using obscure words and we went to Columbia University, people have put all the elements together and prejudged us as privileged white kids, even using the word 'Wasp', which immediately implies privilege," he says. "Those things, juxtaposed with our interest in world music, have made it very easy for people to raise the flag of colonialism or imperialism. But the two main writers in the band are Jewish and Persian, which is a pretty broad definition of 'whiteness'. We're certainly not all fresh off the Mayflower."

Koenig has a theory that his most ardent detractors – "mostly," he guesses, "white, college-educated critics" – are just using Vampire Weekend for some easy point-scoring. "They don't often get the chance to be activists, so when they see us come along, it provides them with a brilliantly simple opportunity to be activists: 'This is an outrage! These people are exploitative!' Of course people should be on guard for exploitation, but . . ." Their argument has one tiny flaw, Koenig suggests: "They're attacking a version of us that doesn't actually exist – the myth of Vampire Weekend."

Critics of the band have often failed to notice that, far from being superior, they use their songs to highlight the contradictions of class and wealth, with Koenig, in particular, adopting the position of the boy in the middle, as likely to gaze up at those with more advantages above him on the social scale as he is at those below. This sense of dual perspective is made clearer on *Contra*, and the music is given more force by a greater use of electronics and more focused arrangements by an increasingly confident Batmanglij, the band's producer.

"Perspective is a huge part of what our band is about," he says. "And I hope we explore it in all the music we make." He cites two Pulp songs as examples of the breadth of vision Vampire Weekend have tried to achieve on *Contra*. "I love Disco 2000: 'Oh Deborah, do you recall/ That your house was very small?' – there he [Jarvis Cocker] is looking down on Deborah, whereas in Common People he's the common one. And there you have it: both viewpoints! There's always going to be someone more oppressed or 'outside' than you."

Koenig remembers feeling that he had "less than other people", growing up in a "pretty modest" home on a street with its fair share of big houses, whose residents were members of exclusive country clubs. "My family," he says, "weren't part of that." Did he long to be living a more privileged life? "To an extent."

He admits that, as a child, he would dreamily draw up intricate floor plans for a mansion that remained forever out of his family's reach. His background and hard-grafting parents have bequeathed him an appreciation of perspective, as well as the importance of context and nuance. The default position of rock music is the easily struck pseudo-revolutionary posture. For Vampire Weekend, life is a little more complex than that. They have called their second album *Contra*, as a gently mocking rebuke to those who might want to adopt a simpler us-versus-them pose.

"On this album, there are songs that deal with wealth and rich girls, but I wanted a more nuanced approach," says Koenig, who writes all the lyrics.

> "They're not pure revenge or you-rich-bitch songs. You can't blame other people, no matter what your upbringing was like. We called the album Contra because it would be very easy to say it's about me versus rich people, but it's more complicated than that. We're trying to have sympathy and compassion, and to be more realistic. There aren't that many people walking about who are a total class stereotype."

The best track on *Contra*, and possibly the best thing Vampire Weekend have ever done, is a sublime slice of digital dancehall with strings and sweet doo-wop harmonies, called Diplomat's Son, the title seemingly flaunting the very thing the band are accused of being: a bunch of old-money toffs. In a way, it's their two fingers up to the tired idea of being a two-fingers-up band. Making the album has given them the confidence to embrace who and what they are.

"It's just as natural for us to listen to music from Africa as it is to Cream or whoever," argues Koenig.

> "There's no reason why Cream should be a bigger part of my heritage – my family is from eastern Europe and grew up in New Jersey and Eric Clapton is a British guy playing the blues. When you break it down like that, the rock'n'roll canon becomes a little less monolithic. Just because I grew up a white guy in America doesn't mean that's the music of my life."

He acknowledges that, when it comes to music and culture, "you have to be careful describing it in racial terms" – but he can't help wondering whether "the electric guitar is a white or black instrument – after all, it's used by people of all colours, in African music and in punk rock. And does that mean punk rock is a white genre? I have to admit," he says, feigning shame, "I do obsess about these things."

Batmanglij has become obsessed with how to cram as many tricksy, original rhythms as possible on to one album, and how to avoid the pratfalls so many second albums succumb to. "There are rules that are so blatantly broken on *Contra*," he says, "like structures of harmony and texture." But the intention has been "to make the catchiest music we can. Classical music can be catchy, so can African instrumental guitar music. It's not just pop songs that are catchy. Rhythms can be catchy, too." He welcomes the prospect of Vampire Weekend's further mainstream penetration, and proudly recalls hearing a group of kids crossing the road in Chicago, humming the guitar solo from Oxford Comma.

It makes sense that Koenig should describe *Contra* as a more "mature" record than the debut, one that deals with what happens when the callow youths of the first album are forced to face the quandaries of life after college. During three days in California, I never see any of the four members behave with anything less than perfect decorum. But maybe that's because the preppy clothes mislead about more than the band's attitudes to colonialism and make observers assume that rejecting the two-fingers-up model of rock music means the band must necessarily reject everything about rock music.

A month after the California trip, following a tour of Japan and Australia, Koenig calls me with a story about how wrong people can be. "I remember once being at a festival in Spain, where people were going absolutely crazy," he says.

> "We played at 2am; there were drugs and alcohol everywhere, and this woman asked if I wanted a beer. And I said sure, and she was like, 'Really?' She said, 'I had such an impression that the people in your band would all be strait-laced virgins.' I was like, 'What?!' It just goes to show what a wrong impression you can get from a buttoned-down shirt."

Source: Paul Lester, "Vampire Weekend: 'They're Attacking a Version of Us that Doesn't Exist'," *The Guardian*, January 7, 2010, www.theguardian.com/music/2010/jan/07/vampire-weekend-contra.

68

"Why Country Is the New Classic Rock"

STEVE LEFTRIDGE

Rock and country have long had a complicated relationship. In the late 1950s the Nashville music industry portrayed rock 'n' roll as a threat to the country audience, but by a decade later Nashville had emerged as an important influence on rock, as musicians such as Bob Dylan and the Byrds traveled to record with the city's top session musicians, and a country rock hybrid soon emerged popularized by west coast groups such as the Eagles. Despite these affinities, by the late 1970s and '80s, the rise of arena rock and heavy metal suggested little, if any, shared ground with country. However, as Steve Leftridge explains in his feature for the online cultural criticism magazine *PopMatters*, in recent decades as alternative and indie rock musicians have rejected many of arena rock's most iconic features—its guitar solos, celebratory hedonism and flare for live spectacles— country artists have begun incorporating these very same classic rock markers into their music. Country stars such as Brad Paisley, Keith Urban and Gretchen Wilson regularly feature classic rock riffs and covers as part of their live sets, and the television show *CMT Crossroads* routinely pairs classic rock bands such as Journey with contemporary country acts such as Rascal Flatts. Still, as Leftridge points out, for all of country's recent classic rock nostalgia, it is still married with the country traditionalism of fiddles and farms. It is thus worth asking whether country audiences have simply embraced rock music as part of their generational experience, or, as Leftridge hints, if country's new legion of stars are primed to fill a void left vacant by rock music itself.

In Mark Wills' 2003 hit "19 Something," Wills waxed nostalgic about the '80s, cataloging Reagan-era American pop-culture touchstones, one of which was "watch[ing] MTV all afternoon." It was a revealing claim, given what aired on MTV afternoons in the late '80s when Wills was a teenager. What he had to have been watching, for the most part, were pop-metal videos, which at that time dominated the *Dial MTV* charts, which counted down the top ten most-requested videos of the day.

The fact that Wills listened to "Livin' on a Prayer" and "Pour Some Sugar on Me" for hours on end and that his '80s nostalgia takes him back to Adam Curry rather than Ralph Emery, shouldn't be entirely surprising, however.[1] After all, anyone who spends time with modern country radio

---

1 Adam Curry was the host of *Dial MTV* in the late 1980s. Ralph Emery was a country music broadcaster and television personality who hosted the talk show *Nashville Now* from 1983 to 1993.

understands that the bulk of today's country hits have way more in common, sonically, with Bon Jovi than they do with George Jones.

Country artists, labels, programmers, etc., have pulled off something of a marketing revolution. It's an industry that's fighting for profitable business models, and that is to corner the die-hard classic-rock market. That's quite a coup, considering the massive shift that has crossed over from rock to country, not just involving '70s and '80s soldiers like Wills—folks now in their 30s and 40s—but their own children, born in the '90s and beyond, who are themselves drawn to the timeless appeal of the big drums, guitar solos, anthemic chants, hedonistic lyrics, giant choruses, and shiny production values that have sold out arenas for the last 50 years.

The accessibility of classic-rock forms defined by an incorporation of country elements is nothing particularly new, since bands like the Eagles and Lynyrd Skynyrd obviously proved such a blend's viability decades ago. What's interesting now is not that rock bands straddle a country-rock line that appeals to country listeners, or that country singers can be pop enough to crossover to pop charts the way, say, Dolly Parton occasionally would. What's remarkable is that we've seen such a wholesale metamorphosis of contemporary country music into arena rock that has left only the slightest tokens of anything traditionally "country" in the music at all.

It's a formula that is paying off, as a quarter to half of the Top 40 albums on the *Billboard* charts over the last three years have been country records, as was the best-selling album of 2009, Taylor Swift's *Fearless*. All of this answers a question on the minds of a major segment of rock fans nostalgic for Van Halen and Journey, which is, "Why don't they make music like that anymore?" The answer, of course, is, "They do. They just call it country music, now."

Remember the scene from *The Wrestler* when Mickey Rourke's character, while partying to Ratt's "Round and Round", extols the glory days of Guns N' Roses until "That pussy Cobain had to come around and ruin it for everyone"? It's one of rock history's great oversimplifications —Nirvana killed hair metal—but the sentiment points to a prevalent notion that big, catchy, accessible "classic" rock has been somehow, inexplicably, washed from the face of the earth in favor of what these fans see as angsty mook-rock, whiny emo-rock, abstruse indie-rock, crass R&B, and atonal hip-hop. Where these fans have found refuge, beyond their old Zeppelin albums, is in modern country radio, the closest thing out there to the music of their rock 'n' roll good-old days.

What these rock fans have to tolerate, obviously, is whatever purely country elements have remained in the music, but in the exodus from a rock radio where Ratt has been supplanted by Rhianna, they're clearly willing to accept a rural drawl or a buried fiddle as long as they can pump a fist to it. The music follows enough tried-and-true hard-rock archetypes to make inroads into a broad audience's pleasure centers. At the same time, Nashville has wisely maintained decidedly red-state concerns in song themes, rolling out a steady stream of hits that celebrate small towns, God, the simple life, the way things used to be, farms, partying in the woods, etc.

In fact, contemporary country is all about looking back, the same kind of nostalgia that fueled Mark Wills' hit about the simpler, innocent days of the '70s and '80s. Part of that looking back reflects the sort of paranoid raving about a mythical American past that the likes of Glenn Beck never shut up about. Political polarization doesn't exactly make for good commerce—just ask the Dixie Chicks—so most of these artists just shut up and sing, embracing a subtle message of yearning for days gone by rather than endorsing anything specific.

The Glenn Becks of punditry confuse the simplicity of their childhoods with a gentler, better country anyway, but that kind of anti-intellectualism works perfectly for a music that isn't spoiling for a fight, but trying to illicit wistful, breezy feelings by focusing on remembering good times, even if they break your heart now. The nostalgia in the lyrics is an important complement to the recapturing of a simulacrum of a beloved arena-rock form.

Take Josh Turner, a nice Christian boy, whose idea of rebellion is his three-day beard. His smash hit, "Why Don't We Just Dance," finds his trademark bass vocal lamenting all the bad news on television. His advice, since the "whole wide world has gone crazy" is to dance in the living room. The dancing that goes on in the song's video depicts a couple dancing through the decades with costume changes—here they're hippies; now they're discoing. It's a song that, true to the new-country aesthetic, laments the present and embraces the music and movements of the past.

Or how about Lady Antebellum, whose current hit "American Honey" is about as nostalgic as it gets. This trio has the #1 album in America as of this writing, likely because they push these same important buttons—the beauty of rural living, fond memories of the past, and singalong choruses. Lady A is especially adept at forging unimaginative but pleasant, melodic songcraft, which springs a bottomless well of commercial appeal of the sort that shipped gold for . . . 80s rock icons.

Lady Antebellum, alongside other contemporary bands like Rascal Flatts, shares an emphasis on bass, guitars, and keys, rather than on fiddles or steel guitar, that is typical of the genre's new, slick rock edge, an element of which is old-fashioned guitar shredding. Indeed, modern country radio is the last bastion in pop music of the persecuted guitar solo.

While country music has long produced guitar legends like Chet Atkins and Jerry Reed, only recently have we seen slingers like Keith Urban and Brad Paisley control a near monopoly over mainstream pop. The flashy guitar solo never did quite survive the grunge years, with even bands like Metallica doing away with it, but Urban and Paisley and Rascal's Joe Don Mooney play the same kinds of fast, dramatic solos that you learned to expect in every song from the guitar-hero-rich metal era.

Despite such wide-net musical appeal, bands like Lady Antebellum also know to keep bringing things back to resonating emotionally with the tens of millions of Americans who grew up in rural areas. After all, if they are going to snare the party-metal lovers, they can't alienate the country base in order to do so. So, while the Zac Brown Band might seem primed for both Parrotheads and Deadheads, they know that if they talk about eating "Chicken Fried" and drinking beer on the farm, then the country fans will embrace them.

Or Luke Bryan, who reminds us that where he comes from, "Rain Is a Good Thing" in one of the year's most exuberant tributes to farming. Or Billy Covington, who champions bar-b-que, beer, fishing, Jesus, Skoal, and giving you the shirt off their backs because "That's How Country Boys Roll". Or Easton Corbin, who recently hit #1 on the singles charts by explaining that he'd never cheat on his girlfriend because he's "A Little More Country than That."

This notion of a simple life where people treat each other right is an essential part of the new-country mythology that attracts a crowd, as long as it comes with a decent dose of shit-kicking, which helps to catch the classic rock lovers at the heart of the recent crossover resurgence. Songs like "Chicken Fried" and Justin Moore's "Backwoods" are all about getting crazy out in the sticks at bonfire parties, and songs like "Backwoods" and Blake Shelton's "Hillbilly Bone" (which sound very similar, all part of the tradition) bring the new country/'80s-metal hybrid to new extremes.

"Hillybilly Bone" is one of those country-boys-lost-in-the-city songs: "I got a friend in New York City / He's never heard of Conway Twitty", it goes. From the sound of the slamming drums and guitars in "Hillbilly Bone," it sounds as though Shelton himself has listened to far more AC/DC than he has Conway Twitty, and it's a solid bet that modern country listeners who've bought this song in droves have, too.

Who do we credit (or blame) for turning country into '80s metal? Perhaps the same guy whom people blamed for taking hard rock and turning it into pop/hair-metal back in the '80s: Mutt Lange. As the producer of both AC/DC's *Back in Black* (1980) and Def Leppard's *Pyromania* (1984), Lange was a key figure in harnessing the strains of '70s heavy rock into the commercial monster that mainstream metal became in the '80s.

By the mid-'90s, however, with the rise of grunge and rap, the metal party was running on its last fumes, so Lange helped revive many of the key elements he helped forge with metal—rounder-than-round choruses, processed instrumentation, walloping drums, layered vocals—but this time on country radio. The album was his wife's, Shania Twain's *Come on Over* (1997), which spawned 12 (!) hit singles and went on to become the greatest-selling country album of all time.

The incredible, unprecedented success of *Come on Over* changed Nashville forever, not the least by redefining the kind of music that could thereafter be called "country." *Come on Over* had almost nothing to do with the honky-tonking of the latest wave of neo-traditionalist country records by Randy Travis and Alan Jackson. Instead, the Twain-Lange formula was only vaguely country at all. Still, it had even less to do with the TLC and Boyz II Men singles that had taken over the pop charts. So, country it became, bequeathing not only the next 15 years' worth of Faith Hills and Carrie Underwoods, her direct descendants, but also the big-rock leather-and-axes of Bomshel and Rascal Flatts.

For instance, Bomshel's new hit "19 and Crazy" is a prototypical example of the kind of nostalgic party metal that Poison would have loved to have had in 1988. In 1991, Alan Jackson claimed that his heart wasn't ready for the Rolling Stones. By 2009, Gretchen Wilson was opening her concerts with "Rock You Like a Hurricane" and Sugarland was covering Pearl Jam. Lester Flatt would be so pissed.

CMT has further capitalized on the hybrid trend by bringing rock and country artists together on its *CMT Crossroads* show. At first, the pairs—Lynyrd Skynyrd with Montgomery Gentry, .38 Special with Trace Adkins—offered little contrast between the two. Lately, however, we've seen an acknowledgment of the pop-metal/country connection with an episode that paired Bon Jovi with Sugarland and another that brought Def Leppard and Taylor Swift together.

For Bon Jovi's part, they made a full-blown post-Shania country album themselves with 2007's *Lost Highway*, their most successful record in years. Other pop-metal artists—Brett Michaels, Kip Winger—have similarly gone country, as have other classic-rock-leaning singers like Darius Rucker and Jewel, who've scored major hits of late in Nashville.

However country purists or rock fans or critics might deride what has become of contemporary mainstream country radio, one thing remains clear—its popularity is growing, particularly among folks like Mark Wills who grew up on rock, and continues to fill a niche for Foreigner fans that doesn't quite exist elsewhere, even if it means that those fans have to tolerate songs about going mudding and swimming in lakes. Furthermore, the major country labels have been far more successful than modern rock or rap labels at nurturing artists for lengthy, multiple-album careers, turning them into the kinds of artists that achieve legendary, arena-filling status.

Here's a fun game. Name a rock or rap artist/band that has made its debut within the last 15 years that has a reasonable chance of headlining arenas 20 years from now.

Today, rock fans still file into basketball arenas to see Paul McCartney, Bruce Springsteen, Elton John, Billy Joel, Fleetwood Mac, Rod Stewart, Eric Clapton, Aerosmith, U2, Tom Petty . . . it's a very long list. However, once those acts are, well, *gone*, what rock acts constitute the next wave? Will John Mayer fill arenas when he's Springsteen's age? Will high school kids 20 years from now be wearing retro Coldplay T-shirts? Perhaps, but it's a very short list.

Over on country radio, they're grooming an army of Underwoods, Swifts, and Antebellums, who are making music modeled closely after those aging rock gods. There are millions of rock 'n' roll true believers who are tuning in, taking their classic rock wherever they can get it, no matter what it's being called these days.

Source: Steve Leftridge, "Pour Some Sugarland on Me: Why Country is the New Classic Rock," *PopMatters*, April 14, 2010, www.popmatters.com/123260-pour-some-sugarland-on-me-why-country-music-is-the-new-classic-rock-2496188121.html.

VII

THE 2010s

69

"Why no Yes in the Rock Hall?"

JOHN COVACH

When the Rock and Roll Hall of Fame inducted its first class of honorees in 1986, the choices were not difficult to justify. Pioneering 1950s icons such as Chuck Berry, Fats Domino, Little Richard, Jerry Lee Lewis, and Elvis Presley were all integral and well-established figures in rock's historical narrative. By the late 1990s/2000s, however, as many major artists from the 1970s and 1980s became eligible, and then repeatedly passed over, for induction, the Rock Hall's induction process and evaluative criteria increasingly became a topic of conversation and debate.[1] Many wondered, for example, if there was a bias against progressive rock, a genre that despite its sizeable fan base, had rarely been received favorably among critics. In his 2010 editorial, published in the *Cleveland Plain Dealer* (the leading newspaper of the Rock Hall's home city), John Covach, a music theorist at the University of Rochester and Eastman School of Music, and a rock historian who has written widely on progressive rock, states the case for one of the genre's most important bands, Yes.[2] Given Yes's stature, Covach believes their absence from the Rock Hall shows a decided lack of historical objectivity. Yes would eventually be inducted in 2017, followed the next year by another progressive rock band, the Moody Blues. Still, there will always be bands whose omission from the Rock Hall raise questions of how exactly one measures musical and artistic value. Is it through record sales? Critical acclaim? Innovation? Influence? Social or cultural context? How do artists enter a canon such as the Rock Hall, and what kind of story does that canon tell?

The 2011 inductees to the Rock and Roll Hall of Fame and Museum have been announced and once again progressive-rock icons Yes have been overlooked. Some prog fans were encouraged last year when Genesis was inducted, though others warned that this recognition probably had more to do with the band's pop success of the '80s than with their prog epics of the '70s. It's not only Yes who has been consistently passed over by the Rock Hall: Jethro Tull; Emerson, Lake & Palmer; King Crimson; The Moody Blues; and Procol Harum are all still outside looking in, and this year's announcement reinforces the suspicion that the Rock and Roll Hall of Fame and Museum is anti-progrock.

---

1 In order to be eligible for the Rock Hall, an artist must have released a record at least twenty-five years prior to induction, and must have "demonstrated unquestionable musical excellence." The induction process and eligibility guidelines are included on the Rock and Roll Hall of Fame and Museum's website http://rockhall.com/inductees/induction-process/ (accessed March 16, 2018).

2 Covach's writings on progressive rock include "Progressive Rock, 'Close to the Edge', and the Boundaries of Style," in John Covach and Graeme Boone, eds., *Understanding Rock: Essays in Musical Analysis* (New York: Oxford University Press, 1997), pp. 3–31; and "The Hippie Aesthetic: Cultural Positioning and Musical Ambition in Early Progressive Rock," in Mark Spicer, ed., *Rock Music (The Library of Essays on Popular Music)* (Burlington, VT: Ashgate, 2011), pp. 65–75. He is also the co-author, with Andrew Flory, of *What's That Sound?: An Introduction to Rock and its History, Fifth Edition* (New York: W.W. Norton, 2018).

Looked at from a music-historical point of view, it is clear that Yes and other prog bands of the 1970s had enormous success and substantial influence. Yes released a series of albums that consistently hit the Top 10 on album charts in the United States and Britain, from "Fragile" through "Close to the Edge" to "Going for the One." Tracks such as "Roundabout" and "Long Distance Runaround" were staples of FM radio during the decade. The band regularly sold out the biggest venues in the country and toured constantly. Yes and its members topped reader polls sponsored by rock magazines (especially in the United Kingdom) and were the frequent subjects of interviews and features. Guitarist Steve Howe won Guitar Player Magazine's Best Overall Guitarist Award five years in a row and was removed from further competition by being assigned to the magazine's Gallery of Greats.

In the 1980s, Yes enjoyed even greater success, fueled by the hit single "Owner of a Lonely Heart" and the album "90125." Other members of the '70s Yes lineup, along with former members of ELP and King Crimson, formed Asia in the early '80s and stormed the charts with an eponymous debut album and the single "Heat of the Moment." In those years, after punk and new wave had declared prog dead, its original practitioners—including Genesis and Peter Gabriel—turned to a more mainstream style and gave the newer, hipper bands a serious run for their money, extending these prog musicians' impact and influence over two decades.

So with all this commercial and artistic success, why is Yes so consistently overlooked by the Rock and Roll Hall of Fame and Museum? Does the fact that it's not only Yes that is passed over, but also most of the other '70s prog bands, point to a pervading prejudice that undercuts the credibility of the entire Rock Hall enterprise? In considering such issues of historical objectivity, it's only fair to point out that the Rock and Roll Hall of Fame and Museum is not primarily a historical institution; those who nominate and vote on the inductees seem to be mostly music industry people and journalists. To the best of my knowledge, none of the academic rock historians I know has ever been contacted about voting or nominating; I know I never have. The voters are thus very knowledgeable about rock music, but are not necessarily historically oriented or trained. Since induction to the Rock Hall can stimulate back-catalog sales, it's also possible that some of the voters have a deep conflict of interest.

The Rock and Roll Hall of Fame and Museum is thus historically flavored entertainment, and perhaps even historically flavored advertisement, but it is most definitely not history. It represents the collective personal tastes of a group of industry insiders and is far less objective than, say, almost any sports hall of fame, after which it is in part modeled. Sports fans at least have statistics to keep them honest. With the Rock and Roll Hall of Fame and Museum, it's not clear what keeps the voters from indulging their personal tastes or dislikes, and as the years go by, it is becoming more and more obvious that there's not much that's objective about it. It's almost as if these folks think they can dictate history with no explanation or supporting argument: rock history by fiat.

I don't mean for any of this to cast aspersions on the current inductees. And it's also important to point out that none of this criticism applies to the Rock and Roll Hall of Fame and Museum in Cleveland, which is in many ways a separate institution. My beef is entirely with the people who determine who's in and who's out.

It is certainly good sport to complain about and debate each year's Rock Hall inductees. A pattern of blatant historical bias, however, seriously and perhaps fatally undercuts the credibility of the institution. After all, few will ultimately pay much attention to the Rock and Roll Hall of Fame and Museum if they cannot take it at least somewhat seriously. Who wants to play if they suspect the game is rigged? There are times when one has to put the fan mentality aside and make decisions based more on evidence than on personal taste.

Give the prog bands the recognition they deserve: Yes in 2012

Source: John Covach, "Why no Yes in the Rock Hall?," *Cleveland Plain Dealer*, December 29, 2010, www.cleveland.com/opinion/index.ssf/2010/12/why_no_yes_in_the_rock_hall.html.

70

A Response to "Why no Yes in the Rock Hall"

LAUREN ONKEY

In her response to "Why no Yes in the Rock Hall?" (Chapter 69), Dr. Lauren Onkey, who at the time was the Vice President of Education and Public Programs at the Rock and Roll Hall of Fame and Museum, addresses John Covach's criticisms of the Rock Hall's induction process. Onkey emphasizes the subjective nature of rock criticism, and how the shifting tides of taste have made the Rock Hall's canon a highly mutable object. As we peer into rock's future, it is intriguing to speculate what different forms the Rock Hall's canon may assume in the years to come. Unlike 1986, when the Rock Hall ushered in its first members, rock is no longer the most dominant presence in contemporary popular music. In recent years hip hop and electronic dance music, each now with its own lengthy history, have both mixed and intermingled with rock, while simultaneously usurping its place at the front of pop music culture. To what extent will the Rock Hall attempt to fold artists from these genres into its canon? Or will we instead witness a retrenchment, and a decision to champion overlooked bands from the 1970s such as Yes, who lie more firmly within rock's historical realm? One significant change has been the addition of a fan vote, beginning in 2012, which has allowed the public to participate in the process. While the weight accorded the fan vote is statistically minimal (the fan vote accounts for only one of 900 total submitted ballots), awareness of this vote has perhaps had an influence on the overall vote. How else to explain that every year since 2014 at least three of the top five winners in the fan vote have ultimately been inducted into the Rock Hall. Regardless of the correlation, the Rock Hall induction process is likely to remain a hotly contested and vital entity in the shaping of rock history.

John Covach's December 29th column in The Plain Dealer, "Why no Yes in the Rock Hall?" offers a provocative view on the Rock and Roll Hall of Fame Induction process. Covach correctly pointed out that the Rock and Roll Hall of Fame has not yet inducted many prog rockers. Only Genesis and Pink Floyd have made the cut, while bands like Yes, King Crimson, and Emerson, Lake & Palmer have not. But Covach uses this fact as evidence that the induction process is "rigged" and that the Rock Hall is "not primarily a historical institution." Those charges are unfair.

Prog rock's status in the Rock Hall is less about bias and corruption than it is a reflection of the changing history of the definition of rock and roll itself. From its inception, prog rock got a mixed reception. As Covach himself has shown in his book *What's That Sound? An Introduction to Rock and Its History,* many critics originally saw the music as pretentious and some rock fans were turned off by prog's lofty subject matter.

By drawing from classical elements, prog rock implied to some that rock itself wasn't artistically interesting or important enough to contain its complex ideas. And for many critics prog strayed too far from rock's African-American origins, reinforcing the stereotype that associated European music with the intellect and African music with the body.

For other critics and fans, prog just got out of hand. The elaborate art work, stage productions and concept albums became emblematic of rock's 1970s excesses, and a perfect target for punk rock's assault.

One could argue that these responses are, in fact, biases, but doing so shuts down an important discussion about artistic standards and objectivity. Standards for artistic merit cannot be objective, precisely because they are historically and culturally constructed.

The standard for artistic value in music, visual art, literature or any art form is fluid, shifting over time and fluctuating with cultural conditions and different audiences. At its birth, rock and roll itself was derided as primitive jungle music. Such a response was motivated by racism and the backlash of major record labels towards the economic threat of rising independent labels like Sun and Specialty.

If prog rockers considered Bo Diddley too simple, or punk rockers rejected ELP as pretentious, it's not bias. It's a debate over how to define the music and the parameters of that debate are always in flux. This is neither a problem nor a failure. While we need to be aware of how our own judgments about value are specific to our own time, interests and taste, we can never truly escape those things.

Prog rock's position in the Rock Hall is similar to heavy metal and girl groups. The Hall of Fame did not induct artists who played these styles at the outset. The Shirelles and The Ronettes were both eligible at the time of the first induction class in 1986, but weren't inducted until 1996 and 2007, respectively. Black Sabbath was eligible in 1995 but weren't inducted until 2006.

Girl group music and heavy metal were not as highly-regarded in the 1980s as they are now. As times passes, our perspective on the past changes. That's how history works.

Unfortunately, Covach did not make a case for Yes based on artistic merit—maybe his own Yes fandom got the best of him. We're all fans, and it's hard to put that aside and focus on the history we're trying to get right.

He argues that Yes should be inducted because they are popular, citing their Top 10 albums, sold out concerts and continued success in the 1980s. This is all true, but in and of itself it does not make Yes worth honoring.

Most importantly, Yes' absence in the Rock and Roll Hall of Fame is not evidence that the Museum isn't a historical institution. Quite the contrary, it's precisely because the Rock Hall is a historical institution that arguments for induction should be founded on musical innovation, influence, and body of work, and a strong case can be made for Yes on those grounds.

Covach accuses the Rock Hall's processes of being rigged and fraught with industry self-interest without providing any evidence other than the fact that Yes isn't inducted. The nomination process is coordinated by the Rock and Roll Hall of Fame Foundation in New York. The selection of Performers is a two-step process. A Nominating Committee consisting of living inductees, journalists, historians, noted musicians, and industry executives put together a ballot. Nominees are publicly announced and sent to a Voting Committee of about 600 people. Those receiving the highest number of votes are inducted into the Hall. Usually, this means five to seven new performing members each year. The Rock Hall inducts many performers and non-performers alike who no longer sell records or who may not be remembered by millions of fans, but who are important to rock history.

For anyone to claim that the Rock Hall is not a historical institution after the inductions of songwriters Jesse Stone, Mort Shuman and Otis Blackwell last year or Art Rupe this year misrepresents the Rock Hall enterprise in the interest of arguing for the value of a single artist. And although groups like Yes and The Moody Blues are not inducted, the Rock and Roll Hall of Fame's education initiatives, exhibits and public programs all explore these artists' music and teach people with programs like our interview last year with Yes's Jon Anderson.

All this controversy and debate is what makes telling the story of rock and roll such an interesting project. Rock fans—including me—feel a powerful sense of ownership over the music and its history. From the start, rock audiences have been uncomfortable with the idea of expertise or specialized knowledge about rock and roll. Fans of Yes and Led Zeppelin flocked to shows and bought tickets despite what the critics said. This tension will likely never get resolved, nor should it. An institution like the Rock Hall—a Hall of Fame and a Museum—lives this every day. So keep the ideas and the criticism coming, but let's not rely on false ideas about objectivity when we're making artistic judgments.

Source: Lauren Onkey, "A Response to 'Why No Yes in the Rock Hall'," *The Rock Hall Blog,* January 13, 2011, http://rockhall.com/blog/post/5442_a-response-to-why-no-yes-in-t/.

71

"Mumford & Sons Preaches to Masses"

ANN POWERS

British folk-rock band Mumford & Sons' debut album *Sigh No More* was the surprise hit of 2010, eventually selling over seven million copies worldwide. Heralded in the press as part of a thriving transatlantic folk revival, ranging from Laura Marling to the Lumineers, Mumford & Sons received crucial exposure in the U.S. through such as avenues as National Public Radio (NPR), where they were featured on influential programs such as "All Things Considered" and "World Music Café." Writing about the band on the release of their second album, 2012's *Babel*, acclaimed *NPR* music critic Ann Powers probes at both the band's appeal and their mixed critical reception, especially as both relate to front man and songwriter Marcus Mumford (born 1987) and his unabashed populist embrace of faith and spirituality. As Powers points out, rock bands from U2 to the present have long seamlessly meshed the sacred and the secular in their music. In the case of Mumford & Sons, the communal singing and participation that their music invites has a direct link to the contemporary worship practices of such congregations as the evangelical Vineyard church, which Mumford's parents founded in the UK in the late 1980s. Does this help explain the music's surge in popularity in the early 2010s? Did the music's spiritual questing in some way speak to the deep societal uncertainties that many young adults felt in the wake of the 2008 Great Recession and the subsequent "Occupy Wall Street" movement of 2011?

Marcus Mumford may not seem like the kind of guy who'd start a bar fight. This apple-cheeked ministers' son, whose weapon of choice is a steel-strung Martin guitar and whose delirious happiness at inheriting the wooly mantle of folk-rock has endeared him to idols from Bob Dylan to Bruce Springsteen and Emmylou Harris, makes music that's all about uplift and carefully borne out catharsis, about honoring tradition while claiming your own space. Such a nice boy seems unlikely to cause trouble on the pop scene.

Yet from the minute the British singer-strummer's band Mumford & Sons started to score big with college kids and music-industry mucky mucks, the backlash against it began. The group's debut album, *Sigh No More*, eventually shifted 2.4 million units on the strength of incessant touring and a well-placed Grammy telecast appearance with old Jack Frost.[1] Critical support, however, pretty much defined "mixed," the indie music tastemakers at *Pitchfork* issuing one of their particularly

---

1 Jack Frost is the pseudonym that Bob Dylan has used in his role as a record producer for his albums beginning with 2001's *Love and Theft*.

vicious swipes and even positive reviewers expressing reservations.[2] The same thing is happening now that *Babel*, Mumford's second studio album, has arrived, with the *Vice* crew making fun of the band's fans, Chuck Eddy at *SPIN* effectively explaining why their spiritual striving strikes him as hollow (I think it's the most knowledgeable negative review of the band) and Steven Hyden at *Grantland* pushing the old deflation button by reminding young Marcus that he'll never be Bob Dylan.[3]

That's right. Marcus Mumford will never be anything like Bob Dylan, really; at least not unless serious life changes wreak havoc on his personality. The great bard is one sort of rock 'n' roll character, a trickster whose wicked sense of play wrings startling new meanings from old texts and traditions. Mumford and his band connect with a different lineage, an approach that honors music's ability to unite and create an aura of ennoblement. It's long proven powerful with audiences and highly problematic for certain music listeners I'd cautiously call elites—people like me, who write about music for a living, or others who've built lives around a particular rock 'n' roll code.

That code values outsider personalities and transgressive acts over the far more common human quest to fit in with conventional society. It's grounded in the real, powerful legacy of popular music as a forum for otherwise unheard voices: African-Americans through jazz, the blues and, later, hip-hop (and really, through most all pop music); rural people through country and early rockabilly; queer people through disco; misfits of various kinds through metal or punk. The idea that popular music should be oppositional is a powerful one and has made it a central conduit for viewpoints that might have otherwise never reached a large audience. But the fact is, plenty of people who aren't rebels or freaks gain insight and sustenance from popular music, too. They even get it from rock 'n' roll.

Marcus Mumford was raised in a devout Christian household, went to expensive schools, and recently married a movie star. He is in no way a social outsider—except perhaps in those dark moments that inspire some of his lyrics, which read very much like the struggles of a person not trying to reject or even remake a time-tested moral code, but to live up to it. When he sings of his unborn sons in "Babel" or of a lover he fears failing in "Not With Haste," the dream that stands just beyond the song is one of family life and personal fulfillment attained through faithfulness and good deeds. Iggy Pop, one expects, would be appalled, or at the very least, bored. How can anyone who's dedicated to loud, raucous music—the stuff that's supposed to rip through life's dull normality—employ it in the service of such commonplace, even orthodox, hopes and dreams? But for many, this emotional stance deeply resonates.

This seems particularly true now, with a new generation of fans emerging not only for Mumford but for acoustic-leaning American bands garnering ever-larger and more fervent audiences on the club and theater touring circuit. A lot of this stuff has unmistakably churchy overtones: The Head and the Heart shares a name with Garry Wills' popular history of American Christianity; The Avett Brothers sing of carpenters and (indirectly) Corinthians; the rousing choruses of bands like The

---

2 The original online article has links in this sentence to a negative *Pitchfork* review and a positive, yet reserved, review in the *New York Times*: Stephen M. Deusner, "Review of Mumford & Sons, *Sigh No More*," *Pitchfork*, February 19, 2010, https://pitchfork.com/reviews/albums/13906-sigh-no-more/; Jon Pareles, "New CDs: Mumford & Sons, *Sigh No More*," *The New York Times*, February 14, 2010, www.nytimes.com/2010/02/15/arts/music/15choi.html?_r=0.

3 The article links in this sentence to the following review and critique: Chuck Eddy, "Reviews\ Mumford and Sons, 'Babel'(Gentlemen of the Road/Glassnote)," *Spin*, September 24, 2012, www.spin.com/2012/09/mumford-and-sons-babel-gentlemen-of-the-roadglassnote/; Steven Hyden, "They Wanna Be Bob Dylan," *Grantland*, September 14, 2012, http://grantland.com/features/why-bob-dylan-better-darker-musical-offspring-avett-brothers-dave-matthews-band/.

Lumineers musically connect to both old hymns and contemporary praise and worship music. It may not be cool on the secular scene to play up these Jesus people leanings, but they're a huge part of what attracts fans to these artists. Many pop fans are or have been churchgoers, and the comfortable feeling of singing along, nurtured in many during childhoods spent in the pews, allows for a form of release that's edifying without proving too scary.

The rise of the megachurch in America (and England, apparently; so Marcus Mumford's Vineyard connections have revealed) has a lot to do with the newest wave of folk-rock taking hold.[4] These institutions are grounded in the principle that religion serves people best when it meshes well with the secular world. Instead of cultivating a separate sphere where mysticism and anachronistic practices prevail, megachurches feel like everywhere else, except with God present (according to the faithful). Dress is casual. Leaders' sermons sound like self-help pep talks. And the music sounds like something that would pour out of your radio.

In the 1990s, megachurches helped spawn a wave of subtly Christian alternative rock bands who leapt onto the mainstream charts. Remember Lifehouse's "Hanging By a Moment"? That band was nurtured by a Vineyard congregation. Switchfoot came out of the contemporary Christian music scene and still has strong connections there. These bands connected the moral questing of alternative rock groups like Pearl Jam to a specifically religious context. Indie artists like David Bazan, and later Sufjan Stevens, found fruitful ways to translate religious introspection into language that spoke to a larger secular audience. The most powerful work by these artists faces up to the fall away from faith as well as celebrating its comforts; dynamic belief always carries plenty of questions, and music offers an immediate and powerful way to confront them.

All of this Godly sound echoes back to the granddaddy of non-sectarian spiritual rock bands: U2. Every U2 album, from 1980's *Boy* (the hit was called "I Will Follow") to 2009's *No Line on the Horizon*, grapples with matters of faith and ethics, sin and salvation. What Bono and his mates figured out early on was how to connect a specific set of concerns formed within religious practice to other cultural forms—literature, soul music, cinema—where similar seekers were expressing themselves. U2 never became a "secular" band; its music simply relies on the fact that religion, for better and worse, is everywhere.

Mumford & Sons does something similar, and by doing it now, it's filling a gap in pop music. I know the feeling that radiates from a room full of Avetts or Mumford fans singing along with every overly sincere, earnest word; I've been there myself. At sixteen, I was a confused Catholic kid struggling to figure out how I could be my parents' daughter and still want to make out with boys, dye my hair funny colors and dance all night to ridiculously loud music. U2's music didn't present an alternative to the church life that had made me, in part, who I was then; it showed me how to struggle within that life, and get to the point where I could either walk on within it or walk away.

I'm not a practicing Catholic now, but when I hear Mumford & Sons or the Avett Brothers, I recognize the same internal fights, the same desire to grapple with impossibly big terms like "sincerity" and "belief," that U2's music helped me through twenty years ago. The frame is different: today's churchy music has more traditional trappings, connecting it with other trends like the crafts revival and sustainable living practices. But the deeper motivations, I think, are the same.

When *Babel* clocks in next week as the biggest *Billboard* album chart debut of 2012 (it's predicted to sell as many as 600,000 copies in its first week), Mumford fans will rejoice and more than a few critics will grumble. How boring! Normal folk like normal music. But there's a reward in really

---

4 The article links in this sentence to an article discussing the relationship of Mumford & Sons to the Vineyard church movement: Christian Scharen, "A Deliberately Spiritual Thing," *The Cresset*, 75, no. 1 (2011): 34–36.

engaging with what this "normal" represents. We should thoroughly examine what's conventional—to question whether, for example, these mostly white male artists really can speak for a broad audience and to point out that there's a lot of baggage attached to Christian-based definitions of morality. But to deny that widely shared notions of being good and strong and fulfilled—the things Marcus Mumford sings about—don't have power is to dismiss a lot of what lives in people's hearts. Some might cringe at the banality of it all; others will celebrate the common chord this band strikes and call it extraordinary. Neither response fully recognizes that the prosaic nature of this music is the point. Mumford & Sons aren't changing the world that much, but they're living loud in their little corner. In that, they're just like most of us.

Source: Ann Powers, "Mumford & Sons Preaches to the Masses," *The Record – Music News from NPR*, September 27, 2012, www.npr.org/sections/therecord/2012/09/27/161883725/mumford-sons-preaches-to-masses.

72

"Making Cents"

Musician Royalties in the Digital Age

Damon Krukowski

As physical music sales declined rapidly over the course of the 2000s and consumers increasingly turned to digital music sites such as Spotify and Pandora, many musicians and songwriters raised serious concerns about the meager royalties generated from these new companies. Explaining his decision to remove both his solo album (*The Eraser*) and recent Atoms for Peace album from Spotify, Thom Yorke of Radiohead proclaimed in a widely circulated 2013 tweet: "Make no mistake new artists you discover on #Spotify will [not] get paid. [M]eanwhile shareholders will shortly [be] rolling in it. Simples." In his feature essay for *Pitchfork* magazine, Damon Krukowski (born 1963), a former member of the influential late 1980s indie rock group Galaxie 500 and part of the current duo Damon and Naomi, compares the substantial business differences between the former model of selling records and the new era of streaming services. As Krukowski concludes, for all their positive attributes companies like Spotify have served to devalue music and contribute very little to the income necessary to support the life of a working musician.[1] If this is indeed the case, then how exactly should today's musicians expect to make a living? Have performing, touring, merchandise sales, and music licensing come to replace the diminished revenue from record sales? Should most rock musicians simply accept that they will most always need a "day job" or some other form of supplemental income to survive?

I'm sure each generation of musicians feels they've lived through a time of tremendous change, but the shifts I've witnessed in my relatively short music career—from morphing formats to dissolving business models—do seem extraordinary. The first album I made was originally released on LP only, in 1988—and my next will likely only be pressed on LP again. But in between, the music

---

1 For a related argument, see David Lowery, "My Song Got Played on Pandora 1 Million Times and All I Got Was $16.89, Less Than What I Make From a Single T-Shirt Sale!," *The Trichordist*, June 24, 2013, https://the trichordist.com/2013/06/24/my-song-got-played-on-pandora-1-million-times-and-all-i-got-was-16-89-less-than-what-i-make-from-a-single-t-shirt-sale/. Lowery's article drew many responses and commentary; see, in particular, Douglas Wolk, "How Ashamed Should You Feel About Using Spotify?," *Slate*, August 21, 2013, www.slate.com/articles/business/moneybox/2013/08/spotify_and_pandora_artist_payments_not_as_exploitative_as_they_re_made.html. For a good summary of the controversies surrounding Spotify and other services during these years, see Lee Marshall, "'Let's Keep Music Special. F—Spotify': On the Controversy Over Artist Royalties," *Creative Industries Journal*, 8, no. 2 (2015): 177–89.

industry seems to have done everything it could to screw up that simple model of exchange; today it is no longer possible for most of us to earn even a modest wage through our recordings.

Not that I am naively nostalgic for the old days—we weren't paid for that first album, either. (The record label we were signed to at the time, Rough Trade, declared bankruptcy before cutting us even one royalty check.) But the ways in which musicians are screwed have changed qualitatively, from individualized swindles to systemic ones. And with those changes, a potential end-run around the industry's problems seems less and less possible, even for bands who have managed to hold on to 100% of their rights and royalties, as we have.

Consider Pandora and Spotify, the streaming music services that are becoming ever more integrated into our daily listening habits. My BMI royalty check arrived recently, reporting songwriting earnings from the first quarter of 2012, and I was glad to see that our music is being listened to via these services. Galaxie 500's "Tugboat," for example, was played 7,800 times on Pandora that quarter, for which its three songwriters were paid a collective total of 21 cents, or seven cents each. Spotify pays better: For the 5,960 times "Tugboat" was played there, Galaxie 500's songwriters went collectively into triple digits: $1.05 (35 cents each).

To put this into perspective: Since we own our own recordings, by my calculation it would take songwriting royalties for roughly 312,000 plays on Pandora to earn us the profit of one—one—LP sale. (On Spotify, one LP is equivalent to 47,680 plays.)

Or to put it in historical perspective: The "Tugboat" 7" single, Galaxie 500's very first release, cost us $980.22 for 1,000 copies—including shipping! (Naomi kept the receipts)—or 98 cents each. I no longer remember what we sold them for, but obviously it was easy to turn at least a couple bucks' profit on each. Which means we earned more from every one of those 7"s we sold than from the song's recent 13,760 plays on Pandora and Spotify. Here's yet another way to look at it: Pressing 1,000 singles in 1988 gave us the earning potential of more than 13 million streams in 2012. (And people say the internet is a bonanza for young bands . . .)

To be fair, because we are singer-songwriters, and because we own all of our rights, these streaming services end up paying us a second royalty, each for a different reason and each through a different channel. Pandora is considered "non-terrestrial radio," and consequently must pay the musicians who play on the recordings it streams, as well as the songwriters. These musicians' royalties are collected by SoundExchange, a non-profit created by the government when satellite radio came into existence. SoundExchange doesn't break our earnings down by service per song, but it does tell us that last quarter, Pandora paid a total of $64.17 for use of the entire Galaxie 500 catalogue. We have 64 Galaxie 500 recordings registered with them, so that averages neatly to one dollar per track, or another 33 cents for each member of the trio.

Pandora in fact considers this additional musicians' royalty an extraordinary financial burden, and they are aggressively lobbying for a new law—it's now a bill before the U.S. Congress—designed to relieve them of it.[2] You can read all about it in a series of helpful blog posts by Ben Sisario of *The New York Times*, or if you prefer your propaganda unmediated, you can listen to Pandora founder Tim Westergren's own explanation of the Orwellian Internet Radio Fairness Act.

As for Spotify, since it is not considered radio, either of this world or any other, they have a different additional royalty to pay. Like any non-broadcast use of recordings, they require a license

---

2 The proposed bill in question, the "Internet Radio Fairness Act," was met with widespread opposition among musicians, most noticeably in an open letter "signed" by 125 prominent artists (ranging from Billy Joel to the Dead Kennedys) that was published as "A Musicians' Perspective on Pandora" in the November 24, 2012 issue of *Billboard* magazine, p. 6. Pandora eventually abandoned their legislative push in late 2013, however, after it became clear that it was not a priority item within Congress.

from the rights-holder. They negotiate this individually with each record label, at terms not made public. I'm happy to make ours public, however: It is the going "indie" rate of $0.005 per play. (Actually, when I do the math, that rate seems to truly pay out at $0.004611—I hope someone got a bonus for saving the company four-hundredths of a cent on each stream!) We didn't negotiate this, exactly; for a band-owned label like ours, it's take it or leave it. We took it, which means for 5,960 plays of "Tugboat," Spotify theoretically owes our record label $29.80.

I say theoretically, because in practice Spotify's $0.004611 rate turns out to have a lot of small, invisible print attached to it. It seems this rate is adjusted for each stream, according to an algorithm (not shared by Spotify, at least not with us) that factors in variables such as frequency of play, the outlet that channeled the play to Spotify, the type of subscription held by the user, and so on. What's more, try as I might through the documents available to us, I cannot get the number of plays Spotify reports to our record label to equal the number of plays reported by the BMI. Bottom line: The payments actually received by our label from Spotify for streams of "Tugboat" in that same quarter, as best I can figure: $9.18.

"Well, that's still not bad," you might say. (I'm not sure who would really say that, but let's presume someone might.) After all, these are immaterial goods—it costs us nothing to have our music on these services: no pressing, no printing, no shipping, no file space to save a paper receipt for 25 years. All true. But immaterial goods turn out to generate equally immaterial income.

Which gets to the heart of the problem. When I started making records, the model of economic exchange was exceedingly simple: make something, price it for more than it costs to manufacture, and sell it if you can. It was industrial capitalism, on a 7" scale. The model now seems closer to financial speculation. Pandora and Spotify are not selling goods; they are selling access, a piece of the action. Sign on, and we'll all benefit. (I'm struck by the way that even crowd-sourcing mimics this "investment" model of contemporary capitalism: You buy in to what doesn't yet exist.)

But here's the rub: Pandora and Spotify are not earning any income from their services, either. In the first quarter of 2012, Pandora—the same company that paid Galaxie 500 a total of $1.21 for their use of "Tugboat"—reported a net loss of more than $20 million dollars. As for Spotify, their latest annual report revealed a loss in 2011 of $56 million.

Leaving aside why these companies are bothering to chisel hundredths of a cent from already ridiculously low "royalties," or paying lobbyists to work a bill through Congress that would lower those rates even further—let's instead ask a question they themselves might consider relevant: Why are they in business at all?

The answer is capital, which is what Pandora and Spotify have and what they generate. These aren't record companies—they don't make records, or anything else; apparently not even income. They exist to attract speculative capital. And for those who have a claim to ownership of that capital, they are earning millions—in 2012, Pandora's executives sold $63 million of personal stock in the company. Or as Spotify's CEO Daniel Ek has put it, "The question of when we'll be profitable actually feels irrelevant. Our focus is all on growth. That is priority one, two, three, four and five."

Growth of the music business? I think not. Daniel Ek means growth of his company, i.e., its capitalization. Which is the closest I can come to understanding the fundamental change I've witnessed in the music industry, from my first LP in 1988 to the one I am working on now. In between, the sale of recorded music has become irrelevant to the dominant business models I have to contend with as a working musician. Indeed, music itself seems to be irrelevant to these businesses—it is just another form of information, the same as any other that might entice us to click a link or a buy button on a stock exchange.

As businesses, Pandora and Spotify are divorced from music. To me, it's a short logical step to observe that they are doing nothing for the business of music—except undermining the simple cottage industry of pressing ideas onto vinyl, and selling them for more than they cost to manufacture.

I am no Luddite—I am not smashing iPhones or sabotaging software. In fact, I subscribe to Spotify for $9.99 a month (the equivalent of 680,462 annual plays of "Tugboat") because I love music, and the access it gives me to music of all kinds is incredible.

But I have simply stopped looking to these business models to do anything for me financially as a musician. As for sharing our music without a business model of any kind, that's exactly how I got into this—we called it punk rock. Which is why we are streaming all of our recordings, completely free, on the Bandcamp sites we set up for Galaxie 500 and Damon & Naomi. Enjoy.

Source: Damon Krukowski, "Making Cents," *Pitchfork*, November 14, 2012, www.pitchfork.com/features/article/8993-the-cloud/.

73

"Top 25 Metal Genres on Spotify"

ELIOT VAN BUSKIRK

Despite, or perhaps because of, all its controversies (as we saw in Chapter 44), heavy metal has long been one of rock's most consistently popular genres, continuously growing and stretching its shape into numerous subgenres. Traditionally, metal's impact has been most visible through its prodigious album sales and concert attendance, where groups such as Metallica and AC/DC have drawn a vast global audience. As Eliot Van Buskirk's blog post for *Spotify Insights* reveals, metal's prominent stature also extends to Spotify's streaming music service, where it accounts for the "most loyal" listenership of any kind of music.[1] Van Buskirk, a long-time music and technology journalist, has been Spotify's "in house data storyteller" since 2014, employing big data and algorithms drawn from their music intelligence platform, the Echo Nest, to illustrate patterns, trends and information about genre and musical taste that emerge from Spotify's usage. Spotify's determined efforts to delineate their listeners' streaming habits across a dizzying array of subgenres (currently at over 2200 and counting) indicates the significance that these categories still hold as they enable music providers and consumers alike to navigate the seemingly unlimited content of the new "celestial jukebox." Examining the descriptions of the "Top 25 Metal Genres" and their corresponding representative artists, how easy or difficult is it to differentiate them from one another? What factors—musical, social, historical, geographical, or otherwise—go towards the determination of each genre? And lastly, how important do you think such labels are to the Spotify listening experience?

We already know heavy metal fans are the most loyal of any of the big genres of music.[2] And it's getting more popular; in a typical week, metal's share of overall Spotify listening increased 13 percent from 2014 to 2015.

Let's delve further into how people listen to Metal by looking at the top 25 genres of metal (out of 91 in total) with the most listeners on Spotify.

---

1 By loyal, Van Buskirk means that heavy metal fans, more than fans of other genres, listen most frequently to the favorite artists in their genre. To determine the degree of loyalty, the Spotify data analysts identified the "core" artists in each genre and then divided the number of streams each one had by their number of listeners. The larger the resultant number, the more loyal the listenership. See Eliot Van Buskirk, "Which Music Genres Have the Loyalest Fans?," *Spotify Insights*, April 2, 2015, https://insights.spotify.com/us/2015/04/02/loyalest-music-fans-by-genre/.

2 The article here links to Van Buskirk, "Which Music Genres Have the Loyalest Fans?"

The top of the list includes some larger, more mainstream and/or contemporary metal genres—including, notably, metal itself at #7 (explanation below). But it quickly wends its way towards the fringes of this incredibly multifaceted genre. We've included an example artist for each genre; click the genre names for the full playlists:

1. **Alternative Metal** mixes the heavy guitars of metal with elements of alternative rock. Emerging in the early '90s, alternative metal includes melodic vocals and unconventional, experimental sounds or song structures (example: *Disturbed*).
2. **Nu Metal** is a form of alternative metal combining groove metal and thrash metal, with elements of grunge, hardcore, hip hop, funk, and industrial. It's a hybrid synthesizing many disparate elements, in other words—just about anything goes, so long as it's modern metal that incorporates influence from other genres (example: *Drowning Pool*).
3. **Hard Rock** uses distorted electric guitars, bass guitar, drums, and often pianos or keyboards to give an extra edge to traditional rock. It has roots in the mid-'60s and influences from garage, blues, and psychedelic rock (example: *Ted Nugent*).
4. **Groove Metal** is a slowed-down version of thrash metal. It has an intense sound but is played at mid-tempo (*DevilDriver*).
5. **Rap Metal** fuses the vocal and instrumental elements of hip hop with those of heavy metal and hard rock (*Linkin Park*).
6. **Funk Metal** is alternative metal that combines the guitar riffs of heavy metal with the bass grooves of funk. Funk metal originated in the '80s and saw a heyday in the '90s (*Audioslave*).
7. **Metal** is where you'll find many of the originators and progenitors of the overarching metal genre (*Iron Maiden*).
8. **Metalcore**, or metallic hardcore, blends extreme metal and hardcore punk. Its sound is distinguished by its emphasis on breakdowns, which are slow, intense passages when the audience can mosh (*Parkway Drive*).
9. **Speed Metal** originated in the late '70s to mid-'80s from the NWOBHM (new wave of British heavy metal) and hardcore punk. It's characterized by extreme speed, staccato drumming, single-note riffing, and technical guitar solos. Speed metal spawned thrash metal and power metal (*King Diamond*).
10. **Melodic Metalcore** is a fusion of metalcore and melodic death metal. It features melodic guitar riffs, blast beats, breakdowns, and vocals that are sung, screamed, or growled (*Killswitch Engage*).
11. **Industrial Metal** takes inspiration from industrial, heavy metal, hardcore punk, and dance music. It usually centers on repeated metal guitar riffs, with samples, synthesizers, sequencers, and distorted vocals (*Marilyn Manson*).
12. **Progressive Metal** is a combination of prog rock and heavy metal that originated in the UK and the US in the late '80s. Progressive metal fuses the aggressive sound of heavy metal with the more experimental, complex structures of progressive rock, using classical and jazz compositional techniques (*Queensrÿche*).
13. **Power Metal** is a melodic form of heavy metal and speed metal. It features fast guitar hooks and bass riffs, as well as guitar solos, keyboards, and high male vocals. Its sound is generally upbeat and anthemic, unlike the doom-like or aggressive sound of other metals (*Avantasia*).
14. **Death Metal** is extreme heavy metal with heavily distorted guitars, growling vocals, blast-beat drumming, tremolo picking, minor keys and atonality, and multiple tempo changes (*Death*).

15. **Thrash Metal** is characterized by fast drumming, complex, shredding guitars, and anti-establishment themes. Thrash originated in the '70s and '80s, influenced by punk and hardcore (*Slayer*).

16. **Glam Metal** is a fusion of hard rock and heavy metal. It features pop-influenced melodies and hooks combined with hard rock and heavy metal elements from the '70s. Glam metal musicians are known for their long hair, tight clothing, and excessive accessories (*Poison*).

17. **Melodic Death Metal** is extreme heavy metal that originated in the '90s. It combines fast, harmonic guitar riffs from the new wave of British heavy metal with death metal elements such as distorted guitars, blast beats, and fast drumming (*Misery's Crown*).

18. **Neo Classical Metal** is heavy metal that is influenced by classical music. Neo Classical metal does not use classical composition techniques, so much as it plays classical themes in metal style and emulates the frills and flourishes of Baroque music, with very technical playing, especially by the guitars (*Symphony X*).

19. **Symphonic Metal**, based somewhat on classical and film music, often features an operatic female lead vocalist; prominent, complex, and technically challenging keyboard parts; and strings (*Delain*).

20. **Death Core** combines death metal's speed, dissonance, blast beats, low screams, and dark tones with metalcore's melodic riffs and heavy, down-tuned breakdowns, minus the clean singing (*Whitechapel*).

21. **Gothic Metal** shares sonic elements with heavy metal and doom metal, and also derives textures from gothic rock. The genre originated during the early '90s in Europe, originally as an outgrowth of death-doom metal (*Sirenia*).

22. **German Metal** is heavy metal from Germany with elements of speed and power metal (*Mystic Prophecy*).

23. **Gothic Symphonic Metal** blends the dark themes of gothic and the hard rock guitars of metal with the grandeur of symphonic classical music. Delicate, usually female vocals contrast with the distorted guitars (*Leaves' Eyes*).

24. **Stoner Rock** is rock with a slower tempo, low-tuned guitars, heavy bass, and melodic vocals. It incorporates elements of heavy metal, blues rock, psychedelic rock, hardcore, and doom metal (*Orange Goblin*).

25. **Folk Metal** features folk elements of the artists' home countries, including lyrical themes, language, instruments, and costumes. It originated in Europe in the '90s (*Eluveitie*).

There they are, the top 25 of the 91 metal genres currently available on Spotify. To see which metal genres sound the most similar to any one metal genre, according to several raw acoustic attributes, go here.[3] Some bands are associated with multiple genres to varying degrees.

Source: Eliot Van Buskirk, "Top 25 Metal Genres on Spotify," *Spotify Insights*, August 5, 2015, https://insights.spotify.com/us/2015/08/05/top-25-metal-genres-on-spotify/.

---

3 The article links here to the ongoing genre list and mapping project "Every Noise it Once" curated by Spotify's "data alchemist" Glenn McDonald: http://everynoise.com/everynoise1d.cgi?root=metal&scope=all.

74

Marginalization in the Music Industry

A Twitter Exposé

JESSICA HOPPER

By the mid-2010s, the social networking service Twitter had emerged as a primary medium of public communication, and a means through which its participants could tweet about and address important societal issues in 140 characters or less.[1] It was in this context that the prominent music critic Jessica Hopper, whose influential writings on punk, emo, rock, and pop have been anthologized in the book *The First Collection of Criticism by a Living Female Critic* (Chicago: Featherproof Books, 2015), posed a query on her twitter account on August 24, 2015: "Gals/other marginalized folks: what was your 1st brush (in music industry, journalism, scene) w/ idea that you didn't 'count'?" Hopper's invitation clearly hit a nerve, as she was met with a flood of responses, retweets, and summary write-ups in various online publications that revealed the devastating extent to which sexism, racism, and discrimination permeated every level of the music industry—affecting everyone from musicians and managers to journalists, photographers, and fans.[2] The tweets compiled below are a small sample of the many hundreds of responses that Hopper received in the first few days. As other social media generated movements, such as #MeToo, have since shown, these gatherings of shared voices wield an undeniable power. To what degree have social media networks like Twitter helped transform the culture of rock and the music industry that supports it?

@jesshopp
Gals/other marginalized folks: what was your 1st brush (in music industry, journalism, scene) w/ idea that you didn't "count"?

10:16 AM – 24 Aug 2015

---

1 Twitter doubled its character limit to 280 on November 7, 2017.
2 Some of the more notable summary write-ups include Paula Mejia, "A Must-Read Twitter Exposé on the Music Industry's Culture of Sexism and Misogyny," *Newsweek*, August 26, 2015, www.newsweek.com/must-read-twitter-expose-music-industrys-culture-sexism-and-misogyny-366046; Amy Zimmerman, "Women's Music Industry Horror Stories: Abuse, Sexism, and Erasure," *The Daily Beast*, August 26, 2015, www.thedailybeast.com/womens-music-industry-horror-stories-abuse-sexism-and-erasure; Taylor Pittman, "This is the Kind of Bullsh*t You Face as a Woman in the Music Industry," *Huffington Post*, August 27, 2015, www.huffingtonpost.com/entry/this-is-the-kind-of-bullsht-you-face-as-a-woman-in-the-music-industry_us_55df67fce4b0e7117ba93ec6.

meagan
@meaganrosae
Replying to @jesshopp
@jesshopp when i used to post on the http://shoegaze.co.uk forums as a TEEN – and was hit on by every single male member

10:20 AM – 24 Aug 2015

Anne T. Donahue
@annetdonahue
Replying to @jesshopp
@jesshopp when a band literally threw the interview to hit on me (on camera). embarrassing/awful – emailed you that night, tbh!

10:22 AM – 24 Aug 2015

Hazel Cills
@hazelcills
Replying to @jesshopp
@jesshopp being told my work as a teenager didn't matter by a much older male writer ON A PANEL that was about writing for teenagers :)

10:30 AM – 24 Aug 2015

Laura Snapes
@laurasnapes
Replying to @jesshopp
@jesshopp the older boys all quit writing for the music pages of our uni paper when I was made section editor

10:30 AM – 24 Aug 2015

---

jes skolnik
@modernistwitch
Replying to **@jesshopp**
@jesshopp one-two punch: guy puts his hands up my shirt to grab my boobs at a hc[3] show/listening to his peers talk about riot grrrl

10:30 AM – 24 Aug 2015

---

3 Hardcore punk.

Best Ex
@CandyHeartsBand
Replying to **@jesshopp**
@jesshopp when I was demoing my first record, the engineer told me to sing it again, but naked this time

10:32 AM – 24 Aug 2015

Sam O' Rama
@samorama
Replying to **@jesshopp**
@jesshopp working at a record store men ignore me & seek out other men to answer questions. Then they're referred back to me.

10:33 AM – 24 Aug 2015

Caroline Moore
@crikitmoore
Replying to **@jesshopp**
@jesshopp Complaints about groping met with shrugs from venue staff, other bands. "Let the pros do their job, sweetie" in the photo pit.

10:36 AM – 24 Aug 2015

Charlotte Zoller
@cz77
Replying to **@jesshopp**
@jesshopp as a TM[4] when a stagehand called me "princess" & I proceeded to breakdown the drumkit in 2 mins flat as retaliation (he apologized)

10:42 AM – 24 Aug 2015

----

clair de lune
@ClaireMPLS
Replying to **@jesshopp**
@jesshopp former GM (he's since retired, new GM is great) at first ave told me majoring in music in college qualified me to "be a housewife"

10:51 AM – 24 Aug 2015

----

4 Tour manager.

Megan Seling
@mseling
Replying to **@jesshopp**
@jesshopp My "favorite," tho, is when a mag pulled me from a story when I refused to ask an all-male band if they jerked each other off.

11:39 AM – 24 Aug 2015

Martin Douglas
@douglasmartini
Replying to **@jesshopp**
@jesshopp The looks I got for being the only black person at the Joanna Newsom show, nerding out over Bill Callahan.

5:20 PM – 24 Aug 2015

Soft Ledges
@shelleymiller1
Replying to **@jesshopp**
@jesshopp Being told at one of my 1st shows that I should wear more makeup and dress like a girl until I learned how to play guitar.

5:31 PM – 24 Aug 2015

Carly Rhiannon
@carlyrhiannon
Replying to **@jesshopp**
@jesshopp When I was at recording school & I heard a guy say, "The girls are just here for affirmative action, to keep the school open."

6:08 PM – 24 Aug 2015

Survival Guide
@SrvvlGd
Replying to **@jesshopp**
@jesshopp my band played warped tour and security wouldn't let me backstage even though I had an artist pass . . .

10:15 PM – 24 Aug 2015

Survival Guide
@SrvvlGd
Replying to **@jesshopp**
@jesshopp . . . until a girl came up & complimented my set & asked for an autograph. :)

10:16 PM – 24 Aug 2015

Father Daughter Records
@father_daughter
Replying to **@jesshopp**
@jesshopp my favorite is when club staff/security think I'm backstage because I'm trying to sleep with a band member

8:46 AM – 25 Aug 2015

Rachel Syme
@rachsyme
Replying to **@jesshopp**
@jesshopp When a man I was interviewing said to me "I hope your writing is as good as your tits"

9:01 AM – 25 Aug 2015

---

amalia
@amalianicholson
Replying to **@jesshopp**
@jesshopp probably being shoved to the back of a rancid crowd as a 13 year old black girl, and being told it wasn't the place for me.

9:15 AM – 25 Aug 2015

Gaptooth
@gaptoothmusic
Replying to **@jesshopp**
@jesshopp While setting up mics for a live band, got asked if I was "helping out the sound guy". Had to tell them I was the sound guy.

9:52 AM – 25 Aug 2015

Jessica Hopper
@jesshopp
Last nite I told another (male) editor about female/non-dude critics I know getting doxxed[5] and threatened over album reviews they wrote.

11:57 AM – 25 Aug 2015

———————

Jessica Hopper
@jesshopp
And if you think these RT's are sad, depressing, awful – go ahead and imagine the DMs I am getting about it, stories too painful to be public

11:58 AM – 25 Aug 2015

———————

Jessica Hopper
@jesshopp
Imagine how many women, queer kids, POC might stick around scenes, industry, journalism if they encountered support not hostility.

12:01 PM – 25 Aug 2015

———————

Kat Bee
@katbeee
Replying to **@jesshopp**
@jesshopp When a college professor teaching "History of Rock" mansplained me after I challenged total lack of women in the syllabus.

3:09 PM – 25 Aug 2015

———————

Wakandana White
@dswhite7
Replying to **@jesshopp**
@jesshopp "we really think the office manager role should go to a man. Would you like to be the receptionist instead?" (Indie label)

5:19 PM – 25 Aug 2015

———————

—————————————

5 Making private information about individuals publicly available on the internet.

Courtney Coles
@kernieflakes
Replying to **@jesshopp**
@jesshopp when i was first starting out, I'd have people tell me that a female photographer is just a glorified groupie.

6:38 PM – 25 Aug 2015

_____

Jill Mapes
@jumonsmapes
Replying to **@jesshopp**
@jesshopp the members of the band Yes once thought I was an assistant + asked if I could fetch them Starbucks. I was there to interview them

8:50 PM – 25 Aug 2015

_____

Izzy Olive
@half_gringa
Replying to **@jesshopp**
@jesshopp I interned for a music ensemble who works w/ guitarist I look up to, member offered to introduce me if I wouldn't "fangirl" him

3:30 PM – 26 Aug 2015

_____

Izzy Olive
@half_gringa
Replying to **@jesshopp**
@jesshopp all of the staff kept equating my professional admiration to a crush, and as invalid, which infuriates me as a young guitarist

3:32 PM – 26 Aug 2015

Izzy Olive
@half_gringa
Replying to **@jesshopp**
@jesshopp I felt so ashamed that when I went to the fest he curates, I saw him around but didn't approach him for fear he'd belittle me

3:37 PM – 26 Aug 2015

_____

Kim Boekbinder
@Kim Boekbinder
Replying to **@jesshopp**
@jesshopp constantly asked to play "female showcases" in a world where festivals with 100s of only male bands are just called . . . festivals.

5:46 PM – 26 Aug 2015

Brodie Lancaster
@brodielancaster
Replying to **@jesshopp**
@jesshopp I was told to pick 3 instruments to try for in school band. drums were my #1 but i was told "girls don't play the drums". I was 9.

8:19 PM – 26 Aug 2015

See Gulls
@SeeGulls
Replying to **@jesshopp**
@jesshopp Guy picked up my guitar on stage, Me: "Please put that down. That's mine.", Him "Oh, you know how to play this?".

7:56 AM – 27 Aug 2015

Rosanne Cash
@rosannecash
Replying to **@jesshopp**
@jesshopp In all-male record label mtg for my 1st record, they said (to me) that the main marketing idea was to make me appear 'fuckable.'

8:24 AM – 27 Aug 2015

Source: @jesshopp. "Gals/other marginalized folks: what was your 1st brush (in music industry, journalism, scene) w/ idea that you didn't 'count'?" *Twitter*, August 24, 2015, 10:16 a.m. https://twitter.com/jesshopp/status/635863142917107712?lang=en.

75

Twenty One Pilots

"The Slippery Appeal of the Biggest New Band in America"

JIA TOLENTINO

Over the course of the 2010s fewer and fewer rock musicians found mainstream success, to the point where only a handful—most notably Coldplay, Fall Out Boy, Imagine Dragons, and Twenty One Pilots—enjoyed multiple hits that crossed over into the *Billboard* Top 40 singles chart. As Jia Tolentino of *The New Yorker* magazine points out in her feature on the Twenty One Pilots duo of Tyler Joseph (born 1988) and Josh Dun (born 1988), their mass appeal is a "slippery" one, based in part on a stylistic pluralism that embraces elements of alternative, emo, rap, reggae, electronic dance music, nü metal, and more. Likewise, this slipperiness extends to their live shows, where Tolentino observes the duo perform a rousing singalong cover of Céline Dion's 1997 power ballad, "My Heart Will Go On," a selection that could easily be read as either ironic kitsch or nostalgic reverie.[1] Lastly, this slipperiness can be seen not only in the duo's adoption of masks, make up, and characters in their performed identities, but also the centrality of their Christian upbringing to their biography, and the question of whether or not one should thus apply religious interpretations to the band's secular music-making. Taken as a whole, to what extent does the pluralism of a group like Twenty One Pilots reflect the broader, more open-ended, listening habits of today's audiences, as well as the more fluid identities of our heavily mediated society?

Last summer, pop radio began playing a fiendish earworm about two young men who feared the ordinary demands of adulthood. A year later, those men have become the biggest new band in America. You may not be familiar with Twenty One Pilots—they're a slippery phenomenon, selling out arenas while remaining nearly invisible to those outside their active fan base—but you'd know the hook of "Stressed Out" if you heard it: the song has enjoyed non-stop airplay for almost a year. Tyler Joseph, the twenty-seven-year-old vocalist and songwriter for the band, composes in hooks; his melodies sound like bar darts swooping toward a bull's-eye, and the "Stressed Out" chorus is as bright as its minor key will allow. "If we could turn back time," Joseph sings, "to the good old da-ays, when our mama sang"—and here's where your ears might prick up in recognition—"us to sleep, but now we're stressed out."

---

1 On the complexities of taste, meaning, and Céline Dion, see Carl Wilson, *Let's Talk About Love: Why Other People Have Such Bad Taste* (New York: Bloomsbury, 2014).

Joseph is a dexterous front man, a chameleon between songs as well as within them. On the verses of "Stressed Out," he raps, with a taut, earnest bounce that recalls Macklemore or Gym Class Heroes. He rhymes "student loans," which are bad, with "treehouse homes," which are good; he bemoans the people who say, "Wake up, you need to make money." Behind his wholesome flow, the instrumentation sweetens; an arpeggiated piano softens the snap of the drummer Josh Dun's beat. The song is so idiosyncratic—a lyrical, emo, rap-rock song about a boy's need for his mommy—that it's got a whiff of the one-hit wonder. But it's not that: Twenty One Pilots keep charting. As of last week, they became the first "alternative" band to land two singles in the Top Ten of the *Billboard* Hot 100 simultaneously: "Heathens," from the "Suicide Squad" soundtrack, and the emo-reggae track "Ride." Meanwhile, "Stressed Out," their calling card, still hovers in the thirties.

All three songs share the dirtbag camaraderie of Joseph's delivery and a certain paranoiac groove. But they become harder to categorize the more you listen. Joseph and Dun are devoted Christians from Columbus, Ohio, and they combine a kind of stalwart Midwesternness with a genre fluidity that feels deployed to confound. The duo is signed to Fueled by Ramen, an imprint probably best known for putting out the work of Fall Out Boy, and they share an insistent puerility and melodic flamboyance with their pop-punk labelmates. But they also switch between E.D.M., dubstep, rap, reggae, nu-metal, ukulele folk, glam rock, and piano balladeering at card-trick speed. They sound like Jason Mraz and Panic! at the Disco, Coldplay and 311, Walk the Moon and Imagine Dragons and Porter Robinson. Name any white-male-fronted musical act from the past two decades that's achieved significant commercial success while inspiring critical apathy, and you will hear that sound in Twenty One Pilots, if you listen long enough.

This amalgamated aesthetic is catnip to a significant portion of American listeners but functions like an invisibility cloak against music writers. Earlier this year, in the *Times Magazine*, Jayson Greene, an editor at Pitchfork, wrote about his realization that the band with the No. 3 song in America was a band he'd never heard of.[2] "What else didn't I know about?" he asked. "Where was I, in relation to everyone else?"

Last Thursday, I met up with everyone else to attend Twenty One Pilots' second sold-out show in Madison Square Garden. It was the last stop of the first leg of their hundred-and-nineteen-night world tour. The arena was full, the crowd was restless, and the air was playoff-game electric. When the band took the stage, in bank-robber ski masks, the audience—which was all ages, with plenty of thirty-year-olds mixed in with the teen-agers—collectively, hysterically screamed. In the pit below me, a buff young man lifted another man on his shoulders. For two straight hours, as men in hazmat suits blasted the crowd with fog and Dun walked on the audience's hands while encased in a red plastic ball and Joseph belted "My Heart Will Go On" as if it were by Queen rather than Céline Dion, these two buff men, along with most of the arena, sang every word.

The name Twenty One Pilots, if you're wondering, comes from the Arthur Miller play "All My Sons," in which a sixty-year-old man named Joe Keller knowingly ships defective airplane parts overseas during World War II, causing the death of—well, you get it. It's a heavy inspiration. So is Blurryface, a character the band created and named its latest album after. Blurryface "represents a certain level of insecurity," Joseph has said, and he sings in character as Blurryface for part of the live set, smearing his face and hands with black paint. The duo's faces, along with those that appear in their onstage visuals, are frequently covered with bandannas or hockey masks or fetish hoods. At times—when a melody mushroomed into panic, or when Dun started going terrifically, precisely

---

2 The article links here to "25 Songs that Tell Us Where Music is Going," The New York Times Magazine, March 10, 2016, www.nytimes.com/interactive/2016/03/10/magazine/25-songs-that-tell-us-where-music-is-going.html?_r=0#/ intro, which includes Jayson Greene's entry on "Stressed Out."

apocalyptic on the drums—I felt like I was listening to the soundtrack for a horror movie sponsored by Hot Topic, in which the great and terrible horror was just learning to be you.

It's a strange aesthetic, another amalgamation—a PG-rated blend of "Mr. Robot" and "The Purge." It also feels a little obvious, this implication that one's face, one's self, is too dangerous to be shown. A religious reading is easy to grasp: Joseph was homeschooled before attending a Christian school where his father was principal, and Dun wasn't allowed to listen to hip-hop or rock. The refrain on their album opener sounds exactly like praise and worship: "Can you save my heavy, dirty soul?" But, watching them, you're left with a simpler impression, and a broader one. What Twenty One Pilots do best, at the center of their suburban musical hodgepodge, is bring certain teen-bait ideas together: guilt with defiance, insecurity with confidence, paranoia with total command.

The arena was full of people who had been waiting for this, and there was, in the air, a sense of adulation and tearful communion that I associate with acts at the level of Beyoncé—a feeling that is particular to a handful of arena-filling musicians each year. I sat down briefly and my seat bounced to perfect eighth notes. Joseph merely had to glance at a section of the crowd and they'd shriek wildly; when he and Dun saluted their longtime tour manager with a plaque and a selfie, a girl in the section beside me did rap hands and cried. Toward the end, they played "Stressed Out," singing the chorus a cappella with the crowd: nearly twenty thousand people with their phones raised like candles, wishing their moms could sing them to sleep.

Source: Jia Tolentino, "The Slippery Appeal of the Biggest New Band in America," *The New Yorker*, August 24, 2016, www.newyorker.com/culture/jia-tolentino/the-slippery-appeal-of-the-biggest-new-band-in-america.

76

"Who Will Save the Guitar?"

MICHAEL MOLENDA

As popular music studies scholar Kevin Dettmar has shown in his book *Is Rock Dead?*, fans, critics, and musicians alike have been declaring rock's demise for decades, to the point where the death of rock almost seems like a necessary correlate to the music's continued vitality and growth.[1] Given this condition, it should come as little surprise that with the waning of rock's mainstream popularity in recent years, many have also expressed concerns about the health of one of its most potent and enduring symbols: the guitar. In their March 2017 issue, *Guitar Player*—the longest running practicing musician magazine devoted to the instrument—addressed the crisis directly with a provocative cover story: "Who Will Save the Guitar?"[2] A few months later, the *Washington Post* followed with a similarly alarming article: "The Slow, Secret Death of the Electric Guitar. And Why You Should Care."[3] In the *Guitar Player* feature, the magazine's editor, Michael Molenda, identifies numerous issues troubling the guitar's future—among them the industry's graying profile, its inability to connect with novice players, and its failure to cater to and cultivate the participation of a growing female base.[4] If the guitar industry is indeed in need of saving, what strategies do you think will work best? And is it the instrument itself, the archetype of the guitar hero virtuoso, or certain styles of rock music that are most in danger?

It doesn't take a genius or a cultural prognosticator to note that today's young people have myriad options for education, entertainment, engagement, and just plain fun. When it comes to our favorite love jones—the guitar—it's also obvious that teens and Millennials don't hold the instrument in nearly as much obsessive awe, wonder, and inspiration as more mature players, who, back in their early days, often wanted to *be* Jimmy Page, Eric Clapton, Jimi Hendrix, or any number of the transcendent guitarists blasting out of radios and television sets in the 1960s and '70s. The intense

---

1 Kevin J. H. Dettmar, *Is Rock Dead?* (New York: Routledge, 2006).
2 This was the not the first time the magazine had raised alarms about the guitar's status. Two decades earlier, during the height of the alternative rock era, another cover story had asked "Who Killed Rock Guitar?" (September 1997).
3 Geoff Edgers, "The Slow, Secret Death of the Electric Guitar. And Why You Should Care," *The Washington Post*, June 22, 2017, www.washingtonpost.com/graphics/2017/lifestyle/the-slow-secret-death-of-the-electric-guitar/?utm_term=.c6884cb8d992.
4 *Guitar Player* has since sought to remedy some of these problems, first by devoting its May 2017 cover story to "50 Sensational Female Guitarists" and second through its September 2017 "Youthquake" issue focused on young up-and-coming players.

pull of that rock-star dream was probably no different than our fervent desires to be astronauts, fighter pilots, or super heroes in our pre-teen years, but acquiring the skills to play guitar was infinitely more achievable than developing x-ray vision or indestructibility. So we got our hands on typically horrendously bad guitars and often suffered our way to competence—and, hopefully, a path to technical and creative excellence. And most of us have stayed dedicated to the guitar throughout the decades, and we will likely continue this devotion until our hands can no longer manage a ragged version of "Hey Joe."

But this is a story of an age gone by.

While society—and history—can be cyclical, there is no current globally seductive force such as "The Beatles," "Jimi-Jimmy-Jeff-and-Eric," "The Sex Pistols," "Stevie Ray Vaughan," "Nirvana," "Unplugged," or "Green Day" to drive an explosion of young people starting bands or solo acts and buying epic numbers of guitars and guitar gear. In fact, even if there were a 2017 version of "The Beatles on *The Ed Sullivan Show* in 1964," would it be compelling enough to inspire Millennials to launch a million bands?

When it comes to guitar playing—and, more importantly, the desire to continue playing guitar for the rest of one's life—the divide between teens and Millennials, and those 45 years old and above, appears to be significant. (One personal aside: I sometimes tell younger players that when I listened to records in the '60s and early '70s, all I did was listen to the records. I didn't do homework, clean my room, talk on the phone, or anything else. I sat in front of my record player like a zombie, utterly transfixed by every sound. They usually think I was a nut case.) In a recent audience-research survey by Brainyard, approximately twice as many Millennials as 45+ individuals are technology "wizards" (tech is life—existing without the Internet or gadgets is unimaginable), stream entertainment, enjoy taking risks, feel advertising is a waste of time, and like to try new things that no one else may be aware of yet. While the survey also found a fair amount of similarities between the two groups, the categories mentioned above may have some effect on guitar culture, both positive and negative.

So, why write a story like this one?

The big guitar and guitar-gear companies are hardly fading into extinction—though many *have* struggled in the current popular-culture climate that is not as conducive to guitar-product sales as other periods in the past when the guitar was more on top of the world, so to speak. Obviously, *Guitar Player*—and all of the other guitar magazines and websites across the planet—still have a ton of guitar players and guitar gear to report on. And cool new players are always popping up in varied stylistic genres, and they're finding audiences the old-fashioned way with record contracts, or via YouTube channels, Instagram posts, or other DIY initiatives.

However, the guitar's relative health as it stands today is not what drove the idea of this cover story. We're certainly aware that some manufacturers are concerned about the dearth of young people staying true to the guitar, and a few companies are troubled enough to actually develop products and other initiatives to keep youthful players playing.

To this end, we are starting out our coverage of the situation by talking to a few music-industry experts who are also monitoring the current state of guitar obsession. Obviously, we couldn't get to everyone in this initial article, but as the year unfolds, we will talk to others who are either concerned about the alleged ebb in committed young guitar players, as well, or who feel such worries are a bit dramatic and unwarranted. We don't want to miss anybody—a manufacturer, a teacher, a media outlet, or anyone else who might shed light on the current guitar culture and its future.

As *GP* celebrates its 50th anniversary this year, we are taking the opportunity to not just celebrate the guitar and its history, but to take incisive peeks at its future. *Guitar Player* has had a fantastic run serving the guitar community since the magazine's inception in 1967, and we'd love to continue that service to all of you for the next 50 years and beyond.

This is the reason we are putting the "patient" on an examination table. If it turns out we're swinging around a big sack of angst with little evidence of a problem, then we've only asked your indulgence for a few pages. (Chalk it up to the whim of a magazine that just hit a monumental anniversary.) But if it's more than that—and we truly need to seriously identify the fact that young, potential players are giving up on us—then we must look at developing strategies as a community to reverse that trend. Tomorrow is never assured—in life, or even in the continued popularity of that plank we adore.

The Article that Kicked Off the Call to Action

In an article filed at bloomberg.com on November 21, 2016, writer Kim Bhasin reported that, according to data from the research organization IBISWorld, the $6 billion United States retail market for musical instruments has been "stagnant" for five years.[5] Even more troubling for the guitar, specifically, is data from Fender—as revealed by its CEO, Andy Mooney, in the article—showing that 90 percent of the people who start playing forsake the instrument within their first year of getting to know it.

"A pretty big milestone for someone adopting any form of instrument is getting them through the first song," Mooney told bloomberg.com. "The industry's challenge—or opportunity—is getting people to commit for life."

For Fender, which believes that approximately half the people buying its guitars are first-timers, cracking that code to player commitment is key. The current strategy is to offer apps and other digital products that keep players engaged and interested in the guitar.

"The guitar is a very intimidating instrument," says Ethan Kaplan, Fender Digital's Chief Product Officer and General Manager. "The way it's sold is intimidating, and the way it's appreciated is intimidating. So we needed to make playing more accessible. For example, when we developed the Fender Tune app, we looked at tuners in the App Store, and they all assumed a level of knowledge most beginning players simply don't have. We'd give tuners to beginners, and ask them to tune up a guitar, and they didn't know what sharp and flat meant—or even the order of the strings from top to bottom—and they tended to break the high E string. So this was critical—we needed to give them a tool to help them want to keep picking up the guitar, and that was a tuner app that could reduce frustration, and educate them without making them feel stupid. We believe that if a beginner can get that first chord sounding great, they'll come back and pick up the guitar again."

Another industry veteran who has sounded the alarm is Rusty Shaffer of Optek Music Systems, whose Fretlight guitar—with its "lights on the fretboard" learning system—was developed years ago to offer a more nurturing educational environment for young and beginning players.

"The guitar industry has been on the decline for decades now, and, unfortunately, guitar manufacturers haven't addressed the problem," says Shaffer. "The guitar industry is basically a ski resort with no bunny slope. Think about that. The industry doesn't embrace the beginner. It's 'good luck and come back when you can play.'

Imagine being a 16-year-old today faced with the prospect of learning guitar. Everything else they touch—a gaming system or their smartphone—allows them to engage instantly. So when a youngster thinks about playing guitar, and he or she sees these antiquated lesson methods that

---

5 Kim Bhasin, "Don't Give Up on the Guitar. Fender is Begging You," *Bloomberg*, November 21, 2016, www.bloomberg.com/news/articles/2016-11-21/don-t-give-up-on-the-guitar-fender-is-begging-you.

haven't changed in almost 50 years combined with the prospect of results, the return on their time investment is just not there. It's not even close."

Shaffer's Fretlight system seeks to offer a more immediate return on that time investment, but worries that the community as a whole continues to look down on instant gratification when it comes to the guitar.

"One of the things that Fretlight does is embrace people who just want to play a riff," he says. "If somebody wants to play 'Smoke on the Water,' they just follow the lights on the fretboard. Now, it's possible that this person is not using the correct fingers to perform the riff. Does that really matter? But let's say the response from industry people is, 'No. You're not *really* playing guitar. You need to learn the notes on the fretboard. You need to learn scales. You need to learn the Circle of Fifths.' I completely disagree. If Fretlight can get someone playing a riff in ten minutes, I believe we've created a new customer for the industry. We helped that person achieve their guitar-playing dreams. Why criticize them? Our industry should embrace *all* interested parties, because it's foolish to think that we don't need to make a lot more players. No one wants to talk about the drop off the cliff that's coming when players my age stop purchasing custom-shop guitars and other high-end instruments."

Can Education & Entertainment Save Us?

The time-honored way to reach new players has been through education. The publishing industry is always a big part of that endeavor, and tech-oriented manufacturers such as BOSS, Fishman, Line 6, and others have long supported their artists and product managers getting out in the field and explaining how to make sounds with their gear. Many times, of course, these seminars correspond to a particular product, but, at times, also share general information on tone creation along with power-user tips. Line 6, for example, offers its Tone Made Pro seminars around its Helix multi-effects processor for guitar, but details the building blocks of some classic tones during the discussion. The nuts-and-bolts details of tone construction by guitar heroes such as The Edge, Stevie Ray Vaughan, Jimi Hendrix, and others can certainly be transferred to digital processors by other manufacturers, and even accomplished in the analog realm if a player has the time and budget to collect a bunch of actual amps and pedals and physically recreate the signal paths learned in the seminar.

"For 20 years, we have analyzed every nuance of the guitar amps, cabs, and effects used to create the most recognizable tones ever," said Marcus Ryle, Line 6's co-founder and President. "Now, we can use this expertise to help guitarists expand their knowledge and create the next generation of legendary tones."

Another route to seduce engagement is to inspire young players to share their music. Again, music publications often run contests where guitar stars and/or editors rate audio files or YouTube videos from solo artists and bands. The idea here is to provide a thrilling "end use" for a guitarist's creative toil and trouble, and hopefully inspire them to continue working their way towards popular acclaim. (*GP* recently relaunched its *Guitar Player* Records imprint in order to provide players a professional venue to distribute their instrumental-guitar music.)

In a similar vein, Ernie Ball has produced its Battle of the Bands program for a few years now, inviting unsigned acts to vie for the opportunity to perform on big stages at major music events. Other companies also have competitions from time to time where bands can win gear, perform with their heroes, or get booked on killer tours—all for simply having the ambition to create some music and share it with either the public and/or their contest judges.

On the face of it, these initiatives are directed at people who already have some facility with their instruments, rather than beginners. But a beginner could be energized by seeing a friend's band win a contest, or intrigued by having someone enthusiastically relate what they had learned at a seminar. The trick here would be the next step: How do we transform that interest into action, and get the novice to risk picking up a guitar and trying it out for themselves?

Women to the Rescue

Look at most magazine content and gear advertising throughout the guitar industry's past five decades, and it's no surprise that the vast majority of it is tailored towards men. For years, the guitar community has been perceived as a "Boy's Club," and we've certainly published stories where female guitarists have commented on the hardships they've endured in their careers due to the situation. But according to recent figures from Brainyard in its "Guitar Searcher Audience Profiles," the past dominance of men and guitars may be changing fast.[6]

Using Experian AudienceView as a source, Brainyard determined that, among Millennials, women were responsible for 49 percent of the web searches regarding information on guitar playing and gear, as compared to 51 percent for men. In the general population (all ages), these figures improved to 53 percent for women, and 47 percent for men.

These are rather earthshaking statistics, as they point out that women are, for the most part, equally active in seeking guitar data as are men. If the trend continues, the industry may need to adjust its perception of men as the movers and shakers and gear drivers, and look to women players as a viable and equivalent market for guitar products, guitar information, guitar marketing, and, well, pretty much all things guitar.

Furthermore, women may already be responsible for a significant increase in guitar sales. Last October, *GP*'s web editor Christopher Scapelliti posted "Is Taylor Swift the New Eddie Van Halen?"[7] Based around on a YouTube report by Phillip McKnight of McKnight Music Academy, the article detailed how his female students have expanded from four percent in 2006, to approximately 60 percent last year.

"We started asking the students, and eight out of ten of them cite Taylor Swift as the reason why they're playing music," stated McKnight. "She's doing the same thing Eddie Van Halen did in the early '80s—causing young players to want to take up the guitar and play."

While McKnight's is not a scientific or comprehensive survey, some manufacturers will affirm that guitar sales to women—especially acoustic guitars—are very strong. Online searches will also confirm that scores of female guitarists are actively promoting themselves on YouTube, Instagram, and other media these days. Where it used to be somewhat difficult to seek out and find awesome female players, this certainly isn't the case anymore, and that's brilliant and timely and wonderful.

Is There a Problem with the Guitar Media?

It's a tough question to ask when you're the editor of a guitar magazine, but is the media somewhat guilty of ignoring beginners? The challenge of keeping mature core readers happy with our content, while simultaneously appealing to the next generation of players is a never-ending discussion at *Guitar Player*. From the feedback we receive, some long-time readers enjoy learning new things from younger artists. There are also those readers who feel that many younger bands can't really

---

6 "Guitar Searcher Audience Profiles: Millennial vs Age 41+," *Brainyard* 2015–16, http://brainyard.com/documents/Brainyard_MI_Audience_Research_Report.pdf.

7 Christopher Scapelliti, "Is Taylor Swift the New Eddie Van Halen," *Guitar World*, October 19, 2016, www.guitarworld.com/artists/taylor-swift-new-eddie-van-halen.

play, sound like crap, and don't put in the educational sweat—even some of the new metal guitarists who wield absolutely crazy technique, and obviously practice like demons. At times, just a young player's look will cause a reader to disregard them. This is actually kind of funny, given how shocking most rockers back in the '60s and early '70s were to our parents and "The Man," and many of these "freaks of their time" are the very same players that readers continue to admire and respect today. But I digress . . .

For the most part, print magazines are favored by the 45+ crowd—and thank goodness for that—which is why the world's guitar publications tend to primarily cover Hendrix-Beck-Page-and-Any-Player-Who-Rose-to-Prominence-in-the-1960s-1970s-and-1980s. And, let's face it, the websites and social networks of these same guitar publications offer similar content—even though online media is where the next generation of players is looking for guitar information. So if you're, say, a teenager who was just mesmerized by a female guitarist who was playing some mad loops on YouTube, would the major guitar media offer that teenager entry into easy and unintimidating information on that particular application of the guitar? Would we even cover that looping guitarist at all?

"In guitar magazines, it's still a lot of dudes, and it's a lot of older dudes," says Kaplan. "The audience that is going to be the next generation of players is more diverse in a lot of ways, and they're pushing away from the thought that guitars are just for making rock and pop music. To them, the guitar doesn't have a demographic, and it doesn't have a gender. It's a tool for making samples, loops, and backing tracks if you're a hip-hop artist—or it's a way to just make noise. There are tons of artists out there using the guitar in ways that were never seen as things to learn. For example, I doubt many guitar classes teach Sigur Ros or My Bloody Valentine, but that's the type of music that turns some kids on to the guitar. Many guitar magazines only cover a certain level of artistic achievement that has nothing to do with the way a lot of young people use the guitar to create."

Shaffer feels that some form of egotism from those who should be open-minded, nurturing, and supportive is partly to blame for keeping beginners at arm's length.

"Sometimes, I think that everyone in the entire chain of players, manufacturers, retailers, and magazine editors feels that they all struggled to learn guitar," he says, "and there's no way they are going to let anybody in the club who takes what they perceive as any kind of a shortcut."

Next Steps

When guitarists talk about getting significantly more beginners into the ranks, there's always that fear that successfully appealing to a mass audience will mean "dumbing down" guitarcraft. I'm not sure that this is necessarily true. There will always be young guitarists who will aspire to scary technique, and we should provide them the tools to take that difficult (and rewarding) quest. But perhaps, as a community, we have focused on those who aspire to that level of accomplishment more than those who simply wish to utilize the guitar as a sound source. The great sonic, textural, and compositional players should be just as respected for their creativity, as those similarly excellent players who are influenced by Yngwie Malmsteen or Jeff Beck. It would be a wonderful reality indeed if both types of players could co-exist within the larger guitar community.

"Some of this work is already being done by some of the artists themselves," says Kaplan. "They are effectively demystifying what it means to be an artist. They are showing that the guitar is not necessarily an intimidating instrument for virtuosos—it's a means of expressing yourself. Someone who knows just three chords can create just as much as someone who knows intervals and Mixolydian modes. The guitar may not be the easiest tool for expression—certainly not as easy as pushing buttons on an iPhone—but once you get past the initial learning curve, it is just as relevant a means of expression as anything out there."

If one keeps an open mind, there are obviously many ways that the guitar can be deployed as a musical and compositional tool. A beginning player might choose a creative option that you or I might find, um, "not to our taste." But if we can still find it within ourselves to support and respect those choices, then perhaps we can help make the guitar less intimidating and imperious, and actually stop some potential players from shoving the instrument under their beds to collect dust. I guess it's our move. *What will we do?*

Source: Michael Molenda, "Who Will Save the Guitar?," *Guitar Player*, March 2017, pp. 48–53.

77

"Where Have All the Rock Stars Gone?"

David Shumway

As rock has gradually ceded its popularity on the charts to hip-hop and pop acts, it has seemed that the rock star is becoming a vanishing breed. In the conclusion to his 2014 book *Rock Star* (included here in a revised and updated version for the *Rock History Reader*), David Shumway, a popular music studies scholar and professor of English at Carnegie Mellon University, argues that it is not simply the dearth of rock stars that is alarming, but rather the inability of today's popular musicians to reach the public consciousness and have a broad cultural impact. As he contends, where iconic rock stars such as Bob Dylan and the Beatles once served as a binding force for a strong countercultural identity and sense of community, popular music has become increasingly fragmented, smashed into thousands of niches that have rendered the galvanizing power of those 1960s stars a thing of the distant past. Similarly, the rise of social media crowdfunding and fan patronage has removed current artists from the very economic support systems traditionally designed to produce and sustain stars. Shumway views these developments skeptically, as a sad commentary on popular music's marginalized cultural position. His polemical essay raises numerous intriguing questions: Have the politicized rock stars that Shumway describes truly disappeared, or can you think of recent artists who have affected contemporary culture in significant ways? Conversely, what are we to make of the many songs from hip-hop and pop artists (such as Shop Boyz' "Party Like a Rock Star," Miley Cyrus/Hannah Montana's "Rock Star," and Post Malone's "Rockstar") that celebrate the rock star as a symbol of excess or individual empowerment?[1] Why have such songs proliferated in recent years? What relevance does this notion of the rock star hold for today's audiences?

The stars I discussed in my book, *Rock Star: The Making of Cultural Icons from Elvis to Springsteen*, remain cultural icons.[1] These performers and others of their era had broad cultural currency; they had meaning for people who did not like, or even hear, their music. They embodied currents of cultural change that emerged in the 1950s and became dominant in the 1960s. Is there any figure who has emerged recently in popular music of whom this can be said? This is not meant as one of those laments about artistic decline, in which the younger generation is compared unfavorably to

---

1 For an insightful consideration of these kinds of songs and the changing nature of the rock star, see Christopher Weingarten, "Grow Up Like a Rock Star," *The Village Voice*, January 15, 2008, www.villagevoice.com/2008-01-15/unknown/grow-up-like-a-rock-star/.

the great achievements of the past ones. I have no doubt that more recent generations of performers are more skilled and at least as talented as their musical forebearers. Rather, my point is that the cultural position of popular music and its stars has been diminished.

Some of this change has to do with social conditions not directly related to either the production or consumption of popular music and its performers. In *Rock Star*, I argued that rock stars contributed to the changes that we associate with the 1960s: the breaking down of hierarchies of race and gender; the new patterns of courtship, love, and marriage; the reintroduction of leftist political perspectives into popular consciousness. But rock & roll hardly caused these changes all by itself. Even the development of a politicized youth culture, perhaps the change most strongly dependent on the music, emerged out of manifold forces and conditions, among them Cold War rhetoric and youth's increasing purchasing power. The ferment of the 1960s was largely over by the 1980s, and, while many of the changes that grew out of the 1960s remain incomplete, the early years of the new millennium have not seen youth in general associated with new movements for social change. Black Lives Matter has many young supporters, but it isn't primarily identified as a youth movement. If the Occupy movement (or was it a moment?) is an exception, we might ask where its impact in popular culture has been felt. While that impact might still come, it is possible that the economic conditions that gave rise to Occupy are not those likely to support cultural innovation. The 1950s and 1960s were defined by prosperity. Thus, we might conclude the time is not ripe for popular music stars to take on the kind of cultural significance that those I've discussed here attained. Athletes have been the prominent of the stars supporting Black Lives Matter.

Other changes have to do specifically with patterns of production, distribution, and consumption of music. The continuing decline in CD sales, the shift first to music downloads and then to streaming, and the difficulty of getting consumers to pay for music have changed the character of the music business and have contributed to (but are also partly a result of) a major shift in the way the pop audience experiences music. Between 1999 and 2015, music sales declined by about two-thirds.[2] The industry blamed illegal downloads and file sharing, and clearly this accounts for some of the change. Since 1987, older buyers have increased their music market share, while the younger demographics' shares, especially those aged 15–19, have decreased. In other words, the young, the group the industry previously counted on to fuel music sales—and at whom promotional strategies continued to be aimed—are no longer buying as much music as they did in the 1960s and 1970s.[3]

Those who do buy music are purchasing CDs less and less. CD sales in the United States have fallen every year since 2002.[4] As of 2016, physical music media, including vinyl and CD albums, accounted for less than a quarter of total recorded music revenues. In 2016 for the first time, paid streaming subscriptions accounted for more than half of recorded music revenues. Beginning in 2013, digital downloads began to decline, as consumers moved to streaming subscriptions.[5] As a result, total album sales continue to decline, even though vinyl LPs have become more popular, sales having grown at an average annual rate of 36 percent since 2007. Still, vinyl only accounts for 5.7 percent of recorded music revenue.[6] Listeners prefer to have the vast music catalogs of streaming services available, rather than to own albums in either physical or digital form. One can conclude from this, that although one can stream albums, listeners are likely to continue the trend of focusing their interest on songs.

This change in purchasing behavior needs to be understood in the context of changes in listening behavior. Where at one time, listening to recorded music was often a social activity, since the advent of the iPod it has become an intensely private pastime. Despite the decline of music purchases by young people, popular music continues to be significant for adolescents. Smart phones have replaced iPods as the main delivery system for music consumption, and many college students seem attached to them as if they were life-support systems. Yet the prevalence of personal listening devices illustrates one reason why popular music has lost its centrality. The 1960s equivalent technology to the smart phone was the car radio, but the radio was public, while a smart phone is private. Not only did young people ride around listening in groups, but everyone listening to a station—or, indeed, during the heyday of the top 40, to almost any station—heard the same records. Now, each listener creates his or her own playlist, taking individual songs and typically ignoring their presentation within an album. With the decline of radio as a major medium for the exposure of new artists and songs, the music market has become fragmented. Young people no longer have a common music culture that defines them against their parents. Rather, they may participate in a particular music culture that exists together with others in which their peers participate, or they may simply pick up tracks more or less randomly. Thus, individual listeners tend to be increasingly isolated users of music, despite social media.

In addition to the overall decline in album sales, there are fewer blockbuster recordings. This is made plain by the occasional exception. In 2015, Adele's *25*, "which was on sale for only the last six weeks of the year, sold 7.44 million copies, more than any album has sold in a calendar year since 2004. About one out of every 32 albums sold [that] year was '25'."[7] Adele's album was not available for streaming. Only three other albums sold over a million copies in 2015.[8] The shift away from albums is not only an obvious economic loss to the industry, but also a significant change in the relationship between audience and artist. In the days of the LP, the album and its packaging allowed purchasers to get to know (or feel as if they got to know) the artist. Streaming a track provides far less of a sense of the producer, turning every artist into the equivalent of the one-hit wonder. It is true that, prior to 2009 and the recession, proceeds from live performance had grown significantly since the mid-1990s, and North American concert revenues grew by one-third between 2011 and 2015.[9] But even this phenomenon reveals the dependence of the industry on older audiences and older acts. It is symptomatic of the current popular music scene that U2's 360° Tour (2009–2011) and the Rolling Stones' A Bigger Bang Tour (2005–2007) were the largest grossing such events in history.[10] Of the top twenty highest grossing tours, only Coldplay's A Head Full of Dreams Tour (2016–2017) came from an act formed after the 1980s.[11]

The conditions specific to the music industry need to be understood in the context of the decline of a genuine mass audience for any medium. What we have long considered to be mass culture has become increasingly a collection of niche cultures. The movies and radio, which had been mass media before World War II, began to lose audience to television in the 1950s, and they responded with the first wave of niche marketing—to youth. Television became the most dominant mass medium of all time by the late 1950s, but by the 1970s, cable began to produce audience fragmentation, which has continued apace as the three broadcast television networks became the 100-plus channels of digital cable or satellite TV. More recently, cable has lost customers to streaming services. The same fragmentation affected print as early as the late 1960s, when mass-circulation magazines such as *Life* gave way to special interest periodicals, and has continued until the present, when people are increasingly reading posts on social media instead of a newspaper their neighbors are also likely to read.

Music was dependent to a great degree on these other mass media for mass-audience exposure, first with radio and later television, with the movies providing powerful, if secondary, exposure. The rise of rock stardom was enabled by the allied media. The mass-print media, which had provided movie stars their primary offscreen connection to the audience, also gave rock fans the most detailed information about the stars' lives offstage. The decline of mass culture means not only that the music reaches smaller groups of listeners but also that performers are less likely to find themselves magnified into stars. Because stars are less visible, their economic clout is much reduced. Young listeners are much less likely to purchase new songs merely because they were recorded by a particular artist, and so the decline of the music star system contributed to the decline in music sales.

Popular music never equaled the mass reach of movies or television, but it may have had its peak mass audience later, in the 1980s, with megaselling albums such as Michael Jackson's *Thriller*. One might equally suggest that these blockbuster records and the mentality they produced in the industry are properly understood in parallel with the similar phenomenon in Hollywood, whereby the enormous sales of a few products tended to mask a decline in the frequency of purchase and experience. Beginning in the late 1990s, however, even the blockbuster strategy failed, and sales declined as the market continued to fragment.

Still, the music industry was also involved in niche marketing much earlier than the other media, with specialized segments going back to the dawn of commercial recording. However, as Elijah Wald has argued, prior to the emergence of rock & roll as the dominant product category, popular music was characterized by a diversity of styles of performance that were heard by a mass audience. What these diverse styles tended to share were songs, which remained the industry's main product until perhaps as late as the 1960s.[12] Thus, up through the 1950s, songwriters—Berlin, the Gershwins, Porter, and so on—had a greater reach than all but a few artists, such as Enrico Caruso or Bing Crosby. On these grounds, it might be argued that popular music lacked a robust star system until the rise of rock & roll. It was then that the experience of music became increasingly dependent on a bond with a performer who was understood as the author of his or her own songs.

I offer this history in order to suggest that the period of popular music beginning in the 1950s with rock & roll, which critics and the industry have accepted as the norm, is in fact just one moment in a continually changing formation. Thus, gurus of a new music business or Internet utopia are right when they caution doomsayers that music will not disappear even if CDs do. But because the experience of music has never been the pure appreciation of the sound apart from a performance context, this change will mean that the listening will change even if the music itself remains the same. In the era of mass culture—what Max Horkheimer and Theodor Adorno described under the heading of the "culture industry"—the various mass media magnified each other.[13] The profits produced from sales to a mass market made the culture industries invest heavily in promotion, and such publicity was a significant condition for the star system in both film and music. Under the new music economics, where niche rather than mass marketing is the rule, heavy investment in promotion no longer makes sense. Indeed, investment of any kind in any particular act must be curtailed, since the likely returns are smaller.

Fortunately for musicians, the costs of recording and distributing music have become radically cheaper. Where at one time, record company resources were necessary to make top-quality recordings, current technology means that high-quality recordings can be made by almost anyone. The Internet, of course, has solved the problem of distribution. The result is that, despite falling music sales, there are more recordings available. Because these recordings are not supported by mass publicity, however—or reflected in mass media—they reach fewer and fewer people. Under these conditions, the beginnings of what has been called by Berklee College of Music administrator Peter Spellman "patronage from the masses" or "crowdfunding" have emerged.[14] Under this model, instead of selling products or performances, musicians are supported by direct contributions from fans.

The Internet is at the heart of this as well, and the new patronage began by artists using it to reach fans to ask for support. Beginning in the 2000s, at least three different patronage sites have appeared: Artist Share, Sellaband, and Slice the Pie. Artist Share offers fans greater access to an artist's music and the creation of that music in return for a small donation. The greater the donation, the greater degree of access a fan will have. Sellaband allows performers to produce a CD through direct contributions from fans. A band must reach the goal of $50,000 to have the CD recorded and distributed, with distribution arranged through Amazon.com. The donations by "believers," as they are called, are not pure charity, however. Believers are investors who receive a percentage of profits from the CD's sales and are entitled to a share of the site's ad revenue. Slicethepie calls itself "the music stock market." Users are paid a small amount for each review they contribute based on how accurately the review reflects the tastes of other investors. In effect, this turns each audience member into an A&R person, and the "review" into a scouting report. The site also allows participants to invest in a band and profit if its "stock" rises. Bands that reach a certain threshold of approval get to make a CD, which their investors receive along with other access privileges, at the band's discretion.

The rhetoric of these crowdfunding services and of the champions of this new model of music commerce like Spellman, Dave Kusek (another Berklee administrator), and Internet prophet, Yochai Benkler, is couched in terms of democracy, meritocracy, community, and artistic freedom. These promoters have different ideologies, which bespeak the ambiguous economic implications of the new patronage. Spellman's rhetoric is clearly neoliberal, and his populism reminds one a bit of the Tea Party in his antipathy to the record companies, combined with a championing of economic freedom. He uses the words *community, audience,* and *fans,* interchangeably with *customers.* Kusek asserts that music is entertainment and bands are entertainers—not artists.[15] Benkler, on the contrary, imagines the failure of copyright protection of musical property to push popular music in the direction of not-for-profit activities such as classical music performances or the academic disciplines of the humanities. He sees the Internet as distancing music from the usual model of commodity exchange and returning it to older models of fee-for-service (for performances) and pro bono. This is not only because the music the artist produces will not earn a significant return when sold as a commodity but also because fans' donations are genuinely charitable in their intent and effect.[16] Spellman and Benkler each capture an aspect of the changes in the music economy, and the latter is helpful in reminding us that even under late capitalism, nonconforming economic activities continue to exist. But, in the long run, I see the neoliberal model as more likely to prevail, producing not, as Kusek has claimed, a new musical middle class but a new musical underclass, as more bands are able to eke out a living, but just barely.

Despite their differing ideologies, both Spellman and Benkler speak of the opportunities available when artists are freed from the domination of the record companies. While it is certainly the case that record companies' "gate keeping" has traditionally been restrictive, and the overhead associated with these businesses has meant that artists have received a tiny percentage of the revenue their work has generated, the companies did offer numerous services to artists, many of which under the new model have devolved back to the artists themselves. For example, in order to raise money on one of the new patronage sites, bands have to promote themselves. As Spellman reveals, crowd-funding is in fact akin to outsourcing, and it reminds one of what Andrew Ross has observed about the trap that knowledge workers fall into of ever-expanding labor justified by one's devotion to the work.[17]

Moreover, since most new patronage schemes involve some form of increased access, artists would seem simply to have exchanged a few masters for many. Under the old system, established stars at least had the freedom to experiment, knowing that one poorly selling record would not mean the end of their contract. Under crowdfunding, the fans must be kept satisfied or they will stop contributing. And access often includes intervention into the creative process. The jam band Umphrey's McGee, for example, has offered small groups of fans concerts where they can text themes or ideas to the band around which it will improvise.[18] This kind of audience interaction may be satisfying to the band, but one could imagine it feeling tyrannical to many artists. Offering increased access itself requires time investments in responding to fans' communications and desires. Singer-songwriter Jonathan Coulton allows anyone to use his recordings as the basis for their own works in any medium, which has helped him to build a paying audience for his music, but he says he spends countless hours emailing with fans about their long-distance collaborations.[19]

After these special access concerts, Umphrey's McGee would hang out with the audience, sharing beers and conversation. To me this epitomizes the upside and the downside of the fan experience under the new model. The upside is that fans have always fantasized about getting to hang out with their idols. Jann Wenner started *Rolling Stone* in order to meet rock stars. But what if the musicians you are hanging out with aren't rock stars but just musicians? Is it still a thrill when you have just spent the last hour telling these guys what to play? Stardom is partly defined by fans' imaginary personal relationships with stars. What happens when they start having actual relationships with them? On the upside, they get a certain degree of recognition from the star; on the downside, they are in an actual relationship, with all of the complications that that involves, including the inevitable disappointments that real—rather than imaginary—relationships entail.

For the artist, the new music economy has meant that it is harder and harder to attain recognition beyond his or her niche. The new patronage model institutionalizes and further narrows the niche to those fans willing to pay more than the cost of a track or CD—or to pay without the certainty of receiving a product in return. One could argue that the term "popular music" has become outdated because no style of music reaches a broad enough audience. My undergraduate students typically know the music of my college cohort—the Beatles, Eric Clapton, Joni Mitchell, Led Zeppelin, and so on—but it is often difficult to find more than a few who are familiar with the same current releases. As a result of this audience fragmentation, popular music and its performers have lost the cultural centrality they once enjoyed, and that means that fewer people are interested enough to pay for the product.

This is not to say that music celebrities now fail to inspire great devotion in their fans. Celebrity has, if anything, become a larger element of popular culture since the 1960s, and the music industry continues to produce it. Yet increasingly, performers seem less to be stars and more to be mere celebrities. The dream of those entering the business since the 1950s has been to become a star, the creation of which was also the aim of the record companies, whose A&R and publicity apparatuses were designed with this goal in mind. But now, as even the most popular music reaches a smaller and smaller fraction of the total audience, the position of the star has, in effect, been eliminated.

Perhaps the bigger issue is that even the music of chart toppers reaches a small fraction of the total audience. Paradoxically, however, as popular music has reached a smaller audience, it has become more pop in form. Those whose recordings now top the charts usually seem to be of the least cultural significance, because their music typically takes no risks. One might argue that Michael Jackson's shift from the rock & roll persona of his years with the Jackson Five to his solo incarnation as the "King of Pop," marks the moment when the pendulum of popular taste began swinging away from the innovation and radicalism of rock toward the familiarity and safety of pop. With the rise of *American Idol* as America's most popular television show after 2002, the new triumph of pop was confirmed. Chart-topping performers going back to Britney Spears and continuing through Lady Gaga and Adele are best understood as entertainers, even though they borrow from the tradition of rock & roll theatrics and may on occasion push the boundaries of decorum.

While contemporary Top Forty hits in general don't sound like pre-rock pop, they share some of its qualities, including a preference for style over substance. "Most of the songs played on Top Forty radio are collaborations between producers like Stargate and 'top line' writers like Ester Dean. The producers compose the chord progressions, program the beats, and arrange the 'synths,' or computer-made instrumental sounds; the top-liners come up with primary melodies, lyrics, and the all-important hooks, the ear-friendly musical phrases that lock you into the song."[20] In this model, the creativity has passed from performer, who doesn't write her own songs, to producer and top line writer. The result is highly crafted recordings that don't sound like anyone's personal expression: "A relatively small number of producers and top-liners create a disproportionately large share of contemporary hits, which may explain why so many of them sound similar."[21] While one might compare this to the work of Berry Gordy or Phil Spector in the 1960s, the great stars were able to enlist producers to help them reach their own artistic goals.

To some extent, the cultural practices associated with rock & roll remain in place. Artists like Chance the Rapper or Beyoncé on *Lemonade* are able to make use of them. The rise of the rock stars in the 1960s meant that popular music would be treated differently afterward, and it continues to receive more serious treatment than it did in the pre-rock era. The new pop is not, therefore, a mere repetition of your great-grandfather's music or style, but it may be equally inconsequential. The age of silly love songs and lavish display has returned. Hence, while lots of people know who Lady Gaga is, I suspect most don't think of her as representing anything beyond sheer spectacle itself. The media remain inclined to assume that popular musicians have something to say about serious matters—and some of them do. But the fragmentation of mass culture has meant that they are able say it to smaller and smaller fractions of the population.

Bono, whose political advocacy in the courts of real-world power has expanded his reach, may have been the last rock star to capture the imagination of a broad spectrum of the public. But even this case reveals a change. Bono's advocacy, in which he presents himself as an equal of diplomats and captains of industry, does not seem to be of a piece with his role in U2, the way, say, John Lennon's antiwar activism seemed perfectly consistent with his role in the Beatles.

The fate of hip-hop may be the best illustration of the increasing marginalization of popular music and its impact on American culture. Hip-hop is arguably the last great innovation in popular music, the successor to ragtime, jazz, R&B, and rock & roll. All of them emerged out of African American culture to change the tastes of Americans of all races. Hip-hop also attracted a large audience of young white listeners, but it did not come to dominate the way its predecessors had. Though several aspects of hip-hop may have made it a more difficult taste to acquire—one could mention the absence of melody and harmony and the often violent and misogynistic lyrics—I would argue that the fragmentation of the market, which was already well under way in the late 1980s, has been a bigger factor. Most Americans didn't hear the music routinely, so it remained foreign to their ears. Earlier hip-hop stars like Grandmaster Flash and Public Enemy were at least as critical of American society as Dylan ever was, and they led some commentators to imagine hip-hop artists as politically efficacious organic intellectuals.[22] But in the last ten years or so, even though hip-hop artists like Jay-Z are popular music's most innovative contributors, the form has become less political and its performers seem less culturally central.[23] In a different market, hip-hop stars might have become leaders like James Brown. As it is, popular music appears to be headed back to the margins of cultural life, and that is a loss for all us.

Notes

[1] David R. Shumway, *Rock Star: The Making of Cultural Icons from Elvis to Springsteen* (Baltimore: Johns Hopkins University Press, 2014).

[2] Mark J. Perry, "Have CD's Have Been Supplanted by Music Streaming," *Newsweek* April 4, 2017, www.newsweek. com/how-cds-have-been-supplanted-music-streaming-588819. See also, Joshua P. Friedlander, "News and Notes on 2016 Shipment and Revenue Statistics," www.riaa.com/reports/.

[3] Stan Liebowitz, "Will MP3 Downloads Annihilate the Record Industry? The Evidence So Far," *Advances in the Study of Entrepreneurship, Innovation, and Economic Growth* 15 (2004): 229–60, www.utdallas.edu/~liebowit/.

[4] Perry, "Have CD's Have Been Supplanted by Music Streaming."

[5] Joshua P. Friedlander, "News and Notes on 2016 Shipment and Revenue Statistics."

[6] Perry, "Have CD's Have Been Supplanted by Music Streaming."

[7] Ben Sisario, "Adele Album Resists the Streaming Trend in Music Sales," *New York Times*, January 5, 2016, www. nytimes.com/2016/01/06/business/media/adele-album-resists-the-trends-in-music-sales.html?_r=0.

[8] Ibid

[9] "The Verdict: 2009's Hits and Misses," *Rolling Stone*, Jan. 21, 2010, 12; Hannah Karp, "Music Industry Sees Growth in Concert Revenue," *Wall Street Journal*, September 16, 2016, www.wsj.com/articles/music-industry-sees-growth-in-concert-revenue-1474250642

[10] Marisa Marcellino, "Here Are the Highest-Grossing Music Tours of All Time," *Entertainment Weekly*, May 4, 2017, http://ew.com/music/2017/05/04/highest-grossing-music-tours/.

[11] Bob Allen, "Coldplay Surpasses Madonna for No. 5 Highest Grossing Tour of All Time," *Billboard*, July 26, 2017, http://www.billboard.com/articles/columns/chart-beat/7881187/coldplay-passes-madonna-no-5-highest-grossing-tour.

[12] Elijah Wald, *How the Beatles Destroyed Rock 'n' Roll: An Alternative History of American Popular Music* (New York: Oxford University Press, 2009), 166–229.

[13] Max Horkheimer and Theodor W. Adorno, "The Culture Industry," *Dialectic of Enlightenment*, trans. John Cumming (New York: Continuum, 1972), 120–67.

[14] Peter Spellman, "Musician 2.0, 3.0. 4.0 . . . Developing Music Careers in Uncertain Times: A Psycho-Spiritual-Musical Manifesto," www.mbsolutions.com/articles/. Spellman runs a company called Music Business Solutions and is director of career development at Berklee College of Music.

[15] Dave Kusek, *The Future of Music: Manifesto for the Digital Music Revolution* (Boston: Berklee Press, 2005).

[16] Yochai Benkler, "Yochai Benkler: The New, Open-Source Economics," filmed July 2005, posted Apr. 2008, TED video, 17:56, www.ted.com/talks/yochai_benkler_on_the_new_open_source_economics.html; Yochai Benkler, "Yochai Benkler—On Autonomy, Control and Cultural Experience," *YouTube* video, 7:53, from an interview for Steal this Film 2, New York, Apr. 2007, posted by "stealthisfilm" on July 24, 2011, www.youtube.com/watch?v=vmiGOQooTNA.

[17] Spellman, "Musician 2.0, 3.0. 4.0"; Andrew Ross, *Nice Work If You Can Get It: Life and Labor in Precarious Times* (New York: NYU Press, 2010).

[18] "The New Music Biz: Letting Fans Direct the Band," *Time* video, 4:44, n.d., www.time.com/time/video/player/0,32068,114797669001_2025840,00.html.

[19] "The New Music Biz: Cracking the Code to Online Success," *Time* video, 5:01, n.d., www.time.com/time/video/player/0,32068,114803516001_2027352,00.html.

[20] John Seabrook, "The Song Machine," *The New Yorker*, March 26, 2012, www.newyorker.com/magazine/2012/03/26/the-song-machine.

[21] Ibid

[22] See, e.g., Tricia Rose, *Black Noise: Rap Music and Black Culture in Contemporary America* (London: Wesleyan University Press, 1994), 99–145; Mark Anthony Neal, "Postindustrial Soul: Black Popular Music at the Crossroads," in *That's the Joint!: The Hip-Hop Studies Reader*, ed. Murray Forman and Mark Anthony Neal (New York: Routledge, 2004), 363–87; *Born to Use Mics: Reading Nas's Illmatic*, ed. Michael Eric Dyson and Sohail Daulatzi (New York: Basic Civitas Books, 2010), passim.

[23] Neal, "Postindustrial Soul," traces this decline all the way back to 1990, and he calls Public Enemy's *It Takes a Nation of Millions to Hold Us Back* (1988) "the apex of politically infused hip-hop," 376.

Source: David R. Shumway, "Where Have All the Rock Stars Gone?," revised from *Rock Star: The Making of Musical Icons from Elvis to Springsteen* (Baltimore: Johns Hopkins University Press, 2014), pp. 205–13.

Copyright Acknowledgments

Every effort has been made to trace and acknowledge copyright holders of the material appearing in this book. The following publishers and individuals have generously given permission to reprint articles and excerpts from longer works. Additions or amendments to this list are welcomed.

Albini, Steve. "The Problem with Music," *The Baffler* 1993. Reprinted by permission of the author.

Alterman Boyle, Loraine. "Record World Forum: Three Artists on the New Consciousness," *Record World*, May 19, 1973. Reprinted by Permission of the Author.

Anderson, Chester. "New Geology of Rock," *San Francisco Oracle*, 1967. Reprinted by permission of Antonia Lamb.

Arnold, Gina. Excerpts from *Route 666: On the Road to Nirvana* (New York: St. Martin's Press, 1993). Reprinted by permission of the author.

Aronowitz, Alfred. "Sweet Baby James." From *New York Post*, March 9 © 1970 *New York Post*. All Rights Reserved. Used by permission and protected by the Copyright Laws of the United States. The printing, copying, redistribution, or retransmission of this Content without express written permission is prohibited.

Bangs, Lester. "How to be a Rock Critic." Reprinted from *Shakin' Street Gazette*, October 1974. © 1974 by Lester Bangs, 2007–12 by Lester Bangs Estate. Used by permission of the Bangs Estate.

Berry, Chuck. "Chuck Berry: the Autobiography" written by Chuck Berry. © 1987 Isalee Publishing Company. All Rights Reserved Used by Permission.

Block, Adam. "The Confessions of a Gay Rocker," *The Advocate*, April 15, 1982. Reprinted by permission of Kenan S. Block.

Bracker, Milton. "Experts Propose Study of 'Craze'." From *The New York Times*, February 23 © 1957 *The New York Times*. All Rights Reserved. Used by permission and protected by the Copyright Laws of the United States. The printing, copying, redistribution, or retransmission of this Content without express written permission is prohibited.

Brown, Ruth and Andrew Yule. Excerpts from *Miss Rhythm*, © 1996 by Ruth Brown and Andrew Yule. Used by permission of Dutton, an imprint of Penguin Publishing Group, a division of Penguin Random House LLC.

Bruford, Bill. Excerpt from *Bill Bruford: The Autobiography* published by Jawbone Press in 2009. Reprinted by permission of the author and publisher.

Bunzel, Peter. "Music Biz Goes Round and Round: It Comes Out Clarkola." © 1960 Time Inc. All rights reserved. Reprinted from *Life* and published with permission of Time Inc. Reproduction in any manner in any language in whole or in part without written permission is prohibited.

Landau, Jon. "A Whiter Shade of Black" from *The Age of Rock* (New York: Vintage Books, 1969). Reprinted by permission of the author.

Leftridge, Steve. "Pour Some Sugarland on Me: Why Country is the New Classic Rock," *PopMatters*, April 14, 2010. Reprinted by permission of *PopMatters*.

Lester, Paul. "Vampire Weekend: 'They're Attacking a Version of Us that Doesn't Exist'," *The Guardian*, January 7, 2010. © Guardian News & Media Ltd 2017.

McNeil, Legs and Gillian McCain. "Why Don't We Call it Punk?" Excerpt from *Please Kill Me*, © 1996 by Legs McNeil and Gillian McCain. Used by permission of Grove/Atlantic, Inc. Any third party use of this material, outside of this publication, is prohibited.

Molenda, Michael. "Who Will Save the Guitar?," *Guitar Player*, March 2017. Reprinted by permission of the author.

Moon, Tom. "Public Enemy's Bomb Squad," *Musician*, October 1991. Reprinted by permission of the author.

Onkey, Dr. Lauren. "A Response to 'Why no Yes in the Rock Hall'," *The Rock Hall Blog*, January 13, 2011. Reprinted by permission of the author.

Paglia, Camille. "Madonna—Finally a Real Feminist," *The New York Times*, December 14, 1990. Reprinted by permission of the author.

Powers, Ann. "Mumford & Sons Preaches to Masses." ©2012 National Public Radio, Inc. News report titled "Mumford & Sons Preaches to Masses" by Ann Powers was originally published on npr.org on September 27, 2012, and is used with the permission of NPR. Any unauthorized duplication is strictly prohibited.

Prato, Greg. Excerpts from *MTV Ruled the World: The Early Years of Music Video*. Lulu.com, 2010. Reprinted by permission of the author.

Rabid, Jack. "The Big Takeover: The Punk Rock Years, 1980–81," *The Big Takeover*, 2000. Reprinted by permission of the author.

Regev, Motti. "Rock Aesthetics and Musics of the World." *Theory, Culture & Society* 14 (3), pp. 125–142. © 1997 by SAGE Publications. Reprinted by permission of SAGE Publications.

Riesel, Victor. "U.S. Musicians' Union Says, 'Beatles Stay Home'," *Delaware County Daily Times* April 3, 1964. Reprinted by permission of Michael Riesel.

Scherman, Tony. Excerpts from *Backbeat: The Earl Palmer Story* (New York: Da Capo Press, 2000). Reprinted by permission of the author.

Schoemer, Karen. "Electronic Eden." From *Newsweek*, February 10 © 1997 Newsweek Media Group. All Rights Reserved. Used by permission and protected by the Copyright Laws of the United States. The printing, copying, redistribution, or retransmission of this Content without express written permission is prohibited.

Schulps, Dave. "The King of Surf Guitar Lives!," *Bay Area Music* magazine, August 13, 1993. Reprinted by permission of *BAM* magazine.

Shumway, David R. Foreword by Anthony DeCurtis, *Rock Star: The Making of Musical Icons from Elvis to Springsteen*, pp. 205–213. © 2014 Johns Hopkins University Press. Revised and reprinted with permission of Johns Hopkins University Press.

Siegel, Jules. "Goodbye Surfing Hello God!—The Religious Conversion of Brian Wilson." Originally published in *Cheetah*, October 1967. © Jules Siegel 1967, 1972, 2005. All rights reserved. Reprinted by permission of the author.

Smith, Evan. "Even Heavy-Metal Fans Complain That Today's Music Is Too Loud!!!." Reprinted with permission of *The Wall Street Journal*, © 2008 Dow Jones & Company, Inc. All Rights Reserved Worldwide. License number 4242060773337.

"So You Wanna Fake Being an Indie Rock Expert?" *SoYouWanna.Com*, www.soyouwanna.com/site/syws/indierock/indierockFULL.html. Reprinted by permission of Demand Media.

Spector, Ronnie with Vince Waldron. Excerpts from *Be My Baby: How I Survived Mascara, Miniskirts, and Madness or My Life as a Fabulous Ronette* (New York: Harmony Books, 1990). Reprinted by permission of the authors.

Sullivan, Kathleen. "2 Live Crew and the Cultural Contradictions of *Miller*," *Reconstruction*, 1990. Reprinted by permission of the author.

Sweeney, Joey. "We're the Younger Generation," *www.Salon.com*, August 31, 2000. This article first appeared in Salon.com, at www.Salon.com. An online version remains in the Salon archives. Reprinted with permission.

Tate, Greg. "It's Like This Y'all," *Village Voice*, January 19, 1988. Reprinted by permission of the author.

Tolentino, Jia. "The Slippery Appeal of the Biggest New Band in America," *The New Yorker*, August 24, 2016. Jia Tolentino/*The New Yorker* © Conde Nast.

Van Buskirk, Eliot. "Top 25 Metal Genres on Spotify," *Spotify Insights*, August 5, 2015. Reprinted by permission of the author.

Walser, Robert. "Highbrow, Lowbrow, Voodoo Aesthetics" from *Microphone Fiends: Youth Music & Youth Culture* (London: Routledge Press, 1994). Reprinted by permission of the author.

Walters, Barry. "The Arson is Blowin' in the Wind: Why Woodstock '99 Devolved into a Frat-Style Free-for-All," *The Washington Post*, August 8, 1999. Reprinted by permission of the author.

Wenner, Jann. "The Rolling Stone Interview: Peter Townshend," pp. 1, 10–15, from *Rolling Stone*, September 14, 1968. © 1968 Rolling Stone LLC. All Rights Reserved. Reprinted by Permission.

Wesley, Jr. Fred. Excerpts from "James Brown" in *Hit Me Fred: Recollections of a Sideman*, pp. 84–115. © 2002, Duke University Press. All rights reserved. Reprinted by permission of the publisher. www.dukeupress.edu

Williams, Paul. "Understanding Dylan," *Crawdaddy!*, August 1966. Reprinted by permission of Cindy Lee Berryhill.

Williams, Richard. "The Sound of Surprise," *Melody Maker*, August 21, 1976. Reprinted by permission of Time Inc UK.

Wolk, Douglas. "Mother, Should I Build a Wall? Now that Radiohead has taken Rock to New Planes, They Face a Bigger Challenge: Taking it to the Stage," *CMJ New Music Monthly*, February 2001. Reprinted by permission of the author.

Young, Jon. "Roll Over Guitar Heroes: Synthesizers Are Here," *Trouser Press*, May 1982. Reprinted by permission of the author.

Index